PENGUIN BOOKS

THE PENGUIN ENCYCLOPEDIA OF
CLASSICAL CIVILIZATIONS

Arthur Cotterell was born in Berkshire in 1942. He was educated at Ashmead School, Reading, and St John's College, Cambridge. Now principal of Kingston College in Surrey, he combines a career in education and after-school training with an extensive interest in other civilizations, many of them ancient. His published works include *The Minoan World*, *A Dictionary of World Mythology*, *The First Emperor of China*, *The Penguin Encyclopedia of Ancient Civilizations*, *China: A History* and *East Asia: From Chinese Predominance to the Rise of the Pacific Rim*. At present he is preparing a dictionary of classical civilizations.

Arthur Cotterell is married with one son and lives in Surrey.

THE PENGUIN ENCYCLOPEDIA OF CLASSICAL CIVILIZATIONS

EDITED BY ARTHUR COTTERELL

PENGUIN BOOKS

PENGUIN BOOKS

Published by the Penguin Group
Penguin Books Ltd, 27 Wrights Lane, London W8 5TZ, England
Penguin Putnam Inc., 375 Hudson Street, New York, New York 10014, USA
Penguin Books Australia Ltd, Ringwood, Victoria, Australia
Penguin Books Canada Ltd, 10 Alcorn Avenue, Toronto, Ontario, Canada M4V 3B2
Penguin Books (NZ) Ltd, 182–190 Wairau Road, Auckland 10, New Zealand

Penguin Books Ltd, Registered Offices: Harmondsworth, Middlesex, England

First published by Viking 1993
Published in Penguin Books 1995
10 9 8 7 6 5 4 3 2

The moral right of the author has been asserted

Printed in Hong Kong

Contents

List of Contributors

John Brockington
Reader in Sanskrit, University of Edinburgh

Arthur Cotterell
Principal, Kingston College, London

Andrew Drummond
Lecturer in Classics, University of Nottingham

J. T. Hooker
Formerly Lecturer in Greek, University College, University of London

E. J. Keall
Royal Ontario Museum, Toronto

Frank W. Walbank
Emeritus Professor of Ancient History, University of Liverpool

T. Cuyler Young, Jr
Royal Ontario Museum, Toronto

A Note on Transliteration

For names and terms in the section on Imperial India the standard transliteration for Sanskrit and Pāli has been adopted. Although this may appear slightly complex at first, it means that each sound has only one representation and so the pronunciation is certain (it will also be found in almost any other scholarly treatment of ancient India to which the reader may turn). Long vowels are distinguished from short by the macron (ā), except that *e*, *ai*, *o* and *au* are regularly long, being diphthongs in origin; *ṛ* represents vocalic *r* (a sort of purring sound). The letter *h* always indicates aspiration, even in such combinations as *th* and *ph* (pronounced roughly as in *coathook* and *uphill*), and *c* is always pronounced as in the Italian *cinquecento* (or like the *ch* in English *church*, but in Sanskrit *ch* is the aspirated form of *c*). A dot below the letter distinguishes retroflex consonants, pronounced with the tongue far back in the mouth, from the dentals (*t*, *th*, *d*, *dh*, *n*) made with the tongue against the teeth. Of the three sibilants, *s* is pronounced as in English *sit*, while *ś* and *ṣ* represent slightly differing sounds, both close to *sh*. However, the usual spellings without diacritics are used for modern place names.

For names and terms in the section on the Unification of China the new Pinyin system of transliteration from Chinese characters has been used.

Preface

When I was preparing the *Encyclopedia of Ancient Civilizations* for publication, late in 1979, it became apparent that a 'classical age' could be discerned for civilization right across the Old World. Whereas the earliest civilizations arose at a few scattered places and pursued largely separate courses, in West Asia, Egypt, India, Europe and China, after 600 BC a change took place, with the result that the various regional civilizations linked up in an almost continuous belt. By the first century of the Christian era four powers dominated the Old World: Rome, Parthia, Kuṣāṇa India and Han China.

Not only were these powers in contact with each other, and quite often in conflict, but they also developed societies with a great deal in common. It is clear how they faced similar problems, devised not entirely different solutions, and in the process of development laid the foundation of present-day Europe and Asia. To list but a few of those who offered guidance is enough to illustrate the formative nature of the period: Confucius, the Buddha, Zoroaster, Christ, Socrates, Plato, Aristotle, Mencius, Shang Yang, Zeno, Diogenes, Epicurus, St Paul, Kautilya, Manu, Sun Zi, Dong Zhongshu, Mani, Kartir, Cato, Cicero, Lucretius, Seneca, Marcus Aurelius, St Augustine, Wang Chong and Hui Yuan.

In order to signify the importance of the period treated in this encyclopedia, approximately 550 BC to AD 600, all civilizations are termed 'classical'. Tradition has hitherto narrowly reserved the word for Greece and Rome. Here the classical features of Greece, Rome, the Hellenistic kingdoms, Persia, India and China are discussed.

Credit for the appearance of this long overdue survey belongs to Penguin, for on the reissue in 1988 of the *Encyclopedia of Ancient Civilizations* as a paperback, they saw the value of following it up with the current volume. Although the *Encyclopedia of Classical Civilizations* cannot hope to be more than introductory, its aim is the encouragement of an approach to antiquity that thinks of the Old World as a whole.

Preparation of this encyclopedia has been overshadowed by the death of James Hooker, who offered its editor sage advice at the planning stage. In gratitude *The Penguin Encyclopedia of Classical Civilizations* is therefore dedicated to his memory.

AC, Kingston

The four great powers at the beginning of the second century: Rome, Parthia, Kuṣāṇa India and Han China.

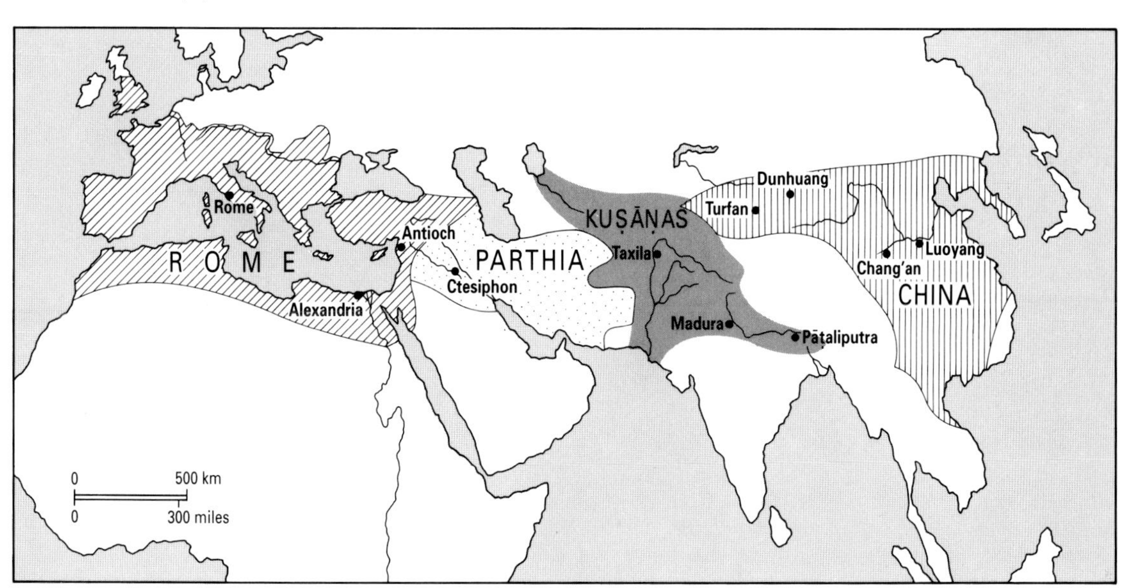

Introduction

Arthur Cotterell

The age of the first civilizations was well past by the time the classical era began, around 550 BC. Of the five cradles of civilization – Mesopotamia, Egypt, India, the Aegean and China – only the last could boast anything approaching political and cultural continuity.

In Mesopotamia the Persian conquest of 539–538 BC marked the close of the ancient period of inter-state rivalries: for the first time in history the Achaemenids had united almost all of West Asia. And in 525 BC the further advance of Persian arms into Egypt brought about an effective end to pharaonic rule. But even before the Achaemenid king Cambyses II inflicted a crushing defeat on the Egyptian army at Pelusium, the Egyptians had been the subjects of the Asiatic Hyksos (*c.* 1652–1567 BC), the Nubians (*c.* 715–663 BC) and the Assyrians (663–651 BC). Although the Persians went on to threaten the Greeks without success in the early fifth century BC, their intended victims were themselves heirs to the Minoan-Mycenaean civilization, which had collapsed about 1200 BC. The destruction of this early civilization meant for the Aegean a temporary loss of literacy. When the Greeks learned how to write again, not later than 750 BC, the writing system was totally different. Not only was it based on an alphabetical form evolved by the Phoenicians, but its users were individuals rather than members of a palace bureaucracy.

India, like China, is endowed today with a strong memory of its remote past. Yet the Aryan invasion of India, which followed hard on the heels of the extinction of the Indus civilization (*c.* 2400–1800 BC), obliterated city life for several centuries. Earlier Aryan raids may well have already undermined the great settlements of Mohenjo-daro and Harappa, if the irrigation system was a casualty. Possibly dams were shattered deliberately. Their warlike god Indra is said to have freed the waters by rolling away stones like wagon wheels. Although they eventually absorbed certain Indus preoccupations – personal cleanliness and worship of the mother goddess, for example – the Aryans were initially destroyers, and given victory over the peoples living in walled towns and fortified cities by Indra in the guise of Purandara, 'the fort-destroyer'.

China suffered no such disruption between its first civilization, under the Shang dynasty (*c.* 1650–1027 BC), and the subsequent one, known as the Zhou, after the new royal house. The longest dynasty in Chinese history, the Zhou was not overthrown until 256 BC, shortly before the imperial unification of the country by the feudal state of Qin. The steady decline of feudalism certainly led Confucius (551–479 BC) to conjure up an ideal past with which to chide contemporary disloyalty, but the philosopher was in no doubt that the Chinese controlled their own destiny. He used to remind his followers of the inestimable service performed by Huan, duke of Qi (684–642 BC), in protecting China from barbarian conquest. And the northern frontier held firm throughout most of China's classical era.

A consequence of Chinese continuity is an unmatched historical record. Not even the notorious destruction of books, ordered by the First Emperor in 213 BC, was enough to expunge this knowledge. For the duration of the repressive Qin dynasty (221–207 BC) it was almost impossible to 'use the past to discredit the present', but as soon as the moderate Han emperor Gaozu (206–195 BC) was secure on the throne, a government-sponsored programme of literary restoration got under way. Illiterate though he was himself, this peasant ruler had the wit to appreciate the value of learned and cultivated advisers and assistants. On their recommendation ancient texts were painfully reconstructed from memory, as well as from damaged copies that had been hidden away at great personal risk. Some 460 scholars had been executed in 212 BC for still daring to oppose Qin imperial will. Only the Greeks and Romans can compare with the Chinese in their surviving histories, and surpass them in terms of inscriptions. The scarcity of stone in north China was a limiting factor when it came to preserving documents. Instead of cutting texts in durable materials, Chinese scribes had to rely on bronze and bamboo.

Chinese inventiveness was to meet the needs of a large bureaucracy through the manufacture of paper, announced by the imperial workshops in AD 105, but this remarkable aid to communication barely disturbed a tradition which, in the classical era, managed with few public documents. Quite typical was Confucius' concern in 513 BC over the publication of a law code. He noted that the punishments inscribed on a tripod by a feudal lord would be learned and respected by the ordinary people above all else. This was undesirable because, Confucius held, the business of government was best left in the hands of those schooled for public service. In contrast to ancient Greece, literacy in China did not take on at once a public purpose; it never disclosed to the people as a whole the workings of government. Only the learned could expect to enter the bureaucracy and exercise power.

The very different political framework of the Greek city-state rested on a much wider degree of power-sharing. In the growth of the Athenian democracy the lawgiver Solon is usually credited with taking the decisive step. Appointed in 594 BC as a mediator between the rich and the poor, Solon cancelled debts, bought citizens out of slavery and prohibited all future loans on the security of the person. The abolition of slavery for debt guaranteed the personal freedom of the humblest citizen; it crystallized as well the concept of fundamental, inalienable civil rights without which citizenship would be rendered valueless. Solon himself considered this measure his most significant reform, but he steadfastly refused to extend the *seisachtheia*, 'the shaking off of burdens', to any redistribution of land owned by the aristocracy. A free peasantry was Solon's ideal, and indeed, throughout the period Athens was a city-state, smallholders comprised the majority of its citizen body. His opening of office to men of substance also marked the end of the nobility's stranglehold on government, although not its dominance.

On the eve of the classical era another aristocrat, Cleisthenes, enlisted the aid of the citizen body in 508 BC to weaken further the power of old families except his own. Yet the effect of his constitutional reforms in distributing political power more widely needs to be seen in historical context. While the ownership of land ceased to be a qualification for citizenship in Athens, the size of the citizen body remained strictly limited. Among others excluded from membership were allies, foreign residents and slaves. That the ancient Greeks took slavery for granted should never be forgotten. For half a millennium the Hellenic and Hellenistic worlds relied heavily on servile labour for their food supply, manufactured goods and public works. In the Laurium silver mines in Attica there were so many Thracian slaves that they outnumbered the total population of some of the smaller city-states. Use of barbarian slaves, however, was a practice most favoured by Rome.

Roman dependence on slaves is apparent by the end of the second century BC. One reason for slavery becoming so widespread in Italy then was undoubtedly the plentiful supply of war captives. Whenever a campaign was launched, or a province added, the late republican armies brought home as booty large numbers of prisoners. These displaced persons were sold for service in agriculture, industry or the home. On occasions a victorious general might be directed by the Senate to sell a whole population into slavery. This happened in 167 BC to Aemilius Paullus, a year after his final defeat of the Macedonians at Pydna. On the Senate's order to deal harshly with the enemies of Rome, the general sold 150,000 Epirotes in northern Greece. But this figure pales into insignificance when compared to the million Gallic prisoners later taken by Julius Caesar (100–44 BC) and the half-million gained as booty by the emperor Trajan during the subjugation of Dacia (AD 101–5).

With the growing size of the slave population, the uprisings from 140 BC onwards were to be anticipated. Starting in the Roman west and spreading to the Greek east, they convulsed the Mediterranean world for several generations, before slowly dying away. The most famous revolt was led by a Thracian gladiator named Spartacus, who between 73 and 71 BC routed five Roman armies and dominated the Italian peninsula. The continued expansion of the early empire maintained the inflow of barbarian slaves almost to the end of the first century AD, but already replacements were having to be found from within the imperial borders – a condition that ultimately brought about a lesser dependence on servile labour. The Graeco-Roman experience was thus entirely different from the situation in China, where an efficient metallurgy combined with irrigation to boost agricultural production to such an extent that rural slavery was in large measure unnecessary. And unlike the Romans, the imperial Chinese were more than willing to redeem barbarian hostages as part of border diplomacy.

Only a small element of those enslaved during the Han dynasty (206 BC–AD 220) were non-Chinese. Though foreign slaves were sometimes presented as gifts and bribes to government officials in charge of supervising allied tribes, the numbers involved remained small. Chinese foreign policy along the northern frontier was dictated by the difficulty of campaigning on the steppe. The endless wastes of the Gobi discouraged any forward strategy other than securing the compliance of the oasis states in the so-called Western Regions of Central Asia. Usually Chinese emperors were inclined to defence in depth. Several lines of fortifications constituted the strength of the Great Wall. As long as these held firm, there was scope for dealing with the nomadic tribesmen of the steppelands on a flexible basis. Even a mass surrender of the Hunnish Xiongnu in 121 BC failed to persuade the belligerent Han emperor Wu Di of the economic advantages to be gained in enslaving barbarian prisoners of war. He treated the Xiongnu ruler and his followers generously, settling them on frontier lands. Perhaps Wu Di's attitude is best illustrated by his treatment of Jin Miti, a Xiongnu who was enslaved for choosing not to surrender with his ruler. So pleased with Jin Miti's service as a groom was the emperor that he freed the slave and appointed him to office immediately. Jin Miti went on to marry a high official's daughter, before ending his own career as a minister.

The majority of the slaves in classical China were therefore native-born Chinese who had fallen into debt. Very poor people with no means of supporting their families had to sell their children into slavery. This was recognized by law and sometimes even encouraged by the imperial government during times of famine or civil disturbance. In 205 BC the first Han emperor, Gaozu, decreed that people living in the environs of the capital might sell their children and emigrate southwards in search of food. Four years later, when the empire was pacified, an edict was issued to free those persons who had sold themselves into slavery because of famine. But general manumissions were rare and the usual method of securing freedom was the generosity of the owner. Pressure from Confucian scholars encouraged the throne to adopt a humane approach to slavery, the philosopher Dong Zhongshu (*c.* 179–104 BC) urging the abolition of enslavement as a punishment and of the right of an owner to kill a slave. By the time of Wang Mang's usurpation (AD 9–23) the argument had been won. Wang Mang even ordered one of his sons to commit suicide when he learned that he had murdered a slave.

Although his attempted abolition of slavery failed, Wang Mang would not have been able to exhibit such a detestation of slave abuse if there had not been a general groundswell of support among the educated. Quite different was the outlook of Cicero (106–43 BC), who gave voice in Latin to the Greek belief about the inevitability of slavery. But then, after the downfall of the Qin dynasty, no Chinese emperor could have repeated Caligula's favourite utterance: 'Remember that I can do anything to anybody.'

It used to be thought that Christianity was an important factor in the manumission of slaves and the amelioration of their conditions. Between 315 and 323 the first Roman emperor to be baptized, Constantine the Great, banned crucifixion and branding on the face as punishments, though these improvements may not have been much solace while slaves could still be forced to drink boiling oil or molten lead. Yet neither the imperial convert nor his bishops were morally outraged by the institution of slavery itself. Christians accepted it as a normal part of society throughout the Roman empire. A well-born lady like Melania could renounce the world in 375 and free the 8,000 slaves working on her Spanish estates without having any impact at all on Church attitudes. Not even the reminder that human beings were created 'in the image of God', a point made around the same time by Gregory of Nyssa, caused any disturbance to the *status quo*. For St Augustine (354–430) the relations between master and slave were divinely ordained, as those between husband and wife. Becoming a Christian did not excuse a slave from his or her duties.

Hardly surprising, therefore, was the amazement of Megasthenes on his arrival in India around 300 BC. Coming from a world in which slavery was commonplace, this Greek ambassador to the court of the Indian king Candragupta was struck by the absence of slaves in the Mauryan empire. 'It is a remarkable thing,' he notes, 'that all Indians are free, and no Indian at all is a slave.' Though the evidence is somewhat slender, there would appear to have been some slavery under the Mauryan dynasty, including the reign of Aśoka (*c*. 268–232 BC). The main cause of enslavement was debt. Numbers remained low throughout the classical and early medieval periods, at least till the arrival of Muslim armies in the subcontinent from the eighth century AD onwards. According to Megasthenes, the reason for the ban on slavery was the teaching of ancient Indian sages which held: 'Those who have learned neither to domineer over others nor to subject themselves to others will enjoy a manner of life best suited to all circumstances.'

Megasthenes represented Seleucus I on several Indian embassies between 302 and 291 BC. The founder of the Seleucid dynasty had already acknowledged the suzerainty of the first Mauryan ruler over north-western India. In 303 BC Seleucus I ceded to Candragupta the satrapies of Aria, Arachosia, Paropamisidae and Gedrosia in return for 500 war elephants. Two years later in Asia Minor these great animals carried all before them at the battle of Ipsus. Their decisive intervention did more than defeat Antigonus, for victory over this would-be successor to Alexander the Great confirmed the division of his vast spear-won realm into separate Hellenistic kingdoms. Luckily for the Ptolemies in Egypt and the Antigonids in Macedon, Seleucus I did not acquire crossbows as well. A lethal Chinese invention, the crossbow was to stay in East Asia for over another millennium. Its eventual adoption in medieval Europe proved an even more startling event than the charge of Candragupta's war elephants. In 1139 the Church was moved to anathematize all those who employed the 'diabolical machine' against Christians.

Warfare was endemic during the era of the Hellenistic kingdoms (336–31 BC). This was probably inevitable, given the extent of Alexander's conquests and the manner of his death in 323 BC. The dying conqueror was asked to whom he left his kingdom. Because his Sogdian wife Roxane had still to give birth to an heir, this was no idle question. 'To the strongest,' replied Alexander, correctly anticipating the prolonged struggle between his generals. With dependent territories stretching from Greece to India, the opportunities for power and booty were too tempting to ignore. As for the mercenary troops of various nationalities who had been serving in Alexander's army, they rallied to whomever paid them most. In a tight spot they would betray their own commander, a fate that overtook Eumenes in 315 BC when a veteran force needed to ransom its captured camp. So Alexander's ex-secretary was exchanged for baggage, women and loot. Yet the very nature of Hellenistic monarchy made success on the battlefield a prerequisite for authority. Lacking the traditional legitimacy of the city-state, a Hellenistic kingdom rested entirely on the military strength of its ruler. Hence the initial advantage enjoyed by Seleucus I with his large elephant corps. The Ptolemies soon added the smaller African variety to their forces, but they proved to be no more effective than Indian imports once infantrymen learned how to sidestep their charges. Slingers and archers were found to be particularly useful in removing their riders, as well as those who guarded the elephants' flanks.

The fundamental importance of warfare for Hellenistic kings was undoubtedly the cause of a greater brutality. Alexander himself showed the way. Although in 334 BC at the battle of Granicus River the Greek mercenaries under Persian command had begged for quarter following the flight of the Persians, nine-tenths of them were cut down, leaving only 2,000 to spend the rest of their lives as slaves on Macedonian estates. Their relatives back in Greece bridled at such savagery, but their own subjugation to Macedon derived from an inability to live together in peace. The Peloponnesian War (431–404 BC), between the rival blocs, headed by Sparta and Athens, had marked the end of brief campaigns in which heavy-armed infantrymen clashed on conveniently sited plains. All expected a short war; no city-state was ready for the full twenty-seven years that it took to bring the conflict to a conclusion. They failed to foresee the dislocation that such a war would bring to Greece: corrosive violence, the decline of moral standards, social unrest and economic stagnation, as well as a chronic instability that was a gift to Alexander's ambitious father, Philip II of Macedon (359–336 BC).

The increased scale of fighting that arose in the Mediterranean as a consequence of rivalry between the Hellenistic kingdoms became even more pronounced with the rise of Rome. Indeed, what distinguished the Romans was their capacity for virtually constant warfare. The struggle against Carthage, from 264 to 146 BC, transformed the Roman army from an essentially part-time force of farmers into a quasi-professional organization in which it was not uncommon for men to serve abroad for years on end. The first emperor, Augustus (27 BC–AD 14), completed the transformation, giving the Roman military system a form which lasted till the imperial crisis of the third century. The professional army was composed of two parts: a regular citizen army of about 165,000 legionaries, supported by a larger number of auxiliary troops drawn from subject peoples resident in the empire. During the final centuries of Roman power, however, the diminished attractions of a military career obliged hard-pressed emperors to rely on conscription and the recruitment of barbarian mercenaries. The *barritus*, the famed battle-cry of the Romans, rising from a murmur to an awesome roar in a long crescendo, was itself of German origin. At the battle of Strasbourg in 356, it was raised by Julian's troops against the Germanic Alamanni.

The composite nature of late Roman armies is nowhere more apparent than in the preliminaries to the ill-fated expedition launched by Julian against the Sasanians (363–4). According to Ammianus Marcellinus, the spirited Gallic contingent within the garrison of Amida, a frontier city on the upper Tigris, had to be locked up for its own safety. It was well suited to the cut and thrust of pitched battles but not to the slow attrition of siege warfare. Its daring night attack on the Persian camp was not enough to deflect Shapur I, whose eventual capture of Amida cost him 30,000 men. After the fall of the city in the autumn of 359, the Sasanian king had the local recruits to the Roman garrison killed to a man, on the basis that as inhabitants of Persian lands the military service they rendered to Rome was treasonable.

The long struggle between the Romans and Persians had been intensified by the foundation in 324 of a New Rome, Constantinople, on the site of Byzantium. The eastward shift of imperial power was bound to make critical the security of the frontier between Sasanian Persia and Byzantium, as the surviving Roman state in the eastern Mediterranean is usually called. The change of name underlines another important difference between the old capital and the new one: the removal to the Bosporus of the seat of imperial authority was intended to signal a break with the pagan past and the foundation of a new Christian empire. Ironically Perso-Byzantine enmity reached its climax on the eve of the Muslim assault. Even though Khusrau II had won the throne with Byzantine support, the Sasanian king chose to renew hostilities on the assassination of his sponsor, the emperor Maurice. In 612 Antioch, Damascus and Tarsus fell; in 614 Jerusalem was taken and the Holy Cross removed to Ctesiphon, the Sasanian capital; in 615 much of Asia Minor was conquered; and in 619 the Persians occupied Egypt as well. Under Heraclius (610–41) the Byzantines rallied and by 622 the tide of battle had turned against Khusrau. Unbeknown to either side, that same year the prophet Muhammed started the campaign which would eventually overwhelm both of them, and take Muslim arms to countries as far distant as Spain and India. But in the bitterness of their final struggle the Byzantines and the Sasanians anticipated something of the fanaticism in the forthcoming Muslim onslaught. Heraclius was indeed styled as a crusader who piously sacked Persian fire temples in revenge for the desecration of Jerusalem.

In Persia a tradition of tolerance had already been challenged, however. During the classical period the Sasanians were unique in systematically attempting to impose a religious orthodoxy. From the start of the dynasty Sasanian kings strove to distance themselves from the less rigorous outlook of their Persian predecessors, the Parthians. The first monarch, Ardashir (226–41), claimed the right to suppress heterodox traditions that had been incorporated in the Avesta, the holy book of Zoroastrianism. A surviving letter from the chief priest Tansar asserts that Ardashir was justified in shedding blood because of the doctrinal errors of his Parthian predecessors. The veneration of cult images was outlawed, although such a practice descended from much earlier Achaemenid times. Under Ardashir's son Shapur I, this surge of iconoclasm first spilled over in the physical destruction of those who did not embrace the state religion. The tidal wave of persecution is associated with the name of Kartir, an astute priest who outlasted several kings. Inscriptions dating from the reigns of Bahram I and Bahram II boast of his successes against Jews, Christians, Manichees, Buddhists and Hindus. Kartir's greatest triumph was the imprisonment and death in 277 of the prophet Mani, to whom Shapur had accorded royal protection. Mani's austere teachings were attractive to followers of both Christ and Zoroaster. For nine years (373–82) before his conversion, St Augustine was to be a Manichee, and long afterwards his own vision of the elect differed little from the chosen few of Mani. But in Persia the dualistic account of the universe propounded in Manichaean scriptures was too close to official orthodoxy for comfort, so Kartir singled out Manichees as the special enemies of Zoroastrianism.

The baptism of the Armenian king Tiridates (274–314) altered the political and religious balance of power in West Asia. Ever a cause of friction, Armenia's emergence as the original Christian state made the new faith a factor to be considered in the foreign policy of the Sasanians for the first time. Fear of fifth columnists goes some way to explain the persecution of Christians, especially when they were seen as agents of Byzantium. It also accounts for the determined effort of the Sasanians to impose Zoroastrianism on Armenia. Defeated though they were in battle, the Armenians resisted fire worship until the Muslim conquest, after which they still clung to their Christian saints and liturgy as the means of preserving a national identity. From the moment the Parthians (247 BC–AD 236) had reasserted Persian influence in West Asia, renewed conflict over a strategically located territory such as Armenia was inevitable with the dominant European power.

Within two decades of the end of Seleucid power in Syria, Rome was put on an almost permanent war footing with Parthia by Crassus, the elderly military partner of Julius Caesar and Pompey. His eastern aims, Plutarch tells us, extended 'as far as the Bactrians and the Indians and the external sea'. They were rudely shattered at Carrhae, a city lying between the Euphrates and Tigris rivers, where in 53 BC the Parthians defeated a Roman army of 40,000 men and slew the would-be Alexander. Although internal difficulties prevented the Parthian king Orodes from exploiting this great victory, 10,000 Roman captives of war were immediately put to work on government-sponsored projects. A tantalizing sequel to this incident may have taken place near the Central Asian city of Turfan in 36 BC, when a Chinese general received the surrender of a mercenary force on the capture of a Xiongnu chieftain. From a description of their drill, the mercenaries look suspiciously like ex-Roman legionaries; quite possibly they were survivors of the Carrhae débâcle.

Both the Parthians and the Sasanians employed military and civilian captives on public works. Their treatment appears to have been less harsh than the lot of slaves in the Graeco-Roman world. The Romans at Turfan, for instance, could have come from the settlements known to have been planted after Carrhae on the eastern frontier of Parthia. One reason for the absence of a large slave class in late classical Persia was the weakness of Seleucid rule, following the death of Alexander. Despite hanging on to large parts of his eastern conquests for a century, the Seleucids never really changed the traditional pattern of subsistence agriculture in the countryside. Because Hellenism was very much an urban phenomenon, it is to be expected that slavery would be concentrated in cities and their environs. Prior to the fall of the Achaemenids in 330 BC, however, there were so many slaves in Mesopotamia that the livelihood of free artisans and labourers was often threatened. Many of those enslaved were the victims of rebellion against the King of Kings. It is recorded how Artaxerxes III increased the size of his own palace staff in 345 BC by the incorporation of numerous Phoenician women. They were the lucky survivors of Sidon, which had been reduced to ashes the same year. So complete was the destruction of this Phoenician city that the victorious Persian general had only the ruins to sell to speculators, who paid him for the right to search for melted silver and gold. A sale of enslaved rebels was the usual climax of an insurrection.

In spite of the typically Indian doctrines of *ahiṁsā*, 'non-violence', and *maitrī*, 'kindness to others', fighting was no more restrained in the subcontinent. Warfare had always been looked upon as good in itself, the natural occupation of the *kṣatriyas*, the aristocratic warriors. Aśoka's patronage of Buddhism did a great deal to check the traditional Hindu warrior ethic, but his plea for peace found few echoes in succeeding centuries. This enlightened Mauryan king laid emphasis on the principle of tolerance, enjoining his subjects to make social conduct a matter of the highest morality. The support given by Aśoka to all sects was intended to encourage debate, always a feature of Indian religious life, without offering offence to any person who sought 'mastery of the senses and purity of mind'. According to Megasthenes, these *sophistai*, or 'wise men', were exempt from any service to the state – a custom which at a later period was to bring Buddhist monks into conflict with the Confucian bureaucracy of China. 'They pass their days naked,' marvelled Megasthenes, 'exposed in the winter to the cold and in the summer to the sun. They eat the fruits of the earth and the bark of the trees, which is no less agreeable to the taste and no less nourishing than dates.'

Already Indian asceticism had made its influence felt on Greek philosophy. Pyrrhon of Elis (*c*. 365–270 BC) adopted an extreme scepticism, holding that judgement should be suspended because of the unreliability of the senses. After his return from India, where he travelled as a member of Alexander's train, Pyrrhon lived in a manner consistent with the view that 'no single thing is in itself any more than another'. Diogenes Laertius also tells us how Pyrrhon's friends had to protect the philosopher from carts, precipices and dogs. When asked by one of them on his deathbed if he were still alive, Pyrrhon is reputed to have replied that he was not sure. Such imperturbability could not, of course, produce a body of thought and, under the sceptic Arcesilaus (268–241 BC), the famous Academy in Athens went into steady decline as a philosophical school. 'According to some,' notes Diogenes Laertius, 'one result of his suspending judgement on all matters was that he never so much as wrote a book.'

Perhaps the attractiveness of Scepticism, like the contemporary popularity of the Epicurean and Stoic systems, was not unconnected with the political impotence of the individual under powerful Hellenistic rulers. In the same way educated Romans were subsequently to espouse Epicureanism and Stoicism as creeds best suited for the pursuit of happiness within the confines of the established order. Except when influenced by Cynic doctrines, Stoic precepts tended to interpret the individual's obligations in terms of the conventional expectations of society.

When Fa Xian reached India shortly after 399, Buddhism was well past its heyday, although the prosperity of Buddhist foundations caused the Chinese pilgrim to wonder. As he points out in his *Record of Buddhist Countries*:

Down from the Buddha's nirvāṇa the rulers of these lands, the nobles and the householders, have raised *vihāras* for the monks and provided for their support by bestowing on them buildings, gardens, fields, labourers and oxen. Engraved title-deeds were prepared and handed down from one reign to another; no person has dared to withdraw them, so that till now there has been no interruption. Monks living in the *vihāras* are thus provided with ample food, drink and clothes.

The maintenance of monasteries by the special allotment of land was an ancient Indian custom inherited by Buddhism. Well-to-do lay believers who had spare land would donate it to the Saṅgha, the order of monks and nuns, in order to earn spiritual merit.

Fa Xian's pilgrimage to India in quest of Buddhist scriptures coincided with the reign of Candragupta II (376–*c.* 412), the peak period of the imperial Gupta age. The greatest classical sculpture was then produced, and the finest literature written, in the poems and plays of Kālidāsa. At Ajaṇṭā, in present-day Mahārāstra, a series of Buddhist caves were cut and decorated with resplendent sculpture and murals. Today a visitor to the semicircular gorge is still amazed at the feat of excavation itself; a single cave can be as much as 100 feet long and 40 feet wide. Yet Fa Xian could not avoid noticing a darker side to Indian society. Whereas the *śūdras*, the peasants, had a somewhat more advantageous position than in the Mauryan age, those outside the class system of the *varṇas* had declined to what was called untouchability. The *candālas*, or 'outcastes', were treated with a lack of humanity only comparable to the segregation of lepers in Europe during the Middle Ages. 'If they enter a town or market,' Fa Xian records, 'the outcastes sound a piece of wood in order to separate themselves.' Even accidental contact with an untouchable was a source of pollution and required ritual ablutions, much to the bewilderment of the Chinese pilgrim. Medieval European society, on the other hand, found a place for lepers in its scheme of salvation: at least the charity shown towards their sufferings in leper hospitals was a means of easing the Christian conscience.

Buddhism was the only outside influence to affect classical China, but its late arrival postponed any impact on Chinese thought till well after the dissolution of the Han empire in 220. At first the new faith was viewed as no more than a sect of Daoism, the philosophical alternative to Confucian orthodoxy and a popular religion in its own right. A notable Daoist development in the 180s had been the semi-independent state set up by the Five Pecks of Grain movement on the borders of present-day Sichuan and Shaanxi provinces. Its resident peasantry was governed with such a conspicuous honesty that on reconquest in 215 even a general as cynical as Cao Cao dared not punish the dominant family. Because of the strength of their local support Zhang Lu and his five sons were ennobled instead. Zhang Lu himself inherited his authority from Chang Daoling, the first heavenly teacher of what was to become the Daoist church. This founding adept had dramatically acquired immortality when, in 156, he suddenly disappeared except for his clothes.

The quasi-religious attempt to build a rural utopia in the borderlands was by no means an isolated event in the final years of Han rule. Where the Five Pecks of Grain movement stood out from other rebel groups was in the clarity of its Daoist inspiration. With the decline of central power, and the incipient fragmentation of China into the Three Kingdoms (221–65), many Chinese turned to the ancient antagonist of Confucianism for solace. Not only did Daoism answer the needs of Zhang Lu's followers, for most of whom Daoist interest in the supernatural chimed with the practices of country magic; it also offered scholars a philosophical system entirely divorced from state-sponsored dogma. Attempts to reinterpret Confucianism in a less scholastic manner were inadequate for the crisis overtaking the Chinese empire: the very role of the scholar-bureaucrat was being questioned when warlords tore the country apart in their never-ending struggle for supremacy. For a few decades one powerful family, the Sima, was able to reunite China, till its own squabbles drew barbarian allies into civil strife and in 316 handed control of the northern provinces to them.

In the middle of the disturbances Buddhism arrived on the Chinese philosophical scene. An entry for the new faith was provided by Daoist scholars, who saw in Mahayana doctrines a reflection of their own concerns. Already the idea was about that the founder of Daoism, Lao Zi, and the Buddha were one and the same. Apparently Lao Zi, after disappearing in the west, went all the way to India, where he converted the barbarians and became the Buddha. That for many years Buddhism and Daoism were regarded as aspects of a single set of beliefs seems almost inevitable when translators used Daoist terms to explain Buddhist concepts. For this reason, in 166 the Later Han emperor Huandi personally sacrificed to both Lao Zi and the Buddha. The ceremony inside the imperial palace was the occasion of a remonstrance from a Daoist astrologer, who warned the throne about the dangers arising from the cruelty of the eunuch administration upon which Huandi relied. 'Now the way of Lao Zi and the Buddha is the way of purity and the emptiness,' the warning said. 'It extols non-action, love of life and hatred of violence, the lessening of desires and the avoidance of excess.' The emperor was unmoved by this attack on eunuch power, which continued unchecked till the military *coup* of 189. Then the killing of a general led to the storming of the imperial palace and the slaughter of the eunuchs responsible for his death.

One of the ironies of East Asian history is the minimal impact that the spread of Buddhism had on the conduct of war. Not untypical as a ruler was the Sui emperor Wen Di (589–604), who in imitation of Aśoka built *stūpas* throughout China. Early in his ruthless campaign of reunification, Wen Di proclaimed his purpose in religious terms when he said: 'With 100 victories in 100 battles, we promote the practice of the Buddhist virtues.' Yet Wen Di's espousal of the Buddhist faith was in all probability no more opportunist than the vision of the Roman emperor Constantine in 312, on the eve of the battle at the Milvian bridge. Neither of them would accept any restraint on imperial power. Miraculously the Church acquired a generous patron, but at the same time it took on a powerful master, for Constantine's subsequent efforts to settle theological disputes foreshadowed the role of the Byzantine emperor as a Christian *pontifex maximus*. Pacifism derived in China not from the gentle teachings of the Buddha, persuasive though these were under certain dynasties, but rather from the non-violent emphasis to be found in Confucian ethics. Since a ruler was expected to attain his ends through benevolence, force was never easy to glorify because its deployment necessarily represented an admission of failure. The Tang emperors, who followed the short-lived Sui dynasty founded by Wen Di, were always reminded by Confucian officials that they would also be unable to cope with internal problems if, like the Sui, they became preoccupied with foreign conquest.

But during the Warring States period (481–221 BC) battles in China were of a size unmatched elsewhere in the classical world. There was an intensification of warfare right down to the country's unification under the Qin in 221 BC and the civil war following the overthrow of this oppressive dynasty. It could be argued that the nationwide peasant rebellion which ended Qin rule so quickly after its establishment as the first imperial house was the reassertion of a traditional disdain for violence. The harshness of the regime can be seen as the last straw for the family-oriented Chinese, who deeply resented the disruption caused by wholesale conscription on public works. The terrible lot of the conscripted labourers who built the Great Wall has been recalled in folk-song ever since. The mildness of Gaozu, the first Han emperor, seems to have been a genuine part of his character and it made his accession something of a popular event. People felt that this commoner would govern in their interests, unlike the previous absolute rulers of Qin.

The handbook for Chinese commanders was Sun Zi's *Art of War*, dating from the late fifth century BC. The earliest known study of warfare, it argues that because success on the battlefield is of vital importance to a state, the ruler must understand all the factors involved. These are morale, weather, terrain, command and supply. By command Sun Zi meant a general's personal qualities – wisdom, sincerity, humanity, courage and strictness. 'Those who master the five factors overcome; those who do not are vanquished.' The armies for which Sun Zi devised tactics were composite forces of infantry, cavalry, chariots and crossbowmen. Their core of highly trained regulars was capable of manoeuvring in the middle of an engagement according to orders transmitted by gongs, drums and flags. For this reason the *Art of War* is able seriously to envisage a victory resulting from very little fighting at all. 'A victor always defeats a demoralized foe.' Even at the height of the struggle between Qin and the other feudal states, the clash of arms was regarded as no more than one option available to a commander in the field. The extermination of the enemy was never a prime objective, although in 260 BC Qin generals took the shocking step of ordering the wholesale slaughter of prisoners after the battle of Chang Ping. The massacre was explained on the basis that the captured troops were restive and a needless hazard in a difficult situation. In reality the Qin army was sending a signal to its feudal antagonists about its own determination to subdue the whole of China.

Imperial unification was undoubtedly intertwined with technical advance, but the ability of a dynasty to endure was also related to the acquiescence of the governed and the means by which they could effect political changes. It happened in classical China that offensive weapons were always superior, the crossbow long before the lifetime of Christ having ruled out any armoured domination by a military élite. No empty threat, then, was contained in the doctrine of justified rebellion against tyrannical government, a formulation of Confucius' greatest disciple, Mencius (372–288 BC). The resolute face Mencius presented to the authoritarian trend in contemporary philosophy came from his own belief in the natural goodness of mankind. Speaking of the inhumanity of feudal rulers, he said: 'A benevolent man extends his love from those he loves to those he does not love. A ruthless man extends his ruthlessness from those he does not love to those he loves.' This singular attitude to military might is probably due to Chinese inventiveness. Early production of cast iron and steel provided efficient hoes, ploughshares, picks and axes; it allowed effective tillage by a peasantry progressively emancipated from feudal bonds. A large population did not inhibit the introduction of labour-saving devices. The hard-headed approach of the authoritarian Legalists, the main rivals of the followers of Confucius, concerned as they were to maximize the state's resources at any cost until the fall of the Qin dynasty, somehow combined later with a Confucian sense of duty towards the people's welfare under the Han emperors to produce a significant improvement in the imperial economy. The famous debate held in 81 BC over the nationalization of the iron and salt industries shows how central an issue the proper exploitation of 'the mountains and the sea' always was for Chinese officials.

In this encyclopedia such a concern is placed within the scope of a whole period of human endeavour, which we term the 'classical age'. By looking at the ways in which the Greeks, the Macedonians, the Romans, the Persians, the Indians and the Chinese dealt with the problems their various civilizations threw up, it is hoped that a more general understanding of a very important period of the past will evolve. This is an ambition all the contributors share.

HELLENIC CIVILIZATION

A Corinthian helmet, an essential piece of equipment in the close-packed phalanx.

Chronology

BC

508	Cleisthenes' political reforms at Athens
499	Beginning of Ionian Revolt
494	Battle of Lade
	Persians capture Miletus
493	Suppression of Ionian Revolt
490	Persian expedition to Greece
	Sack of Eretria
	Athenian victory at Marathon
c. 485	Death of Darius; accession of Xerxes
480	Persian invasion of Greece
	Battles of Thermopylae, Artemisium and Salamis
	Battle of Himera
479	Battles of Plataea and Mycale
477	Confederacy of Delos formed
477–473	Successful campaigns by Cimon
c. 468	Battle of the Eurymedon
467	Democracy established at Syracuse
464	Helot revolt at Sparta
461	Ephialtes' political reforms at Athens
	Ostracism of Cimon
457	Battle of Tanagra
454	Transfer of allied treasury from Delos to Athens
	Failure of Athenian expedition to Egypt
451	Citizenship law at Athens
	Five-year truce between Athens and Sparta
	Thirty-year treaty between Argos and Sparta
449	Peace of Callias
	Death of Cimon
445	Thirty-year peace agreed between Athens and Sparta
433	Alliance between Athens and Corcyra
432	Revolt of Potidaea
	Megarian decree
431	Beginning of Peloponnesian War (first phase)
429	Plague at Athens
	Death of Pericles
425	Spartan overtures rejected at Athens
422	Battle of Amphipolis; death of Cleon and Brasidas
421	End of Peloponnesian War (first phase)
	Fifty-year alliance between Athens and Sparta
420	Alliance between Athens and Argos
418	Spartan victory at Mantinea
415	Athenian expedition to Sicily
413	Beginning of Peloponnesian War (second phase)
	Spartan occupation of Decelea
	Athenian catastrophe in Sicily
412	Negotiations between Sparta and Persia
411	*Coup* of the 400 at Athens
410	Democracy restored at Athens
409	Carthaginian invasion of Sicily
406	Athenian victory at Arginusae
405	Athenian defeat at Aegispotami
	Dionysius comes to power at Syracuse
	Sicily divided between Syracuse and Carthaginians
404	Surrender of Athens
	End of Peloponnesian War (second phase)
	Destruction of Long Walls
	Coup of the Thirty at Athens
	Death of Alcibiades
403	Democracy restored at Athens
401	Revolt of Cyrus
c. 400	War between Sparta and Elis
c. 398	Accession of Agesilaus at Sparta
397	Conon admiral of the Persian fleet
396–394	Campaigns of Agesilaus in Asia Minor
395	Beginning of Corinthian War
	Death of Lysander
394	Battle of Cnidus
392	Union of Corinth and Argos
387	Operations of Antalcidas at Hellespont
386	King's Peace
	End of Corinthian War
382	Phoebidas seizes Theban acropolis
379	Capitulation of Olynthus
	Liberation of Thebes
378	Sphodrias' incursion into Attica
	Alliance between Athens and Thebes
377	Second Athenian alliance formed
376	Battle of Naxos
371	Peace of Callias
	Battle of Leuctra
370	Jason of Pherae assassinated
	Arcadian League formed
	Expedition of Epaminondas to Peloponnese
	Foundation of Messene
369	Alliance between Athens and Sparta
	Expedition of Epaminondas to Peloponnese
367	Persian proposals for peace
	Death of Dionysius in Syracuse
366	Expedition of Epaminondas to Peloponnese
	Alliance between Athens and Arcadia
364	Theban naval success at Hellespont
362	Battle of Mantinea
	Death of Epaminondas
360	Death of Agesilaus in Egypt

359	Philip II comes to power in Macedonia
c. 356	Beginning of Sacred War
355	Independence of eastern allies recognized by Athens
353	Death of Mausolus
352	Advance of Philip to Thermopylae
348	Olynthus capitulates to Philip
346	Athenian embassy to Philip
	Peace of Philocrates
343	Timoleon restores democracy at Syracuse
340	Athens declares war on Philip
339	Philip seizes Elatea
	Timoleon's victory over the Carthaginians
338	Battle of Chaeronea
	First meeting of Hellenic League at Corinth
337	Second meeting of Hellenic League
336	Philip assassinated
	Accession of Alexander

Hellenic Civilization (500–338 BC)

J. T. Hooker

History

The ancient Greeks regarded themselves as a people apart. They differed in some acute sense from the non-Greek races with whom they had dealings, however cultivated these might be. To the Greeks they were all 'barbarians'. For the Greeks laid claim to a common ancestry, in which no barbarians participated. And the Greek stock itself was threefold, comprising Aeolians (in north-western and central Greece), Ionians (in Attica and central Asia Minor) and Dorians (in the Peloponnese, Crete, Thera and southern Asia Minor, including Rhodes).

For most Greeks the local community was everything. In some states, like Thessaly, Locris or Arcadia, the sense of community was not highly developed; those regions contained loose associations of rural settlements. But in much of Greece the local community was equivalent to the polis, a self-centred, autonomous city with a political structure and religious observances peculiar to itself.

The polis, in short, overlaid the concept of Greekness with another: that of belonging to a specific city. In religion and language, for instance, there was a polarity between what was pan-Hellenic and what belonged to each individual city. There did not exist any such entity as 'the Greek language', any more than there was a Greek nation, but only a multiplicity of local dialects. And each state maintained its own cults, while participating in those which were common to all Greeks.

Language and religion formed two criteria in differentiating one city from another. A third lay in the nature of the political system. In theory, each city was fully independent, though as we shall see presently, practice failed to accord with theory. As certain cities increased in power at the expense of others, freedom and independence became words enshrining (more or less remote) aspirations rather than describing the actual state of affairs.

The physical differences between one polis and another are really irrelevant. What made a polis was the presence of certain civic and religious institutions which gave shape to the community of citizens. Citizens did not comprise all, or even most, of the inhabitants of the polis. Barbarians, women, slaves and members of other states resident in the city were in principle excluded from the citizenship; and still other restrictions, differing from city to city, were often imposed.

The institution of slavery was endemic in the Greek states. Most slaves were unransomed prisoners-of-war or the offspring of other slaves. Although formally the chattels of another, slaves did not completely lack juridical rights. The state too was a slave-owner. At Sparta the state slaves, the helots, formed a numerous and economically essential class. But among the Greeks (including the Spartans) slaves did not form a separate caste: citizens could be enslaved, while slaves were sometimes granted their freedom.

Vase painting of an early warship. The Greeks used these vessels to colonize the Mediterranean shores.

The Rise of the City-state

Long before the start of the classical period, Greeks had spread beyond the limits of Old Greece. After the great migrations to the coasts of Asia Minor and the Aegean islands (*c.* 1000–800 BC) there were extensive colonizing movements, in which settlers from individual Greek cities founded a new city either in a different part of Greece or in a barbarian land. The main colonizing age lasted from the eighth century to the sixth century BC, although colonies were still being founded in the classical period. The colonies were so widespread and, once in existence, took on such vigorous life that by the beginning of the fifth century it was not only Greece and the Aegean Sea, with their long coastlines and multitudes of islands, that were thoroughly Hellenized; Greeks had settled in southern Italy and Sicily and as far west as Massilia (Marseilles). Thera had two colonies in Africa, at Cyrene and Naucratis. To the north-east there were powerful thrusts through the Hellespont to Byzantium and to the shores of the Black Sea.

These colonizing movements were accompanied by changes in the cities themselves. The hereditary kings lost their monopoly of power, sharing it with aristocratic families or abandoning it altogether to a combination of noblemen and the emergent mercantile class. Merchants and entrepreneurs were the beneficiaries of colonization and the expansion of trade. The orientalizing style in art and the adoption of writing arose from trading relationships with Asia Minor, Phoenicia and the eastern empires. The use of coinage to a regular standard was learned in the rich empire of Lydia, bordering the Ionian cities.

In their chronic warfare with one another, the Greek cities originally placed great reliance on units of cavalry, accompanied by light-armed archers and missile-throwers. This essentially aristocratic method of fighting underwent a change early in the seventh century BC. The cavalry declined in importance and was supplanted as the principal arm by a body, or phalanx, of closely knit ranks of infantry. The soldiers comprising the phalanx were heavy-armed hoplites, wearing helmet, corslet and greaves, and armed with sword and thrusting-spear. The combination of phalanx with fast-moving, light-armed infantry units became the chief military instrument of the Greek cities; cavalry lost its former supremacy, except in Thessaly. The hoplite took the field as his own man: although subject to the discipline imposed by the city, he provided his equipment and maintained himself out of his private resources. Hoplites, and hoplite tactics, became possible because a greater number of citizens acquired economic independence. And this independence was now gained as often from commercial enterprise as from the traditional source of wealth, ownership of land.

To this pattern Sparta is the outstanding exception. Her citizens, forbidden to engage in commerce, lived on the produce of their estates. In a purely political sense also, the Spartans differed from other cities. In many of them, as we have seen, the collapse of monarchy was followed by aristocratic rule. But in some – Athens, Corinth, Sicyon, Samos – a despot seized power and ruled arbitrarily. The despots of some cities kept courts of unprecedented brilliance. Their rule proved to be not long-lasting, however, and was abolished everywhere except in Sicily, where it persisted into the classical age. Sparta held aloof. She never fell under a despot, and was instrumental in suppressing despotism elsewhere.

Except in despotic regimes, the body of citizens formed one of the chief institutions of the city. In a democracy, such as Athens was to become during the fifth century BC, this body acquired day-to-day jurisdiction in the conduct of public business; but even at Sparta, not usually classified as a democracy, important matters were referred for discussion by the popular assembly, which also had responsibility for making the laws. Another institution was the council. In a democracy this acted as the executive arm of government, with responsibility to the assembly; but in an aristocratic regime the council was often the true repository of power, containing representatives of the ruling families. Third came the magistrates, the civil and military officials who, in a democracy, gave expression to the popular will. In some Dorian states, however, a small board of magistrates had more extensive powers: for instance, the *kosmoi* in Crete and the ephors at Sparta. Sparta was unique in retaining its two hereditary kings, who had an important military and ceremonial role, and were sometimes influential in shaping policy.

As the horizons of many Greek cities grew wider, their relations with one another and with the world outside Greece took on a new dimension. During the archaic age of the sixth century BC, Athens and Sparta began their rise to pre-eminence in Greece and, for the first time, affected each other's internal affairs. When, in 510 BC, the Spartan king Cleomenes invaded Attica and brought down the despotic regime, his action was not specifically anti-Athenian but formed one facet of a general trend towards expansion and intervention. It was in furtherance of her diplomatic policy that Sparta formed an alliance with cities in the Peloponnese and in central Greece. At the outset, she was merely the most influential of the allies, without a decisive voice; only in the fifth century BC did the alliance grow into a league under Spartan control.

With the end of despotism at Athens, a vacuum was left at the centre of political life. The state was torn by the rivalry of aristocratic families, eager to fill this vacuum, until the leader of one of them, Cleisthenes, prevailed upon the popular assembly to introduce constitutional reforms in 508 BC. These had the effect of distributing political power more widely and more equitably. The number of citizens was enlarged, and ownership of land ceased to be a requirement for

The Aegean.

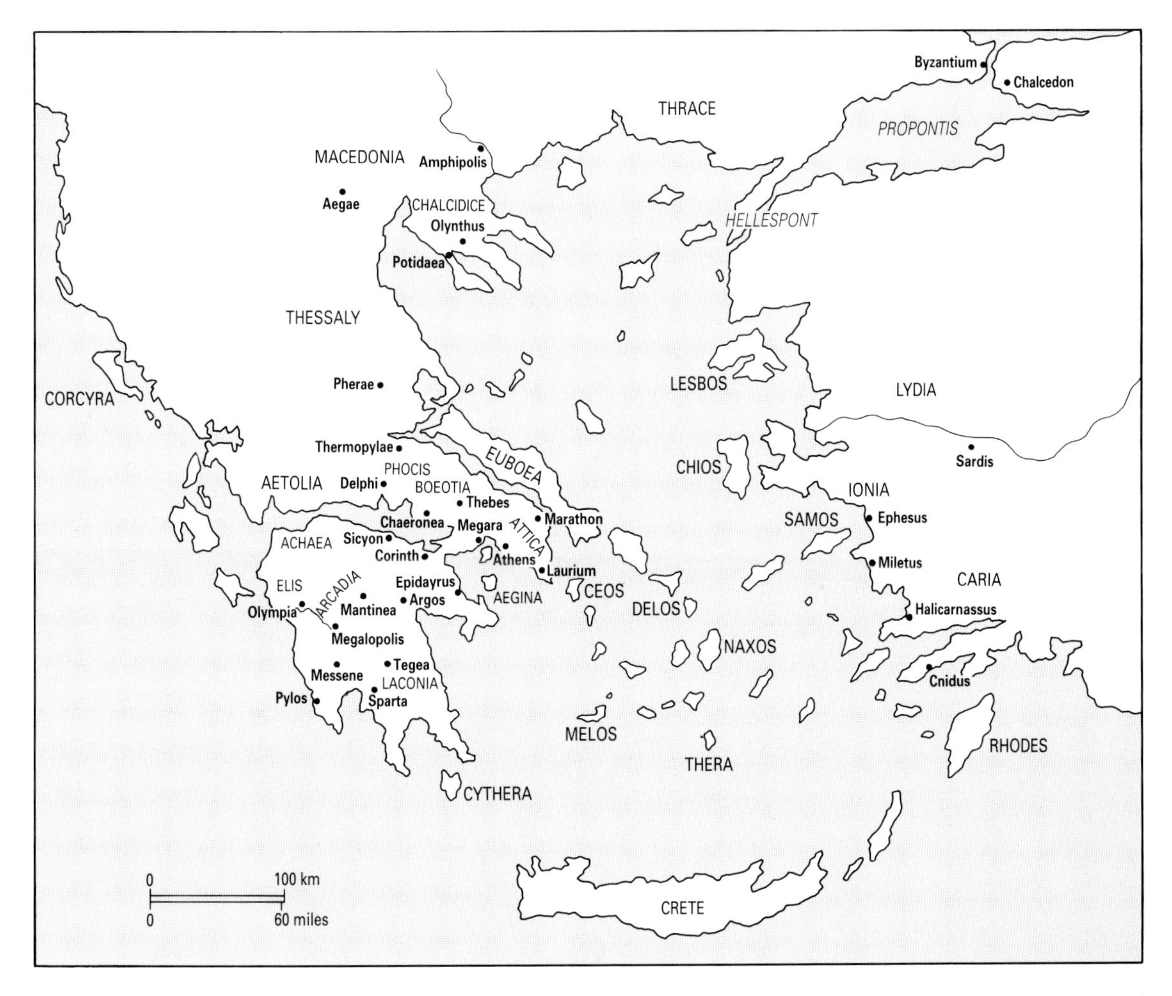

citizenship. The citizens were grouped into ten tribes, based not on kinship but on locality. Each tribe consisted of a number of *demes*, or 'parishes'. The council was now to consist of 500 members, fifty from each tribe. By a further reform, not attributable to Cleisthenes himself, the practice of ostracism was established, whereby a majority of citizens could exile a politician for ten years. Ostracism was intended to frustrate the ambitions of a potential despot; it was later extensively abused.

During the sixth century BC Greek settlements in the west and the east came into conflict with expanding barbarian powers. Little is known for certain about the course of warfare in Sicily. It was a matter partly of fighting among the Greek settlements themselves and partly of the Greeks trying to beat off invasions from Carthage. This north African city had been founded by Phoenicians in a commercial enterprise parallel to that of Greek colonization. Events in the east, on the other hand, can be traced in greater detail. Greek cities in Ionia had an ambiguous relationship with Croesus after he became king of Lydia. Although a professed phil-Hellene, he brought their independence to an end and made them tributary subjects. In 546 BC Croesus was forced to yield to the Persian king Cyrus. Lydia was incorporated into the Persian empire and Croesus' capital, Sardis, became the seat of a Persian satrap. Persian power swelled to monstrous size with the absorption of Lydia, the defeat of Babylon, the invasion of Egypt and a movement into Thrace.

Themistocles (*c.* 528–462 BC), the founder of Greek naval supremacy. In 483 BC he persuaded the Athenians to build a fleet of 200 triremes.

The Struggle against the Persians

In 499 BC the Greek cities in Ionia rebelled against Persian rule. This Ionian Revolt was doomed, given the lack of a unified plan, the strength available to the Persians and the inadequate response from the cities of Old Greece. Only two of these, Athens and Eretria, offered practical help. Assisted by their Athenian and Eretrian allies, in 498 BC the rebels made their way to Sardis and set fire to the city. The news of this action won further adherents to the rebel cause, but the Persians recovered and methodically put down the rebellion. The decisive defeat of a combined Greek fleet at Lade near Miletus, and then the capture of Miletus itself, formed the prelude to the suppression of the revolt in 493 BC.

Athens was now in a perilous situation. But among her citizens were two men of extraordinary ability, through whose talents danger was fought off and the foundations of future power laid. Miltiades (*c.* 550–489 BC) had been despot of the Thracian Chersonese, but in 493 BC he returned to Athens in consequence of a new Persian invasion of Thrace. He combined political experience with military skill and an intimate knowledge of Persian tactics and strategy. In the year of Miltiades' return, Themistocles (*c.* 528–462 BC) was chosen as a magistrate. Two perils appeared to him to threaten Athens by sea. One was posed by the neighbouring island of Aegina, a naval power ruled by a Dorian aristocracy of old-fashioned type; the second by the Persians' freedom to sail the seas at will. He accordingly persuaded his countrymen to establish a new naval base at the Piraeus, applying for the purpose silver from the mines at Laurium in southern Attica. These works were not completed for some time; meanwhile, a further initiative by Themistocles led to the Athenians greatly augmenting their fleet of triremes.

When, or where, the trireme (Greek *trieres*) was invented is not known for certain. During the entire classical period it was the principal warship at the disposal of the Greeks and of their adversaries the Phoenicians. Its crucial importance in the history of Greece, and especially of Athens, was twofold. The Athenian mastery of trireme-fighting led directly to their building, and retaining, an extensive maritime empire. But the trireme also provided a means of rapid communication, and this was an important asset for a city at the head of widely dispersed subject territories. At the same time, the use of the trireme was subject to certain limitations, imposed by its design. It was, in essence, a long, narrow craft propelled by three banks of rowers – about 200 men in all. The bow of the ship formed a beak for ramming.

With the Ionian Revolt put down and Egypt and Thrace made secure, in 490 BC the Persian king, Darius, sent a powerful fleet into Greek waters. The

Persians sailed to Euboea unopposed, settling old scores *en route*. Disembarking near Eretria, they sacked the city and enslaved its inhabitants.

The Persians now crossed to Attica and landed a contingent in the Bay of Marathon. At Miltiades' insistence, Athenian troops marched out and offered battle there. In the fighting that followed Miltiades was himself one of the Athenian generals who, with their Plataean allies, inflicted a defeat on the Persians. At this the Persian ships gathered up the remnant of their force and sailed to Phalerum; but, making no further attempt to land, they then drew off.

Persian ambitions, however, had received only a check. The task of making an outright invasion fell to Darius' son Xerxes. Elaborate preparations were made for leading the army overland from Lydia to Thessaly, the plan being that the ships should keep pace with the advancing army. Xerxes reviewed the Persian and allied host at Sardis, as it was about to set out in the spring of 481 BC. Those Greek cities which were determined to resist Xerxes sent delegates to a congress at Corinth, with a view to coordinating defensive measures.

Their work was excessively difficult. Feuds and suspicions smouldered between various cities. Some states

The Persian invasion of Greece, 480–479 BC.

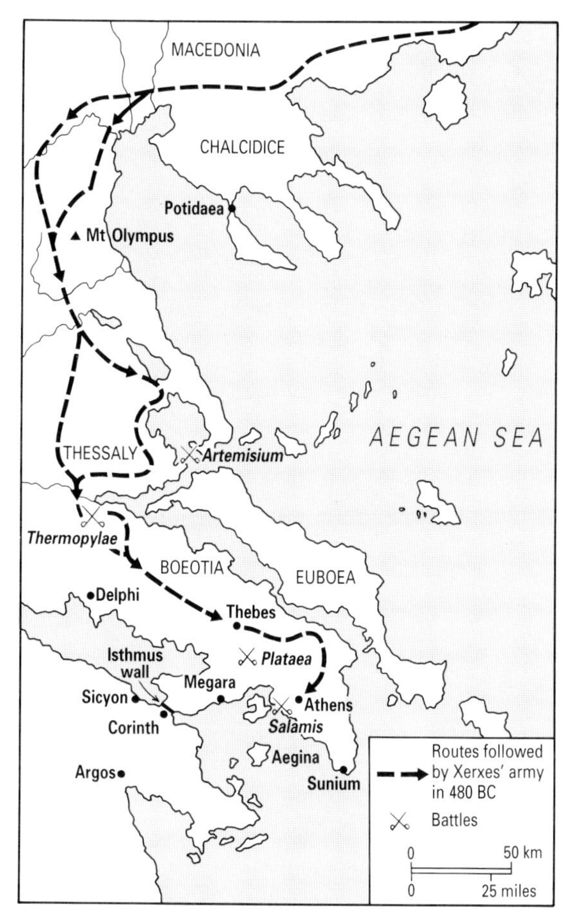

Small bronze statue of a Spartan hoplite showing tresses. At Thermopylae in 480 BC the Spartans dressed their hair before resisting Xerxes' army.

either took a neutral line or actually sided with the Persians. And Gelon, the despot of Syracuse, when asked for assistance, could give none, as he was expecting another invading force from Carthage (it arrived in the following year and was crushed at the battle of Himera). In spite of these obstacles, the congress, with Sparta and Athens taking the leading part, cobbled together a rough plan, which involved forming a line of defence first in Thessaly and then at Thermopylae, a narrow pass in central Greece.

At Xerxes' coming, the Greeks found that they had insufficient force to defend Thessaly, and the Spartan king Leonidas attempted to hold Thermopylae. The king and his army were betrayed and, in 480 BC, fighting with exemplary bravery, were overwhelmed by the Persians.

True to their policy of shadowing the land forces, the Persians had their ships (chiefly manned by Phoenician and Ionian subjects) standing off Artemisium. The Greek triremes which engaged them were not able to prevent their sailing southwards in support of Xerxes' army.

Vase painting of a Greek warship somewhat smaller than the trireme, the vessel used to such effect against the Persian fleet at Salamis in 480 BC.

No further resistance was offered in central Greece. Thebes took the Persians' side and Attica now lay open to the invader. The Athenians evacuated their city and took to the ships. Meanwhile, the Persian fleet had sailed round Sunium and was at Phalerum, waiting for the Athenian and Aeginetan ships to emerge from the straits between Attica and Salamis. But they did not emerge. It was Themistocles' plan to lure the Persians into the straits, where the greater weight of the Athenian triremes could be brought to bear, and they would be able to ram the enemy in narrow waters. And, when the Persians at last moved, everything turned out according to plan. One day's fighting off Salamis put paid to the Persian fleet as an effective force. Its remnants made for home, while the army was withdrawn northwards to winter in Thessaly.

Little attempt was made at sea to follow up the advantage gained at Salamis. On land, the interests of Athens and Sparta diverged dangerously as the Persians marched through Boeotia and into Attica. The Athenians trusted that a Peloponnesian army would come to their assistance, but as none seemed to be coming, they again evacuated their city. When the Spartans eventually dispatched a hoplite force, the Persians withdrew to Boeotia, where they took up a well-fortified position. The combined Greek army then followed. Our sources fail to elucidate the movements of the two armies, but the conclusive Greek victory at the battle of Plataea in 479 BC seems to have been won despite effective deployment of Persian cavalry and despite lack of cohesion on the Greek side. But the decisive nature of the victory was not in doubt. It had the effect of denying to the Persians any future intervention in the Greek homeland; there was even a Greek counter-attack in the same year. A naval victory off Mycale reversed the effects of the battle of Lade and began the process of detaching the eastern Greeks from dependence upon Persia.

The leading Greek cities in Sicily, Syracuse and Acragas, were not affected directly by these events. Gelon's victory at Himera in 480 BC secured a period of relative peace in which the great despots, Gelon himself, Hieron and Theron, held court. In splendour and taste they surpassed the despotic regimes of the sixth century BC, and nor were they inferior in military vigour, as Hieron showed when he defeated the Etruscans at Cumae in 474 BC. But the arbitrary and oppressive nature of despotic rule was blatant – never more so than when Hieron uprooted a whole population in order to found his new city of Aetna. In 467 BC, a year after his death, despotism at Syracuse was put down and a democracy established.

The cities of Old Greece had found it hard enough to sink their differences when the Persians were in their very heartland. There can be no wonder, then, that after a short while only lip-service was paid to the idea of a Hellenic confederation. The two great powers reacted in opposite ways to the removal of the Persian threat. Apart from one final act of collaboration, in which she helped Athens liberate Byzantium and the cities of Cyprus, after 477 BC Sparta abdicated the larger role she had played in the Persian Wars. Although her military strength ensured that she remained head of the Peloponnesian League, she reverted to the state she had been before Xerxes' invasion. Eschewing commerce and the higher arts of civilization, the Spartan citizen class lived, as before, on the produce of Laconia and the subject state of Messenia. The strict course of military training obligatory on all citizens provided a corps of hoplites to intimidate external enemies and also to keep down the helots.

The Rivalry of Athens and Sparta

The Athenians were quick to exploit the situation in which they found themselves. Instead of allowing the eastern Greeks to resume their former independence, they established an alliance based on their own maritime supremacy and having as one of its aims the protection of their grain route through the Hellespont. This alliance comprised many Aegean islands and cities in Asia Minor, Thrace, the Chersonese and Propontis. Some states were admitted to the alliance on equal terms, but from the inception of the confederacy in 477 BC most allies were obliged to pay a monetary tribute. The common treasury of the alliance was kept on the island of Delos, although the treasurers themselves were all Athenians. The chief naval base was the Piraeus, which the Athenians now fortified in accordance with Themistocles' proposal.

The external policy of Athens was conceived in highly aggressive terms. An ally was not allowed to secede; those who tried were forcibly brought back. The Athenians conducted two successful campaigns against Persian strongholds. In command was Miltiades' son Cimon, who was repeatedly elected one of the ten generals by the Athenian assembly. The generals (*strategoi*) formed a board for the prosecution of war; and, since naval power formed the basis of the Athenian alliance, a general could acquire exceptional prestige and, with it, strong political influence. This was certainly the case with Cimon (died 450 BC) and, after him, Pericles (*c.* 500–429 BC). Cimon, an aristocrat, was content with the Cleisthenic constitution, which left the conduct of affairs largely in the hands of the great families. As Athens took a tighter grip on her alliance, and controlled an increasing volume of trade in the Aegean, the lowest class of citizens (those who did menial work, tilled the soil and manned the triremes) still had little effective political power. A radical party arose in opposition to Cimon, determined to enhance the role of this class. Ephialtes was leader of the radicals, to whom the young Pericles adhered. Like Cimon, both of them were aristocrats; but their paths to the apex of power differed from his. The first part of their programme involved the emasculation of the Council of the Areopagus, the chief repository of aristocratic privilege: in 461 BC most of its functions were transferred to the Council of 500, or the popular lawcourts. The assassination of Ephialtes, and also the ostracism of Cimon, followed shortly afterwards.

After these events the way was clear for Pericles to pursue his political career. His ascendancy in the Athenian state, which lasted for the next thirty years or so, must not be mistaken for absolute dominance. Although to our eyes the events of those years seem to fall into a definite pattern, we cannot be sure to what extent Pericles was personally in control of them.

Pericles (*c.* 500–429 BC), the leading Athenian statesman during the bitter struggle with Sparta.

A series of measures completed the process begun by the reform of 461 BC. The radical democracy which evolved during the Periclean period became the hallmark of the classical Athenian polis, except for brief interludes in 411 and 404 BC. The functions of the popular courts were extended at the expense of magistrates' powers, and payment for jury service made it possible for poorer citizens to participate in the work of the courts. The assembly still elected the generals, but minor officials were chosen by lot in the tribes. All public affairs, including relations with the allies, now came within the purview of the assembly. While democracy advanced, the citizenship was made more exclusive. A law of 451 BC provided that only the legitimate offspring of two Athenian parents could be enrolled as citizens.

In their operations abroad, the Athenians showed themselves the same brash interventionists they had been in Cimon's time. Many of their actions now had a distinctly anti-Spartan tendency. In 457 BC, for the first time, Athens and Sparta came into military collision. The battle of Tanagra (between Peloponnesians and a joint Athenian-Argive force) was

A silver coin of Athens showing the goddess Athena and her owl. This was the standard coinage of the Athenian empire.

inconclusive, but a few weeks later the Athenians were back in Boeotia, winning a battle and taking hostages. They also completed the long walls from Athens to Phalerum and to the Piraeus, so removing their city from the danger of direct assault by land.

Athens had now reached the high-water mark of her power. She received the capitulation of Aegina, who became a tributary ally. An Athenian fleet sailed round the Peloponnese and set fire to Spartan dockyards, while an army with Pericles landed near Sicyon. In 454 BC, the treasury of the alliance was transferred from Delos to Athens – an open acknowledgement that one Greek city had acquired imperial power over others.

Cimon, recalled from exile, negotiated a five-year truce with the Peloponnesian League in 451 BC. While it was in force, the Athenians abstained from attacking Sparta directly, but they found other outlets for their energy. On his last expedition, trying to detach Cyprus from Persian control, Cimon died and, despite some Athenian victories, the main aim was not achieved. By the terms of the Peace of Callias in 449 BC, Athens recognized Persian rule in Cyprus and secured a guarantee that her eastern subjects would not be molested.

On the expiry of the five-year truce, the Athenians overreached themselves in central Greece and lost control of Boeotia. Soon afterwards, both Euboea and

Athens and the Piraeus. At the end of the Peloponnesian War in 404 BC the Spartans demolished the long walls.

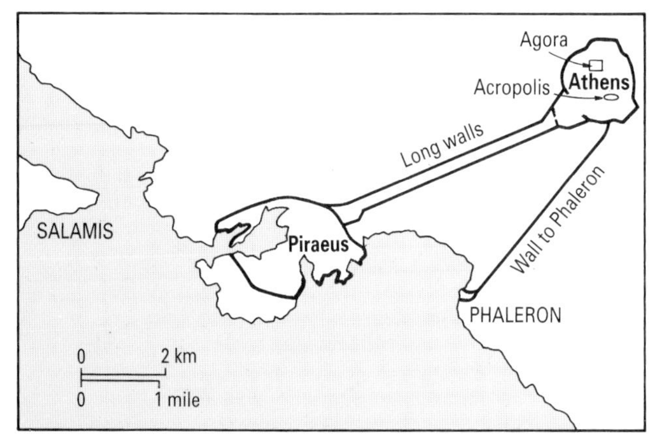

Megara seceded. The island of Euboea was won back, but Megara returned to the Spartan League. A Peloponnesian army marched but never made contact with Pericles' forces. The situation, however, was potentially dangerous, and called into being a solemn thirty-year treaty between Athens and the Spartan alliance (445 BC).

Two incidents involving Corinth and Athens were later cited as pretexts for the war between the power blocs. The first concerned the Athenians giving aid to Corcyra, a colony but now the enemy of Corinth. And then another Corinthian colony, Potidaea in Chalcidice, was a tributary of Athens. The Potidaeans, assured of Spartan support, left the Athenian empire in 432 BC, whereupon an Athenian force began to invest the city.

Later that year, Corinthian delegates spoke at a meeting of the Spartan alliance and urged a declaration of war, on the ground that the Athenians had violated the treaty. Two other delegates made complaints against Athens: the Aeginetan claimed that his city had been refused autonomy and the Megarian, that his countrymen were denied access to the centre of trade at Athens, the market, or *agora*. These arguments, when referred to the Spartan assembly, were thought sufficient to justify Sparta in declaring war on behalf of her alliance. The conflict itself, later known as the Peloponnesian War, had two distinct phases, the first lasting from 431 to 421, the second from 413 to 404 BC.

The Peloponnesian War (431–404 BC)

The early years of the war belonged largely to Athens. Despite two setbacks in 429 BC – the great plague and the death of Pericles – the Athenians carried out many successful operations, especially at sea. Spartan strategy consisted of an annual invasion of Attica to destroy the growing crops – an irritant, no more, since Athens went on importing supplies with impunity. It was at this time that the demagogue Cleon (died 422 BC) acquired an influential voice in the Athenian assembly.

Two brilliant strokes brought the war close to Sparta herself. The capture of some hoplites at Pylos, on the south-western side of the Peloponnese, was regarded as so serious by the Spartans that they sent envoys to negotiate a treaty. However, the terms dictated by Cleon were far too stringent to be acceptable. In 425 BC Cleon himself inflicted a humiliating reverse on Sparta by going to Pylos and ignoring the usual 'rules' of hoplite-fighting. The following year the Athenians established a base on Cythera, from which they carried out raids on Spartan territory. But their attempt to gain advantage from a democratic rising in Boeotia ended in disaster, and some tributary cities in Chalcidice and Thrace were lost to the Spartan general Brasidas. After a year's armistice, hostilities were resumed in the north, where Cleon fell in the fighting at Amphipolis. Brasidas also received a fatal wound. The Athenians were now ready to discuss terms. A fifty-year treaty between the two sides was ratified in 421 BC; at the same time Athens and Sparta, as individual cities, formed an alliance, also to last for fifty years.

It proved impossible to carry out the terms of the treaty, and the alliance was unpopular with Sparta's own confederates. Moreover war-parties in both Athens and Sparta kept things on the boil. Among the Athenians, the most forceful advocate of anti-Spartan measures was the nobleman Alcibiades (*c.* 450–404 BC), a kinsman of Pericles. At the insistence of Alcibiades, the Athenians concluded an alliance with Argos and other enemies of Sparta in 420 BC.

The treaty might still have been rescued had the Athenians not embarked, in the summer of 415 BC, on a grandiose scheme which was bound to lead to fresh hostilities. Their real object was the absorption of Sicily into the empire. Alcibiades was one of the generals leading the expedition to Sicily, but he was recalled to face charges at Athens. Instead, he made his way to Sparta, where his febrile energies were turned against his own countrymen. He persuaded the Spartans to give help to Syracuse, a Corinthian colony now in danger of an Athenian attack. In response, Sparta sent as general Gylippus, who took up his command in 414 BC, at a time when Athenian forces were also making provocative attacks in the Peloponnese.

The following year saw the formal reopening of the Peloponnesian War, with the Spartan king Agis advancing into Attica and making Decelea, some miles north of Athens, into a permanently manned fortress. In Sicily the Athenians besieging Syracuse tried to wall in the city and starve out the defenders. In this, however, they were unsuccessful, and Gylippus, with the Syracusans, broke through the besiegers' lines. The Syracusans next engaged the Athenian fleet in the great harbour and won a complete victory. The land forces of Athens, trying to make their way to a friendly Sicilian city, were cut off and forced to surrender.

So within a few months Athens was deprived of the powerful armada she had sent to Sicily. Her defeat fundamentally affected the course of the Peloponnesian War, and also had important consequences for Sicily itself. The continuing differences among the Greek cities in Sicily encouraged the Carthaginians once more to attempt the conquest of the island. To this end they deployed mercenaries, with archers and slingers wearing down the defenders' resistance before storm-troops made a frontal assault. In the course of the fighting a Syracusan, Dionysius, displayed military talents above the rest. He was given the title 'general with absolute powers', and for many years he ruled Syracuse as a despot (405–367 BC).

At first, Dionysius I was obliged to recognize Carthaginian overlordship. This accommodation enabled him to perfect the various warlike arms that in time he would use to expel the barbarians and then establish his own supremacy. His battle-fleet was manned partly by mercenary crews. The army, also containing a large mercenary element, was reorganized in a scientific manner. The catapult was invented and the siege engine made more versatile and more powerful. In his defensive measures, Dionysius consulted his personal position as much as the safety of the city.

In repeated conflicts with the Carthaginians, Dionysius greatly weakened their grip on Sicily, but could not drive them out altogether. On his death a confused power struggle followed in which his son was unable to resist other claimants. Timoleon, a Corinthian, finally put down despotism at Syracuse and in 343 BC restored the democracy. Four years later he defeated another invading army and made peace with Carthage.

The Athenian defeat at Syracuse in 413 BC left the initiative with Sparta, and the next two years saw a contraction of Athenian power. When some subject states of Athens showed a willingness to secede, Alcibiades procured the dispatch of a Peloponnesian fleet. Several important cities joined the Spartan side. While Athens was doing her level best to shore up her empire, Sparta was also showing signs of desperation. The character of her alliance was changing. A resident magistrate was appointed to govern Lesbos, while Rhodes had to render tribute – indications that the alliance of free states was being turned into an empire of Athenian type. Moreover, Sparta entered into negotiations with Persia. The eastern cities were abandoned to her, in return for money and ships.

The Persian satrap in Ionia played a devious game. Alcibiades had now left Sparta and joined the satrap's court. He wished to resume his prominent place at Athens, but rightly considered this impossible so long as the democracy held firm. His intrigues, aimed at the establishment of oligarchy, were conducted through Pisander, then serving with the fleet at Samos. Alcibiades was unable to secure a promise of Persian help, but still Pisander's faction thought the time ripe to set up an oligarchic regime both in Athens and at Samos. After preparing public opinion and resorting to terrorist methods, the conspirators engineered a *coup d'état* at Athens in the summer of 411 BC. The government was now in the hands of a clique of 400 men. While the oligarchic *coup* succeeded in Athens, it foundered at Samos. There, the fleet and army declared for democracy and also brought back Alcibiades. The men at Samos called for the 400 to be deposed and an assembly of 5,000 to be constituted. This proposal was put into effect, Alcibiades was recalled and a limited democracy established. On the naval front, thanks to Alcibiades' energy, there were some brilliant successes, culminating in his action at the Hellespont in 410 BC. A few weeks later the oligarchy came to an end and the assembly of all Athenian citizens regained the government of the state.

Despite their continuing victories at sea, the Athenians could now only postpone defeat, not avoid it altogether. In 407 BC the Spartans formally coordinated their war effort with Persia and sent Lysander (died 395 BC) to Rhodes as admiral. He got the better of Alcibiades' fleet at Notium, near Ephesus, whereupon, in 406 BC, Alcibiades was superseded by Conon (*c.* 444–392 BC). He in turn won an important victory in the same year at the battle of Arginusae.

The destruction of the Athenians' fleet, and with it the loss of their sea power and empire, resulted from

The Parthenon in Athens, the chief temple and the imperial treasury until the city's surrender to Sparta in 404 BC.

Lysander's seizing an opportunity suddenly presented to him in 405 BC. While engaged in operations in the Hellespont, he saw the Athenian ships beached on the northern shore at Aegispotami, with their crews some way off. It did not take long for Lysander's own men to take possession of the ships and round up the crews.

Lysander brought back Byzantium into the Spartan alliance, claimed Lesbos for Sparta and sailed for the Piraeus with a large fleet. Anchoring in the harbour, he was able to deny the Athenians all imports of food. Agis was still at Decelea, and now the other Spartan king, Pausanias, led an army into Attica. The citizens held out for a few months, but in early 404 BC they were forced to accept the terms dictated by Sparta. She insisted on the destruction of the long walls, the recall of political exiles, the surrender of all but twelve triremes and the conclusion of an alliance between the two cities – which left Athens the tributary partner. In other respects Athens was to retain her autonomy. On the Athenian acceptance of these terms, the war was concluded by the withdrawal of Lysander and the Spartan kings.

Fourth-century Struggles for Hegemony

Material losses and the blows to her self-confidence meant that Athens would never again be so rich or so powerful as in the days of Pericles, although in time she was able to establish a new maritime alliance. The years from 404 to 370 BC are often known as the era of Spartan hegemony, but it was only intermittently that Sparta enjoyed undisputed mastery over the other Greek states.

Subsequent to his stunning victory at Aegispotami, Lysander set himself the task of dismembering the maritime empire of Athens. He established Spartan governors and garrisons in some cities; others he brought under the control of oligarchs. His influence was greater than that of the regularly constituted authorities at Sparta and, as such, was much resented there.

Shortly after the capitulation at Athens, a second *coup* brought to power a government of Thirty, imposed upon the Athenian assembly by Lysander. Under the protection of a Spartan garrison, the Thirty conducted a sickening rule of terror. War broke out between them and certain democrats who had taken up a position in the Piraeus. A clash left the leaders of the Thirty dead and caused their replacement by a more moderate board of ten in 403 BC. Lysander again intervened with an army and a blockading fleet, whereupon Pausanias took an army of his own into Attica. After complex negotiations, Pausanias managed to reconcile the chief parties in contention. A general amnesty was proclaimed and the full democracy brought back.

By the beginning of the fourth century BC a great change had come over the Greek world. The Spartans' conduct showed the hollowness of their claim to be the liberators of Greece. In the event, they had used the eastern cities as bargaining counters with Persia, and imposed on the other subjects of the Athenian empire a rule just as oppressive as that of Athens herself.

King Agis punished with a heavy hand the citizens of Elis, on the ground that they had taken the anti-Spartan side (*c.* 400 BC). He was succeeded by Agesilaus, who pursued an equally imperialistic policy. And Sparta was again drawn into Persian affairs. Cyrus, who had helped Sparta during the war, led a rebellion against his brother Artaxerxes II in 401 BC. The Spartans gave Cyrus the requisite naval support. His army contained mercenaries from various Greek cities, and his march up-country saw the use of Greek mercenary troops on an unprecedented scale. The Greeks were successful in the fighting, but Cyrus himself was killed. The collapse of the revolt left a large Greek army stranded deep inside hostile territory. They managed to force their way northwards to the Black Sea, whence a long route brought them back to the Bosporus. Their experiences had made of them a corps of hardened veterans.

After suppressing Cyrus' rebellion, Artaxerxes thought to assert his claim over the Greek cities in Ionia. Sparta intervened with a considerable force, including many troops who had seen service with Cyrus. The Persians were forced on the defensive and in 397 BC a truce was agreed. But within a year a larger expedition was launched against Persia. Agesilaus' campaigns on land had a degree of success, but no intelligent plan underlay them and he left Asia with little accomplished. A Spartan fleet sustained a crushing defeat at the hands of Conon, the Athenian admiral who was now in the pay of the Persians. This battle, fought off Cnidus in 394, led to a weakening of Spartan influence in Ionia.

While Agesilaus was prosecuting his fruitless designs in Asia, anti-Spartan sentiments erupted at home. The so-called Corinthian War (395–386 BC) consisted of a series of collisions between Sparta on the one side and her allies Athens, Corinth and Thebes on the other. An action at Haliartus, in Boeotia, resulted in the death of Lysander and Pausanias' return to Sparta in disgrace (395 BC). The balance was restored in the following year, when Agesilaus brought his army back to Greece and inflicted a defeat on the anti-Spartan coalition on the plain of Coronea. But the victory had no consequence and, shortly after winning it, Agesilaus simply went home. In the remaining years of the Corinthian War, the Spartans vainly tried to break into the stronghold which their enemies had established at Corinth. The circumstances were unsuitable for hoplite-fighting, so mercenaries and light-armed troops came into their own.

In 393 BC Athens at last felt strong enough to rebuild her long walls. A serious threat to Sparta was posed by the fleet under Conon, which made raids upon the Peloponnese from its base at Melos. Since Pharnabazus, the Persian satrap, was giving strong support to the enemies of Sparta, the stalemate could not be broken by purely military means. The Spartans therefore took a diplomatic initiative. In an attempt to turn Persia against Athens, they sent Antalcidas to the satrap at Sardis, who promised to take proposals for a peace treaty to Artaxerxes. The focus of military operations now shifted once more to the Hellespont. At first Athenian power was strengthened by the operations of her light-armed troops. But in time a reverse was effected by the same Antalcidas who had gone on the embassy to Asia. He found the means (contributed in part by Dionysius of Syracuse) to cut off the Athenian fleet and so cause a stranglehold on the trade route through the straits. In 386 BC Athens was therefore willing to accept Artaxerxes' proposals, which formed the basis of the King's Peace: the Greek cities in Asia were declared to belong to Persia, while the rest were to be free and autonomous.

Five years later the Spartan authorities acted to protect their interests in Chalcidice, which, they said, were threatened by the city of Olynthus. A Spartan fleet duly arrived at Potidaea. But as the Peloponnesian army marched through Boeotia, its general became aware that a strong pro-Spartan faction existed at Thebes. He therefore seized his opportunity and brought the city under Spartan control. All this time, the Spartans kept up their pressure on Olynthus, forcing it to capitulate in 379 BC. Later that year a counter-revolution at Thebes ended the Spartan occupation and put in power a regime hostile to Sparta. The Spartans made repeated attempts to retrieve the situation by sending armies into Boeotia, but these were not able to attack Thebes directly, and so left garrisons to inflict what damage they could. An incursion into Attica by the Spartan Sphodrias in 378 BC only helped to draw Athens closer to Thebes.

Circumstances now favoured the formation of a new Athenian alliance, and its programme, based on the King's Peace, was announced in 377 BC. This alliance, unlike that of the fifth century, was to be an association of free and sovereign states, with Athens at their head. Conversely, the Spartans exercised a tighter control over their own alliance, in preparation for the forthcoming war against Thebes and Athens.

The war, when it came, saw further incursions into Boeotia by Peloponnesian forces, which were, however, unable to prevent the resurrection of the Boeotian League under Theban hegemony. In 376 BC an Athenian fleet with Timotheus in command won a naval victory off Naxos; the following year Timotheus sailed round the Peloponnese and won Corcyra for Athens. In 374 BC Jason of Pherae was elected overlord of Thessaly. His ambition was boundless, and he had at his disposal powerful forces of ships and cavalry. But Sparta was too hard-pressed to deal with this threat.

In response to the aggressive conduct of Thebes in central Greece, the Athenians sent ambassadors to Sparta to explore the possibility of renewing the King's Peace. One of the Theban envoys was Epaminondas (*c.* 420–362 BC), who had already shown the quality of his generalship against Spartan forces. The basis of the proposed peace (the Peace of Callias) was that alliances should be dissolved and all cities left autonomous. But an unbridgeable gap opened between Thebes and Sparta. Agesilaus forbade Epaminondas to take the oath in the name of the Boeotians, since to do so would have recognized the existence of a confederation. The Theban delegation accordingly left for home in 371 BC, excluded from the peace agreement.

Sparta now determined to make an end of Thebes. The Spartan king Cleombrotus led an army into Boeotia and encamped near Leuctra. With his numerically superior forces, he might have won a hoplite engagement of traditional type. But Epaminondas deployed his cavalry so effectively and made of his left wing such a powerful striking force that he routed the Peloponnesians, killing Cleombrotus and decimating his army. More Spartan troops were mobilized, but before they could reach Boeotia Jason had already arrived from Thessaly. He assumed the role of arbitrator and caused the two sides to disengage. Returning north, he made further far-reaching plans, but these were frustrated by his assassination in the following year. With Sparta more or less impotent and the Athenians' movements greatly curtailed, Thebes was able to enjoy a brief hegemony. Epaminondas continued to take a leading part in formulating and executing policy, but after his death Thebes lost her commanding position.

The period of Theban supremacy falls into three phases. During the first, the tide of anti-Spartan feeling in 370 BC led to the reconstitution of Mantinea under a democracy and the formation of an Arcadian League. When Sparta took up a threatening posture, Epaminondas brought an army into the Peloponnese. A career of destruction brought him almost into Sparta itself, the first recorded invasion of the Eurotas valley. There a new city, Messene, was founded, so depriving the Spartans of their territory west of Taygetus and establishing an entity perpetually hostile to them. Sparta now turned for help to Athens and in 369 BC formed an alliance with her. Although their joint action hindered another expedition of Epaminondas, he did establish Megalopolis as the capital of the Arcadian League. Yet another invasion of the Peloponnese, far from enhancing Theban prestige, actually drove the Arcadians into the arms of Athens three years later.

In the second phase of their hegemony, the Thebans were engaged in a struggle with Athenian maritime power. Both Thebes and Athens had tried, with varying success, to influence the course of events in Thessaly and Macedonia. Now Athens took the initiative in the eastern and northern Aegean, and Timotheus secured the adherence of a number of cities, including some at the Hellespont. For the first time the Boeotians built a sizeable fleet and sent it, with Epaminondas in command, to break the connection of the maritime states with Athens. Considerable success attended this expedition. The defection of Byzantium from Athens in 364 BC was followed by unrest in other cities.

Serious dissension arose among the members of the Arcadian League, with the result that Epaminondas again had to invade the Peloponnese. At the battle of Mantinea in 362 BC, Epaminondas won a great victory over the Arcadians, with whom Sparta and Athens had allied themselves. The tactics adopted by Epaminondas were the same as at Leuctra; again his cavalry proved far superior, and again his powerful hoplite wedge drove deep into the enemy lines. But Epaminondas was killed in the battle. With his death, Athens and Sparta regained a certain freedom of action. Agesilaus led a force of mercenaries to Egypt, in support of an ultimately successful rebellion against the Persian king. Agesilaus raised some funds for his city, but died on campaign in 360 BC.

The Rise of Macedon

The Athenians set about restoring their power in what they regarded as their sphere of influence. While they recovered cities in Euboea and in the region of the Hellespont, their expansion westwards into Thrace was checked by the emergence of Macedonia, where Philip II had come to power in 359 BC. His first task was the reorganization of the army, the instrument by which he then subjugated the neighbouring peoples. Having welded together the disparate tribes into a great military power, ruled absolutely by himself, Philip set out on a course which was to bring him the mastery of Greece.

Athens could not bring her full force to bear upon Philip (even if there had been a unanimous wish to do so), because she found it necessary to deal with a series of secessions in the eastern Aegean. Revolt among her allies was fomented by Mausolus, the nominal satrap of Caria, who between 377 and 353 BC established a strong base at Halicarnassus. Chios and Rhodes were lost to Athens, and her naval operations to reclaim them ended in failure. She was still able to intervene effectively among the warring satraps, but this intervention did nothing to win back the rebellious cities. This 'War of the Allies' was concluded in 355 BC by a peace which recognized the independence of the eastern cities.

Philip derived enormous benefit from the distractions of Athens in the east. He seized a number of important cities in Chalcidice and Thrace and took possession of the gold-fields and forests in the region round Crenides. This place he settled with Macedonians and renamed Philippi. During Philip's campaigns in the north, the so-called Sacred War had broken out in central Greece, probably in 356 BC. This took the form of a discontinuous series of conflicts, often degenerating into acts of brigandage by mercenary troops, which did not really come to an end until the conclusion of peace in 346 BC. The council which had charge of Apollo's sanctuary at Delphi fined the people of Phocis in consequence of an act of sacrilege. Far from paying the fine, the Phocians took control of the sanctuary and helped themselves to more and more of the temple

Demosthenes (384–322 BC), the outspoken opponent of Macedon in Athens.

treasures. Many other Greek cities were drawn into the conflict. Athens and Sparta took the Phocian side. After some successes, the Phocian general Philomelus was killed in a confused engagement. In 354 BC Onomarchus inherited the war from Philomelus and pursued it with equal vigour, but on going to help his Thessalian ally, he became embroiled with Philip and was killed in his turn. Philip then advanced as far as Thermopylae, where he was checked by the presence of an Athenian force. Further fighting resulted in a great decline of Phocian power.

During the next few years there were skirmishes between Macedonian and Athenian ships. The best efforts of Philip were concentrated on Olynthus, an important city in the Chalcidice. The Athenians were roused by Demosthenes, the leader of the anti-Macedonian party, to intervene in defence of Olynthus, but they failed to prevent its capitulation to Philip in 348 BC. The result was that Chalcidice now passed altogether under Macedonian control. At the same time a movement in Euboea led to the secession of most of the island from Athens, a blow much closer to home. The steady increase in Philip's prestige led to his being invited by the Thebans for help against Phocis in the Sacred War. At Athens, the desire for peace drove out other considerations and an embassy was sent to negotiate with Philip. The resulting Peace of Philocrates (346 BC) excluded the sacrilegious Phocians.

Whereas Philip's mastery in northern Greece was recognized by his assuming the overlordship of Thessaly, in Thrace he established fortresses owing allegiance to Macedonia. Only the Chersonese and Propontis were denied him for the moment. Penetrating the Hellespont, the Macedonians seized a convoy of merchant ships bound for the Piraeus, an act which caused the Athenians to declare war in 340 BC. Despite a protracted siege, Philip was unable to take the cities of Perinthus and Byzantium, to which not only the Athenians but also the Persians gave support.

The political acumen of Philip enabled him to make up for this rebuff by intervening once more in central Greece. Another case of sacrilege had been alleged: this time the culprits were the people of Amphissa in western Locris. Philip accepted an invitation to become general in a war against them. While prosecuting this war, he made for Elatea, the principal city of Phocis, which he turned into a fortified base of operations. The threat to Athens was immediate. Both Philip and Athens tried to court the Boeotians, who in the end decided to renounce their alliance with Philip and make common cause with Athens.

The decisive battle was fought at Chaeronea in the summer of 338 BC. A fatal gap was opened between the Athenian hoplites and the Theban 'sacred band', a picked corps of troops. The latter were cut down in a cavalry charge led by Philip's son Alexander. Philip's defeat of his enemies was absolute, but his treatment of them differed. Thebes lost her primacy in the Boeotian League and her men were sold into slavery. The Athenians, on the other hand, were spared the threat of invasion or military occupation so long as they dissolved their alliance and became the allies of Philip. His settlement of the Peloponnese was accepted by all the states concerned, except Sparta.

Philip followed his victory by a political settlement more far-reaching than any which had preceded it. He instituted a confederation of Greek states, in which they were all autonomous but at the same time lost the power of initiating action outside their own borders, since Philip reserved to himself the presidency and military command of the league. The new league met at Corinth in 338 BC and again in the following year, all the major states except Sparta sending delegates. The fragility of the league was demonstrated when cities began to fall away immediately on Philip's death in 336 BC. Nevertheless, the fact that such a league had been imposed on the Greek cities by a Macedonian king announced the approaching end of the system of independent city-states. The decline of the system was accelerated in the reign of Alexander.

Religion and Its Rivals

A pre-eminent mark of Greekness was the possession of a common religion. The shrines of Zeus at Olympia and Dodona, and those of Apollo at Delphi and Delos, were the great cult centres of the Greek world, existing alongside those which each city possessed. Zeus' shrine at Dodona in Epirus was of immense antiquity, but as a place of oracular response it was overshadowed by the shrine of (Pythian) Apollo at Delphi, to which even non-Greeks had recourse. Replies were delivered by a priestess while in a state of divine possession and were recorded in writing. Questions of both personal and public import were put to the Delphic oracle, and its answers were sometimes manipulated for political reasons, with the result that the reputation of the oracle began to decline after the Persian Wars. In its greatest days, however, Delphi contained many choice offerings, which were kept in the treasuries belonging to the various cities.

The importance of Olympia and Delphi was not confined to their role as cult-places. The Olympic and Pythian games held there were the principal pan-Hellenic gatherings. And these games were intimately connected with religious festivals: the magnificence of the games and the competitors' prestige, together with the offerings they brought, increased the honour of the presiding god. In classical times these games formed a recurrent group together with the Nemean (in honour of Zeus) and the Isthmian (in honour of Poseidon) games. An Olympiad was the four-year period between one celebration of the Olympic games and the next: the Olympiads were a convenient pan-Hellenic method of dating complementary to local systems, which were usually based on magistracies.

By the classical period the temple had become a ubiquitous mark of Greek civilization. But sacrifices to the gods did not of their own nature require temples and for many centuries had had none. The burnt sacrifice of an animal in the open air was the norm, although bloodless offerings (as of barley) were also made. Divination formed an ingredient of some sacrifices. Once temples were founded, they provided an impressive background for the open-air ritual and a fitting home for the god's cult image. The image was adorned at festival times, so forming the centrepiece of religious observances, but it remained only an image and was never identified with the godhead. Temples and sacrifices were in fact the outward manifestations of the traditional, or Olympian, religion.

Gods and Men

One component of this traditional religion, the family of anthropomorphic deities, formed part of the Indo-European heritage and was represented in the earliest poetry of India and Iran. And the succession myth, told in Hesiod's *Theogony*, whereby the supreme god (Zeus) ousted his father (Cronus), was not original to the Greeks but had been borrowed from West Asia. Furthermore, the Greek system, once formed, lay open to influences from Egypt and Asia Minor. From these and still other sources there emerged a diversity of myths, most of them anchored to specific places in Greece or abroad. Such myths comprised a treasure-house of story, still available to the classical painters, sculptors and poets. Myth gave shape to episodes in the past which most commonly concerned the ancient communion between men and gods. But myth also had an irrational element, a dark side of the human consciousness, which was never entirely forgotten even in the brilliant creations of the fifth century BC.

The Olympian system of gods and goddesses is displayed with consummate clarity in the *Iliad* and *Odyssey* of Homer. These are not in any sense religious documents, but epic poems relating exploits of heroes and the gods' part in them. Although of Ionian growth (*c.* 700 BC), the Homeric poems became a common Greek possession, and perhaps the most precious of all. They bestowed upon the Greek race, and the Greek language, an identity never subsequently lost, and they gave definitive shape to the Hellenic gods and to the gods' relations with one another and with mankind.

There is in Homer a universal belief in the existence of a supernatural order of beings. The high gods dwell on Olympus under the sovereignty of Zeus; Hera, his sister-wife, is concerned with the sanctity of marriage. The sea is Poseidon's domain. The earth contains swarms of lesser divinities: spirits of the mountains, woods, springs and rivers. Below ground is the kingdom of Hades and Persephone, who rule over the souls of the dead.

The Olympian gods form a family, often a quarrelsome one. Apart from Hera, they were born from the union of Zeus with lesser goddesses or mortal women. His progeny includes Demeter, Hermes, Artemis and her brother Apollo, Aphrodite and Athena, who sprang directly from the head of Zeus. The gods are passionately concerned with human affairs and use their power to assist favourites and to harm enemies. The hero and his family are under the care of an Olympian god, who in return requires sacrifices, offerings and prayers. The realm of the dead is set apart from the Olympians and is abhorrent to them, especially to Apollo, the god of light. Unlike Olympus, the underworld is imperfectly realized, but there are hints of eternal punishment for certain offenders, while the primitive race of Furies have power to exact vengeance.

A bronze Zeus, the supreme deity of the Greeks. He was 'father of the gods and men'.

There is a total lack of any feeling we could call 'moral' in Homeric religion. Nor are its sanctions derived from any revelation; it has no sacred book and its priests are the humble servitors of the shrines, without power to teach or to reprove. It is the warrior-kings themselves who offer formal prayer and sacrifice.

The method of divine working found in Homeric poetry is not lost sight of in the classical period, although by then the gods have become the champions and protectors of cities rather than of individuals. The power of the gods to help or to harm has not diminished: they jealously guard the holy places and still crave animal sacrifices, due portions of the harvest and libations. No powerful priestly caste arises and no writings take on a sacred character. As a result, there is no concept of religious orthodoxy, and while abundant examples of piety and superstition are recorded, the Greeks to a large extent remained free from religious fanaticism and intolerance. Nobody, for example, will mistake the Sacred War (356–346 BC) for a struggle between religious factions: it was a purely political conflict. The Greek world seems always to have contained communities in which speculation of the most fundamental sort was tolerated: forced to leave one city, the inquirer could find a refuge, and sometimes even adherents, in another.

Two aspects of classical religion are only extensions of the Homeric system. One is the hero-cult, whereby the virtue inherent in a dead hero was invoked to help his city. The other is divine possession. Often in Homer the hero goes into battle 'filled with' a god. In the post-Homeric *orgia*, bands of women dance and rave in the open air, possessed by Dionysus – also called by his Lydian name, Bacchus. This god, though known to Homer, is not well integrated into the Olympian pantheon, but remains an ambiguous figure. In one aspect, he belongs on the fringes, just as the raving women, the Bacchae, themselves belong on the fringes of civilized society, where the forces of wild nature are focused on his worship. He is often attended by silens or satyrs, part-animal, part-man. But under another aspect he becomes one of the presiding divinities of the city of Athens.

As well as the pan-Hellenic observances already mentioned, each city gave expression to the worship of various Olympians by means of temples, cults and festivals. These were official institutions, reflecting the god's presence and continuing care in the heart of the polis. Immense numbers of state cults are attested, some going back to a time before the foundation of the cities, others deliberately established or magnified as part of a political programme. At Athens, we may point to three festivals which had come in classical times to mark the exalted place held by the city in Attica and in Greece generally. The Great Panathenaea, held every four years on Athena's birthday in high summer, took on some attributes of the Olympic festival: as well as a cult celebration proper, it encompassed processions, games and the awarding of prizes. In late March the Great Dionysia (in honour of the ambiguous god just mentioned) likewise gave the Athenians an opportunity of displaying to a pan-Hellenic audience the wealth of their city and its achievements in poetry and music. A different kind of observance, involving rites of initiation, is exemplified by the Eleusinian Mysteries, connected with the corn goddess Demeter and her daughter, Persephone.

The civic and private lives of the Greeks were governed by two closely connected feelings: a fear of ritual defilement and the need for purification, also in ritual form. These feelings were known to Homer, but never held a central place in his outlook. By the classical period, however, the boundaries between sacred and profane had taken on greater significance, and the worship of the immortal gods became quite separate from the cycle of human, mortal life. This separation was realized, in practical terms, by the 'defilement' incurred at death, at birth and in sexual intercourse.

Philosophical Speculation

There were attempts to find some meaning in the Homeric system: in other words, to give it a moral content. Prominent among such moralizers were Herodotus and the tragic poets of the fifth century BC. These writers were questioners, not iconoclasts. It was otherwise with the thinkers in Ionia and, after them, in the Greek cities of the west. Such men suggested an explanation of the universe which either did away with the Homeric gods or, if it retained them, did so as the mere cement of popular religion without giving them intellectual credence. The Ionian philosophers of the sixth century BC had attempted to explain the structure and composition of the universe in purely rational terms, without reference to any polytheistic belief. They postulated, rather, a single, all-embracing divinity. So also did two writers who lived into the classical age: Xenophanes, who explicitly repudiated the Homeric gods and advocated monotheism, and Heraclitus, with his insistence on the primacy of reason (*logos*), the essential unity of contrary notions, and fire as the primal form of matter.

Different from Xenophanes and Heraclitus, and in the end more influential, were the early thinkers and teachers in the Greek west. At the beginning of a remarkable series stands Pythagoras, an immigrant to Italy from Samos around 531 BC. It is easier to judge the strength of his personality than to assess his doctrines with any confidence. By the end of the fifth century BC his name was already legendary, with many strands of belief adhering to it. But it seems certain that he founded a sect of like-minded disciples who revered him as a sage. Although he was later credited with highly sophisticated doctrines involving the immortality and transmigration of souls and the place of number in sustaining the harmony of the universe, his true originality lay in showing the right way for people to live in a community. In this respect he marks a shift away from the Ionian thinkers, and seems closer in spirit to Socrates (469–399 BC) and Plato (*c.* 429–347 BC). Like these, he advocated a life of moral purity and unremitting intellectual activity and contemplation in which attention to the soul, the divine part of man, was crucially important.

Elea in southern Italy was the city of a master and a pupil, Parmenides and Zeno respectively. Their teaching raised serious challenges to common sense which modern thinkers, like the ancient Greeks themselves, have found it difficult to meet. Parmenides (died after 450 BC) adopted a poetical form, expressive of his exalted mood and divinely inspired teaching. This teaching, said in his poem to have been confided by a goddess, turns on the nature of reality. Whatever can be contemplated must, for that very reason, necessarily exist; and whatever exists must necessarily be one, whole and entire – it never came into being and will never pass away. Parmenides' monism, if accepted, makes irrelevant all the speculations about the nature of the universe that the Ionians had entertained. Zeno (born *c.* 490 BC) constructed no system of Parmenidean type. Instead, his challenge took the form of paradoxes. The most famous of these, and the hardest to refute, are concerned with motion and time. An arrow is at rest even while moving through the air, since at any given moment (the 'now') it occupies its own space; and Achilles never overtakes the tortoise, because the faster runner must always reach the point from which the slower began, with the result that the slower is always in front.

Parmenides' position was in time contested in Ionia, especially by Anaxagoras, but it was also contested by an admirer and emulator of his own in the west, Empedocles. Writing in verse, as Parmenides had done, Empedocles (*c.* 493–433 BC) reasserted the power of human perception to penetrate at least some way into the essence of things, and that perception informs us that the universe is only apparently the perfect whole, uncreated and eternal, of which Parmenides spoke; in reality it is instinct with dynamic change – elements are all the time coming into being and falling away, love consummates unions while strife dissolves them. In his radiant vision of the universe as a diverse and beautiful whole, Empedocles perhaps showed himself a truer poet than Parmenides.

Yet Parmenides had given such forceful expression to his monistic belief that it came to form a dominant concept in Greek thought. It provoked a powerful reaction among the philosophers of the Greek east, even though they were not able to assail it fundamentally. Plato himself considered Parmenides the most important of his predecessors, and devoted his dialogue entitled *Parmenides* to a searching examination and refutation of the doctrine of 'the one'.

Before Plato, the most far-reaching criticism of the Parmenidean position was voiced by Anaxagoras (*c.* 500–428 BC), the first philosopher to reside in Athens. While agreeing with Parmenides that 'coming to be' and 'passing away' are erroneous concepts, he asserts (in direct contradiction of Parmenides) that in the past 'all things were together, infinite in number and smallness, for the small also was infinite'. Not only, then, did Anaxagoras postulate the infinite divisibility of matter, but he saw the universe as a blending of all available components. For him, as earlier for Heraclitus, there was a controlling intelligence, or *nous*. Other aspects of Anaxagoras' intellectual activity were concerned with cosmic speculation and the nature of perception.

The last achievement of Ionian philosophy to be considered here, the atomic theory of Leucippus and Democritus, was worked out in an attempt to reconcile Parmenides' teaching with the evidence of our senses. According to Aristotle's exceptionally clear account, Leucippus held that the universe consists of two parts, matter and void, matter comprising an infinite number of particles moving through the void. These particles are so small as to be invisible; their collision causes things to come into existence, while their parting brings existence to an end. It is not clear exactly what Democritus contributed to this radically new doctrine.

All the thinkers named so far are known as pre-Socratics. The term is, however, inapposite for two reasons. In the first place, these philosophers formed no conscious school, but on the contrary pursued their thought along highly individual lines, often in opposition to one another. And in the second, they did not all even live before Socrates. Still, there is some justice in demarcating them from Socrates, as the Greeks themselves did. Their concern was mainly with abstract speculation; Socrates, like his opponents the Sophists, made man the focus of his interest. Abstract thought, though still important, was no longer an end in itself but became subordinate to the evaluation of human conduct in society. This intellectual readjustment took place in fifth-century Athens, and so will best be considered in its context in the final section. A few words, meanwhile, about some general intellectual tendencies of the classical period.

Nearly all states, including some of the most conservative, came to adopt new approaches without discarding the old ones completely. The art of writing, which Greeks had known for about 200 years, was now practised much more widely. Potsherds, animal skins and tablets of wood or lead formed the most common media for short inscriptions. Literary works were written on rolls made from the papyrus plant. The fifth century BC saw the copying of such rolls for private use, at least in Athens, where a book trade gradually grew up. Public texts, however, were usually inscribed on stone. These comprised many types – dedications, epitaphs, treaties, title to privileges, assessments of tribute, declarations of inter-state alliances. But no Greek city seems to have set out the whole body of its laws in monumental form. The lawgivers of earlier days continued to receive extraordinary veneration: Lycurgus of Sparta, Zaleucus among the Locrian colonists in Italy, Solon and Draco at Athens. Special interest concerns Draco's legislation on homicide (first promulgated *c.* 620 BC). Even after the constitutional upheavals of the next two centuries, Draco's work held an honoured place. His enactment was republished in 409 BC as part of the general revision of law after the fall of the 400.

The longest legal inscription to survive comprises the laws of the city of Gortyn in southern Crete, dating from about 450 BC. This is not a true code but a restatement of archaic procedure in which the oath was all-important and written testimony played a minimal part. The judge fulfilled his office by awarding damages to the injured party. Many provisions apply to the family, and they contain both primitive and more advanced elements. Among the former we note the attitude towards adultery. This was a private injury, like any other, and the issue could be settled by the payment of a fine. By a striking innovation, on the other hand, women had come to enjoy far more extensive rights of inheritance than was usual in Greek states.

Medicine, like law, did not escape the intellectual revolution of the fifth century BC, although its roots in the cults of an earlier age were never entirely lost sight of. Asclepius, a son of Apollo, had long been regarded as the god of healing; his devotees, the Asclepiads, formed a quasi-priestly body dedicated to the theory and practice of medicine. By far the most famous Asclepiad was Hippocrates (469–399 BC), from the island of Cos. A large collection of some sixty medical treatises, the so-called *Hippocratic Corpus*, has come down to us under his name. Hippocrates cannot possibly have written all of these works; in fact it is not certain that he wrote any. Nevertheless, he is a much less shadowy figure than, say, Pythagoras. He taught first that the practice of medicine should have an ethical basis – hence the Hippocratic oath, still regarded as an ideal statement of doctors' duties towards their patients; and second, that close and detailed observation was all-important in the treatment of disease.

Two works of the *Corpus* exemplify the Hippocratic approach. The first, entitled 'Airs, Waters and Places', is addressed to those going to practise medicine in a strange city. It takes a broad and humane view of the doctor's interest in people's surroundings; the writer already displays much of our present-day concern with the environment and its effect on health. More specialized, and written with a strong polemical bias, is the treatise on 'The Sacred Disease'. The very title is ironical. The author's purpose is to show that there is nothing sacred about the disease in question, epilepsy; its sacred character has been given it by priestly charlatans, for their own purposes. Whether or not Hippocrates wrote 'The Sacred Disease', its clear-headedness and rationalizing approach are emphatically Hippocratic, as that term was understood by the Greeks.

The Aristocratic Vision

We saw earlier how tenaciously the aristocratic idea maintained itself in classical Greece. The democracy at Athens and a few other states represented, in fact, a divergence from the norms of Greek life. Even in Athens the noble families still formed an élite during the fifth century, possessing more than their fair share of political influence. The aristocratic families of the various states formed a self-perpetuating network transcending local boundaries and local prejudices. The institution of *xenia*, or 'guest-friendship', subsisted between noblemen, even when their cities were ranged on opposite sides. Pericles himself was the *xenos* of the Spartan king Archidamus, while Alcibiades' noble birth gave him admission to the upper reaches of society at Sparta. Athens also retained her cavalry, recruited exclusively from the sons of noble or wealthy houses.

What enabled the nobles to exercise such a commanding role in Greece until well into the fifth century BC? It was partly, but only partly, the self-confidence that comes with a long use of power and ownership of landed estates. No less important was the careful cultivation of an aristocratic ideal through training and example. Intellectual attainments and practical skills counted for little beside the desired combination of physical and moral qualities. The offspring of a good family expected to take a leading part in civic and religious life and, at least in theory, placed his surplus wealth at the service of the city. Schools, as known later in Greece, were not yet common; nevertheless the education of boys proceeded along well-established lines. The two most formal parts of education were called by the Greeks 'gymnastic' and 'music', terms which approximate to their modern derivatives but differ in some important respects.

Education and Training

Music meant literally any art over which one of the Muses presided, but the word was often applied to the production of a sequence of notes by a man-made instrument. Although the Greeks used a variety of instruments in military and country life, only two played any large part in musical performances strictly so called: the lyre and the aulos, a species of oboe. Like all the other treasured possessions of the Greeks, both lyre and aulos were given a legendary pedigree, the lyre being Apollo's (or Hermes') invention and the aulos Athena's. Down to the classical period, there was virtually no independent development of instrumental music in Greece. Aulos and lyre were employed solely to accompany the human voice. The resulting compositions ranged from the simplest marching-songs to choral lyric. The latter, which flourished between the mid-seventh and mid-fifth centuries BC, was the most intricate musical genre, and the most highly esteemed. It consisted of a fusion of song, dance and musical accompaniment. A choir of older or younger men, or sometimes of girls, sang an ode to words especially composed for a festive occasion. Their dancing likewise followed a pattern laid down by the author of the ode. He also indicated the notes to be played on the lyre or aulos, or sometimes a combination of these.

Despite its considerable diversity, choral lyric possessed some constant properties, which made it so apt for training the young. There was, above all, the religious component: either the song actually formed part of a religious festival or it invoked the divine presence at some more secular occasion or, at the very least, it recounted former deeds of the gods. Then again, music was commonly believed to affect its hearers in a discernible manner. The Greeks distinguished various harmonies according to the sequence of intervals they contained. Each harmony created an impression of its own: the Dorian induced martial vigour, the Phrygian restraint, the Lydian melancholy, the Ionian languor and so on. In the third place, performances of choral lyric often took on the aspect of an *agon*, or 'contest'. Choirs competed for a prize at the Panathenaea, the Pythian Games, and other important religious gatherings. There were, in short, several ways in which a musical education prepared the young for their future place in society: it taught them knowledge of the gods and reverent participation in the city's cults, it moulded their character in accordance with the harmonies employed and it encouraged the spirit of competition.

Bronze charioteer from Delphi, a celebration of the most aristocratic form of competition, chariot-racing.

According to a widespread Greek concept, the gymnastic part of training was very closely allied to the musical part and was inseparable from it. In their system of gymnastic exercises, taught by a gymnasiarch, naked youths and men engaged in boxing and wrestling, running and long-jumping, and throwing the javelin and discus. The last five of these sports formed a group, the *pentathlon*. The *pankration*, on the other hand, was a contest in all-in wrestling and boxing. Not only were all these exercises complementary to musical performance, but they shared with it the element of competition. Throughout boyhood and early manhood, the winning of a prize at the hands of one's fellow citizens remained an object of life's effort. And winning was all; the prize itself usually had only symbolic value. Apart from at Sparta, women took no part in gymnastic exercises.

A milieu which saw the display of the naked body and the intimate association of boys and men allowed the formation of homosexual pairings. These relationships, if stable, were approved of, as bringing a boy under the moral guidance of an older lover. Nor did the Greeks fail to find among their own legends divine exemplars of homosexual affection: Apollo, it might be, or Poseidon, or Zeus himself. Thus, by a transformation which may strike us as peculiarly Greek, the banal affairs of every day came to be idealized; the result was classical art and poetry that projected an image of the perfectly formed male body, refined and yet apt for the most strenuous physical endeavours, beautiful but not wanton.

The pick of contestants at local festivals made their way to the pan-Hellenic games at Olympia and Delphi.

Delphi, the greatest Greek oracle.

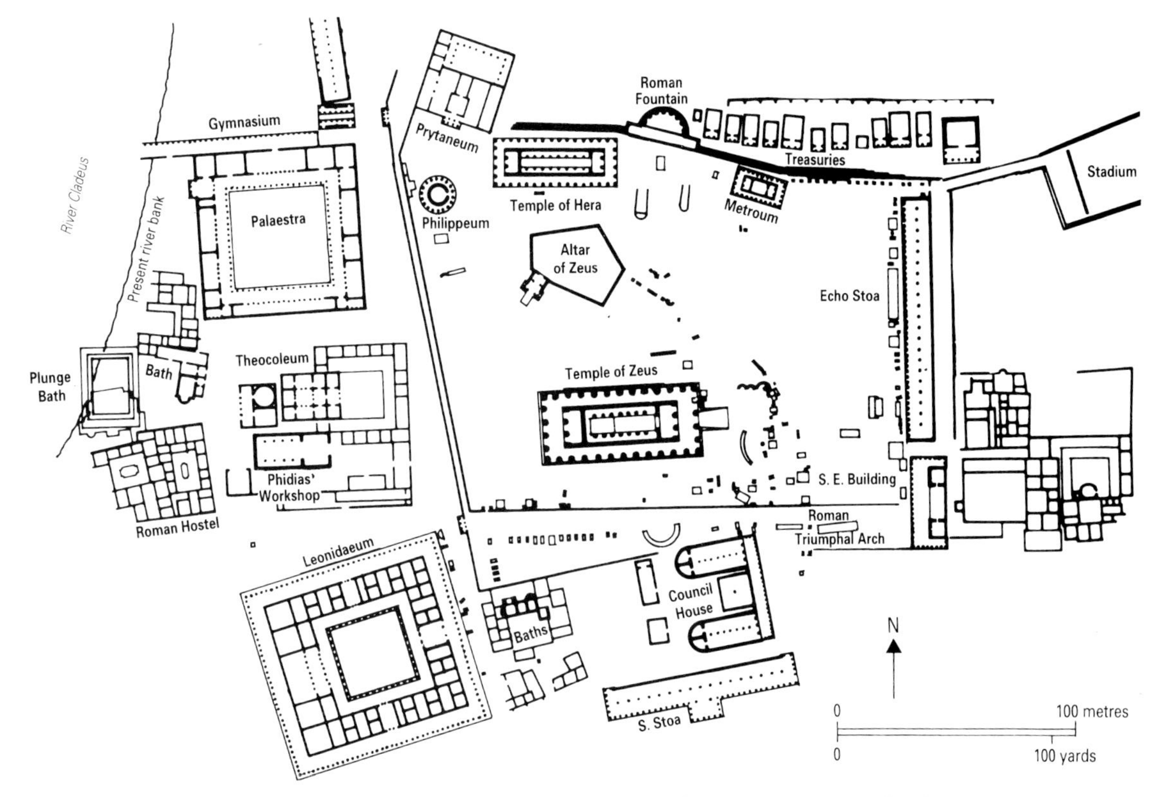

Plan of Olympia showing Greek and Roman buildings.

At the outset, these seem to have been simple in character and of short duration. But in the course of time new events were added, no doubt in response to pressure from noble families. For example, the race of hoplites in armour was a mark of military ideology not otherwise prominent in the games. Other additions were chariot-races and horse-races, which plainly reflect an aristocratic preoccupation with the rearing and training of horses. Naturally, only rich men could participate in such events; and very often the owner of a successful horse or chariot was held to have won the race, even though he had merely paid the riders or drivers. To win at any of the national games conferred great prestige on the victor, both in his own city and in Greece as a whole. Certain families gained renown by breeding, generation after generation, winners in the games. An Olympic victory counted above all. This, the greatest of pan-Hellenic festivals, was said to have been inaugurated by Heracles, the greatest of pan-Hellenic heroes. The sacred ground at Olympia held temples of Zeus and Hera, as well as gymnasia, wrestling-schools, the treasuries where victors dedicated their offerings, and the stadium and racecourse. Extraordinary measures were taken to ensure the integrity and security of the Olympic festival. Any cities at war observed a month's truce, while the games themselves were conducted under the strict eye of Hellenic judges, with penalties for fouls. The presence of crowds of onlookers and of embassies from the Greek states added to the festal air and presented a forum for the declamation of literary works and political programmes.

In the evening, the focus of interest moved from gymnasium and council-house to the symposium. The literal meaning of the latter word, 'drinking-party', conveys only a faint notion of its central place in Greek life. In the sixth and early fifth centuries BC it was mainly the resort of aristocratic families. Later, its scope grew wider until, like the gymnasium itself, it became an institution in democratic Athens. For institution it certainly was. Its precise character varied with the participants. These might simply be young bloods, intent on getting drunk and pursuing the attendant slave girls, but to men of political weight it gave an opportunity for private meetings not to be undervalued. Certain formalities were involved in the symposium. Its members, garlanded and anointed with oil, reclined on couches to drink their wine, usually mixed with water. They elected a president, who established the rules of the proceeding. One unvarying rule was that libations should be poured to the gods, in a set order. The rest of the time was passed in conversation or in playing various games which had come to be associated especially with the symposium. There was, for example, the capping of verses: one guest would accompany himself in a short song, and it was up to his neighbour to sing an appropriate sequel. Some of these drinking-songs, or *skolia*, have survived. They have an air of high-minded piety which perhaps was not a mark of all symposia. The setting of riddles was another favourite pastime. The *kottabos*, too, was a game played at drinking-parties. It involved the shooting of drops of wine at a mark; success or failure here indicated success or failure in a love affair.

Poetic Celebration

Several distinct types of choral lyric had been developed in Greece. These included dithyrambs and paeans (hymns in honour of Dionysus and Apollo respectively), processional odes, dirges and victory songs. A poet admired for his many-sided talent was Simonides (died *c.* 468 BC), an Ionian from the island of Ceos. His fame was derived not least from the epitaphs, dirges and dedications he wrote for the Greek dead in the Persian Wars. Younger composers, who unlike Simonides seem to have confined themselves to choral lyric, were Simonides' nephew Bacchylides (also from Ceos) and Pindar of Thebes (518–438 BC). All three were pan-Hellenic poets, and they were all professionals, willing to execute commissions for public performance from cities or individuals. The extant work of Pindar and Bacchylides consists mainly of victory songs – namely, choral odes celebrating an athletic victory at one of the great national games. The victory songs of Pindar, above all, embody the aristocratic vision most fully and most richly. They were later collected into four books, containing respectively Olympian (*O*), Pythian (*P*), Nemean (*N*), and Isthmian (*I*) odes.

The victory song is a highly formal, and often very intricate, work of art. Although we know nothing directly of the musical or choreographic components, we catch a hint of their nature from the triadic structure of the surviving, poetic part: that is to say, a victory song was composed (like many choral lyrics) in three-stanza groups. Within each group, the first two stanzas correspond very closely in metre. We may be sure that there was a close correspondence also in the music and dancing. The last of the three stanzas, the epode, was metrically related to the first two but did not correspond exactly. The song itself might consist of any number of triads, from one only (*O* 11) to thirteen (*P* 4). Despite these very strict formal requirements, each song and each triad within it were entirely new; the arrangement of long and short syllables in a triad was never exactly repeated in any other. No doubt the same was true of the dance steps and musical notes. The content of the ode, like its formal structure, was determined to a large extent by traditional practice. Praise of the victor was, of course, mandatory. There were also maxims of a moral or proverbial type. The myth, as it appears in the victory odes, often forms the mainstay of the whole poem. The poet chooses from the vast Greek repertory a legend which is in some way relevant to the present victor, either as describing an ancestor of his or as relating some past episode in the history of his family or city. The composer's talent was chiefly revealed in the selection of the myth, and in the telling of it.

With Pindar's victory songs, Greek choral lyric (at least in its non-dramatic form) reached its final, brilliant flowering. The conditions in which such a rarefied form of art could flourish did not survive his own lifetime. The patrons who commissioned his victory odes belonged to a wealthy and powerful élite, who had the means to indulge their taste for magnificent display, both at the games and at the subsequent festivities with their accompaniment of revelry and song. Sometimes the festivities were held at the scene of the victory, sometimes back home in the victor's own city. Nearly all those who commissioned victory songs from Pindar came from Sicily and Aegina, two islands where the aristocracy still held sway. The most magnificent of these patrons was Hieron the Sicilian despot, whose horse won the race in the seventy-sixth Olympiad, in 476 BC. The victory forms the theme of *O* 1, in which Pindar looks forward to Hieron's winning the supreme prize, victory in the chariot-race. This he did in the Pythian Games of 470 BC, and the event was celebrated in another of Pindar's masterpieces, *P* 1.

Although (except in *P* 5) Pindar shows little interest in the details of the games, or in the circumstances in which athletic victories were actually won, he dwells lovingly on the aspects of aristocratic life which most appealed to him: striving for success, the giving of wise advice in the council-hall, opulence, magnanimity and hospitality. But the great families have a still higher claim on his gratitude. It is they who have given shape to the history of Greece, first by founding her cities and then by endowing them with their own exalted ideals of excellence. For the most part, the aristocrats are nowadays content to live at peace; the warlike spirit of the past has been sublimated in the contest for glory that is seen in the games. But, in case of need, the aristocrat can still fight and win; and Pindar places Hieron's defeat of the barbarian at Himera on an equal footing with the victories of Plataea and Salamis (*P* 1).

Pindar is deeply committed to an ideology which holds that the true aristocratic virtues of character and physique are bred in the race. Training may heighten these attributes but it cannot impart them. 'What comes from a man's own nature is in every way superior; yet many have striven to win fame by the merit acquired from mere instruction' (*O* 9). And again: 'It is by inherent glory that a man prevails; those who have to be *taught* their skills walk in darkness' (*N* 3). The charmed, aristocratic circle does not exclude Pindar, for he is part of it. His descent from an ancient Theban family puts him on familiar terms with the first men in other parts of Greece: for instance, at Syracuse (*O* 6, *P* 1, 2, 3), at Cyrene (*P* 4, 5) and in Thessaly (*P* 10). Pindar, an aristocrat commemorating the athletic achievements of other aristocrats, practises as high a skill as theirs, since it re-creates on earth the music which gladdens the gods on Olympus and brings them repose (beginning of *P* 1). The power of song outweighs even the splendour of athletic victories. 'When a man comes to Hades' house, having done noble deeds uncelebrated in song, he has spent his breath in vain and won little pleasure by his toil' (*O* 10). 'Mighty deeds of valour are plunged in deep shadow, if they lack songs of praise' (*N* 7). 'When men are dead, only the voice of praise lives on to proclaim the manner of their life' (*P* 1).

Confident in his social position and in his mastery of song, Pindar acts as teacher as well as poet. The two functions are not always easy to distinguish from each other. The odes contain many reflections on the divine order and man's place within it. Man must not aim too high, for the gods resent any attempt to encroach upon their own domain: hence a modest, reserved, courteous demeanour is required of the aristocrat as he goes about his business. At the same time, the gods have a gracious care for the families and cities they love, a care which causes them to bring even apparent disasters to a happy conclusion.

The Arts of the Greeks

In his victory odes Pindar speaks of several arts as adorning the cities and sanctuaries of Greece. For him music and dance naturally hold the highest place, but beautiful objects shaped by human hand add to the radiant display – perhaps half-idealized by Pindar but not wholly distorted from reality. He compares his cunningly constructed, gleaming ode with a great temple (*O* 6); an adornment of temples, as of sacred precincts generally, was the statue, its repose contrasted by Pindar with the dynamic movement of his own odes (*N* 5); and then there are the painted clay amphorae containing olive oil given at Athens as Panathenaic prizes (*N* 9). These three arts, architecture, sculpture and vase-painting, are the most prominent in Greece, but artistic skill of a high order was lavished on small objects of everyday use, such as gems, coins and mirrors or statuettes made of bronze.

We gather from descriptions in Greek writers that wall-painting was an art much admired in ancient times, and we know the names of two classical masters, Polygnotus and Micon, whose works embellished buildings at Delphi and Athens. Of the works themselves we have nothing.

All the arts considered here had been taken to a high pitch in archaic Greece. In sculpture, further study of human anatomy resulted in the statuesque figures, in stone or bronze, of women (*korai*) and men (*kouroi*); but there were also sculptured groups of people in action – for example, the Treasury of the Siphnians at Delphi. A corresponding interest in human, and also in animal, figures is seen in the arts of the gem-engraver, especially in Ionia, and the maker of dies for the silver coins now issued by the wealthier cities. The two so-called orders of temple architecture, Doric and Ionic, were developed, with large buildings of both kinds erected in the sixth century BC. In vase-painting, the black-figure technique attained perfection at Athens in the hands of Exekias and the Amasis Painter. The classical age was to produce no finer drawing than theirs, but the red-figure ware of classical Athens allowed the representation of a wider range of subjects, and of postures, than had been possible before.

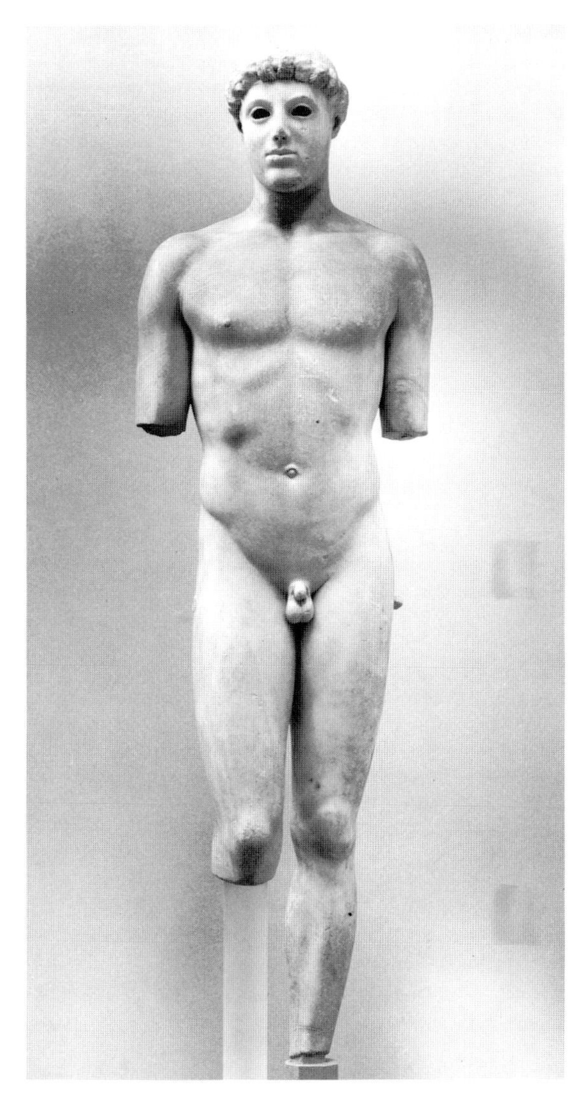

The Critian Boy, dating from the 480s BC.

Architecture and Sculpture

In architecture the temple is our main concern. The nucleus of the Greek temple, and its only strictly essential part, was a hall which modern writers call by its Latin term, *cella*. Here was kept the cult image of the god to whom the particular temple was dedicated. The cella had in front of it a porch, and often behind it a false porch, inaccessible from the cella. Columns supported the ceiling of the cella and its porch. Further rows of columns formed a colonnade round all four sides of the central complex. A gabled, tiled roof covered the entire structure.

The two orders of Greek architecture relate not so much to the ground-plan, which remained similar in all temples, as to the elevation. In the Doric, which predominated in mainland Greece and the western colonies, massive columns stood directly on the floor. Each column was topped by a plain capital. Upon the row of capitals rested the architrave, a beam of stone which in turn supported a row of metopes alternating with triglyphs. The former were plain or sculptured panels, the latter formed blocks divided into three vertical sections. The pediment was the triangular area at either end of the temple, enclosed by the metope–triglyph frieze on the lower side and the sloping roof on the upper sides. Each pediment was filled with more or less elaborate sculptured figures, which were not merely decorative but tended to lighten the otherwise rather heavy effect. Ionic columns, typical of the eastern settlements but introduced at Athens during the fifth century BC, were more slender than the Doric and, unlike the Doric, rested on richly carved bases and were finished on top by capitals formed of graceful scrolls, or volutes. Above the architrave ran a frieze composed of formal patterns or sculptured figures. The pediment was usually left plain, however.

The Corinthian style (not an order in its own right) is an offshoot of Ionic, invented in the later fifth century BC. In its capital, moulded acanthus leaves replace volutes. Corinthian columns were occasionally placed in the interior of temples (first attested in the Temple of Apollo at Bassae in Arcadia), but did not comprise temple colonnades in the classical period.

Quite apart from its main function as the house of a god, the Doric temple of classical Greece satisfied exacting demands: it had to suit the terrain available; it had often to form an element in a sacred precinct; and its proportions had to please the eye of a distant spectator, and its details and decoration that of a worshipper or visitor.

The Temple of Aphaea in Aegina, dating from the early fifth century BC, was the third to occupy the precinct of that goddess. The building, of stuccoed limestone, can be reconstructed from the substantial remains. The form is canonical, an elegant feature being the double storey of columns which span the cella. Sculptured figures in the round occupied both the east and the west pediment. Athena with spear and shield stands, calm and majestic, in the centre of each group. Helmeted warriors bearing shields are engaged on either side of her; their size diminishes gradually to fit the space available. The sculptors gave much thought to the representation of the human body in movement. The attitude of the fighting warriors is accurately rendered, that of the wounded less so. By a convention observed generally in the art of the period, the female figure is clothed in a long dress or robe; males, except musicians and charioteers, are nude.

By the time of the Persian Wars, Greek sculptors had mastered many of the problems presented by the form of the human body. The marble statue of the Critian Boy (*c.* 480 BC) is often, and with good reason, cited as a decisive advance on the stiff pose of the archaic *kouroi*. The advance had been made by imparting a number of corrections to the schemata of the archaic style so as to approach reality more closely (the terminology is that of Emanuel Loewy). That the process was effected within a single generation we may certainly wonder at, but it is impossible to explain in the absence of any of the textbooks of fifth-century-BC sculpture.

Copies of early classical statues abound, but original works are fewer. Attica and the islands contribute fine reliefs. One of these, the Giustiniani Stele, combines a conventional pose with sensitive rendering of details.

The Giustiniani Stele, an example of the growing sensitivity of sculptors to detail.

There are some masterpieces in bronze. The Delphi Charioteer, weary at the end of the race, offers a striking contrast to the (later) Zeus in the act of hurling his thunderbolt. In this piece, an unsurpassed rendering of the angry god, strict representational accuracy has been sacrificed in order to achieve the greatest impact, from whichever angle the statue is viewed. Virile strength of a similar order is displayed in the two Riace Bronzes recovered from the sea in 1972.

Two events during the fifth century BC mark the rapid progress of sculpture in intimate association with architecture, and the subordination of both arts to an overriding concept. The first is the building of the Temple of Zeus in the sanctuary at Olympia; the second, the wholesale reorganization of the Athenian Acropolis.

At Olympia the worship of Zeus had long centred on his altar. The new temple was completed by 456 BC, except for the cult image. That, a colossal chryselephantine statue (now lost), was provided later by the Athenian master Phidias (born 490 BC). The temple itself is a large building of normal Doric type (210 x 90 feet), with a colonnade of thirteen by six columns. Stuccoed limestone was used for the building, Parian marble for the sculptures.

Both pediments contain carved groups in which the figures are about one and a half times life-size. An underlying theme is the establishment of a moral order controlled by the pan-Hellenic gods, and this theme is continued by the metopes inside the temple. Apollo stands in the centre of the west pediment, flanked by the fight between lapiths (upholders of civilization) and centaurs, half-man and half-horse, who have assaulted women and boys at the wedding feast of Pirithous. The mastery in depicting the monstrous creatures is equalled only by the successful indication of passion in the faces, and the very attitudes, of the participants: rage, lust or an agony of pain. Apollo holds aloof, yet his outstretched arm spells defeat for the centaurs. On the east pediment there is no struggle, only the intimation of one. We are to envisage the forthcoming race, which Pelops wins by treachery. On one side is Oenomaus, his chariot team and members of his household; on the other, Pelops stands with *his* team, and human figures. The eye is drawn to Zeus, the arbiter, in the very centre.

The grand design was completed by twelve sculptured metopes inside the colonnade. Each of them is about 5 feet square and depicts one of the famous labours of Heracles, who was not only the founder of the Olympic festival but, like the lapiths, also carried out a civilizing mission by grappling with monsters. He is also a folk-hero who fulfils seemingly impossible tasks. The contents of many of the metopes can be conjectured from the broken remnants. They present the same fine carving, indication of changing mood and satisfying composition as the pedimental sculptures. Heracles, naturally, figures in all the metopes; his tutelary goddess, Athena, is in four. The features of Heracles change as he ages: he begins as a beardless youth, and is a grizzled but still powerful giant at the end of his long toils. Athena, too, is seen under diverse aspects. When Heracles presents her with the Stymphalian birds, she leans towards him, a confidante rather than a patroness; but in another metope she stands by, an august witness, as Heracles in the centre bears the weight of the world on his head, and to the right Atlas (temporarily relieved of his burden) offers the apples of the Hesperides.

The figure of Apollo from the west pediment of the Temple of Zeus at Olympia.

A few years after the dedication of Zeus' temple at Olympia, in 450 BC Pericles proposed an ambitious scheme of building for the Athenian Acropolis. The largest element in the scheme was to be a new temple of Athena, later known as the Parthenon (begun 447 BC, Phidias' 40-foot-high cult statue dedicated 438 BC; pedimental sculptures in place by 432 BC). Of all the Doric temples standing in Old Greece, or in the western colonies, the Parthenon is incomparably the finest in both conception and execution. The material throughout is Pentelic marble. Minute attention was paid to every detail, so that a system of deliberate distortion, already worked out for Doric architecture, was applied here with unusual subtlety.

Under the supervision of Phidias, Ictinus was architect and Callicrates master mason. Enormous expense and practical difficulty attended the work, which no city save Athens could have contemplated. The plan

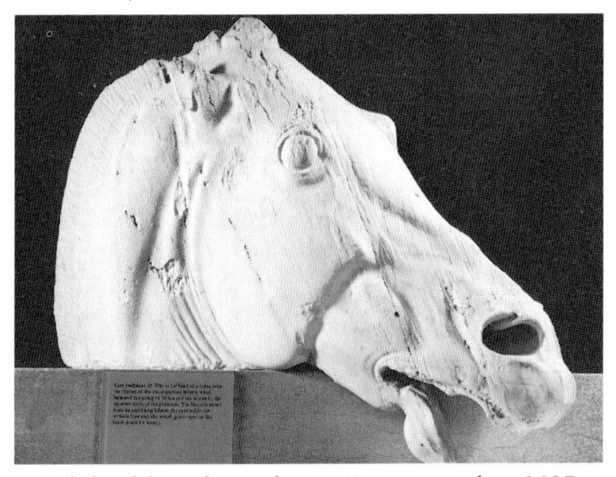

Horse's head from the Parthenon. Disaster struck in 1687, when a Venetian shell set fire to the gunpowder stored in the temple by the Turkish garrison.

measures about 228 by 100 feet; the colonnade is long and narrow for a Doric temple, with sixteen by six columns. The larger of the two rooms was intended to accommodate Athena's statue, the smaller to hold the treasury of the Athenian alliance.

Although almost entirely ruined by the indifference or stupidity of later ages (including our own), the Parthenon still conveys in outline something of its original appearance. But much of its abundant sculpture has been lost or disfigured. The sculptures occupied three areas: the east and west pediments; the metopes; and a continuous frieze, 525 feet long, running round the outside wall of the cella. The last is an Ionic feature, here exceptionally adopted for a Doric building.

The metopes, each about 4 feet square, are badly weathered. The standard of workmanship varies greatly, and no overall scheme is followed. Some depict lapiths and centaurs fighting, others Greeks and Amazons, others again Greeks and Trojans. Little remains of the pedimental sculptures, but their general design is known from drawings and descriptions made when they were intact. The centrepiece of the east pediment, we are told, was formed by Athena's birth from the head of Zeus. Of the gods present at this epiphany, some are watching it and others look away. A few fragments attest the quality of the work in different subjects: the draped figures of three goddesses or a horse belonging to the moon goddess Selene. The west pediment depicted Athena's contest with Poseidon for the land of Attica. The horses of a chariot team rear up behind each of the angry deities. The remainder of the space is crowded with local worthies, heroic or divine, including a nude male at the far left, often identified as the river god Ilissus.

The greater part of the Parthenon frieze is extant, and in fair condition. This immense work was executed to a master plan by many craftsmen, most of them of great ability. The usual, and most plausible, interpretation of the frieze is that it depicts (of course in a selective and idealized manner) the Panathenaic procession, in which a new robe was dedicated to Athena. The culminating ceremony appears on the east side. The robe itself is being given by a youth to an older man, possibly a magistrate; meanwhile, the Olympian gods are present, reclining at their ease. Two processional streams converge upon them, having both begun at the south-west corner of the temple: one moves along the south side, one along the west and north sides. The bustling scene unwinds impressively along the two long sides, with here and there a standing figure to interrupt the movement. There are groups of musicians, older citizens, bearers of various offerings to the goddess, and heifers and sheep for the sacrifice. Most brilliant of all are the charioteers and riders, with every detail in the complex relationship of horses and men rendered with perfect clarity.

Comparing the Parthenon sculptures with those of the Temple of Zeus at Olympia, we see that the ideological commitment found there has been sharpened to the point of making a distinct statement about the city of Athens at the height of its power. Even at the time of building, voices were raised against the expenditure of so much treasure in self-glorification; but the Periclean vision prevailed, with the gods and heroes of the pediments complemented in the frieze by crowds of citizens. The Parthenon marks the culmination not merely of Athenian prestige but of classical Greek art, as we now understand the term. Whereas the masters who fashioned the Olympia sculptures had sought, in their restrained and disciplined way, to allow full play to the emotions, Phidias and his circle attained an ideal type of beauty, serene and timeless, subsuming individual characteristics and transient passions.

The Periclean Acropolis was approached by the Propylaea (built 437–432 BC), which forms an incomplete entrance, with both Doric and Ionic columns. Upon the Acropolis itself, two Ionic temples were brought to completion after the death of Pericles. The first of these, Athena Nike, is elegant and compact, with four columns at either end of its cella. The Erechtheum is more elaborate, comprising three elements built to a unified plan. The central part has an east-facing porch with six columns, a pediment and an Ionic frieze; this part contains the rooms with the cult images. The second element takes the form of a large north porch, placed at a lower level; this also has a pediment and frieze. A much smaller porch projects on the south side, looking towards the Parthenon. Its flat roof is sustained by six caryatids (draped girls), instead of columns.

Throughout the fifth century BC Doric temples were built of local stone at sites in Sicily and at Paestum in southern Italy. None of them compares in subtlety or refinement with the best work of Old Greece. Impressive effects have to be gained by great size and unusual architectural features, as in the Temple of Zeus at Acragas. This measures 361 by 173 feet, with fourteen by seven columns. Walls the height of the columns

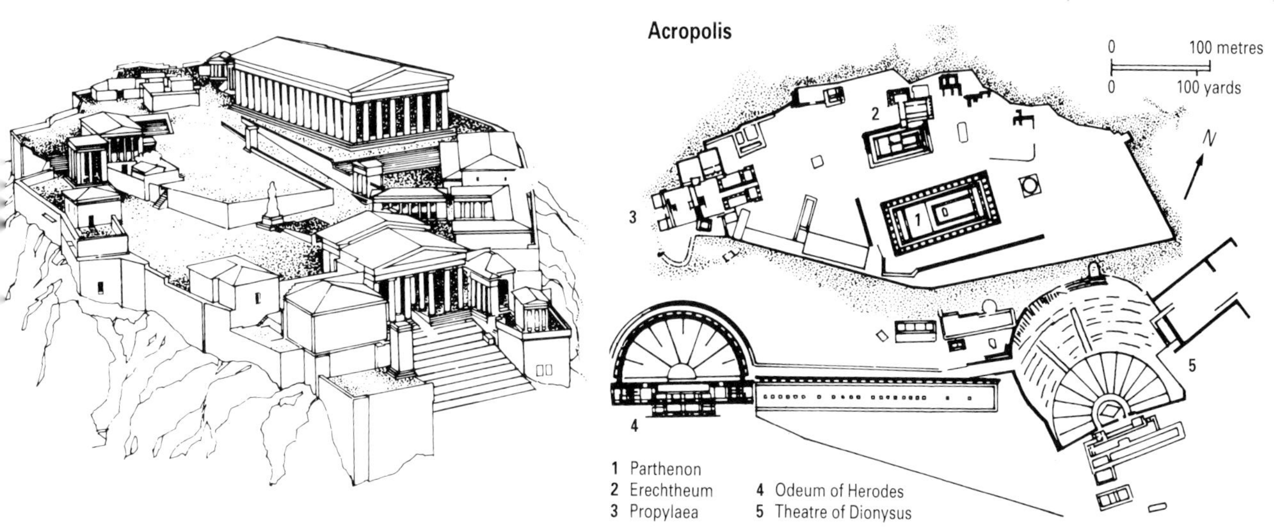

Reconstruction of the Athenian acropolis.

contain Atlas-type figures, which appear to hold up the entablature.

At Athens the well-preserved Temple of Hephaestus (miscalled 'Theseum') was designed to overlook the west side of the Agora. This open space, crossed by the Panathenaic Way, formed the financial quarter of the city. Long colonnaded buildings, or *stoas*, formed commodious places for the transaction of business. Close to Hephaestus' temple were the meeting-place of the Council of 500 and the *tholos*, a circular structure with six internal columns. Here stood statues of the heroes after whom the ten Cleisthenic tribes were named. The architect of the Temple of Hephaestus also (probably) designed the marble Temple of Poseidon at the headland of Sunium.

The Doric idea, in its canonical form, did not long outlive the end of the fifth century BC. Different proportions were adopted and more lavish decorative schemes employed. One brilliant adaptation of temple architecture to a round building is represented by the marble *tholos* at Delphi (diameter *c.* 49 feet). Inside the circular cella stood a ring of ten Corinthian columns, outside it a ring of twenty Doric columns. The Delphi *tholos* is dated to just before 400 BC; some thirty years later, a larger *tholos* (in limestone) was built at Epidaurus to a similar plan. Large temples, especially in the east, were now built on the Ionic principle. Two of the most impressive, well known from their ground-plans and from bases and capitals, are the Temple of Artemis at Ephesus and that of Athena at Priene. The architect of the latter was engaged to design Mausolus' tomb at Halicarnassus. This grandiose Mausoleum, with its Ionic colonnade and pyramidal roof surmounted by a chariot team, was quite alien to classical Greek taste. A completely different type of building, and an indispensable component in any Greek city of standing, was the theatre. That at Epidaurus has lasted the best, so far as seating and orchestra are concerned.

Although (to our knowledge) a large sculptural design of the quality of the Parthenon frieze was never

Reconstructed Atlas figure in the Temple of Zeus at Acragas (Agrigento), Sicily.

Mausoleum at Halicarnassus.

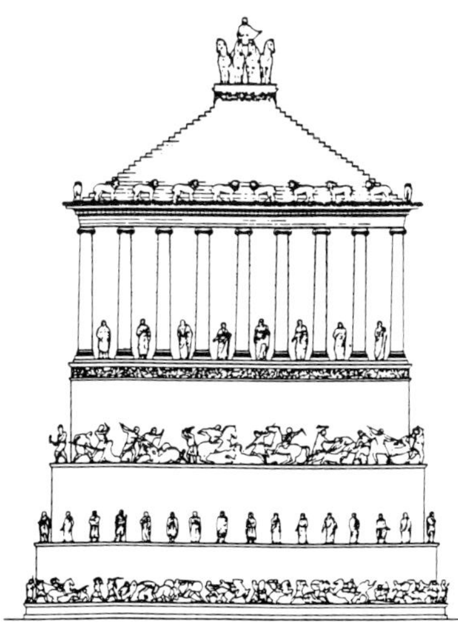

This colossal figure of Mausolus, ruler of Caria, was sculpted for his mausoleum at Halicarnassus around 353 BC. It reveals the penetration of Greek influence in art and architecture prior to Alexander's conquests.

again attempted, that frieze left a kind of afterglow in Attic grave reliefs which continues into the fourth century. A noble example is the monument, carved around 400 BC, for a woman named as 'Hegeso [daughter of] Proxenos'.

Sculptured figures were still applied to the pediments of Doric buildings: for instance, the Temple of Asclepius at Epidaurus and the Temple of Athena at Tegea (early fourth century BC). The former contained an assortment of Trojan themes, the latter Achilles' fight with Telephus. There was no political or religious programme here. Scopas, from the island of Paros, designed the Tegea temple and its sculptures; he also contributed some sculptures to the Mausoleum at Halicarnassus. His is one of several names of fourth-century artists, famous in their day, whom it is now difficult to assess, since very little of their original work is extant. We hear of Leochares and Praxiteles, both Athenians, and a little later the Peloponnesian Lysippus. Leochares created a renowned bronze Apollo; a marble copy, known as the 'Apollo Belvedere', is now in the Vatican. Praxiteles' nude Aphrodite, carved for the people of Cnidus in Asia Minor, caused a sensation: we have only a copy of this, as of other celebrated works, including his 'Satyr Pouring Wine' and 'Apollo Killing the Lizard'. His statue of Hermes holding the baby Dionysus survives in what is largely its original state. Some may find attractive the sweet fulsomeness of the two figures. Lysippus was known for his portrait sculptures of Heracles and of contemporary athletes. He lived beyond the classical age and sculpted Alexander, the new master of Greece.

Vase-painting

To move from architecture and sculpture to vase-painting may seem like leaving the major arts for a minor one. Apart from the difference of scale, however, there was nothing minor about vase-painting as practised by the classical Greeks, or for that matter by their archaic predecessors. A virtual monopoly of the production of fine painted ware was enjoyed by Athens, where the potters and pot-painters (the two were rarely identical) occupied their own quarter north-west of the Agora. Many thousands of vases were taken from here by merchants and middlemen to other Greek cities and their colonies, and even beyond the Greek world. Most places were content to import and use Athenian ware, but some local workshops in Italy and Sicily began by imitating Athenian models and later went their own way, showing a marked taste for theatrical scenes.

Many products of the potters' quarter at Athens survive. Thanks to this, and to modern scholarship, it is possible to attribute many vases to individual painters, or to individual workshops. The names of only a few painters are known, so vases are called either after the potter (Brygos Painter, Cleophrades Painter, Midias Painter), or after the place where an important pot is kept (Berlin Painter), or after the subject of a typical vase (Achilles Painter, Niobid Painter).

Water pot with scenes from the sack of Troy, a favourite Greek topic, by the Cleophrades Painter.

At about 530 BC the red-figure technique of pot-painting was invented at Athens. The painters of the following generation used the new method alongside the prevailing black-figure style. Some pots even combined the two methods. Athenian black-figure survived into the fifth century BC, but was eventually supplanted by red-figure, except on Panathenaic amphorae. These, owing to their special status as state prizes, continued to be painted in the black-figure style with which they had been associated since the first Panathenaic contest. The new method is a mirror image of the old. The artist working in black-figure draws his subjects in glossy black paint, leaving the pale colour of the clay as background; red-figure technique, on the other hand, involves the sketching of figures in outline, adding black relief lines for important detail, and filling in the background with black paint. A third method, white-ground painting, was sometimes used. Outline figures were drawn on a white background, with washes of various colours emphasizing certain features such as hair and clothing. Inscriptions were occasionally written on Athenian vases, either identifying the characters depicted or describing a certain youth as *kalos* ('handsome').

Although the three types of painting differ greatly in method and in the impression they convey, they share some noteworthy characteristics. In all of them, as in Greek sculpture, the human body remains the centre of interest. To explore its contours, in action and at

Interior of cup showing a drunken reveller and a courtesan, by the Brygos Painter.

rest, and to display the encounters of men and women hold unending fascination. And, as with the best sculptors, so with the best vase-painters a crisp, clear outline was all-important. Several limitations were imposed on these painters by their material and by the conventions of their art. True perspective was out of the question, nor could narrative be shown, except by somewhat clumsy expedients.

In determining the subjects of their scenes, the classical vase-painters largely followed their sixth-century-BC predecessors. Skill is displayed less in discovering new themes than in treating old ones in an original manner. The part played in the selection by the patron's preference or by the painter's own taste we can hardly determine; perhaps the size and shape of the vessel in question had more influence than either. It is possible that, especially on *kalos* vases, a scene carried some hidden significance in addition to the obvious one.

The range of subjects was very wide. Representations of gods, heroes and legendary episodes remain common throughout the fifth century BC, but there are also scenes of contemporary fighting. Many peaceful aspects of everyday life make their appearance: the home, the workshop, religious observances, the wrestling-school, the symposium, the revels of young men. The various stages of a love affair are sometimes explicitly rendered, from shy courtship to full intercourse. Satyrs, with horse tail and permanent erection, pursue their female prey with only intermittent success.

The prolific output of the fifth century BC must be indicated here by a very few pieces. Two important pot-painters were at work in Athens before, and for some time after, the Persian defeat in 479 BC. The Berlin Painter's vases present beautifully drawn, statuesque figures, as it were brilliantly illuminated in the centre of a black field. Such compositions are not entirely eschewed by the Cleophrades Painter, but he more often displays his power in scenes of action, particularly those based on the Trojan cycle. A little later, the specialized art of cup-painting was practised with impressive skill by the Brygos Painter, who preferred incidents of the symposium and the athletic contest. Towards the middle of the century, the circle of the Niobid Painter, under the influence of Polygnotus and his followers, painted mythological friezes on large vessels. A reaction was led by the Achilles Painter, who, like the Berlin Painter, liked to set individual figures against a black ground, with the minimum of accessorial decoration. His figures, even when static, can yet give the promise of intense activity; the Achilles of his 'name vase', for instance, is poised on one foot, with a look of expectancy and alertness. The Achilles Painter also showed the power of his drawing, and his imagination, on the white-ground *lekythoi*, or 'oil-flasks', dedicated in tombs. Towards the end of the century, such severity and restraint were abandoned in favour of a voluptuous, over-decorated style, typified by the Midias Painter. A decline sets in thereafter.

Coinage

Each of the great commercial cities of Greece had begun to mint its own silver coins before the classical period. But coinage of the fifth century BC served much more than a merely commercial purpose. The expertise of the best die-engravers was put at the service of political propaganda. Large coins were struck in 480 BC at Syracuse to commemorate the victory over the Carthaginians at Himera; the symbol of Syracuse, Arethusa's head, dominates the reverse. Athens likewise marked the expulsion of the barbarians by an issue of coins bearing her own symbol, Athena's owl. The dominance of Athens in the later fifth century BC ensured that her coinage became the commonly accepted currency in Greek commerce. The Sicilian cities were still able to call upon artists of great distinction, who now began to represent Arethusa full-face. But Syracusan coinage never again reached such heights, and in the fourth century BC generally, although more cities minted their own coins than in the time of the Athenian empire, their quality was rarely outstanding.

The Athenian Democracy

The prodigious energies released at Athens after the victories of 479 BC over the Persians were only partly directed along the channels of political change, imperial expansion, mercantile supremacy, and mastery in the arts of building, sculpture and painting. Still other modes of expression were created there or, if already in existence, were given definitive shape. These modes are, first, poetical drama and then (in prose) oratory, history and philosophical discourse.

The Theatre

Four Athenian dramatists are our concern: Aeschylus

(*c.* 525–*c.* 456 BC), Sophocles (*c.* 496–406 BC) and Euripides (*c.* 486–406 BC) for tragedy; and Aristophanes (*c.* 450–385 BC) for comedy. Tragedy and comedy formed separate genres. The so-called satyr plays written by tragedians cannot be classed as tragedies, but neither are they comedies in the Greek sense.

The plays were performed at the civic festivals of Dionysus, and so belonged to the whole citizen body. These festivals embodied a contest in which dramatists and actors competed for a prize. Only a single performance was envisaged, although sometimes the city decreed the revival of a popular play. Plays were produced at the public expense: wealthy citizens regarded it as an honour, or at least a duty, to defray the cost.

All the Athenian plays known from the fifth century BC contain, besides the actors' speeches, a number of songs performed by a choir of about twelve to the accompaniment of music and dance. The presence of a choir is indispensable, but the extent of its participation varies greatly. In most plays the choir acts as an observer and commentator whose sympathies are often engaged on behalf of one of the actors. A choir, especially in comedy, can change its viewpoint in the course of the play. The choir leader had a special part: as well as his role as principal singer, he communicated with the actors in spoken verse. Conversely, at moments of highly charged emotion, the actors sometimes burst into song. The actors in tragedy numbered no more than three, and so many roles had to be doubled or even trebled – a practice facilitated by the wearing of masks by actors and choir. All parts in the plays were taken by men.

Dramatic performances were given in the Theatre of Dionysus, near the god's temple on the southern slope of the Acropolis. The very long and very narrow stage was slightly raised above the circular orchestra, where the choir sang and danced. The auditorium accommodated a large proportion of the citizen body, together with visitors. Nearly all the extant plays require the presence of a stage building, which provided a means of entry and exit for important characters through a large central door.

The highly formal structure of the plays, together with features of production such as masked actors and the necessity to declaim before a large audience in the open air, shows that the poets never had any naturalistic aspirations. For the power of Athenian drama lies in a different direction altogether.

Although we possess no tragedy by any poet before Aeschylus, the titles of some have survived. We hear of a *Pentheus* by Thespis, and also works by Phrynichus taken from the legends of Tantalus and Heracles and a play based on Darius' capture of Miletus in 494 BC. Aeschylus and his successors likewise used chiefly heroic legend, but sometimes a real event, such as the battle of Salamis, which forms the background of Aeschylus' *Persians*. Like Pindar, the Athenian tragedians interpreted the legends so as to express a certain point of view, and their attitudes differed widely, as a brief examination of some extant plays will show.

The Athenian playwright Aeschylus (525–456 BC), a veteran of the Persian Wars. In *The Persians*, produced in 472 BC, he ascribed Greek victory to divine will, not to native prowess.

In 458 BC, Aeschylus produced the *Oresteia*, comprising a trilogy of linked plays (*Agamemnon*, *Libation-bearers* and *Eumenides*), together with a lost satyr play, *Proteus*. At the most superficial level, the *Oresteia* is a melodrama, showing how Agamemnon, on his return from the sack of Troy, is murdered by his wife, Clytemnestra, and her lover, and how the guilty pair are slain in their turn when the king's son Orestes grows to manhood. When Aeschylus comes to refashion this legend, the motives underlying the murders come under searching examination in the choral songs. Zeus himself prescribed the expedition against Troy, but Agamemnon could not set sail without sacrificing his daughter Iphigenia. In doing so, he fulfils the ancient curse on his house, and when Clytemnestra kills Agamemnon she simply takes the operation of the curse a stage further. Yet she is no mere puppet, but a passionate woman with reasons of her own for wishing her husband dead.

In *Libation-bearers* divine demands again place the characters in an irresolvable dilemma. Orestes is driven to murder Clytemnestra not only by filial piety but by the urging of Apollo. However, in obeying his command, Orestes falls foul of the Furies. They undermine Orestes' reason, and he rushes out on his way to Delphi in order to get ritual purification from Apollo.

The god does purify him and he is now free from guilt, so far as the Olympian gods are concerned. But in *Eumenides*, the Furies pursue Orestes to Apollo's temple, where ensues a confrontation between the radiant god and the primitive agents of vengeance.

Aeschylus resolves the dilemma by shifting the scene from Delphi to Athens. The choir of Furies appeal to Athena to let justice take its course. She cannot decide and appoints a tribunal to sit upon the Areopagus. There is to be a normal trial for homicide, with Athena presiding, Athenian citizens acting as jurors and Apollo testifying on Orestes' behalf. At this point, legendary past and actual present come together. The opposing claims cannot be reconciled except by submitting them to arbitration, as was done in Aeschylus' own city. Athena appeases the Furies by promising them honour for all future time. They accept this offer and, now changed to Eumenides, 'the gracious ones', they establish their cult in the city. The old cycle has been brought to an end and the cry of blood for blood has lost its power, superseded by a nobler concept of justice, thereafter celebrated in the Council of the Areopagus.

Rather differently, Sophocles achieves his effects by the remorseless accumulation of small details. A single key to Sophocles' art does not exist; there are, however, certain recurrent themes, notably the conflict between illusion and truth and the experiences of people after all pretence has been torn away. These themes are present most powerfully in *Oedipus Tyrannus*, performed in 425 BC. *Oedipus at Colonus*, produced near the end of the fifth century BC, brings the old legend into close relationship with contemporary Athens; despite many differences in outlook, Sophocles is thereby revealed as no less profoundly Athenian a dramatist than his older contemporary Aeschylus.

At the beginning of *Tyrannus*, Oedipus' prestige stands high. He once came to Thebes from abroad and, by solving the riddle of the Sphinx, broke her power over the Theban people. They, in gratitude, made Oedipus king and married him to the widowed queen Jocasta. Now they beg Oedipus to avert a plague. First, an oracle declares that the plague is caused by the presence of an unpunished murderer. And the murdered man is Laius, the previous king and Jocasta's husband, who was assassinated while travelling to Delphi. Stung by the words of the prophet Tiresias, Oedipus resolves to investigate the whole mystery. By relentless cross-examination, he then gradually becomes aware that an older oracle has been fulfilled: not only is he the murderer of his own father, Laius, but he has married his mother, Jocasta. Laius had been told by yet another oracle that he would be killed by his own son. His attempt to frustrate this prophecy was of course a failure.

Up to this point in the drama, Sophocles keeps control of the developing plot. Striking subjects are introduced, only to fade away. At the end, one alone remains: Oedipus' desire to learn his own identity. When he does learn it, events take a predetermined course. The choir of elderly Thebans are aghast at Oedipus' fall; he puts out his own eyes, while Jocasta hangs herself. By a strange paradox, it is only now that the true greatness of Oedipus is seen. He accepts his destiny without self-pity. But the role of the gods remains unexplained. That men should be pious goes without saying, for Sophocles' own piety was a byword; when first Jocasta and then Oedipus pour scorn on Apollo's oracles, they are rapidly undeceived. It seems that Oedipus acted as he did in obedience to some fate which the gods could expound only through their oracles.

Oedipus at Colonus concerns the exile's last hours, pre-ordained like so much else. On reaching the Grove of the Eumenides, near Athens, Oedipus recalls the old oracle mentioned in *Tyrannus*. We now hear that, among the woes foretold by Apollo, there was something of good: Oedipus should die at peace when he reached this very spot and received asylum. He is given refuge by Theseus, the king of Athens, and in return Oedipus promises that his burial place will be a perpetual source of benefit for the Athenian people, assuring them safety from Theban attack. In thus connecting the Attic shrine of the Eumenides with a legendary cycle, just as Aeschylus had done, Sophocles added a further element: that of hero cult. The widespread belief in the power of a dead hero enabled Sophocles to link a number of previously separate strands and compose a play more diffuse than *Tyrannus* but just as pathetic.

Sophocles' younger contemporary Euripides shows greater interest in everyday life than the other two tragedians. He appreciates the feelings of women in their plight, which must sometimes have been a desperate one in Greek communities. In *Medea* (431 BC) we even hear observations made by slaves and learn something of their views and emotions; and, of course, there is Medea herself, who emphasizes her precarious position at Corinth as both a woman and an alien. Euripides' concern with women's feelings and humble life comes to the forefront in his *Electra*. The opening of that play, in fact, is defiantly anti-heroic. Electra (not, as in Aeschylus' play, her brother Orestes) is the dominant personality; and her home is no palace, but a peasant's hut out in the countryside.

Euripides' highly sceptical attitude towards legends is seen in such plays as *Alcestis*, *Iphigenia among the Taurians* and *Helen*. We witness, in others, the impact of vast, destructive forces upon guiltless people. The sufferings of *The Trojan Women* are those of conquered people everywhere, not only at Troy. Hippolytus, in the play of that title, is caught up, a helpless pawn, in a clash between Artemis and Aphrodite. Once he has aroused Aphrodite's enmity, he, and all around him, are brought to ruin by her malice. In the *Bacchae*, Pentheus, a mere human being, and not an admirable one, pits himself against Dionysus, and again the uncontrollable force incarnate in a god works terrible havoc in the everyday world. So with *Medea*. Euripides here embarks on a daring re-evaluation of a famous legend. Jason, one of the most illustrious Greek heroes, has outlived his glorious deeds. All he now wishes to do is contract a conventional marriage and bring up his children by Medea in orderly surroundings.

She represents an elemental, devastating force, 'a lioness, no woman'. Her anger falls first upon Jason's intended bride, who dies in agony after putting on a poisoned robe sent by Medea. Such scenes were never enacted in view of the audience but had to be related by a messenger. Euripides retained this convention and in *Medea* he even exploited it, causing Medea to gloat over the details of the murder as they are told her.

Medea's revenge culminates in the murder of her children. Jason is a broken man at last, unaware of the nature of the power which has struck him down. He is soon confronted by that power, in the shape of Medea, who is seen on top of the stage building. The part she now plays is a ghastly parody of the *deus ex machina*, a god who appears near the end of a play, resolves discord and foretells the future. The fact that it is here Medea who takes such a part again points to her dual nature: the passionate woman who was deeply in love with Jason and the semi-divine sorceress able to shape events according to her will.

About the Athenian satyr play we know nothing directly except for a few fragments, a large part of Sophocles' *Trackers* and the complete *Cyclops* of Euripides. The thematic association of a satyr play with a tragic trilogy (usual in Aeschylus) did not always hold with Euripides, and in the fourth century BC satyr plays were produced independently. The aged Silenus took a major part, together with his sons, the satyrs: these comprised a choir remarkable for braggadocio, cowardice, drunkenness and lewdness. Silenus and choir are brought into connection with some incident from earlier literature; the result is a kind of tragic burlesque, lower in tone than a true tragedy but not entirely different in spirit. In *Trackers*, the satyrs go in search of Apollo's cattle, which, it turns out, have been stolen by the infant Hermes. The sound of Hermes' lyre, which he has just invented, causes the satyrs inordinate alarm – an incident recorded in the 'Homeric' *Hymn to Hermes*. The theme of Euripides' play comes from the *Odyssey*. In Euripides Odysseus blinds the one-eyed giant, so saving himself and releasing the satyrs from servitude. They make much noise but give no practical help. Euripides has created a Cyclops different from Homer's. He displays a philosophical bent and, like some contemporary Sophist, justifies the supremacy of brute force over law.

Political allusions, of this veiled sort, are found in Athenian tragedies as well. We cannot be surprised by their presence, considering the civic nature of dramatic contests. After all, the Old Comedy, produced at Dionysus' festivals during the fifth century BC, is political through and through: it forms an element in democratic debate by taking up a certain position with regard to issues of the day. Only comedies by Aristophanes have survived entire, but fragments by other dramatists suggest that he adhered to the main conventions of the genre.

The structure of Old Comedy was built according to a highly formal pattern. In the prologue, a current evil is identified and a solution proposed for it. The evil is all too real, but the solution lies in the realm of fantasy. In its working out, all laws of nature are suspended, yet the participants comment on actual people and events. Most of the painful situations arise out of the long Peloponnesian War. Fact and fiction are thus mingled in the prologue of *Acharnians* (425 BC). Dicaeopolis, an ordinary Athenian citizen, is suffering the discomforts of war while others line their pockets at the public expense. His remedy is to conclude a private peace with Sparta. The *Peace* (421 BC) envisaged an even more grotesque remedy: a citizen goes to Olympus on the back of a huge dung beetle to beg Zeus to show mercy to the Greeks. *Lysistrata*, a decade later, is also concerned with peace, and again an unthinkable solution is proposed: women will not sleep with their husbands until the latter put an end to the war. *Frogs* (405 BC) contains two prologues: the first shows Dionysus on his way to the underworld to bring back Euripides from the dead; the second introduces a poetic contest between Euripides and Aeschylus, and in the end Dionysus takes back Aeschylus, as better qualified to give the city good advice.

Aristophanes' comedies combine escapism and a preoccupation with the realities of life. The hero is often an ordinary individual who gets the better of authority and brings his plan to triumphant success. Among the traditional attributes of Old Comedy is the extreme licentiousness of language in referring to sexual activity and bodily functions. The licentiousness is in keeping with the occasion: a time of high festival, sanctioning the removal of usual constraints. The festal atmosphere sometimes invades the action of the play, as when in *Acharnians* a large phallus is carried in procession in honour of Dionysus.

Aristophanes' political opinions are easily elicited from his plays. He venerates the city and her democratic institutions, while detesting warmongering demagogues, profiteers, informers and litigious busybodies. The arch-enemy is Cleon, the target of sustained satire in *Knights* (424 BC) and other plays. Euripides and the philosopher Socrates embody, for Aristophanes, intellectual tendencies which are wholly pernicious. They encourage immorality and impiety, Euripides scorning the sanctity of oaths and Socrates proclaiming that the reign of the gods has come to an end.

The Old Comedy was a unique product of fifth-century-BC Athens, which allowed its poets a freedom of expression otherwise unknown. That freedom did not outlast the Athenian defeat in the Peloponnesian War. Aristophanes' *Ecclesiazusae* (392 BC) and *Plutus* (388 BC) are still concerned with the realization of an impossible dream: respectively women's acquisition of power and the unblinding of Wealth, so that he visits the righteous and avoids the wicked. The satire, however, is less political and individual, more social and generalized.

Historical Writing

Before Herodotus, there existed in Greece oral traditions and simple written records. He wove them together in

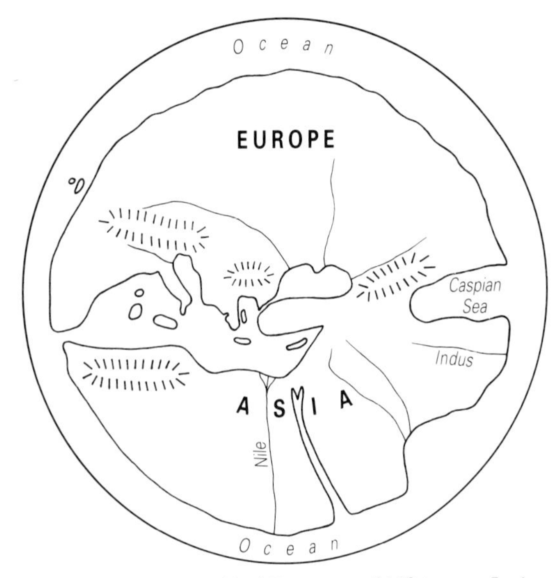

The two-continent world of Hecataeus of Miletus, an Ionian city long associated with learning. This is how he imagined the classical world around 500 BC.

a convincing literary whole, aided by his own curiosity and philanthropy. Two of the springs of his art lay in Ionia: the Homeric epics and the short, self-contained descriptions of various peoples and regions composed in the early classical age, the *logoi*.

Herodotus was born at Halicarnassus a few years before Xerxes' invasion of Greece. He was a much-travelled man, making journeys to Egypt, Phoenicia and Mesopotamia, and possibly other countries. He settled for a time at Athens, and died at Thurii, an Athenian colony in Italy, around 430 BC.

Herodotus' *History* has come down to us in nine books. Its climax is reached in the last three, with the war between the Persian king Xerxes and the Greeks. Possibly the plan of writing an account of the Persian Wars occurred to Herodotus at an early stage of his inquiries. On this assumption, his curiosity led him to seek the causes of the conflict, first in Darius' expedition, then further back in the foundation and expansion of the Persian empire, and further back still in the Lydian empire and its overthrow by the Persians. And all the time the pattern of Greek history was unfolded as a counterpart to the happenings in Asia. An alternative hypothesis holds that Herodotus began by assembling materials for *logoi* of traditional type. These are exemplified by the accounts of Lydia (Book 1), Egypt (Book 2) and Scythia (Book 4). The *logoi* which treat the development of Athens and Sparta in the sixth century BC (Books 1, 5) are strongly political in content. Other easily detachable elements are genealogies and other records of noble families.

Humanity shines through the whole work. When Herodotus describes the manners of various peoples, as he frequently does, he refrains from censuring or patronizing them. This attitude seems so natural to him that he never feels the need of justifying it. Also literary skill is displayed in things small and great. So many well-told stories occur in the *History* that the work could be treated as a collection of tales loosely strung together. And perhaps some readers do treat it in that way. Although the stories which congregate in the earlier books contribute little that is strictly historical, they enhance the grace and brilliance of the whole composition, besides affording Herodotus a vehicle for expressing his own belief in the divine government of the universe and the inevitability of fate.

Such stories foreshadow the great themes of the *History*. The men of destiny follow one another like actors crossing a well-lit stage. In Book 1 attention is concentrated first upon Croesus and then, after his fall, on Cyrus. Darius is the prominent figure in Books 3–6, but the Spartan king Cleomenes too has an important part. In Books 7 and 8, Xerxes naturally takes the central role. After the defeat at Salamis, he loses grip on the direction of events. We hear of him only once more, in an episode typical of Herodotus the moralist. The arrogance of his earlier conduct recoiled on his own head, as it had in the case of Cleomenes and Cambyses: they had become insane, while Xerxes fell into the depth of moral degradation (Book 9).

Herodotus' critical judgement makes him truly the 'father of history', as Cicero described him. It is by means of inquiry that he seeks to establish the 'cause' of things (beginning of Book 1). The recognition that there are different versions of events and that the choice between them can be made on grounds of general probability forms the basis for the writing of history. Herodotus' critical acumen is accompanied by an engaging candour in taking the reader into his confidence; not only is the evidence fairly presented, but the sifting of it takes place in full view.

At about the time of Herodotus' death, Thucydides (460–*c.* 400 BC) began his work on the Peloponnesian War. He was an Athenian, and his intellectual background lay in the Sophistic movement. He searches for causes as relentlessly as Herodotus had done, without sharing Herodotus' interest in the marvellous or his predominantly theological outlook. Thucydides' *History* of the rivalry between Athens and Sparta is furnished with an elaborate preface, setting out the causes of the conflict; but the narrative of the Peloponnesian War itself is unfinished, breaking off at the end of Book 8. The difference between Thucydides' work and that of Herodotus is due partly to outlook and temperament, partly to selection of material.

Thucydides' personality is graver and more sombre. He has studied history, especially political history, more profoundly and more systematically, but his range of interests is narrower. He avoids 'romantic fiction' of

The Temple of Athena Nike, 'Victorious'. This tiny building was erected near the entrance to the Athenian acropolis between 427 and 424 BC.

The Temple of Hera at Paestum, southern Italy. Founded about 600 BC, this Greek wealthy city eventually acknowledged Roman authority in 273 BC.

Herodotean type. His work is an 'everlasting possession' (Book 1), since human beings tend to behave similarly in similar situations. Book 3, for instance, deals with the revolution in Corcyra and the civil war which followed (427 BC). Terrible as the consequences were, they were even worse considered as the first instalment of sufferings: 'Revolution brought many disasters which occur and will always occur so long as human nature remains the same.'

In inquiring why the Peloponnesian War broke out (Book 1), Thucydides transmits to the reader the truth as he sees it. Despite a common supposition, the Corinthian grievances did not constitute the 'truest cause' of the war; that, Thucydides has established for ever, was the fear aroused at Sparta by Athenian imperial aggrandizement.

In its broader aspects, Thucydides' *History* is closely related to that of Herodotus. Both derive their momentum from a certain polarity: in Herodotus, that between east and west; in Thucydides, that between Sparta and Athens (expressed most eloquently in Pericles' funeral speech in Book 2). Both give their narrative a satisfying shape on a broad scale and in the vivid realization of individual scenes. In reporting speeches and debates, Thucydides does not allow himself Herodotus' freedom of invention. One debate recorded by Thucydides, the Melian Dialogue (Book 5), goes to the root of the nature of power and the responsibilities resting on those who exercise it. In this debate there is no recourse to comfortable formulae. The Athenians have gained the upper hand and now dispense with all pretext: 'You know, and we know, that a just result is reached in human dealings when the balance of power is equal; the dominant side effects what it can, and the weaker submits.'

Thucydides had successors, but none with his intellectual grasp. The unfinished *History* was continued down to 362 BC by the Athenian Xenophon (*c.* 430–354 BC). This continuation in seven books, the *Hellenica*, recounts political and military history, with the rise and fall of Sparta forming the central theme. But some outstanding matters – for instance, the re-emergence of Athenian power – are not adequately treated. While still in Athens, Xenophon became a member of Socrates' circle, and afterwards wrote some Socratic works. These hardly amount to serious philosophy, but they provide opportunities for the author's homespun reflections on life. His Spartan sympathies led to his banishment from Athens. A strong streak of hero worship appears in the *Cyropaedia* (a romantic view of the founder of the Persian empire) and in the biography of the Spartan king Agesilaus. Military matters were Xenophon's forte. He joined the rebellion of Cyrus the Younger in 401 BC, and the expedition forms the subject of his ablest work, the *Anabasis*.

The Theatre at Epidaurus, *c.* 350 BC. One of the largest theatres to survive, it measures 390 feet across the top.

Leonidas, the Spartan king who fell with his men in 480 BC at Thermopylae, resisting the invading Persians.

Oratory

Rhetoric, the art of persuasion through speech, is displayed in works of Greek literature from the *Iliad* onwards. It became established at Athens as a subject with its own rules; a subject, moreover, that could be taught in schools and used in the service of any cause. The recognition of rhetoric as a separate discipline is accompanied by the ascendancy of prose, with poetry coming to occupy a less important place in public life.

The beginning of the formal study of rhetoric is dated to 427 BC, when the Sophist Gorgias arrived in Athens from Sicily. Little of his work survives, and that little has no conspicuous merit. We have to believe that he was an effective orator, but one without principles, for whom persuasion counted for everything. Two orators of considerable reputation, Antiphon and Andocides, were in fact involved in the political upheavals at Athens late in the fifth century BC; but it is in the speeches of Lysias, delivered in the first twenty years of the following century, that we encounter Athenian oratory in its soberest and most lucid form. Such was the fame of Lysias (*c.* 459–*c.* 380 BC) as speech-writer and legal adviser that a great number of orations (not all genuine) circulated under his name. Skill in framing a speech so as to exhibit the character of the particular litigant and in setting forth a chain of probabilities, on Antiphon's model, justifies his reputation.

Isocrates (436–338 BC) was a man of different stamp. In his youth he wrote speeches for others to deliver in court, but his true importance lies in his foundation of an oratorical school. He codified the art of oratory by prescribing the parts of a speech and by paying minute attention to the arrangement of words. Isocrates was the earliest significant writer of *epideixeis*: that is, works cast into the form of speeches, but not intended for actual delivery. However, Isocrates' own *epideixeis* are predominantly political. They lack profundity or originality, and show little awareness of what was practical. The *Panegyricus*, dating from 380 BC, for instance, is addressed to an imaginary pan-Hellenic assembly. It advocates an expedition against Persia as a way of uniting the Greek people. This dream of re-creating a past golden age colours the subsequent political writings of Isocrates, but it is plainly insufficient to form the basis of a constructive programme.

Demosthenes (384–322 BC) was regarded as the supreme orator, in both the forensic and the political sphere. The overriding theme of his public speeches was that Philip of Macedon was patiently but relentlessly making himself the master of the Greek world. From this idea grew the unifying power of Demosthenes' political oratory. First he awoke the Athenians to a realization of Philip's true aims. Then he advocated the requisite military and diplomatic measures. Finally he felt driven to deal with the covert or open sympathizers of Philip. Demosthenes was not only a visionary, in seeking to preserve the independence of the Greek cities, but a practical politician who thought that if the resources of Athens were applied intelligently and wholeheartedly, then Philip could be thwarted.

His last years were overshadowed by the failure of his policy and by a long quarrel with Aeschines. In 336 BC, Ctesiphon proposed that the Athenians should recognize Demosthenes' services by the award of a golden crown. Aeschines entered a writ against this proceeding, alleging technical breaches of the laws. The case was not brought to trial until 330 BC. Aeschines' speech *Against Ctesiphon* was answered by that of Demosthenes, *On the Crown*. Aeschines frames his arraignment with great skill. Demosthenes' material is arranged in three main parts: in the first and second he defends his own public career, which was Aeschines' real target; in the third he goes over to the attack. *On the Crown* has many impressive attributes: besides the careful structure, a rapid shift from one topic to another – legal arguments, narrative sections, self-justification, personal abuse (essential to the genre), lofty encomia of the city, prayers to the gods. Throughout, Demosthenes pursues the central point that he had perceived the magnitude of the threat to Greek freedom and had taken the part of an honest statesman in meeting the threat. Looking back on the course of events, he can still ask (not unjustifiably): 'What else could I have done? How else could my countrymen have acted, if they were to keep their self-respect?' The jury had no doubt about the answer and found against Aeschines by an overwhelming majority.

Contending Schools of Thought

Intellectual life at Athens in the later fifth century BC was expressed in many contending movements. Debate between two of them, the Sophistic and the Socratic, was especially fruitful. The debate is not concluded yet, and never will be, so long as the purpose of human life can be seen from opposite points of view. At its most abstract level, the debate concerns appearance and reality. What we perceive by the senses is constantly changing. Can we look beneath this shifting surface? No, answered the Sophists. If any deeper reality exists, it lies beyond our reach. Hence there is no validity in any ethical or religious system; immediate usefulness constitutes the sole end of teaching. Socrates and his followers took the contrary view. There are absolute truths; these are never perceived directly, but their existence can be verified by reason. It follows that a moral code, based on right or justice, has justified claims on human obedience.

A Sophist was an itinerant teacher who provided instruction, especially rhetorical instruction, for money. At Athens the Sophists found their golden opportunity, for, as the democracy took deeper root there, a politician's career was advanced by an ability to persuade his fellow citizens. Most Sophists were non-Athenian: Protagoras came from Thrace, Gorgias from Sicily, Prodicus from Ceos, Hippias from Elis, and so on. The very term 'Sophist' took on a pejorative meaning through Plato's hostility, but the positive achievement of the Sophists in enlarging the old educational curriculum should not be underrated.

The exact opposite of a Sophist was personified by Socrates, born in 469 BC. He was, in the first place, an Athenian, and one passionately devoted to the city, rarely leaving it, except on campaign. Unlike the Sophists, he made no claim to be a teacher – least of all a professional teacher. He rejected the two basic Sophistic contentions, that there existed a body of knowledge and that this could be imparted to others. The Socratic method was to engage in inquiry along with friends. Socrates himself wrote nothing, but we gather from Aristotle (384–322 BC) that he used inductive arguments, whereby particular examples were examined and sifted. On this basis, he sought to attain universal definitions. For example, from a number of instances of 'the just', 'the pious', 'the courageous', he arrived (again in opposition to the Sophists) at fixed concepts of justice, piety, courage. These procedures, though often conducted in a bantering spirit, were not for Socrates a mere intellectual game; on the contrary, they formed the essential preliminary to the establishment of an ethical basis for life in the polis.

A certain cast of mind is attributed to Socrates. He equated right conduct with knowledge; hence all wrongdoing arose from ignorance, and could be cured by enlightenment. Possessed of a conventional piety and punctilious in religious observances, he had no doubt that the universe was divinely governed. There was an irrational side to Socrates, complementing his earnest search for truth and contributing to his well-rounded character. He sometimes said (only half humorously) that he had acted in such and such a way in response to the monition of a *daimonion*, or 'inward voice'. This word denotes a spiritual component, superior to reason.

Socrates, though a notable lover of his city, was convinced that the cobbler should stick to his last and not lay claim to political skills. Whether because he thus called into question the extreme democracy, or from some private malice, two trumped-up charges were brought in 399 BC: that Socrates had introduced strange gods and had corrupted young men. He was condemned to death by a popular court and executed in the same year.

Socrates' bearing at his trial and in the face of death was even more impressive than his intellectual and moral excellence. A large Socratic literature grew up, and schools were established in several parts of Greece to propagate his views. The leading associate of Socrates, the writer of the greatest Socratic works, and the founder of the most influential Socratic school was Plato, who was born into a noble Athenian family in 429 BC.

After the execution of Socrates, Plato's life was punctuated by three visits to Italy and Sicily. On the first of these, when he was about forty, he made the acquaintance of the despot Dionysius I in Syracuse. Returning to Athens, he founded and endowed the Academy, which was to remain a centre of Platonic teaching for the rest of his life and for centuries afterwards.

For all the reverence he owed Socrates, Plato was unlike him as man and philosopher. He was deeply versed in mathematics, and drew copiously on the work of thinkers other than Socrates. He abandoned the Socratic example entirely in founding a school and in committing so much to writing, although, to judge from the *Phaedrus*, he shared Socrates' preference for the give and take of live discussion.

Apart from the *Letters* (not all of them authentic) and the *Apology* (Socrates' speech of defence at his trial), the extant works of Plato are couched in dialogue form. A character called 'Socrates' takes a part, and usually the leading part, in all Platonic dialogues except the last, the *Laws*. The personal traits of this Socrates recall the living man, remembered with painful vividness for so many years. But, as he grew older and especially when he discoursed on a subject outside the Socratic sphere, Plato used this Socrates as a mere peg on which to hang his own opinions. The Socratic dialogues of Plato actually constitute a major Greek art form, without any obvious predecessor – or any descendant, save pallid imitations. The dialogues are often conceived in highly dramatic terms, with the scene carefully set, most often in the Athens that Socrates knew. Each of the earlier dialogues is dominated by a particular theme, an inquiry in which Socrates clears away much mental confusion by the method of question and answer. A solution is not always attained, or even sought. A number of major dialogues contain a myth, in which the dramatic illusion is broken and Socrates embarks on a monologue of exalted tone. In the telling of the myth we escape the restrictions of the dialogue form and follow Plato as he communicates, through the mouth of Socrates, the sublime vision of a higher truth than can be reached by argument alone.

Protagoras and *Gorgias* stand out among the earlier dialogues for their examination, and refutation, of the Sophistic position, especially that concerning 'the good' and its teaching. The *Meno*, too, considers the possibility of teaching the good; here we see the application of a positive Platonic doctrine, the 'recollection' of something learned in a previous existence. The next group of dialogues sees the development of a cardinal part of Platonic teaching: that of the 'forms'. These constitute the only true reality. They are perfect, eternal, indivisible, inhabiting a sphere of their own and yet participating in the perceptible world. As there is a hierarchy of excellence in the perceptible world, so there is in their world. The form of the good stands at the pinnacle, and the human soul can aspire to nothing higher than communion with it.

Colourful biographical material about Socrates is found in three important dialogues. *Symposium* contains a series of virtuoso speeches in praise of love; its climax comes with Socrates' myth concerning the 'form' of beauty, which is the object of all true love. *Phaedo* concerns the immortality of the soul. Forms and recollection are again important in the argument. The work draws unbearable pathos from its taking place on the last day of Socrates' life. The starting point, but only the starting point, of *Phaedrus* is instruction in rhetoric. The discussion follows a number of different, though related, paths (nature of love, 'divine frenzy', tripartite nature of the soul), reminding us that Plato did not demarcate between the various branches of philosophy.

The most elaborate Platonic dialogue is the *Republic*, in ten books. Book 1 resembles an early dialogue in which Socrates inquires into the nature of justice, without reaching any conclusion. Books 2–9 form a discourse by Socrates, to the effect that the problem of justice can be resolved only in the context of the polis. He accordingly traces the emergence of an ideal state, with its three classes (rulers, guardians, workers), reflecting the three parts of the soul (wisdom, courage, self-restraint). In the state as in the soul, that which maintains equilibrium is justice. The type of state envisaged here, and the curriculum of the rulers' education, arouse repugnance in some modern readers, less alive than Plato to the dangers of rhetorical blandishments. The myth of Er in Book 10 is framed to meet a specific need. Socrates has demonstrated that justice must be cultivated in and for itself, not because of any advantages that may accrue. But for Plato a full definition of justice will never be attained by examining a person's deeds in this world; we must inquire also into the life of the soul.

Some of Plato's later works explore more purely philosophical problems: *Theaetetus* inquires how we come to know what we know; *Parmenides* confronts some of the difficulties arising from the theory of forms; and *Philebus* seeks to identify the nature of true pleasure. And towards the end of his life, Plato wrote two dialogues which supplement the *Republic*, but in disparate ways. The *Timaeus* performs for the cosmos what the *Republic* performed for the human community. Timaeus, a Pythagorean, relates in a myth how the Demiurge, by working on formless matter, shaped the universe after an imperishable model (presumably a complex of forms). As the Demiurge was a supremely rational being, his creation displayed a perfect proportion and order in all its parts – these qualities are capable of being expressed in mathematical terms. The twelve books of the *Laws* are more practical, and also more pedestrian, than the *Republic*. An Athenian stranger, patently Plato's mouthpiece, instructs his two interlocutors in the most desirable aspects of a new city which is to be founded; emphasis is now placed more on the rule of law than on the elaborate structure envisaged in the *Republic*.

Plato, then, ventured on intellectual voyages never previously attempted. His journeys did not always end in a secure landfall, and readers expecting a reasoned defence of an intelligible position will often retire from his dialogues in bafflement, or even disgust. If Plato was a daring adventurer, his pupil Aristotle set himself the task of mastering, and classifying, the sum of human knowledge. How nearly he succeeded is seen in his extant treatises, which bring a strictly logical method to the investigation of an unparalleled range of subjects.

In 367 BC Aristotle came from his birthplace, Stagira in Chalcidice, to Plato's Academy when he was about seventeen. He remained there, in close association with Plato, until the master's death in 347 BC, whereupon he became a teacher in his own right, first at Assus, then in Lesbos. Philip summoned him to Macedon in 343 BC to help in Alexander's education. But after the accession of Alexander, Aristotle returned to Athens, where he founded his own school, the Lyceum.

We possess only some of the immense number of Aristotle's writings. He is known to have been productive in all the stages of his career, beginning with his time in the Academy. His earliest, or exoteric, works transmitted the teaching of the Academy to a wider audience. At first he seems to have adopted Plato's philosophical position, and even wrote philosophical dialogues in the Platonic manner. Different in character, and of uncertain date, are the vast collections of diverse materials: biographical, literary, politico-historical (among the latter is the *Constitution of the Athenians*). Upon the basis of these and other collections, Aristotle constituted the pedagogical works which he used for instruction in the Lyceum. These were not published until long after the author's death. The pedagogical writings concern the following subjects (among others): logic, natural and human sciences (physics, astronomy, meteorology, zoology and psychology), metaphysics, ethics, politics, rhetoric, poetics. Simply by drawing up such a list, we gain an inkling of the extent to which Aristotle had come to diverge from Plato. His arguments were based on observation and experience. Only when facts had been established did he have recourse to abstract reasoning. His works, accordingly, are untinged with Platonic myth-making or mysticism. He reveals no blinding truth, as Plato and Socrates had done.

In the *Physics* and *Metaphysics*, Aristotle brings powerful arguments against the existence of the Platonic 'forms'. There is, he insists, no such system of transcendental qualities inhabiting some sphere remote from our world. For Aristotle, the important questions are: how do things come to be what they are and where are they leading? The answer to these questions, he thought, lay in the assumption of four 'causes': material, formal, efficient, final. The objects we perceive (and, as always with Aristotle, these must be the starting point) represent a mingling of pattern (formal cause) and matter (material cause) by the operation of movement (efficient cause). Nor is movement ever haphazard. Whenever the 'potential' is realized in the 'actual', there is a purpose (final cause) in the mind of 'nature' or 'god'. God is identified as the unmoved first mover, in whom all movement has its end.

Aristotle (384–322 BC), philosopher and tutor of Alexander the Great, was the son of a Macedonian doctor and a pupil of Plato.

Passing over the prolific works on natural science – so influential in later times – we may mention two which concern the place of human beings in society. This topic interested Aristotle no less than Socrates or Plato. His analysis, however, leads him to far different conclusions. In the *Nichomachean Ethics*, he has no thought of founding a new society. Since the Platonic forms do not exist, men cannot be called upon to fashion their life according to an abstract form of good. What, then, is the nature of human happiness? Various types of virtue are considered in detail, and the contemplative life is finally recommended. Not an exalted aim, perhaps, but neither is it an ignoble one.

Closely allied to this treatise is the *Politics*, which investigates the different kinds of Greek state from a historical point of view and proposes an ideal constitution. The *Politics* has often been thought to show Aristotle in a somewhat parochial light. For this tutor of Alexander (the man who was to blur the distinction between Greek and barbarian) could not see beyond the venerable forms of the polis, or imagine that the highest human faculties could be exercised in any other environment. In this respect, certainly, Aristotle was a prisoner of his age, and his attitude brings us back to our starting point: namely that the ancient Greeks regarded themselves as a people apart.

THE HELLENISTIC AGE

The Alexander sarcophagus from Sidon, showing a battle between Greeks and Persians.

Chronology

BC

339	Xenocrates head of Academy
338	Philip II defeats Athens and Thebes at Chaeronea
337	Philip founds Hellenic League
336	Philip assassinated; accession of Alexander III (the Great)
335	Aristotle founds the Lyceum
334	Alexander crosses to Asia; Battle of Granicus; conquest of Asia Minor
333	Battle of Issus
332	Siege of Tyre
331	Alexandria founded Battle of Gaugamela
330	Burning of Persepolis Death of Darius
330–328	Alexander in Bactria and Sogdiana
327	Execution of Callisthenes
326	Battle of Hydaspes
325	Alexander reaches Indian Ocean
325–324	Alexander returns to Susa by sea and land
323	Death of Alexander
323–322	Perdiccas regent in Asia Lamian War in Greece
322	Death of Aristotle; Theophrastus head of the Lyceum
321–292	Menander active at Athens
320	Perdiccas murdered Meeting at Triparadeisus
319	Death of Antipater
317–307	Demetrius of Phalerum governor of Athens
317	Philip III Arrhidaeus murdered
316	Cassander executes Olympias He founds Cassandreia and Thessalonica
316/15	Death of Eumenes
315–311	Coalition of satraps against Antigonus the One-Eyed (Monophthalmus)
314	Polemo succeeds Xenocrates as head of Academy
311	Peace between Antigonus and the satraps
310	Zeno establishes the Stoic school in the Stoa Poikile at Athens
309	Alexander IV murdered
307	Epicurus sets up his school at Athens Demetrius Poliorcetes expels Demetrius of Phalerum from Athens
306–304	Antigonus, Ptolemy and Seleucus take the title of king
305–304	Demetrius' siege of Rhodes
303	Seleucus cedes Indian possessions to Candragupta and acquires 500 elephants
301	Battle of Ipsus Death of Antigonus
c. 300	Museum founded at Alexandria;
300	Zenodotus first head of the Library at Alexandria
297	Death of Cassander
294	Demetrius king of Macedonia
c. 293	Berossus' *History of Babylonia*
288	Lysimachus and Pyrrhus partition Macedonia
287	Death of Theophrastus; Strato head of the Lyceum
285	Demetrius surrenders to Seleucus (and dies in 283)
283	Death of Ptolemy I; accession of Ptolemy II Philadelphus
281	Lysimachus killed at Battle of Corupedium Seleucus assassinated Ptolemy Ceraunus king of Macedonia
281/80	Refounding of Achaean League
280	Duris of Samos active Bion of Borysthenes active
279	Gauls invade Macedonia and Greece
277	Antigonus II (Gonatas) defeats Gauls at Lysimachia
276	Antigonus king of Macedonia Death of Polemo, head of Academy
274–271	First Syrian-Egyptian War (Ptolemy II and Antiochus I)
274	Pyrrhus invades Macedonia
272	Pyrrhus' death at Argos
271/70	Death of Epicurus
c. 270	Callimachus, Theocritus, Aratus all active Manetho engaged on history of Egypt
269	Death of Strato, head of Lyceum
268–261	Chremonidean War of Athens and Sparta against Macedonia
268–241	Arcesilaus head of Academy
263	Euemenes I succeeds Philetaerus at Pergamum
263/2	Cleanthes succeeds Zeno as head of Stoa
261	Death of Antiochus I; Antiochus II succeeds Antigonus takes Athens
260–253	Second Syrian-Egyptian War (Antiochus II and Ptolemy II)
260	Death of Hieronymus of Cardia Death of Timaeus of Tuaromenium Apollonius Rhodius and Herodas active Erasistratus active
260–212	Archimedes active at Syracuse
256	The Mauryan king Aśoka (269–232) proclaims his Buddhist mission
255	Naval victory of Antigonus over Ptolemy II off Cos
251	Aratus frees Sicyon and brings it into the Achaean League

249	Alexander of Corinth revolts from Antigonus and allies himself to Achaea
246	Deaths of Ptolemy II and Antiochus II; accession of Ptolemy III and Seleucus II
246–241	Third Syrian-Egyptian War (Ptolemy III and Seleucus II)
246	Eratosthenes head of library at Alexandria
245	Antigonus II recovers Corinth
	Antigonus' naval victory over Ptolemy at Andros
244–241	Agis IV attempts social reforms at Sparta
243	Aratus seizes Corinth
241	Attalus I succeeds Euemenes I
240	War of Seleucus II against Antiochus Hierax
239	Death of Antigonus II; Demetrius II succeeds
239–229	War between Macedonia and the Achaean and Aetolian Leagues
238–227	War of Attalus I against Hierax and the Galatians (Gauls); Attalus becomes master of Asia Minor and takes royal title
235–222	Cleomenes III king of Sparta
232	Chrysippus becomes head of Stoa
229	Antigonus III succeeds Demetrius II Athens independent
229–222	War of Sparta against Achaea
226	Death of Seleucus II; Seleucus III succeeds
	Death of Hierax
225/4	Achaeans call in Antigonus III
224/3	Antigonus sets up the Hellenic Symmachy
223	Seleucus III assassinated; Antiochus III succeeds
222	Battle of Sellasia and flight of Cleomenes to Egypt
	Death of Ptolemy III; accession of Ptolemy IV
221	Death of Antigonus III; accession of Philip V
220–217	War of the Hellenic Symmachy against the Aetolians (Social War)
220	Antiochus III suppresses the pretender Molon
219–217	Fourth Syrian-Egyptian War (Antiochus III and Ptolemy IV)
217	Battle of Raphia
	Peace of Naupactus ends Social War
216–213	Antiochus suppresses Achaeus
215	Alliance between Philip V and Hannibal against Rome
212–205	Antiochus III's expedition to the Far East
206–185	Upper Egypt in revolt
204	Ptolemy V succeeds Ptolemy IV
203–200	Fifth Syrian-Egyptian War (Antiochus III and Ptolemy V)
200	Battle of Panium
	Palestine becomes Seleucid
c. 200	Aristophanes of Byzantium head of the library at Alexandria
170–168	Sixth Syrian-Egyptian War (Antiochus IV and Ptolemies VI and VIII and Cleopatra)
168	Battle of Pydna; end of Macedonian monarchy
167	Maccabean revolt against Seleucids
	Polybius arrives in Rome
166–159	Building of the Great Altar to Zeus and Athena at Pergamum
155	Carneades (head of Academy) visits Rome
149–148	Suppression of Andriscus' revolt in Macedonia
146	Macedonia becomes a Roman province
	Achaean War against Rome
	Sack of Corinth
145	Expulsion of intellectuals from Alexandria by Ptolemy VIII
144	Panaetius arrives in Rome
138	Attalus III succeeds Attalus II
135	The poet Nicander active
133	Attalus III dies and bequeaths his kingdom to Rome
100	Slave revolt in Laurium mines in Attica
88	Athens, under restored democracy, joins Mithridates of Pontus against Rome
87–51	Poseidonius active in Rhodes and Rome
87	Sulla campaigns in Greece
85	Athens stripped of all political privileges
79	Cicero in Athens and Rhodes
66	Pompey hears Poseidonius lecture in Rhodes
48	Caesar defeats Pompey at Pharsalus in Greece
42	Battle of Philippi
31	Battle of Actium

The Hellenistic Age (336–31 BC)

Frank W. Walbank

History

In August 338 BC Philip II of Macedonia (359–336 BC) defeated the armies of Athens and Thebes decisively at Chaeronea in Boeotia. The victory secured his domination over most of Greece. Thebes was treated harshly but Athens more generously. Philip went on to invade Laconia; Sparta was humbled and eventually deprived of some border territories. More important, Philip summoned the various Greek states to Corinth, where a confederacy was set up with the express purpose of making war on the king of Persia, whose dominions extended to the Aegean seaboard of Asia Minor. The League of Corinth was to be the instrument of Macedonian control over Greece and Philip was to lead the Persian expedition in person. Some advance forces were sent over to Asia Minor under Parmenion, but in 336 BC Philip was assassinated as he entered the theatre at Aegae (modern Vergina). He was succeeded by his twenty-year-old son Alexander III in 336 BC and he, after two years' campaigning against Illyrians and Triballians on his northern and western frontiers, crossed the Hellespont with an army of about 37,000 men, including 5,000 cavalry. With this act Alexander opened a fresh chapter in the history of Europe and Asia and set the stage for a new world of territorial states that was to endure for 300 years.

Alexander the Great (336–323 BC)

In order to give his expedition, which included a contingent of 12,600 Greeks, a pan-Hellenic flavour, Alexander began with a romantic visit to Ilium, thus conjuring up memories of the Trojan War. But the hearts of the Greeks were never in either the League of Corinth or the Persian expedition. An early victory in 334 BC at the River Granicus in north-west Turkey opened up Asia Minor to the Macedonians and during the following winter Alexander seized the western provinces – Caria, Lycia, Pamphylia and Phrygia. In 333 BC a second great victory at Issus (near Iskenderun) enabled him to advance south through Palestine, where the city of Tyre resisted him for six months, and on into Egypt. There he founded what was to be one of the world's great cities and called it Alexandria. He also visited the oracle of Amon, whom the Greeks identified with Zeus, at Siwah in the western desert. In 331 BC, leaving a governor in charge of Egypt, he marched north and east to win his third

Philip II, the architect of Macedon's rise as a world power.

Alexander the Great, conqueror of Persia and deified monarch.

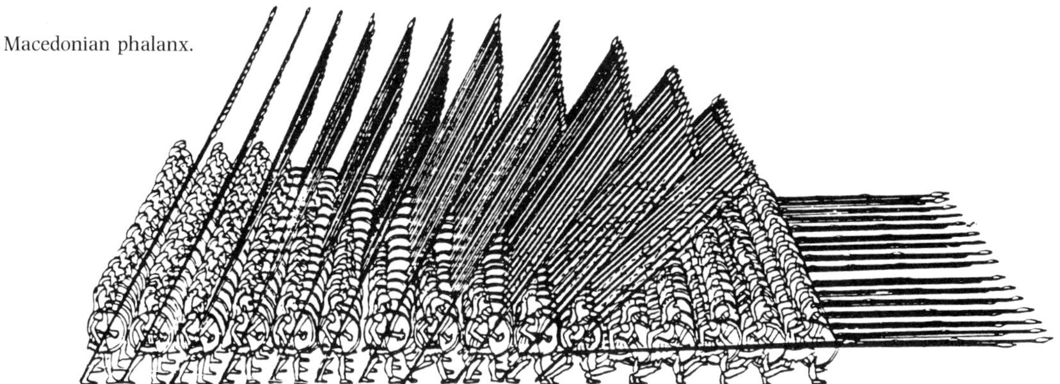

Macedonian phalanx.

decisive victory at Gaugamela, beyond the River Tigris. Darius, the Persian king, fled east, leaving Babylon and a treasure of 50,000 gold talents to the victor.

From Babylon Alexander advanced to Persepolis and Ecbatana, where he dismissed the Greek contingent. The pan-Hellenic crusade was over; henceforth it was to be a war of personal conquest. In 330 BC Darius was deposed and murdered by a usurper, Bessus, and Alexander assumed the title 'King of Asia'. Pressing on through Hyrcania, Aria and Drangiana (eastern Iran and Afghanistan), he reached Kabul by December. In 329 BC he crossed the Hindu Kush mountains into Bactria, advancing as far north as the Jaxartes (Syr Darya), where he founded a city, Alexandria the Furthest (Eschate), on the site of Leninabad in modern Tadjikistan. By this time his general Ptolemy had seized Bessus; after a flogging and oriental-style mutilation, Alexander sent him back to Ecbatana for execution.

Alexander spent the years 329 and 328 BC in northern Bactria and Sogdia where the local population had risen against him. After suppressing their revolt he married Roxane, the daughter of a Sogdian noble, Oxyartes. In 327 BC he returned over the Hindu Kush and, following the Kabul River down to the Punjab, crossed the Indus, made an alliance with a local prince, Taxiles, and defeated his rival Porus at the River Hydaspes (Jhelum). At this point his men refused to go any further. He was therefore obliged to abandon his expedition. From the mouth of the Indus he sent some of his forces in a newly built fleet by sea to Babylon, while he himself led the rest overland, with great losses, through Baluchistan into southern Iran, where the two halves of the expedition were reunited. On his arrival at Susa, in 325–324 BC Alexander held a great feast to celebrate his long campaign; and to make a start of a new policy of fusing Macedonians and Persians into a master race, he, his friend Hephaestion and eighty officers took Persian wives, and 10,000 soldiers with native partners were given dowries. In spring 323 BC, in Babylon, Alexander received embassies from many parts of the Greek world and began preparations for new conquests in the west and various campaigns of exploration, including one to the Caspian Sea. But, shortly afterwards, following a prolonged bout of feasting and drinking, he suddenly fell ill and died on 13 June in his thirty-third year.

The Significance of Alexander's Conquests

Many aspects of Alexander's career look forward to the so-called Hellenistic age which came into existence after his death. First, there was the character of his army, which was in marked contrast to those of the city-states such as Athens, Thebes, Syracuse or Sparta. In the ten years he was campaigning in Asia he had transformed the Macedonian and Greek force with which he set out into a multiracial army, including oriental troops, which owed its allegiance to him personally. In this he was to be followed by the generals who succeeded him. At the same time he effected a gradual change in his relationship with those about him. By Macedonian tradition relations between king and people were free and easy. But as he marched eastward and became King of Asia, Alexander grew more autocratic. This trend was underlined by a series of incidents. In 330 BC he executed Philotas, the son of his general Parmenion, on a charge of treason and followed this up with the death of Parmenion himself. In 328 BC he murdered his friend Cleitus in a drunken frenzy. In 327 BC, while at Bactra (modern Balkh), he tried to introduce an oriental form of obeisance (*proskynesis*) which Greeks and Macedonians practised only before a god; by ridiculing this proposal and causing Alexander to abandon it, the Greek historian Callisthenes, the official historian of the expedition, thereby signed his own death warrant. Somewhat later, both in India and after his return to Mesopotamia, Alexander showed himself ruthless in disciplining and purging various governors who he felt had betrayed his trust.

His autocracy also displayed itself in his relations with the Greek cities. Inscriptions show him interfering arbitrarily in local affairs, though indeed his actions were sometimes favourable to the city in question: for example, at Ephesus, where he restored democracy but ordered the city to pay to the temple of Artemis the taxes previously due to the Persians. In a particularly blatant example of interference he decreed in 324 BC the restoration of all exiles to the Greek cities, a measure which caused many complications involving rights and property. As we shall see, such autocratic acts were to be characteristic of the relationship between Hellenistic kings and the cities within their domains.

Another measure, which clearly foreshadows the

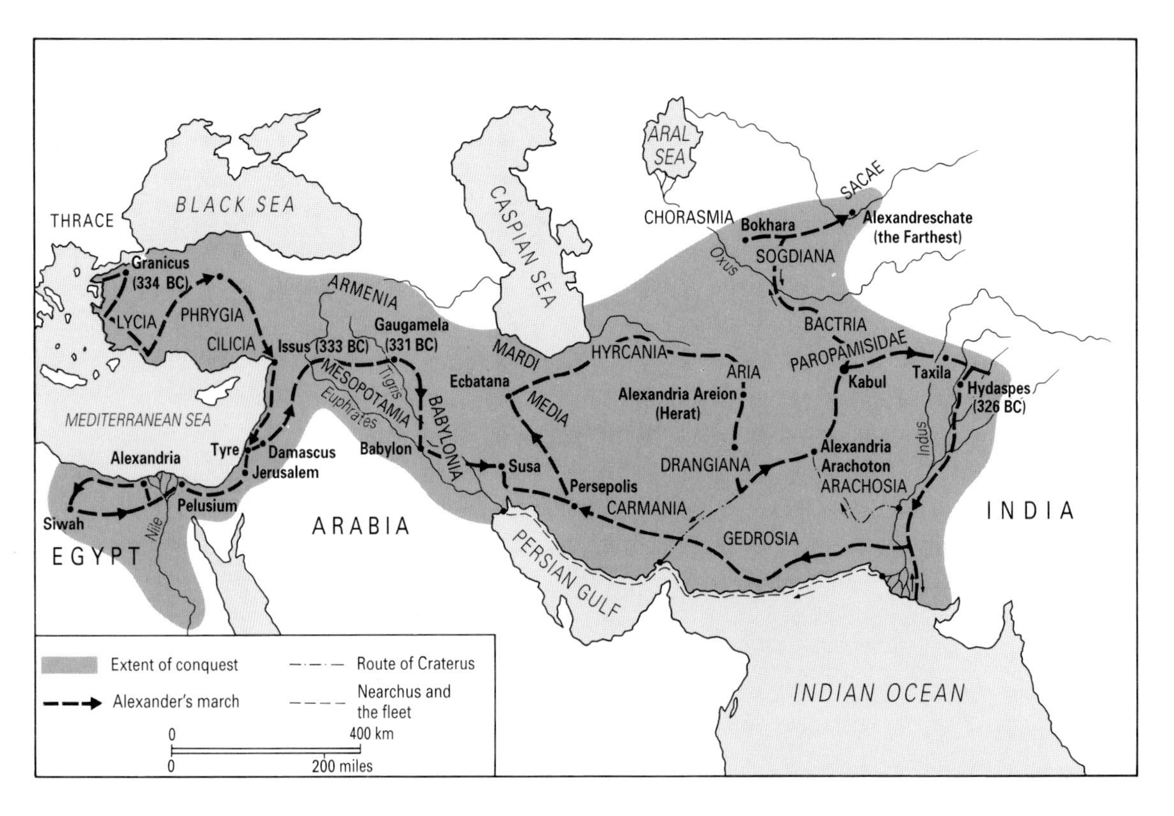

Alexander the Great's Asian campaigns.

atmosphere of the new age (though it had Greek precedents in the city-states of the fourth century BC and also in certain honours accorded to his father, Philip) was Alexander's demand, probably made at the same time that he called for the return of the exiles, that he be declared a god. He had evidently been considering this for some time. In Egypt, where he was accepted as pharaoh, he was a divine being. At Siwah he had been saluted as the son of Amon, and his attempt at Bactra to insist on *proskynesis* was interpreted, though perhaps wrongly, as a demand for worship. For the time being Alexander's death brought this development to an end, but ruler-worship soon crops up again.

Finally, there were Alexander's many city foundations. Apart from Alexandria in Egypt and Alexandria-by-Issus, these all lay east of the Tigris, and were designed to guard key points, supervise regions and serve as administrative centres, and were settled mostly with Greek mercenaries. With these foundations Alexander was anticipating the policies later characteristic of the Seleucid kingdom in Asia. Many of Alexander's cities decayed and perished, for their inhabitants were often reluctant colonists who seized the first opportunity presented to try and return to Greece. But some flourished and they were reinforced later by the Seleucids. Their role was central to the civilization of the centuries that followed.

The Struggle for the Succession

The fifty years following Alexander's death saw a protracted struggle between his leading generals either to win overall power for themselves or to carve out separate kingdoms from the whole. This struggle ended with three major dynasties in power: the Antigonids in Macedonia, the house of Seleucus in Syria and the east, and the Ptolemies in Egypt. The period falls into three sections of unequal duration.

The first of these, from 323 to 320 BC, is dominated by the attempt of Perdiccas, Alexander's senior cavalry officer, to devise a compromise settlement leaving effective power in his hands. Alexander's death had been followed by a fierce dispute between the cavalry and the infantry. The former, under Perdiccas, wanted to postpone appointing a successor to the throne till an expected child of Roxane should be born, but the infantry, under the chief phalanx-leader Meleager, wanted to appoint Arrhidaeus, a feeble-minded bastard son of Philip II, as king immediately. Thanks to the intervention of Alexander's secretary, a Greek named Eumenes, a compromise was reached. Roxane's baby proved to be a boy and the two nominees were made joint kings as Philip III (Arrhidaeus) and Alexander IV. Both were fated to become pawns in the struggle of others for power. Meanwhile, the commands were shared out. Antipater was to be general in Europe, Craterus was 'protector' of Arrhidaeus, and Perdiccas was in effect in charge of the whole, with the title of chiliarch. Ptolemy received Egypt, Antigonus western

Asia Minor, Lysimachus Thrace; and Eumenes was to take over Cappadocia and Paphlagonia. The first stage in the struggle between these strong and ruthless competitors for power ended in a coalition against Perdiccas, who was murdered in Egypt in 320 BC. Craterus had already died and at Triparadeisus in north Syria Antipater was made guardian of the kings and Antigonus general of Asia.

The second period, from 320 to 301 BC, was dominated by Antigonus, whose aim to the end of his life was to gain the whole empire for himself. The struggle was carried on in both Europe and Asia. In Europe Antipater died, leaving in charge another of Alexander's generals, Polyperchon; but a coalition of Antigonus, Ptolemy and Antipater's resentful son Cassander made war on Polyperchon. In the course of this conflict in 317 BC Alexander's mother Olympias (who supported Polyperchon) had Philip III and his wife put to death, but she was herself executed a year later by Cassander, who was by this time master of Macedonia. In Asia Antigonus eliminated Eumenes (316–315 BC), extended his power into Iran and expelled Seleucus from Babylonia. Ptolemy, Cassander and Lysimachus now combined against Antigonus, presenting him with an ultimatum to surrender most of his gains, together with other unacceptable demands. Antigonus replied with counter-demands against Cassander and, as a bold propagandist stroke, declared in 314 BC that all Greeks were to be free, without garrisons and self-governing. It was probably now that he also organized the island cities of the Aegean into a confederation, the Nesiote League, which later fell under Ptolemaic domination.

The war continued for two more years, during which Ptolemy soundly defeated Antigonus' son Demetrius at Gaza in southern Palestine and Seleucus seized the opportunity to recover Babylon. In 311 BC peace was made on the basis of the *status quo*: Cassander was recognized as general in Europe (till Alexander IV came of age – but he was soon assassinated, perhaps in 309 BC), Lysimachus as lord of Thrace, Ptolemy of Egypt and Antigonus of all Asia. Neither Polyperchon nor Seleucus was mentioned. This peace did not last. Over the next ten years there were frequent changes of alignment among Antigonus' various rivals. Seleucus was involved in war in the east against the Mauryan king Candragupta, with whom he made peace in 303 BC, ceding at least eastern Afghanistan, Baluchistan and the upper Indus valley; in return he received 500 elephants, a notable addition to his military strength. In 307 BC Antigonus' son Demetrius took advantage of Cassander's absence in Epirus to seize Athens, expelling Cassander's protégé, Demetrius of Phalerum, who fled to Egypt. The next year he defeated Ptolemy's governor of Cyprus in a naval battle off Salamis and annexed the island. This victory had momentous consequences. Antigonus celebrated it by taking the title of king for both Demetrius and himself, whereupon Ptolemy, Seleucus and Cassander very soon followed suit – a further step in the break-up of Alexander's empire.

A coin probably struck by Seleucus I Nicator to celebrate his victory at Ipsus. Indian elephants were a factor in its decisiveness.

Antigonus was now in buoyant mood and in 305 BC Demetrius attempted to reduce the powerful independent commercial city of Rhodes. The naval siege lasted until 304 BC and, though it brought Demetrius the nickname Poliorcetes, 'the Besieger', it ended in a compromise peace. In 304–303 BC Antigonus carried the war to the Greek mainland, where he resurrected the Hellenic League of Philip and Alexander against Cassander. But it was only a flash in the pan, for in 301 BC Cassander, Lysimachus and Seleucus forced Antigonus and Demetrius to battle at Ipsus in Phrygia. There father and son were defeated and Antigonus perished. Ptolemy now took most of Palestine, together with parts of Cilicia and Pisidia, Lysimachus the rest of Asia Minor as far as the Taurus mountains and Cassander was confirmed as king in Macedonia.

Ipsus marked the end of Antigonus' vain attempt to unite Alexander's empire under a single ruler and so confirmed the future pattern of separate kingdoms. The third stage in the struggle of Alexander's successors was marked by momentous changes in Macedonia and by the disappearance of Lysimachus' kingdom straddling the straits between the continents of Europe and Asia. It lasted from 301 to 276 BC and also saw the appearance of a new contestant, Pyrrhus, the king of the Molossians in Epirus. The years 301 to 285 BC were dominated by Demetrius' partially successful efforts to recover from the shock of Ipsus. He was helped in this by Cassander's death in 297 BC; and in 294 BC, after a period of weak government under Cassander's young sons, Demetrius seized the Macedonian throne. During a six-year reign he founded an important city on the Pagasean Gulf in Thessaly and named it Demetrias after himself. He also acquired

Corcyra in a marriage settlement with Lanassa, the divorced wife of Pyrrhus and daughter of Agathocles, the tyrant of Syracuse.

In 289 BC Demetrius invaded Aetolia, but the campaign went disastrously wrong and within two years Pyrrhus, who was allied to the Aetolians, had joined Ptolemy, Seleucus and Lysimachus in a coalition which forced Demetrius out of Macedonia. This setback was followed by the loss of Athens. Demetrius now invaded Asia Minor to attack Lysimachus, but without success. In 285 BC he surrendered to Seleucus and died two years later in captivity. Macedonia, meanwhile, had been divided between Pyrrhus and Lysimachus, but Pyrrhus failed to win the loyalty of the Macedonians and in 285 BC Lysimachus seized control of the whole country.

Lysimachus was now in a strong position, for he enjoyed much goodwill in Greece. But he wasted it all through palace intrigues in which, instigated by his third wife Arsinoe, the daughter of Ptolemy I, he executed his own son Agathocles for treason. Agathocles' widow, Lysandra, and her brother Ptolemy Ceraunus (they were also the son and daughter of Ptolemy I by a different mother) incited Seleucus to attack Lysimachus. In 281 BC Lysimachus was defeated by Seleucus at the battle of Corupedium in western Asia Minor, but the latter, after crossing the Hellespont into Europe, was assassinated by Ceraunus, who was now hailed king in Macedonia. Seleucus was succeeded in Asia by his son Antiochus I (281–261 BC), who at first became involved in an obscure war with Demetrius' son Antigonus Gonatas. In 278 BC, however, the two made a peace which was to be a lasting feature of relations between the two dynasties for the rest of the century. Ceraunus' rule in Macedonia was brief. In the early months of 279 BC he was obliged to face, without adequate preparation, a body of invading Gauls and was defeated, captured and decapitated. The following winter another body of the same Gauls, who formed part of a large migration, penetrated as far into Greece as Delphi, but were defeated and scattered by the Aetolians, who subsequently exploited the prestige of their victory to the full. A third group set up a kingdom in Thrace, while others crossed into Asia Minor and eventually settled in the area to be known as Galatia, becoming renowned as mercenaries. Meanwhile, Antigonus Gonatas, who still held strongpoints in Greece – at Corinth, Chalcis and Demetrias – was able to exploit the chaos in Macedonia following Ceraunus' death to win, in 278 BC, a much-publicized victory over the Gauls at Lysimachia. Within two years he was king in Macedonia and Thessaly.

The Hellenistic World up to the Coming of Rome (276–200 BC)

Antigonus' seizure of Macedonia completed the dynastic pattern which was to last for three-quarters of a century, until the arrival of Rome upon the scene. Among the main political features of these years were the peaceful relations between Macedonia and the Seleucids, and the prolonged rivalry between the latter and the Ptolemies. This hostility went back to Ptolemy's seizure of Palestine as far north as the River Eleutherus (Nahr al-Kabir, north of Beirut) at the time of Ipsus. It lay behind a succession of Syrian-Egyptian wars, five in the third century BC. Though the main bone of contention was Palestine, both powers had an eye on Greece and both had possessions in Asia Minor. There was also rivalry between Macedonia and Egypt, and this turned partly on the question of naval power in the Aegean and control over the islands there through the Nesiote League. The Ptolemies sought to protect the approaches to Egypt by holding Palestine to the east (and were successful in this until Antiochus III secured it in 200 BC) and Cyrene to the west, while the northern approaches were secured by the possession of Cyprus (permanently from 294 BC) and a number of coastal points in Asia Minor and the area towards the Hellespont; around 310 BC Ptolemy also made an alliance with the island city of Rhodes. A powerful Ptolemaic fleet linked these possessions together.

The Ptolemies were no doubt primarily concerned with Syria. But the kings of Macedonia were also hostile to Alexandria over long periods and the reigning Ptolemy was always ready to subsidize potential enemies of Macedonia. Since the days of Philip II, control of Greece had been a traditional Macedonian concern and the Antigonids sought to secure this in various ways. Demetrius Poliorcetes first resuscitated the council of states that had met at Corinth, and Antigonus III Doson (229–221 BC) similarly set up a Greek confederacy, this time consisting of federal bodies as members. But in addition Antigonus II Gonatas and his successors down to Philip V (221–179 BC) held various strongpoints with Macedonian garrisons, in particular Demetrias, Chalcis, the Piraeus (with or without Athens) and Corinth. Gonatas also encouraged pro-Macedonian tyrants in several Peloponnesian cities and his fleet was twice victorious over those of Ptolemy II and Ptolemy III, probably on the pretext of intervening in two of the Syrian-Egyptian wars on the Seleucid side. But the Antigonids were partly handicapped in their ambitions in Greece by the need to keep constant watch over their northern and western frontiers, which were always at risk from warlike barbarian neighbours in Illyria, Dardania and Thrace – as indeed the Ptolemies were, in turn, obliged to keep a watchful eye on Nubia.

From an early date Seleucid power was in retreat in both the far east and Asia Minor. At both ends of their extended dominions separate kingdoms arose, carved out of the unwieldy empire of Alexander. Already much of the east was lost to Candragupta, the aggressive Indian ruler, and in about 275 BC Philetaerus, the governor of Pergamum in north-western Asia Minor, who had deserted Lysimachus for Seleucus shortly before the battle of Corupedium, declared himself independent and founded a separate state, which he held until his death in 263 BC. His successor, Eumenes I (263–241 BC), considerably expanded its territory, but

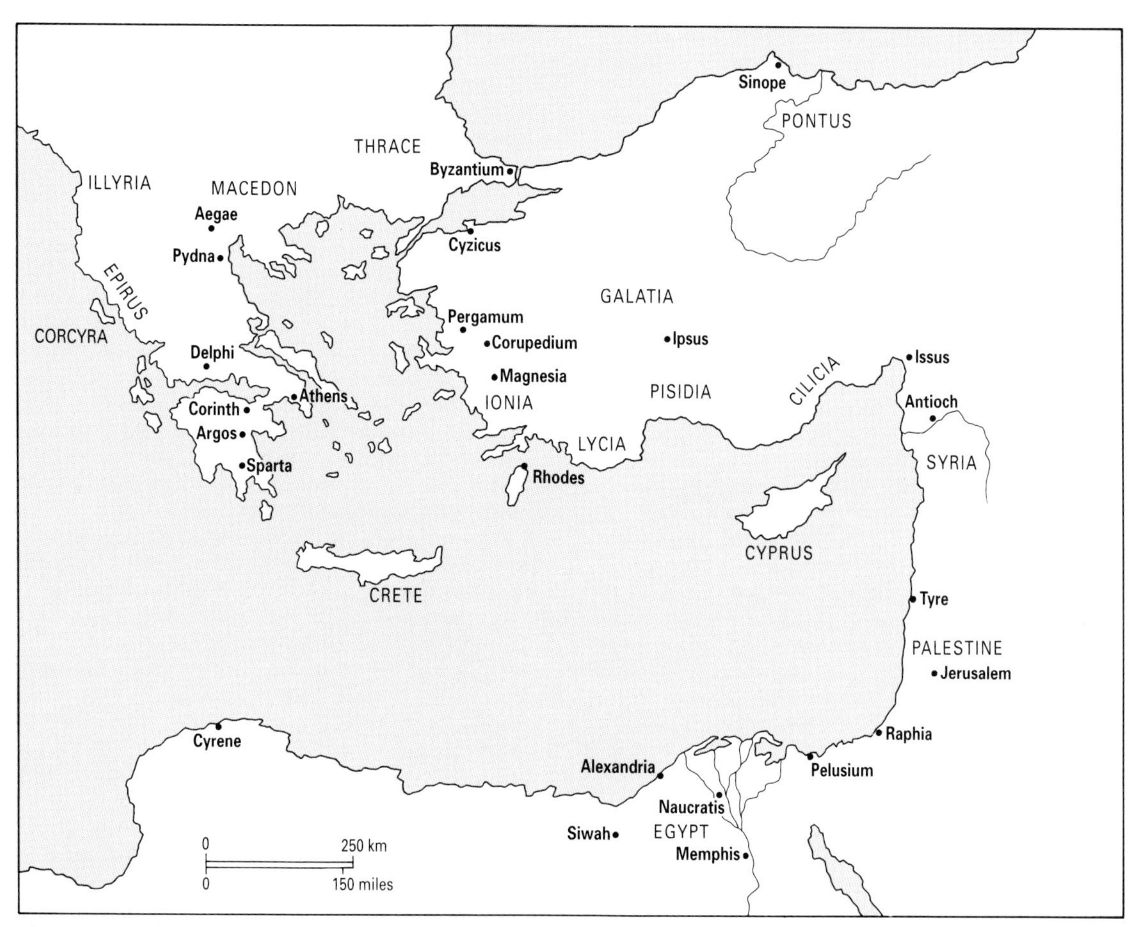

The eastern Mediterranean during the Hellenistic Age.

it was his successor, Attalus I (241–197 BC), who first took the royal title and gave his name to the dynasty. Under the Attalids Pergamum was to develop, eventually with Roman support, into a kingdom of equal status with those of the Antigonids, the Seleucids and the Ptolemies.

The central position in the Hellenistic world was held by the Ptolemaic dynasty, with its various outlying possessions forming a ring around Egypt. The Greek historian Polybius regarded these possessions outside Egypt as basically a defence – primarily against Syria, no doubt, but also perhaps against the kings in Macedonia. The situation was in fact less simple, not least because the Hellenistic world recognized no formal doctrine of a balance of power. When the opportunity offered itself, Hellenistic kings usually took what they could get and hold. So defence and offence are concepts that merge one into the other to suit changing circumstances.

Macedonia and Greece (276–261 BC): The Chremonidean War

Between 276 and 200 BC four kings sat on the Macedonian throne: Antigonus II Gonatas (276–239 BC), Demetrius II (239–229 BC), Antigonus III Doson (229–221 BC), and Philip V (221–179 BC), whose reign ran well into the second century. Gonatas' first four years were unstable. He had to bring order to a country in chaos and his royal tenure was threatened by Pyrrhus, who, after returning from a war in Italy (where the Romans defeated him, together with his allies, in Tarentum), now invaded and for a short time held Macedonia. But in 272 BC Gonatas followed him into the Peloponnese and defeated him in a battle fought in the streets of Argos, where the Epirote king was killed (by a tile thrown from a roof). Antigonus now consolidated his hold on Thessaly and strengthened his position further south with strongpoints on the island of Euboea, at both the Piraeus and Athens, at Corinth and even perhaps at Megara. There were also tyrannies at Elis, Megalopolis, Argos and Sicyon, although not all were necessarily sponsored by Macedonia. To break this Macedonian control was the object of the so-called Chremonidean War, waged by Sparta and Athens against Antigonus and named after the Athenian statesman Chremonides, who introduced the war measure at Athens. It was sponsored by Ptolemy II Philadelphus (283–246 BC) and, besides Athens and

Sparta, was joined by Elis, Achaea, Tegea, Orchomenus, Phigalia, Caphyae and certain Cretans allied to Sparta. The war lasted from 268 to 261 BC. Few details have survived. Areus I, king of Sparta (309–265 BC), made two vain attempts to break through the Macedonian line at the Isthmus of Corinth and at the third attempt was killed. Ptolemy sent some aid, but not enough, and in 261 BC Athens was forced to surrender. Macedonian control over southern Greece was resumed and lasted for another decade.

Syrian-Egyptian Conflicts (261–242 BC)

In 260 BC, a year after the end of the Chremonidean War, the Second Syrian-Egyptian War broke out. It seems likely that Antigonus was involved at sea in this conflict. There had already been one Syrian-Egyptian War during the 270s BC, when Antiochus I took advantage of the revolt of Magas, the governor of Cyrene, against Ptolemy II to attack his rival. The result had been in Ptolemy's favour. The second war probably arose out of an attempt by Ptolemy II to exploit the arrival of a new ruler upon the Seleucid throne, Antiochus I having died and been succeeded by his son Antiochus II (261–246 BC). Antigonus' naval victory over Ptolemy's admiral Patroclus off Cos is probably an episode in this war, in which the Macedonian king intervened briefly on the Seleucid side. The war ended in Antiochus' favour in 253 BC. As part of the settlement he divorced his wife Laodice and married Ptolemy's daughter Berenice, a move which laid up trouble for the future.

The strong position of Antigonus in central Greece rested on his possession of Corinth and its formidable citadel, the Acrocorinth. So it came as a severe blow that Alexander, the son of its loyal commander and Antigonus' own choice as the latter's successor, revolted and declared himself independent. The event was indeed the last of a series of setbacks. These included the expulsion of Nicocles, the tyrant of Sicyon, who was well disposed towards Macedonia, by a young man named Aratus, who in 251 BC then took the imaginative step of bringing Sicyon into the lately reconstituted Achaean League. Pressure from Aratus and the Achaeans may have helped to precipitate Alexander's revolt. But the latter died shortly afterwards and in 245 BC Antigonus managed to trick his widow into surrendering the fortress. His triumph, however, was short-lived. Two years later, in a brilliant *coup*, Aratus seized the Acrocorinth and this time it was to be lost to Macedonia for almost twenty years. It was probably between his recovery of Corinth and his loss of it a second time that Antigonus once again intervened with his fleet in a war between Egypt and Syria, and dealt a blow at Ptolemaic naval power with a victory off Andros.

The Third Syrian-Egyptian (or Laodicean) War, like the second, followed on a change of rulers, for both Antiochus II and Ptolemy II died in the same year and were succeeded respectively by Seleucus II (246–226/5 BC) and Ptolemy III Euergetes (246–222 BC). Seleucus II was the son of Antiochus by Laodice, his divorced wife, and Ptolemy III answered an appeal from his sister Berenice, Antiochus II's widow, to intervene on behalf of her son. Very soon, however, both mother and son were assassinated and although Ptolemy III advanced as far as the Euphrates and made territorial gains in Asia Minor, he could not prevent Seleucus II consolidating his position as king. It was probably early in this war, in 245 BC, shortly after Antigonus' recovery of Corinth, that his fleet defeated Ptolemy's off the island of Andros. This defeat cost Ptolemy his control of the Cyclades, and in consequence Antigonus felt able to celebrate his victory by establishing two special annual festivals, the Soteria and the Paneia, on Delos. But this was his last triumph. After 241 BC he tried in various ways to avenge himself on the Achaean League. Ever since the Aetolians' much-publicized success in driving the Gauls from Delphi in 279–278 BC, they had been gaining prestige and territory in central Greece. Antigonus now entered into an alliance with them in order to attack Achaea. But despite more than one Aetolian raid into the Peloponnese, Aratus kept up pressure on Athens and Argos, until 240 BC brought a peace settlement. In the ensuing year Antigonus died and was succeeded by his son Demetrius II (239–229 BC).

The Macedonian Recovery

Shortly after Demetrius' accession the Achaean and Aetolian Leagues made an alliance against him. The Aetolians had their eyes on western Acarnania, which belonged to Epirus, and their alliance with Achaea was a reply to Demetrius' action in making an agreement with Olympias, the widow of the Epirote king Alexander. The war of Macedonia against the two Leagues lasted for ten years and its most important outcome was the collapse of the Epirote royal house, followed by Demetrius' appeal to Agron, king of the piratical Illyrians, to come to the aid of Acarnania against Aetolia. The Illyrians compelled both Acarnania and Epirus to join them, and in 229 BC Teuta, the widow of Agron, who had recently died, sent a fresh naval force south to defeat a joint Achaean and Aetolian fleet off Paxos. Illyrian piratical outrages in the Adriatic had, however, led Greek cities there to appeal to Rome and in 229 BC this growing power in central Italy sent its first expedition into Greek waters, thoroughly defeated the Illyrians and made a treaty with them, by which they were forbidden to sail with more than two light unarmed vessels south of Lissus (modern Lezha in northern Albania). But, more important, this First Illyrian War left the Romans with a protectorate along the Albanian coast, which included Apollonia, Epidamnus and the Genusus valley, as well as the islands of Issa and Corcyra. In Greece Demetrius' reign was mainly important for the expansion in the Peloponnese of the Achaean League, which now incorporated Argos and Megalopolis.

Demetrius was succeeded by Antigonus III Doson (229–221 BC), his cousin and a descendant of Deme-

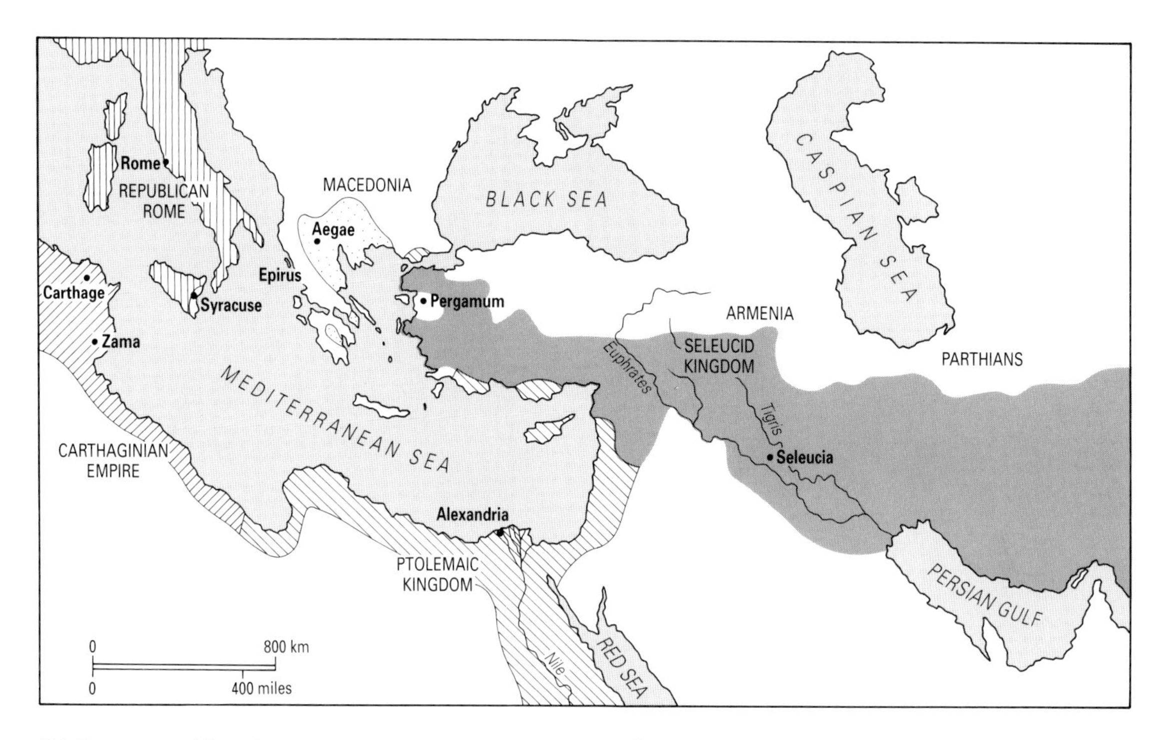

Chief international boundaries in 238 BC.

trius I, first as general and then as king, for Demetrius' son Philip was only a child. After putting down internal revolts, expelling the Aetolians, who had invaded Thessaly, and retaliating with a raid into Doris and Phocis, Antigonus mounted a naval expedition to Caria and established some strongpoints there. But his aims in Asia Minor are obscure, since they were overtaken by events in southern Greece, where a new king of Sparta, Cleomenes III (235–222 BC), now set out to disrupt the Achaean League and take over its cities piecemeal. In 227 BC Cleomenes strengthened his position at Sparta with a revolutionary *coup* and the introduction of a programme of land reform and debt cancellation, designed to swell the citizen body (and the army). Foreseeing further disasters, Aratus opened private and secret negotiations with Antigonus, who readily agreed that, if Aratus gave the word, he would march south and assist the league against Cleomenes. The price of his help would be the surrender of the fortress of Corinth.

During the next two years the Achaeans lost city after city to Cleomenes, who eventually became master of Argos and Corinth. In autumn 224 BC Antigonus received the awaited call and very soon arrived at the Isthmus of Corinth with his army. The return of Argos to the Achaean fold compelled Cleomenes to abandon his position at Corinth. Two years later he was decisively defeated at Sellasia, on the hills to the north of Sparta, and fled with all his family to Alexandria. Cleomenes' meteoric rise had been noted in Egypt, and between 225 and 222 BC Ptolemy III had transferred to the Spartan the subsidy that he had been giving to the Achaeans, evidently regarding him as a more useful counterweight against Macedonia. But once Antigonus had responded successfully to the Achaean appeal, Cleomenes was useless and Ptolemy withdrew his subsidy. Refuge in Alexandria had little to offer Cleomenes and in 219 BC he perished in an abortive rising against the new king of Egypt, Ptolemy IV (222–204 BC).

Before the battle of Sellasia Antigonus had already set up a new version of the Hellenic League originally founded by Philip II and briefly revived by Antigonus I and Demetrius I in 302 BC. Antigonus' alliance consisted of federal states, with the Macedonian king as commander-in-chief and president. Its original members were the Achaeans, Macedonians, Thessalians, Epirotes, Acarnanians, Boeotians and Phocians. It was partially crippled by possessing no treasury and by the fact that its decisions had to be ratified by the component states. This Symmachy, as it is generally called, was to last for over twenty years, during which it involved its members first in a war against the Aetolians and after that in a much more disastrous one against the Romans. The latter marked a significant stage in the process which was to end in Roman domination over the whole Hellenistic world.

The First Roman-Macedonian War (214–205 BC)

When Antigonus died in 221 BC he was succeeded by Philip V (221–179 BC), the young son of Demetrius II. The first four years of his reign were occupied with a war between the Hellenic Symmachy and the Aetolian League, which was allied to Elis and Sparta in the

Peloponnese, the so-called War of the Allies. In 219 BC Demetrius of Pharos, an Illyrian protégé of the Romans, had broken the treaty of 229 BC by sailing south of Lissus with a squadron of his warships. As the Romans swiftly crossed the Adriatic against him, Demetrius took refuge with the Macedonian king and it was allegedly at his instigation that Philip, hearing of the victory of the Carthaginian general Hannibal over the Romans at Lake Trasimene in Etruria, brought the fighting in Greece to an end and opened negotiations with Hannibal. In 215 BC a treaty was made between the two. The Romans in reply secured an alliance with the Aetolians and for over a decade there was renewed conflict in Greece, fought largely between the Greek allies of the two powers, Rome and Macedonia. In 206 BC the Aetolians were driven to make a separate peace and a year later, at Phoenice in Epirus, the Romans made their own peace with Philip and the Symmachy. Philip's aim, to control the area beyond Pindus down to the Adriatic, had been thwarted and he now took up an old Antigonid policy by building a fleet to serve for expansion in the Propontis and the Aegean. His ambitions there were conveniently fuelled by the sudden death of Ptolemy IV and the accession of his six-year-old son, Ptolemy V Epiphanes (204–180 BC). In the winter of 203–202 BC Philip and Antiochus III of Syria (223–187 BC) made a compact to exploit the new situation by seizing Ptolemaic possessions (the existence of this agreement has been queried, but unjustly – though its contents were certainly exaggerated, once it became known).

Antiochus III the Great (223–187 BC)

Antiochus III had succeeded in 223 BC to find Seleucid power seriously reduced. Iran, together with areas to the east, had been lost. Bactria and Sogdiana became an independent kingdom under Greek kings, probably around 250 BC, and Parthyene was annexed by nomads, who set up the kingdom of Parthia there. Added to these difficulties on the eastern frontier was the catastrophe of a revolt in Asia Minor, which lasted from 240 to 237 BC and cost the Seleucids the lands west of the Taurus mountains. These were seized by Attalus I of Pergamum, who also won some remarkable victories against the hardy Galatians. Nor was his the only kingdom now established in Asia Minor. Since the early years of the third century a Thracian dynasty had ruled in Bithynia beside the Propontis, and further to the east, on the Black Sea, Mithridates I was proclaimed king of Pontus in 281 BC. Around the middle of the century Ariarathes II took the title of king in Cappadocia in the heart of the peninsula.

Antiochus had first to deal with the revolt of two of his generals. Molon he defeated, but he was obliged to leave Achaeus in possession of the diminished Seleucid holdings in Asia Minor while he campaigned against Ptolemy IV. Ptolemy defeated Antiochus at Raphia on the borders of Palestine and Egypt, thus bringing to an end the Fourth Syrian-Egyptian War (221–217 BC). It took Antiochus another four years to capture and execute Achaeus and between then and 205–204 BC he was busy with an ambitious expedition into the eastern provinces, designed to reassert Seleucid power there. The results of this campaign were disappointing. Armenia and Iran were both restored to Seleucid authority, but elsewhere, in Bactria, India and the satrapies of Arachosia, Drangiana and Carmania, Seleucid control was entirely nominal. After returning to the west in 205 BC, Antiochus spent two years extending his power in Asia Minor. In 203–202 BC came his agreement with Philip V of Macedon; and shortly afterwards he attacked Egypt for a second time. In 200 BC the defeat of Raphia was avenged at Panium, near the source of the Jordan, and as a result of this battle Palestine became Seleucid – a significant change in the power relations and one which reflects the weakening of Egypt in the last decades of the third century BC. For though the earlier war with Antiochus had ended in the victory of Raphia, Ptolemy had been obliged to enrol 20,000 native troops in his army and subsequently had to make concessions to the native priesthood. An inscription in Greek and in Egyptian, both hieratic and demotic, which records the celebration of Raphia by a synod of priests in November 217, gives Ptolemy the full titulature of a pharaoh, an indication of the strength of Egyptian influence. This in itself need not necessarily have weakened the king's position. But from 207 to 186 BC Egypt was rent by a civil war marked by the appearance of a separate pharaoh of Nubian origin in Upper Egypt and by continuous brigandage elsewhere. This had a serious effect on the revenues received in Alexandria and the accession of a boy king only added to the difficulties.

Roman Intervention

Between 203 and 201 BC Philip V of Macedon used his newly built fleet to continue his aggressive policy, intriguing against Rhodes, advancing in the Propontis and finally in 201 BC engaging in full-scale naval warfare against Rhodes and Pergamum. The Romans became alarmed and presented Philip with an ultimatum, which was soon followed by war. The Second Roman-Macedonian War (200–197 BC) marks a further decisive stage in Roman intervention in the Hellenistic world. Both the Achaeans and the Aetolians sided with the Romans and the war ended with Philip's defeat at Cynoscephalae in Thessaly. Although

The reconstructed Stoa of Attalus I, king of Pergamum. He built this in Athens during the 150s BC.

'Fortune', Tyche of Antioch. The statue was commissioned shortly after the city's foundation in 300 BC by Seleucus I Nicator, one of Alexander's successors.

Chrysippus (280–207 BC), the third head of the Stoa and the elaborator of its system of philosophy.

The Rosetta Stone is a triscript, containing a decree in honour of Ptolemy V Epiphanes. Because the hieroglyphic and demotic versions translate the Greek, the stone proved crucial in the nineteenth century to the decipherment of ancient Egyptian.

Antiochus' secret agreement with Philip was never directed against Rome, the Senate took alarm when Antiochus invaded Europe in order to recover lost territories in Thrace. After a confused diplomatic exchange, war ensued and Antiochus was defeated in 189 BC at Magnesia in Asia Minor. In the years 171–168 BC, incited by Eumenes of Pergamum (197–159/8 BC), the Senate also launched the Third Roman-Macedonian War against Philip's son and successor, Perseus (179–168 BC), defeated him at Pydna in southern Macedonia and brought the Macedonian monarchy to an end. At the same time the invasion of Egypt by Antiochus IV (175–164 BC), who had succeeded his elder brother Seleucus IV (187–175 BC), led to the Sixth Syrian-Egyptian War (169–168 BC). This ended in humiliation for Antiochus, who, on the brusque orders of a Roman officer, Popillius Laenas, was compelled to leave the country.

The Hellenistic states now looked more and more towards Rome. We need not follow in detail the rise and fall of Pergamum, favoured with new territories after Antiochus III's defeat in 189 BC, at war with Pontus and Bithynia in the following decade and, after the Third Roman-Macedonian War, in disfavour at Rome. In 133 Attalus III (139–133 BC) died and bequeathed his kingdom to Rome. Meanwhile, the Seleucids had been weakened by a long period of Jewish revolt under the Maccabees (165–141 BC). At the root of this movement was a strong current of Jewish orthodoxy resisting the spread of Hellenization, as we see it illustrated in the book of *Ecclesiastes*, composed around 250 BC. The *Wisdom* of Jesus ben Sirach (*Ecclesiasticus*), first written in Hebrew but in 132 BC translated into Greek at Alexandria, was a counterblast to this trend and was extremely popular among Jews resisting Hellenism. After 200 BC the Seleucids proved less understanding towards the Jews than the Ptolemies had been. The Jewish rising was a reaction to the attempt by Seleucus IV to seize the wealth of the Temple in Jerusalem and that of a hellenizing High Priest, Jason, under Antiochus IV, to turn Jerusalem in some sense into a Greek city-state, or at the very least to establish a Greek community there. There was fighting from 165 BC onwards, first under Judas Maccabaeus and later under his brothers Jonathan and Simon, until in 141 BC substantial concessions were extorted from Demetrius II (145–140 BC). By then Jerusalem was in Simon's hands. This Jewish conflict dragged on to weaken an already enfeebled line of Seleucid rulers.

In mainland Greece the Romans consolidated their power. A Macedonian pretender, Andriscus, was defeated in 148 BC and, two years later, a Roman province of Macedonia was set up. In the same year the Achaean League was crushed in a short war and forcibly disbanded. Egypt was disrupted by dynastic struggles and, after his restoration from exile in 145 BC, Ptolemy VIII carried out a massacre of Greeks and an expulsion of intellectuals which, together with more violence, degraded the quality of life in Alexandria.

A silver coin of Euthydemus I of Bactria, a Greek kingdom on the borders of India.

A silver coin of his son, Demetrius I. Greek rule in Bactria and north-west India ended around 50 BC.

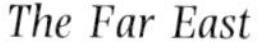

The Far East

One part of the Hellenistic world, however, lay outside the field of Roman influence. In Sogdiana and Bactria, around 250 BC, a break-away kingdom had been set up. Here two rulers named Diodotus, father and son, reigned for a considerable time. Later we find a new dynasty, that of Euthydemus and his son Demetrius, ruling and extending Bactrian power at the expense of Parthia and across the Hindu Kush into Paropamisadae and Gandhāra (southern Afghanistan and the Punjab). In the absence of any consecutive literary account our knowledge of these kings rests on a remarkable coinage. From this we learn of Eucratides (known to the historian Justinus, third century AD), who probably ruled Bactria from 171 to 155 BC, and of Menander (recorded as Milinda in the Buddhist tradition), who greatly extended Greek rule and commanded from Kabul to Chandrigarh and from Swat to Kandahar. The obscure history of the Greeks in Bactria and India ended around 50 BC at the hands of nomad Da Yuezhi, Śakas and Pahlavas (Scytho-Parthians). But its intensity and continuity is demonstrated by a coinage which reveals the names of some forty kings throughout a period of two centuries, and recently too by the excavation of Aï Khanum on the Oxus.

The First Century BC

Apart from the far eastern kingdoms, the history of the Hellenistic world in the century before Christ simply merges into that of Rome. Here we need only mention briefly the remarkable career of a king who may be regarded as the last and dubious defender of an independent Hellenism. Mithridates VI of Pontus (120–66 BC) presented the only serious challenge from the

A silver coin of Mithridates VI of Pontus, the enemy of Rome, struck in 75 BC.

The reverse side of a Roman gold coin struck in 27 BC to celebrate the fall of Egypt.

east during the last century of the Roman republic. After military successes in Asia Minor, he built up a strong alliance of fellow kings, reputedly massacred 80,000 Romans and Italians, and raised up a revolt in Greece. But the Roman general Sulla recovered Athens, which had fallen into his hands, and defeated his general, Archelaus. A first war (88–85 BC) ended with a treaty requiring Mithridates to give up all his conquests. A second war, provoked by the Roman officer, L. Licinius Murena, went in Mithridates' favour. But in a third war (74–71 BC) he was defeated at Cyzicus (74/3 BC), while the Roman general Lucullus was victorious over his fleet near Lemnos. After a final defeat by Pompey in 66 BC, Mithridates took refuge in the Crimea and soon afterwards committed suicide. The general settlement of the east which Pompey now carried out brought the Seleucid monarchy to an end. The Ptolemaic dynasty survived until 31 BC, when, as the culminating event of the civil war between Octavian (the later emperor Augustus) and his rival Mark Antony, Cleopatra VII (51–31 BC) avoided sharing in the latter's naval defeat off Actium in Acarnania by flight and the next year committed suicide rather than face being paraded in Octavian's triumph. The year that saw the disappearance of the last great Hellenistic dynasty, the Ptolemies, also marked the end of the Roman republic and in its place initiated a disguised monarchy at Rome. The Roman empire by this time incorporated within itself most of the Hellenistic world. The former kingdoms were the basis of Roman provinces and the Hellenistic cities remained essential units in their administration.

A silver coin of 34 BC showing Antony and Cleopatra VII, the last Ptolemy.

The Character of Hellenistic Society

The word *Hellenismus* was coined by the German historian J. G. Droysen early in the nineteenth century to describe the Greek civilization of the three centuries we are considering. The English equivalent, Hellenism, is sometimes used, but it has never really caught on. Instead we employ circumlocutions such as the Hellenistic age. Whatever words we choose, though, the implication is that we are dealing with a single civilization, different from that of classical Greece with its city-states but one basically still Greek – even though some, including Droysen himself, have taken the view that the Greek element was so fundamentally modified by the admixture of Anatolian, Iranian, Babylonian and Egyptian strands as to form a sort of cultural compost, in which the religion of Christianity was destined later to take firm root, blossom forth and spread over Europe and eventually most of the rest of the world. Modern scholars see the situation differently. Few would now seek to impose such a purposeful pattern upon history. But, more to the point, although there are aspects of the Hellenistic age in which we detect a cultural mix, it is generally more helpful to see that world as a multicultural society in which men and women of many races, religions and traditional cultures lived side by side, interacting with each other but not merging.

If that is so, can one speak of homogeneity, or indeed of a single Hellenistic society at all? An affirmative answer to this question must be a qualified one. As the word Hellenism implies, the unifying element is undoubtedly Greek, or, more accurately, Graeco-Macedonian. Such homogeneity as society possesses comes from the dominant class of Greeks (and later, 'culture-Greeks' – that is, assimilated non-Greeks), who had the upper hand everywhere and most of the wealth. How that homogeneity was created and maintained is the main topic of this section. At the outset one should note that the majority of the population were non-Greeks and non-city-dwellers, slaves or serfs or peasants of some kind living on the land, and that there were also non-Greeks of substance, such as the Egyptian or Babylonian priesthood, often resistant to Hellenization. It goes without saying that the peasants were usually indigenous and so non-Greeks – barbarians, as the Greeks chose to call them. From kingdom to kingdom they were naturally of different races and cultures, and indeed often within the same kingdom these differences still existed. And over the centuries the relationship of non-Greeks to the Graeco-Macedonian ruling class

The Olympeium in Athens, essentially a Hellenistic construction not completed until the reign of the Roman emperor Hadrian (117–38).

changed in response to changes in the power structure. But with this qualification, it remains true that we are dealing in the main with a homogeneous Hellenistic civilization.

The Mediterranean and the Greek Language

One obvious factor encouraging that homogeneity was the Mediterranean Sea itself. Despite the extension of Seleucid rule as far east as Afghanistan and India and the great Seleucid power base in Mesopotamia, all three major Hellenistic kingdoms looked towards the Mediterranean, and, as we have seen, the political and military interaction between them took place around that sea. More and more is now coming to light about the Seleucid concern with Babylonia and the nature of Hellenism further east, and the importance of both these aspects of Hellenistic civilization should not be underestimated. But the great centre of Seleucid urban development was in Seleucis, the area around Antioch in Syria; and the Mediterranean was the great highway of trade, opening up paths for the spread of ideas, art forms and new religious cults.

Another powerful element making for homogeneity was the Greek language, usually in the form of the *koine*, the 'common tongue', based on Attic Greek and superseding earlier dialect forms. The *koine* was used all over the Hellenistic world and would take a traveller from southern Spain to central Asia without serious problems of communication. It was the *lingua franca* throughout these centuries, and basically the Greek of the Septuagint and the New Testament. The Greek language was the foundation of Greek culture, often exclusive and self-conscious, and the hallmark of a dominant class which in most areas formed only a minority living in the midst of non-Greeks. Vivid illustration of this has come from the excavations at Aï Khanum, a Greek city on the Afghanistan side of the River Oxus, where ink traces left in the hardened sand from a perished papyrus roll have been identified as part of a Greek philosophical dialogue, and from Kandahar, where in the mid-third century BC the Mauryan king Aśoka, a convert to Buddhism, set up an inscription containing moralizing edicts in Greek and Aramaic. Aï Khanum has also revealed the foundations of a gymnasium, with its dedication to the usual gods of the gymnasium, Hermes and Heracles – proof that this remote city possessed the most central and typical institution of Hellenistic urban life.

The gymnasium was not simply a place of exercise. It was the centre of Greek education, where adolescent Greek youths studied Greek literature (especially Homer and Euripides), as well as mathematics. More than that, it was a focus of social life and Hellenic culture. Gymnasia were to be found in all Greek cities and also in the district capitals of Egypt – and even in the countryside. The one at Pergamum was built on three levels and catered for boys, youths and young men. It contained lecture rooms, porticoes useful for informal discussion and libraries. One at Teos in Ionia was unusual in admitting girls as well as boys. Those who had grown up and, as it were, graduated from the gymnasium remained attached to it through supporters' institutions and were referred to as 'those from the gymnasium'. As time passed, however, and especially in the remote parts of the Hellenistic world such as Bactria, the racial restrictions may have been relaxed and 'culture-Greeks' admitted. But in the main, by its emphasis on Greek culture the gymnasium served to reinforce traditional Greek feelings of superiority over all other races.

Hellenistic Kingship

The form of government to be found in most parts of the Hellenistic world was monarchy. In classical Greece monarchy was habitually rejected as something antiquated (as at Sparta), barbarian (as in Persia) or characteristic of fringe areas of Greece such as Macedonia and Epirus. But Macedonian monarchy, in the person of Alexander, had conquered the world, and later on his generals set a cachet upon their power by taking the title of kings. There was a bonus for them in this, for the lands which the Ptolemies and Seleucids controlled had an indigenous population – Persians, Babylonians and Egyptians – accustomed to monarchic rule. In Babylonia Seleucus inherited a traditional kingship, while in Egypt Alexander and after him the Ptolemies were easily accommodated as pharaohs. Once the cards were down, lesser dynasts followed suit. We have noted the growth of several small monarchic states in Asia Minor, and at Syracuse in Sicily Hiero II (269–215 BC) also created a monarchy of a Hellenistic stamp.

Kings were distinguished by several standard outward marks common to most dynasties. They wore Macedonian military uniform with boots, a flowing cloak, a broad-brimmed hat (or a helmet, sometimes with horns attached) and a diadem made of a white or purple headband with two loose ribbons behind. Their royal status was also indicated by a sceptre, a throne and a ring with a seal-stone. They established certain rituals and their features were made widely known throughout their dominions through the medium of idealized sculpture.

Except in Macedonia, where the kings normally took account of certain traditional rights invested in the people – at any rate, when it suited them – Hellenistic monarchy was by its nature absolute. Kings were kings by reason of their martial prowess and they ruled over 'spear-won lands'. They were not kings of a country but kings by status, regardless of where they ruled. Though after the battle of Ipsus Demetrius Poliorcetes had no realm at all (apart from one or two cities in Greece), he still continued to be a king. No one, however, can govern a kingdom alone and a characteristic institution of Hellenistic monarchy was that of the king's 'Friends', chosen by him personally and taking only secondary account of class, birth and state origin. These men often rose to high positions through favour or ability in a world of swift changes. As a body, the Friends formed a royal council at which they tendered advice, to be accepted or rejected as the king saw fit. They held army commands and offices of state, they went on embassies and they sometimes smoothed relations between the king and their city of origin – though indeed many were refugees from their original city, seeking a new career at a royal court. They were men of many different types, including artists, writers, doctors and scholars. The sole requirement was a combination of some skill and a willingness to put it at the king's disposal. On inscriptions the Friends are officially recognized alongside the army as sharing power within the kingdom. Later, as the dynasties became more established and their rule was legitimized by time, the Friends hardened into a more hierarchic institution, though it is only in Egypt that we have evidence of their development into a regular bureaucracy. In general they formed an element of government common to the whole Hellenistic monarchic world and yet another indication of its structural homogeneity, at least in the upper echelons.

One problem common to all the kings other than those in Macedonia (and perhaps those in Pergamum, which had the form of a city-state with a monarch superimposed) was to gain acceptance for their rule over both Greeks and native peoples and to minimize the offence given to the independent Greek cities within their realms. The growth of ruler cult, which implied public recognition of the king as a deity, the recipient of worship, helped in the solving of this problem. We shall be looking at this phenomenon more closely later, in the context of religious thought and practice. Here it may be noted that ruler cult, an institution already foreshadowed in the fourth-century world of the Greek cities, acquired a special role in Egypt. There a dynastic cult designed primarily for the dominant Greek class had its counterpart in the Egyptian temples, where the Ptolemies were associated in traditional cult and ritual with the local gods.

A silver coin showing Alexander the Great with a ram's horns and elephant-scalp headdress. It was minted by Ptolemy I Soter in 305 BC so as to associate his own rule in Egypt with Alexander's divine mission as a conqueror.

Cities and Federal States

Greek cities were to be found both within and in proximity to the new kingdoms, and the kings usually enjoyed an ambivalent relationship with them. There were of course the old cities of the Greek mainland, whose chief concern was to ward off the attentions of the kings of Macedonia. There were also those around the Aegean and in western Asia Minor and the Greek colonies of an older epoch, spread out along the shores of the Mediterranean, the Adriatic, Sicily and the Black Sea. Of the newer foundations further east, established by Alexander himself or later by the Seleucids, and of the few Greek cities in Egypt, we shall have something to say under Science and Technology. It was still the aim of all Greek cities to be fully free and independent, even though this ambition had rarely been achieved even in classical times, when smaller cities were apt to fall under the control of the more powerful, such as Athens, Sparta or Thebes, while those of Asia Minor had at most times been under the king of Persia.

During the wars of Alexander's successors the freedom of the Greek cities had become a propagandist slogan to be used by each general against his enemies. It had meant very little. Though kings might declare cities 'free, ungarrisoned and autonomous', they did not hesitate to intervene in their internal affairs, as Antigonus I of Macedon did when he set up a court in Cyme, or sent detailed instructions to Teos to regulate a union between that city and Lebedus – a measure which, as his letters, preserved on stone, make clear, was extremely unpopular in both places. Many cities were forced to receive a royal garrison and pay taxes to the king in whose realm they were situated. It was only a favourably placed city such as Byzantium or the island city of Rhodes that could maintain a genuine independence. On the other hand, proclamations made by a king for propagandist purposes could sometimes be exploited so as to extract concessions. A whole series of inscriptions from Asia Minor records exhortations to Seleucid kings to underwrite freedom and democracy or applaud them because they have done so. The difficulty is to decide what, in practical terms, 'peace', 'freedom', 'democracy' or 'autonomy' means in a particular case. In many inscriptions democracy seems to be used simply as an equivalent of freedom – but from what? Certainly it is a qualified freedom and need not exclude the imposition of taxes or even garrisons.

This ambiguity in their status relative to the kings did not, however, hinder the development of a very active civic life in most cities of any size, whether they lay inside or precariously outside one or other of the kingdoms. To compensate for the loss by many cities of an earlier genuine political freedom (which had often meant freedom to wage war) they now enjoyed a vigorous range of activities linked with athletic contests, literary festivals and religious celebrations, involving the sending of frequent embassies to and from kings and other cities. In the course of these, spurious mythological connections and bonds of pretended kinship were often paraded. Activities of this kind helped to bind the Hellenistic world together and could assume considerable political importance. An example is that of the Dorian city of Cytinium, which invoked an ancient kinship with the Lycian town of Xanthus in south-western Asia Minor in order to solicit a contribution to the cost of rebuilding its walls, destroyed by the Macedonian king Antigonus III after they had already been damaged by an earthquake. Similarly, the town of Ilium presumed on its links with Troy to claim special consideration from the Romans, the supposed descendants of Aeneas.

Many inscriptions also record the sending of embassies to secure for temples grants of immunity from attack and pillage. Such grants were often accorded by kings and also by cities, and were one way of limiting the effects of constant warfare and, in particular, of the right to reprisals, which Greek custom allowed the citizens of one city to exercise against anyone from another city which had in some way provoked a grievance in the first. By negotiating a declaration of *asylia* – 'freedom from reprisals' – it was possible to limit the damage inflicted by this disastrous practice. In this way an immunity originally attached to temples was extended in scope to whole cities, and by persuading one or more of the important kings to associate himself with such a grant a city strengthened the likelihood that it would hold.

Another way in which Hellenistic cities reduced the danger of war breaking out was by the growing practice of seeking arbitration on issues – usually the disputed ownership of land – most likely to lead to conflict. In all these activities an important part was played by rich citizens prepared to expend time and wealth on their city's behalf. Many inscriptions refer to the efforts of such men being rewarded with honours in their native city and often too by concessions and honorific awards in the city they had visited – in particular *proxenia*. The word originally described the position of a representative of a foreign state abroad (rather like a modern consul, but a citizen of the host city) and was linked to the older institution of *xenia*, a ritualized personal and family relationship running across state boundaries and often translated as 'guest-friendship'. *Proxenia* was now frequently accorded for services rendered, sometimes in combination with a grant of citizenship. Such awards served to break down the traditional particularism of the Greek cities and to knot them together in a web of formalized interchange. A modern parallel might be the growing practice of twinning cities in different countries.

Internally the cities of the Hellenistic world provided their citizens with an active private life at various social levels, centring on clubs and societies (*thiasoi* or *eranoi*, as they were called), which carried out the functions of a modern burial club, dining club and friendly society. At the centre of each such organization there would be the religious cult of a particular deity. These clubs fulfilled an important function, especially in the new cities in the east. They were less exclusive than the upper-class gymnasia, and frequently contained both Greeks and non-Greeks, men and women, and even slaves among their members.

Proxenia linked men and women individually with cities other than their own. But the cities themselves often grew closer to each other with mutual grants of *isopoliteia*, by which citizenship was interchangeable between them. A citizen of one city who went to live in another city linked in this way acquired citizenship in the latter. Sometimes this trend was carried further and two cities were actually combined in an act of *sympoliteia*, or 'political union'. Examples are those of the two Phocian cities of Stiris and Medeon, for which the act of union survives, specifically mentioning the political, economic and judicial rights covered, or the transfer of the inhabitants of Colophon and Lebedus in Asia Minor to Ephesus. Such moves made for additional security and broke down exclusiveness, but when enjoined by a king, as they often were, they fired considerable resentment.

This trend towards combination took a very large step forward in the growth of federal states, especially in mainland Greece, where those of Aetolia (in the north-west) and Achaea (in the Peloponnese) provided a useful pooling of resources and initiative to oppose the military might of the kingdom of Macedonia. The Aetolians, as we have seen, gained great prestige from their defence of Delphi against the Gauls in 279–278 BC, and in the following decades they extended their federation to take in most of central Greece south of Thessaly. The earlier Achaean confederacy had become moribund but reorganized and revitalized itself from 280 BC onwards and, through the initiative of the Sicyonian leader Aratus, burst its ethnic limits to become an instrument of Peloponnesian unity – only to founder upon the resistance of Sparta under the leadership of its reforming and imperialistic king Cleomenes. Both leagues were democratic in form, with full assemblies, deliberative and executive councils and annual magistracies. Federalism was not a discovery of the Hellenistic age; there had been many confederacies even in the fifth century BC, and more particularly in the fourth. Nor was the institution confined to mainland Greece, for there was an important federal body in Lycia in Asia Minor and another in southern Italy. But Aetolia and Achaea stand out as the most active non-monarchic participants in the power struggles of the third and second centuries.

One World?

After this short survey of some of the characteristic institutions of the Hellenistic world, we may return to the question of how far it was indeed homogeneous. We have considered the geographical scene centring on the Mediterranean (though with its outposts stretching far into Asia); the unifying effect of a single tongue, the Greek *koine*; the similarity of institutions, with monarchy – reinforced by the religious implications of ruler cult – accommodating itself to the different world of the Greek cities; and finally a whole series of political and social institutions, common to cities throughout the Hellenistic world, which unified and reconciled particularly those who belonged to the dominant ethnic groups of Greeks and Macedonians. The forces making for homogeneity within the élite can be extended if one thinks of the various categories of people who for one or another reason travelled around from court to court and from city to city. There were mercenary soldiers (coming especially from poor areas such as Aetolia and Crete), envoys from kings or city authorities, actors (the so-called Craftsmen of Dionysus) organized in guilds and moving from festival to festival; and individuals – philosophers (like Clearchus, who brought a copy of traditional gnomic sayings from Delphi and had them set up in the founder's shrine at Aï Khanum in Afghanistan), doctors (who found a ready clientele wherever there was fighting), military engineers (especially welcome if they possessed skill with artillery), artists, musicians, poets giving readings of their works (with flattering references to the city in which they were performing), slave-dealers and merchants of every kind. For the dominant class it was indeed one world. But if we look below the surface, especially in the kingdoms away from Greece and Macedonia, the picture is somewhat more complicated.

Mixed Societies in Egypt and Asia

Ptolemaic Egypt

The third century BC saw the high point of Graeco-Macedonian domination in Egypt. From its last decades onwards, Egyptian influence grew stronger. In 207–206 BC a native rising broke out in Upper Egypt and lasted, under native kings, for twenty years. Henceforth one can detect an increase in Egyptianizing tendencies, which found expression both in art and in a more accommodating royal policy towards the great native power base, the Egyptian temples and the priesthood. However, this is no more than an accentuation of a trend of which signs were visible much earlier, indeed from the very beginning of the Ptolemaic dynasty.

The family occupying the high priesthood of Ptah at Memphis, the old capital, can be traced through ten generations and was active throughout three centuries of Ptolemaic rule. One can also follow the shifting relationship between the kings and the native temples throughout much of that period. The priesthood was not an institution to be ignored. It exerted economic power as well as religious and social influence and the Ptolemies, if reluctantly, had to make concessions to it. It was inevitable that some tension would exist between the Egyptian temples and the Ptolemaic government, since both sought to control the output of Egypt in their own interest. In the fourth century BC Ptolemy I Soter, new to the country, tried to hold a balance between Greeks and Egyptians. He needed the educated priests and Egyptian scribes to enable him to organize and control a land where most of the population was illiterate and he therefore displayed a conciliatory attitude towards the temples. For some decades demotic Egyptian was used within the administration. Under Ptolemy II Philadelphos (283–246 BC) Greek influence and the Greek language gained the upper hand and a concerted attempt was made to intensify the exploitation of Egypt. This was partly to

A silver coin of the first Macedonian ruler of Egypt, Alexander's general Ptolemy.

Pharos at Alexandria.

finance the holding of Cyrene and a ring of outlying possessions in Asia Minor and the Aegean, to pay the soldiers stationed there and to meet the cost of fighting the Seleucids. But that was only one factor in a policy of subordinating the whole economy of Egypt to state power.

A determined effort was now made to accumulate precious metals in Alexandria by comprehensive control of production and taxation. The system has been described as a planned economy, but that is misleading. The Ptolemies built on what was there before, adding new measures to underpin the Graeco-Macedonian ruling class and the army. The resultant system contained many compromises and was often incompetent. How it worked out in practice can be seen from the rich harvest of administrative documents preserved on papyrus which have been recovered from the sands of the Fayum (an area freshly developed under the Ptolemies) and of Upper Egypt. From these it is clear that the ordinary Egyptians fared badly. If one disregards occasional fine words, the fiscal system took little account of their basic needs and welfare.

The Ptolemies took over the pharaonic divisions of Egypt into forty main districts, or *nomes*, subdivided into areas (*toparchies* or *merides*) and villages (*komai*), with officials in charge at each level. While troops were stationed throughout the country under the command of generals (*strategoi*), a tax-collecting system operated under the control of *dioiketai*, 'financial overseers'. One of these officials who served under Ptolemy II, Apollonius, is known particularly well from an extensive dossier, found at Philadelphia (modern Darb el-Gerza) around 1912–13 and containing the files of the Carian Zeno, who worked under Apollonius during the period 261–246 BC. From these and other comparable documents, including some recorded on *ostraka*, or potsherds, we learn of the wide variety of taxes imposed. The most important of these were the ones affecting the land and its products. Ptolemy I treated the whole land of Egypt as his personal property, since, to quote the historian Diodorus, it was 'spear-won and the fruit of his own bravery'. But these were only words. In practice much land was held by the temples. From Ptolemy II onwards the government tried to control the cultivation and sequestrate the revenues that came from this temple land. But in the second century BC the temples once more extended their estates and the priests increased their influence. The conciliatory attitude of the Ptolemies towards them is evidenced by the many Egyptian temples – at Denderah, Karnak, Edfu and Kom Ombo – built during the Ptolemaic period.

The royal land was farmed mainly by free peasants holding plots on short leases. Papyri provide a lively picture of the dealings of these people with minor village officials, often themselves Egyptian. A schedule laid down the crops that were to be planted, and the seed corn was provided on loan by the government and repaid out of the harvest. In addition some land was made over as a gift to the temples or to favoured individuals, such as the *dioiketes* Apollonius, or Andromachus, 'owner of 10,000 *arourai*' (rather under 7,000 acres), who is mentioned on some of these papyri around 250 BC. In addition, the land was used to attract settlers and to this end a new form of land-holding was introduced. Land allotments varying between 3$\frac{1}{2}$ and 70 acres were assigned to *klerouchoi*, 'lot-holders', mostly immigrants, who were to farm the land, either in person or through tenants, and serve in the army when called up. By the early second century BC cleruchs were treating their land as private property. As reservists they were from time to time called up and we frequently hear of their being billeted on native Egyptians, a source of great friction and bitterness. In the late second century BC, however, there were also Egyptian cleruchs, who had received their land at the expense of larger Greek cleruchic allotments.

For all these categories there was a wide range of taxes – on rents, sales, corn, cattle, slaves and on vineyards, orchards and gardens. The last group of these, valued at one-sixth of the product, was diverted to pay for the posthumous cult of Arsinoe Philadelphus, the wife of Ptolemy II, and the temples were allowed to keep that part of the proceeds of this tax which was derived from temple land. There were also local customs dues and a poll tax. In all, crown peasants had to pay

A silver coin of Ptolemy V Epiphanes, the first Macedonian ruler to be enthroned as pharaoh at Memphis.

about 50 per cent of their harvest in taxes. The cleruch was a little better off, since he fulfilled part of his obligations in military service. In addition to the income from rents and taxes, the government drew large sums from the leasing of monopolies – especially for oil-producing plants, mines, quarries, salt and the extraction of nitre and alum (used for fulling). These, together with licences for many occupations – bee-keeping, pig-keeping, fishing and trading – added to the fiscal burden and the government's gain.

The court and the king's chief ministers lived in Alexandria but the reservist soldiers, as we have seen, had homes scattered about the countryside, especially in the newly developed Arsinoite *nome*, present-day Fayum. The foundation of Greek cities was not favoured. Alexandria, with its large population of Greeks, Macedonians, Jews and native Egyptians, was an exception. Unfortunately the damp soil in the Nile delta has destroyed any papyrus records from the capital. Apart from Alexandria there were only two other Greek cities, Naucratis, an ancient Greek settlement long used as an outlet for foreign trade, and Ptolemais in Upper Egypt. There were, of course, several venerable Egyptian cities like Memphis and Thebes, but the tradition of the land and the inclination of the Ptolemies themselves were both against the founding of Greek cities like those set up by Alexander and the Seleucids. It was perhaps feared that they might make an unwelcome claim to some form of limited autonomy.

Outside Alexandria the Greeks lived of necessity in the villages alongside the native Egyptian peasants. These included the minor priests, who besides their religious duties worked on the land. On the whole, there is little evidence of hostility between the two races, at any rate during the earlier reigns. There were royal judges called *chrematistai*, with jurisdiction over both races, but the Egyptians kept their own laws and courts. The king, however, from time to time published royal decrees with the force of law (*prostagmata*), and these applied equally to native Egyptians and to Greeks. To that extent Greek decisions were imposed upon the native population, which also suffered along with the Greeks from the increasing tendency of administrative power to encroach upon that of the judiciary. Moreover, the new establishment, consisting of the upper ranks of the bureaucracy, the Greek priests, the cleruchs, the holders of gift estates and the king's Friends, constituted a single caste from which for a long time even the richest Egyptians were excluded. It is only in the middle of the second century BC, under Ptolemy VIII Euergetes II, that we hear of Paos, a general of the Thebaid and 'one of the First Friends', who is an Egyptian.

In the close confines of village life private personal quarrels between Greeks and Egyptians tended to take on a racial aspect. Thus an Arab camel-driver who has not been paid complains that this is because he is a 'barbarian who does not know how to play the Greek'; and an Egyptian priest, involved in a lawsuit against a cleruch billeted on him, complains of being despised because he is an Egyptian. But it would be wrong to make too much out of a few examples of this kind. In the main the two races seem to have got along reasonably well together, though the Egyptian peasants, who in the absence of a slave class of any importance in the countryside occupied the lowest ranks in the social scale, naturally found themselves in conflict with the Greek representatives of authority. They had their own traditional weapons, however, especially the long-established practice of running away (*anachoresis*), usually in a group, and taking refuge in a temple offering asylum. This ancient equivalent of the strike often secured improvements in the peasants' conditions of work and these concessions are sometimes published in official pronouncements by the king himself.

There was probably more intermarriage between Greeks and Egyptians than at first sight appears to be the case, for it is now known that many people bore double names, Greek and Egyptian, either of which they might use to fit the occasion. Hence it is not always clear whether a particular individual is a Greek or an Egyptian. Some Egyptians, however, undoubtedly used double names as a sign that they were on their way up the social ladder and in the hope of breaking into the exclusive Greek society – sometimes successfully, for Egyptian influence increased from the end of the third century BC onwards. The flow of Greek and Macedonian immigration had by this time ceased (except in the hiring of mercenaries) and social pressures, which frequently took a racial form, compelled the kings to make concessions and sometimes to publish amnesties, withdrawing earlier demands made on the peasantry. Land allotments were made to Egyptian troops and Egyptians entered the bureaucracy. Increasingly Egyptian gods were worshipped by non-Egyptians, and there was more intermarriage. Thus gradually the passage of time and changed circumstances combined to reduce the gap between the races.

Seleucid Asia and the Far East

In many ways the Seleucid kingdom in Asia provides a striking contrast to Ptolemaic Egypt. It involved very different territories at different times, since its frontiers fluctuated violently between 312 BC, when Seleucus

A silver coin of Antiochus I Soter, the son of Seleucus and the saviour of his realm.

A silver coin of Antiochus III the Great (223–187 BC). On the reverse an elephant recalls his reduced eastern territories.

first seized Babylonia, and the late second century BC, by which time the Seleucid realm had shrunk to a small area in north Syria. To Babylonia, his original fief, Seleucus had soon added the provinces in the far east but he then lost India. In the early third century BC he and his son Antiochus I Soter acquired most of Syria, Mesopotamia and Asia Minor, but by the middle of that century everything east of the Caspian Sea had been lost, either through revolt or defeat by the Parthians. In 200 BC Antiochus III took Palestine from the Ptolemies, but after his defeat in 189 BC by the Romans he had to relinquish everything in Asia Minor west of the Taurus mountains. Whatever its boundaries at any particular time, however, the Seleucid kingdom offered a complete contrast to Egypt in the variety of the peoples and cultures which it embraced. The Seleucids could draw on the administrative procedures of the Persian empire, of which their realm was the successor. But any unity the realm possessed had to be imposed by means of the bureaucracy and the army.

Seleucus I was a Macedonian and he governed with the help of his Friends and a Graeco-Macedonian élite, though, like the Ptolemies in Egypt, he was obliged to employ native personnel at the lower levels of administration. Our current picture of the Seleucid kingdom may suffer some distortion from the preponderance of Greek evidence and the fact that many cuneiform documents from Babylonia are yet to be published and evaluated. But even allowing for this, statistical evidence shows that, if one can judge from the names recorded, for about two generations the higher ranks of the administration were almost exclusively Greek and Macedonian; subsequently Syrians, Jews, Persians and other Iranians never amounted to more than around 2.5 per cent of those employed.

The Seleucids encouraged immigration from Europe and the Greek world generally by granting land and founding cities in a conscious policy of colonization which, in Asia Minor, is probably a continuation of methods employed by Antigonus I when he was in possession of the area in the late fourth century BC. Because of the disparate nature of the Seleucid dominions it is even more difficult to make generalizations about land tenure and economic conditions than it is for Egypt. The evidence at present depends mainly on a handful of Greek inscriptions and is only really valid for the areas to which it applies. But, such as it is, it gives us a glimpse into a system in which there are *laoi*, 'royal peasants', living in villages, gift estates (as in Egypt) granted as rewards for loyal service to the king and large temple estates. The royal peasants were apparently attached in some way to the land and villages where they lived. When land was granted or sold, or in some other way made over to another owner, the *laoi*, like serfs, were included in the transaction. The recipient of a gift estate was urged or required to attach it, along with the villages included in it, to some nearby city – though this was not true everywhere, for it is known that there were some estates of this kind in Palestine (after it became Seleucid) which were not attached to any city. There is evidence of villages combining to pass decrees, thus implying a degree of administrative independence, perhaps the first step towards what might ultimately develop into a city. In short, conditions varied very considerably from district to district.

An important institution inherited by the Seleucids, especially in Asia Minor, was the temple state with its lands, temple peasants, a hereditary high priesthood and often eunuchs and temple prostitutes. Relations between these states and the monarchy followed no universal rules. On the island of Icarus off Kuwait in the Persian Gulf the king treated temple land as if it were his own to dispose of, and in north-western Syria a Seleucid king Antiochus (it is not known which) assigned the village of Baetocaece to the Temple of Zeus (Baal). Though the position almost certainly varied from one area to another, it is likely that with the passing of the years the temple states grew stronger, both in the Seleucid kingdom and generally throughout Asia Minor, where after 189 BC the Attalids of Pergamum controlled much of the territory that had belonged to the Seleucids.

In the Seleucid dominions, as in Egypt and the Attalid kingdom, there were many settlements of a military nature, known as *katoikiai*. The settlers were active soldiers (not retired veterans, as in Alexander's foundations), and these men, like the cleruchs in Egypt, provided a reserve of trained troops whom the king could call up in time of war. In peacetime they served as garrisons, spread out over the countryside, maintaining order and available in the event of trouble or revolt. In addition, like cleruchs, they cultivated the land. Indeed, not all settlements described as *katoikiai* were military. Several dozen civilian settlements with this title are known, especially in western Asia Minor, in both Seleucid and Pergamene territory. In practice the difference cannot have been very great, since in times of emergency civilian *katoikoi* will also have been liable to call-up. *Katoikiai* of either kind approximated closely to the more traditional villages, inhabited by peasants, and in favourable circumstances both contained the seeds of further development into cities.

The planning of Greek cities is one of the great achievements of the Seleucids and in this they followed in Alexander's footsteps. The new cities in the far east were laid out in the rectilinear pattern which had become regular practice in the Greek world from the fourth century BC onwards. This can be exemplified at

Ruins of Alexander's foundation at Aï Khanum in modern Afghanistan. The city was settled exclusively by Greek and Macedonian colonists.

Aï Khanum on the Oxus or at Priene on the shores of the Aegean, a city which was refounded and laid out along those lines in 350 BC. Most Seleucid colonization took place under the first three kings, Seleucus I (305–281 BC), Antiochus I (281–261 BC) and Antiochus II (261–246 BC); a few cities in the far east are the work of Antiochus IV (175–164 BC). Many of these settlements are to be found in northern Syria, where the names of both cities and regions betray the presence of Greek and Macedonian settlers. There one finds areas called Pieria and Cyrrhestice and cities with the names of Europus, Beroea, Edessa, Cyrrhus, Perinthus, Maronea and Apollonia. Similar names occur elsewhere: in Palestine Dium and Pella, in Mesopotamia Anthemusia, Ichnae and Aenus, in Media Europus, in Persia Tanagra, in Bactria and Sogdiana Thera and Rhoetea and on the Arabian Gulf Arethusa, Larisa and Chalcis. These names were probably given spontaneously, to recall their homeland, by the men who settled there. But direct Seleucid policy can be seen reflected in such dynastic names as Antioch, Seleucia-in-Pieria, Laodiceia and Apamea, which celebrate Seleucid kings or their queens. Seleucia-on-the-Tigris was Seleucus I's earliest foundation and served as the administrative centre for Mesopotamia. Further east a host of Seleucias, Antiochs and Apameas controlled vital communication points or served as administrative centres far into Asia. By their names they advertised the achievements of the Seleucid dynasty.

The cities of the Seleucid kingdom were of more than one kind. First, there were the ancient Greek cities on the Aegean coast, such as Smyrna, Miletus and Ephesus; secondly, there were new foundations like Seleucia-on-the-Tigris; thirdly, some ancient cities were given dynastic names, like Jerusalem, renamed Antioch; and finally, and especially in the east, there were Hellenized native cities which received functionaries and a garrison and served as administrative centres. Cities were identified by their possession of the normal Greek forms of organization: tribes, a council, magistrates, a territory, a code of law and some (often rather primitive) financial provisions. An assembly was usual but was not to be found everywhere. Though situated within the kingdom and often founded or refounded by a royal act, all these cities behaved as if they were independent, engaging in a very full range of activities both internally and in the international field. Their apparent independence was, however, largely illusory and, unless specifically exempt, all could expect to be required to pay royal tribute. This situation later provided a precedent for the Romans, when they took over the role of the Hellenistic kings. The newer cities in the east do not usually issue their own coinage – not at least before the second century BC, when under Antiochus IV a municipal coinage emerges, as indeed a regional coinage had appeared a little earlier in Macedonia under Philip V (221–179 BC). The far eastern cities lacked even the pretence of freedom, and the only known example of a 'grant of freedom' to one of these occurs in a letter sent by a Seleucid king to Ptolemy IX at the end of the second century, which records such a grant to Seleucia-in-Pieria.

Science and Technology

In classical Greece no clear frontier was drawn between science and philosophy; after Alexander that was no longer true. The Hellenistic age saw a wide diffusion of creative energy which resulted in the planting of Greek cities over large parts of central Asia and the setting up of Graeco-Macedonian monarchies in areas that had hitherto been barbarian. But at the same time it encouraged a concentration of cultural activity at a high level in the new royal capitals, in particular Alexandria and Pergamum. This is especially true of what we should today term 'the sciences'. Philosophy continued to flourish in the city-states, and chiefly at Athens.

Both pure and applied science registered noteworthy developments during the centuries we are considering, especially in the great Hellenistic capitals. Impressive though these developments were, one should not ignore their limitations. The Hellenistic world proved no more able than the earlier city-states to harness scientific discoveries to the practical use of human beings. The extension of scientific knowledge was one of degree and not of kind. Nevertheless, it was real and substantial. Our assessment of it rests mainly on accounts contained in later writers whose works enshrine the new advances made in mathematics, astronomy, biology and medicine.

Even though most scientists were Greeks, undoubtedly the scientific thought of the Hellenistic age received some stimulus from the cross-fertilization of cultures and the general shake-up in traditional ideas which accompanied Alexander's conquests and the establishment of the new kingdoms. But even more it benefited from the leisure and resources made available by royal patrons and, at Alexandria, from the research facilities of the great library and the famous museum, where, according to the sceptic philosopher Timon of Phlius (*c.* 320–230 BC) – himself a practitioner from the world of the city-state – 'well-propped pedants could quarrel endlessly in the Muses' bird-cage'. Timon's criticism should not be taken as evidence that scientists all lived in isolation from the everyday world. Though many had private means or enjoyed the welcome fruits of patronage, others earned their living in the professions, as doctors, architects or engineers, thus combining theory with practice. Here we can only glance at what was achieved in some of the sciences.

Astronomy and Geometry

One field in which great progress was made was astronomy. An early exponent, Aristarchus of Samos (*c.* 310–230 BC,) wrote a treatise on the relation of the sun and moon to the earth and propounded the theory that the sun was at the centre of the universe – whether as a fact or merely as one among several hypotheses is not clear. In any case, this theory did not win assent for a variety of reasons, which at the time seemed compelling. A rival hypothesis, which kept the earth at the centre and postulated a combination of epicycles and eccentric circles to explain the apparently erratic movement of the planets, seemed to give a more satisfactory explanation of the observed phenomena and was therefore preferred. For the true answer to some of the objections to the heliocentric theory, one would have needed optical instruments more refined than any then available. The more popular, though false, theory was the work of Apollonius of Perge (mid-third century BC) and Hipparchus of Nicaea (*fl.* 161–129 BC). The former was also famous for his work on conic sections; the latter devised an apparatus for counting the stars and also discovered the precession of the equinoxes.

An achievement no less distinguished than that of Aristarchus was the calculation made by Eratosthenes of Cyrene (275–194 BC), the head of the Alexandrian library under Ptolemy III and ironically nicknamed 'Beta' to indicate, quite unfairly, that he always came second in every field. By reading the angle of a shadow cast by a stick at Alexandria at midday on the day that no shadow at all was registered at the same hour by a similar stick at Syene (modern Aswan), Eratosthenes employed geometry to calculate the earth's circumference. Though his calculation proved to be somewhat too large, the accuracy of the result is less significant and impressive than the mathematical imagination shown in the simplicity of the method employed.

But the most celebrated work in ancient geometry was that of Euclid (*fl. c.* 300 BC), the thirteen books of whose *Elements* represented a systematic exposition of the subject and brought together much earlier work. Later in the third century Archimedes of Syracuse (287–212 BC) wrote extensively on optics, statics, hydrostatics, astronomy and engineering. He is remembered especially for his calculation of the value of *pi* and was probably the inventor of the so-called Archimedean screw, which is still widely used to raise the level of water for irrigation. Archimedes perished in the Roman sack of his native city of Syracuse in 212 BC.

The world according to Eratosthenes of Cyrene around 200 BC. He also managed to calculate the earth's circumference by means of geometry.

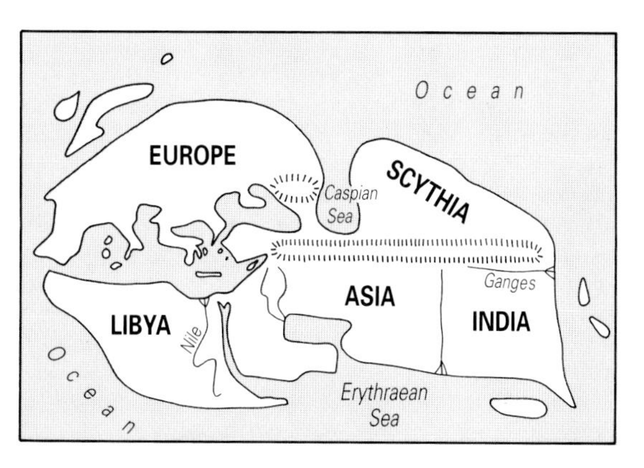

Medicine

Alexandria was famous for its medical schools and especially for those led by Herophilus of Calchedon (*fl.* early third century BC) and Erasistratus of Ceos (*fl. c.* 250 BC). The former did work on the eye, the brain, the duodenum, the liver and the reproductive organs, the latter on the digestive and vascular systems. According to the Roman writer Celsus (active under the emperor Tiberius, 14–37) both employed what is to us the repulsive practice of human vivisection on criminals provided from the prisons of Ptolemaic Alexandria.

Engineering

In applied science progress was rather less impressive. Ctesibius of Alexandria (*fl. c.* 270 BC) invented several mechanical devices, including a pump, a water-clock and certain improvements to artillery. Another Hellenistic inventor was Philo of Byzantium (*fl. c.* 200 BC), the author of a compendium of technology in nine books. In addition, a good deal of Hellenistic applied mechanics is incorporated in the work of the Roman architect and engineer Vitruvius (*fl. c.* 40–20 BC), entitled *On Architecture*, and in various works by Hero of Alexandria (*fl. c.* 60). Pappus, the author of a fourth-century AD work listing technical devices and assessing their relative practical importance, concludes that two fields of activity were particularly highly regarded: those ministering to the needs of warfare and 'wonder-working machines' – pneumatic devices, automata and the like. He also mentions with approval machines used in weight-lifting and irrigation and a kind of forerunner of the planetarium. This evaluation of technical advances – and it does not stand alone – may appear surprisingly limited in view of the capacity (as with hindsight we now know) of mechanical devices exploiting non-human and non-animal sources of power to change the whole basis of material existence.

Despite the striking intellectual achievements of its scientists, no such development occurred in the Hellenistic period, nor indeed in the whole of antiquity. By 300 BC several basic technical devices were already known and utilized. They included the lever, the pulley, the wedge and the windlass. But little besides the so-called Archimedean screw was added in the third century BC. The water-mill was discovered in the first century BC, the earliest known example being installed by Mithridates VI of Pontus at Cabeira, on the River Lycus in what is now north-eastern Turkey. Vitruvius described an undershot wheel. The windmill, however, was unknown throughout antiquity and steam power, though familiar, was not put to any practical use. In fact, little change in the material level of life took place during the period we are considering. Transport by land remained slow and expensive. Water transport was more important and effective, but ships were not helped by having a square sail, set athwart the hull, which created serious difficulties with anything but a following wind, and by the absence of the compass, which was not yet known – a serious matter in bad visibility. The development of sea trade with India from the second century BC onwards was due to the discovery and exploitation of the monsoons and not to any technical improvements in the ships themselves.

The reasons for this sluggishness in applying technical knowledge in a practical context are complex. One limiting factor is the interdependence of various techniques one on another. The jet-propelled revolving ball central to Hero's steam engine must have been extremely inefficient, owing to leakage at the point where the pipe carrying the steam entered the ball, since a loose joint leaked steam and a tight joint created serious friction. Hence the overall efficiency of the device has been estimated at no more than 1 per cent. It was, moreover, incapable of practical development without the ability (which was not there) to make a strong metal cylinder and some form of piston to convert direct force into circular movement. Another factor was economic. In the Hellenistic world labour was so cheap that saving it seemed scarcely worth while. For this attitude slavery has often been blamed. But whether the labour was that of the slave or of the free man or woman does not seriously affect the issue. In either case the outlay to the employer was small. Furthermore, the invention of new devices and their development so as to achieve practical ends is not simply a matter of whether there are economic incentives. Such a development depends very much on men's attitude of mind and on their being willing to take a long view and invest resources in something likely to take some time to show a return. In antiquity generally, men were conservative in their material affairs and preferred old and tried ways. Thus the simple rotary mill worked by donkeys and mules spread throughout the whole Mediterranean area in the course of the second century BC, whereas the water-mill, which was far more costly to install (and, of course, required an adequate available head of water) spread only slowly over the first three centuries of our era.

Along with this conservatism went a contempt for manual labour and the crafts which, in the fifth century BC, the historian Herodotus believed to have been taken over from the barbarians and which later found expression in many writers, Aristotle among them; he quotes approvingly the view that 'the best form of state' will not admit artisans into its citizenship. This attitude of mind, perpetuated within the governing class of both the city-states and the Hellenistic kingdoms, had as its accompaniment a set of values which regarded wealth as a measure of status and prestige, preferably wealth in the form of the ownership of land. In a society without the expectation of continually increasing productivity it is not surprising that there should be no programme of research towards that end. The inventor himself – Archimedes, for example, if we can believe Plutarch (*c.* 50–120), writing in his *Life of Marcellus* (17.3) – was disposed to value his inventions more for their intellectual quality than for their practical utility and any benefit they might bring to his fellow men.

Warfare and Invention

This failure to apply intellectual discovery to the attainment of practical ends was not due to any lack of ability to make the jump. That is clear from the one field in which great technical progress was made – in warfare. The central role which fighting occupied in the philosophy and practice of Hellenistic kings meant that their military engineers had a great incentive to come up with ever more powerful and accurate artillery and ever stronger and more sophisticated defences to set against the artillery of their opponents. Alexander's chief engineer, Diades, the inventor of mobile, transportable siege towers, was the head of a department of the Macedonian army which went back to the time of Philip II. Already under Philip great progress had been made in the development of torsion catapults. Later, under the Ptolemies, Alexandria became the centre where, as early as 275 BC, the problem of devising formulae for the calibration of these machines, so as to obtain increased accuracy at a given range for a specific weight of missile, had been systematically tackled and a solution reached. It is clear from Philo's work *On Artillery Construction* (15.14–29) that this was achieved as the result of an organized work project. In contrast to the affairs of everyday life and the financial prosperity of merchants, warfare was basic to the very existence of any Hellenistic kingdom and a primary concern of those controlling its wealth and government. It is therefore hardly surprising that this status was reflected in the practical achievements of military technicians.

Hellenistic warfare was highly developed. The phalanx of heavy-armed infantry bearing a 21-foot pike and advancing in close formation, in which each man occupied a space 3 feet wide, presented the enemy with a formidable front, in which the spears of the front five ranks protruded in advance of the first line. But this force, which took the shock in battle, was only part of a mixed army, in which it was supported by other types of infantry, considerable bodies of cavalry, special corps of bowmen and slingers, including such mercenary forces as the treasury could afford. This was the standard pattern. But Seleucid armies also included many kinds of eastern troops, all fighting after their own native fashion. Elephants too played an important part in Hellenistic armies and were used to break up the enemy line. But experience showed that they were a vulnerable and dubious weapon and could often inflict as much harm on their owners as on the other side. In the first century camels appear in Parthian armies, but these beasts were not a feature of Hellenistic warfare generally. Armies based on the developed Macedonian phalanx remained the basic Hellenistic force of war until, in the early second century BC, the Romans arrived on the scene to demonstrate the superiority of the looser formation characteristic of their highly disciplined legionary armies.

Siegecraft played an important part in warfare and usually the defence had the upper hand, except when faced by so determined an enemy as Alexander the Great. More typical was the successful Rhodian resistance to Demetrius I in 305–304 BC in one of the most famous sieges in Greek history, which brought Demetrius the additional name of Poliorcetes, 'the Besieger' – but not victory. The techniques of naval warfare also profited from Hellenistic kings being prepared to subsidize research in order to achieve greater efficiency at sea. The classical trireme with its three banks of oars now gave place almost entirely to the quadrireme, the quinquereme and even larger ships, the exact arrangement of which has not yet been satisfactorily worked out. But new kinds of naval warfare were also exploited, manning cheaper and lighter ships similar to those used effectively by Illyrian pirates. Thus naval as well as land warfare showed what could be accomplished by engineers given enough motivation and financial support. In other fields, as we have seen, these preconditions were lacking.

Despite these shortcomings, Hellenistic scientific theory had considerable achievements to its credit. In particular it was successful in developing two important conceptions which had already been formulated in the fourth century BC. These were the use of mathematics as a method of investigating natural phenomena and the use of empirical research to prove or disprove a hypothesis. In the period we are considering knowledge was greatly advanced by the application of these notions in various fields of scientific activity. Where development stops short the cause lies not in any failure of intellectual grasp but in the absence of any organizational drive within society as a whole.

Patterns of Society

As we have seen, the Hellenistic world was not devoid of material progress, though this was uneven. Land was, of course, fundamentally important to the lives not only of countrymen but also of the people in the towns, and there were some improvements in land use. Recorded is Alexander's work on the canals of Babylonia, where he constructed dams and devised methods to prevent silting, and similar work is known to have taken place in Thessaly and in the Crimea. In early third-century BC Egypt the Arsinoite *nome* (the modern Fayum) was developed for agriculture by a system of irrigation control which rendered it one of the most fertile parts of the country. The Ptolemies in Egypt and the Seleucids and Attalids in Antioch and Pergamum introduced new fruits and improved cereals. But most of these crop improvements were designed to provide luxury products for the courts and the upper classes, and not to bring about any substantial change in the quality or yield of basic commodities. More use was made of iron ploughs and there were some improvements in farm equipment, such as oil- and wine-presses, and perhaps even a threshing-machine was used. But as achievements all these do not add up to very much.

How far the Hellenistic world sought or needed to make substantial changes in the availability of everyday commodities such as wheat is debatable. Governments certainly showed a real interest in grain and in ensuring a regular supply of it, for corn shortage could easily lead to rioting and civil disturbance. But shortage of wheat need not necessarily imply overall shortage of food, for barley often provided an adequate substitute. Barley was the usual crop and probably the main item of diet throughout the countryside in all the lands around the eastern Mediterranean. But city-dwellers seem to have developed a marked preference for wheat, which consequently formed the staple of the vast grain trade. Funds set up to provide grain are known from Messenia and Delos, but they do not appear to have been designed to subsidize the population: the evidence is rather against the assumption of widespread food shortages calling for special measures. From time to time cities will have taken action to cope with local bad harvests and dislocation due to war. But there is no firm evidence that people were either better or worse off for food than they had been in the days before Alexander.

One change brought about by Alexander's conquests and the founding of cities in the far east by the Seleucids was an extension of the areas penetrated by a monetary economy. This trend was also assisted by Alexander's release of quantities of precious metal from the treasuries of the east, a development which caused a fall in the value of both gold and silver. It is doubtful, however, if this had much effect on the native peoples living in their villages. For them barter is likely to have remained the usual means of commodity exchange and they probably paid their taxes largely in kind.

As in the period before Alexander, trade and industry continued to be on a small scale. Businesses usually consisted of a working master and one or two slaves. There were no factories or anything like mass-production. The city of Rhodes was exceptional in basing its prosperity consciously on the maritime commerce from which its ruling aristocracy derived its wealth. Apparently the Rhodian government warded off popular discontent by a system of supplying foodstuffs to the poor at the expense of rich benefactors, who undertook such obligations as a *leitourgia*, or 'liturgy', a public office carrying financial obligations but also bringing its holder prestige. Rich benefactors, known to us from many honorary inscriptions, had an important role to fill in most cities. Such men won the esteem of their fellow citizens, and the satisfaction of seeing that publicly expressed in official decrees and privileges, having met out of their own resources payments that had to be made to the kings, the cost of subsidizing festivals, the institution of charities and, in some of the Black Sea cities, the payment of 'Danegeld' to threatening barbarian kings living in the neighbourhood. The existence of such a system of benefactions played an important and often symbolic role in Hellenistic society. It also implies the presence in the cities of a class of very rich men. How their wealth was acquired one can only speculate. Doubtless the circumstances varied from city to city. But in the Black Sea area a likely source may well have been the slave-trade, operated in conjunction with those same barbarians whose attentions had on other occasions to be bought off. This picture of material life in the cities is necessarily sketchy and only applies to the older urban centres of Greece proper, the Aegean lands, and those of the Black Sea and Syria. Evidence on material conditions in the new foundations in the east is almost entirely absent.

In Greece proper literary sources point to a growth in debt and a population decline from the third century BC onwards. The assertion of the historian Polybius (*c.* 200–*c.* 118 BC) that there was a widespread refusal to marry, accompanied by the practice of infanticide, is valid only for his own class of rich landowners. The existence of a widespread demand for land redistribution implies a shortage of land among poor farmers rather than a shortage of men to work it, and the flow of mercenaries to the various kingdoms from areas such as Aetolia and Crete tells the same story. Moreover, recent archaeological surveys in several parts of the Greek mainland have provided evidence for a fall in the number of inhabited sites from the end of the third century BC. Such a development is consistent with changes in land tenure, the growth of larger estates and the prevalence of less intensive cultivation by tenant farmers, and this in turn would imply the dispossession or disappearance of many peasant smallholders. Of such a development there is well-documented evidence from Sparta, where an ambitious king attempted to impose social revolution in order to reverse the trend.

At Sparta a concentration of land in a few hands had resulted from the fourth century BC onwards in a catastrophic decline in the number of full citizens (Spartiates), whose status and ability to serve in the army depended on their ownership of a plot of land. By the third century BC Sparta had abandoned its traditional communal messes and had become a city of little importance. A first attempt to reverse this trend was made by king Agis IV (244–241 BC) but was thwarted by his enemies, and he was assassinated. In 235 BC Cleomenes III succeeded to the other throne – from the earliest times there were always two kings at Sparta, from different houses – and, as already described, he set out to break up and take over the Achaean League. In 227 BC, in furtherance of this plan, he overthrew the regular magistrates and turned the kingship into a form of tyranny. The land was divided up, 4,000 new citizens were thus created and trained to fight in the phalanx, and the old traditional Spartan discipline was reintroduced. Cleomenes went further, also liberating those members of the serf class of helots who could pay five Attic minae for their freedom and arming 3,000 of them to add to his forces. As we saw, Cleomenes was defeated at Sellasia in 222 BC and was forced to take refuge in Egypt, where he soon perished.

The reforms were cancelled, but the revolutionary movement persisted at Sparta under subsequent leaders: Lycurgus, Machanidas and Nabis. The movement eventually deteriorated into an oppressive sort of dictatorship and failed to restore Sparta to her old dominion in Greece. Backward-looking and ultimately impotent, the Spartan revolutionary movement collapsed soon after the arrival of the Romans. Henceforth the social problems of the Hellenistic world were increasingly absorbed into those of an expanding Roman imperialism.

Intellectual Life

Scholarship

Although it produced no writers of the calibre of the greatest names of the fifth and fourth centuries BC, the Hellenistic age displays a wide range of noteworthy scholars, poets, historians and artists. Not all of these were connected with the Ptolemaic court. Nevertheless, in all these fields, as in that of science, Alexandria dominated the intellectual life of the enlarged Greek world. The museum – the Muses' sanctuary – and the great library were set up in that city under the first two Ptolemies. If we can believe the twelfth-century Byzantine scholar John Tzetzes, the library eventually contained around 500,000 scrolls, but whether these were lodged in a separate building or in rooms off a *stoa* or off the museum itself is uncertain. Together, the museum and the library constituted a unique research facility and an important centre of philological activity, especially in the field of Homeric criticism. Under three distinguished chief librarians, Zenodotus of Ephesus (*fl. c.* 284 BC), Aristophanes of Byzantium (*c.* 257–180 BC) and Aristarchus of Samothrace (*c.* 217–145 BC), Homer's text was examined in detail. Their commentaries and studies, which also took in the historical and geographical background of the poems, laid the foundation of all later Homeric scholarship.

Possibly Attalus III of Pergamum, who in 133 BC bequeathed his kingdom to Rome. The Attalid dynasty encouraged intellectual life in both Pergamum and Athens.

Similar patronage to that of the Ptolemies was also exercised by the Attalid kings at Pergamum. The Pergamene library was second only to that at Alexandria, and Pergamum too attracted a group of distinguished artists and scholars, whose names are known especially from the anecdotal biographies of Antigonus of Carystus (*fl.* 240 BC), a writer on art who was himself a sculptor. Other Pergamene scholars were Crates of Mallus (*fl.* mid-second century BC), who had the misfortune to break his leg in an open sewer while visiting Rome in 168 BC and stimulated great interest by lecturing there during his convalescence. Crates tried to explain away inconsistencies in Homer by assuming allegorical meanings in his narrative. Another scholar, Polemon of Ilium (*fl. c.* 190 BC), collected and published information on works of art and also epigrams on monuments, which he assembled in the course of extensive travel from Asia Minor to Sicily and Carthage. He engaged in scholarly polemic against both Antigonus of Carystus and Eratosthenes.

Literature

Compared with the literature of the classical period, that of the Hellenistic age assumed a much greater variety. New or freshly developed genres which now emerged were biography, usually of an anecdotal kind, romantic fiction and popular moralizing, as exemplified in the so-called diatribes associated especially with Bion of Borysthenes (*c.* 325–*c.* 255 BC), who wandered from town to town lecturing. In the new political climate scope for independent politics was much reduced and with it political oratory like that of Demosthenes, but the many embassies which went from city to city and between the cities and the royal courts (and later Rome) still gave plenty of opportunity for oratory of a practical or epideictic sort.

The work of the poets was more impressive. Beginning with Philitas of Cos (*fl. c.* 300 BC), who became tutor to the future Ptolemy II, the Alexandrine school produced verse that was highly polished, learned, spattered with recondite mythological references, witty (sometimes over-clever), urbane and superficial. New literary forms appeared, in particular the mime, developed out of a rough popular kind of prose sketch into a polished verse product by Herodas (*fl.* third century BC) and Theocritus (*fl. c.* 300–*c.* 260 BC). Herodas' poems were recovered from a papyrus published in 1891. They contain dramatic sketches portraying often risqué social situations, in which women frequently figure in unflattering roles; they were perhaps designed to be recited. Theocritus, a native of Syracuse, was only briefly in Alexandria, preferring his own city or Cos to the Ptolemaic capital. He was the inventor of pastoral, a style with a long later history reaching down through Virgil to Spenser and a wide range of writers in all the lands and tongues of Europe, in which a highly elaborate wit is projected on to rustic characters. In his *Idylls* Theocritus provides racy vignettes of country and city life, which never wholly lose sight of reality behind the artifice. One of his best poems, the *Syracusan Women* (*Idyll* 15), recounts a conversation between two Syracusan women living in Alexandria and out for the day as spectators of the festival of Adonis. This poem is exceptional in being located in Alexandria.

The epigram, brief and well adapted to capture a mood or make a point with wit and urbanity, also flourished in the third century BC. Its most famous practitioner was Asclepiades of Samos (*fl.* 290 BC), who revived the so-called Asclepiad metre formerly used by Alcaeus and Sappho, and wrote mainly on the themes of love and wine; his poems conjure up the atmosphere of the symposium and the banquet. His contemporaries Hedylus and Poseidippus, both resident on Samos and later at Alexandria, pursued similar themes and together with Asclepiades formed a small literary circle. More distinguished than any of these, however, was Callimachus of Cyrene (*fl.* 305–*c.* 240 BC), who was a master not merely in epigram but in several other literary genres as well, and who stands out as one of the leading figures in Alexandrine literature, perhaps not least because of his influence on later poets at Rome towards the end of the republic. Knowledge of his work has been greatly extended as a result of discoveries of fragments on papyri, the disproportionate number of which reflects his popularity in Egypt.

Callimachus emigrated from Cyrene to Alexandria, where he was for some time a schoolmaster before obtaining a post as cataloguer in the library; he never rose to be the head of that institution. Callimachus' most famous work *On Causes (Aitia)*, in four books, dealt with various aetiological legends strung together in a continuous form. Only fragments survive. These suggest that in the first two books he represents himself as holding conversations with the Muses on various puzzling, often trivial, topics – for example, why the Parians do not use flutes at sacrifices – but that in the third and fourth books he dispensed with such artifice. Some of the longest fragments are those preserved on papyri and these include the story of Acontius and Cydippe. The last *Aition* records how Queen Berenice's lock of hair was detected as a new constellation in the heavens, a fanciful conceit later copied by Catullus and adapted by Alexander Pope in his *Rape of the Lock*.

Only Callimachus' *Hymns* and *Epigrams* have survived in the manuscript tradition. The *Hymns*, six in all, are set in various cities, and though they recall the Homeric *Hymns*, they have a more playful touch. Some scholars have interpreted them as works of serious piety, but it seems more likely that they should be thought of as literary compositions of a highly sophisticated kind, designed for recitation. There are about sixty *Epigrams*, many in the form of epitaphs, of which the best known is perhaps that to Heraclitus: 'They told me, Heraclitus, they told me you were dead ...' Apart from several studies in prose, often on topics which strike the modern reader as highly pedantic, Callimachus produced many other works, including lyrics in a variety of metres, love poems to boys (never women) and, of especial interest, the *Hecale*, an epyllion, or 'small epic', relating the entertaining of Theseus by an old woman of that name on his way to fight the bull of Marathon. The emphasis is on Hecale and on the meal she prepared for Theseus rather than on the epic hero himself and this poem was much imitated – by Ovid, for instance, and by the author of the *Moretum* attributed to Virgil. The epyllion became a very popular and typical Alexandrine verse form, which afforded all the possibilities for a romantic and witty treatment and consequently appealed strongly to the taste of the public of that period. Another noteworthy example is the poem on Europa and the bull, who was Zeus, by Moschus of Syracuse (*fl. c.* 150 BC), a pupil of Aristarchus.

Several details from the *Hecale* were borrowed by a pupil of Callimachus, Apollonius (*fl.* mid-third century BC), for incorporation in his epic on the Argonauts, written around 260 BC. Apollonius, a native of Alexandria – though he is usually known as 'the Rhodian', as he later settled on Rhodes – was head of the library between Zenodotus and Eratosthenes. Epic had its own place in the literature of the Hellenistic age, though it was often turned to didactic ends, in such poems as the *Phaenomena* of Aratus of Soli (*c.* 315–240 BC), a study of the stars and the heavens, and two tedious poems on snakebites and their antidotes by Nicander of Colophon (*fl.* second century BC). Developed at Rome, the didactic epic was later to produce a masterpiece in Virgil's *Georgics*. As a genre, epic was detested by Callimachus: 'A great book,' he wrote, 'is a great scourge.' A perhaps untrustworthy tradition records a bitter quarrel and lasting animosity between Callimachus and Apollonius, which ended in the latter's withdrawal to Rhodes, where he stayed for the rest of his life. But, as many papyrus fragments demonstrate, Apollonius continued to have a considerable following. His *Argonautica* displayed many of the most typical characteristics of Alexandrine literature. Charming in its descriptions and seasoned with wit and irony, it was distinguished above all for its description of Medea's initial involvement with Jason and its portrayal for the first time of the emotions and agitation of a young girl in love. This episode was later taken up and used to good effect by Virgil in his description of the awakening of Dido's love for Aeneas in the fourth book of the *Aeneid*. But Apollonius' work as a whole is episodic,

Menander (342–*c.* 293 BC), the most famous exponent of the New Comedy which inspired the later Latin playwrights Plautus and Terence. A mosaic portrait from a Roman villa on the Aegean island of Lesbos.

badly balanced and lacking in structural unity; its characters are flat and it suffers from its author's excess of erudition.

One important branch of literature remained in Athens. New Comedy, represented by Philemon (*c.* 368–*c.* 267 BC) and Menander (342–*c.* 292 BC), was the final form of Attic drama to be supported in the Athenian national theatre of Dionysus. It was a comedy of manners, cosmopolitan in its themes, concerned no longer with politics but rather with domestic intrigue, and built up around a number of standard roles. These included the miserly old man, his spendthrift son who, assisted by the clever and unscrupulous slave, outwits the villainous pander and secures for his young master the girl with whom he is in love. She, apparently a slave and brought by misfortune to the brothel, turns out, as the plot is unravelled, to be in reality the freeborn daughter of a neighbour of good lineage, and all ends happily. The ingenious intricacies of plots such as this and the delineation of character are brilliantly worked out on the stage. Menander has been largely restored to the modern world as a result of papyrus finds and it is now easier to compare him with the Roman writers Plautus and Terence, who drew on him. His works are highly entertaining, but they also reveal a deep sense of humanity, which made a strong impression on his audience.

Historical Writing

Even before the death of Philip II of Macedon in 336 BC, the pattern of the Hellenistic age had thrown its shadow ahead in the historical work of Theopompus of Chios (born *c.* 378 BC), who first wrote *Hellenica*, but later, recognizing the new power visible in the Greek world, turned to writing *Philippica*, in which history became the measure of one man's achievements. Alexander's expedition had its court historian, Aristotle's nephew, Callisthenes (died 327 BC), who was, truly or falsely, accused of conspiracy against the king and executed. His work contained extravagant glorification of Alexander. Not surprisingly Alexander's extraordinary career produced a crop of histories soon after his death. None of these has survived, though their use can be traced with varying degrees of certainty in later authors. The best surviving account of Alexander's expedition, by Arrian (*fl.* second century AD), was based chiefly on the histories written by Aristobulus, a Greek military engineer, who accompanied the army, and the Macedonian general Ptolemy, the founder of the Ptolemaic dynasty in Egypt. Other eyewitness accounts were those of the Cretan Nearchus, admiral of Alexander's fleet which brought part of his forces back from the Indus to the Persian Gulf, and author of a description of India used by Arrian; and of Onesicritus, the helmsman of Alexander's flagship on the River Jhelum. The Alexandrian Cleitarchus probably did not take part in the expedition himself, but he was the author of what was perhaps the most popular history of Alexander and was later to become a major element in the *Alexander Romance*. This work went back to an original manuscript, falsely attributed to Callisthenes, which is no longer extant. In its various versions it was to become immensely popular for many centuries, surrounding the whole adventure with an atmosphere of wonder and unreality.

The Alexander-historians represent a response to a unique occasion and they had little influence on the next generation. Within the Hellenistic kingdoms historians continued to write chronological accounts of political and military events after the fashion of Thucydides and Xenophon, often taking up the thread where a predecessor left off. Many of them were of little consequence and almost nothing of their work survives. An exception is Hieronymus of Cardia, who was an active administrator under various successors of Alexander for about sixty years and who died at the court of Antigonus Gonatas (276–239 BC). His work has also perished, but with the help of Diodorus (*fl.* first century BC), who drew on it, supplemented by a few attested fragments embodied in other writers, it is possible to form some impression of Hieronymus' history, which lies behind the best tradition of the wars of Alexander's successors. Strangely, there was no school of historians devoted to chronicling the history of particular dynasties. A few such writers are known: Neanthes (*c.* 200 BC) wrote on Attalus I, Ptolemy of Megalopolis on Ptolemy IV and Strato on Philip V and Perseus of Macedonia. But usually it is unclear whether such works were genuine histories or simply encomiastic biographies similar to several written by the Athenian Isocrates in the fourth century. A more interesting development is the positive encouragement given in Egypt and in the Seleucid kingdom to native historians

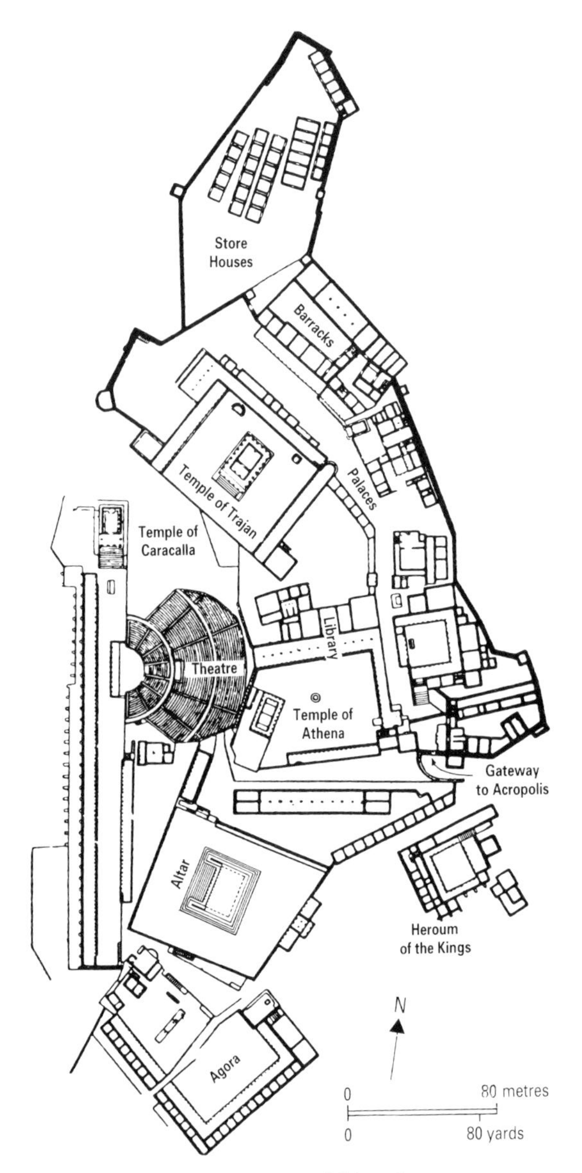

Pergamum, the capital of the Attalid kingdom.

such as Berossus, a priest of Bel at Babylonia, and Manetho, high priest at Heliopolis (both early third century BC), to produce histories of their own civilizations in Greek, which served the political ends of the new rulers of those lands.

Many historians of the early Hellenistic period, as we know from later criticism of their work, wrote in a sensational and emotional manner, designed to entertain rather than to instruct the reader. One such writer of some importance was Duris (*c.* 340–*c.* 260 BC), a pupil of the Aristotelian scholar and writer Theophrastus (*c.* 370–*c.* 285 BC) and tyrant of Samos. Included in Duris' considerable literary output was a history in this vein covering the period from 370 to around 260 BC. Later Phylarchus of Athens wrote a history covering the period from the death of Pyrrhus of Epirus in 272 BC to that of Antigonus III of Macedonia in 221 BC, a work criticized by the historian Polybius for its patent pro-Spartan bias and the sacrifice of accuracy to emotional appeal.

Though he wrote as an exile in Athens, the thirty-eight books of the Sicilian Timaeus of Taormina (*c.* 356–260 BC) dealt primarily with the western Mediterranean. Timaeus was violently attacked by Polybius, who, while conceding his accuracy in chronological matters, accuses him of falsification and rhetorical writing. Nevertheless, Timaeus won a reputation as the acknowledged historian of the western Greeks and Polybius himself chose to begin the preliminary books of his own history from the point where Timaeus left off.

Polybius (*c.* 200–*c.* 118 BC) is the greatest Greek historian of the Hellenistic period. Significantly, he sprang, like so many other historians, not from the milieu of any Hellenistic court but from that of the city-state. His birthplace was Megalopolis, an important member of the Achaean League. Unlike many literary genres, history seems to have flourished mainly within the older world of the city-states. Polybius, like Thucydides, Xenophon and Hieronymus before him, was a statesman and a general before he took to writing history; and, like the first two of these, he spent many formative years in forced exile. His work originally consisted of forty books, but of these only Books 1–5 survive intact, the rest being made up mainly out of fragments assembled in Byzantine times. The whole work covered the years from the outbreak of the First Punic War between Rome and Carthage in 264 BC down to 146–145 BC. The central part (after two introductory books) originally set out to relate the events of the years 220–168 BC, the fifty-three years during which, as Polybius claimed, Rome rose to be 'the mistress of the inhabited world'. Later he added the last ten books to cover the next twenty-three years, from 167 to 145 BC, the aftermath of the catastrophic year, 146 BC, which saw the destruction of Carthage and in Greece the Roman sack of Corinth and the dissolution of the Achaean League. Thus Polybius' *Histories* strike a new note in recognizing the importance of the Romans, who had put an end to the Macedonian monarchy, which still carried an aura from the great days of Alexander, and had driven the Seleucids beyond the Taurus mountains. His work indeed sounds the knell of the Hellenistic world.

Polybius' work is admirable on several counts, not for its style, which is jejune and prolix, but for its firm rational outlook (apart from some wavering on the role of Fortune in human affairs), its emphasis on practical experience in public life, its rejection of rhetorical and emotional writing and its determined attempt to establish both what happened and why. Like several other writers of this period, Polybius was deeply interested in the geography of the world he was describing. With the assistance of influential friends at Rome he had personally explored the Atlantic coast of North

Africa and he took some pride in having sailed further than the legendary Odysseus. But his main purpose, conceived during the seventeen years he spent as a detainee at Rome (from 167 to 150 BC) was to alert his fellow countrymen to the rise of power and the source of strength of the Roman republic. It was, he averred, their incomparable army and their mixed constitution that had enabled this people to conquer the known world. History was to be in the most literal sense the school for political action; since the Greeks could not hope to throw off the Romans, they must learn to live with them. Polybius' *Histories* were continued down from 145 BC by Poseidonius (*c.* 135–*c.* 50 BC), who migrated from Apamea on the Orontes in north Syria to Rhodes and later to Rome. He was a philosopher and a polymath, whose *History* in fifty-two books was basically a justification of the Roman empire, but at the same time pointed to a process of increasing degeneration at work.

Before we leave the subject of history-writing in the Hellenistic age, mention should be made of memoirs and autobiographies, which, though not strictly history, are akin to history and often provide the historian with his material. Examples of this genre are the apologia for his ten years' rule at Athens by Demetrius of Phalerum (*c.* 350–after 283 BC), the *Memoirs* of King Pyrrhus of Epirus, the *Memoirs* of Aratus of Sicyon, the hero of the Achaean confederacy, and twenty-four books of *Memoirs* written by King Ptolemy VIII, Euergetes II. These varied in character from works of personal self-justification to official journals or pure reminiscences.

The Aphrodite of Melos (120–100 BC), an outstanding example of Hellenistic sculpture.

The Winged Victory of Samothrace, which was sculpted *c.* 200 BC to celebrate a Rhodian naval triumph over Antiochus III.

Art and Architecture

In the field of art the Hellenistic world produced some masterpieces, of which the most famous are probably the Victory of Samothrace (*c.* 200 BC) and the Aphrodite of Melos (late second century BC), both now in the Louvre in Paris. But these are only two out of a large number of works of sculpture known from this period – though the history and dating of Hellenistic works of art are far more difficult than those of works belonging to the classical period, owing to poorer literary records. It is clear that after Alexander the great centres for art shifted to where patronage was strongest – to Pergamum, Antioch and Alexandria, and to Rhodes, which until the mid-second century BC drew great prosperity from its trade. In these new centres art no longer existed to express the identity of the city-state but conformed to the taste and purses of kings and courtiers. The religious aspect receded, even statues of gods were humanized and new themes emerged. Sculptors now provided a realistic portrayal of sleeping figures, ugly old women, female nudes – a genre first made popular in Praxiteles' Cnidian Aphrodite (*c.* 340 BC) – children at play, like the famous third-century boy with a goose (known from a Roman copy) and various hermaphrodites; some of these types were exaggerated to the point of caricature.

A new realism found expression in life-like statues of famous people, including philosophers and statesmen. Examples are the bronze statues of Demosthenes, set up at Athens in 280/79 BC, and known from many later copies, and the marble statue of the philosopher Chrysippus, now in the Louvre. But private patrons would often have their own likenesses perpetuated, and a study of Hellenistic domestic architecture has demonstrated that these statues were frequently placed in a position designed to make the greatest impression upon visitors entering the house.

At the other end of the scale Hellenistic kings devoted great attention (as did Roman emperors later) to familiarizing their subjects everywhere with their features. The Sicyonian sculptor Lysippus (*fl.* 320 BC) made a famous bronze statue of Alexander, which is known from a Roman marble copy now in the Louvre: the head is tilted and the eyes gaze slightly upwards, creating a highly romantic impression, of which the king, who favoured Lysippus, was obviously not unconscious. A series of battle scenes portrayed on sarcophagi, such as the late-fourth-century Alexander-sarcophagus from Sidon, now in Istanbul, culminated in the baroque frieze on the Great Altar of Zeus from Pergamum, now in Berlin, which represents a battle between gods and giants, no doubt symbolizing the victories won by the Attalids over the Gaulish barbarians.

Most Hellenistic painting is lost. But some notion of its merits can be gained from the painted Macedonian tombs at Levkhadia and Vergina, from painted gravestones at Alexandria and at Demetrias in Thessaly, from Roman copies and from mosaics of Hellenistic inspiration at Pompeii. Hellenistic painters had fully mastered the art of perspective and they made increasing use of landscape as background when treating such topics as the scenes from the *Odyssey* portrayed on the wall of a house on the Esquiline at Rome and dating to the first century BC. At Pella in Macedonia a remarkable pebble-mosaic has been revealed, representing a lion-hunt, and displaying great virtuosity. Other forms of art included jewellery, glassware, ceramics and engraved gems.

The Hellenistic age brought great variety to architecture, as it did to so much else. The classical orders were no longer kept distinct. Buildings accommodated both Doric and Ionic columns and a new order, the more florid Corinthian, was widely employed. Elements of one order were grafted on to buildings belonging

The Great Altar of Zeus at Pergamum, erected about 180 BC as an assertion of Hellenistic culture in Asia Minor.

essentially to another. The result was a greater fluidity, which did more than reflect the kind of undisciplined eclecticism one encounters in California today. Buildings were now often built to fit a particular site within a planned whole. Hellenistic cities were often laid out on a grid plan where the ground was level, but where it was uneven or adjacent to the sea, the streets and levels were carefully adjusted to fit the site. This resulted in some spectacular urban complexes, such as those at Miletus and Priene, begun before the Hellenistic age but developed further in the third and second centuries, and above all at Pergamum, where a large theatre spanning several levels and a long columned *stoa* served to round off a rising group of terraces and a way leading past the Altar of Zeus to further temples clustered around the summit of the hill. Individual buildings were now more elaborate. Theatres were of stone and with a high proscenium. There were public baths with hypocausts for heating and monumental staircases. At a more basic level there were granaries supported on vaults and arches; arsenals were often harmonious and elegant buildings.

The new monarchic regimes demanded palaces. The main ones to survive are Macedonian: an impressive example was built by Cassander at modern Vergina on the hill-top overlooking the plain. There are also two palace-like buildings at Pella, the capital, and Philip V used the one at Vergina as a model for his palace at Demetrias in Thessaly. The Macedonian pattern of rooms around a rectangular courtyard was also followed at Aï Khanum in distant Bactria.

Theophrastus (322–287 BC), the pupil, collaborator and successor of Aristotle.

Philosophy and Religion

Like New Comedy, philosophy resisted the attractions of the courts and remained at home in Athens, with its traditions of Socrates, Plato and Aristotle, for Athens, like Rhodes, Cos and (at the very end of our period) Tarsus, maintained a cultural tradition independent of the new monarchies. In the years after Alexander philosophers from all over the Greek world chose to settle and teach there. The old schools continued to flourish, but the emphasis of their teaching changed. Plato's Academy, under the direction of Xenocrates (339–314 BC) now turned primarily to questions of practical morality, rather than theories of ethics. In his doctrine that one must try to eliminate all disturbing elements from life Xenocrates brought the school near to the position taken up by Epicurus; and under his successor, Polemo (314–276 BC), there was a move away from the Socratic dialectic. Thereafter the Academy, under Arcesilaus (268–241 BC), became associated with scepticism and the doctrine of suspending belief, a practice which, it was argued, created an equanimity of mind conducive to happiness. This trend was continued until the death of Carneades in 136 BC, after which such views were abandoned and the school ceased to exercise any significant influence.

Aristotle's school, the Peripatetics, with their seat in the Lyceum, was also important until about 270 BC. After Aristotle's death in 322 BC it came under the control of Theophrastus (322–*c.* 287 BC) and maintained its founder's interest in biological research. With its intensive work on the description and classification of plants, and its investigations into the physiology of plant life, the Lyceum thus kept up the old connection between philosophy and what would now be thought of rather as science. But the school also maintained its interest in ethics, and Theophrastus is perhaps mostly remembered for his *Characters*, impressionistic sketches of various 'types' of character, not without their practical use for students of rhetoric. In the main Theophrastus continued to work along the lines already indicated by Aristotle. His successor, Strato (*c.* 287–269 BC) was exceptional among Hellenistic philosophers in retaining the earlier interest in natural science; he also wrote books on ethics, psychology, logic, zoology, physics and cosmology. His name is associated with an important doctrine asserting the existence of the void within the cosmos, which was later to be influential at Alexandria in physiological theory (under Erasistratus in the mid-third century BC) and in mechanics as pursued by Hero (first century AD).

New Schools of Thought

The philosophical schools which brought distinction to Athens from the third century BC onwards were, however, those of the Epicureans and the Stoics. Epicurus (341–270 BC) was a native of Samos who set up a school at Athens in about 307 BC. This very soon fell into bad odour, on the grounds that it taught a hedonistic philosophy which regarded pleasure as the greatest good. In fact to the Epicureans pleasure was

Epicurus (341–270 BC) set up his own school of philosophy in Athens in about 307 BC.

Tradition says Zeno arrived in Athens from Cyprus in 310 BC. There he founded Stoicism.

specifically defined as not sensual enjoyment, but rather freedom from pain and mental anxiety, to be achieved by sober reasoning and the considered rejection of anything liable to give rise to those evils. Pleasure was to have one's desires satisfied, not the act of satisfying them; the aim was *ataraxia*, or 'imperturbability'. The Epicureans believed that there was no life after death, that the gods existed but had no interest in us, and that the universe ran of its own volition according to the atomic theory propounded by Democritus of Abdera in the fifth century BC. Political action was to be avoided; the ideal in life was a gentle friendship within a small group. Not unnaturally, the exclusiveness of Epicurean communities, which included women and slaves, and the ambiguity of the word 'pleasure', which could so easily be misconstrued, led to popular suspicion; apart from a short period at Rome towards the end of the republic in the first century BC, Epicureanism never became wholly reputable.

In popularity and influence Epicureanism was soon outstripped by the teachings of the Stoics, who took their name from the Painted Hall, the Stoa Poikile, where, around 310 BC, Zeno of Citium in Cyprus set up his school. Stoicism was a complete philosophical system embracing a theory of knowledge (with logic and rhetoric), a theory of the physical world (including theology) and a doctrine of ethics. With some modifications Stoicism flourished throughout the whole of the Hellenistic period and was to become the dominant philosophy under the early Roman empire; indeed, as a philosophy, it lasted well into the third century AD. The Stoics taught that the only good was *arete*, or 'virtue', and that virtue was based on knowledge – that is, on mental conceptions which agree with reality and are therefore unmistakable. Certainty about them can be attained by a 'perception conveying direct apprehension' (*kataleptike phantasia*), that being the Stoic jargon used to describe accepting the evidence of one's senses. Basing his knowledge (and conduct) on such perceptions, the Stoic wise man can live in accordance with the will of god (or nature, since the two very soon became identified). This and only this constitutes true virtue, and only true virtue is good. All else, if not positively evil, is indifferent. True, there are also certain things which the wise man will choose (such as health) or avoid (such as pain or death), if he can, but these are not essential to the achievement of happiness. The truly wise man is not dependent on the vicissitudes of fortune.

These views became widespread outside the confines of the Stoic school. Under Zeno's successor Cleanthes (263–232 BC) Stoic doctrine was further developed and popularized in a famous *Hymn to Zeus* (Zeus being here identified with the Stoic idea of nature); and Cleanthes' successor, Chrysippus (280–207 BC), a convert from the Academy, finally shaped Stoic doctrine so decisively that it is now difficult to separate his contribution from what went before. One aspect of Stoic doctrine was the belief in a periodic world conflagration. That was rejected by the so-called Middle Stoa under Panaetius of Rhodes (129–109 BC) and his successors. But, more important, Panaetius modified the earlier Stoic view that only the absolutely wise man can be virtuous. On the contrary, it was possible by one's own efforts to make progress towards both wisdom and virtue, and to help one's fellow men in this was an important part of the philosopher's task. Before assuming the headship of the Stoa, Panaetius had travelled widely and had become closely associated with P. Scipio Aemilianus, the Roman statesman and general, who had destroyed Carthage in 146 BC. Panaetius sought, and not without success, to adapt Stoic teaching to the minds of his Roman friends, by emphasizing the positive virtue of liberality, benevolence and magnanimity. His work *On Duty* exercised great influence and Cicero drew on it for his own work on the subject, *De Officiis*.

If we may follow the fortunes of this influential school of philosophy a little further, we find it adopted by many members of the group around Scipio Aemilianus, who was a close friend of Polybius, and, a couple of generations later, by the last defenders of the Roman republic, M. Porcius Cato (95–46 BC), whose suicide at Utica in North Africa won him lasting renown, and M. Brutus (*c*. 85–42 BC), who organized the assassination of Julius Caesar. During the first century of the Roman empire a modified Stoicism, which concentrated on ethical teaching, became the philosophical doctrine of the aristocratic opposition to the imperial autocracy; and in the second century AD, under Marcus Aurelius, Stoicism became the creed of the emperor himself.

Though pre-eminent among the schools, Epicureanism and Stoicism did not cover the whole range of Hellenistic philosophy. A school of extreme scepticism was founded by Pyrrhon of Elis (*c*. 365–*c*. 270 BC). In advocating that one should refrain from all judgements, the Pyrrhonists insisted that sense impressions are unreliable. Pyrrhon himself had taken part in Alexander's expedition and he may have been influenced by forms of asceticism which he met in India. The scepticism of his school has much in common with the views of the Academy under Arcesilaus and the object of its teaching was close to that of the Epicureans: that is, to secure tranquillity of mind.

Two other schools which exercised some influence were the Cyrenaics and the Cynics. The Cyrenaics preached the doctrine falsely attributed to the Epicureans, that bodily pleasure was the greatest good. How far that doctrine derived from Aristippus of Cyrene, an older contemporary of Plato and an associate of Socrates, and how far from his grandson of the same name, is disputed. Antisthenes (*c*. 445–*c*. 360 BC), another follower of Socrates, and Diogenes of Sinope (*c*. 400–*c*. 325 BC) were together regarded as the founders of a school not without influence in the Hellenistic period. Diogenes taught that happiness consisted in satisfying one's natural needs as simply and as cheaply as possible. Nothing natural was shameful, hence all natural acts could be performed in public. Many anecdotes related how Diogenes carried out this doctrine of 'shamelessness' in his everyday life. It led to his being nicknamed 'the Dog' (*kyon*, genitive *kynos*) and his followers Cynics.

Religious Development

Philosophy was no recondite pursuit in Hellenistic times. Theophrastus is said to have lectured to audiences of 2,000. But religion counted for much more, being less intellectual, more universal in its influence and more fundamental to men's thought and behaviour. Religion in the Hellenistic age covered a wide spectrum of beliefs and practices, ranging from official cults associated with rulers and governments to the popular creeds which permeated every aspect of people's lives. Though it had been under attack since the sophistic movement of the fifth century BC, the Olympian pantheon still survived and probably commanded a wide spread of tepid belief – though many were no doubt agnostics at heart. The difficulty is to penetrate beneath the established rituals and to discover what they really signified to those who participated in them. The expansion of the boundaries of the Greek world exposed people to new forms of religious experience and introduced them to non-Greek deities. At the same time the heads of the new monarchic regimes encouraged specific cults, some traditional, some novel; for reasons of state and for a variety of other motives, these were taken up and even anticipated by their subjects. At the same time and at a different level, many sought comfort in cults offering the promise of personal salvation. These various strands combine to create a kaleidoscopic picture of change in religious patterns not easy to analyse or bring into focus.

The new rulers, all of whom were in a sense usurpers, turned to Olympus for validation of their rule, claiming the support of some protective deity. Thus the Antigonids in Macedonia (like the previous dynasty of Philip II and Alexander, with whom they claimed a probably spurious kinship) traced their ancestry back to the hero Heracles. The Seleucids put out the story that their founder Seleucus I was under the special protection of Apollo and carried the symbol of that god, an anchor, as a birthmark on his thigh. The Ptolemies specially cultivated the worship of Dionysus; Ptolemy III claimed descent from both Heracles and Dionysus. Alongside this adoption of certain patron gods was the institution of the official cult of the ruler, by which the dead kings and their queens – and later the living ones as well – were accorded worship in a special state cult. Thus in Egypt a cult for Alexander was instituted perhaps as early as 290 BC, and after the deaths of Ptolemy I and his queen they were given a similar cult. Subsequently each pair of Ptolemaic rulers was declared divine, with special distinguishing titles, and eventually they were incorporated in a portmanteau list containing all the Ptolemies and Alexander.

The native Egyptians were also drawn in. Arsinoe, the wife of Ptolemy II, was admitted into all the Egyptian temples as a 'temple-sharing deity' alongside

The Ptolemaic temple of Horus at Edfu, built between 116 and 57 BC. It shows the Macedonian rulers of Egypt after the manner of the pharaohs.

the native gods, and her cult was financed out of a tax on vineyards, orchards and gardens. Towards the end of the third century a similar state cult, including himself and all the earlier members of the dynasty, was instituted by Antiochus III (223–187 BC) in the Seleucid kingdom. Neither the Antigonids in Macedonia nor the Attalids in Pergamum set up a dynastic cult in the true sense, though there were city cults to the rulers of both houses.

Dynastic cults of this kind cannot in fact be wholly divorced from the less official cults to Hellenistic rulers and others which were everywhere established in the Greek cities. The origin of such cults can be traced back to isolated occasions in the fourth century BC, when for instance oligarchs in control at Samos set up altars to the Spartan general Lysander and instituted a festival in his honour entitled the Lysandreia, or the people of Syracuse offered prayers and libations to Dion, their liberator, 'as to a god'. There is also some evidence pointing to the worship during their lifetime of the Macedonian kings Amyntas III (*c.* 393–370 BC) and Philip II (359–336 BC) in Macedonia, but it is not entirely conclusive. The change came decisively with Alexander the Great and in particular with his demand that the Greek cities should accord him divine honours, an order followed reluctantly and quickly forgotten

The first Macedonian ruler of Egypt, Ptolemy I Soter, with the regalia of a pharaoh.

after his death. But by the early third century BC such city cults had multiplied and were by no means always a response to pressure from above. Many causes combined to ensure their growing popularity: for example, a desire to keep on the right side of kings with great powers for good or ill and a recognition that kings could often accomplish what had in the past seemed the prerogative of the traditional gods. 'The other gods are far away or have no ears or do not exist or do not heed us: but you we can see present among us, not in wood or stone but in truth' – so ran the welcoming hymn sung by the people of Athens to Demetrius Poliorcetes in 290 BC, when they hoped to enlist his help against the Aetolians. Ruler cults served to oil the wheels and to reconcile kings and cities. But in what sense men felt the kings to be gods and what 'a god' meant in such a context is hard for us to apprehend.

For the individual man or woman the official cults of the cities and dynasties cannot have meant a great deal. The decline in the power of the city-states and the accompanying decline in the prestige of the traditional gods was balanced by a growing interest in mystery religions involving secret initiations and promises of personal salvation, such as the rites of Eleusis or the cult of the Cabiri on Samothrace. At Epidaurus in the Peloponnese the cult of Asclepius was an object of pilgrimage, which reached its height in this period, and countless inscriptions testify to the miraculous cures vouchsafed there. Simultaneously attempts were made to explain and define the nature of the gods in terms acceptable to those who were basically sceptical about their existence in anything like their traditional form. One theory asserted that the gods were originally men, who had been raised to godhead in recognition of their services to mankind in the role of rulers, seers or inventors. This line of thought, which recalls the similar attempt to give rational interpretations of no longer acceptable myths (such as the reversal of the sun's course by Atreus), was associated with the name of Euhemerus (*fl. c.* 300 BC), the author of a Utopian account of a visit to an island in the Indian Ocean, where an inscription attested the former presence of the later gods as kings. But Euhemerus doctrine did not really take off until Roman times. A perhaps more common development in the Hellenistic period was the depersonalization of divinity and the worship of abstractions, in particular that of *Tyche* or 'Fortune', whose cult was widespread and who is shown intervening in human events in the pages of many historians, including the usually materially minded Polybius. Visualized as wearing a crown and holding a cornucopia signifying abundance, this ambivalent force for good or evil was portrayed hopefully and apotropaically as benevolent. But how far such abstract objects of worship were really thought of as gods in men's minds it is hard to say. Then, as now, beliefs concerning such matters were probably highly confused and inconsistent.

Perhaps more important to ordinary people were the oriental cults, which increasingly penetrated Greek communities. From Egypt came the worship of Sarapis, a manifestation of the sacred bull Apis, identified after his death with Osiris. His cult was set up by Ptolemy I, probably to provide the Greeks in Egypt with a new patron deity linked with their new home. But whereas the cult of Sarapis achieved only a modest popularity in Egypt, it spread fairly rapidly throughout the Greek and later the Roman world. The worship of the native Egyptian goddess Isis also made great progress in Hellenistic times, probably because it embodied the principle of the mother goddess, always the object of devotion

A silver coin of Philip V of Macedon, who was defeated by the Romans at Cynoscephalae in Thessaly in 197 BC.

A silver coin of Perseus, the eldest son of Philip V and the last king of Macedon. He was defeated by the Romans at Pydna in 168 BC.

in Mediterranean lands. Isis is certainly found identified by syncretism with many goddesses, both Greek and barbarian. But Egypt was not alone in contributing candidates for inclusion in the new pantheon. From Asia Minor Cybele, the Great Mother, accompanied by Attis, and the Phrygian god Men took firm root in Greek lands (and by the end of the third century BC Cybele had been introduced with official approval into Rome). Atargatis and Hadad from Assyria were identified with Aphrodite and Zeus, Melqart with Heracles, Astarte with Aphrodite. And especially in such cosmopolitan cities as Rhodes, Delos or Demetrias in Thessaly, gravestones reveal the presence of such non-Greek cults as those of Sabazius and Adonis. It was especially those cults which offered a personal religious link with divinity or the promise of personal survival after death that now took root.

Finally, mention should be made of the Jewish experience during the Hellenistic period. We have already touched on the Maccabean revolt against the Seleucids, which embodied a combination of religious and nationalist motives and created in Judaea the fertile soil in which 200 years later the new world religion of Christianity was to take root. But the Jews of the Hellenistic world were not confined to Palestine. Already in the fourth century BC there were Jews at Elephantine in Upper Egypt and under the Ptolemies Jews settled in large numbers in the countryside and more especially in Alexandria, where they probably lived alongside Greeks until the establishment of a ghetto in the mid-second century BC. In Egypt, as in Palestine, orthodox Jews were exclusive and resisted all concessions to Greek polytheism or forms of the ruler cult. But there existed a substantial body of Hellenizing Jews both in Egypt and in Palestine, and it was largely in the context of Hellenized Jewry outside Palestine that Christianity made its first advances.

St Paul's missionary journeys took him to the Greek or Hellenized communities of Asia Minor and to Greece proper, and scholars have detected Stoic ideas in his first letter to the Corinthians. Later, in the second century AD, many Christian writers drew on the teachings and the language of Greek, and especially Cynic, philosophy to put the Christian case. In the early fourth century, under the Christian emperor Constantine, it became the religion of the Roman empire, although the faith always continued to reveal its mixed Jewish and Hellenistic parentage.

THE WORLD OF ROME

A bas-relief of the Roman army, with legionaries in the centre. They were the key to Rome's military success.

Chronology

BC

c. 510–509	Expulsion of last king (Tarquinius Superbus) and institution of the republic
494/3	First plebeian secession Creation of plebeian tribunate
493	Defensive alliance between Rome and the Latins
451–450	Compilation of Twelve Tables Second plebeian secession
390	Gauls defeat Romans at Allia and sack city
366	Consulship opened to plebeians
343–341	First Samnite War
340–338	Latin War results in dissolution of Latin League and reorganization of relations between Rome and individual Latin states
326–304	Second Samnite War
321	Samnites force Roman surrender at Caudine Forks
298–290	Third Samnite War forces final submission of Samnites
280–275	Pyrrhus of Epirus fails to keep the Romans out of southern Italy
264–241	First Punic War (against Carthage) results in Roman acquisition of Sicily
238	Rome seizes Sardinia
218	Hannibal's invasion of Italy at start of Second Punic War
214–205	First Macedonian War
202	Carthaginians defeated at Zama (in north Africa) by P. Cornelius Scipio Africanus the Elder
201	End of Second Punic War; consequent Roman occupation of Spain
200–197	Second Macedonian War ends with defeat of Philip V by T. Quinctius Flamininus at Cynoscephalae
191–188	War against Antiochus III of Syria
171–167	Third Macedonian War – defeat of Perseus by L. Aemilius Paullus at Pydna (168)
149–146	Third Punic War, resulting in destruction of Carthage and establishment of province of Africa
146	Subjugation of Greece Creation of province of Macedonia
133	Ti. Gracchus as tribune pushes through land bill but is lynched by senatorial opponents
123–121	Further reforms by C. Gracchus, who is suppressed by the consul Opimius
112–106	War against Jugurtha in north Africa finally concluded by C. Marius (107–106), who for the first time enlists the propertyless as regular recruits
91–88	Social War between Rome and her allies results in granting of Roman citizenship to all Italy up to River Po
88	Sulla marches on Rome to recover the command against Mithridates of Pontus and butchers his opponents
83–80	Sulla returns to Rome after making peace with Mithridates. He seizes power, proscribes political opponents and muzzles the plebeian tribunate
79	Retirement and death of Sulla
73–71	Slave revolt of Spartacus finally suppressed by M. Licinius Crassus
71	Pompey returns victorious from Spain and is elected consul with Crassus
65–62	Pompey defeats Mithridates and reorganizes Eastern empire
59	First consulship of Caesar, now in alliance with Pompey and Crassus ('First Triumvirate')
58–50	Caesar's campaigns in Gaul and (55–54) in south-eastern Britain
55	Second consulship of Crassus and Pompey Pompey given major Spanish command Crassus attacks the Parthians but is defeated and killed at Carrhae (53)
49	Caesar crosses the Rubicon and invades Italy
48	Defeat of Pompey at Pharsalus; he is murdered in Egypt
44	Caesar becomes dictator for life but is murdered the same year
43	Caesar's heir, Octavian, makes agreement with Antony and Lepidus ('Second Triumvirate') and they take formal charge of Roman world; proscription of their enemies (including Cicero)
42	Defeat and suicide of Brutus and Cassius at Philippi
31	Defeat of Antony and Cleopatra at Actium leaves Octavian master of the Roman world
27–23	Octavian is given governorship of most military provinces and overriding authority elsewhere; assumes name Augustus
12–7	Campaigns of Augustus' stepsons Drusus and Tiberius in Germany and Pannonia

AD

6–9	Pannonian revolt suppressed by Tiberius
9	Three legions under Varus destroyed in Germany

14 Death of Augustus and accession of Tiberius
31 Fall and execution of the powerful praetorian prefect Sejanus
37 Death of Tiberius and accession of Gaius (Caligula)
41 Assassination of Caligula and accession of Claudius
43 Invasion of Britain
54 Claudius poisoned by Agrippina, whose son Nero succeeds him
64 Fire at Rome and execution of Christians for alleged responsibility
67 Vespasian appointed to suppress Jewish revolt
68–9 Galba (in Spain) proclaimed emperor
Suicide of Nero
Galba superseded by Otho, who is in turn defeated by Vitellius
Vespasian hailed as emperor in east
Vitellius' army defeated at Cremona
79 Death of Vespasian; accession of Titus
81 Death of Titus; accession of Domitian
96 Murder of Domitian by 'palace' conspiracy; accession of Nerva
98 Death of Nerva and accession of Trajan
105–6 Trajan annexes Dacia
113–17 Trajan campaigns in the east; annexation of Armenia and Mesopotamia
117 Death of Trajan and accession of Hadrian, who vacates Armenia and Mesopotamia
132–5 Jewish revolt
138 Death of Hadrian; accession of Antoninus Pius
161 Death of Antoninus and accession of Marcus Aurelius and Lucius Verus
162–6 Campaigns of Verus to repulse Parthian aggression in the east.
167–80 Campaigns of Marcus Aurelius on the northern frontier against Germanic tribes
169 Death of Lucius Verus
180 Death of Marcus Aurelius; accession of Commodus
192 Death of Commodus
193 Accession of Septimius Severus, who campaigns in the east (197–9), in north Africa (203–4) and Britain (209–11)
211 Severus dies at York; accession of Geta and Caracalla
212 Murder of Geta
Roman citizenship given to all free inhabitants of the empire
217 Caracalla murdered; accession of Macrinus (the first equestrian to become emperor)
218 Defeat and murder of Macrinus; accession of Elagabalus
222 Murder of Elagabalus; accession of Severus Alexander
226 Persian king Ardashir becomes ruler of Parthian empire
230–32 Persian offensive and unsuccessful Roman response
234–5 Campaigns against the Alemanni on the upper Rhine
235 Death of Alexander Severus
237–8 Persian invasion of Mesopotamia
238 Goths and Capri attack across lower Danube
250–51 Decian persecution
252–3 Renewed Persian attack on Asia Minor
253 Accession of Valerian; his son Gallienus appointed co-emperor
254 Marcomanni invade Pannonia and reach Ravenna
258 Gallienus defeats Alemanni near Milan
260 Valerian captured by Persians
Revolt of Postumus in Gaul initiates 'Gallic empire'
268 Murder of Gallienus
Major Gothic inroads in Thrace and Greece
270 Accession of Aurelian, who then suppresses Queen Zenobia of Palmyra
274 Aurelian recovers control of Gaul
275 Murder of Aurelian
284 Accession of Diocletian
288 Peace agreement with Persia
293 Galerius and Constantius I appointed as subordinates to Diocletian and Maximian
303 Start of Diocletianic persecution
305 Retirement of Diocletian and Maximian ushers in dynastic conflict
312 Conversion of Constantine, who defeats his rival Maxentius at the Milvian bridge and takes control of the western empire
324 Constantine defeats Licinius and takes control of the eastern provinces
325 Council of Nicaea
330 Foundation of Constantinople
337 Baptism and death of Constantine
340 Constans becomes sole emperor in the western provinces, while Constantius II rules in the eastern provinces
350 Constans killed
353 Constantius II establishes himself as sole emperor
360 Accession of Julian, who withdraws the privileges of the church and actively promotes revival of traditional pagan cult
363 Julian killed in battle against the Persians
364 Accession of Valentinian I and Valens, emperors in the west and east respectively

365–75	Campaigns against the Alemanni on the Rhine
367	Gratian (son of Valentinian I) declared co-emperor
369–71	Prosecution of leading senators at Rome
370–77	Campaigns of Valens in Armenia
375	Death of Valentinian I
	Valentinian II joins Valens and Gratian as co-emperor
376	Visigoths given permission to settle south of Danube but settlement delayed
378	Visigoths defeat and kill Valens at Hadrianople
379	Theodosius appointed emperor for the east
382	Visigoths settled as federates
386	Gratian overthrown by Magnus Maximus
388	Maximus killed by Theodosius
391–2	Measures of Theodosius to prohibit pagan rituals
395	Death of Theodosius, succeeded by Arcadius (in the east) and Honorius (in the west)
405–6	German band under Radagaesus invades Italy but is defeated at Faesulae
406/7	Alans, Sueves and Vandals invade Gaul
408	Death of Arcadius, who is succeeded by Theodosius II
	Overthrow of Honorius' chief minister, Stilicho
409	Alans and Vandals enter Spain
410	Alaric sacks Rome
423	Death of Honorius
425	Accession of Valentinian III in the west
429	Vandals cross to north Africa
438	Promulgation of Theodosian Code
450	Death of Theodosius II
451	Council of Chalcedon
452	Huns under Attila invade Italy, where Attila later dies
455	Assassination of Valentinian III
457	Accession of Leo in Constantinople
473	Leo recognizes Theoderic as king of the Goths in Thrace
474	Accession of Zeno in Constantinople
476	Deposition of Romulus Augustus, last western Roman emperor

The Capitoline she-wolf suckling Romulus and Remus, the legendary founders of Rome. The bronze dates from the early fifth century BC.

The World of Rome (510 BC – AD 476)

Andrew Drummond

History

Along the west coast of central Italy there is a sequence of volcanic complexes, most long extinct, which have had a decisive impact on the landscape and its resources. Once the cover of forestation had been removed, the primary and alluvial volcanic soils of the three major regions concerned (Etruria, Latium and Campania) proved agriculturally productive – above all those of Campania, the most fertile region of peninsular Italy. Settlement was further encouraged by the ready availability of water resources, in the form of springs, streams and major rivers, and of well-delimited and defensible sites for occupation. In Etruria magmatic intrusions created important deposits of iron and copper, most especially on Elba, in the Colline Metallifere and in the Tolfa hills, and these both facilitated local metallurgical development and attracted outside interest.

Situated on the southern banks of the Tiber, Rome itself stands at the interface between Etruria and Latium, although geographically and historically it belongs to Latium, the coastal plain which stretches south to Anzio and Terracina and which is dominated by the major volcanic complex of the Alban hills (last active *c.* 30,000 BC). The hills themselves are no formidable geographical barrier and the plain is readily traversed, with two major corridors of land communication into Campania to the south (inland along the valleys of the Trerus and Liris, and along the coast over the spur of the Apennines that meets the sea at Terracina). But Rome's situation also ensured constant contact and interchange with the regions to the north and east. As the first bridging point on the Tiber it held a key position in land communications with southern Etruria, and the river itself acted as a major artery of intercourse with the interior. Its flow regulated by the reservoirs of the Apennines, the Tiber was navigable well inland in antiquity. Thus Rome enjoyed ready access to the agricultural and material resources of the hinterland, as well as a potentially important role in transit trade. In turn, there were major salt deposits at the Tiber mouth and the land route running inland along the Tiber became known as the Via Salaria (the 'Salt Road'). Moreover, Rome's position close to the Tiber mouth meant that she had ready access to seaborne traffic, without being vulnerable to piratical depredations.

The site of Rome itself is not exceptionally strong, apart from the natural barrier which the Tiber provides on its northern fringe. The hills that comprised the heart of the ancient city surround a central depression that was initially marshy and prone to flooding. Although the Capitoline and Palatine hills offered natural strongholds, to the east the hills of the Quirinal and Esquiline melt into the tableland of the Campagna, leaving them exposed to external attack. In practice, however, this seems not to have been a major concern: earthwork defences may have been installed at vulnerable points in the sixth or fifth centuries BC, but it was not until the Gallic sack of Rome in 390 BC that a stone-wall circuit encompassing the entire city was constructed. For initial settlement the key considerations were workable and productive soils, and reliable and easily accessible water supplies. From the perspective of Rome's future history it was her strategic location that was all-important: not only did it offer some limited potential for market development but it ensured that Rome's horizons were not narrowly delimited, socially, culturally or militarily. The Romans' own legends reflect both the peaceful assimilation of outside personnel, ideas and influences, and the early involvement of the city in hostilities with her neighbours to the north, east and south: integration and conquest represented two fundamental poles of Roman history from a very early date.

The Early Development of Rome

In explaining the origins and early growth of their city later Romans deployed an array of popular and learned stories – of the Greek exile Evander, who created a temporary settlement on their site and entertained the saviour-hero Hercules; of the Trojan fugitive Aeneas, who founded Lavinium, to the south-east of Rome; of his descendant Romulus, who founded Rome itself and became its first king; of the early absorption of a motley array of outsiders; of the rape of the Sabine women and the ensuing conflict with their menfolk, eventually resolved by the absorption of some of them into the new community. The process whereby these various legends were created and combined was complex, but none of them is to be taken as historical fact in a literal sense: they are later constructs that tell us only how Romans wished to portray themselves at the time in question or how they were seen by others. To trace the actual development of the city, we have to turn to the evidence of archaeology.

A significant permanent settlement at Rome is first attested in the late Bronze Age (eleventh–tenth centuries BC). From this period on there is a progressive development in the size and number of sites in Latium, and although the material culture of the region belongs broadly to the traditions of the Villanovan culture of Etruria, it assumes its own distinctive form, most clearly seen in the characteristic hut-urn used for cremation burials. This progressive upsurge in occupation and population is probably linked to an increasing predominance of agriculture over pastoralism, which in turn may correlate with improved metallurgy. In certain places in Etruria, where parallel developments are observable, several village settlements are found close together on a given site; and perhaps by the eighth century BC these have crystallized into a single unified community which represents the later city-state in embryo. A similar development probably occurred at Rome, fostered not only by the growth in population but by new military needs and opportunities, by the incipient development of surplus agricultural production and craft specialization, and by the closely associated emergence of dominant social and military élites.

A key factor in all of this was the growth of external contacts with Phoenicians and Greeks after the eighth century BC. The earliest Greek colonists settled on Ischia, probably attracted in part by the metals of Etruria; Greek and Phoenician trading points were established on the coast of southern Etruria; and some Greek and Phoenician craftsmen actually settled in central Italy. The influence of Greek and oriental forms, techniques and decorative schemes is clearly apparent in local pottery and metalwork from the eighth century BC, and Greek pottery in particular was imported on a considerable scale through to the early fifth century BC. But Greeks also brought new modes of agricultural activity (notably wine production and olive-growing), new methods of recording (writing and inscriptions), new types of armour and warfare (hoplite weaponry and tactics), new models of social activity (such as the banquet, chariot-racing and athletic contests), new forms of monumental structure (such as the temple), sculpture and painting. And Greek ideas probably also had a significant impact on political, religious and legal institutions and practices. These new influences were not received passively but were accepted only in so far as they could be accorded a positive value in the recipient culture and society, and they were freely modified as individual needs or preferences dictated. And in such modified form they might then be transmitted to others, who would further adapt them in their turn. That was perhaps particularly true at Rome, because of its geographical position: Greek influence came both directly and via Etruscan intermediaries, and then might be shaped to local requirements.

Early Rome.

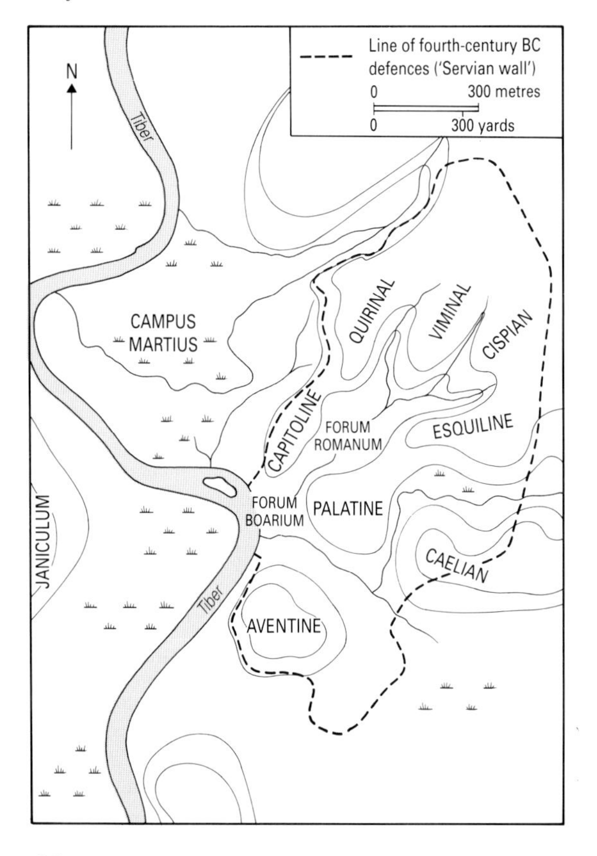

Such new influences (Greek, oriental and Etruscan) were embraced above all by aristocrats. The presence of élite individuals is clearly documented by the rich burials that appear in Etruria and Latium from the eighth century BC onwards and reach their pinnacle in the great orientalizing tombs of the seventh century BC. The sheer wealth of the metal and ivory work deposited testifies to the social prestige and power of their occupants, for whom such lavish disposal itself, as well as particular items such as chariots, was a demonstration of their status. This was a highly competitive aristocratic society whose lifestyle and modes of display represent a localized version of the preoccupations and rivalries of their Greek counterparts.

At Rome also we see clear signs of social and economic differentiation from the eighth century BC, indicating the self-assertion of élite individuals or groups. These were the nascent leaders of what was now very probably a single unified community, with settlements scattered over all the hills, with adult burials banished to the periphery on the Esquiline, and with the Forum area perhaps already a focus of political and religious activity. That was certainly the case in the later seventh century BC, when the Forum area itself was paved, the assembly area (Comitium) was laid out, a meeting place for the council of elders (the Senate) may have been created, and the cult of Vesta was already established. This new monumental development (evident also in the parallel transition from huts to houses) continues in the next century, culminating in the vast and grandiose Temple of Jupiter, Juno and Minerva on the Capitoline Hill. By the same period Roman territory and power had apparently expanded to the point where she was by far the largest community in Latium, and indeed claimed hegemony over many of her Latin neighbours, none of which approached her in size, power or resources. This position had probably been created by a progressive expansion from the eighth century BC at least, as Rome absorbed the smaller communities in her immediate vicinity and then sought to assert her authority over those further afield.

Such an expansion presupposes well-established political and military institutions. In the military sphere Rome probably adopted hoplite armour and tactics along with the southern Etruscan cities in the late seventh century BC. Then or subsequently she created the political institutions needed to ensure that the maximum manpower was available for the new force, where numbers, equipment and discipline were all-important. Military leadership was the prime function of the community's leader, although he also had important judicial and religious responsibilities. He is conventionally called a king but is perhaps better regarded as a type of chieftain. His position was not hereditary, and military capacity was very probably a key factor in his selection. Indeed, there are signs in the sixth century BC of individual aristocratic adventurers in central Italy, able to assemble bands of followers for autonomous military enterprises, including even the seizure of power in individual communities; and one or more of the kings of Rome may have owed their position to such acts of 'usurpation'.

Republican Rome

The last king of Rome, Tarquinius Superbus, was expelled around 510 BC. The circumstances of his departure are uncertain but the aristocratic political system, or 'republic', which now replaced the monarchy clearly represents an act of determined self-assertion by a group of aristocratic lineages (the patriciate), which sought to monopolize political power and to preserve that monopoly, not least against attempts at individual usurpation. The power of these lineages must already have been well established and probably rested on a number of factors: wealth, the adherence of dependants (clients), their own network of kinship and friendship relationships (outside as well as inside the Roman community), and a major (or even exclusive) role in filling the priesthood, the Senate and important military posts. The patriciate was not ethnically exclusive but included men of Etruscan and Sabine as well as Latin extraction, reflecting the apparent receptiveness of central Italian communities to individual migrants in the sixth century BC. Politically the principal collective vehicle of the patriciate was the Senate, which acted as the advisory council to the chief executive magistrates. These were two consuls, charged with broadly the same military, religious, political and judicial functions as the kings but subject to two crucial restrictions: their term of office was limited to a year and each consul had the same powers as his colleague, whose actions and orders he could therefore countermand if necessary. So fundamental was this principle of collegiality that in the period from 444 to 367 BC, when the two consuls were often replaced by three, four or even six consular tribunes, all of them were still given identical powers; and the same principle was also applied to other offices that were progressively created to relieve the consuls of some of their burdens. The only exception was the dictatorship, an office created to provide unified military leadership for a major campaign, but with a maximum tenure of six months.

In this system there was little political role for the ordinary populace. At most an assembly based on the army organization (the so-called centuriate assembly) may have elected the chief magistrates and been consulted on issues of war and peace. This lack of real political power and therefore of effective means of redress provoked reaction among the non-patricians (the plebs). They comprised men of widely disparate social and economic status, and their grievances and concerns were correspondingly diverse. Although they were perhaps united by a fundamental sense that as members of a common citizen community they were entitled to protection from abuse and even to some positive political rights, their particular objectives did not necessarily coincide. The poor were afflicted by the twin evils of land shortage and debt bondage. Those who served in the hoplite forces had no redress against the arbitrary actions of patrician magistrates, whether in military or judicial matters, and no doubt resented their restricted political role. And at their head there emerged individuals and families with the wealth and status to claim admission to the magistracies themselves.

It was above all service in the main infantry force which gave plebeians both a sense of their own common purpose and a weapon by which their claims could be pressed. The first major act of plebeian self-assertion was reputedly a military strike or 'secession' in 494 BC, which resulted in the establishment of two (eventually ten) officers (the plebeian tribunes), appointed specifically by the plebs to defend and represent them. This was crucial, for it created a potentially permanent, institutionalized structure whereby the plebeians could protect and advance their interests; and it also gave them a potent rallying point, since the power of the tribunes rested ultimately on the readiness of the plebs to come to their defence. Initially the principal role of the tribunes was to protect individual citizens against the oppressive acts of patrician magistrates, but they soon emerged as spokesmen for positive acts of reform. In particular, plebeian agitation must have been primarily responsible for the publication in the mid-fifth century BC of the Twelve Tables. This was a collection of legal procedures and penalties, primarily in the civil sphere, and was clearly designed to prevent arbitrary modification and application of the law by patrician magistrates or judges.

As the fifth century BC drew to a close, the pressure for the admission of non-patricians to the chief magistracy apparently intensified, and indeed some such men did secure election sporadically from 400 BC onwards. However, the decisive breakthrough came in 367 BC. At that date the magistracies were radically overhauled: instead of the system of six consular tribunes, Rome reverted to appointing two consuls, now supplemented by a praetor (who had chiefly judicial functions but could if necessary assume military command), and by two curule aediles (charged with supervisory

The early expansion of Rome: Italy and Sicily.

administrative duties in the city itself). It appears that as the price for their acceptance of this reform, the plebeians extorted the formal right to hold one of the two consulships, and from 342 BC one consulship was always held by a plebeian. Already in 356 BC a plebeian had held the dictatorship and by the early third century BC most of the other political and religious posts hitherto reserved to patricians had been opened up to plebeian aspirants.

The plebeians who benefited by this political advancement enjoyed essentially the same economic and social status as many patricians and progressively the distinction between patrician and plebeian lost much of its importance. Not only did patricians and high-status plebeians intermarry and establish relations of friendship, but over time the more successful plebeian families (including some from the local élites of enfranchised communities outside of Rome) were able to establish their own political dynasties. Although this new patrician-plebeian aristocracy was constantly enlarged as new families progressively made their way up the ladder of political office, by the early third century BC a majority even of plebeian consuls were themselves of consular ancestry; and they had as much vested interest in the preservation of their position as their patrician counterparts. It was largely because of the common economic and political interests of this patrician-plebeian aristocracy that political competition continued to focus on the individual pursuit of office rather than the proposal and implementation of particular programmes. There were no political parties or even long-term groupings, and the outcome of elections for office depended on the personal support that candidates could muster from kinsmen, associates and dependants and from the electorate at large, which had to be wooed on the basis of the candidate's own ancestry, achievements, conduct and liberality. Once in office, even consuls seldom initiated major reform: they were usually concerned rather with military glory and with the more material rewards of military success.

With the opening up of political office, plebeian tribunes no longer had the same incentives to advocate popular reform as in the days when this had been

The tomb of Scipio Barbatus, consul in 298 BC.

The Senate House, Rome.

necessary to mobilize support for their separate ambitions. In the later fifth and early fourth centuries BC in particular, tribunes may have been active in measures for the distribution of newly acquired territory to poorer citizens; and in 367 BC they reputedly secured popular support for the opening of the consulship only by linking that proposal to measures which provided for debt relief and limited the amount of public land any one individual could occupy. With their own admission to office, however, this stimulus to popular reform largely disappeared. None the less, the tribunate was not immediately neutered as a popular mouthpiece: through to the early third century BC tribunes and others saw political advantage to themselves in promoting popular measures of various kinds. Moreover, during this period the tribunate's powers were progressively enhanced, and not purely in the aristocratic interest. As a result of a secession provoked by debt grievances in 287 BC, measures proposed by a tribune and passed by the plebeians' own assembly became binding on the whole community; tribunes also came to acquire the right to attend, summon and consult the Senate; and they increasingly exercised rights to prosecute offenders (particularly ex-magistrates) for misconduct before the popular assemblies. Their long-asserted right to protect individuals against oppressive magisterial action was no longer contested in principle and they acquired a recognized prerogative to veto magisterial proposals to the Senate or assembly, including those of fellow tribunes. That these powers were used less and less in a specifically plebeian interest does not merely reflect the class interests of the holders of the office. Socio-economic tensions themselves eased as a result of the recurrent resettlement of poorer citizens on conquered territory in Italy and the emergence of chattel slavery (of outsiders) rather than debt bondage (of fellow citizens) as the principal source of dependent labour. And politically the aristocracy's position was strengthened and validated by the military successes achieved under their leadership and the profits that flowed from them.

Roman Expansion in Italy

For much of the fifth century BC Roman military activity had been concentrated on defensive actions, undertaken in concert with the other Latin communities against the inroads made into Latium by Sabines (from the north-east), Aequi (from the east) and especially Volsci (in the south). It was not until late in the century that significant advances were achieved. However, these successes encouraged Rome to a major effort against her Etruscan neighbour Veii, which was stormed after a prolonged siege in 396 BC. The territory of Veii, and that of the neighbouring Capenates and Faliscans, was seized and, although a good number of the original inhabitants were probably left in possession of their land and given citizenship, the rest was distributed to existing citizens or left as public land. As a result, Roman territory was virtually doubled and her manpower substantially enlarged. All this heralds the initiation of a major sequence of conflicts which by the early third century BC established Rome firmly in control of peninsular Italy. She asserted her control definitively over the Latins in 340–338 BC, over the individual Etruscan cities progressively from the mid-fourth century BC, and over Campania and the Samnites of the southern central Apennines in three wars (343–341, 327–304 and 298–290 BC). After the vigorous but ultimately unsuccessful attempt by the Epirote king Pyrrhus to curb Rome's advance into southern Italy (280–275 BC), Roman dominance was established here too. And the same century also saw a progressive Roman advance into central northern Italy, culminating in 225 BC in a major defeat of the Gauls of the Po valley at Telamon, to be followed by deep inroads into their territory.

The story was not one of unremitting success. There were major defeats at the hands of the Samnites (at the Caudine Forks in 321 BC) and of Pyrrhus; and there were the recurrent Gallic raids, beginning with the famous 'sack of Rome' in 390 BC by a Gallic war band. None the less, both the persistent Roman engagement in warfare and the general level of success are themselves remarkable. Of course, one fed off the other: military success brought not only increased military experience and, above all, military morale, but increased incentives and resources, in the form of glory, power, security, slave labour, land, other booty and indemnities. Above all, it brought increased manpower. Unless defeated enemies were enslaved, they were normally either incorporated directly into the Roman state as citizens (and were therefore liable both for conscription and for taxation) or forced to conclude separate individual alliances with Rome by which they were obliged to supply and finance troops for Rome's wars from their own resources. From a military viewpoint, this meant an ever increasing pool of available manpower at no extra cost to the existing citizenry. As a result, in most, if not all, her Italian wars Rome was able to call on larger military resources than her enemies, and the concentration of the organization and direction of her forces in her own hands gave her the capacity to adopt a consistently aggressive military strategy. At the same time, Roman power was consolidated by the progressive establishment of military settlements (colonies) at key points in conquered territory, by allocations of confiscated land to citizens, and by the grant of Roman citizenship to numerous communities, particularly in the Latin and Sabine areas. Initially this may have been a penalty for disloyalty, for although these citizen communities retained a local administration, they were deprived of all effective independence, and in some cases their members were excluded from political rights at Rome. However, these policies of integration and settlement were a key factor not merely in ensuring that the citizen element in Rome's armies remained a substantial one in proportion to that of her allies but in fostering the spread of Roman institutions, values and identity, while leaving Rome's own city-state institutions essentially intact.

The Acquisition of a Mediterranean Empire

The extension of Roman power into southern Italy brought her not only into the orbit of the Greek cities there and in Sicily but also threatened to impinge directly on the interests of Carthage, with whom she had hitherto had friendly relations. As at other sites in Sicily, Sardinia and Spain, a small initial settlement was established at Carthage, probably in the mid–late eighth century BC, and received a major influx of fugitives from the Levant in the mid-seventh century BC. However, in contrast to the other settlements, Carthage had a restricted hinterland: it was not perhaps until the late fourth and early third centuries BC that she acquired control of substantial territory in Africa, and hence long-distance trade (and perhaps marauding) had been dominant factors in her economy from an early date. By the later sixth century BC she had developed powerful naval forces and gradually assumed a hegemonial position in relation to the other Phoenician settlements of the western Mediterranean. She was effectively able to prescribe the conditions under which external commerce was conducted within their borders and to conclude alliances with Etruscan cities and with Rome which defined their rights to trade within her sphere of influence. Initially she seldom engaged in major territorial wars, but from the early fourth century BC the need to preserve her hegemony (and the other rewards of successful warfare) led her into increasing involvement in the intermittent conflicts between the Phoenician settlements in western Sicily and the Greek colonies of the rest of the island. The vigorous defence of her interests in Sicily became a cardinal element of Carthaginian policy, and it was in defence of those interests that she went to war with Rome in 264 BC, in the first of the so-called Punic Wars.

The conflict originated in internal divisions in the strategic port of Messina, which was under threat from Hiero of Syracuse. Initially a Punic garrison was installed, but it was then ejected when a pro-Roman faction took control and appealed successfully for Roman intervention. In the conflict that ensued, Roman ambitions rapidly expanded to embrace the expulsion of the Carthaginians from the whole of Sicily, a goal they pursued with extraordinary tenacity. That was shown above all in their creation and successful deployment of major naval forces. These were built virtually from scratch, and were replenished or replaced on three separate occasions before the final victory in 241 BC off the Aegates Islands. Under the treaty then concluded, Carthage was forced to evacuate Sicily, and shortly afterwards Rome seized control of Sardinia also. The two islands became territorially defined administrative areas, or 'provinces'. From 227 BC each was governed by a praetor, charged with major jurisdiction, the maintenance of order and any necessary military activity, although local administration remained in the hands of the pre-existing communities, whose institutions were left intact. This typical *ad hoc* extension of her existing magisterial apparatus was to provide Rome with the model for the organization and control of all those territories outside peninsular Italy which she annexed in the course of her expansion.

Deprived of Sicily and Sardinia, from the late 230s BC Carthage diverted her energies to the creation of a land empire in southern Spain, and it was the mineral and manpower resources thus acquired that emboldened Hannibal (246–183 BC) to seize the military initiative in a renewed dispute with Rome in 218 BC. He marched over the Alps into Italy and inflicted three major defeats on Roman forces in as many years. Weakened by the defection of many of their allies in Italy, the Romans fell back on a strategy of attrition, designed to reduce the insurgents and preclude them from giving active succour to Hannibal. Roman control of the sea and successful campaigns in Spain also cut the Punic general off from reinforcements and he was slowly penned into the south of the Italian peninsula. After the charismatic P. Scipio Africanus (*c.* 235–183 BC) successfully landed an invasion force in Africa in 204 BC, Hannibal was finally recalled; but even he was

A silver Carthaginian coin showing Hannibal, the scourge of Rome. It was struck in 221 BC.

unable to prevent a Carthaginian defeat at Zama (202 BC) and the imposition of humiliating peace terms that effectively ended Carthage's role as a Mediterranean power. And a half-century later Rome took advantage of a breach of the treaty terms to besiege, storm and ultimately (in 146 BC) destroy Carthage itself, its territory becoming the new province of 'Africa'.

The war against Hannibal had stretched Roman manpower and finances to the limits. It also threatened to involve Rome in the tangled world of the Hellenistic kingdoms of the eastern Mediterranean, which had been created on the death of Alexander the Great. Philip V of Macedon had already sought to ally himself with the Carthaginians in 215 BC and Rome, with her Aetolian allies, had fought an intermittent war against him that was only finally concluded in 205 BC. Three years later Philip turned his attentions to the Aegean area and, after initial hesitation, Rome answered an appeal for assistance from Rhodes and from King Attalus of Pergamum. The ensuing war concluded with the defeat of Philip by T. Quinctius Flamininus (228–174 BC) at Cynoscephalae in 197 BC, but it was swiftly followed by a confrontation with the Seleucid ruler Antiochus III of Syria (*c.* 242–187 BC). With his defeat, however, and enforced evacuation of much of Asia Minor, Roman influence and interests appeared well entrenched, not only in Greece and Macedonia but also in the Aegean basin. And when Philip's successor, Perseus (*c.* 212–165 BC), threatened to undermine that Roman hegemony by his successful courting of the Greek cities, Rome responded decisively. Perseus was defeated in 168 BC at the battle of Pydna, and the kingdom of Macedonia was broken up into four republics. Twenty years later, after a vain show of independence by the Greeks of Achaea, Rome had determined on direct annexation and the province of Macedonia was created.

The process of expansion did not stop here. Throughout the first half of the second century BC Roman control was progressively extended in northern Italy and in Spain. Towards the end of the century the strategic coastal strip between Spain and Italy was annexed as the province of Transalpine Gaul, and from here Julius Caesar (100–44 BC) launched the series of campaigns that established direct Roman control over the whole of Gaul to the Channel coast. In 133 BC the kingdom of Pergamum was bequeathed to Rome and was transformed into the province of Asia. Elsewhere in the first century BC, Bithynia, Cyrene, Syria and finally Egypt were all brought under direct Roman administration. However, it was the crucial century from the outbreak of the First Punic War to Pydna that established Rome as mistress of a Mediterranean empire. This empire was not limited to those regions directly under Roman administration: the system of individual alliances so successfully employed in Italy was extended here also to embrace kingdoms and peoples which Rome preferred to leave nominally independent, but which in reality served Roman interests

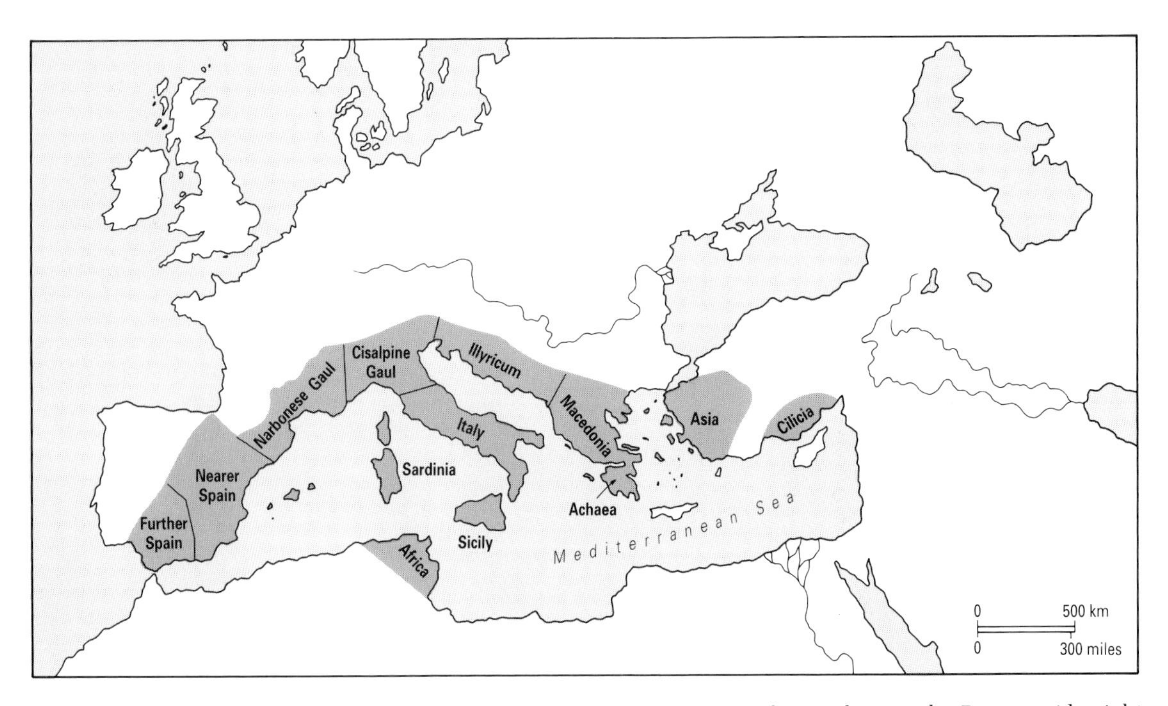

Roman provinces in 100 BC. Thirty-three years earlier the kingdom of Pergamum had been bequeathed to Rome; it became the province of Asia.

and were often called upon to supply auxiliary military forces for Roman campaigns.

As in the earlier phase of Italian expansion, it is seldom easy to determine the precise motivation that prompted particular decisions for war, and indeed a combination of factors was probably often involved. On different occasions, and in different combinations, individual ambition, prospects of booty or new natural resources, the need to reassure and retain allies, communal power, prestige and security may all have been involved. Rome was a society whose whole value system and institutional structure reflected the priority given to military success, and Romans regarded the extension of Roman power as an eminently desirable and laudable objective. Moreover, the sheer perception of that power and Rome's readiness to employ it had itself encouraged outside states to seek her aid or to forge alliances in which they were or became the subordinate party, and this had been a key factor in the comparative ease with which Rome came to dominate the eastern Mediterranean.

Romans naturally sought to justify their wars within their own terms, as a response to hostile actions against themselves or more particularly their allies, but that does not imply that once war was declared, they regarded it as essentially defensive. Wars were regularly fought on enemy territory and with the objective of reducing that enemy to whatever state of impotence seemed feasible or desirable; and Roman methods of subjection were frequently brutal, particularly against defectors. Even those who sought Roman aid might first be required to make an unconditional surrender, so that any ensuing treaty was on Rome's own terms. If the catalyst of Rome's major wars was usually an appeal for Roman assistance, Rome's own expansion itself regularly resulted in the adhesion of new allies, and that increased the likelihood of future requests for intervention, which preservation of Rome's credibility might make it difficult to resist. Similarly, where Rome annexed conquered territory, her methods of administration and especially the exaction of taxes (itself a cause of native revolt) required secure conditions both within and beyond the provincial boundaries; and individual governors showed few scruples in devising pretexts for aggressive campaigns in their pursuit of glory and booty. Moreover, when successful, war came relatively inexpensive: armies could live off enemy resources and the treasury was enriched by indemnities and (in the case of provinces) fresh revenues.

None of this should cause surprise. The Romans were certainly not alone in taking an essentially aggressive view of their own interests or in preferring to eliminate what they perceived as a potential threat, however remote, before it actually materialized; and they certainly had few illusions about the realities of inter-state relations. What distinguishes Rome is her capacity for virtually constant warfare (in terms of commitment and resources) and her success (due to her formidable logistical capabilities, as well as the effectiveness of her forces and their commanders). And though the inherent weaknesses and divisions of her opponents often contributed to their own defeat, in essence it was the political stability of Rome herself, the general agreement among the citizen body on communal priorities and objectives, and the ability to mobilize the military and financial resources of Italy in the pursuit of Roman goals that, along with accumulated military expertise, were the key factors.

The Fall of the Republic (133–31 BC)

For all the comparative ease and rapidity of Rome's acquisition of a Mediterranean empire, it carried a high price, as economic and political problems emerged which heralded a century of political upheaval and civil war. Among the most fundamental was rural impoverishment, itself a recurrent phenomenon which Rome had largely met by resettlement on conquered territory. However, with the Roman conquest of Italy more or less completed, little new land had become available for settlement since the early second century BC. Large tracts had been confiscated from rebel communities in southern Italy after the Second Punic War and become public land; but this and other public land had been increasingly cornered by the wealthy of Rome and Italy, who thus precluded its exploitation by poorer individuals. At the same time numbers of the peasantry faced new and additional difficulties: the burdens of conscription fell heavily and unevenly, with individuals required to serve abroad for years; and there was increased competition for Italian land from the rich, intent on investing some of the new wealth of empire in slave-run estates and ready to buy up, or force out, peasant proprietors in the process. The scale of the problem is impossible to assess and certainly large numbers of peasant proprietors survived into the first century BC and beyond, but it was perceived as sufficiently serious to prompt essentially palliative measures of reform by two aristocrats, Ti. and C. Gracchus (who were plebeian tribunes in 133 and 123–122 BC respectively). These achieved only temporary success

A coin depicting the surrender of Jugurtha, the Numidian leader. Army reforms in Rome were introduced by C. Marius to deal with this determined opponent, who was executed in 104 BC.

in the face of Roman and Italian vested interests: rural poverty, exacerbated in the first century BC by civil war, a major slave revolt and land confiscations for distribution to veteran troops, remained a serious problem to the end of the republic.

Some of the poor migrated to the towns, which experienced a rapid growth, particularly from the second century BC. This was above all true of Rome, whose population grew vertiginously, to perhaps three-quarters of a million or more by the mid-first century BC. Slaves and ex-slaves account for much of this growth and featured prominently among craftsmen, artisans and shopkeepers. The indigenous free-born rural immigrant was often dependent on casual labour, particularly in the harbour and in the building trade. Survival for many must have been precarious, their living conditions those of slum-dwellers, and problems of high grain prices and rent-debt were recurrent. The formal political power of both ex-slave and free-born was strictly limited, but their sheer numbers and concentration made them a potent force for agitation, violence and riot. As early as 123–122 BC C. Gracchus sought to win their allegiance by the state provision of a monthly ration of grain at a fixed price. Although this was temporarily abolished by Sulla (138–78 BC) in the late 80s BC, it was progressively restored and ultimately, in 58 BC, made free by the tribune Clodius (*c.* 92–52 BC), who capitalized on his popularity to organize street gangs for systematic political agitation and violence until his own murder in early 52 BC.

The attempts of the Gracchi at land reform also highlighted and intensified the growing resentment of the Italian allies. It is not clear whether impoverished Italians benefited from the Gracchi's agrarian reforms, but it is certain that wealthy Italians (whose local interests Rome had usually actively supported) found themselves threatened with deprivation of their excess holdings of public land. Precisely to reconcile them to the land programme, proposals were made in 125 and 123–122 BC to upgrade the status of the Italian allies, whether by grants of full citizenship, of so-called Latin rights (a kind of semi-citizenship) or of protection against arbitrary coercive actions by Roman magistrates. As with a similar attempt by the tribune Drusus in 91 BC, these proposals foundered largely on popular and senatorial apprehension of the consequences for their own privileges and position, and many of the allied peoples, especially those of central and southern Italy, rose in revolt. The land issue exposed with appalling clarity their vulnerability to decisions taken at Rome without reference to themselves. They also lacked any formal protection against oppressive magisterial actions and there were notorious instances of arrogant humiliations inflicted on individuals and communities by Roman officials. They had perhaps been required to make heavier contributions to Roman military forces and certainly to finance those contingents themselves, whereas war-tax had ceased to be levied on Roman citizens since 167 BC. And both the virtual cessation of fresh grants of citizenship in Italy over the previous century and the rejection of legislative proposals to enhance their status only served to entrench their sense of resentment. For some there may have been hopes of establishing independence from Rome entirely, but probably most sought a major enhancement of status within the Roman framework and the political rights and opportunities this would entail. In and after a brief but savage conflict (the Social War of 91–88 BC), Rome was forced to concede citizenship, first to those non-citizens that remained loyal and then to the rest of Italy up to the River Po. An incipient sense of Italian identity, due in the last analysis to Roman hegemony, had already been apparent in the second century BC, which had also seen a spontaneous, if sporadic, spread of Roman institutions, law and language in non-Roman communities. With the concession of citizenship that process was accelerated: formerly independent communities now became *municipia*, organized on the Roman pattern and administering Roman law; by the early first century AD Latin had become the common language, certainly of the towns, superseding the other native tongues of Italy; service in the legions further developed the role of the army in spreading knowledge of Roman ways and in developing a Romano-Italian identity; education on the Roman model disseminated Roman values and traditions; new opportunities opened up for local élites to develop ties with members of the Roman political class and, eventually, to embark on a senatorial career themselves.

Initially the more affluent of these local gentry swelled the ranks of the equestrian class, which begins to acquire a more definite identity in the later second century BC. Although the *equites* had originally formed the Roman cavalry, the term now denoted a status group. This could be variously defined but it effectively comprised the wealthy élite minority outside the Senate and the vast majority of its members were drawn from the landed gentry of Italy. Some of the more prominent were involved in running the companies of *publicani* that bid for profitable public contracts, including from 133 BC onwards that for the collection of the taxes of Asia; senators were restricted to taking shares in such companies. In general, however, equestrian economic interests coincided with those of senators, with whom socially they often contracted ties of marriage, friendship and hospitality and with whom they regularly stood firm in the defence of the established property regime. However, from 123 BC, when C. Gracchus gave them exclusive rights to man the juries in one or more of the new criminal courts, a sense of their own corporate identity and status seems to have developed that could, on occasion, bring them into conflict with the Senate. This did not get anywhere near the point of a standing conflict, the establishment of a specifically equestrian programme or a concerted effort to get candidates favouring equestrian interests into office; and the most consistently contentious issue, membership of the juries in the criminal courts, was largely defused by a compromise settlement in 70 BC. Yet among some of this class there may have remained a lack of fundamental commitment to a political order that made it difficult for them to achieve high political office and where decisions directly affecting them were made by a body (the Senate) or individuals (city magistrates and provincial governors) that could easily appear insensitive to their interests.

Finally, there were the military dynasts, who undermined and ultimately destroyed the republican political system itself. A crucial feature of that system had been the fierce competition among individual aristocrats for office and for its rewards (in terms of personal standing and military glory). And aristocratic ideology necessarily endorsed such a pursuit of *dignitas*, or 'status', and *gloria*, or 'renown', as the proper objectives of individual activity. Yet the stability of the system and collective aristocratic interest also required curbs on individual self-aggrandizement. That was achieved in three principal ways: by careful organization of the executive offices to avoid an unacceptable concentration of power in the hands of any one individual; by the imposition of detailed requirements and restrictions on the tenure of magisterial office; and by giving a central role in political decision-making to the Senate. Certainly by the third century BC, and probably very much earlier, the Senate was the regular forum of debate and decision on most major issues, even where these were subsequently put to a vote of the popular assembly. In particular, the Senate handled issues of foreign policy, finance and the allocation of military

Pompey the Great (106–48 BC). After his defeat by Julius Caesar in 48 BC, this military commander fled to Egypt and was assassinated there. It is an irony of fate that four years later Caesar himself was killed in Rome, in Pompey's Theatre.

Julius Caesar (100–44 BC), the most successful of the late Republican army commanders.

commands, as well as usually passing an initial verdict on legislative proposals. In character the Senate was an essentially aristocratic body: by the late republic it comprised ex-office holders who sat for life and were answerable to no one for their opinions. Conservative aristocrats in particular came to regard its pre-eminent and independent political role as the key factor in the preservation of the traditional political order; outsiders viewed it with more jaundiced eyes, as a bulwark of aristocratic interests and power.

Spasmodically through the period of Roman expansion the delicate equilibrium of individual ambition and collective aristocratic interest had been threatened by the exigencies of war, as some of the normal restrictions on office-holding were temporarily removed and individual commanders acquired new opportunities to enhance their prestige and status. What was new about the late republic was, first, the scale of the military problems which Rome periodically faced and which required, or could be used to justify, large-scale, long-term military commands (with all that implies for enhanced wealth, political prestige and power); second, the increasing attachment of Roman troops to their commander, whom they saw as the chief potential upholder of their own interests; and, third, the occasional ability and willingness of those commanders to use military force for their own political ends. It was such ruthless pursuit of their own interests that determined the bloody conflicts between Sulla and his enemies in the 80s BC; it was the intense political rivalry of the two great military conquerors, Pompey (106–48 BC) and Caesar, which prompted a renewed resort in 49 BC to civil war; and after Caesar's assassination in 44 BC it was the unwavering self-assertion and ambition of his adopted son, Octavian (63 BC–AD 14), that brought about, first, the defeat and suicide of Caesar's murderers, Brutus (85–42 BC) and Cassius (*c.* 85–42 BC), at Philippi in 42 BC, and then the eventual elimination of his principal remaining rival, Mark Antony (82–30 BC), in the Actium campaign of 31 BC.

Although these wars were conducted principally in the interest of the individual commanders and their immediate followers, they could not have occurred without the active support of their troops. Many of these, volunteers or conscripts, were drawn from the rural poor, whose difficulties were now translated into the hope (occasionally realized) that their commander would secure them land on discharge, albeit at the expense of other peasant proprietors. These expectations, and other material benefits, could only reinforce the existing ties of loyalty which bound them to their commander and which a peculiarly successful, charismatic or persuasive general could mobilize to his own ends if he could convince them of the justice of his cause and his prospects of success. Others, of higher rank, looked equally to their own interests: some saw support of one or other dynast as a means to wealth and advancement (or as a way of avoiding financial and political ruin); others sought simply to preserve their property and status as best they could. For those who looked beyond their immediate interests, the intensely personal character of aristocratic political and social life meant that personal obligation and allegiance could influence or determine a decision to support one side or the other. At the same time, issues of political principle were often compromised by their entanglement with questions of individual advantage or prestige, and by the way in which Roman political institutions had themselves come to be perceived as vehicles for the promotion of sectional interests and therefore as instruments of personal or collective political power. Aristocratic ideology itself fostered these processes: the ingrained acceptance of the pursuit of rank and status, for example, made it easier for Caesar to advance the defence of that status, earned in the 50s BC by his achievements in Gaul, as a legitimate motive for civil war; and the 'freedom' championed by Caesar's murderers was essentially the independent power and privilege of the senatorial class. Caesar's veterans and the urban plebs of Rome could be forgiven for their coolness towards such notions of liberty: they and others could recall the ruthless senatorial elimination of popular tribunes like the Gracchi or Saturninus and the Senate's consistent opposition to virtually every measure of popular reform. When it had enjoyed a brief period of virtually unchallenged political control in the 70s BC, the Senate and its appointees repeatedly showed themselves inept and corrupt, and the political life of the following two decades was disfigured by bribery, intrigue and violence. When in 30 BC, after nearly twenty years of civil war, Octavian emerged as master of the Roman world, most seemed prepared to accept a victor who was more responsible than most for the turmoil which had torn that world apart but who now offered all social classes – but especially men of property – prospects of order, security and tranquillity that Rome and Italy had not known for more than two generations.

The Principate (27 BC–AD 235)

After the defeat and suicide of Mark Antony, Octavian as the emperor Augustus determined to remain sole ruler of the Roman world, like Caesar before him. But Caesar's murder in 44 BC had posted a warning: though some of his assassins had personal grudges, the principal cause was the deep revulsion felt by many of the senatorial class at his naked assumption of autocratic power, itself a negation of senatorial status and freedom. In the new political system which he progressively evolved from 27 BC, Augustus sought a more subtle solution to the problem, and clothed his control in forms that were not so deeply offensive to senatorial sensibilities. The old republican political institutions were left ostensibly intact and Augustus' formal position came to rest on the conjunction of a number of powers, each of which could claim some kind of republican root or precedent, but which cumulatively gave him a unique position and overriding authority throughout the empire. And this Augustan settlement was rapidly consolidated into the basic framework of imperial rule through into the early third century.

It was Caesar Augustus (63 BC–AD 14) who benefited from Julius Caesar's victories on the battlefield. His own supremacy was secured in 31 BC at Actium with the defeat of Mark Antony.

Two key elements in the emperor's power were his control of the army and of finance. Emperors became the governor-in-chief of all the provinces with military forces (which they governed through deputies). The armies swore an oath of loyalty to them and looked to them for any amelioration of their conditions or remedy of grievances; all wars fought were formally their wars and major campaigns of conquest were usually fought by them or members of their immediate family; and they monopolized the major honours that were the reward of military success, whether or not they had actually been responsible for the victories concerned – even more important than their formal command of the armies was the need to prevent the emergence of rivals in military achievement and prestige.

Their responsibility for the military forces and provinces, as well as for the other disbursements from public funds for which they were responsible, gave emperors a key role in the supervision of public finance. Technically there remained a distinction between the public treasury, the public funds available to emperors and the emperors' own private resources. In practice, however, knowledge, control and management of the finances of the empire became largely concentrated in the hands of the emperors and their staff, while the emperors' own wealth grew to vast proportions.

Effective control of military and financial resources gave emperors the opportunity to develop much more cohesive military and foreign policies than had usually been the case under the republic. Under that system both the structures of political decision-making and the difficulties of exercising effective central control over the military activities of provincial governors had made it virtually impossible to conceive and implement long-term strategies. That now became possible to some extent, although the slowness of communications in the Roman world still made it essential to give local commanders discretion to deal with emergencies and it is doubtful whether many emperors engaged in more than short-term forward planning. In the provinces themselves emperors from the first gave instructions to their own deputies and at least occasionally to other provincial governors; and from the late first century there are signs of a paternalistic readiness to institute more positive intervention and regulation of the affairs of individual provincial communities. All this, however, was aimed simply at ensuring the continued smooth working of the system; it was not part of a radical overhaul of that system itself. At home the initiatives of the emperor were few, and usually confined to traditional concerns, such as the curbing of individual extravagance, the reinforcement of social morality and the social hierarchy, or the encouragement of child-rearing. In the administrative sphere new posts and commissions were created both to serve the emperor's own needs and to supervise key public concerns at Rome, such as the grain supply, fire brigade and aqueducts. In general, however, most of the emperor's activity was individual and/or reactive: receiving reports and requests for guidance on particular issues from officials, making a vast array of appointments, responding to requests for assistance, privileges or redress from individuals, communities or provinces, or hearing civil and criminal cases. This limited and particularistic character of the emperors' activity reflects the restricted functions of the state in antiquity, which lacked the resources, expertise and institutional structures to engage in the large-scale support and interventionist roles that characterize their modern counterparts. Even public finance was little more than a simple exercise of balancing income against expenditure and (ideally) building up public reserves to meet future emergencies; economic policy as such simply did not exist. As in the days of the republic, the primary role of the authorities was to provide internal and external security, to dispense justice, and to maintain the proper working of the existing order, above all in the interest of the privileged classes, to whom radical structural change was anathema.

Over time the real losers under the new system were the lower classes, at least outside Rome itself. At the capital the urban plebs received preferential treatment, through repeated imperial liberality, games and shows, the provision of the grain ration, and other amenities and services. That simply reflected the need, of the élite in general as well as the emperor, to keep quiescent a population whose capacity for violent demonstration was still apparent in the fourth century – as late as *c.* 375 a leading senator was supposed to have arrogantly refused to sell his wine at the price anticipated and his house was set ablaze by the outraged mob. However, the privileges of the city populace remained exceptional; the more significant development is the steady erosion of the political and then legal prerogatives of the ordinary citizen. Under the republic the popular assemblies had acquired the right to elect magistrates, try political offenders and enact measures binding on the whole community. Admittedly, citizens had to travel to Rome to vote at all and the assemblies could not initiate, modify or debate measures put to them. Only a magistrate could propose legislation and many decisions were made by the Senate without reference to the populace at large. At public meetings it was the presiding magistrate who determined who should speak, and the assembly itself could only accept or reject measures presented to it. None the less, the mere existence of these powers ensured that some account had to be taken of popular opinion, and they had been used at various times during the republic to defend or secure popular rights, most notably protection against summary flogging or execution by the magistrates.

The judicial role of the assemblies had already largely disappeared under the late republic and in the early principate their legislative and electoral functions rapidly lost any real significance. In addition, the plebeian tribunes ceased entirely to act as upholders of collective and individual popular rights; and although emperors stressed their own permanent tenure of the

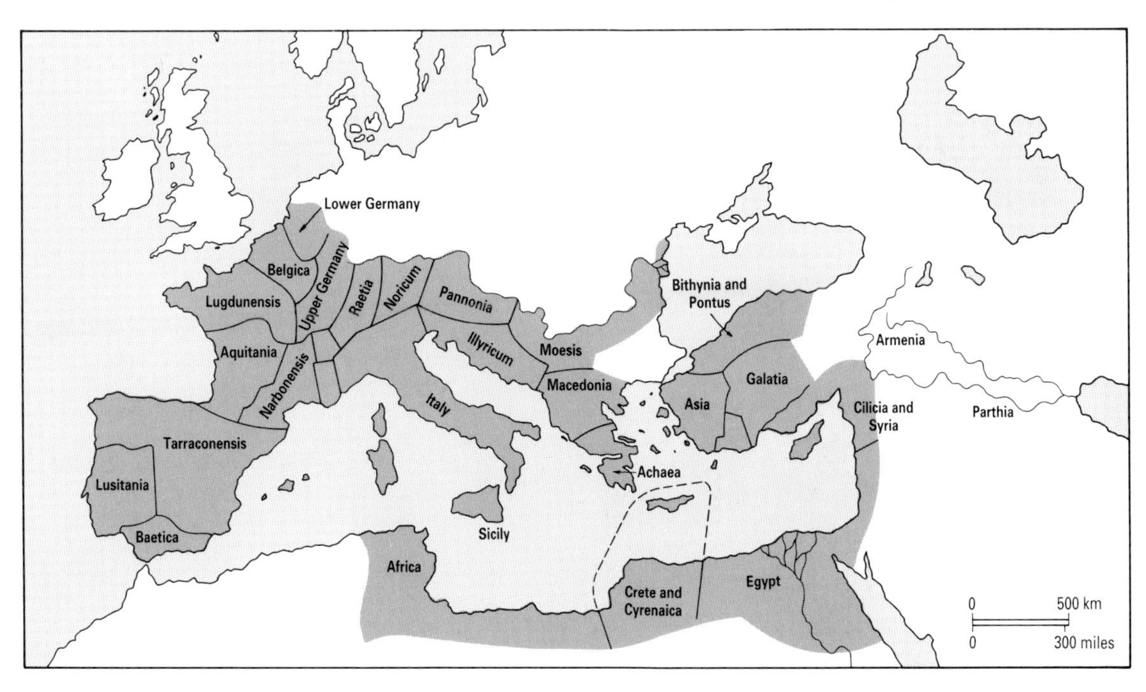

The Roman empire on the death of Augustus (AD 14).

powers of the tribune as a talisman of their concern for popular interests, they had even less reason to encourage popular political participation. The process was undoubtedly facilitated by Augustus' creation of a professional army, serving in the provinces with fixed terms of service and rewards on discharge. Henceforth the interests, privileges and rights of troops and veterans were kept clearly distinct from those of other Roman citizens. The resultant loss of political power for those citizens encouraged the development of other forms of discrimination and humiliation. By the mid-second century a formalized distinction had developed between 'those of higher status' (senators, equestrians, town councillors and army veterans) and 'those of lower status', who were subject to more severe penalties in criminal trials, to flogging by magistrates and governors at their own discretion and to torture (hitherto reserved for slaves). As a result, the value of citizenship to the ordinary individual was substantially diminished, and when it was conferred on all free-born residents of the empire in 212, this had little real impact on their status and was itself motivated by fiscal considerations.

In contrast, emperors had to deal much more carefully with the élite classes, above all the Senate. Nominally the Senate's powers (and those of the old republican magistracies) remained intact and, indeed, the emperor himself derived his own powers and provinces initially from a senatorial decision (subsequently rubber-stamped by the assembly). But it was clear from the outset that he was the effective ruler of the Roman world, accountable in practice to no one and removable only by force. That left little room for the Senate to exercise its traditional republican role as the major independent decision-making body of the Roman state or for magistrates to act as independent executive officials. In addition, emperors had a vast patronage at their disposal that could materially affect the careers of individual senators. They acquired exclusive control over the filling of the consulship and could similarly secure the election of their nominees to other regular magistracies; and they had in their gift an array of other posts, from deputy governorships in their own provinces downwards. Equally, it became clear early on that emperors could, and often would, use their power to destroy senators and others whom they regarded as a threat to their security or otherwise wished to eliminate. Most commonly, this was done by a prosecution for treason, itself often brought by other senators who were at odds with the defendant or anxious to secure imperial favour.

There were, however, powerful incentives to emperors to maintain good relations with the senatorial class. Senators were broadly the most privileged, wealthy and influential stratum in imperial society and it was from their ranks that many of the most powerful positions in the empire were filled and any potential rivals would emerge. In general, therefore, emperors attempted to conciliate senatorial opinion, although not at the expense of their own power or security. In some respects the Senate's powers were actually extended: senators acquired the right to try their own peers on criminal charges and in 14 they were given a decisive role in the outcome of elections for those magistracies not filled by the emperor's own candidates. Indeed, Augustus and, in his early years, his successor, Tiberius (emperor 14–37), regularly used the Senate as a vehicle for decisions on a wide range of matters and attempted to encourage genuine debate. But it rapidly became clear that the emperor's pre-eminent power made this impossible on any matter of substance, though it remained important for emperors to justify their actions or proposals to the Senate and to secure senatorial approval. The realities seem to have been accepted by most of the senatorial class itself. Though the right of the Senate to determine at least some secondary matters remained important, there was little serious attempt (or even perhaps active desire) to redraw the boundaries of power and responsibility between emperor and Senate. What tended to alienate senatorial opinion were overt demonstrations of autocratic power, the courting of extravagant honours, the neglect of constitutional forms, the scouting of senatorial privilege, the influence, wealth and honours sometimes enjoyed by imperial wives, slaves and freedmen, the destruction of men of their own class or encroachment on their property. What they valued was the effective maintenance of the established order (above all, their own privileges) and actions that stressed the emperor's status as a fellow citizen, rather than an all-powerful monarch: the refusal or only reluctant acceptance of honours, the discouragement of exorbitant flattery, personal accessibility and affability, adherence to traditional norms, conferment of office on men of the appropriate rank, connections and qualities, demonstrations of respect to the Senate itself and to (self-censored) senatorial freedom of speech. Implicitly these expectations acknowledge the emperor's supremacy, for they are all concessions on his part and none represents a real delimitation of his authority. Rather, they are ritual symbols, demonstrating respect for senatorial traditions and prerogatives; and as such they offer reassurance about the manner in which the emperor's own power will be exercised in a system where that was of direct and vital concern to senators' own advancement, security and self-esteem.

The senatorial class itself, however, did not remain immune from change: indeed, one of the most remarkable and significant developments of this period is the increasing recruitment to its ranks of men drawn first from Italy, then from provinces of the western Mediterranean and finally from the Greek provinces in the east. Italian representation at the lower levels of the Senate had probably increased significantly in the first century BC, but it was the civil wars that effectively ended the dominance of the older aristocratic families. They suffered particularly heavy casualties and no other substantial core of families emerged to replace them as an entrenched senatorial élite. Under the principate there is a rapid turnover of senatorial families, with comparatively few able to sustain their position for more than a generation or two. Those newcomers who benefited were, of course, men of established wealth and standing within their own communities and they attest the progress of Romanization at the élite level in Italy and the western provinces. Numbers of such men were themselves ultimately of Italian stock, the descendants of veteran troops or others who settled in considerable numbers in the western provinces, particularly from the mid-first century BC. Others were of native extraction and their citizen status reflects the growing enfranchisement of provincials in the west, achieved through individual grant, service in the auxiliary units of the Roman army, incorporation in a citizen community or the tenure of office in a community that had itself been raised to 'Latin' status. Such an enhancement of communal status itself, however, often presupposed cultural Romanization, especially of the local élite. That was sometimes directly fostered by Roman authorities, but there was no systematic attempt to impose Roman political, religious, legal or cultural institutions on native communities. More often, Romanization reflects the spontaneous attempts of the local upper class to absorb not merely the Latin language but Roman practices, lifestyle, attitudes and values – a process in which education played a key role.

Provided they could secure the right patronage, the more prosperous and able of such families could hope to make their mark in the wider Roman world, and this was often done first by the tenure of posts reserved to equestrians. A hierarchy of these evolved over the first and early second centuries: junior army officers, administrative agents (or 'procurators') of the emperor, principals in the imperial administrative bureaux, and finally major posts of high responsibility and no little power (including commander of the Praetorian Guard, the emperor's own standing force in Italy). Career patterns in these posts varied considerably and tenure of them did not depend on particular expertise or professional qualifications: the approved élite qualities and status, along with patronage, were the key considerations and they offered both a mechanism whereby those below senatorial rank could enhance their status (and fortunes) and a stepping stone by which families might advance to senatorial status in a subsequent generation.

These twin processes of the Romanization of western élites and their integration into Roman public life are most graphically illustrated by the occupants of the imperial throne themselves. Formally, it was for the Senate and people to designate the emperor and confer his powers. In practice emperors regularly attempted to determine the succession, and where they were violently removed, the effective decision usually rested not with the Senate but with the Praetorian Guard and its commanders or with the armies. The four emperors who succeeded Augustus – Tiberius, Caligula (37–41), Claudius (41–54) and Nero (54–68) – were all related to him, though not all were blood relatives or designated by their predecessor. In 68 Nero fell and

The emperor Trajan (99–117) annexed Arabia Petraea, Dacia and Mesopotamia. The Roman empire was then at its widest extent.

four rival army commanders (Galba, Otho, Vitellius and Vespasian) in turn seized power. Like Augustus himself, Vespasian (69–79) was of Italian extraction, but of a new senatorial family; and when his second son, Domitian (81–96), was assassinated in 96, his stop-gap replacement, Nerva (96–8), adopted as his successor the powerful military commander Trajan (98–117), who was from Italica in Spain. Trajan's reign ushered in a sequence of emperors – Hadrian (117–38), Antoninus Pius (138–61), Marcus Aurelius (161–80) and Lucius Verus (161–9), and Marcus' son Commodus (180–92) – whose immediate origins lay in Spain or (in the case of Antoninus) southern Gaul. And when Commodus was murdered in 192, the eventual beneficiary and founder of a new imperial dynasty was Septimius Severus (193–211), from Lepcis Magna in Africa.

The period of the principate also saw the consolidation of Roman military power. The military ethos remained strong, and was actively fostered by Augustus, whose reign was marked by a systematic series of campaigns of pacification and expansion, particularly in Africa, Spain, the Danube basin and, above all, Germany. The process of expansion was brought to an abrupt halt in Augustus' last years, first by a major revolt in Pannonia (6–9) and then by the calamitous loss of three legions in Germany (9), but was resumed by later emperors with a taste for aggressive warfare or a need to consolidate their new political position. Claudius' invasion of Britain in 43, for example, was

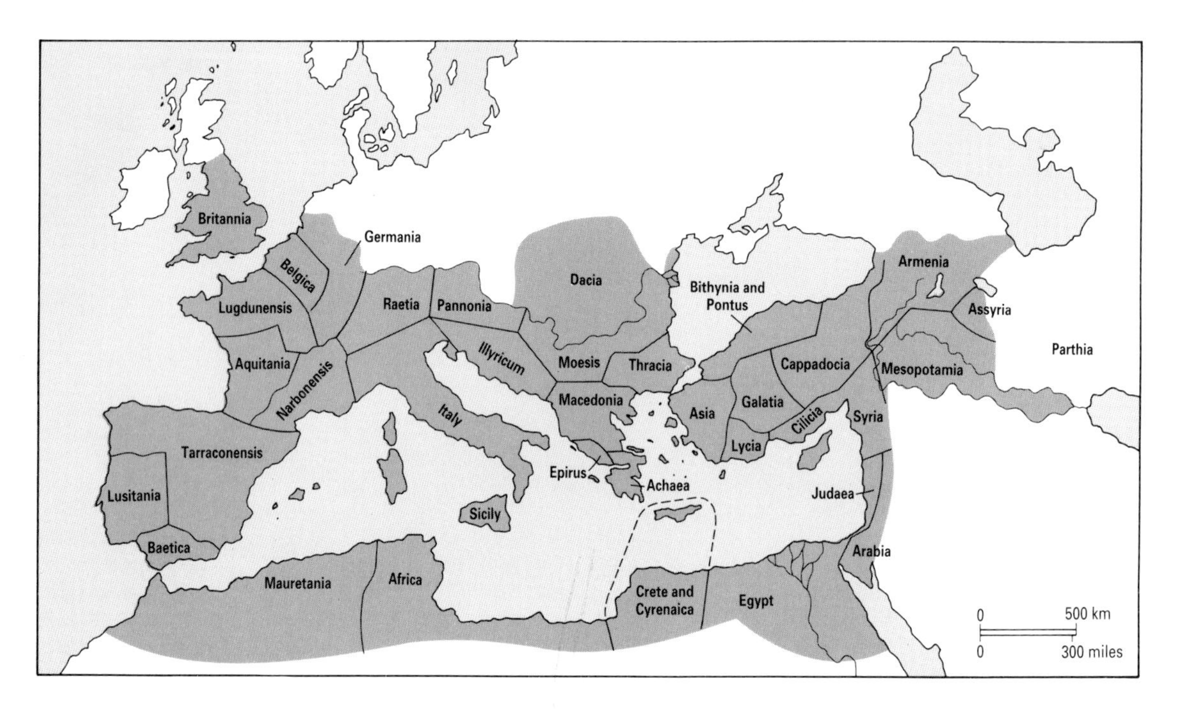

The Roman empire on the death of Trajan (116).

due to his desire to establish his own military credentials after his sudden and unexpected accession. Trajan sought prestige and booty by his annexations north of the Danube and on the eastern frontier, and Septimius Severus by renewed campaigns in the east, in Africa and in Britain. A number of other emperors,

The tomb of Julius Classicianus, procurator of the province of Britain. Classicianus' reports to Rome led to the recall of the aggressive governor Paulinus in 61.

however, showed little interest in extending Roman power. In some cases this was because of the need to direct available resources to deal with existing external threats or internal revolts. In others personal aversion or political caution may have been partly responsible, since few emperors could risk the political fall-out of a major defeat and there seems to have been little active political pressure for expansionist policies, whose main political beneficiary would be the emperor himself. But there were also strategic difficulties that tended to inhibit expansion. In the course of the first century the vast majority of the legions had come to be stationed in the frontier provinces and became rooted in the local population, with the deterrent defence of those provinces against external attack their primary function; and the overall burden of frontier defence had been significantly increased by the occupation of part of Britain, by the annexation of client kingdoms in the east and by the emergence of new threats from the peoples across the Danube. Major new campaigns in one sector required either the weakening of forces elsewhere by the withdrawal of individual units or the raising of new forces, which was often difficult and unpopular. The problems were graphically illustrated in the 160s, when the diversion of troops from the Danube to meet a Parthian invasion of Syria and Armenia opened the way for a massive barbarian incursion across the river.

That incursion was ominous for other reasons also. It seems to indicate a growing capacity of the barbarian peoples of the north to combine into larger agglomerates, at least for particular campaigns of aggression.

Traditionally, Rome had sought to neutralize such peoples by honours and subventions to their rulers but their inherent instability and the frequent political insecurity of their chiefs had always made it difficult to establish a nexus of reliable border dependencies that could distance or at least initially absorb external threats. There was always the possibility of the emergence of powerful figures among these peoples who could temporarily unite them and who would take advantage of Roman weakness, not least to reinforce their own position through the rewards that a successful incursion would bring. And the perception of such Roman weakness would itself be a major incentive to concerted action in the pursuit of booty and plunder. After an unsuccessful Roman foray across the Danube in 170, marauding bands penetrated deep into Greece and to the northern frontier of Italy. Roman control was gradually re-established but the potential fragility of the Roman system of defence had been clearly exposed.

Crisis and Recovery (235–305)
None the less, the empire survived in its old form for another fifty years until a combination of internal instability and external attack instituted a half-century of chaos. In the period from 235 to 284 more than twenty rulers received senatorial recognition and numerous others laid claim to the imperial purple. There were recurrent incursions deep into the empire by barbarian peoples from across the Danube and Rhine, and in the east Rome had to confront a new aggressive Persian dynasty that had replaced the old Parthian ruling house in control of a loose-knit empire that stretched from the Indus to the Euphrates. These developments were closely interlinked. The diversion of troops to settle internal conflicts weakened the frontier provinces and encouraged outside attack. If an emperor was unsuccessful in dealing with the intruders or lost the confidence of his troops, his position rapidly became untenable. Equally, the prospect or realization of military success under a particular commander could lead immediately to calls for him to assume the purple. The multiplicity of military crises often made a division of command, with all the attendant political dangers, inevitable and the concentration of forces impossible. Legions themselves had come since the second century to acquire a regional character, since they were recruited largely from the area in which they were stationed. That perhaps fostered their commitment to any general who seemed able to afford effective leadership against invasion of their territory. In particular, the low priority given to the defence of Gaul allowed the emergence and survival there, for some fifteen years (260–74), of a separate imperial regime which enjoyed the support not only of the troops but of local élites as well. It was Aurelian (270–75) who eventually brought this Gallic empire to an end and reasserted

A coin of Aurelian, whose five-year reign as emperor (270–75) saw the reunification of the empire after a period of chaos.

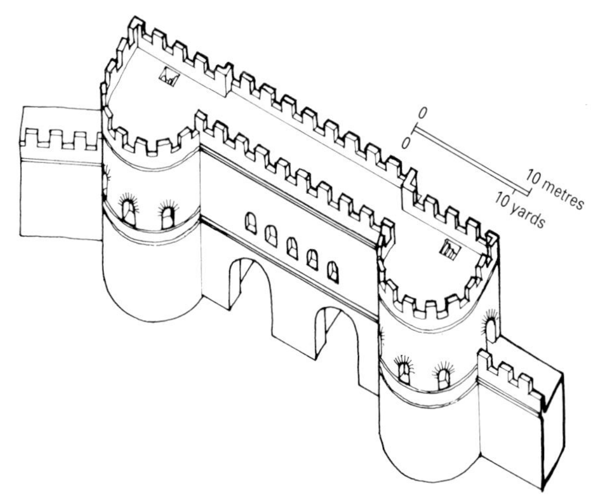

The Porta Appia, part of the new defences of Rome, built after the crisis of the third century.

A sculpture of Diocletian (284–305), his fellow Augustus and their two Caesars. Despite the show of outward harmony, the late Roman empire remained under great strain.

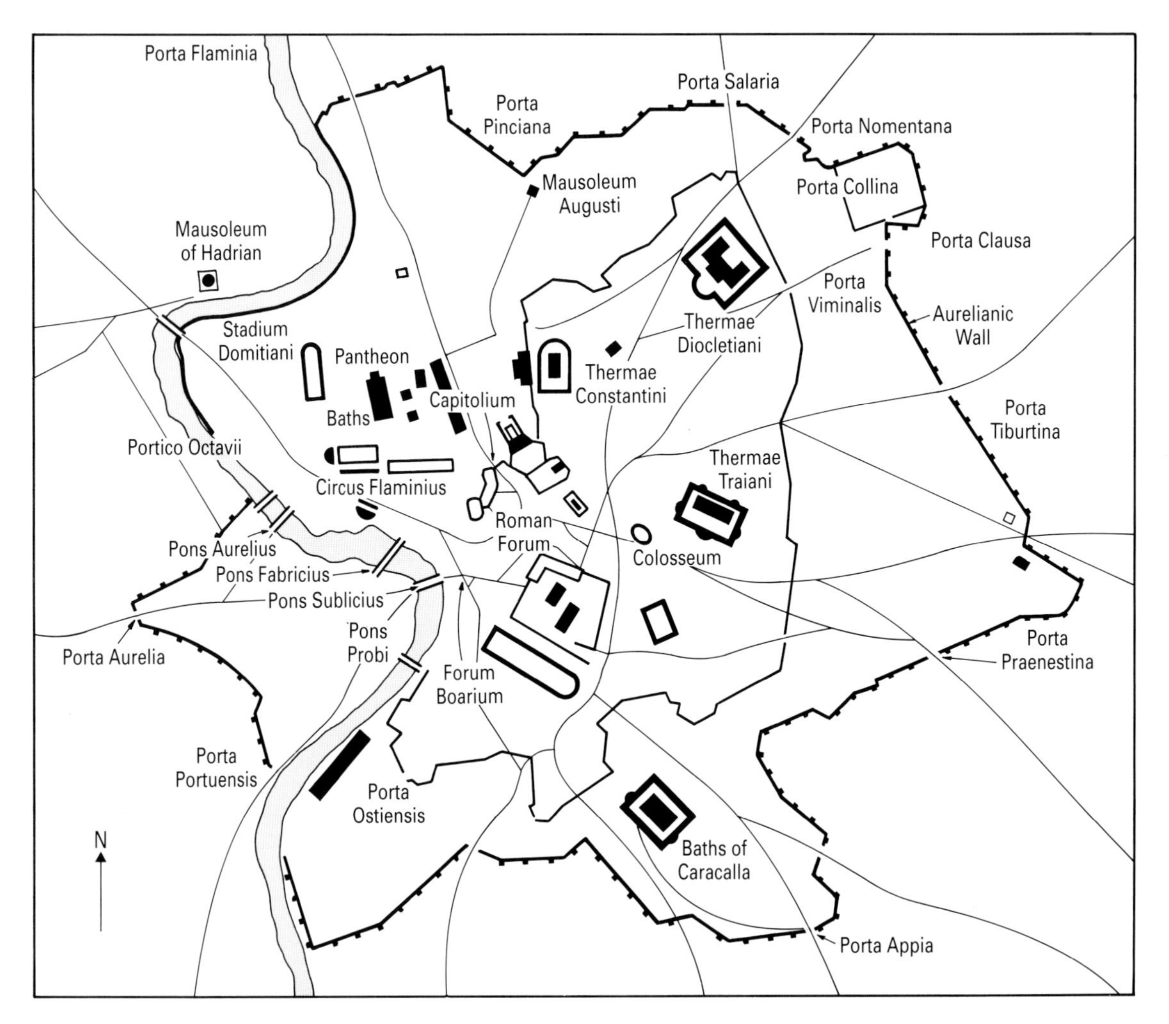

Imperial Rome.

full control of the Roman east by the suppression of the similar independent regime of Zenobia, queen of Palmyra. He and his two most notable immediate successors, Probus (276–82) and Carus (282–3), also did much to restore Roman control both in the east (where Persia was pushed on to the defensive and Roman suzerainty of Mesopotamia reasserted) and in the north (although the Trajanic conquests north of the Danube and the territory between that river and the Rhine were abandoned). But it was only with the accession of Diocletian (284–305) that a greater political stability returned.

The crisis of the third century produced or intensified a number of difficulties and developments that were to have important consequences for the empire's organization and government in the fourth century. Economically there was severe inflation, at least in the later part of the third century. This was caused largely by imperial attempts to meet increased military expenditure through a debasement of the coinage. Its effects on ordinary economic activity may have been limited but it eroded the real income of those (particularly troops and officials) whose regular remuneration was on a fixed cash basis. Partly as a consequence, extraordinary requisitions in kind grew in frequency and under Diocletian such requisitions became the regular form both of direct taxation and of the salaries of military and administrative personnel – a system only gradually reversed by a return to monetary payments from the late fourth century. Under Diocletian's arrangements the quantities of produce and goods required each year were assessed in advance and levied accordingly. Payment in terms of a given number of rations and units of fodder replaced monetary remuneration, thus offering recipients protection against

The Forum, the heart of Rome. It contained the chief public monuments of the city.

The Pont du Gard. This Roman aqueduct, built in 19–18 BC to supply Nîmes, was originally 25 miles long.

The impressive remains of the Roman city at Timgad in modern Algeria.

inflation, but with the attendant difficulty of realizing the value of their surplus provisions. The chief beneficiary was the imperial government itself: the new system was inevitably more expensive and cumbersome to organize and inhibited the accumulation of reserves, but it promised a more flexible and potentially reliable form of exaction that made it possible to maintain the value of disbursements, to draw up an annual budget and to use the same machinery for supplementary exactions as these became necessary.

The disruption and exactions of the period also severely affected the basic local administrative units of the empire, the cities. From the first Rome had governed its overseas territories by the imposition of a layer of political control (in the form of governors) over the existing local administrative apparatus. In many parts of the central and eastern Mediterranean this was already focused on urban centres, usually of very modest size, which in turn controlled the surrounding territory; and Rome actively fostered the further development of similar politico-administrative centres in the west also, albeit with greater success in the Mediterranean provinces than in Gaul, Germany or Britain. The cities were not merely responsible for local administration; they became the agents of the central government for important purposes at the local level, in particular for the collection of direct taxes and requisitions and for the supply of military conscripts. Within the cities Rome fostered the power of local élites. These formed the curial class, which manned the local council and held local office. They were usually drawn from the free-born propertied class and were expected to apply some of their wealth for communal purposes, whether in funding shows or sacrifices or in the provision of public buildings, entertainments or other benefactions. Among their wealthier members there was often intense competition in such public liberality since it brought the benefactor enhanced status and prestige in the community.

In the first and more especially the second centuries the cities of the empire had experienced an unprecedented upsurge in public building, much of it financed by wealthy individuals. From the 240s, however, there is a marked and rapid decline, part of a more general crisis apparent in the cities and clearly due to the disruption and exactions of the period. Once the crisis was past there was some recovery, especially in the east; in Africa, which largely escaped external attack, city life remained vibrant well into the fourth century; and even elsewhere in the west, where the wars of the third century had caused the worst disruption, cities continued to be a significant element in the political, administrative and religious landscape. But imperial encroachments on municipal taxes and lands in the fourth century seriously weakened the cities' own resources, and especially in the Balkans, Gaul, Britain and Spain the idea of the city as distinguished by its public buildings, monuments and amenities was eroded, so that local munificence no longer operated on the earlier scale. Particularly in the west, numbers of local magnates become semi-detached from the cities, preferring to live on their estates, and although competition in local munificence is still attested in various centres, it seems often no longer so important as a major vehicle for status enhancement. It was the titular or actual tenure of posts in the emperor's service, and the rank that went with them, that came to assume a dominating significance.

This not only had obvious implications for the social and economic life of the cities; it also exacerbated longstanding problems within the curial class itself. In contrast to voluntary benefactions, the various obligatory financial demands of curial membership were already regarded as a burden. Richer councillors might attempt to load a disproportionate share on to their poorer colleagues, who often in any case found them oppressive. Particularly from the late third century emperors used exemption from curial obligations as a cheap means of rewarding favoured individuals or groups, to the obvious detriment of the councils themselves. Evasion of curial responsibilities inevitably increased the burdens of those who remained and changes in the distribution of landed property, together with reduced opportunities for individual enrichment, may have diminished the pool of lesser propertied families that qualified for curial membership. Already in the third century membership of the curial order had become compulsory for those who qualified by wealth and were nominated; in the fourth the erosion of the status of councillors themselves – who might now even be subject to flogging – further encouraged individuals to make their escape by pursuing careers in the army or the imperial administration. These difficulties were most acute in the Latin west and even here varied in their intensity, but they caused increasing concern. The most serious casualty was the political vitality of cities themselves, but there was also a potential threat to the ability of the central government to tap the resources of the provinces, since cities were the instruments used for this purpose and councillors were ultimately liable personally for the taxes they collected.

Militarily, losses of manpower both in the armies themselves and in the frontier provinces from which they were recruited, together with the diminished attractions of a military career to many ordinary

The hapless Roman emperor Valerian, who was captured by the Persians in 260 at Edessa. Here he is shown at Bishapur as Shapur I's captive, although his consequent fate is unknown.

A gold coin of Constantius Chlorus, the senior Augustus after Diocletian's abdication in 305. He was the father of Constantine the Great, who succeeded him at York. Constantius is shown here in London, following his reconquest of Britain in 297.

recruits and a possible enlargement of the military forces themselves, led to a much greater use of conscription and to the compulsory service of veterans' sons. Even so, Roman armies had to rely increasingly on barbarian recruits to maintain their strength, especially from the reign of Constantine (306–37). There were also significant changes in army organization and equipment, with smaller units, a larger proportion of cavalry and the abandonment of the traditional heavy armour of the legions. Under Diocletian frontier defences were strengthened, and Roman strategy continued to rely on locally deployed forces to meet the various external threats. But under Constantine and his successors the frontier forces were reduced to allow the creation of separate regional field armies, and to transform the troops immediately at the emperor's disposal into a comparable force. The regional field armies represented a permanent concentration of forces, to be moved wherever a major threat became apparent, although in conditions of slow communications and mobility their effectiveness would depend on good intelligence. But the praesental armies at the emperor's own immediate disposal had a primarily political purpose – the protection of the emperor's own position.

The wars of the third century had made the military responsibilities and effectiveness of the emperor paramount. Since the middle of the century most had come from the Danubian regions, the chief recruiting ground of the Roman army. Some were from families of wealth and standing, but others had risen from relatively humble origins to positions of high command through military service. Their military commitments ensured that they were seldom in Rome itself, which from this period ceased to be the normal domicile of the imperial court. The court moved with the emperor, who, when he was not campaigning, tended now to reside in centres much closer to the areas of potential military concern. In the fourth century Trier, Milan and Serdica all served as his headquarters in the west; in the east Nicomedia was soon replaced by a new second capital of the empire, Constantinople.

This physical divorce of the court from Rome contributed materially to the political isolation of the Senate. Much of the latter's residual prerogatives had been progressively undermined with the consolidation of the imperial system, but until the mid-third century senators as individuals had continued to fill most of the important military positions in the empire. After 260, however, they were virtually excluded from such posts and from military commissions in general; these positions were now reserved for equestrian officers, men with military experience who were potentially more effective. This policy was largely maintained by Diocletian in his systematic overhaul of provincial administration. Senators were limited to the traditional magistracies and offices at Rome itself, and to governorships in Africa, Asia, Greece, Sicily and Italy. With the notable exception of Valentinian I (364–75), later emperors were more conciliatory. The range of appointments open to senators widened again; senators established good working relations with members of the imperial court; and at the end of the fourth century, the Senate itself briefly achieved a new political significance as the support and resources of the senatorial aristocracy became more crucial to the survival of the western government and Rome and Italy themselves became the setting of barbarian demands and aggression. But the senatorial aristocracy of Rome continued to be restricted to civilian posts in an age when real political power was exercised by the military commanders, men who had risen by the now entirely separate ladder of military promotion and were themselves sometimes barbarians. The Senate's purview remained limited to matters of direct interest to itself and its members; and senatorial rank was now regularly conferred on higher-ranking officers and officials in the emperor's service, so that a much wider senatorial order emerged, many of whose members took little or no interest in the activities of the Senate at Rome.

This quasi-marginalization of the Senate went hand in hand with an exaltation of the emperor's own person. Although on their rare visits to Rome emperors might be expected to observe some of the old rituals of civility and affability with senators or the urban plebs, the court became the centre of an elaborate ceremonial, admission to the imperial presence a rare privilege, and the emperor's public appearances few and carefully orchestrated. In every way the ruler was set apart from his subjects. Everything to do with him became sacred. Already in the early third century obeisance was expected in the emperor's presence. By the time of Diocletian a still more extreme act of reverence was required. In their public posture on formal occasions emperors adopted a studied pose of lofty dignity, reflected in the expressionless, hieratic character of their images. The insignia of imperial rule became more splendid and more potent: under Constantine, the diadem, the symbol of monarchy that even Caesar had rejected, became a regular part of the imperial regalia.

This process represents primarily an attempt by successive emperors to create around their person and office an aura of majesty and power in an age when their own tenure of power was frequently precarious. It capitalized on a more general feeling that such remote splendour was properly appropriate to the ruler of the Roman empire, and it offered some reassurance that the emperor was not the servant of his armies. It also, however, reflects the more overtly autocratic nature of imperial rule, which begins to adopt a more authoritarian attitude and to play a more interventionist role in the affairs of the empire. Diocletian in particular, with his thorough overhaul of the system of taxation and army recruitment, his attempt to control prices, and his radical provincial and military reorganization, showed a new taste for far-reaching reform. And he adopted a similar approach to the problem of imperial rule. In an effort to reconcile the need for multiple army commanders with political

A relief from the Arch of Constantine, recalling the earlier victories of Trajan. The triumphal arch was erected in 315 by the Romans to commemorate Constantine's victory over Maxentius at the Milvian bridge.

stability, he developed the tetrarchy, a system of two senior and two junior emperors (one each in east and west), which he clearly intended to be self-perpetuating. Like others of Diocletian's measures, this had a tidy logic to it but ignored realities. When Diocletian retired in 305, it rapidly foundered on the rocks of individual rivalry and ambition, and by 312 Constantine had taken possession of the west and in 324 brought the whole empire under his sole rule.

Collapse in the West (305–476)

For the rest of the fourth century the central power remained comparatively strong under the family dynasties of Constantine, Valentinian I and Theodosius I (379–95). The increasing practice of brothers or others dividing the responsibilities of imperial rule was translated at the death of Theodosius into a definitive division of the empire between east and west, with the Balkans as the effective boundary. This had already been foreshadowed by the elevation of Constantinople to second capital of the empire by Constantine's son Constantius (337–61), by the concomitant enhancement in the status of the Senate there, and by the development of regional army commands and administrative machinery. Nominally the empire remained a unity and, after an initial decade or so of friction (395–408), relations between the two halves were generally good, primarily because the external pressures on both excluded any alternative. There was, however, virtually no assistance rendered by one half to the other, and no mechanism for the transfer of resources: each retained, and was essentially reliant upon, its own logistical base.

This arrangement proved to the advantage of the eastern provinces. Less ravaged by outside attack, they were both more prosperous and more populous than those in the west. The strategic position of the eastern empire was considerably stronger. Although it had to confront periodic incursions from the Danube region, its lines of defence and communication were short and the natural barrier of the Bosporus was supplemented by heavily reinforcing the defences of Constantinople itself. On its eastern frontier it was potentially more vulnerable, but although there were intermittent conflicts with Persia, the Persian kingdom was too preoccupied with its own internal weaknesses and with the preservation of its own territorial integrity to constitute a consistent or seriously aggressive threat. As a result, the resource base of the eastern empire remained unimpaired, and by prudent financial and political management, coupled with a preference for diplomatic rather than military solutions to its external problems, it managed to survive intact until largely swept away in the Arab invasions of the seventh century.

By contrast, the division of the empire could only weaken the west, which already faced critical difficulties and could no longer tap the revenues of the richer east. Throughout the fourth century there had been recurrent campaigns in the north, designed to repel or preclude attack from across the Rhine and Danube. For the most part these had achieved their aims, but the pressures remained and were to some extent fostered by Rome's own success and policies which encouraged barbarians to see in the Roman lands a variety of opportunities for themselves. The third century had exposed the potential vulnerability of frontier defences, which were perhaps further weakened in the fourth century with the creation of the new field armies. Long acquaintance and contacts across the frontiers had familiarized the barbarians with Roman material culture and way of life. Since the principate, there had been a recurrent practice of voluntary or compulsory settlement of barbarians within the empire itself, to occupy abandoned land or supply additional dependent labour. Such people were liable for service in Rome's armies, which had also frequently incorporated barbarian volunteers. In the fourth century Germans became an increasingly important element in Roman military forces as conscription, unpopular with both peasant recruits and their landlords, failed to produce the requisite manpower, and some of their leaders rose to positions of high command and status within the Roman army. As a consequence, the patterns of interaction between Roman and barbarian were varied and often complex. The barbarian 'invaders' were not uncommonly men invited in initially by the Romans themselves and ready to serve Roman interests, provided their own expectations were met. Others sought admission, settlement and incorporation within the empire, which they would then help to defend. Even those who entered in hostile fashion usually comprised war bands intent on booty and plunder – objectives which might then give way to mercenary service in the Roman cause and/or seeking land for settlement. Far from being determined on the destruction of the empire, the satisfaction of the barbarians' needs depended on its continued existence. Indeed, some of their leaders expressed positive admiration for Roman traditions, professed willingness to support the Roman cause or sought positions of power within the Roman system itself. But increasingly they saw the preservation and enhancement of their power as dependent on the continuing separate identity of their followers. These were to remain subject to their own exclusive authority and command, not absorbed into the Roman population.

The Roman fortress of Divitia (Cologne), built to resist barbarian pressure.

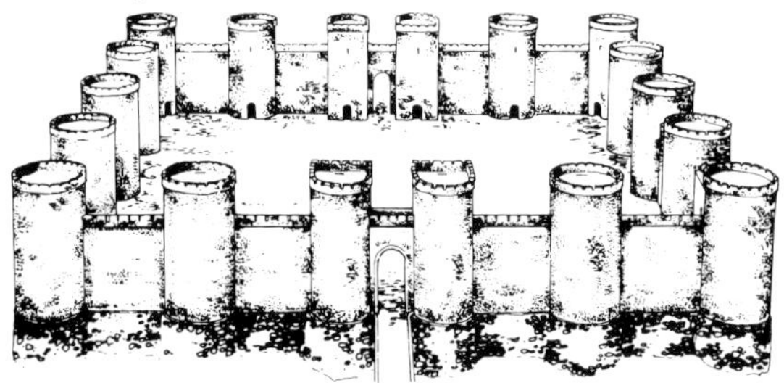

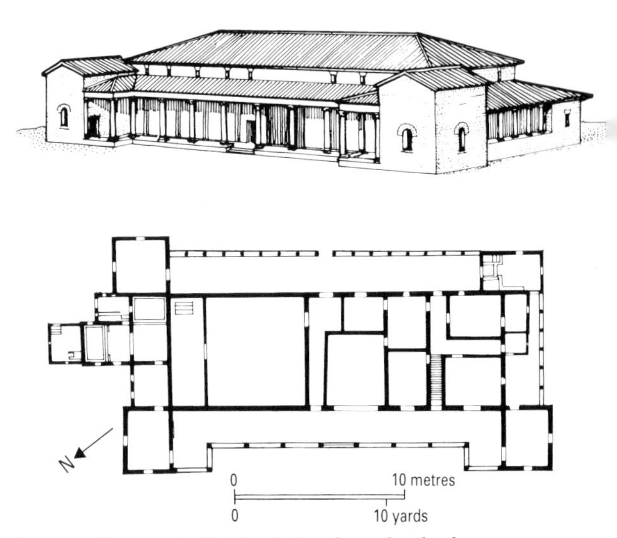

Roman villa near to Divitia, dating from the third century.

In this sense there was no overthrow of the western empire but rather a long process of progressive transformation, with the late fourth and early fifth centuries as the most decisive phase. In 378, at Hadrianople in Thrace, the emperor Valens (364–78) suffered a shattering defeat at the hands of Visigoths, frustrated in their desire to receive lands within the empire. The defeat not only left the barbarians out of control inside the frontiers but caused severe difficulties of military manpower from which the western government never fully recovered. Four years later Rome was forced to resort to a new mode of controlling the barbarians and securing their military assistance. Hitherto, barbarian settlers had come under direct Roman control and barbarian soldiers had served under officers appointed by Rome as part of the Roman chain of command. Now Visigoths were settled in Thrace, liable for military service, but living and fighting under the command of their own chiefs, the first in a succession of allies or 'federates'. This policy carried self-evident dangers. Far from being assimilated like their predecessors, the separate identity of these peoples was retained and their cohesion potentially intensified. The authority of their chiefs depended in large part on their prowess in war and their ability to provide for their followers. That could readily lead to demands for enhanced rank or new subventions or to action independent of the imperial power. The most notable such figure was Alaric, who so successfully built up a personal following of disparate barbarian elements that in 410 he sacked Rome itself when his demands were not met; and although he himself died soon afterwards, his brother Athaulf led his followers to south-western Gaul, where they eventually established a separate Visigothic kingdom.

However, the decisive event in the fortunes of the western empire was the massive invasion of Gaul and Spain by bands of Vandals, Sueves and Alans from 406 to 407, and the subsequent Vandal occupation of Africa. The very limited mobile forces at the government's disposal proved hopelessly insufficient to expel the invaders and the government was eventually forced to recognize many of the immigrants – and numerous others – as federates, allocating them a proportion (usually a third) of the lands of existing property-holders. Progressively these immigrant German peoples began to establish their own kingdoms, effectively independent of the imperial power (the Franks, Burgundians and Visigoths in Gaul, the Vandals in Africa), depriving the Roman government of vital resources and forcing it to rely more or less entirely on federates for its defence. Ultimately, in 476 the last vestige of Roman imperial power disappeared when the Gothic federates, who for a generation had supported puppet emperors, deposed the last of their number, Romulus, and established their own kingdom in Italy. The significance of this was little more than symbolic and it did not entail the immediate abandonment of the Roman inheritance. On the contrary, to a greater or lesser extent all these barbarian kingdoms maintained a clear structural division between the barbarian rulers and their followers on the one hand and what remained of the pre-existing population on the other, with each preserving its separate identity, culture and traditions. Hence the Roman population continued to live under Roman law, the Roman administrative machinery often remained intact, and even the Senate not merely survived but was actively cultivated by the Ostrogothic kings who ruled Italy from 493. The conflicts, insecurity and devastation of the period caused severe disruption for many of the propertied class, particularly in Gaul and Africa; but the survivors retained the bulk of their estates in the new dispensation and made their peace with their barbarian rulers. Indeed, some of these rulers themselves showed a ready appreciation of the claims of Roman culture and the traditions of Roman aristocratic life, which local magnates throughout the west continued to preserve and perpetuate.

The progressive destruction of Roman imperial power in the west resulted ultimately from the failure of its military, political and administrative structures to maintain continued resistance in the face of recurrent barbarian pressure. There were inherent weaknesses in those structures or their operation which made it more difficult to develop effective military responses. The financial resources of the government were limited by the resistance and evasion of wealthy taxpayers, by depopulation in some areas, by the division of the empire, by the progressive loss of revenue from areas that became lost to the central government, and by expenditures not directly related to the administration and defence of the empire. Conscription was similarly difficult to implement effectively. Much of the empire had long ceased to supply recruits and men feared and resented service on distant frontiers, while their landlords were reluctant to lose much needed labour. Western manpower resources were themselves eroded by successive wars and depredations, and by the intensified exploitation of the peasantry. The effective demilitarization of much of the empire meant that there was comparatively little effective local resistance to barbarian war bands once they had broken through.

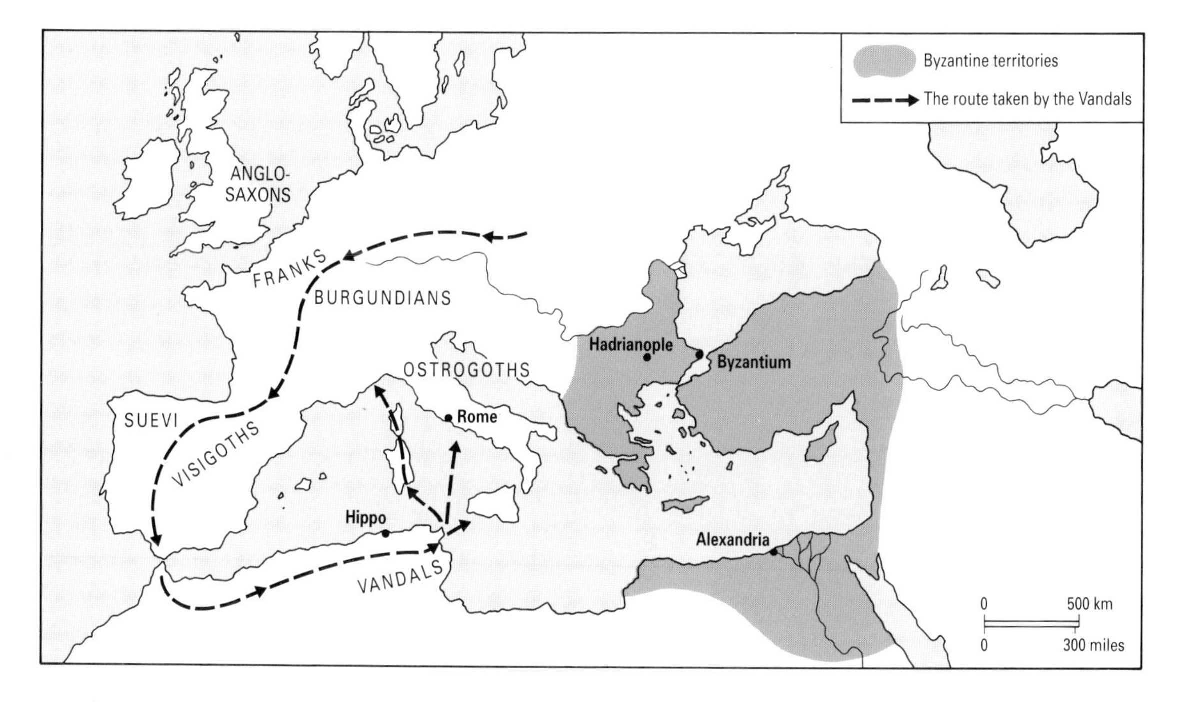

The barbarian powers about 500. Rome was first sacked in 410 by Alaric, a Visigoth ally who was discontented with the treatment of his people.

Corruption was rife in both the central and the provincial administrations. And the military dispositions of the government were weakened by the political need to maintain a major force at the emperor's immediate disposal. Most of these problems were not specific developments of the fourth and fifth centuries: their roots lie much further back. Nor would their recognition and solution necessarily have saved the western provinces. The existence of that empire and the prospects it offered, combined with the internal dynamics of the Germanic and other peoples themselves, encouraged sustained barbarian pressure along the long, vulnerable northern border and made the establishment of stable and peaceful dependencies beyond it impossible. Once those societies, themselves often profoundly modified by contact with the empire, developed to a stage, militarily and politically, where they were capable of forming large-scale, loose-knit, offensive agglomerates, the defence of the Roman west was always going to be a Herculean task.

Economy and Society

Throughout its long history the Roman world remained for the most part obstinately agrarian. The overwhelming majority of its population was engaged in agriculture and most urban centres were little more than market towns, closely integrated economically with the surrounding countryside and with correspondingly localized horizons. So far as possible, foodstuffs and raw materials were drawn from that territory and the territory's own need for artisan products or other goods was supplied by local production. Except for luxury goods or vital resources (such as metals or salt), which had to be acquired from further afield, external exchanges were predominantly regional in character. Only in a few cities were large-scale manufacture or long-distance trade items of major economic significance, and some of the greatest owed their growth and continuing prosperity to their role as major political and administrative centres rather than as foci of productive economic activity.

The key limiting factors were the low level of ancient technology and the absence of major technological advances. That failure is rooted primarily in the social values and attitudes of the élite classes of the Roman world. They assigned a low status to manual labour of all kinds and to scientific knowledge and its practical application. While not indifferent to profit, they developed no proper means of calculating it and no ideology of its systematic maximization. They frequently took no active interest in the detailed running or improvement of their estates, generally finding that their own needs and aspirations could be satisfied within the parameters of existing technology, and they saw no reason to provide or encourage education of any kind for the great mass of the working population. Hence, although some Roman writers realized the importance of technological discoveries to the development of human civilization and showed a casual awareness of the possibility of new advances, there was little serious incentive to technological innovation and little progress was made.

The most important consequence was the failure to develop more efficient forms of power. Apart from the use of wind at sea, power remained almost exclusively animal or human. That made the large-scale carriage of goods by land slow and expensive, while seaborne transport was at the mercy of the elements and usually precluded in winter. It also severely restricted the potential for surplus agricultural production and the large-scale output of cheap manufactured goods. Economies of scale, in both agriculture and manufacture, were feasible only to a very limited degree and the prevalence of subsistence or near-subsistence agriculture further restricted demand. As a result, most artisan production continued to operate at the level of a cottage industry. The key resources remained land and labour, and élite wealth depended heavily on their exploitation.

That had probably always been true, despite the Roman political moralists of the second and first centuries BC, who fondly recalled an earlier Rome, a community of peasant soldiers in which there had been no great disparities of wealth and in which leading senators ploughed their own lands alongside their humbler neighbours. This was a potent myth, but more a critique of their own society than a serious re-creation of historical reality. Even in the days when it was no more than one of a number of city-states in central Italy, Rome had been a strongly stratified society, marked by significant differences of wealth and with the powerful exploiting the dependent labour of the powerless, in particular that of debt-bondsmen. The competition between members of the élite already found expression in the acquisition of luxury items and in public and private liberality.

The Increase in Wealth

None the less, the moralists were right to the extent that progressively over the republican period the wealth of the élite classes increased prodigiously, as part of a nexus of developments that had a significant impact on the economy of both Rome and Italy. These developments were the outcome of a massive transfer of resources, human and material, both within the Italian peninsula and, subsequently, from the empire and beyond. Military war and conquest brought booty and plunder, often on a vast scale. Mass enslavement of captives and the Mediterranean-wide growth of the slave trade opened up a new reservoir of exploitable labour. In Italy itself territorial confiscations had paved the way for the development of larger property-holdings. Much of the more regular profits of empire, in the form of requisitions, taxes, perquisites, rents and debt interest, found their way to the capital or elsewhere in Italy, as did many of the profits of official or semi-official corruption. And its role as the seat of government and as the focus of aristocratic life meant that the capital itself attracted an increasing number of visitors and residents from Italy, the provinces and beyond.

It was chiefly the élite classes of Rome and Italy who disposed of the new resources, which they used both for investment in landed property and to fund new forms of display and self-indulgence. Large-scale pasturage developed in the south, while central Italy in particular saw the emergence of new medium-size estates on which agriculture was geared towards the production of a marketable surplus and the permanent workforce, chattel slaves, was intensively exploited. In the pursuit of status and pleasure, enormous amounts were expended on new private residences and on an increasingly luxurious lifestyle in both town and country. Status was also to be achieved by liberality, both public and private, and men sought constantly to outdo each other in their largesse, in the lavishness of their public spectacles and in their provision of public buildings and amenities. Communal resources too were deployed on games and shows, and on the construction and repair of major public works and monuments.

If Rome benefited most spectacularly from these developments, the same pattern is observable on a lesser scale elsewhere, and in many of the towns of central Italy especially the new patterns of investment and consumption were integrally linked to urban economic development. Much of the surplus production of the estates went to the urban markets. The profits were themselves often spent in the towns as part of the increasing lavishness of élite lifestyles, which, with private liberality and other public expenditure, radically increased the demand for a wide variety of urban trades, skills and labour. In turn the expansion of Roman power brought new opportunities for long-distance trade. This involved some export of Italian surplus production, like wine, and the bulk import of some basic commodities (alongside requisitioned grain) particularly into the vast urban conglomerate of Rome. But apart from slaves, the most significant item was the import of luxury or semi-luxury items of all kinds from the Mediterranean littoral and beyond.

In these different ways Rome became economically parasitic on the empire. But the establishment of that empire also stimulated economic development in the provinces, albeit again often at the cost of major dislocation and individual human suffering. In most of the eastern provinces the existing cities remained the basic local administrative unit and were simply supplemented as need or occasion arose, but in the west there were more fundamental changes. In Provence, Spain and Africa there were numbers of urban centres already well established, but both here and, to a lesser extent, in the rest of Gaul, Germany, Britain and the Danubian region, there was a significant growth in fully developed urban communities, beginning in the late first century BC and first century AD. Some new centres were themselves Roman colonial foundations; others (especially in the frontier provinces) grew out of the presence of major concentrations of Roman troops; others again reflected the transformation of native proto-urban settlements, sometimes encouraged by direct Roman intervention or by the presence of Roman administrative or other personnel. In all these cases, as in the pre-existing urban centres in both west and east, the power and ambitions of local élites followed the familiar Graeco-Italian model of the accumulation of wealth and its deployment in the pursuit of status through imposing domiciles, elegant lifestyle, and public and private liberality. Such social and cultural patterns spread particularly rapidly in the Mediterranean provinces of the west, and the progressive admission of men from these areas into the senatorial and equestrian orders implies that a significant minority possessed or acquired considerable fortunes.

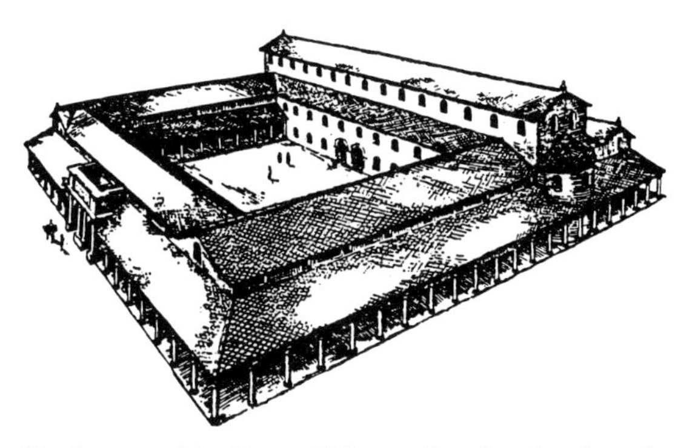

The forum and basilica at Silchester. Together they formed the centre of the Roman settlement there, Calleva Atrebatum.

A brass coin showing the rebuilt Colosseum around 81. Wild animals were brought from many provinces to be pitted against men in its vast arena.

The core element in the wealth of these local élites – as of their counterparts in the eastern provinces – must have been landed estates in their region of origin. That presupposes the exaction of rents or labour in the production of marketable surpluses, and so far as the proceeds were spent locally, they had much the same effects in increasing urban demand as in Rome and Italy. Furthermore, so far as rents were settled in cash, they required of the tenant that he sell surplus agricultural production to the relevant value; and the same was true for those provincials (in east and west) whose taxes were levied in cash rather than in kind. Both processes had the effect of encouraging the monetization of local economies and market exchange. Partly as a result, Roman currency progressively established itself as a common medium of exchange throughout the empire. In addition, there may also have been some stimulus to long-distance trade. For a proportion of private and public provincial revenues – and other exactions – was not spent locally within the province itself but at Rome or elsewhere (there was, for example, considerable investment in provincial estates and moneylending by members of the Roman and Italian élites); and in so far as the resultant deficit to the province as a whole was not met by the inflow of other funds, it was (if at all) counterbalanced by exports beyond the province's own boundaries.

In other ways too the establishment of Roman control may have fostered or facilitated market exchange and development, including long-distance trade. The mere establishment of a direct Roman presence increased knowledge of new potential markets, not least because Roman armies were themselves regularly attended by camp followers and suppliers. The establishment of Roman authority gave greater protection for investment and trading activity. For much of the imperial period piracy in the Mediterranean was kept at a localized and small-scale level; some curbs were imposed on brigandage, at least until the third century; and Roman military roads made a significant contribution to the improvement of land communications.

The expenditure of revenue and associated government activities also affected local economies. The presence of Roman officials and administrators, in assize towns or (later) provincial capitals, naturally had significant effects on local prosperity. Most spectacular of all was the development in the late empire of those cities where the court itself took up residence. The stationing of Roman troops, especially on a permanent basis, created a demand which could result in the creation of a well-defined local market structure. The government also had a large and regular need for army supplies. In the case of foodstuffs, much of this may have been raised by direct requisition (in place of money taxes), but arms, clothing and other equipment had to be purchased through contractors and suppliers or (in the late empire) be produced in the government's own factories.

The cumulative economic impact of Rome's political and military aggrandizement was therefore considerable. But although the acquisition of new resources (especially land, slaves and other booty) may sometimes have been a factor in Rome's wars, the economic changes of the Roman period were largely a by-product of military, political and administrative developments, not a consequence of policies or actions undertaken by the Roman state in the interests of commercial or industrial expansion. There was no substantial class of men primarily engaged in private commerce or manufacture with the wealth, standing and political influence to establish the promotion of these activities as a key element in Roman policy, nor were private trade and industrial production perceived as vital to the strength and prosperity of the Roman state. Rome's wars were not fought to protect or advance commercial interests. The legal and institutional framework of commercial activity of all kinds remained crude and unsophisticated, and even Roman coinage (first minted in the late fourth century BC) was issued for the disbursement of state revenues, not as a means of facilitating market transactions or as an instrument of economic policy. Indeed, the economic consequences of varying the volume and quality of different issues were neither appreciated nor even considered.

If, none the less, the Mediterranean world came to enjoy an unrivalled prosperity in the first two centuries, this was above all the prosperity of the élite classes, whose basic resource remained landed property. Artisans and craftsmen, traders, shippers and merchants, bankers and usurers, building and other contractors all benefited, as did other professional and service personnel. But those directly involved in such activities were of lower social status and, though the more enterprising, able or fortunate could significantly improve their economic position, their prospects of rapid large-scale enrichment were remote. Occasional fortunes might be made – for example, in long-distance trade – by those with access to the necessary capital, and some of those engaged in such activities were men of substance. But the élite classes of the empire remained overwhelmingly landowners. Their incomes were not drawn exclusively from their estates – loans at interest and the rents of urban properties were two popular supplements – but landed property remained

During the late empire Rome had need of strong defences: these walls were built by the emperor Aurelian (270–75).

the core of their wealth, and its profits derived from the sustained exploitation of dependent labour.

In the earliest period such labour had taken predominantly the form of debt bondsmen, but from the fourth century BC chattel slavery was increasingly prevalent, and by the end of the second century BC it was employed on a vast scale in Italy and Sicily. It was used elsewhere in the empire also, but there other forms of labour, both compulsory and voluntary, were widespread, and even in Italy itself slavery lost some (though by no means all) of its importance to tenantry over the course of the imperial period. The erosion of the rights of ordinary citizens made possible the more ruthless exploitation of small tenants, who, in one way or another, were no longer able to preserve their independence and who now appear as an ever more important source of dependent labour throughout much of the empire. In the late imperial period, as a side-effect of Diocletian's new taxation system, a class of tied tenants emerged, permanently bound to their land and their landlords. Interested writers of the fourth and fifth centuries write graphically of the oppressive conditions of the small tenantry in general, subject to the exactions and brutality of landlords and to the crushing burdens of imperial taxation. As a generalized portrait that is certainly exaggerated, but the only effective constraints upon landlords were those of prudential self-interest, and throughout the Roman period the propertied class showed a complacent readiness to engage in the relentless and often ruthless exploitation of their fellow human beings.

The Social Hierarchy

The reliance of the Roman élite on landed property had a solid economic basis in that land was the most secure (if not necessarily the most immediately profitable) form of investment available. But it also reflected the role of land as a guarantee of relative stability in the distribution of wealth (and therefore of status) and was correspondingly translated into an ideology that regarded land as the most socially acceptable form of wealth-holding. Other occupations were viewed as socially degrading (to various degrees), and any who made fortunes by commerce or trade could best achieve respectability by investing their wealth in landed property. Equally, Roman satirists and others regard the acquisition of wealth by men of low birth, origins or profession as itself an incipient threat to the social order.

Such prejudices reflect the delicate relationship between wealth and status among the Roman aristocracy in particular. Wealth was a fundamental prerequisite for the maintenance and enhancement of aristocratic power. Not merely was it, in the right forms, a source of status in its own right but it made possible the cultivation of an aristocratic lifestyle, the exercise of largesse and munificence, and the pursuit of office. Partly in consequence, property rights and property transmission were an obsessive concern of Roman law and of Roman lawyers, for bequest and inheritance remained the principal modes by which basic wealth was acquired at all social levels. But wealth was neither the sole criterion of social status nor the sole bulwark of the Roman aristocracy's social and political power. Other factors came into play, reflecting and maintaining that power and helping to define and control access to it.

The most fundamental aspect of the social hierarchy was a series of quasi-formal ranks which were determined by individual rights, the possession of particular qualifications or the achievement of political office. The principal categories under the empire were, in ascending order, slaves, freedmen (freed slaves), freeborn citizens, local town councillors (the curial order), equestrians and senators. Within these broader divisions considerable individual differences of status were often acknowledged, but these remained fundamental ranks within society, publicly distinguished from each other in various ways. Costume was one important mechanism. Only citizens (whether or not of free birth) were entitled to wear the toga; and both equestrians and senators wore distinguishing forms of dress or other adornment. In a piecemeal process that began as early as 194 BC, senators and then equestrians were given separate seats at public spectacles, a practice followed for town councillors in the municipalities; and both senators and equestrians acquired other distinguishing privileges and ceremonies. Particularly from the second century AD, equestrians and senators appropriated to themselves particular titles denoting preeminence ('most distinguished' and the like) and these became the basis also for formal distinctions in status within the two orders. In the case of the equestrian order, this was based on the grade of post in the emperor's service (actual or honorary) that the individual had held; for equestrian rank in a formal sense gradually ceased to depend purely on the earlier criteria of birth and wealth (and perhaps imperial recognition) and became restricted to those who had occupied procuratorial and other posts in the imperial administration or were deemed to have done so.

The preservation and reinforcement of this sociopolitical hierarchy was always a dominant concern of the Roman élite classes. When the first emperors, Augustus and Tiberius, wished to reassure those classes of their commitment to the established order, measures to defend and articulate that hierarchy were one of their principal weapons. These included not only enhanced public ceremonial and privileges for senators and equestrians, but also the prohibition of connections and conduct deemed incompatible with senatorial or equestrian rank. Thus men of senatorial family were forbidden to marry freedwomen and, by a senatorial decree of 19, senators, equestrians and their families were barred from appearing on the stage or in the gladiatorial arena: because actors and gladiators were traditionally drawn from low-status categories, these were not activities consonant with élite status, even if the popularity and fame of individual performers tempted some to participate.

As with the categorization of other occupations in terms of their social standing, this reflects a long process whereby the élite classes sought to differentiate themselves from the rest of the population not merely by formal recognition of rank but in terms of lifestyle, conduct and culture. That was already true of the early aristocracy, which by the sixth century BC had adopted a form of lifestyle, focused on hunts, feasts, chariot-racing and other forms of display, that clearly marked them off from their inferiors and owed much to Etruscan and Greek models. But it was the fruits of imperial expansion and the new scale of exposure to Greek culture which, from the third century BC especially, enabled the upper classes of Rome and Italy to create new social and cultural identities for themselves. These were embedded in every aspect of élite life: in the scale and splendour of houses and their furnishings; in the development of an elaborate etiquette that covered every mode of conduct, speech and deportment; in the cultivation of a life of leisure and in the forms such leisure took. Above all, it manifested itself in the growing importance attached to literary and rhetorical culture, both Greek and Roman. Despite some initial hostile reaction from individuals like the elder Cato (234–149 BC), who feared the dilution or destruction of traditional Roman values and priorities, a veneer at least of literary culture became fashionable, and for many literary pursuits of various kinds were an integral part of aristocratic leisure. In part this reflects an increasingly high valuation put on literary activity in its own right, but also the implicit acknowledgement of the role of literary culture as a social differentiator.

This perception in turn stimulated the spread of such culture (and the education which supplied it) among those who saw its acquisition as a prerequisite for social or political recognition and advancement in the world of Rome. It was this that was the primary factor in the spread of the Latin language and Roman culture, first in Italy and then in the western provinces. Here too it was predominantly local upper classes who were involved and the process made a fundamental contribution to cultural, social and political integration of the western élites. And at the local level it brought a new dimension to the gulf that separated the ruling class from much of the rest of the population, many of whom now literally spoke a different language from that of their superiors, especially in the rural areas. It was only in the late empire, for example, that Latin began to supplant Celtic in much of the Gallic countryside, largely as a concomitant and consequence of the processes of Christianization.

Both the high prestige that literary culture came to enjoy and the social grading of particular pursuits and occupations reflect the way in which the Roman élite's own ideology and values were permeated by issues of status. Their perceptions were not necessarily shared by those lower down the social scale. On their tombstones, for example, skilled craftsmen, traders and others sometimes advertise and proclaim their professions in terms which imply that they were to them a source of pride and no doubt of status also within their own social milieu. But for the likes of architects or doctors to achieve full recognition in élite terms, they had to show that their occupations were an aspect

A relief from Trier showing a dinner party, an essential part of social life for the rich.

of, or required knowledge of, liberal studies and that they were not hired (which effectively compromised their independence) but gave their services voluntarily as 'benefits'. In this élite value system the key factors were birth, inherited rank, wealth, occupation (or rather the lack of it), education, individual qualities and mode of life; and ideally the highest orders of society were restricted to those who met all these requirements, some of which were incorporated in the formal prerequisites for the rank concerned. Equestrians, for example, had not only to possess a certain minimum of capital wealth but, by a senatorial decree of 23, to have three generations of free birth behind them.

It is a further consequence of this hierarchical system, and of the centrality of individual status and competition to Roman political life, that there is no sharp division drawn between social, moral and political norms, and indeed that such distinctions are not recognized. The maintenance of the established order requires not only that the normal moral constraints of any society are observed but that men keep to their proper station and behave in the ways appropriate to it. Sexual immorality, for example, may be castigated not merely because of its general disruptive effects but more specifically because it threatens to override proper distinctions of status. Similarly, a man's whole standing depends on a complex of attributes, qualities and achievements. At one and the same time, a senator may be attacked in equally virulent terms for his low birth, for conduct inappropriate to his rank, for immorality and for misconduct in office: all such deficiencies violate established norms and threaten the socio-political order.

In such critiques the past (or a particular image of it) regularly features as a criterion by which contemporary behaviour is assessed. As with any established socio-political hierarchy in which power is largely vested in the propertied classes, the ideology and values employed to sustain the current order were regularly presented in terms of adherence to ancestral tradition. That was always a potent consideration in a society where the past served as an essential point of reference for defining the community's identity, values and achievements. This does not mean that Roman usages were static and immutable. On the contrary, for all the stress on adherence to ancestral tradition, Rome was necessarily dynamic in modifying her practices and institutions to meet new situations and new eventualities. But the élite naturally preferred such change to be *ad hoc* and piecemeal, accommodated within the established framework in ways that did not threaten the existing social and political structures. In addition, they usually had a vested interest in emphasizing the value of those structures and the norms which upheld them since their own collective power was embedded in them. Hence, when (as in the late republic) an explanation is sought for the current failures or ills of society, it is regularly found in a supposed decline from the standards of the past. Far from inadequacies in the inherited framework being seen as potentially responsible for contemporary political turbulence, the responsibility is laid at the door of individual conduct and a return to the norms and conduct of an idealized past may be paraded as the Utopian cure.

In other ways also the senatorial élite of the republican period used the past to validate its own values and power. Monuments recording the military exploits of individual aristocrats provided a constant visible reminder of their contribution to Rome's past successes. Aristocratic funerals were an elaborate piece of political theatre in which not merely the dead man but his forebears and their deeds were paraded before the populace. Aristocratic houses similarly recalled their distinguished ancestry and military exploits. And as Rome's own history itself came to be recorded, in verse and prose, from the late third century BC, it was written either by aristocrats themselves (most Roman historians were senators) or by others writing from an aristocratic standpoint.

All this reinforced the dominant ideology of the republican aristocracy, in which the magistracies were the prerogative of men of family, wealth and status who demonstrated their fitness for office by their military, oratorical or judicial capacities, who put their services freely at the disposal of friends, dependants or others, who engaged in public liberality and largesse, and who were rewarded for their services to the Roman state, and in particular for their miltary exploits, by enhanced prestige and personal standing. This was necessarily a highly competitive ethos in which individual self-assertion was a major element, and with the advent of the principate it soon had to be modified. Such fierce self-aggrandizement by senators was inimical to the security and interests of the ruler. Not that competition for advancement diminished or that office itself ceased to be a major source of enhanced status, but senators had to find new ways in which their role could be evaluated without appearing to threaten the emperor's own dominance. Partly through the imperial monopoly of key honours like the triumph, partly through senators' own self-limitation, some of the old forms of self-advertisement disappear from the senatorial repertoire and new ideologies emerge in which office is regarded as a burdensome duty, the holders of magistracies or commands are simply honest servants of the Roman state, and the emperor has taken on himself all the major cares of government. By the fourth century this had been translated among the senatorial aristocracy of Rome into a professed aversion to public office as such and a preference for that life of cultivated leisure which had long been an alternative to the humiliations, dangers and frustrations inherent in a political career. Even in the late empire, however, this remained something of a façade, designed to make the best of a situation in which fewer appointments of real substance were awarded to the traditional senatorial class but in which it remained important to allay any lingering imperial suspicions of senatorial ambition.

Friendship and Patronage
When Roman writers complain of contemporary moral decline, they frequently remark with particular force on the decay or perversion of key social bonds which were central to Roman society as a whole but particularly to the élite classes. These relationships – of kinship, marriage, friendship and patronage – enhanced the aristocracy's own internal cohesion, reinforced its power and prestige, and helped to control the entry of outsiders. All of them carried obligations of mutual assistance that in turn reflected the constant need for personal aid, again at all social levels. Thanks partly to the low cumulative surplus of ancient economies, partly to the vested interests of the élite classes in a system where men often looked to them for assistance and support, there was little or nothing in the way of regular public or private agencies for individual aid or protection. There were, for example, no public institutions of law enforcement concerned with the defence of the rights and interests of the individual citizen: even for ordinary assaults on his person, he had himself to initiate and pursue legal action, and if successful to execute the judgement. That posed particular difficulties for those of low status, who were in any case seriously disadvantaged by the procedures of the law and the way in which they were operated, especially when confronted with an adversary of higher social standing. In this and in many other spheres the individual was regularly thrown back on whatever resources he himself could muster: hence the particular importance of a network of individuals bound to render you assistance as and when it was needed, and the ubiquity of such bonds throughout Roman society.

Within the élite such attachments predominantly took the form of 'friendship'. This might vary both in the relative status of the two parties and in its origins, objectives, cordiality and intimacy. It could, for example, involve the feelings of affection and common interests that we associate with the term, but it does not necessarily do so. Friendship need be no more than an abiding obligation of mutual respect and assistance, and the duty to provide services as and when they were needed was always a central element. Close kin and marriage connections might be regarded as similarly obligated, and in all these cases the bond could entail assistance in any or all of a number of different spheres – legal, financial, social and political.

Such relationships all had potential strains and tensions built into them. To a greater or lesser extent they all had a significant utilitarian dimension, but yet were not to be reduced to a simple *quid pro quo* exchange of services; and in principle they imposed a long-term duty of assistance that might, in particular circumstances, conflict with the individual's other obligations or with his perception of his own self-interest. Since the only external sanction was that of public opinion, such ties were often fragile, and moralists regularly complain of their neglect. None the less, precisely because of their continuing importance to the defence and promotion of individual interests, they necessarily remained a crucial social phenomenon through to late antiquity; and the ethos of a relationship that was based on mutual gifts and services freely offered, rather than on a straight commercial exchange, was potent and pervasive.

Like friendship, patronage entailed an enduring obligation of mutual aid whenever and in whatever form it was required, and the boundary between the two was not always sharply defined. Indeed, both embrace a partly overlapping spectrum of relationships, depending on the relative status and situation of the parties concerned and on the way in which each chooses to regard them. Like friendship also, patronage was deeply embedded in Roman social and political life and may have operated at different levels, with men who were clients of one or more superior in turn acting as patrons for others less well placed than themselves. Inevitably, however, we are best informed about the patronage exercised by members of the senatorial class. They could be patrons of individual citizens, of provincial notables and even (at least in the republican period) of rulers and others beyond the provinces (and the same practices had been adapted to the patronage of cities, provinces, companies of *publicani*, and other corporate entities). Most such relationships were not exclusive: the dependant might enjoy multiple patronage – indeed, it was to his obvious advantage to do so. But in all cases the critical factor was the grandee's own ability to provide or secure privileges, advancement, protection or redress for his dependants.

Such patronal assistance might take many different forms, according to the status, situation and needs of the dependant, and again the services concerned often coincide with those which would be accorded to friends. Loans, gifts and other forms of economic assistance might be afforded, as might entertainment, hospitality and even accommodation; patrons might deploy their powers of advocacy or influence in legal proceedings or in the Senate; they might serve as witnesses or guarantors of legal undertakings; particularly when in office senators could offer a range of specific posts and perquisites to their own nominees, as well as use their powers to the more general advantage of friends and dependants; and they could use their own network of connections to secure particular benefits, favours and appointments. In return the patron might himself receive specific gifts or services, but precisely because of his superior power these were not on a par with those which he provided, and the principal benefits to himself were less tangible. Not only did he acquire enhanced esteem from his readiness to put his time and resources at the disposal of his dependants but a perceived ability to advance the interests of many friends and dependants contributed materially to his reputation; and the number and range of those friends and dependants were themselves an index of his social power. At Rome this was exemplified by the morning greeting ceremony (*salutatio*), at which clients, lesser friends and others would attend on the great man, and by the entourage of such individuals who would accompany him on his progress through the public spaces of the city.

There were also collective benefits to the aristocracy as a whole from the exercise of patronage and the prevalence of patronal values and attitudes. By channelling access to key goods and services through the beneficence of individuals, the aristocracy was able to strengthen, validate and make more palatable its own privileged position. Patronage served as a vehicle whereby particular benefits could be distributed to individuals, groups and communities in a way that fostered their social and political integration while reinforcing rather than undermining élite power. For such beneficiaries (and others) were encouraged to see the winning of patronal support as the key to their own protection and advancement rather than collective action among themselves or the establishment of public mechanisms by which assistance was provided by right or appointments were made on the basis of independently proven capacity.

Furthermore, patronage could serve to control entry into the élite itself by limiting it to men of the right social status and background, and it could foster the imitation and assimilation of élite values, behaviour and lifestyle by those who sought such advancement. Even under the republic, where office was properly elective, the entry of new families to the senatorial class owed something to the readiness of existing members to form connections of hospitality, patronage, friendship or marriage with outsiders and to promote their political careers. Under the principate, where the emperor controlled a vast array of senatorial and equestrian appointments, the role of patron-brokers became much more crucial in securing advancement; and much of the energy and credit of senators was expended in promoting the interests and claims of their protégés. Posts in the imperial administration – magistracies and other offices – were not in general allocated on the basis of specific expertise, nor were they decided by open competition on the basis of objectively assessed capacity for the duties involved. Such impersonal systems of appointment would themselves militate against élite privilege and control, and even in key military appointments a man's own connections, patrons and status usually played at least some role. In general specialist expertise was provided by subordinates: the most that was expected of office-holders was industry and integrity. What was sought was the right birth, family, status, education and élite qualities, and in commending men for privileges or posts senators were concerned above all to emphasize that their candidate was indeed 'one of us'. The whole patronage system was therefore a critical factor in the reconciliation of élite privilege and power with the progressive integration of outsiders – including, increasingly, provincials – into the Roman ruling class. So far as the existing members of that class were themselves the medium of such integration, their ability to effect such advancement demonstrated their own influence and enhanced their own prestige; and those so advanced were men of whom they themselves had approved and who could be expected to share their outlook, to show them due deference and gratitude, and to accept their conception of traditional élite conduct and attitudes.

Patronage was at once an outcome, manifestation and source of élite power. Under the republic the senatorial class in particular controlled much of the judicial, religious and political activity of the Roman state. As well as comprising, by definition, the principal decision-making body, they occupied the major magistracies and priesthoods; they served as presidents for civil and criminal cases at Rome and supplied a significant proportion of judges and jurors; and in the provinces senatorial governors themselves heard and determined all major cases in their own right. Control of these roles also gave them control of specialist knowledge. The priests were the ritual experts of the community, regularly consulted on matters vital to its relations with the gods, and one college of priests, the *pontifices*, had originally been the community's legal experts also, not merely providing advice on the interpretation of the law but actively involved in its further development. Over the last two centuries BC knowledge of the law (itself ever more complex) became increasingly concentrated in the hands of outside specialists, but these too were men of status (initially senators, joined subsequently by some equestrians). All of this – and their wealth – meant that senators were especially well placed to attract dependants. Equally, the adhesion of such dependants itself consolidated and enhanced the power of the individual patron and, cumulatively, of the aristocracy as a whole, and helped to perpetuate their control of key goods and resources. Already in the early republic the patriciate had been able to rely on the support of clients as a counterweight to the political self-assertion of the plebs, and although clients as such do not play so critical a role in the preservation of senatorial power in the late republic, the operation of the patronage system as a whole remained an important instrument of élite primacy.

The advent of the imperial system inevitably brought significant changes. Senatorial political power was severely eroded, and although their economic and social leverage remained largely intact, in the public arena the patronal role of individual senators had to be adjusted to the new political framework. Emperors themselves controlled much of the effective political and religious power of the state, and exercised an important judicial role. As with the dispensation of favours and privileges, therefore, the effectiveness of senatorial patrons often depended on their ability to influence the emperor's own decisions. Admittedly, others now had a still greater incentive to court them if they appeared to have access to imperial patronage, but in exercising such brokerage senators had inevitably to reckon with the influence of others who were in regular contact with the emperor: members of his family, close personal attendants, administrators and advisers. In the middle of the first century the emperor

A bronze head of the emperor Claudius (41–54), found in Suffolk.

Claudius, for example, was popularly supposed to be putty in the hands of his wives and freedmen secretaries, who used their influence to destroy their enemies (regularly of senatorial or equestrian rank), to advance those who courted them and to accumulate exorbitant wealth, honours and power for themselves. From the reign of Tiberius on, a number of equestrian prefects of the Praetorian Guard came to exercise preponderant influence as a result of their own proximity to the emperor and the importance of their functions. And under the later empire the non-senatorial origins of most key administrative and military personnel, and the physical divorce of the court from Rome, meant that senators at Rome were seldom those with most influence on, and regular access to, the emperor. Even more than before, therefore, it became essential for them to cultivate the acquaintance of men at court if they were to maintain their own role as patron-brokers in the political arena.

Social Mobility

For all the intensification of the socio-political hierarchy and its increasingly complex elaboration at the higher levels, the Roman world was, to varying degrees, socially dynamic. That can be seen in the steady inflow of new families into the curial and equestrian orders in the late republic and the early empire, but it is most graphically illustrated by the progressive changes in the composition of the senatorial class, after the early patrician monopoly was broken. Under the republic the entry of new families was gradual and on a restricted, though still significant, scale; during the empire it gathered momentum rapidly, with a continuing high turnover of senatorial families; and in the fourth century senatorial status was increasingly bestowed as a favour on individuals or attached to offices in the military and civil administrations; indeed, in the early fifth century it entirely absorbed and superseded the equestrian rank and itself became largely dependent on the actual or honorary tenure of positions in the emperor's service.

None the less, such advancement was strictly limited in its scale and scope. Even in the late empire, when there was greater opportunity to reach high office from a relatively humble background, there was no prospect of such advancement or of rapid enrichment for the vast mass of the population, who lived at, or not far above, subsistence level. Wealth, education and rank were the privilege of a small minority and, though there were significant numbers of men of intermediate status, there was no substantial middle class as that term is now understood. Opportunities for personal enrichment for the vast majority were closely circumscribed or non-existent, and, for reasons already explained, there were no impersonal institutionalized mechanisms by which large numbers of men could rise from lowly origins to positions of power.

Moreover, even for those of higher status rapid improvement in their fortunes was usually the result of special circumstance; individual enhancement, in terms of wealth or status, tended to be essentially gradual and progressive. That can be traced to some extent in the higher echelons of society, where, for example, successful equestrian careers in one generation of a family can pave the way for entry to the Senate in the next; but it will also have applied, within much narrower parameters, lower down the social scale. There must at all periods have been peasants, artisans, traders or others who, by initiative, industry, good connections or sheer good fortune, secured a modest but appreciable improvement in their fortunes which they or their heirs might build upon. One avenue by which such advancement might be achieved was through the tenure of sub-equestrian positions. Thus, from the late republic at least, the different categories of magisterial attendant begin to be exploited by men below equestrian level both as a source of enhanced status in their own right and as a springboard for access to still higher offices; and in the late empire literate men from below the curial class are similarly prepared to accept lesser posts in the imperial administrative bureaux and utilize them to much the same ends.

However, the most important regular channel of social mobility, particularly under the empire, was the army. In the period of the principate (27 BC–AD 235) not only might those of established equestrian status hold commissions before moving on to higher equestrian or senatorial posts but the centurionate and/or equestrian officer posts were an important instrument of advancement for men of relatively modest social status. Even ordinary legionaries could look forward to a secure position in local society on retirement. The minority who caught the eye of their officers and were promoted to the post of centurion secured much larger

A terracotta relief plaque of a racing chariot, first century. This expensive sport was as important to Romans as it had been to the Greeks.

financial rewards, with leading centurions acquiring equestrian wealth and rank. The most successful of all were recruited from the centurionate into equestrian officer posts from where, exceptionally, they too could rise to the higher equestrian administrative positions; and even those who retired as leading centurions left their sons enhanced prospects of direct entry into the centurionate or an equestrian commission, from where they or their offspring might sometimes rise to senatorial rank itself.

The political and military changes of the third and fourth centuries tended to accentuate still further the role of the army as a medium of advancement both for the fortunate few from the ordinary ranks and for those of higher status who secured equestrian commissions. Indeed, from the mid-third century service in equestrian military posts could lead on to governorships and other positions previously reserved for senators, and even to high command and, ultimately, the imperial purple itself. This development heralded the definitive separation of civilian and military careers in the fourth century, which itself increased the possibilities of advancement. As equestrian and, progressively, senatorial status became dependent on the actual or honorary tenure of particular military or civilian offices or on service in particular grades or bureaux of the imperial administration, new opportunities opened up, especially for some humbler individuals of curial status. Service in the higher reaches of the administrative bureaux, a career at the bar and/or acknowledged literary or rhetorical expertise became avenues of economic and social advancement for such people, and occasionally for those of still lower origins who had managed to acquire the necessary education and patronage, while with the recognition of the Christian Church others found an entirely new arena for the realization of their ambitions.

As we have seen, the working of patronage was an important factor in mitigating the strains that such social mobility might otherwise have engendered. So also was the concomitant eagerness of candidates for promotion to acquire the values, culture, lifestyle and modes of conduct deemed appropriate to élite status. Indeed, the possession of such qualities, especially high literary or rhetorical expertise, was itself one of the most powerful recommendations for advancement in the first place. Even the provincial and barbarian military men who rose through army service into key positions at court in the fourth century placed a high value on the traditional elegances of senatorial life, sought to acquire them themselves, and took good care that they were inculcated in their sons. That did not preclude their caricature as uncultivated illiterates by senators resentful of the power and influence of men who had risen without the need for their patronage and who occupied positions once the preserve of senators. It was in fact precisely when the established occupants of a particular rank felt that their own status, power or privileges were being debased, diminished or destroyed by the indiscriminate promotion of outsiders that tensions became most apparent. If in the late empire that is most commonly expressed with regard to the military men, in an earlier period it was perhaps a more surprising category, that of ex-slaves, which caused the greatest anxieties.

The Dependence on Slavery

Slavery was practised at Rome as far back as we can trace but it grew in scale and significance from the fourth century BC as it became the dominant source of labour for the creation of marketable surpluses and provided the extensive domestic and administrative staff increasingly required by the élite classes. By the second century BC slaves were not only widely employed on the larger agricultural estates in Italy and Sicily but were also widely used in mining and in those few larger manufacturing enterprises which developed, such as pottery, tile and brick production. With the growth in demand for specialist urban products, slaves were also commonly trained in a particular handicraft, trade or service occupation and set up in business on the owner's behalf. In addition, a large domestic establishment became itself a source of status and therefore display. By the early empire households of 400 are attested at Rome, with slaves employed in a wide variety of domestic functions. And slaves come to provide most of the administrative and other assistance required by the wealthy, serving as secretaries, stewards, financial or political agents, literary aides and so forth.

As was emphasized earlier, by the late republic Rome was emphatically a slave society, in the sense that slave labour was the primary mode by which the rich extracted surplus value, at least in Italy and Sicily. Slaves were employed elsewhere in the empire for these purposes, sometimes extensively, but they were perhaps never so dominant here over other forms of voluntary and involuntary dependent labour and even in Italy their importance seems gradually to have diminished over the course of the imperial period, although they remained a significant element in the agricultural and urban workforce to the end of antiquity. The principal cause of the change was probably a progressive reduction in the availability of slaves from external sources. In the late republic war captives, the slave trade and, to a limited extent, piratical kidnapping were the principal sources of supply, but the suppression of large-scale piracy in the first century BC and the overall decline in offensive military activity after the reign of Augustus meant a greater reliance on the slave trade and, especially, an increase in home-breeding. We do not have the data, and ancient owners did not have the accounting techniques, to assess the expenses and profitability of slave labour – and, indeed, both are likely to have varied considerably even in a given period. But the reduced external supply and increased reliance on home-breeding will certainly have pushed up costs. A larger proportion of female slaves will have been needed, especially in rural contexts, where they had hitherto been largely absent, and the development of slave-breeding may have encouraged the practice of setting slaves up on their own plots of land as quasi-tenants, liable for the payment of rent or a quota of their produce. Once military conscription had been largely eliminated from Italy, the use of slaves may have lost most of its distinctive advantages over that of small-scale tenants, particularly given the constant supervision which the direct use of slave labour required, and for reasons already discussed such small-scale tenantry seems to have become a dominant form of exploited labour throughout the Roman world by the late imperial period.

The best-preserved of the Saxon Shore forts, at Portchester, Hampshire. These fortifications were built by the Romans in the fourth century to deter sea-raiding Saxons.

The conditions of slaves varied enormously according to their mode of employment and the attitude of owners. Those employed on mining endured some of the worst treatment, as emphasized by the Greek historian Diodorus in the mid-first century BC, in his description of the Spanish silver-mines:

> Those employed in the mines create astonishing profits for their masters but their own physical constitution is progressively destroyed by the constant labour, day and night, in the workings underground. Indeed, many die under the intensity of their suffering (for they are given no respite or remission from their toil but are forced by the overseers' whips to submit to their plight in all its barbarity and surrender their lives in the most wretched manner). And although their physical strength and resilience of spirit enables some others to hold out and endure their afflictions for a considerable time, the scale of those afflictions is such that they regard death as preferable to life itself.

Many agricultural slaves were also treated as no more than another item of farm equipment. Through into the empire they were often subject to a brutal regime, worked in chaingangs and deprived of any possibility of family life or the prospect of significant amelioration of their position. The ruthless exploitation of their owners had provoked two major slave revolts in Sicily in the late second century BC and many rural slaves joined the great uprising of Spartacus in Italy

The Porta Nigra, the gateway at Trier. In the late Roman empire the city was of strategic importance for the north-western defences.

(73–71 BC). In fact these were to be the only large-scale revolts in Roman history. The multiplicity of ethnic backgrounds, the slowness of ancient communications, the logistical problems of organizing and arming a rebellious force and the ruthlessness of the Roman authorities were all powerful deterrents to coordinated slave resistance. But together with a realization that merciless exploitation did not necessarily yield the best returns, these revolts may also have encouraged the appreciation that a less savage agricultural regime was in the owner's own interest. But even if this was the case, conditions improved only very patchily and slowly, the fear of slave revolts remained and fugitive slaves were a regular phenomenon to the end of antiquity.

Fear was inherent in the slave–owner relationship and found its most potent expression in the savage legal provisions designed to deter the murder of owners, a prospect that might haunt even the relatively humane. Often forcibly deracinated, slaves were without rights. Legally they were treated primarily as property, entirely at the disposal of the owner. Even slave families were liable to be broken up at the owner's whim, or if the parents were given their freedom, their children might be retained in servitude in their place. The owner's control was total and largely unaccountable, a situation which itself encouraged some to gratify their sense of dominance and power. Even urban slaves could find that proximity to their owner exposed them to sexual exploitation, to arbitrary punishment and to sadistic victimization. Although individual emperors sought to curb some of the worst barbarities of treatment, not least in the interests of public security and the general maintenance of the regime of slavery itself, they were careful to make clear their respect for the general principle that individual owners could treat their own slaves as they saw fit. In consequence, the effectiveness of their measures is highly dubious, and there was no major institutional reform of slavery itself. When Roman writers advocate more humane treatment it is commonly on the basis of enlightened self-interest and seen essentially as a matter of individual discretion. Nor was slavery itself ever seriously questioned, even by the adherents of creeds which might have encouraged a reassessment of an institution that so explicitly denied individual human dignity and value. Stoics and Christians alike sometimes advocate better treatment of slaves, but even then their primary concern is often the moral stature of the owner. With their belief that what matters is the disposition of the soul, external circumstances being irrelevant, adherents of both creeds regularly show a complacent indifference towards the morality of the institution itself.

It is no palliation of Roman slavery that some slaves enjoyed a relatively fortunate lot and might even form close bonds with their owners or be given opportunities denied to the free-born poor. In general, urban slaves fared best, although many (including the vast majority of female slaves) were restricted to menial domestic occupations. Even so, they had some chance of family life and might, with their owner's permission, participate in social and religious activities outside of the household. But it was the skilled craftsmen and professionals set up by their owner, and still more his trusted administrators, agents and aides, who had the best prospects. They alone had usually been given or acquired a particular expertise or a measure of literacy and numeracy; their own occupations often gave them a measure of independence and responsibility, and a clearly enhanced status within the household itself; and the most successful could come to enjoy a position of high trust and affection with their owner.

The nave of S. Maria Maggiore, built by Pope St Liberius (352–66) as one of the great basilicas of Rome.

The most extreme example of this development was the growth of the emperor's personal administrative staff. For all the limited and often individual character of their responsibilities, emperors retained both a large household staff and an increasing body of administrative subordinates. Initially they followed the pattern set by republican officials, who had regularly used their own slaves and freedmen to supplement the skeleton personnel provided by the state itself. Specialist bureaux, to handle matters of finance, correspondence, petitions, judicial hearings and cultural activities, gradually emerged, all staffed and headed by the emperor's slaves and freedmen. No objection was raised by senators or others to the exercise of these and other quasi-public functions by such traditionally low-status individuals. What concerned them rather was the wider influence with the emperor that some of the more important came to acquire and the enhancement of their status that ensued. Partly as a consequence, from the later first century the most important positions in the emperor's own service came to be held by equestrians. But the permanent staff were still to be supplied by the emperor's own slaves and freedmen (who were not entirely superseded even in the late empire) and they continued to enjoy exceptional financial and social prospects for men of servile origin. Imperial slaves, for example, might accumulate considerable wealth (including other slaves) which they could treat effectively as their own; from the mid-first century AD they were far the most likely to persuade free-born women to cohabit with them or (on receiving their freedom) to marry them; and once freed they were especially well placed to advance themselves and their families within the overall restrictions to which all freedmen were subject.

Freedmen

Although the majority of slaves in all periods died in slavery and Augustus introduced formal restrictions designed to curb the indiscriminate freeing of slaves, substantial numbers regularly received their liberty by the process of manumission. Slaves might purchase their freedom from personal savings they had been allowed to retain or they might be given their freedom by their owner during his lifetime or in his will. Such gifts might be a reward for loyal service, an ostentatious display of the owner's generosity or motivated by affection. Few rural slaves could hope to benefit in this way: it was principally those in domestic and other urban occupations, above all those with specialist skills, those employed in positions of trust and those who otherwise enjoyed their owner's favour that profited. Female slaves might even be set free to marry their masters, although for men of status it was more appropriate to keep them as concubines and Augustus formally forbade intermarriage between freedwomen and men of senatorial family. Rather more common was the practice whereby a freed male slave would purchase and then liberate his own slave partner, so that they could contract a full Roman marriage and any subsequent children would be free-born.

This apparent generosity in granting manumission might work as much to the owner's advantage as to that of the slave. Most obviously, it did much to reinforce the institution of slavery itself, since the prospect of manumission was a powerful incentive to slave quiescence and industry, and manumission by will created an impression of liberality whose costs were effectively borne by your heirs. Even when freed during the master's lifetime, many slaves continued in their former occupations, including those within the household, often because they lacked the capital to establish themselves independently, and where they purchased their freedom, the price may have been calculated on the basis of the cost of a replacement. There were also various ways in which individual freedmen or particular categories of freedmen might remain legally obligated to their former owner (for example, in the provision of labour services) or in which their former owners would retain inheritance rights to part or all of their property. More generally, the bonds between the freedman and his former owner were regarded as analogous to those between patron and client: the owner became the freedman's patron and the freedman owed him a general duty of respect and assistance, which might be reinforced by an oath at manumission in which he acknowledged a general obligation of compliance towards the patron.

Provided that he received his freedom by one of the recognized formal procedures, the slave secured not only personal liberty but full Roman citizenship. Admittedly, freedmen's political power was carefully limited. They were normally (and from the time of Augustus legally) debarred from holding office at Rome or in the municipalities; and they could not serve in the legions. Yet this most striking example of the Roman integration of outsiders remains a significant phenomenon. Its roots probably lie far back in Roman history, when most slaves were themselves of Italian stock and their integration therefore presented few problems. Later freedmen were of more diverse ethnic origins, although if not home-bred they most commonly derived from the Greek east. None the less, the process of integration continued. That not only obviated the social dangers inherent in excluding freedmen from full membership of the Roman community; it also made manumission itself still more valuable and channelled freedmen's own ambitions and behaviour in the direction of positive social and cultural assimilation, to their own benefit and that of their local community in particular.

It was one of the paradoxes of Roman society that slaves and freedmen could secure access to skills, expertise, capital and opportunities often denied to the free-born poor. Many freedmen had already been given the training for, and been set up in, skilled occupations before manumission. And even when they had set them free, owners were naturally more ready to make capital available to men over whom they retained some control rather than to the independent free-born, who in any case often lacked the expertise required. Hence in Rome and Italy slaves and freedmen came to be prominent in a range of service, professional, artisan and commercial activities, with their owners or patrons creaming off some of the proceeds and thus tapping some of the profits of enterprises or occupations which were socially below their notice. The more successful of such freedmen became rich enough to rival the local curial class and, although they were always a small minority among freedmen, they became a significant social phenomenon by the early imperial period.

Still more prosperous were many of the trusted agents, administrators and others who continued to enjoy the favour of their former owner. They grew rich (to varying degrees) on gifts and bequests and on the perquisites and other opportunities which came their way as a consequence of their duties and the influence they enjoyed with their patrons. Some of the most trusted freedmen of the great figures of the late republic gained spectacular wealth and no little power, forerunners of the great imperial freedmen of the early principate whose fortunes might outstrip those of most senators. Of course, the position of such men remained individual and derivative, owed to their patron's favour and often dependent on him for its continuation. None the less, it highlighted with peculiar clarity the emergence of freedmen whose wealth might be represented as potentially disruptive of the established social hierarchy, at Rome as well as in the municipalities.

One symptom of this is the creation by the élite of a conventional image of the freedman as an ostentatious upstart, perhaps of eastern origin, vainly attempting to acquire a veneer of aristocratic culture. The stereotype is adroitly elaborated by Petronius in the depiction of the fictional freedman Trimalchio in his anarchic comic novel the *Satyricon* (mid-first century AD). In this case the narrator is able to adopt an air of detached and superior amusement, mingled with a growing revulsion, for Trimalchio represents no threat. He lives within the confines of his own self-enclosed world in which he can work out his own absurd pretensions and live out the grotesquely inflated self-image which he has created. In the real world the accommodation of wealthy freedmen was a more contentious problem, and understandably some freedmen were only too ready to parade their material success. Yet some individuals of servile extraction could demonstrate a high literary culture and, though their own circumstances had probably precluded most from acquiring it, the notion of freedmen's essential vulgarity remains a canard, a myth designed to validate their continued exclusion from the higher ranks of society.

That exclusion was formalized in the early empire when freedmen were legally barred from municipal office and they and their descendants for two generations were disqualified from equestrian (and thereby senatorial) rank, but it should not be allowed to obscure the quieter processes by which affluent individuals of freedmen descent were gradually assimilated, particularly into the curial order. Both at Rome and in the municipalities wealthy freedmen found new vehicles to establish and enhance their status. Numbers of them are found, alongside free-born individuals, in the ranks of magisterial attendants; from the reign of Augustus wealthy ex-slaves begin to use tenure of an annual local priesthood of the imperial cult (the Seviri Augustales) as an alternative to the municipal office, from which they were excluded; and they are found also utilizing some of their wealth on benefactions, not least to accelerate the entry of their sons into local politics. All this betokens the freedmen's desire for status within the established framework. They do not constitute a class carefully harbouring their own separate identity and pursuing their own independent objectives. As the aping of élite values, culture and lifestyle indicates, the socially ambitious sought, to varying degrees, to accommodate their behaviour and that of their offspring to élite norms. How many men of servile extraction succeeded in entering the curial class it is impossible to estimate; but cumulatively they seem to have been a significant source of recruits, particularly in the western provinces, and the overall contribution of the freedmen's enterprise to urban prosperity under the principate was very considerable. Equally, it is perhaps both a symptom and a cause of the decline of many cities in the west that far fewer of them are in evidence on the urban scene in the later empire.

The Position of Women

Of all the categories of Roman society women remain the most elusive, at least outside the level of the élite, to which most of our evidence refers. Virtually all that evidence derives from male writers and reflects male perceptions and values; and when it concerns individual women, it focuses principally on those who, for whatever reason, stood apart from the norm. We can form little notion of how women viewed their position, the roles that were assigned to them and the restrictions to which they were subject. For the most part we must be content with a generalized picture of their social, economic and legal status, though that too may be seriously misleading. Even within a given period the position of individual women may vary significantly, both from one individual to another and from one stage in life to another.

Throughout its history Rome was a male-dominated society. Women had no formal political rights: they could neither vote nor hold office. Male power was also deeply entrenched in the structures of this gerontocratic and patriarchal society. The basic unit of Roman society was the household, under the potentially autocratic and lifelong control of its male head, the *paterfamilias*. He had the power of life and death over his descendants and the right to determine whether a new-born child should be reared (a power which was probably used to discriminate in favour of male offspring). He was also the sole owner of the household property and those subject to him could not own property in their own right. These restrictions applied to male and female descendants alike, but whereas sons achieved full independence at the death of the *paterfamilias*, during the republic at least women never fully escaped from male control, that of their *paterfamilias* giving way only to that of their husband or a guardian.

Men viewed the primary functions of women as the supervision of the household and the bearing of legitimate children. Women were married early, usually in their teens and sometimes even before puberty, to husbands who might be considerably older than themselves. Marriages were regularly controlled by parents. Among the élite, for example, marriage was a key stratagem in the maintenance and enhancement of wealth and status and not, therefore, to be trusted to the vagaries of youthful infatuation. Marriage entailed the provision of a substantial dowry to assist the new household, a system that itself helped to preserve the overall social hierarchy while facilitating limited social mobility within it. How far the girl's wishes were consulted no doubt varied, but in the case of first marriages especially her role must commonly have been a passive one. While intensity of mutual love is sometimes advanced as a possible and even desirable element in marriage, moralists could deprecate passionate physical response to love-making in wives, whose function was to conceive children, not to provide pleasure to their husbands, let alone themselves (Lucretius, *On the Nature of the Universe* IV. 1263); and in marriage a common, and no doubt often more realistic, hope was simply for harmony between the partners. Even that did not guarantee the permanence of the marriage if it did not fulfil its other functions (above all, the production of heirs) or new circumstances made its dissolution desirable. Before the Christian era at least, marriage had no sacramental character. It was essentially a social instrument, to be contracted, maintained or discarded as circumstances dictated. Hence, although there were strict limitations on the justifiable grounds of divorce down to the third century BC, those restrictions were subsequently discarded (in concert with other changes in marriage arrangements), and in the late republic and early empire the *paterfamilias* commonly retained the right to initiate the girl's divorce whenever that suited his purposes.

The male concern with legitimate heirs entailed

considerable stress on the importance of female chastity and the severe punishment of adultery. Men did not subject themselves to the same rigorous demands. Their extramarital sexual activity was generally tolerated, provided it did not involve other men's wives or free-born virgins. The wife's domestic role was also enshrined in male values and expectations. Women are regularly praised for their thrift, industry, reliability and alertness, and for their deference and obedience to their husbands. But the most potent expression of this aspect of the woman's role was the symbolic importance attached to wool-working as a characteristic female activity and accomplishment. The potential of women for more positive and heroic action was recognized, but such action was proper only in the absence of men or in their support, or in defence of female virtue or (occasionally) the communal interest. Female initiative and self-assertion purely on their own account were deprecated, when not positively abhorred as an incipient threat to male control.

None the less, the position of upper-class women was more subtle, varied and complex than this simple stereotype suggests, and may in general have improved over time, particularly in the late republican and early imperial periods. As ever, a central factor is the control of property. As far back as we can trace, women could own property in their own right, provided they were not subject to the power of their *paterfamilias* or under the formal authority of their husbands. Moreover, the rules governing intestate inheritance treated male and female claimants equally, so that daughters who were still under their father's power inherited equally with sons at his death, and wives under the formal authority of their husband inherited equally with his children on his demise. Down at least to the fourth and third centuries BC wills were rare and such intestate inheritance therefore common. But women who so inherited came automatically under the guardianship of their own or their husband's nearest male relative in the male line. Such 'statutory guardians' would commonly stand to inherit the woman's property themselves if she died intestate, and they could both veto her disposal of key assets (above all land) and preclude her from making a will.

This regime was self-evidently designed to encourage the retention of property within the male line of descent and, although women could and did administer their property themselves, they regularly found their freedom of action seriously circumscribed. Over the course of the republican period, however, there were two major developments which together radically transformed the picture. First, the form of marriage by which the wife effectively passed from the power of her *paterfamilias* or the control of her guardian into the formal authority of her husband became progressively less frequent. It was increasingly superseded by a 'free' form of marriage in which the wife remained subject to her *paterfamilias* or the supervision of her guardian and the husband therefore had no legal rights over her or her property (if any). Secondly, as wills became ever more popular, at least among the élite, many women ceased to be subject to a statutory guardian on the death of their *paterfamilias*, but had a guardian appointed for them in his will or, failing that, by a magistrate. Such a guardian was not necessarily the woman's own prospective heir and the control he exercised over her affairs was much looser. Indeed, by the second century AD such guardians could be compelled to give their assent to her actions if they were deemed to be withholding it unjustifiably.

The upshot of these developments, and of the continuing practice of bequeathing substantial amounts of property to women (despite some attempts at legal restriction), was to leave many élite women, even if married, in effective control of substantial property once their *paterfamilias* had died. Indeed, in the early imperial period statutory guardianship for free-born women was abolished by the emperor Claudius and total exemption from guardianship was granted as an incentive and reward to specific categories of women, especially those who had produced a certain number of children. Not all these developments resulted from a positive desire to enhance the independence of women. The 'free' form of marriage originated as a mechanism by which a woman's family could prevent her property being absorbed into that of her husband and thus lost to them for ever. The popularity of wills was due to the increasing desirability of making detailed dispositions of one's property, not only to prospective heirs but to other friends and connections. Legacies became yet another aspect of the exchange of gifts and services between friends, with the consequence that legacy-hunting, the deliberate courting of the wealthy and (preferably) childless, became a recognizable if despised means of enrichment. However, the increasing freedom exercised by women in the disposal of their property does also represent a deliberate male decision, if only by default. It is probably closely linked with a more general development whereby kin in the female line acquired increased inheritance rights, at the expense of some of the priority previously enjoyed by kin in the male line of descent. This was a long and complex process, but it reflects a gradual reordering of (male) strategies. At its simplest and crudest, fathers now often preferred that their daughter's inheritance should go to her future children rather than to a kinsman in the male line, particularly perhaps where the daughter was the sole heiress. The only way in which that could be achieved was to give the daughter effective control over her property and its bequeathal.

It follows that women's independence of action varied very considerably, with ownership of property and the form taken by male control the key determinants. The daughter subject to her *paterfamilias*, owning no property in her own right and given in marriage to a husband of her parents' choosing, was in a very different position from the elderly aristocratic widow Ummidia, sniffily described by the younger Pliny (*Letters* 7.24) in the early second century AD. She enjoyed apparently unrestricted control of her property and its disposition, could engage in extensive local benefactions to the family's home town of Casinum, could indulge her own plebeian tastes in entertainment and could generally pass her time in whatever way she chose, albeit in an essentially private context. Not only that, but she exercised considerable *de facto* authority over her grandson and prospective heir, whose upbringing and education she supervised and who came to be known by her family name because of its greater distinction.

Such a situation was no doubt all the easier to accept when men discovered that it did not in practice undermine their own collective social and political control. But it did give some women new opportunities for independence of action. Whatever the form of guardianship to which they were subject, women administered their property themselves. The guardian's role was simply to give or refuse his sanction to the disposal of particular categories of assets (not to any and every action taken with respect to her property); and women are found investing in a variety of enterprises. Women who had effective control of their property must also have acquired a considerable say in their marriages (and remarriages) and have potentially enjoyed greater independence in their relations with their husbands, particularly given their own ability to initiate divorce. Significantly, women are now commended if they allow their husbands to administer their property. At least occasionally women could choose sexual partners on the basis of their physical attraction, even where that scandalized polite society, and the married woman who pursued her own independent life of leisure and dalliance became a recognizable figure in both literature and life.

Women of the élite classes enjoyed other advantages. As far back as the rich female tombs of the eighth and seventh centuries BC women's rank was manifested in elaborate display, not merely of jewellery and dress but of other symbols of status such as chariots. Indeed, a key factor in the whole development of women's property rights may have been the role that aristocratic women could play as vehicles of family status, particularly in a society where the production and survival of male heirs was often problematic and where marriage itself was not uncommonly a means of social advancement. From at least the second century BC some aristocratic men found it convenient to stress their maternal ancestry as well as their paternal, especially where it was the more distinguished, and the funerals of aristocratic women become themselves occasions of family display.

The fact that women were not kept in seclusion socially may be linked with this. Women could attend dinner parties with their menfolk (though they did not necessarily do so regularly), could witness popular shows and entertainments, and from the late republic at least could participate in individual cults and rituals independently of their husbands. One particularly significant indication of male attitudes to, and expectations of, their wives and daughters is the fact that numbers of élite women acquired not only the literacy that would make them better equipped to administer their property and household but at least the elements of literary culture. This enabled them both to share in this increasingly important aspect of male élite interests and lifestyle, and sometimes to engage in the active encouragement of literary works and literary men on their own account.

In addition, aristocratic women especially could act as social and political patrons and brokers. Their property could itself be an instrument of social power, but they also stood at the centre of a web of connections which they could mobilize to advance their own interests, those of their menfolk or those of other acquaintances or dependants. Wives, relatives, concubines or others could acquire considerable personal influence with the powerful which could be exploited in this way. It was one of the scandals of the new imperial regime that such influence, and the public role and privileges enjoyed by imperial wives and others, opened up the possibility of women exercising real political power and influence, and powerful and even dominant women were a sporadically recurring feature of imperial dynasties to the end of antiquity.

Such women remain, of course, exceptional. Even among the élite classes most women's lives are shrouded in silent anonymity, reflected even in the lack of individuality of their portraits. Moreover, the power and influence even of the most successful is regularly derivative from their status and connections in the male world and commonly exercised through and on behalf of their menfolk. And that too is exemplified by the way in which portraits of imperial women sometimes include items borrowed from the emperor's own iconography. Even when the advent and eventual triumph of Christianity, with its high valuation on virginity, its recognition of female martyrdom and sainthood, its eager acceptance of female subvention and charity, and its recognition of female salvation and female standing in the sight of God, opened up new ways in which women could find self-dignity, exercise influence and even resist the traditional social pressures to which they were subject, there was no radical transformation in the essentially secondary and subordinate status of women. The Church preached a new doctrine of marriage (and of male sexual fidelity) but not one of partnership based on parity; and far from promoting any new social or political status for women, its own structures and practices largely mirrored the patriarchal world of secular society. Women could be deaconesses, but among the orthodox the priesthood and the episcopacy were, and remained, the exclusive preserve of men.

Philosophy and Religion

Philosophy was and remained a Greek import, part of the Greek cultural heritage to which the Roman élite were exposed on a new scale in the second century BC and to which they responded with varying degrees of enthusiasm. To a limited extent Greek philosophical doctrines were mediated through books, but oral instruction remained the principal mechanism, whether through the visits of philosophers to Rome, through study with resident philosophers in Campania or later Rome itself, or through visits to the great centres or particular distinguished figures in the east. And the Greek language remained the principal medium of philosophical exposition, oral and written, through to the end of antiquity.

This did not entirely exclude the ordinary populace from some acquaintance with philosophical ideas. Stage references or the dramatic use of particular philosophical ideas or language offered one avenue of superficial familiarization; there were popular philosophical preachers, often with Cynic leanings, who addressed their gospel to any who would listen; and (very exceptionally) one of the most distinguished Stoic philosophers of the imperial period was the ex-slave Epictetus (*c.* 55–135), who had been permitted to attend the lectures of Q. Musonius Rufus (born before 30). None the less, serious study of philosophy remained largely the preserve of an élite minority, and some of its devotees could revel in their superior knowledge that set them above and apart from the ignorant masses. Even so, the doctrines and practice of philosophy were often viewed with distrust. Philosophical teaching might challenge and undermine established norms and modes of behaviour, social organization and political authority; the pursuit of philosophy might distract the individual from engagement in public and social life; or his philosophical principles might be incompatible with the pragmatic requirements of such activity. It was commonly held, therefore, that philosophy should be at best a leisure activity, cultivated only in so far as it was consonant with the traditional order and with the individual's own responsibilities and obligations. Though by the late first century BC many of the cultured élite may have acquired some knowledge of the more important schools and doctrines, committed adherence to a particular philosophical creed was always confined to a small minority.

Philosophy at Rome

Hence few Romans became professional philosophers themselves (Musonius was the most notable exception) and there was little specifically Roman input into the development of philosophical doctrine. The only new school to be created by a Roman (the Sextians of the Augustan period) was essentially an ascetic amalgam of Stoic and Pythagorean teaching. Such Roman philosophical writing as there was confined itself largely to the presentation of Greek doctrines in Latin dress, with the author's role restricted to their selection, combination, modification, illustration or specific application, in response to his own predilections or the needs of his Roman audience.

Moreover, some of the strongest advocates of philosophical study stress its subordination to the inherited values and institutions of Roman society. That is explicitly the view of the orator and politician M.

The world according to Ptolemy around 150. In rejecting the ancient Greek idea of a circumfluent ocean, he assumed the existence of a large sub-equatorial continent. But he correctly gauged the size of Asia, adding China at last to ancient European maps.

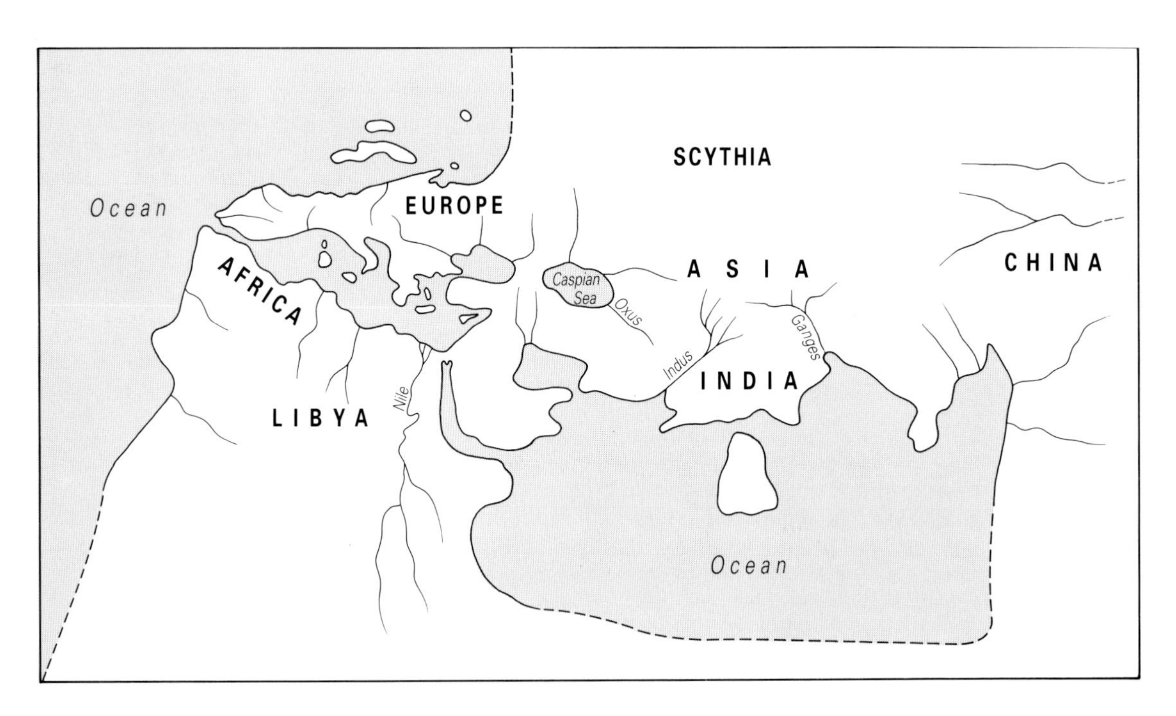

Cicero (106–43 BC), whose philosophical works were a buttress for the traditional order.

Tullius Cicero (106–43 BC), who wrote a cycle of works expounding and criticizing key doctrines of the major schools (the first major philosophical prose-writing in Latin). Not only does Cicero emphasize that his own philosophical activity is secondary to his political involvement, but he sees the central task of philosophy as the justification and reinforcement of the traditional order – economic, social, political and religious. Philosophy's role is not to challenge that order but to provide it with secure intellectual foundations, to foster positive adherence to its norms and to encourage active participation in its social and political life. If it does not do so, that represents a failure on its part, not a reason for questioning the traditional order itself – a view virtually all Romans of the élite classes would readily have endorsed.

As a result both of this and of the wider Roman cultural aversion to abstract inquiry, the main focus of such writing – and of Roman philosophical engagement – was ethical. Although the physical doctrines of Epicurus were the subject of perhaps the most powerful poem to survive in Latin (Lucretius' *On the Nature of the Universe*) and Roman gentlemen could show a dilettante interest in physical curiosities, systematic interest in natural philosophy or mathematics was rare, and even logic was studied (if at all) mainly for its usefulness to the orator. The concrete applicability of philosophical teaching to the individual's own conduct and pursuit of well-being was always the dominant concern.

All the principal Hellenistic schools of philosophy won adherents at Rome, but the two most popular, at least into the second century AD, were Stoicism and Epicureanism, both of which originated in Athens. With its stress on the secluded pursuit of tranquillity, Epicureanism appealed especially to those equestrians who turned their back on a political or military career, preferring to devote themselves entirely to that cultivated leisure which had become an increasingly accepted part of the aristocratic lifestyle. Critics misrepresented Epicureanism as naked hedonism, subversive of the social order as well as hostile to engagement in politics. Yet in fact Epicureans regarded the maintenance of society, and therefore the observation of its norms, as essential to the conditions of security in which alone the life of tranquillity could be pursued; and far from preaching a new economic, social or political order (except as a distant Utopia), Epicureans sought their objectives within the context of the established framework. Indeed, it was perhaps on the grounds that the whole existence and fabric of society were under threat that a number of Epicureans justified their active engagement in Roman politics in the 50s and 40s BC. And if Epicureans retreated from the public arena thereafter, they could be as assiduous as any in the fulfilment of their social obligations and firm in their commitment to the social virtues.

If Epicureanism as such offered no substantive positive challenge to the established order (even traditional religious activity was readily accommodated), Stoicism too was primarily concerned with the well-being of the individual's own soul. It had no clearly defined political creed and failed even to develop criteria by which the propriety of particular social or political institutions could be judged. The primary concern in the political arena was the moral conduct of the ruler, and its Roman adherents neither advocated nor implemented any serious institutional reforms. Except when influenced by Cynic doctrines, much Stoic teaching could be seen as supportive of traditional socio-political norms and structures. In Stoicism the practice of the social virtues was itself a constituent of individual self-

The Pantheon in Rome. Hadrian's building has proved one of the most durable of Roman temples.

fulfilment and well-being; and mainstream Stoicism always advocated political participation where circumstances permitted. Moreover, as Stoic teaching tended to interpret the individual's obligations in terms of the conventional expectations of society, Stoic ethics might readily be regarded as largely coinciding with traditional Roman aristocratic values and norms, particularly in the form in which those ethics were presented by Panaetius of Rhodes (born 185 BC). Panaetius was himself a friend of Roman aristocrats and his detailed application of Stoic teaching to ordinary conduct was so consonant with Cicero's ideas of the proper conduct of a Roman gentleman that he used it as the basis for his quasi-philosophical exposition of those ideas in his *De Officiis*, a work on the proper or appropriate conduct which consistently upholds the regime of property, privilege and power, sometimes in the most forthright terms. In fact, however, Stoic teaching was predominantly oriented towards the co-operative virtues and, for all the emphasis on 'greatness of spirit' in both Panaetius and Cicero, it was not easily reconciled with the self-assertive, success-oriented dynamics of Roman political life. Office, power and popular acclaim were regarded as of no intrinsic value and certainly not as goods to be sought in their own right. Men who found their satisfaction in the traditional goals and rewards of aristocratic activities might find little in the Stoic rejection of those values to attract them, and it is no accident that none of the great political-military figures of the late republic espoused the Stoic creed.

With its focus on the inner moral self-sufficiency of the individual, particularly in the face of hostile circumstances or misfortune, Stoicism appealed especially to those who found themselves at odds with their world or oppressed by its transience and uncertainties, and there is often an air of dreary melancholia in Roman Stoic writing of the imperial period. The highly personal *Meditations* of the eclectic Stoic emperor Marcus Aurelius (121–80) are a prime example of the way in which even social and political duties can come to be regarded as an unwelcome burden. But Stoicism offered also a source of moral strength and self-reliance which might steel men to resistance and opposition. In the second half of the first century AD a sequence of senators of Stoic conviction engaged in implicit or overt criticism of the immoral, tyrannical or autocratic acts of emperors and paid for that opposition with their lives. Stoics had no quarrel with monarchy as such and none of these men sought to overthrow the imperial system itself. Even their limited and occasional advocacy of senatorial freedom, status and dignity represented no more than the assertion of traditional senatorial ideals: their Stoicism might endorse such a stance, but did not positively require it. Yet their Stoic beliefs were not irrelevant to their conduct or their fate. By implication they claimed the right to judge the emperor's conduct by standards that had objective external validity; their creed denied intrinsic value to the offices, honours and gifts by which emperors expressed and maintained their power; the actions of some of them in withdrawing from political life exemplified their own indifference to such levers of power, and that in turn enhanced their own moral stature; above all, their creed encouraged resolute open (if often passive) opposition, based on issues of principle alone, and gave them the moral fortitude and resolution required to sustain it.

A bronze statue of the philosopher-emperor Marcus Aurelius (121–80).

Few of any philosophical persuasion could match the commitment of such men. Many even of those who professed adherence to a particular school probably wore their philosophical principles lightly. It was not only the Stoic tutor and adviser of the emperor Nero, M. Annaeus Seneca (*c.* 1 BC–AD 65), who was accused of conduct inconsistent with the teaching of his numerous treatises. The extent to which a man's philosophy (if he had one) determined his choices and actions will clearly have varied from one individual to another. In many instances that philosophy would offer no specific guidance, but at most a set of terms or principles within which to debate the issue. Even that, however, might have some influence on the outcome, particularly for those who took their philosophy seriously; and the fact that a particular course of action could be justified in philosophical terms may sometimes have enhanced its potential attractions or acceptability. In general, however, the major function of philosophy for the committed was a wider one. It provided a world view, a definition of man's role in the scheme of things, an account of the means by which individual well-being could be achieved with little or no reference to externals; and it offered a broad creed to live by, an exhortation to the exercise of virtue, and a source of consolation, reassurance and resolve in times of adversity, affliction or distress.

Seneca (*c.* 1 BC–AD 65), the Stoic tutor and victim of Nero.

Roman Religion

It will be apparent from what has just been said that philosophy performed many of the roles which we associate with religion but which traditional religious activity at Rome did not fulfil. Roman religion had no theology and no world-view; it afforded no definition of man's role in the universe and no prescriptions for his social conduct or the organization of society; and it offered no doctrine of individual survival in a world to come. It was not a religion of belief and faith, but one of ritual. It had no authoritative book or creed setting out doctrines which its adherents were required to accept: its books were concerned with ritual observances and technical issues of religious practice and law. It even had little in the way of native myth. The myths of Roman literature are overwhelmingly Greek myths and though Greek myth may have acquired some vogue among the ordinary populace by the late republic, they made no more than a marginal impact on cult practice itself.

It is only our preconceptions and assumptions about religion that encourage us to regard this as a serious deficiency in Roman religious activity. It was not a view shared by Romans themselves. They did not in general feel the need to endow social morality with a religious sanction – other social and legal mechanisms were usually preferred. Individual goals and patterns of action were satisfactorily evolved within the context of communal or group values, expectations and rewards. And the prospect and realities of individual extinction were similarly comprehended within existing social and cultural horizons.

The objectives of religious activity were essentially different: to mobilize the positive assistance of deities in specific undertakings or in the prosecution of general goals, to obviate divine hostility or the intervention of potentially destructive divine forces, to neutralize prodigies, and to ascertain the will of the gods or secure their sanction for particular activities. These objectives were secured by ritual actions: prayers, vows, sacrifices, offerings and a variety of divinatory techniques. The rules that were elaborated to ensure the correct performance of such rituals concerned the technicalities of the rite itself, not the moral conduct or religious beliefs of the participants. Even the nature – and precise identity – of the recipient deity could be left undefined.

The form and structure of Roman sanctuaries reflect these ritual priorities. Temples are regularly set within areas ritually defined to mark off their separate status and that of the actions performed within them. They are in some undefined sense the 'dwelling' of the deity and may contain his cult statue, but their form and monumentality again emphasize his distinctness. The characteristic 'Etrusco-Italic' temple, which was the dominant type throughout Roman history, is distinguished by its elevation on a podium, the strong monumentality of its frontal aspect and its ordered axial symmetry. Even so, it was not the sole or predominant focus of the sanctuary (indeed, it is not a necessary constituent). That was the altar, set in front of the temple building and along its principal axis, and the location for the principal cult acts.

Religious activity was always, therefore, particularistic, and geared to the goals and needs of the

Roman legends spread widely. This fourth-century mosaic of Romulus and Remus with a she-wolf was excavated in Yorkshire.

A brass coin of the emperor Nero (54–68), showing the Temple of Janus in Rome. This issue celebrated one of the rare periods of peace during which the temple doors were traditionally closed.

worshipper, whether individual or collective. Far from offering its own distinctive values or priorities, it articulated those already dominant within the community, particularly at the public level. Nor could it be insulated from the rest of social, economic, military and political life. Since it was concerned with the achievement of specific goals in all those spheres, it was an integral part of such activities. Before most major political or military actions, for example, divinatory procedures (the auspices) would be observed to ascertain whether the gods approved of such action being taken on that particular day, and in general the achievement of the community's goals (above all, its military victories) was contingent on the scrupulous observance of ritual, while failure was regularly ascribed to its neglect. Consequently, religious activity was woven into the fabric of communal life at every turn and its maintenance regarded as essential to the preservation of the established order. It was itself part of the community's own self-identity and the Roman gods were in every sense the gods of Rome – one ancient practice in war was to 'summon forth' the principal deity of an opposing city in an effort to entice him or her to change sides in return for a new sanctuary and cult at Rome itself.

The most visible expression of this role was in the building of grandiose temples to the chief local deity as a source of communal prestige and a material demonstration of communal identity and power. In the second and first centuries BC especially, monumental sanctuary buildings at Praeneste, Tivoli and elsewhere in central Italy testified to the scale of local pretensions, while Rome's own power had been signalled in this way as far back as the sixth century BC, by the construction of the huge temple to Jupiter, Juno and Minerva on the Capitol. And in the imperial period the adoption of that cult became a key mechanism by which communities in the empire could express their Roman identity. The institution of such a cult, usually dominating the community's civic centre, became a regular response to an enhancement in the city's formal status.

The integration of religious action into the life of the community went hand in hand with its incorporation into the existing power structures. There was no distinct church organization, with its own separate resources and its own independent authority. Most of the important ritual actions on behalf of the community were performed by the magistrates. They were guided and advised by priests and the different priestly colleges might be asked to give their opinion on religious issues – religious expertise was concentrated in their hands and the frequent need for religious correctives of various kinds gave them a position of high authority. It was also the priests (above all the *pontifices*) who worked out the prescriptions for different ritual acts, with an assurance and in a detail that increased both their own prestige and popular confidence in the efficacy of the ritual itself. But the priests did not form a separate caste. The more important were drawn from the senatorial class and most were able to combine their priestly duties with the continued pursuit of a political career. Moreover, most major decisions on religious matters (including especially significant public innovation) were taken by the Senate itself, acting in concert with the priestly college concerned. This is not a case of a 'political' body (the Senate) taking 'religious' decisions. Rather, the Senate's role in guarding the interests of the community necessarily covers both 'religious' and 'political' matters, not least because the two spheres are inextricably intertwined.

Religion at the public level is therefore fundamentally political. Its prime purpose is the interests of the community and it must serve those interests to be of any value. That justifies the use of religious mechanisms for political purposes by those who consider this to be in the wider interest; and it ensures that strong political action is taken against any religious activity that is deemed to conflict with that interest. Religion is also an integral part of the community's power structures, and it contributes to their continued maintenance. Under the republic, for example, religious decision-making at the public level was concentrated in the hands of the senatorial class, who naturally identified the preservation of their own power with the interests of the state. The concentration of ritual expertise in the hands of senatorial priests itself increased their standing and validated their pre-eminence. Religious celebrations, such as the triumph, the thanksgiving ceremony or the games, provided a spectacular stage for advertising individual liberality and military success, and for acquiring prestige and status. These were still further enhanced by the fact that such ceremonies

Games, including chariot-racing, were an important part of religious festivals in Rome.

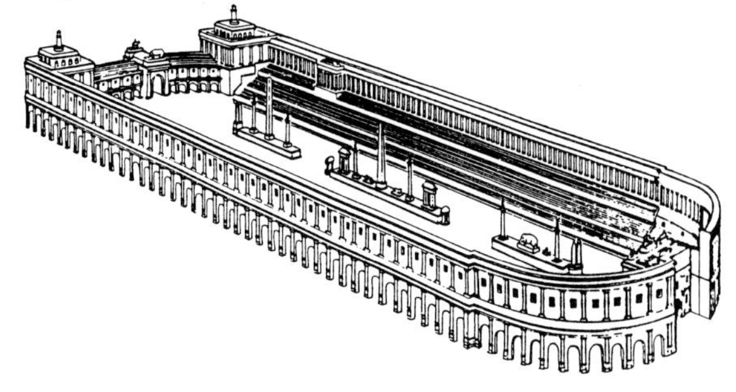

were set within an on-going tradition of divine favour to the Roman community. The most common permanent memorial of military victory was a new temple building, constructed and dedicated by the successful commander out of the spoils, with both him and his achievement commemorated in the dedicatory inscription.

In other ways also religious structures enunciate and reinforce élite or more general communal values – for example, by the institution of the cult of key abstract qualities or objectives, or by the careful articulation of the religious activities of particular social groups. Thus women's cult activities at the communal level focus pre-eminently on deities of fertility and chastity. And in this and other ways also religious activity could act as a means of communal integration. For although many state cult acts required no public participation, all sought to secure by public rites the welfare of the individual citizen as a member of the Roman community, and some festivals and ceremonies directly involved the populace at large or particular sectors within it.

One consequence of this political character of religious activity is that political changes regularly have religious correlates. That is most apparent in the developments consequent upon the establishment of the principate. Emperors became members of all the great priestly colleges and (from 12 BC) occupied the most important position of *pontifex maximus*, or 'chief priest'. Religious initiatives and decision-making become effectively concentrated in their hands. Altars and temples are dedicated to their virtues, record their achievements or celebrate their safekeeping, further fashioning their image and reinforcing their pre-eminence. The protection of particular deities may be invoked as an earnest of their continuing success. Their welfare and that of their families, their anniversaries and their successes become a central focus of public vows, games, prayers and sacrifice, not only at Rome but in the provinces and cities of the empire, emphasizing that the fortunes of the Roman people and of the empire as a whole are necessarily dependent on their further survival and prosperity.

Furthermore, cities and provinces themselves progressively instituted cults of the emperor, a continuation of the Hellenistic Greek practice whereby communities acknowledged individual or general benefactions of Greek kings or Roman officials by paying them religious honours and establishing their cult. This was neither simply an extravagant use of language nor a theological statement about the ruler's ontological status. It was a ritual means of evaluating the benefaction (and therefore the benefactor) on the scale of services which the community might receive, of establishing a permanent mechanism for communal acknowledgement and gratitude, and of legitimizing and integrating the ruler and his power within the city's own religio-political framework. In principle – and usually in practice – such cults of the emperor were the result of civic or provincial initiative and recognized his role as an individual or universal benefactor. They became a focus of communal identity and prestige and of élite display and liberality and, along with imperial statues and images, they were an enduring manifestation of the ruler himself and of the imperial power. Embedded within the community's own structures, they served as an institutionalized acknowledgement of the emperor's authority and as a demonstration of loyalty, and as such they offered a means by which provinces in particular could commend their interests and concerns to the emperor himself. The rationale and function of these cults required that they should usually appear to be voluntary expressions of local gratitude and there was no general policy of imposing the imperial cult on the empire. None the less, individual emperors from Augustus on were well aware of the political advantages

A view of the Palatine, the hill on which, legend says, the she-wolf suckled Romulus and Remus. In imperial times the palace stood here, and even after the foundation of Constantinople the Palatine was still officially the emperor's residence.

to themselves of such a ritual institutionalization of their power and actively encouraged the creation of such cults at the provincial level in the west wherever such a means of expressing loyalty both to themselves and to Rome seemed requisite.

At Rome itself such initiatives were out of the question. Although, for example, the emperor's patronage of the urban plebs found a religious correlate in the worship of his *genius*, or 'protective spirit', by slaves and freedmen at the crossroad shrines of the city, there could be no public cult of the emperor during his lifetime. This was not due to any theological objection (there was no theology), but rather to the incompatibility of such a cult with the ideology that the emperor was no more (but no less) than the *princeps*, or 'first citizen'. Nevertheless, Augustus, who had traded heavily on his status as the son of the deified Caesar, saw the value of posthumous deification as a final public acknowledgement of the legitimacy and achievements of his own rule and as a means of easing the path of his own adopted son and successor, Tiberius. Not all emperors received such divine honours – the Senate could and did refuse to vote them to emperors they regarded as tyrannical. And such deification should again be seen from a functional, not a theological, viewpoint. Indeed, in various ways deified emperors are set apart from the regular pantheon and even potential recipients of divine honours may go out of their way to emphasize their own mortality.

Change and Innovation

The particularistic character of Roman religious activity makes it in some senses inappropriate to speak of a 'Roman religion', as if it were a closely coordinated system of religious beliefs and practices. Pluralism was always a central feature and development piecemeal and often haphazard. That, however, facilitated the processes of change which were always an inherent aspect of Roman religious practice and indeed essential to its survival. Particular rituals may be given a new interpretation, individual deities new functions. Some cults may achieve increased importance, others suffer progressive neglect, whether through loss of confidence in their efficacy, changed priorities, changes in patterns of settlement or other causes. And there was a regular influx of new rituals and new divinities, at the public as well as at the private level, in response to particular crises or new needs or as a correlate of social and cultural developments.

In the public sphere such innovation was carefully controlled and legitimized, and, where necessary, potentially disruptive elements in new cults or rituals were discarded or carefully segregated. Moreover, those cults deemed in some sense foreign were kept outside the sacred boundary of the city. But the integration of such cults, predominantly from the Greek world, into the public religious activity of the Roman state was a regular resource, particularly when crises arose with which the existing religious apparatus seemed unable to cope. Such new cults did not, however, directly supplant or replace existing ones. They simply supplement the inherited complex of cult activity and their introduction does not imply or require the discarding of other established ritual action.

The Temple of Isis, excavated from the remains of Pompeii, the city overwhelmed by lava in 79.

Much the same is true also at the private level. Here the authorities could and did intervene to suppress activity they deemed undesirable, particularly where forms of religious organization or authority emerged that were independent of the existing religio-political structures. But there was no consistent suppression of new cults and, particularly as a result of urban development, of social and political changes within the towns, and with the movement of people and ideas within the empire, new Greek or Graecized cults, such as those of Isis and Serapis or, later, of Mithras, became established at various localities, sometimes incorporating new religious ideas, practices and ceremonies, or even offering hope of an afterlife for initiates. Such cults were not, however, universal and although they enlarged the menu of religious options and sometimes advanced grandiose claims for the power of their deity, they did not exclude the simultaneous retention of other gods or observances. Indeed, some (such as Isis) were eventually incorporated in the public pantheon and all were effectively integrated into the existing framework, alongside those numerous older cults that continued to maintain their vitality.

The Rise of Christianity

In all major respects Christianity differed fundamentally from the diverse ritual-focused religious activity of Rome and the cities of the empire. It was monotheistic and therefore exclusive. Its adherents had to renounce all pagan gods and ritual. Strictly, therefore, they were debarred from participation in the numerous political, military and social activities of the Graeco-Roman world of which such ritual was an integral part, and in particular were precluded from political office. Christianity was a universal and individual religion; it was not the religion of a particular political community and membership required a sustained act of positive personal commitment. Its worship was congregational in character, with participation open to all believers irrespective of social status. Its individual churches were clearly defined communities whose internal cohesion was reinforced by obligations of regular attendance and financial contribution and by outside hostility. It laid especial stress on charity and almsgiving, on provision for the material needs of poor and destitute brethren. It offered a theocratic interpretation of history, of the world and of man's place within it, in which the fortunes even of Rome were at best an instrument of God's wider purposes, and worldly goods, offices and status were of no account. It taught the believer to attend not to this world but to the next, and it offered specific doctrines of individual salvation leading to a state of bliss in the life to come.

Such salvation required both an act of faith and observance of a strict code of conduct. This covered all spheres of life, was reinforced by a systematic regime of penitence and in some respects differed from the established practices of the Graeco-Roman world. Christian teaching recoiled from the taking of human life, denounced public entertainments, preached a much more restrictive code of sexual ethics and put a high valuation on celibacy and virginity. Indeed its emphasis on the value of the unmarried state seems deliberately designed to highlight its distinctive (and superior) morality in a manner that offered no positive threat to the social order as such, and it led readily and frequently to the pursuit of asceticism as a necessary consequence of the rejection of the world and its values.

The basilica at Trier, dating from the early fourth century: A) reconstructed view of exterior; B) plan.

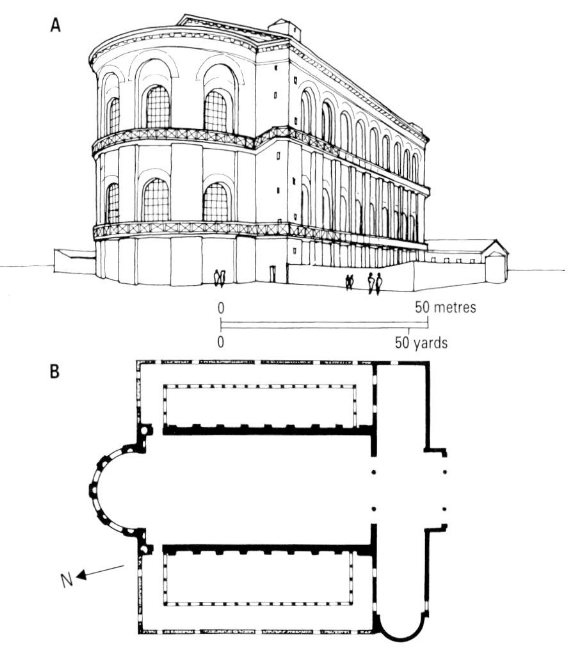

Salvation also demanded the acceptance of specific key beliefs. Correctness of doctrine, its definitive formulation and its defence became central concerns; and the notion of orthodoxy implied the possibility of heresy, of which ritual religion could know nothing. Inevitably the problems of orthodoxy became bound up with issues of revelation and authority. The Christian gospel claimed to be based on divine revelation and the question of the possibility of further revelation, as a source of teaching on the 'true' faith, continued to exercise the Church, and in particular its leaders, who periodically found their own authority threatened by those who claimed privileged access to God's will. Already in the late first and second centuries much of the Church's energy was devoted to confronting these various challenges. To maintain the internal cohesion of the churches, particularly in the face of doctrinal and other dissensions, a strong power structure had developed in many Christian communities by the early second century. This was focused on the person of the bishop, who had the right to suspend or even excommunicate both clergy and laity; and his authority was further reinforced by the notion of apostolic succession, which also played a key role in the progressive establishment of the New Testament canon in response to the heretical claims of Gnostics and others in the second century. At the same time the emergence of bishops reinforced the strong organizational base of the Church, which was to be a key factor in its survival and growth. With direct clerical encouragement, the financial resources of the individual churches increased steadily, especially in the third century, and the churches themselves formed part of an intercommunicating network that could be expanded to take in every part of the empire and beyond.

Christianity was also in principle a proselytizing religion, and although the Church was precluded from public preaching and does not seem to have engaged in systematic missionary enterprise after the apostolic age, its numbers and geographical extension increased progressively. However, the scale, speed, stages and causative factors of its growth are uncertain. It seems to have been predominantly an urban phenomenon (and its own organization was largely based on the cities), and by the third century most cities in Syria, Asia Minor, Egypt, Greece, Africa and Italy had their own bishop. Elsewhere, and generally in the countryside, its success was apparently more sporadic, and even in those centres where it was established Christians remained a minority, and often probably a small minority, until Constantine. Socially Christianity seems to have made most headway among urban artisans and others of similar status, though it attracted men, and especially women, of all social strata, including some from the higher ranks of local and even Roman society (particularly perhaps from the later second century). Predictably, however, males of the élite classes, whose own ambitions and careers were intimately bound up with the public – and therefore the religious – life of their cities or of Rome, were seldom to be found in its midst.

The prime mechanism for the conversion of outsiders must have been the persuasion of existing Christians, but conversion was always an individual decision and consequently the occasion, motives and strength of commitment will have varied considerably. Indeed, Christianity's success may have been due in part to the very diversity of its appeal. The inner strength and mutual affection of individual Christian communities, their lack of social exclusivity, their doctrine of the accessibility of the Christian god and Christian moral excellence to all alike, their teaching on individual salvation and the life to come, their advocacy and sometimes practice of high morality, their fusion of religion and philosophy and their admission of ordinary men to the knowledge and study of such matters, their miracles and exorcisms, together with the steadfast resolution of individual martyrs, may all have contributed. We do not in fact begin to have the evidence on which to formulate a judgement about the relative significance of these and other factors. But if we had, speculatively, to point to one consideration above all others, it should perhaps be the sense of individual worth which Christianity gave to the convert, as a sinner for whom Christ had suffered the agony and degradation of crucifixion and who was now one of the elect, 'set apart' from his or her fellow men and destined to stand in God's own presence. Other religious and social organizations flourished at this politically emasculated level in the imperial period, partly as a source of individual identity in a communal context, but none gave participants so potent a sense of their own significance or that of their faith and none had the rigorous organizational structure or internal dynamics of growth which Christianity possessed.

In or by 64 Christianity was proscribed and Christians who persisted in their faith could be executed for that reason alone. Roman officials probably had only the most sketchy knowledge of what Christianity entailed, but their distaste for it is readily explicable. So far as they knew anything about its doctrines, these must have seemed incomprehensible, and the worship of a Jew executed for political crimes no less absurd and outrageous. As a separate and secret sect, Christians were themselves widely accused of criminal activity. They rejected the Roman and all other gods (readily interpreted as a denial of prior social and civic bonds and allegiances), and, in contrast to the Jewish religion (regarded with equal distaste), their faith could claim no high antiquity or national basis. No less important was the potentially disruptive effects of Christianity within those cities where it had taken root. 'New superstitions' were always suspect precisely because they could easily threaten the existing order. Moreover, once they had become distinguished from Jews, Christians themselves were popular targets of local hostility, as 'atheists' who denied the gods, withdrew from much social and public life, and met in their own self-contained communities. The accusations levelled at Christians at different times included cannibalism, incest, political disloyalty and, above all, responsibility for calamities and disasters through their denial of the gods.

Such local hostility was, in fact, responsible for the sporadic persecution of Christians in the first two centuries AD. Except where Christians were accused of specific crimes, the initiative was not taken by magistrates or governors. Christians were not regarded by Roman authorities as in the same category as brigands and assassins, men whom governors had a positive duty to hunt down, and individual governors could show considerable reluctance to punish those who were brought before them. Prosecution of Christians was a matter of local initiative and much depended on relations with the local community. Consequently it was sporadic, unpredictable and relatively small-scale, and those accused could always escape punishment by renouncing their faith. Only in the third and early fourth centuries did a few Roman emperors attempt to eliminate Christianity systematically, perhaps because it was deemed incompatible with a Roman identity in an empire where all were Roman citizens and because its adherents refused worship to the emperor when it was pressed upon them – this was an age in which the empire's own integrity was threatened by external and internal conflict, and the survival of emperors themselves often hung by a tenuous thread. However, even the persecutions of Decius (250–51) and Diocletian (303–5) were short-lived, partially implemented and ineffectual. If the Church had grown to a size to attract positive hostility from the central government, popular antagonism may generally have weakened. When in 312 Constantine embraced the Christian faith (for reasons that are uncertain), there was no backlash among his followers or in the empire at large. With imperial recognition and endorsement the Church's progress now quickened, meeting comparatively little serious popular opposition or protest except when pagan interests were directly attacked.

Constantine proved an enthusiastic convert, parading the faith as the source of his military successes, actively intervening in Church affairs and providing extensive patronage in the form of buildings, resources and privileges. High-ranking converts were the recipients of gifts and honours, and petitioning communities found it advantageous to stress their Christian character. But though they cannot have been indifferent to Christianity's potential as a source of cohesion to the empire, neither Constantine nor his immediate successors tried to impose the faith on their subjects or to bar pagans from office and government. Indeed, Julian (360–63) attempted to stem and reverse the Christian tide, not least by introducing into traditional religious practice some of the institutional apparatus, the charitable and moral concerns, the definition of basic beliefs and the social integration that characterized the new faith. But Julian's death on a Persian campaign in

Constantine's basilica at Trier. Originally a large hall used for public business, the basilica in the late Roman empire became a characteristic form of the Christian church.

363 ended this crusade and within twenty years first Gratian (367–83) and then especially Theodosius I embarked on a more positive policy of Christianization, culminating in the formal (if never fully implemented) prohibition of all pagan sacrifices and of access to all pagan sanctuaries in 391. And both Theodosius and his successors also enacted a series of measures against, and occasionally actively persecuted, schismatics, heretics and Jews.

This new phase of policy was encouraged, and to some extent made possible, by the progressive (though still partial) Christianization of those classes from whom emperors drew their advisers and officials. But much of the impetus came from the Church itself, from influential or zealous bishops (such as Martin of Tours) and from fanatics in the eremitical and monastic movements. Monks and hermits first appear in the early fourth century in Egypt, and are subsequently found, in considerable numbers, in other parts of the east and then in the west also. Their withdrawal from the normal structures, and often the physical environment, of Graeco-Roman civic life into a calling of ascetic devotion was a declaration that only thus could the Christian ideal be achieved, and they were believed by the faithful to have special powers of intercession with Heaven in consequence. They were naturally among the most fervent opponents of all idolatry and, from the late fourth century, are in the vanguard of violent attacks on pagan shrines and property in the east.

The recognition of Christianity also brought major changes for the Church itself. Clerical posts became respectable, many desirable for the rank and wealth they brought, and they come to be filled predominantly by men of the curial class. The size of congregations and the public dimension of Christian worship revolutionized Church architecture. Previously Christians had tended to meet for their regular services in specially modified rooms in private houses. Now they adapted the secular basilica, the multipurpose internally arcaded hall, to serve as the basis of a Church architecture in which grandiose monumentality was often a dominant concern. Other types of Christian structure (such as the baptistery or martyrium) also acquired more imposing designs appropriate to their liturgical function, while the long-established repertoire of Christian symbolism was itself deployed to inspire, and give enhanced meaning to, particular architectural schemes.

Such symbolism was also freely employed in the decorative schemes that became a dominant feature of Christian sanctuaries. In contrast to most pagan ritual, Christian worship was a corporate act normally carried out indoors, and that was not only a major factor in the adoption of the basilica form but determined the emphasis on its internal aspect. The interiors of the principal churches were lavishly adorned and

The Basilica of SS Giovanni e Paolo, Rome. It was probably built at the beginning of the fifth century by Pammachius, a prominent senator.

sumptuously furnished, to provide a dazzling visual accompaniment to the now elaborate ceremonial, in which there was an increasing physical differentiation of clergy and laity; and the insignia and dress of the clergy themselves assumed a quasi-magisterial distinction. The Church itself and its services, festivals, parades and processions became a form of religious theatre, designed to impress and to awe, and to encapsulate the universal power and meaning of its mysteries.

Its new public dimension, with rapidly increasing wealth and status, posed also the question of the Church's relations with the state. The Church did not intervene directly in the political order. Church sermons, for example, regularly avoided even the most urgent political topics. Yet churchmen could not remain indifferent to the political world. Emperors from Constantine on took an active interest in Church affairs, seeing it as their duty to ensure that orthodoxy was established and defended. In their turn churchmen had from the outset sought to engage the emperor in their own concerns and disputes, in which questions of doctrine became increasingly intertwined with issues of power and status between the major sees, particularly in the east. Major Church appointments were often a key instrument in such conflicts and could be the focus of bloody competition. And the more general defence and advancement of the interests of his Church made it important for a bishop to retain influence with the secular power and to maintain as extensive a network of powerful contacts as he could.

At the same time bishops became men of some significance in their own right, not least those in the major capitals, who were likely to be in close and regular contact with members of the imperial family and court. They could become important channels of patronage and their religious authority could make them particularly suitable as emissaries or intermediaries of the government. At the local level also bishops were naturally involved in the life of their communities. The Church itself may be a focus of civic pride and identity. The fourth century especially saw the rapid spread of the cults of saints and martyrs, reverenced as local patrons and protectors and paraded as local heroes. Much local munificence was now funnelled into church-building and other religious expenditure. Church services became an important focus of communal life in which all members of the community, of whatever status, participated. As the old civic political leadership was progressively eroded in many places, bishops frequently emerged as the real leaders of their community. They would engage in local benefactions, dispense patronage, petition the local governor or central authorities, seek redress for local grievances (individual or collective) and might even organize defence against external attack or negotiate with barbarians.

All this, however, was conducted within the context of the existing socio-political framework, which Christianity never sought to modify in any serious fashion. Indeed, St Augustine (354–430) could use the defence of that order as a major argument for the suppression of the one major Christian sect (the Pelagians) who did subject it to radical criticism. Although offering some distinctive moral teaching, the Church had long lived at the margins of organized communal life and its priorities had always been individual salvation and the life to come. As a consequence (and to avoid further jeopardizing its survival), it had accepted the existing political and social structures of the cities and the empire itself (which, as even Augustine implicitly recognized, had provided an essential framework for the Church's growth). That policy was inevitably maintained once Christianity spread among the élite classes.

Admittedly, sources of social and political tension remained. A long-standing strain of Christian thought continued to regard service in political office or the army as incompatible with Christian principles. The Christian exaltation of charitable giving could conflict with the normal patterns of property transmission. Individuals like Paulinus of Nola (*c.* 353–431) could be tempted to abandon a public career in favour of a purely Christian vocation. The frequent identification of Christian faith as the source of military victory by emperors and others meant that for the first time Christianity had to be justified in terms of its contribution to the success of the ruling power. This was a subject which provoked bitter pagan comment after Alaric's sack of Rome and prompted Augustine in turn to produce a critical and revisionist account of Rome's history and its significance in his *City of God*. Moreover, though the Church's power was not yet such as to challenge that of the secular authorities (even the papacy was still largely preoccupied with establishing its own primacy within the Church itself), its wealth, personnel and scale of operation made it potentially a force to be reckoned with; and the temporary excommunication and regime of public penitence which Ambrose (*c.* 337–97), the imperious bishop of Milan, imposed on Theodosius I after a massacre at Thessalonica in 390 showed how the Church might use its independent moral authority and its own autonomous instruments to brand, chastise or coerce the powerful.

As yet, however, such conflicts were exceptional, and the Church's own influence on political decision-making and policy remained extremely restricted. There was a little imperial legislation on matters on which Christian teaching had always been insistent (for example, the abolition of gladiatorial games), but even in some of these areas emperors stopped short of a thoroughgoing implementation of Christian principles, and some of their measures were only slowly put into effect (gladiatorial games survived in the west until the end of the fourth century). In general the legislation, policies and actions of emperors seem singularly unaffected by their Christian professions. This was not due simply, or even primarily, to political weakness on the Church's part, but rather to a general indifference to questions of institutional reform. Thus, although there were occasional protests at oppression of the poor or the perceived victimization of Catholic communities, and although large numbers of charitable institutions were created from Church funds and private endowments to relieve the individual hardship of the sick, the poor and the orphaned, there was no attack on the social order and its injustices as such. Indeed, one prelate could urge on the wealthy the advantages of churches as an instrument by which to strengthen control of their workforce, while other landowners helped to finance them as a form of personal investment.

Latin Literature

In its earliest phases Latin literature was entirely inspired by Greek and it remained heavily indebted to Greek models. Livius Andronicus (*c.* 240–207 BC), the 'father' of Latin literature, was himself a Greek, reputedly from Tarentum, and wrote Latin adaptations of Homer's *Odyssey* and of Greek tragedies and comedies. Such adaptations, performed in Greek dress and with a notional Greek setting, rapidly became a staple element in public dramatic performances from the late third century, but their dependence on Greek predecessors did not preclude individuality of treatment, as the surviving comedies of Plautus (died 184 BC) and Terence (*c.* 190–159 BC) show. Plautus' work is characterized by a free combination of material from different Greek originals, a replacement of the complexities of a tightly-knit plot with a rapid sequence of individual scenes, a colourful riot of exuberantly inventive language and imagery and an importation of a Roman dimension to this loosely delineated Greek world through unsystematic allusion to Roman practices, institutions, values and ideas. In contrast, Terence eschews Plautus' boisterous dramatic style and Roman imports for a more universal treatment in which details of plot construction, the careful depiction of the characters and their relationships, a greater refinement of language and accommodation to the modes of colloquial speech are all central concerns. As was always true of Latin literature, the extensive use of earlier literary material (increasingly Latin as well as Greek) did not exclude an individual creative voice.

Alongside versions of Greek originals there were also specifically Roman comedies and specifically Roman historical dramas, but the most significant original Latin compositions were in epic. Here the initial themes were nationalistic. Cn. Naevius (died 201 BC) wrote a celebratory narrative of the First Punic War, but this was rapidly overshadowed by the *Annales* of Q. Ennius (239–169 BC), which chronicled Rome's history from its origins to Ennius' own day. For all its characteristically Roman solemnity and power of style and

The theatre at Leptis Magna in present-day Libya. The statue is of Sabina, wife of the emperor Hadrian (117–38).

language, the mode of the *Annales* showed strong Greek influence. Ennius not merely adopted the conventions of Homeric epic but asserted that Homer's soul had passed into him. His narrative focus and technique show clear Hellenistic traits and he claimed that, in contrast to the primitive rusticity of his Latin predecessors, he had acquired the expert knowledge associated with the Greek scholar-poets of urban Alexandria. All this did more than establish Ennius' own poetic credentials; it also implied that Rome's history was a subject on which the full resources of the Greek literary tradition could be properly deployed and that it was a subject worthy of Homer himself. But that Greek literary framework served a specifically Roman ideology. The predominantly military narrative celebrated Rome's victories and largely minimized her defeats. It reiterated the fundamental importance of Rome's own moral, political and religious traditions. And it both celebrated the deeds of individual Roman aristocrats and endorsed the aristocratic goals of individual renown and status, won through the service of the commonwealth, above all in war.

In its broad adherence to prevailing Roman norms and values, particularly those of the aristocracy, the *Annales* is typical of early Latin literature in general, seldom advocating alternative values, questioning traditional ideas or challenging the socio-political hierarchy. The early poets themselves were all outsiders in some sense (both Livius Andronicus and Terence, for example, were ex-slaves) and all of more or less low status. They had every reason to accommodate themselves to the pre-eminence and ethos of the aristocracy, particularly in works intended for a popular audience. Indeed, they and their views were likely to receive a hearing only in so far as they served, or at least did not conflict with, the dominant ideology. And if, like Ennius, they wished sometimes to explore unconventional viewpoints, this was best done by subsuming them within a more conventional framework or by confining them to works for a more restricted and potentially sympathetic audience.

Although some aristocrats maintained a posture of suspicion or antagonism towards Greek culture and its potentially disruptive and enervating effects, both the writing and the reading of literature became increasingly a part of élite culture. Prose writing of all kinds was largely monopolized by senators and much of it was directly relevant to their own public activities and concerns. History (initially written in Greek and partly to justify the ways of Rome to a Greek audience) required political and military experience, commonly reflected the outlook and concerns of the aristocracy as a whole and celebrated the exploits of its individual members. Political biography, autobiography and personal memoir became popular forms of individual aristocratic propaganda, of which Caesar's account of his Gallic campaigns and the initial stages of the civil war are a particularly artful and refined example. Works on law and estate farming rehearse essentially élite interests and expertise. Oratory, the lifeblood of both political and forensic argument and persuasion, was progressively refined and was destined to find its greatest exponent in the person of Cicero.

There were few senators among the great poets of Rome, but already in the late second century we encounter the first major poet of equestrian status: C. Lucilius (died 102/1 BC) from Suessa Aurunca on the southern border of Latium and a friend of high Roman aristocrats, including the younger Scipio (185/4–129 BC). Lucilius adapted the poetic medley essentially as a vehicle for individual self-expression in a way that only his own status and connections permitted. His 'Satires' explored diverse facets of the poet's own experiences, attitudes, views and culture with exuberant verve, and their attacks on major political figures of the day themselves exemplified the uninhibited freedom of speech enjoyed by members of the élite.

The increasing literary culture of the élite classes went hand in hand with the progressive adoption, over the last two centuries BC, of a pattern of education which was based on the Hellenistic Greek model and conducted in Greek as well as in Latin, so that those who followed it became (to varying degrees) bilingual. The focus of such education was linguistic, literary and (increasingly) rhetorical, and it was largely limited to the affluent. Even in the imperial period there was little public subvention, particularly at the earlier stages, and such education was in any case of benefit only to those who aspired to participation in élite society (though as such it could attract the would-be socially mobile, particularly in the imperial period, when it might facilitate access to posts in the imperial administration). Partly as a result, literary culture remained first and foremost an élite accomplishment and hence of itself an important social indicator and differentiator. Though the populace at large was not entirely excluded from high literary culture, particularly through oral performances, their access to it was essentially occasional. Even when a book trade developed at Rome in the first century BC, the purchase of books would have involved a heavy outlay for the ordinary working population; most were in any case illiterate, even in the towns, and the literate skills of the minority would often have been inadequate for all but the most superficial appreciation, especially of poetry. Hence the primary audience for all poetry of any pretensions was the élite. Even most serious drama was now written to be read rather than performed. Cicero's brother Quintus once knocked up four such pieces in sixteen days while on Caesar's staff in Gaul, and the surviving tragedies of Seneca a century later were similarly designed for literary recitation rather than for the theatre.

Catullus and Lucretius

The increasingly self-conscious sophistication of Latin poetry itself enhanced its élitist character. This is particularly true of the so-called New Poets, who appeared in the 50s BC. They reacted against the turgid derivative character of contemporary epic and tragedy, and turned instead to the practices and polemics of the third-century Alexandrian poets, above all Callimachus, who had championed an essentially private, highly cerebral poetry, whose full subtleties could be appreciated only by an educated few of exquisite literary sensibility. The sole surviving representative of this coterie is Catullus (*c*. 84–54 BC). He and his friends were men of wealth and standing. A number came from northern Italy (Catullus himself was from Verona) but the capital was the focus of their literary activity and many of Catullus' poems breathe the metropolitan lifestyle and snobbish sophistication of the gilded youth of Rome. This was a highly individualistic society in which elegance, refinement, discrimination and wit are paramount and the self-absorbing pleasures, hopes, disappointments and agonies of love a recurrent preoccupation.

It is Catullus' shorter lyrical poems and epigrams that most vividly conjure up this milieu, above all the innovatory cycle of poems that explore the ebb and flow of his relationship with the aristocratic 'Lesbia' and his own, often ambiguous, emotional reactions to its successive delights and frustrations. Deceptively simple and immediate in their appeal, they are a supreme example of art concealing art. Catullus' epigrams, for example, regularly depend for their effect on a sophisticated interaction of sense, sentence structure and metrical unit, and on the opportune deployment of rhetorical and other literary devices. But it is in some of the longer, narrative poems that the 'Alexandrian' influence is most evident. What Catullus and his friends advocated, above all for narrative poetry, was the small-scale masterpiece, highly wrought with a total mastery and coordination of language and metre to achieve both elegance and precise literary effects, the result not of uncontrolled inspiration but of self-critical dedication to a highly exacting craft. The poetic focus itself was commonly on the individual episode or tableau, where the emotional reactions of the participants could be explored in depth and often expressed with dramatic intensity; elaborate structural patterns may give order and introduce a creative interweaving of diverse themes whose interrelationship is left unstated or even ambiguous; and the texture and thematic development of the poem may be enriched by a complex web of literary and mythological allusion, adaptation and reference. A full realization of such poetry's potential makes heavy demands on the listener or reader. He or she has to be alert to the implications and overtones of its often recondite allusions, to the larger narrative framework (often implied rather than stated), to the sophisticated interweaving of theme and imagery, to the manipulation of established literary motifs and forms, to the implications of its structural patterns and to its inherent tensions, ironies and ambiguities. Such poems do not yield up their secrets on a single reading; they create a sense of engagement or dialogue between author and reader, and require a correspondingly creative response.

In that such highly self-conscious literature depends on an essentially individual act of interpretation and on repeated perusal, it is much more private and bookish than traditional grand poetry, and it seems correspondingly to eschew a public, pedagogic voice. Yet a close contemporary of Catullus, Lucretius (94–55 BC), showed how a large-scale poetic discourse on the apparently unpromising theme of Epicurean physics and cosmology could become the vehicle for some of the most powerful and profound poetry in Latin. The style of his (unfinished) *On the Nature of the Universe* is elevated, rich and sonorous, with vivid descriptive power and compelling visual images. The mode is resolutely didactic. Traditional poetic myth, no less than the sexual passion and associated imagery of love poetry, is deliberately denied and reversed to highlight the distinctive character and value of Epicurus' intellectualist message. Yet at the same time there is a constant tension between the philosopher's stress on reason and the poet's emotional engagement with man's predicament. If the impassioned denunciation of the fear of death at the end of Book III consorts with the basic optimism of Epicureanism, it is more than counterbalanced by the desolate account of the great plague at Athens, with which the poem now concludes. And while Lucretius has a lively appreciation of the achievements of human civilization, few have matched his sombre despair at the futility of man's moral self-destruction, his sense of the tenuous and precarious character of human society or (most remarkable of all) his abhorrence of war.

Horace and Virgil

The Catullan poetic ideas were widely endorsed and practised by the major poets of the next generation, including Horace (65–8 BC) and Virgil (70–19 BC). But in part as a reaction to contemporary political upheavals and civil war, they and others came to espouse also a social and political role for poetry and to regard the major genres of epic and tragedy as still poetically viable. Thus in their smallness of scale and technical perfection, their subtleties of texture, their narrative techniques and their concern with individual experience and sensibility Virgil's pastoral poems, the *Eclogues*, exemplify the continuing vitality of Alexandrian/Catullan principles. Yet Virgil's pastoral does not confine itself to escapist fantasy but rather sets the conventional idealization of the countryside against the contemporary distress and dislocation caused by the land confiscations that followed the battle of Philippi (42 BC). Moreover, for all the patronizing metropolitanism of their treatment of simple rustics, the *Eclogues* are the first-known Latin poems to confront the plight of ordinary peasants, and from an Italian perspective, while the poet himself reflects on the powerlessness of poetry in the face of contemporary brutalities. Such a marginalization of poetry is itself a symptom of the loss of civilized values.

Similarly, Horace's *Conversation Pieces*, usually known as his *Satires*, and also published in the 30s, espouse Catullan principles of poetic composition but employ them for an overtly didactic purpose, in a characteristically urbane, detached, often ironic exploration of individual ethics and the pursuit of personal well-being. For Horace the composition of such poetry is itself a social act (and therefore subject to moral

Virgil, the poet who celebrated Roman imperial power.

constraints), and the disciplined, self-critical qualities of writing it requires offer significant parallels to the proper approach to conduct in general. Such ethical questions remained an important preoccupation of Horace's later poetry also, but they were increasingly joined by more public concerns, and he, above all his contemporaries, was most explicit in seeking a role for the poet as guide and mentor of society.

After the battle of Actium (31 BC) this public dimension becomes closely associated with the celebration of the successes of Augustus and with the concerns and ideology of his regime. The most obvious manifestations are Horace's so-called Roman Odes (*Odes* III, 1–6), which set Augustus' role as a saviour-hero against the moral decay that has brought Rome to the verge of self-destruction, and Virgil's *Aeneid*, where the emperor's pacification of the world is the final summation of Roman history and of Rome's divinely ordained destiny. Such eulogies of the deeds of great men were a long and honourable poetic tradition (Greek as well as Latin), provided the subject merited it. Far from subverting its author's poetic credentials, such poetry helped to confer on the beneficiary the renown which was his due reward and which might stimulate emulation in others. Moreover, both poets clearly welcomed Augustus' proclaimed revival of moral and religious traditions, not least because it capitalized on entrenched Roman attitudes and sentiment; and though they enjoyed the generous patronage of Maecenas (died 8 BC), one of Augustus' principal aides, they cannot be reduced to hired propagandists for the new regime, nor was their work necessarily designed for immediate political purposes. Significantly, neither joined in the propaganda war between Octavian and Mark Antony in the 30s and their own poetic principles precluded rapid or superficial composition. What their poetry offered was not so much short-term political advantage as the prospect of undying fame among posterity.

Even so, their work goes far beyond uncritical eulogy of the emperor. In the *Aeneid*, for example, Augustus' own deeds are themselves subsumed within a universalizing interpretation of Roman history and of the Roman destiny as the imposition of peace and order through military conquest. More than that, the poem urges a distinctive view of the Roman identity in which the Italian dimension becomes paramount, and advances a revisionist definition of the relations between Greek and Roman. It rejects the old competitive self-assertive values of the republican aristocracy (or their Homeric counterparts) in favour of a conception of service and obedience at whatever personal cost. The poem's hero is himself a vulnerable, isolated figure, traumatized by the destruction of his city and the guilt of his own survival and brought only gradually, and at considerable personal cost, to assume the role that destiny has assigned him. In turn Juno, Dido and Turnus exemplify the self-destructive irrationality of intense emotion or frenzy, whether in the form of defiance of the decrees of Fate, passionate love, war-lust or an obsession with personal honour. Above all, the poem is shot through with a sense of individual human suffering, much of it apparently pointless. The tragedies of Dido and Turnus are not merely the ultimate outcome of divine interventions over which they have no control, but those interventions are themselves unnecessary to (indeed, in part a vain bid to frustrate) Aeneas' achievement of his mission and the realization of the Roman destiny. Even Virgil's treatment of war is complex and ambivalent. Alongside the jingoistic extolling of Rome's imposition of order through conquest, war is itself the destroyer of order. It cuts down the young on whom the future depends, yet also offers a stage for youthful prowess, devotion and self-sacrifice. Death in combat enables the deposed tyrant Mezentius to achieve a dignity and moral stature that eluded him in life; but equally the emotions and violence of war can brutalize even the normally disciplined Aeneas. There is no easy resolution of these complexities; they are all inherent in the human condition, and readers must formulate their own judgements and responses.

Propertius and Ovid

Not all Augustan literature, however, saluted the emperor's achievements or endorsed his traditionalist programme. Already in the 20s BC the love elegies of Propertius (died 16 BC) espoused a lifestyle in which there was no place for military or other public service, for conformist marriage or the procreation of future legionaries. Politics and, above all, war (itself the product of greed) are anathema to the lover; if men had adopted the poet's own predilection for women and wine, the Battle of Actium and its useless waste of Roman lives would have been avoided. Even the normal relations of social power are reversed in the lover's obsession with his mistress. Not merely does the poet become her slave, to be scorned, excluded or admitted as she chooses, but he seems sometimes to revel in his servitude.

Since Catullus such defiant non-conformism had become a familiar means whereby the poet established his credentials as a lover and the consequent individuality of his viewpoint. But such poetry did not systematically challenge the established order (on which it was in fact parasitic), nor were the humiliations and disillusionments of its lifestyle likely to prove generally attractive. And even where it betrayed scepticism about Augustan achievements or ideals, it at least took them seriously.

The same cannot be said of Ovid (43 BC–AD 17), who could adopt a more subtly subversive mode, in which an undercurrent of mockery is often a key constituent. Ovid's poetry consistently displays a determined metropolitan modernity of outlook, and he himself took the unprecedented step of deliberately rejecting a public career in favour of poetry as a surer route to immortality. His extensive output served above all as a demonstration of his own literary virtuosity. In the *Amores*, for example, the love elegy and its conventions become the vehicle for literary play; and the illusion of a real affair engendering profound emotions gives way to an admiration of the literary elegance, sophistication and sensibility of the poet himself.

It is, however, the *Metamorphoses* that represent Ovid's art at its highest and most complex. Like all his poetry (and that of Propertius), it is heavily indebted to the Alexandrian-Catullan traditions, in subject matter and narrative mode as well as in the apparently effortless perfectionism of its technique. Metamorphosis myths were themselves a favourite Alexandrian subject, appealing to the taste for the bizarre and permitting a detailed exploration of individual psychology. Ovid follows that lead, not least in exploiting themes (such as rape and incest) that were largely avoided in poetry which purported to deal with the real world. The work has a loose chronological progression and a variety of structural devices link together individual sequences of stories, but there is no overriding theme, or central moral or psychological concern. Although there are passages of intense emotion and percipient observation, the immediacy and self-contained character of Ovid's narrative serve principally to entertain the reader through a succession of episodes, each elaborated in its own right but also integrated into a poem which flamboyantly flaunts traditional epic conventions and concerns. Throughout the work variety of manner and mood is pervasive. Ovid regularly shifts stance and tone within an individual narrative, so that the reader is constantly aware of the storyteller's own role, and the poem itself celebrates the poet's autonomy within his own universe. Feats of literary bravura, sophisticated remodelling of early literary material, rhetorical *tours de force*, irrepressible resourcefulness of narrative and verbal invention, all manner of literary conceits and the constant suffusion of literary wit similarly keep the narrator at the forefront of our attention. Ovid has himself become a second Orpheus.

Tacitus and Lucan

In 8 Ovid was exiled to Tomis on the Black Sea coast, principally for his presence at some scandalous incident affecting the imperial house. Additionally, however, his *Art of Love* was belatedly held against him, presumably for its flippant and frivolous dismissal of traditional concerns and morality. There followed sundry attempts to suppress other literary works regarded as subversive (initially writings abusive of men of rank, subsequently attacks on the deified Augustus and his successor, Tiberius). Such action was not wholly successful and was largely discontinued after 24, but the warning was clear and in relation to the reigning emperor self-censorship became the norm, at least in mainstream literature.

As a result, political dissent took refuge in the past. Historians (still usually senators) were particularly assiduous in extorting posthumous revenge on rulers deemed hostile to the senatorial class. The effects are still visible in the surviving portions of the account of the years 14 to 96 written by Tacitus (born *c.* 56), who was a senator himself and largely relied on sources which adopted a senatorial viewpoint. Yet despite this narrowness of perspective, his *Annals* and *Histories* afford by far the most penetrating political analysis to be written in Latin. Magisterial in their command and deployment of their material, they are unremitting in their dissection of the character of autocratic rule, the reversal of traditional social values, norms and relationships which it engendered, and the ethico-political dilemmas it posed, above all for the Senate and its individual members. Immune from illusions about the realities and pretensions of power, sombre in their prevailing mood, Tacitus' works none the less evince a resolute belief in individual dignity, courage and integrity, even in the most adverse circumstances. Above all they represent some of the most powerful prose ever written in Latin: language, sentence structure, forms of thought and expression are integrated into a dramatic style of intense and vigorous grandeur that is at the same time subtly modulated according to the historian's own narrative concerns and objectives.

If Tacitus makes little specific reference to his own times, other literature (biography or memoir, drama or epic) might use the past more directly for contemporary commentary. In particular the Stoic martyr of the dying republic, the younger Cato (95–46 BC), or the Stoic victims of Nero and Vespasian might be commemorated in terms that implicitly criticized the current regime and promoted their heroes as role models for contemporary senators. For all its ostensible initial eulogy of Nero, the unfinished epic on the civil war between Caesar and Pompey by Lucan (39–65) belongs in this category, reflecting its author's own growing political disillusionment. In his *Civil War* (or *Pharsalia*) Caesar's victories usher in a tyranny under which Lucan's own generation still lives. The poem is pervaded by a sense of the overturning of the established order, natural as well as political, at the behest of a capricious and malevolent Fortune; and that sense is reinforced by the author's own baroque reversal or denial of the conventions, motifs and disciplines of Virgilian epic. The poles of Lucan's simplistic political ideology are represented by Cato and Caesar, who are transformed into mythic symbols of an interlocking complex of moral and political antitheses (freedom and tyranny, virtue and material success, public service and personal ambition, real self-knowledge and megalomaniac self-deception); and if Nero does not lurk directly behind Lucan's Caesar, he remains by implication Caesar's political heir.

The Social Context of Early Imperial Literature

Dissent of this type was essentially political, senatorial and focused on the conduct of the emperor. Far from challenging the traditional order, it tended to assume its essential rectitude and all literature continued to reflect traditional aristocratic values, even when not written by senators. Poets were themselves commonly drawn from the local élites, first of Italy and then of southern Gaul, Spain and Africa, and many were, or became, equestrians. Far from questioning the established social hierarchy, what they sought was their own advancement within it. As with others who strove for enhancement of status, the patronage of the powerful was an important means to this end. Indeed, their literary talents may be only one of a complex of factors that enable such men to secure patronage and determine its (highly variable) form. Such patronage was not regarded as compromising the writer's integrity. The notion that the poet should speak without regard to his personal situation or to those to whom he was indebted was largely absent. The poet's work could not be divorced from his social context and obligations, and some literature was written directly in the interests of patrons – not merely laudatory epic or historical drama, but a wide range of occasional poems and complimentary verses, such as the *Silvae* of Statius (*c.* 45–96) or many of the epigrams of Martial (*c.* 40–104). In other instances, however, dedicatory references sufficed, as in Statius' mythological epics; and though patronage doubtless encouraged much second-rate versifying, it cannot be held generally accountable for the deficiences of imperial literature.

Alongside the patronage of men of literary talent and ambition, the social dimension of literary culture was further emphasized in the development of recitation. From the outset most Latin poetry was written partly or principally with a view to oral performance, and formal or informal reading to friends or to a wider audience was a long-established practice. From the late first century BC this became institutionalized in the *recitatio*, an organized reading to an élite audience, which became an increasingly central aspect of cultural life, with attendance itself often a social obligation. Not surprisingly, writers increasingly composed with a view to recitation, by which their reputations might be most gratifyingly established. This was not always beneficial to their work. Not only aural effects but the pursuit of the arresting, the pointed and the witty acquired a higher priority; overall structure and coherence might be sacrificed to the composition of purple passages; and immediacy of literary effect could be preferred to subtle elegance and allusion and to the complex interweaving of recurrent imagery and theme.

These tendencies were reinforced by the growing influence of rhetoric. Despite the emasculation of political oratory which the establishment of the imperial system entailed, forensic and other forms of rhetoric remained a major instrument of social and political advancement, the study of rhetoric assumed an increasingly dominant role in élite education, and rhetorical expertise, demonstrated through showpiece declamations, became a valued accomplishment in its own right. Inevitably, the modes of thought, forms and techniques of rhetoric came to exercise a pervasive influence on literature of all kinds. At its best rhetorical education could inculcate a clear analysis and careful deployment of complex material, sophistication of thought, argument and expression, a keen sense of stylistic and linguistic nuance, imaginative identification with situation and character, a rich repertoire of literary resources of all kinds, and clarity and succinctness of narrative style. In practice its effects were often less salutary. It encouraged concentration on the immediately striking at the expense of real intellectual engagement or the subtle coordination of structure, theme and imagery. It fostered the tendency to see literary composition in terms of the novelty and skill with which stock motifs were handled; the writer's perceptions could readily become the prisoner of rhetorical stereotypes; and an often superficial ingenuity of thought supplanted any attempt to grapple with the complexities of profound and serious issues. Above all, the rhetorical mode inspired the adoption of a clearly defined didactic stance in which there was little room for the ambivalences, tensions and ambiguities that had been so central a feature of some of the best Latin poetry. The effects are perhaps most clearly seen in the tragedies of Seneca and in Lucan's *Civil War*, where the rhetoric creates immense declamatory colour, dynamic and power, yet also fosters a harsh, externalized, didactic mode and a one-dimensional shallowness of thought. These are very much works for declamatory performance and concomitant immediacy of impact.

In the central role accorded to rhetoric in literary composition, as in so much else, Ovid had been very much the pivotal figure. His *Letters from Heroines*, for example, are themselves a poetic version of a well-established rhetorical exercise. No less significant was Ovid's exploitation of the sense of literary composition as an autonomous act. Ovid's projection of the poet's role in orchestrating his material made it difficult to recapture a sense of immediate engagement with real experiences, especially in personal poetry, and it further encouraged the sense that, though poetry might draw on real life, it operated in a self-contained domain that possessed its own traditions, imperatives and dynamics. In the novelist Petronius or the satirist Juvenal (*c.* 60–130) this can be exploited successfully by the exercise of a rare and distinctive literary wit. But it could also lead to much derivative versification, sometimes bordering on pastiche.

Literary attitudes and educational practice tended to foster such verse. The emphasis on individual authors as the model exemplars of their genres might encourage a potentially sterile classicism, which the minute attention paid to 'proprieties' of language, style and characterization would only reinforce. Established conventions and stock themes offered a ready formula for writing in a given genre without the need for real creative imagination. An obsessive concern with individual verbal effects and the detailed articulation of individual thought tempted writers to see these as pre-eminent concerns, at the expense of serious intellectual engagement. Above all, only in the best writers is there a real sense of response to a creative challenge, whether in terms of style, form, mode, material or viewpoint. Yet the literature of the age cannot be uniformly dismissed as second-rate. Lucan, Juvenal, Petronius and, above all, Tacitus are serious literary artists of high calibre, and their lesser contemporaries are not all negligible.

The Late Imperial Period

Juvenal was the last major Latin poet for over two centuries and most forms of secular Latin prose found few practitioners of note before the mid-fourth century. This is not simply a matter of the quality of the literature which was written. It must in part result from the second-century archaizing reaction against the dominant literary tendencies of the early principate, from a decline in the value attached to contemporary composition of poetic and other work in Latin, and from a diminished perception of such composition as a channel of social advancement. It was not until the fourth century that secular Latin literature saw a major revival, and this was itself perhaps primarily a response to the progressive division of the empire between east and west, and to the need to express in cultural terms a Roman identity that had barely survived the third-century crises and was still under barbarian threat. For a number of senators scholarship and letters became an integral element in a highly cultivated and distinctive lifestyle, in which studied formalism and elegance were highly valued and consciously pursued as part of the etiquette of aristocratic life. But their literary culture was also a bridge, over the chasm of the third century, to the traditions of an earlier Rome in which they sought their own cultural identity and whose perpetuation was synonymous with the survival of Rome itself. Both the major secular poet of the period (Claudian (died 404)) and the last great Roman historian (Ammianus Marcellinus (*c.* 330–95)) exemplify this tendency, all the more notably in that both were Greek by birth. In Ammianus a specifically Roman ideology determines his admiration for the city of Rome itself, his preoccupation with the survival of the Roman empire and his emphasis on the recapture of traditional virtues as the key to the achievement of that objective. Claudian similarly proclaims a traditional ideal of Rome and Roman virtue derived from the Latin classics and, like Ammianus, readily cites great figures of the republican and imperial past as a yardstick for the conduct of contemporaries. Indeed, Claudian's verse itself could almost be mistaken for that of an earlier age, so heavily indebted are his style, language, metrical and narrative techniques to Virgil, Ovid and their immediate successors.

Claudian spent most of his career in the west at the court in Milan, in the service of Honorius and, more especially, Honorius' chief minister, Stilicho. Patronage of Latin letters was no longer restricted to senators at Rome. Court circles sought cultural legitimation by the pursuit and encouragement of letters; provincial aristocrats frequently regarded literary attainments as part of their socio-cultural identity; and literary talent was again an instrument of advancement. Yet much of the literature of the period is essentially undemanding, and its restricted capacity for a profound engagement with personal issues is most forcibly exemplified by the convention that excluded all Christian reference, even where the writer was himself a believer. By contrast, Christian writing necessarily confronted what it saw as the real problems of the human condition, and much of the most significant Latin literature of the middle and late empire is that of Christian exponents. In prose the pioneer was Tertullian (170–212), who sought to legitimize Christian belief and practice by the deployment of a vast erudition and the classical rhetorical strategies of argument in a characteristically vigorous, mordant style. In poetry the most significant figure was Prudentius (348–after 405). He likewise adopted the language, metrical norms and techniques of the great pagan poets (whom he frequently echoes) but his organization of material and subject matter again reflects specifically Christian concerns and practice, and he employs a complex Christian symbolism and a distinctively Christian form of allegory that was entirely alien to classical poetic practice.

In their different ways Tertullian and Prudentius exemplify the ambiguities that characterized Christian attitudes to classical culture, which could easily be represented as a threat to the purity of the faith. Yet it was Christian practices and institutions which preserved the great classical writers. Already in the fourth century their works were being transcribed from (largely papyrus) rolls on to the (largely vellum) codex which Christians had used for ease of reference in their own writings from the first century AD. And when the western empire disintegrated, it was monasteries and cathedrals that became the repositories of the Latin classical inheritance. Much was lost and the survival of some works was tenuous. Yet enough remains to justify Ovid's defiant faith in his chosen art:

> Even rocks, even the enduring ploughshare,
> Perish with age, but poetry lives on, untouched
> by death.

THE EMPIRES OF PERSIA

A head of Darius I (521–486 BC), from the Bisitun relief. In 490 BC his attack on Greece was thwarted by the Athenians and their allies, the Plataeans, at Marathon.

Chronology

BC

559 Cyrus II (the Great) enthroned as a vassal of the Median king Astyages

550 Having united the Persian tribes, Cyrus overthrows Astyages and conquers Media

547 Cyrus defeats Croesus, king of Lydia, and subdues the Greek cities of Ionia

539–538 Conquest of Babylon

526–525 Cambyses II conquers Egypt

522 Darius I (the Great) enthroned
He puts down the 'great rebellion', annexes north-western India (518), starts building Persepolis (515) and attacks Scythians beyond the Danube (513)

499–494 Ionian Revolt

490 Battle of Marathon ends in first Persian defeat

486 Death of Darius and succession of Xerxes

485 Xerxes crushes Egyptian rebellion, then another in Babylonia (482)

480–479 Persian invasion of Greece
Battles of Thermopylae and Salamis (480) and Plataea (479) repulse the invaders

459–454 Rebellion in Egypt

449 By the Peace of Callias the independence of the Greek cities of Ionia was guaranteed, Persian suzerainty over Cyprus recognized and hostilities ended between Athens and the King of Kings

431–404 The Peloponnesian War
After the failure of the Athenian expedition to Sicily (413), Persia switches sides and backs Sparta with gold
From 407 onwards the Spartans and Persian satraps combine militarily against Athens

424 Xerxes II, son of Artaxerxes I (464–425), killed in a drunken brawl
Palace intrigue rife
The murderer executed by his successor, Darius II (423–404)

401 The Spartans gave backing to Cyrus, the brother of Artaxerxes II and their ally in Asia Minor against Athens

400 The death of Cyrus leads to a war between Sparta and Persia
For a time Artaxerxes II tries to reconquer Ionia
In 394 the Athenian admiral Conon, who was in the pay of the Persians, sinks the Spartan fleet off Cnidus

386 The King's Peace
A partly restored Athens, along with a weakened Sparta, forced to accept Persian domination of the Greek cities of Ionia

343 The restoration of Egypt to the Persian empire after a rebellion lasting from 405

338 Battle of Chaeronea makes Macedon supreme in Greece
The victor, Philip II, announces a pan-Hellenic invasion of Persia

336 Accession of Darius III, the last Achaemenid king
He suppresses yet another Egyptian revolt

334 Battle at Granicus River opens the Asian campaign of Alexander the Great

330 Persepolis fired by Alexander's order
The fugitive Darius murdered by his own followers

The Achaemenids (559–330 BC)

T. Cuyler Young, Jr

History

Some would argue that the Achaemenid or first Persian empire represents the last ancient West Asian state; others insist that Cyrus the Great's conquest of Babylon was the beginning of something entirely new. Whichever position one prefers, it remains certain that important and lasting changes in the history of both West Asia and Europe have their origins in Achaemenid times.

For the first time in history almost all of West Asia was united politically. The Persian empire surpassed in size any previous polity in the region: the Great King's writ ran from central Asia to Libya and from the western shores of the Black Sea to the banks of the Indus. The Achaemenids also introduced, with much success, entirely new ways of ruling. Thus a convincing argument can be made that the Persians created the first true empire in the Mediterranean world.

Finally, and most importantly, Europe and West Asia were brought into contact in ways and with an intensity never experienced before. Greeks in Asia Minor and in Europe itself came under direct Persian rule for long periods of time. The Persians were actively engaged militarily in Europe for almost 100 years, beginning in the late sixth century BC, and Persian political and diplomatic involvement in Europe continued to the end of the empire. Furthermore, Asians and Europeans travelled regularly back and forth between the two continents throughout Achaemenid times. The modern forms of both Europe and West Asia had their birth in the Hellenistic period, following the conquest of the Persian empire by Alexander the Great. It can be argued that those forms had their gestation period in Achaemenid times.

The Early Achaemenids

Cyrus II (559–530 BC) and Darius I (521–486 BC) both provide us in their inscriptions with a genealogy of the early Achaemenids. Cyrus says that he is the son of Cambyses, the son of Cyrus, the descendant of Teispes. Darius reports that he is the son of Hystaspes, the son of Arsames; and that Arsames' father was Ariaramnes, the son of Teispes, whose father was Achaemenes. Darius also informs us that he is the ninth of the Achaemenid family to rule in Persia.

A comparison of the two genealogies raises serious historical problems. Ariaramnes and Arsames, whom Darius claims were kings, must have been roughly contemporary with the kings Cyrus I and Cambyses I in the genealogy of Cyrus II. This means that the family of Achaemenes must have ruled two kingdoms prior to Cyrus II. None of the proposed solutions of this puzzle is entirely satisfactory. Our inability to document any of the early kings listed outside of these two genealogies is critical. Some argue that Cyrus I is mentioned in a cuneiform record from the time of Ashurbanipal of Assyria, and that he is also the original owner of an inscribed cylinder seal which appears in impressions on the so-called Fortification Texts from Persepolis, but both of these identifications can be challenged. The gold tablets from Hamadan naming Arsames and Ariaramnes are forgeries. Finally, we are left with only the statements of Cyrus and Darius regarding their ancestors.

Probably in the end the contradictions need not disturb us greatly. Kings sometimes have difficulty keeping their genealogies straight and, furthermore, they often find it useful to alter them for political purposes. Darius, a usurper, may well have done just that; Cyrus had no such need. This may also explain why Cyrus apparently had no knowledge of the namesake for the dynasty, Achaemenes.

According to the Greek historian Herodotus, when Cyrus the Great came to the throne of Persia in 559 BC he was a vassal of Astyages, king of the Medes. The Medes, another Iranian people, were one of the four principal powers of West Asia. Allied with Babylon in the overthrow of the Neo-Assyrian empire, they had shared the spoils of that victory. They ruled over much of the Iranian plateau, traditionally controlled Anatolia westward to the Halas River, and may have been masters of parts of northern Mesopotamia and Syria.

The Lydians, controlling western Asia Minor, the Egyptians and the Babylonians were the other three major powers of the day. Peace had been maintained in the area since the fall of Nineveh in 612 BC because these four great powers were relatively equally matched. However, this delicate balance was about to be totally broken by the arrival of Cyrus and the Persians on the international scene. Within twenty years of coming to the throne, Cyrus would defeat Astyages and the Medes, overrun most of the eastern Iranian world as far as the borders of India, conquer Lydia and the Greek city-states of Ionia, and overwhelm the Babylonians.

Cyrus' first step on this road of conquest was to unite under his leadership all of the various tribes of Persia and south-western Iran. His local power thus expanded and ensured, war broke out between the Medes and the Persians. Unfortunately, our sources on the war between Cyrus and Astyages are somewhat contradictory. Herodotus naturally reports that it was Cyrus who rebelled against his Median overlord. The Babylonian sources for these events, on the other hand, do not mention Cyrus as a Median vassal, and the Babylonian Chronicle specifically states that Astyages attacked the Persians. In any case, all sources agree

A cylinder with cuneiform inscription of a proclamation issued by Cyrus the Great (559–530 BC), founder of Achaemenid power.

that the battle, which occurred in 550 BC, was short because the majority of Median troops deserted to the Persians. Thus power on the plateau passed from one Iranian group to another. However, because the Medes became so closely allied with the Persians in their rise to world domination, the Greeks often had difficulty distinguishing between the two.

In 547 BC Croesus, king of Lydia, invaded Cappadocia. Cyrus reacted immediately and marched westward through northern Mesopotamia and into Asia Minor. An indecisive battle was fought in Cappadocia, after which, since it was November, Croesus decided that the campaign season was over. He withdrew to Sardis, disbanded his non-Lydian troops, and sent messengers to Sparta, Egypt and Babylon requesting military help in the spring. But Cyrus continued to march westwards and, after winning a brief cavalry battle before Sardis, laid siege to the Lydian king in the city's citadel. The Persians discovered a way to climb to an undefended section of the walls and, after a daring assault, captured the citadel, Croesus and presumably all of his famous gold. The Greek cities of Ionia appealed to Cyrus for clemency, which he refused, with the apparent exception of Miletus. Cyrus then returned to the east, leaving his Median general, Harpagus, in command. He soon subdued Ionia, with the result that the whole of Asia Minor was now firmly under Achaemenid control.

For some seven years following the conquest of Lydia our sources on Cyrus are silent. Probably during this period he extended his kingdom in the east. Parthia, Drangiana, Aria, Chorasmia, Bactria, Sogdiana, Gandhāra, Scythia, Sattagydia, Arachosia and Maka were most probably conquests of Cyrus. On reaching Gandhāra, modern Afghanistan, he had marched his troops as far to the east from Persia as Lydia was to the west.

In the meantime, Cyrus mounted a very effective propaganda campaign in Babylon in order to facilitate its eventual conquest. Nabonidus, king of Babylon, had managed to lose both the respect and the affection of his people. A fanatical devotee of the Mesopotamian moon god Sin, he consistently neglected to perform the necessary religious rituals involving Marduk, which the Babylonians knew were essential to their economic and spiritual survival. He was also usually resident in Teima in north Arabia rather than in Babylon. Nabonidus' behaviour thus created a climate of opinion in Babylon which was easy for Cyrus to exploit. The success of the Persian propaganda campaign is perhaps best recorded in second Isaiah, where the great Hebrew prophet declares that Cyrus has been chosen by the Lord to conquer Babylon and to permit the Jews to return to their homeland. Clearly a similar message was conveyed to the people of Babylon: if you will open the gates of your city to me I will, unlike Nabonidus, be a faithful servant of the god Marduk and a proper king for the Babylonians.

In October 539 BC, Cyrus marched into Mesopotamia with one wing of his army under the command of Ugbaru, possibly a Babylonian deserter. The only battle, a Persian victory, occurred at Opis early in the same month. Ugbaru was dispatched to Babylon, which he entered unopposed on 12 October. Again without a battle, Cyrus had taken the important city of Sippar two days earlier. Nabonidus was captured after fleeing to Babylon, and Ugbaru stood guard over the city until Cyrus entered it at the end of the month.

The Babylonian Chronicle records how Ugbaru controlled the city so peacefully and so well that all religious festivals were properly observed. Thus when Cyrus entered the city he was received with considerable rejoicing. The king then proceeded to do exactly what he had promised. He performed the necessary royal rituals to ensure the prosperity and well-being of the city, announced himself as the legitimate king of Babylon chosen by Marduk himself, and assumed the traditional Babylonian royal title. Cyrus returned to all the cities of Mesopotamia the statues of their gods which Nabonidus had gathered up and collected in Babylon. In 538 BC Cyrus installed his son, Cambyses, in his stead as king of Babylon, and Cambyses is reported by the Babylonian scribe to have performed all of the ancient and necessary rituals prescribed for a true Babylonian king. That same year Cyrus issued his famous decree, recorded in Ezra (I:1–4), permitting the Jews to return to their homeland and rebuild their temple.

Our sources are entirely silent on the last eight years of the life of Cyrus. It is logical to assume that he spent the time putting in place those government mechanisms needed to rule so vast an empire. Yet we cannot speak with any certainty on such developments. What we do know is that Cyrus' policy for the governance of the empire was one of remarkable tolerance, as demonstrated by his treatment of the Medes, the Babylonians and the Jews. In short, his policy was such that if you paid your taxes, gave appropriate homage to the Great King, were a loyal subject of the empire and, in some cases, did your military service, you were permitted to maintain your own customs, and to a considerable extent your own forms of government and law. The vision was of a partnership in empire. This policy remained in force, with notably few exceptions, to the end of the empire.

Herodotus reports that Cyrus died fighting against the tribe of the Massagetae on the north-eastern frontier of the empire. In a reign of just under thirty years this king, undoubtedly the greatest of the Achaemenids, had conquered the Medes, the Lydians and the Babylonians. Of the four kingdoms that held the balance of power in West Asia at the time of his accession, only Egypt remained.

Herodotus characterizes Cyrus' son and successor, Cambyses II (530–522 BC), as a madman. Among other claims, it is stated that he murdered his brother, Bardiya, before leaving for the invasion of Egypt, that he mocked Egyptian religious beliefs and that he totally neglected properly to provision military expeditions sent out from Egypt. Our primary sources on his reign, however, strongly suggest that Herodotus must have received his information from prejudiced sources, for it would appear that Cambyses was a military commander of considerable skill and that he carefully followed his father's policy of ethnic and religious tolerance.

Before coming to the throne, Cambyses had successfully ruled in Babylon, and for some years had been his father's chosen heir-apparent. The transfer of power from father to son had gone smoothly. Thus when he marched against Egypt in 525 BC, we have no reason to assume he was not a talented and worthy successor to his father.

The campaign against Egypt was well organized and swift. Apparently there was a certain degree of disaffection among the Egyptian defenders. Phanes of Halicarnassus, an officer of mercenaries in the Egyptian army, defected to Cambyses, and Uzahor-resenet, the commander of the Egyptian navy, seems to have arranged for the fleet to stay in port. Cambyses made careful plans with the Arab tribes of Gaza and the Sinai to supply water for the dangerous crossing of the desert to the eastern delta. The Persian advance went smoothly, and the invaders swiftly defeated the Egyptians at the battle of Pelusium. Egypt was then organized as a province within the Persian empire. That task, along with further military conquests, kept Cambyses in Egypt for almost three years. Persian troops captured the oasis of Kharga, but failed to take the oasis of Siwa (Ammon) thanks to an overwhelming sandstorm. A Persian drive to the west added Cyrene and Barca to the empire, but plans to capture Carthage were abandoned when the Phoenician sailors refused to attack their own colony. Cambyses himself led an expedition up the Nile into Nubia. Although Herodotus reports this as a total military disaster, our Persian sources make it perfectly clear that Kush or Nubia was firmly under Persian control in the reign of Darius. As it could have been brought into the empire only under Cambyses, his campaign can hardly, therefore, be described as a failure.

As for Cambyses' treatment of the conquered Egyptians, while it is clear that he in part reorganized the bloated and overly wealthy religious establishment,

The Persian empire of the Achaemenids on the eve of the invasion of Greece in 480 BC.

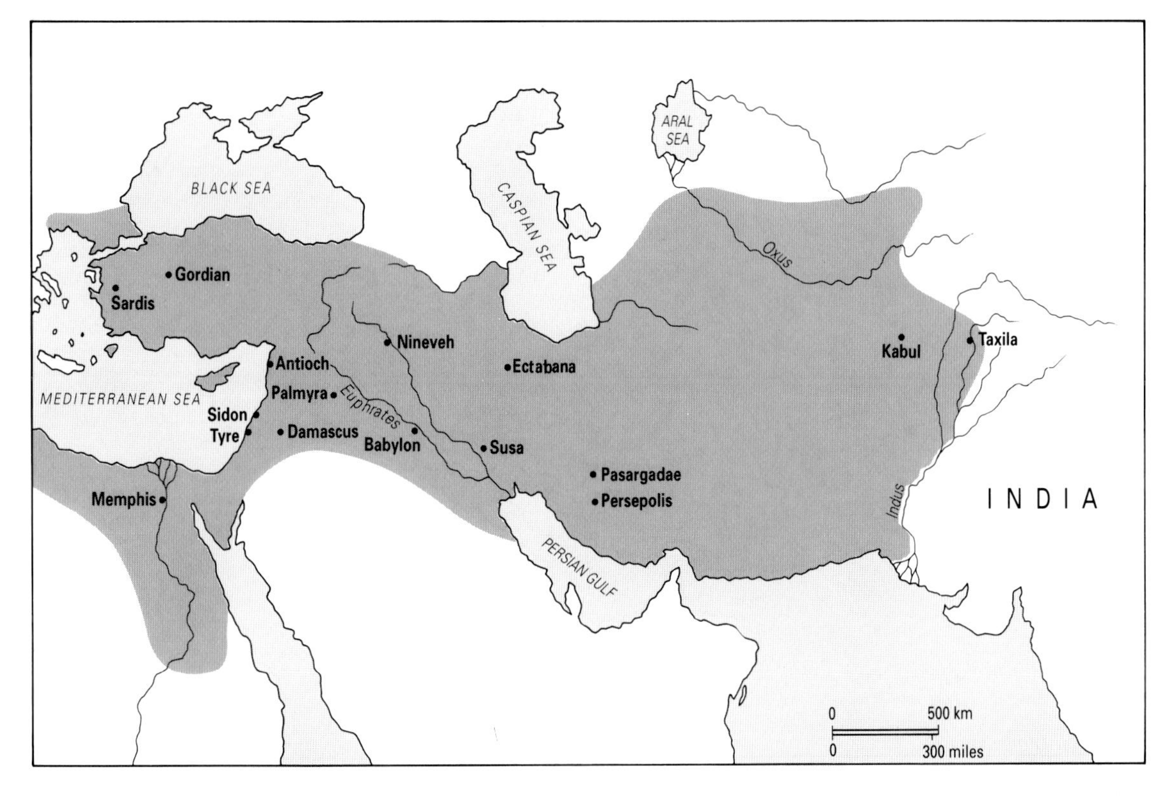

he nevertheless assumed authority in Egypt as the legitimate pharaoh. He also carefully observed both the secular and the religious rituals that accompanied that kingship. Despite Herodotus' report that he stabbed the sacred Apis bull with a sword and then laughed at the Egyptians for worshipping it as it bled to death before their eyes, there is good evidence to indicate that the Apis bull died in 524 BC when Cambyses was in Nubia, and that the next bull lived until the fourth year of his successor, Darius I. Furthermore, an inscription on the coffin of the bull tells us that Cambyses ordered it to be made in honour of his father, Apis-Osiris, and a stele which accompanied the sarcophagus records that all due honours were ordered for the bull by Cambyses, as pharaoh of Egypt. In the end, one suspects that Herodotus got his information on Cambyses in Egypt from disaffected priests who remembered Cambyses' religious reforms.

Cambyses began his return journey to Persia in 522 BC. We do not know whether he was aware that rebellion had broken out at home. Some have argued that he committed suicide on the return journey, but our Iranian sources make it clear that Herodotus' story that he died of an accidental wound caused by his sword falling from its scabbard is correct. Thus it was left to Darius to crush the rebellion in Persia and restore the Achaemenid family to kingship.

Crisis and Expansion under Darius I

Probably our only source on the rebellion of Gaumata or Bardiya (Smerdis in Greek), and on Darius' seizure of the Achaemenid kingship is the story Darius tells in his famous Bisitun inscription. Much the same story is, of course, in Herodotus, but he was most probably using as his source one of the copies of the Bisitun inscription which Darius ordered distributed throughout the empire.

On the surface the story of these events is fairly straightforward. Darius tells us that before Cambyses left for Egypt he killed his only brother, Bardiya, to forestall any rebellion in Persia during his absence. No one in Persia knew that he had done this. Gaumata, a Magian priest, then claimed that he was in fact Bardiya and stirred the people into rebellion against Cambyses. On his return to Persia Cambyses died. Darius, who had been serving in the army as bow-bearer to Cambyses, and six fellow conspirators were the only people not afraid to dispute Gaumata's claim to be Bardiya. They deposed Gaumata, who fled to Media, where he was captured and killed in the fortress of Sikayauvati in late 522 BC. The supreme Persian deity, Ahura Mazda, then bestowed the kingship on Darius, who went on to declare that he had re-established his family, the Achaemenids, restored the sanctuaries which Gaumata had destroyed, returned to the people the pastures, the herds, the household slaves and the houses which Gaumata had taken away, and 're-established the people on its foundation, both Persia and Media and the other provinces'.

Even on a simple level of analysis, however, it is difficult to separate fact from fiction in this story. In the end one concludes that while in part Darius may be telling the truth, he is at times at least doctoring that truth for his own propagandistic purposes. After all, it was his word against Gaumata's, and Gaumata was mute.

On a deeper level of analysis it is clear that extremely important events lie behind Darius' account. Clearly, whether the rebellion had been led by Bardiya or Gaumata, the empire had been shaken to its foundations, for political, social, economic and religious issues of fundamental importance were raised. First, from a political point of view there seems to have been in the event a definite element of Persian versus Mede. Gaumata is stigmatized by Darius as being a Magian, or Median priest, and in fleeing Persia he seeks sanctuary in Media. It had, after all, been less than thirty years since Cyrus the Persian defeated Astyages the Mede, and there may well have been many Medes not yet reconciled to the resultant shift in imperial power. Secondly, there seems to have been much disagreement between the protagonists on social and economic issues. Gaumata's appeal may well have been to disaffected economic and social groups within the empire. Certainly Darius and his immediate allies were all from the highest classes of society, and were supported by the regular army. There is good evidence, particularly in the Aramaic version of the Bisitun inscription, that when Darius speaks of restoring 'the people' he is not speaking of the masses of society, but rather of people of some considerable economic and social standing. And in Babylonia at least the lands which he restored were the so-called 'bow lands' awarded to military personnel for faithful service. Thus it would appear that the rebellion may well have contained an element of conflict between 'haves' and 'have-nots'. Finally, there is clearly a religious aspect to these events. Darius makes a special point of telling us that Gaumata was a Magian, a priest. Herodotus elaborates and tells us that ever after the revolt the Magi were in poor repute among the Persians. And what were the sanctuaries which Gaumata destroyed and Darius restored? Clearly, there was at least some quarrel between the factions over religious behaviour, if not theology.

Whatever the complexities of our sources, it is clear that Darius did succeed in placing himself firmly on the throne of the Achaemenids. Whether he could maintain authority over the empire, however, was an issue severely tested in the first year of his reign. Troubles at the succession had been the signal for widespread rebellion throughout the empire. Elam and Babylon were the first to declare their independence, the new native king of Babylon, Nebuchadnezzar III, being recognized at least by 3 October 522 BC, only a few days after the execution of Gautama. The rebellion in Elam collapsed quickly and Darius himself marched to Babylon with the regular army in November. Two battles were won by the Persians, and the rebellious king was captured and executed. Our first cuneiform tablet from the reign of Darius is dated 22 December

522 BC. In the meantime, however, revolts on a grand scale had broken out in Armenia, Persia, Elam, Media, Assyria, Parthia, Margiana, Sattagydia and Scythia.

Darius responded to this challenge with great skill. Independent contingents of troops were sent at once to Elam, Armenia, Media and Persia. The second revolt in Elam collapsed at once, but battles were fought in Persia, Media and Armenia which, though not decisive, managed to hold the rebels in check. In April Darius himself, presumably in command of the core of the army, went over to the offensive. He concentrated his efforts on the Median rebellion, which was probably the most dangerous. At the same time that Darius was thoroughly defeating the Medes and their rebel king, Phraortes, reinforcements sent under separate command to Armenia and Persia made possible complete victory on both those fronts. Success there provided sufficient manpower to reinforce the king's supporters in the north-east of the plateau, and the stubborn rebellion in Parthia was crushed. In the meantime, rebellions elsewhere in the east had been successfully suppressed by provincial governors who remained loyal to Darius.

Thus in little over a year Darius had succeeded in deposing the usurper Gautama and thoroughly defeating the largest rebellion of subject peoples ever experienced, or to be experienced, by the empire. The reasons for this remarkable success are fairly clear. Darius had retained the loyalty of the professional army, with which he had served in Egypt. He used his control of the central position to great advantage, primarily by preventing any efforts at coordination among the rebels. And finally, he succeeded because he was clearly a dynamic young man, a mover of men, and an outstanding general. In short, he was a worthy successor of Cyrus the Great.

Having crushed rebellion, Darius could now turn his attention to enlarging the empire he had seized. Campaigns of expansion were conducted successfully both to the east and to the west, although towards the end of his reign efforts in Europe were temporarily checked at the battle of Marathon (490 BC).

In the east, in India, at some time between 520 and 513 BC, Darius conquered the whole of Sind and probably the greater part of the Punjab. Thus the rich river valley of the Indus was brought under Achaemenid control. Curiously enough, we know next to nothing about this event, even though it added to the empire one of its richest provinces – India is reported to have contributed 360 talents of pure gold dust per year to the royal treasuries. No mention of this significant event is made in the Old Persian sources other than simply to list India as one of the peoples of the empire. Classical sources do not mention the conquest at all.

Fortunately, we know a great deal more about Darius' expansion of the empire to the west. Perhaps as early as 517 BC Persian control had been established over several important islands off the Ionian coast. In 513 BC the Persians, under the direct command of Darius and ably assisted by their Ionian Greek subjects, crossed the Bosporus into Europe and, *en route* to a campaign against the Scythians north of the Black Sea, conquered large sections of Thrace. Just how far to the north the Scythian campaign carried is not clear. The picture we have of it from Herodotus is of an organized army chasing elusive nomads further and more fruitlessly into an endless steppe. And yet the Scythians of this region are mentioned for many years among the subject peoples of the empire, so the campaign cannot in fact have been the total failure that Herodotus describes.

At the end of the Scythian campaign the competent general Megabazus was left on the scene to continue the conquest of Thrace. Megabazus was succeeded by Otanes, who completed the work in hand, giving the

A cylinder seal of Darius I. The King of Kings is depicted as a hunter, a traditional pose for West Asian monarchs.

Persians total control of the whole of the north Aegean. Several years of peace then followed between the Persians and Greeks.

That peace was rudely interrupted by the Ionian Revolt (499–494 BC), involving almost all of the Greek cities of Asia Minor. The Persians were taken by surprise and at first the rebellion prospered. In 498 BC, having received limited assistance from the Athenians, the Ionians took the offensive. On the one hand, the Persians negotiated with individual city-states, with partial success in some instances, in order to disrupt the cohesion of the rebellion. On the other hand, they prepared for a counter-attack, which, when it came, was only partially successful. 496 and 495 BC were years of respite for the Ionians, but in 494 BC the renewed Persian offensive was successful. The Greek fleet was defeated at Lade, near the city of Miletus, and soon after the Persian army completed a systematic reduction of the rebel cities. Initially the Persians renewed their long-standing support of the tyrant rulers in the Ionian cities, but in 492 BC Mardonius, a son-in-law of Darius, was sent as a special commissioner to Ionia, where he suppressed the local tyrants and established democratic government in many cities. In that same year Mardonius also started and finished the systematic restoration of Persian power in Thrace and Macedonia, temporarily disrupted during the Ionian revolt. The stage was now set for an expanded Persian attack on mainland Greece, ostensibly in retaliation for the assistance the Athenians and the Eretrians had earlier given the Ionian city-states.

The first step in the new campaign was for Darius to demand of the mainland city-states of Greece their submission to his authority. From a Greek point of view a frightening number of those states did voluntarily submit to the Persians, but Sparta and Athens steadfastly refused. Under the command of a Mede, Datis, the Persian army and navy moved to the attack. The invasion fleet progressed first slowly along the south coast of Anatolia and then turned north up the coast of Ionia. The Greeks probably expected the invader to continue to hug the coast around the north Aegean, but were thoroughly surprised when the Persians suddenly turned and sailed directly across the Aegean, capturing the island of Naxos and the city of Eretria on the island of Euboea.

The Persians landed unopposed on the plain of Marathon, north of Athens. The Athenians decided to challenge the invader immediately, even before the Spartans could join them, and with a small number of Plataeans force-marched to Marathon. For nine days neither army attacked. Then, roughly at dawn on 12 August 490 BC, while the Persian cavalry was apparently watering and feeding its horses, the Greeks attacked. The Persians were pushed back on both wings, but the Greek centre had to give ground. The Persian cavalry, returning to the scene, failed to check the Greek successes to right and left, and the Greek flanks were able to close in on the rear of the Persian centre, which after fierce fighting finally broke. In the rapid retreat to their ships many Persians were drowned in a nearby swamp. Though Persian casualties were high (the Greek sources report 6,400 Persians dead), most of the army got away safely to sea and apparently only seven Persian ships were lost; 192 Greeks were killed. Thus ended the first Persian attempt to conquer southern mainland Greece.

The Greek counter-offensive, after some initial successes, failed. Thrace and the northern Aegean remained firmly under Persian control. Darius was determined to try again, but preparations were interrupted, first by rebellion in Egypt and then by his death. In the event, his son Xerxes was unable to take up the cause until 480 BC.

The Reign of Xerxes (486–465 BC)

Apart from his wars with Greece, our sources tell us little about Xerxes. He was not Darius' eldest son, but the first son born after Darius came to the throne. His mother, the Great Queen Atossa, is said to have persuaded her husband to make Xerxes crown prince some years before Darius died. The transfer of imperial power from father to son must have gone smoothly: Darius died in November 486 BC and the first Babylonian tablet from the reign of Xerxes is dated 1 December 486 BC.

Rebellion had broken out in Egypt some four months before the death of Darius. Persian authority was not re-established until early 484 BC. Herodotus claims that the Persian forces were led by Xerxes himself, but this is unlikely. Herodotus' report on a change of style of Persian rule in Egypt, on the other hand, may be correct. He tells us Xerxes put Egypt under a far heavier burden than it had borne before the rebellion, including the confiscation of temple lands. And contrary to his father's practice, Xerxes apparently constructed no royal monuments in Egypt, and we have no evidence of his having ruled as pharaoh.

In 484 BC rebellion broke out in Babylon. Xerxes put the rebellion down with, according to Greek tradition, a firm hand. It is said that the Persians systematically destroyed the symbols of Babylonian nationality. The walls of the city were razed, the temple of Esagila and the great ziggurat may also have been torn down, priests of the local gods killed, and the great statue of Marduk taken away and melted down. Our local Babylonian sources, both epigraphic and archaeological, however, do not bear witness to any such systematic destruction. If, on the other hand, it is possible to associate the famous 'Daiva' inscription of Xerxes with his crushing of the Babylonian rebellion, then it is clear that there was indeed a religious element in these events. In that inscription Xerxes tells us that when he became king there was one country of the empire 'in commotion', and there was another country where 'previously false gods were worshipped'. Xerxes destroyed the sanctuaries of these demons, the false gods, and then tells us, 'Where previously the demons were worshipped, there I worshipped Ahura Mazda and Arta reverently.' Egypt was probably the country 'in commotion', and Babylon was most likely the country where false gods and demons were worshipped.

In rapidly suppressing rebellion in Egypt and Babylon Xerxes displayed all of the characteristics of a strong king. In preparing for a new invasion of mainland Greece, and in the first year of the campaign itself, such impressions of strength were confirmed. But after the Persian defeats at the battles of Salamis and Plataea, the character of Xerxes appears to change, and the last fourteen years of his reign, of which we know all too little, suggest a weak and ineffective king.

Massive preparations for the invasion of Greece were under way by at least 481 BC, with large numbers of troops being mustered in Asia Minor. Just how many troops there were in the Persian army of invasion has been a matter of much argument. Herodotus gives a number of over 5 million, which is of course impossible. Modern scholarship on the question divides essentially into two groups: those who wish to maximize the number to the greater glory of Greece, and those who argue from the military and demographic realities of the time for a much lower figure. Given our sources, disagreement will continue. It is suggested here, however, that perhaps no more than 120,000 Persian soldiers in 480 BC crossed the Hellespont into Europe.

The Persians accomplished that crossing on two remarkable floating bridges in part supported by enormous ropes. Ahead of them they found abundant supplies stockpiled along their routes of march all the way from Doriscus, the main Persian supply base in Europe, south to the limits of Persian control on the mainland. The first battles of the invasion were on land at Thermopylae and on sea at Artemisium. Immediately prior to the naval battle on 17 September, the Persian fleet suffered severe damage and considerable losses in a major storm. The engagement at Artemisium itself was indecisive, the Persians losing some thirty ships. They then lost 200 more in another storm on the night of 17/18 September. A second major clash between the two navies took place on 19 September. The Greek losses were heavy and their fleet withdrew southward all the way to Salamis, albeit in part because, given the events at Thermopylae, they no longer needed to maintain contact with the Greek land forces.

The Persians had attacked the Greeks at the famous pass of Thermopylae early in the morning of 17 September. These frontal assaults cost the Persians dearly, but they then learned of a track through the mountains which permitted them to turn the Greek position in the pass. Crack Persian troops were sent over this path on the night of 18/19 September. Many of the Greeks, about to be surrounded, withdrew, but the Spartan king, Leonidas, and his stalwart troops stayed and fought until they were all dead. Their bravery is remembered in the following famous lines: 'Tell them in Lacedaemon, passer-by: obedient to our orders, here we lie.' The Greeks lost 4,000 men killed, the Persians undoubtedly many more.

Athens was then abandoned, and the Persians marched in on 27 September, setting fire to large parts of the city and the acropolis. The Greek fleet was concentrated at the island of Salamis and the main Greek land defences were now based on fortifications rapidly under construction on the Isthmus of Corinth. Preparations by both sides for a naval battle lasted until 29 September. There was much dissension and discussion among the Greeks as to what were the best tactics to undertake in the circumstances, but eventually, in part by ruse, they lured the Persians to battle in the very narrow straits between Heracleum on the mainland of Attica and Cape Tropaea on Salamis. Though the Greeks were outnumbered, the Persians were unable to manoeuvre with advantage in the narrow water and the Greek victory was complete.

The campaign season was now at an end and both sides withdrew and in part disbanded for the winter. Xerxes himself, in fact, returned with part of the Persian army to Sardis, leaving a contingent of troops sufficient to subdue the Greeks in the new campaign in winter quarters in Thessaly under the command of Mardonius. Contrary to our sources, there is no reason to suppose that the Great King's withdrawal was anything but orderly, and that he had every intention of returning in the spring.

In the event, Xerxes did not return, the Persian fleet remained inactive at the island of Samos and the decisive land campaign of 479 BC was left to Mardonius. At the end of June he marched into Attica, disrupting such harvest as the Athenians had hoped to make. Sparta then responded to Athens' plea for the Greeks to fight north of the isthmus and sent her troops out from behind their fortifications. Mardonius concentrated the Persian forces in Boeotia, taking up a defensive position facing the town of Plataea.

The Greeks arrived from the south, and there followed several days of manoeuvring, each side trying to draw the other on to the attack from strong defensive positions. One of the most effective of these manoeuvres was the 'battle of the baggage trains', in which Mardonius sent the Persian cavalry on raids into the rear of the Greeks, capturing and destroying enough of their supplies to threaten them with hunger. The Persians then attacked the Greek position with cavalry and managed to capture their enemy's water supply. With his troops now thirsty as well as hungry, the Spartan commander of the Greek coalition, Pausanias, ordered a tactical withdrawal during the night. Unfortunately for the Persians, when the Greek manoeuvre became visible at dawn Mardonius completely misinterpreted it as a rout of the enemy and gave foolish orders for an all-out Persian attack. In fact, the Greeks had withdrawn in an orderly fashion to a new, highly defensible position. Even so, the fighting was particularly ferocious, and it was only when Mardonius was killed, leaving the Persians leaderless, that they broke and fled from the Spartans in great disorder, seeking sanctuary in the large stockade which had earlier been constructed behind their original lines. In the meantime, the Athenians on the left of the Greek line succeeded in defeating the Theban allies of the Persians, who broke and retreated to their own city. Artabazus, who was said to be in command of some 40,000 Persians, and who had not attacked with Mardonius, retreated immediately with his troops all the way to Asia. The Persians in the stockade fought valiantly but were overwhelmed. Total Persian losses are unknown, but they must have been enormous. The Greeks are said to have lost 1,360 men.

In the aftermath of victory Thebes was taken by the coalition forces, and the leaders of those allied with the Persians, though they had been promised a pardon, were led off and summarily executed. Then the Greek fleet, which had hung back thus far like the Persians, crossed the Aegean to attack the Persian fleet at Samos. The Persians withdrew without a battle to the mainland, where they took shelter on land within the shadow of Mount Mycale. The Greeks came in behind them, attacking from the landward side and defeating them completely.

The Greeks then sailed on to the Dardanelles, where they found the bridges connecting Asia and Europe already destroyed. The Spartans sailed for home, but the Athenians and others stayed to put the satrapy's capital, Sestus, under siege. After several months the town was captured, and the satrap was executed. The Greeks sailed home; the war was over and their victory complete.

The decade which followed the battle of Plataea witnessed the nadir of Persian power and influence on the west coast of Asia Minor, the end of Persian naval ambitions in the Aegean, the formation of the Delian League and the rise of the empire of Athens.

Effectively, Xerxes is not heard of again. Some have argued that he lost interest in the affairs of the empire and sank ever deeper into the comforts of his court. He has the honour to be the first Achaemenid king to be assassinated, killed by Artebanes, a royal favourite, in his bedchamber. Thus a reign which began with great promise ended in dynastic intrigue and murder.

The Late Achaemenid Kings

The half-century following the death of Xerxes was a period of considerable weakness and confusion within the Achaemenid empire. Three kings reigned in this period: Artaxerxes I (464–425 BC), Xerxes II (425–424 BC) and Darius II (423–404 BC).

Apart from a rebellion in Egypt in 459 BC, put down only in 454 BC, the important event in the reign of Artaxerxes I was the signing in 448 BC of the Peace of Callias with Athens. Thus the war with Greece, which had begun under Darius, officially ended. The terms of the treaty required the Persians to stay out of the Aegean, while in return the Athenians agreed to leave Asia Minor to the Achaemenids. The peace, however, was fragile. Athens attacked Samos in 439 BC, and in the follow-up to that attack the Persians made some military gains in the west.

Artaxerxes died peacefully in bed (unusual for a late Achaemenid king) and was succeeded by his son, Xerxes II. Court intrigue immediately broke out. Only forty-five days after his accession Xerxes II was killed following a particularly drunken party. The assassin was himself killed by Darius II, who then managed to hold on to the throne for the next nineteen years.

The principal event of all three of these reigns was the Peloponnesian War between Athens and Sparta, which was largely fought out between 431 and 404 BC. These troubles in the Greek world were ably exploited by the Persians, primarily through bribery and diplomacy. The Great Kings mustered the famous 'Persian archers', the gold coins of the Achaemenids with an archer on their obverse, and sent them off to battle against the Greeks. First of all the Persians backed Athens against Sparta, but following the disastrous Athenian attempt to invade Sicily in 413 BC, the Persians switched their support to Sparta, in return for which Achaemenid control over the whole of western Asia Minor was reconfirmed. The Spartans used the money they received to pay sailors in the Peloponnesian fleet. Thus the combination of Persian gold and Spartan might brought Athens to complete defeat in 404 BC.

Artaxerxes II (405–359 BC) had a long and, one could argue, reasonably profitable reign, the principal events of which were a successful war with Sparta, the revolt and loss of Egypt to the empire, the rebellion of Cyrus the Younger (his brother) and the so-called Revolt of the Satraps.

Shortly after her triumph over Athens, Sparta became involved in war with the Persians, the main cause being again the Greek city-states of Asia Minor. As so often the satraps of Ionia were unable to present a united front to the Spartans, while the central government spent gold in Greece in support of Sparta's enemies. The war lasted from 400 to 387 BC, with Sparta more or less continually falling back, particularly in the face of a revitalized Athens supported by Persian gold. Eventually a balance of power was achieved in Greece, and Artaxerxes was actually invited by the Greeks to mediate their internecine quarrel. The result was the so-called King's Peace of 387–386 BC. Once again the mainland Greeks relinquished all interest in Greek Asia Minor, and agreed to maintain the *status quo* on the mainland itself. In a certain sense Artaxerxes II had accomplished with his golden archers much of what Xerxes had failed to achieve with the real thing almost 100 years earlier.

Cyrus the Younger had attempted to assassinate his brother, Artaxerxes II, at the time of their father's death. Thanks to the fervent pleadings of the queen mother, he had been forgiven and returned to his satrapial duties. But his ambitions continued. In 401 BC he rose in revolt against the Great King and, supported by 10,000 Greek mercenaries, invaded Mesopotamia. The culminating battle of Cunaxa was a very near-run thing. The satrapial and native troops broke and fled only when Cyrus himself was killed. The Greek mercenaries stood firm, however, and managed to depart in good order. Xenophon's *Anabasis* records their famous march northwards across the highlands of

Anatolia to the Black Sea and their return to Greece. The ability of such a group of Greek mercenaries to march through the heartland of the empire with comparative impunity no doubt impressed upon their countrymen that empire's growing weakness.

Persia had been unable to respond to another rebellion in 405 BC in Egypt. As late as 373 BC Artaxerxes II, assisted by numerous Greek mercenaries, attempted the reconquest of Egypt, but he failed. Shortly thereafter the Revolt of the Satraps began. Several satraps joined in the rebellion, and Aroandas even defied the Great King to the extent of stamping his own gold coinage. The rebels planned a combined attack. Coming from the western parts of the empire, they were to march eastwards through Syria with an Egyptian attack supported by Greek mercenaries on their flank. The latter effort never materialized because of dynastic difficulties in Egypt. In the meantime, as might be expected, bickering and quarrelling amongst the rebellious satraps resulted in the collapse of any efforts at co-ordination. Artaxerxes, with the help of loyal satraps, was able eventually to crush the rebellion. The Great King, however, was yet so unsure of his power that he actually forgave several of the rebels, including Aroandas, and returned many of them to their governorships. Such is the behaviour of the ruler of a decaying empire.

Artaxerxes II was succeeded by his son, Artaxerxes III (359–338 BC). On his accession fresh revolts broke out throughout the empire. All were successfully put down, and another attempt was made to win back Egypt in 351–350 BC, but that failed too. This reversal led to revolt in Sidon and later to the rebellion of all of Palestine and Phoenicia. While some parts of Cilicia joined in the rebellion, it was nevertheless successfully suppressed in the very year it began, 345 BC. There followed a third attempt to recover Egypt, led by Artaxerxes III himself and supported by Greek mercenaries. Remarkably, this effort succeeded in 343 BC, but the local Egyptian dynasty escaped to Nubia, where it maintained an independent kingdom. Artaxerxes failed to support any of the Greek city-states, particularly Athens, in their efforts to resist conquest by Philip II of Macedon. As a result the Macedonians won the battle of Chaeronea in 338 BC, giving Philip effective control of Greece.

Artaxerxes was poisoned at the command of the eunuch Bagoas, who made Arses king (338–336 BC). Arses then attempted to poison the king-maker, only to be killed himself in retaliation, and Bagoas arranged for Darius III (336–330 BC), the grandnephew of Artaxerxes II, to become king. Darius put down yet another rebellion in Egypt under Khababash in 337–336 BC, but very soon Alexander the Great, not internal rebellion, became the Great King's principal concern.

Alexander won his first battle against the Persians at Granicus in May 334 BC. A second battle was fought shortly afterwards in the neighbourhood of the Cilician gates and, though commanded by Darius himself, the Persians were once again defeated. Alexander spent the next two years conquering the Levant and Egypt, while Darius attempted, unsuccessfully, to bribe him into going away. In 331 BC Alexander marched to the east. A final and conclusive battle was fought on 1 October 331 BC at Gaugamela, near the modern city of Erbil. The Persians, once again commanded by their king, were beaten. Alexander captured Persepolis in April 330 BC, and Darius was murdered in the summer of the same year while fleeing from the conqueror.

Though the history of the Achaemenid empire following the death of Xerxes is, in the main, a sad tale of gradual decay, it is nevertheless a tale that took over a century to unfold. Our sources for this story are predominantly Greek and must, therefore, be prejudiced. Also, they tell the story of life at the top of the empire, and thus tend to focus on only a limited range of concerns. One suspects that beneath these lay a well-organized and relatively peaceful and smoothly functioning polity. If this had not been the case, it would not have taken so long for the empire to fall.

In turning now to examine aspects of Achaemenid government and society, religion, and art and architecture, we may be able to discover some of those hidden strengths.

Government and Society

The royal court was the centre of government in the empire, and at the centre of the court was the king. Thus the capital of the empire at any given time was where the king was. Most often that was at Susa, but also, seasonally, at Ectabana (modern Hamadan), Persepolis and, sometimes, Babylon. Since the king was all-powerful his word was law, and often even the smallest details of government required his decision. Much of the time he remained in considerable seclusion, and access to him was tightly controlled. Thus his power was based in part on a degree of mystery, illusion and institutional charisma which lifted him in society well above the levels attained by even the highest ranks of the nobility. Much of his real power, on the other hand, lay in his complete control of patronage and finances. The highest officers of the empire were appointed by the king, and even the lowest ranks of the bureaucracy were financially dependent on the king's treasury.

The Royal Court

Of the court surrounding the king we know little. Certain officials, such as the 'spear-bearer', the 'bow-bearer' and the 'commander of the 1,000' appear to have performed governmental roles often unrelated to their titles. It is possible that the commander of the 1,000, the imperial guard, functioned in the later years of the empire as a grand vizier. All such high officials, and lesser ones as well, were paid from the king's treasury.

A major component of the court was the harem. The Achaemenid king always had several wives, one of whom was his principal queen, and many concubines. While such a set-up had the advantage of ensuring numerous relatives for appointment to imperial offices, it also provided endless opportunities for social and political intrigue. As the Book of Esther makes clear, the women of the harem often played an important role in imperial decision-making.

The king, court and government were supported by an extensive scribal bureaucracy concentrated in the treasuries of the empire, best documented by the records of the one at Persepolis. These treasuries were both repositories of imperial wealth and offices from which massive stores of wealth in kind were administered. A wide range of economic activities took place within the territory under the authority of the treasury. The texts from Persepolis inform us of regular provisions issued to various kinds of work parties, craftsmen, travellers, treasury officials, members of the royal household and even the king himself. While it has often been argued that the central government of the empire conducted its affairs in a loose, informal and tribal manner, the evidence from the treasury texts makes it clear that the opposite was, in fact, the case.

Provincial Government

The organization of most of the empire into provinces (satrapies) under the authority of a governor (satrap, or 'protector of the kingdom/kingship') is attributed by Herodotus to Darius I. While Darius may have reorganized the provincial structure following his successful crushing of rebellion in his first regnal year of 521 BC, there is good evidence that the system as such was in place as early as the reign of Cyrus II. The satrap, often a close relative of the king, was appointed and removed by the king. He commanded royal resources within his province, and, usually wealthy himself, supplemented those resources out of his own pocket. With the exception of certain royal fortifications, the satrap seems also to have had control over imperial military forces within his province. None the less, representatives of the central government, referred to as the 'king's eyes' or the 'king's ears', travelled throughout the satrapies and reported directly to the Great King. Under a strong central authority such officials clearly represented a major check on the exercise of any independent authority by the satrap.

Control of the empire and its provinces was much facilitated by the construction and maintenance of an extensive system of 'royal roads'. The texts from Persepolis inform us of the regular provisioning and maintenance of way stations along these roads, and they also mention the 'élite guides' and the 'express couriers', who conducted travelling officials and carried messages for the king over the length and breadth of the empire.

Xerxes' Gate of the Nations at Persepolis, the great ceremonial city founded by Darius I.

The Military

Within the military establishment there was a clear division between the army and the navy, and within both units a distinction was made between standing forces and the levee, called up at times of major conflict. At the core of the standing army were the 10,000 Immortals, the élite of whom formed the 1,000-troop bodyguard of the king. It is also likely that there were 10,000 cavalry in the regular standing army. These well-trained men provided the core around which the levee and irregular troops were organized, and it was this standing army which provided the force behind the Great King's dictates. Troops of the standing army, made up exclusively of Persians, Medes and Elamites, were often permanently stationed in the satrapies. In the provinces these were augmented by native troops and long-term mercenaries, such as the Jewish troops who protected the Egyptian frontier of the empire at Elephantine on the Nile.

The standing forces of the navy were probably provided by Phoenicians and Egyptians, and perhaps by Cypriots. In war these naval forces were supplemented by conscription, often involving Ionian Greeks. But all marines were Persians, Medes or Scythians.

While it is clear that in a crisis the empire could send to war masses of men and ships, the command of these forces must have been a military nightmare. Such a diversity of troops, speaking many different languages, armed in a wide variety of ways and trained, if at all, in widely varying tactics must have presented the enemy with anything but a coherent challenge.

An inscription of Darius I at Bisitun, one of the few surviving Achaemenid government documents.

Law and Economics

The Achaemenids, as well as the Medes, had a reputation for laws which were firm and 'unalterable'. Unfortunately, we know all too little of even the broad outlines, let alone the details, of ancient Persian law. Our evidence indicates that the Achaemenids governed the empire with tolerance of, and respect for, the customs, traditions and laws of the various ethnic groups over whom they ruled. Our best evidence in this regard comes from Babylonia, where, in the main, legal affairs continue to be conducted throughout the Persian period according to long-standing Babylonian custom and practice. We do find, however, in certain legal and semi-legal texts written in the Semitic language of Babylon the appearance of the Old Persian words *datā* and *datābarā*, meaning 'law' and 'bearer of the law' respectively. The word *datā* might refer to a specific law code imposed by the Achaemenids, but could simply mean 'decree' or 'royal command'. *Datābarā*, sometimes interpreted as meaning 'judge', could equally mean simply 'law officer' or 'constable'. Given that most of the texts in which these terms appear are documents concerning economic transactions and contracts, it would appear that, in Babylon at least, the Achaemenid authorities were much more involved in introducing some form of new economic and administrative arrangements than in rewriting the law.

The wealth of the empire was founded on agriculture, although manufacturing and particularly commerce played important roles in the economy. The government naturally taxed with vigour; it has even been suggested that over-taxation was a major cause of the empire's downfall. On the other hand, the government did much to encourage and strengthen the economy.

Taxes were collected in a variety of ways. Specific tax obligations were levied on each province, with the exception of Persia itself. State and royal properties were rented, funds were collected from citizens in lieu of obligations, tribute was paid by subject peoples outside the provincial structure, customs charges were levied and, at least in Babylonia, some form of a sales tax was collected. The vast majority of these levies were paid in kind, held in storehouses near their point of origin and administered by the appropriate royal treasury.

Some of the wealth, however, went back into the economy. The treasuries issued seed grain for use on both government (royal) and private estates. The latter suggests some kind of government subsidy to private agricultural enterprise. The treasury also issued to various estates large numbers of seedlings, probably fruit trees, and Darius commends one of his governors for having arranged for the transplanting of fruit trees from Syria to Asia Minor. There is also good archaeological evidence for a rapid expansion of agriculture in Babylonia in Achaemenid times, and for efforts by the government elsewhere to improve irrigation in those parts of the empire where it was absolutely essential for the development and growth of agriculture. In sum, there is strong evidence that the government was deeply concerned with, and involved in, agricultural activity throughout the empire, whether public or private.

Finally, we also have evidence for government support of both manufacturing and commerce. Texts describe issuing rations from the royal treasury to various workforces which are involved in a variety of at least cottage industries. Some of these groups are predominantly female, and one suspects either the weaving of cloth or the manufacture of rugs. In support of commerce, the government funded a number of sea voyages of exploration, the construction of ports on the coast of the Persian Gulf and, under Darius I, the digging of a canal linking the Red Sea with the Nile. On land the system of royal roads also provided pathways for the smooth and efficient movement of goods and products, strongly supporting the economic life of the empire. Thus the people of the empire must have experienced some of the economic benefits of, for ancient times, a very large common market.

The Social Structure

Because of the religious, ethnic and social tolerance with which the Achaemenids chose to rule, one cannot speak of an imperial social structure. That Persian willingness to tolerate the customs and social structures of conquered people may, however, have in part derived from the social structure and organization of the Persians themselves.

Earlier attempts at empire in ancient West Asia had been anything but tolerant. Why, therefore, were the Achaemenids so different? The answer to the question is twofold. On the one hand, tolerance was a realistic policy. Given the size and diversity of their empire, probably no other approach would have worked. On the other hand, such a policy probably fitted their own idealized traditions of social structure, which had a vertical view of society, beginning at its base with the family, progressing upwards through the levels of clan, tribe and country, and culminating in a people or a nation. Viewed horizontally, Persian society was divided into four classes: priests, warriors, scribes/bureaucrats and artisans/peasants. At the summit of the structure was the king, surrounded by the concept of kingship. This concept of *khvarna*, or 'kingly glory', attached itself both to the office of the king and to the individual who held that office, and brought the king and kingship into touch with the mysterious, thus assuring his position at the summit of society.

Thus the Great King and his government functioned only at the highest social and political levels. He was a king of countries, peoples and nations, and it was entirely logical that imperial policy interfere as little as possible in the concerns of tribes, clans and families. If peasants, artisans, priests and warriors, all at the lower end of the social scale, functioned well, then how they did so was entirely their own business, and it was only right for the state to be tolerant of their social organization.

Religion

Less than a century before Cyrus the Great came to the throne, the great ethical prophet Zoroaster had preached his singular message in north-western Iran. In the early years of the Achaemenid empire that reforming message was gradually being turned into an organized religion which would eventually, in post-Achaemenid times, triumph over the pre-Zoroastrian Iranian religions and the various non-Iranian polytheisms of pre- and early Achaemenid times. Eventually, of course, Zoroastrianism became the state religious orthodoxy of Sasanian times.

The critical question is, were the Achaemenid kings Zoroastrians in terms of the beliefs and practices that would have defined evolving Zoroastrianism in the sixth and fifth centuries BC? We can say nothing of Cyrus, for we have no data. There is, however, good evidence that Darius and Xerxes practised an early form of Zoroastrianism. Their inscriptions reveal beliefs that were theologically compatible with those of the great Iranian prophet. *Arta*, or 'truth', being in conflict with *druj*, or 'falsehood', is a theme constantly stressed in royal inscriptions. Ahura Mazda is also clearly the supreme god of the Achaemenid pantheon, and is the only deity named in official inscriptions by Darius. Xerxes, in his suppression of Daeva (Devil) worship, is thoroughly Zoroastrian in belief and practice. He does, however, elevate Arta to the level of a deity alongside Ahura Mazda in his inscriptions, and this slight lapse into polytheism is carried further by his successors when they also mention Anahita and Mithra as deities. Finally, from a theological point of view, the adoption of the Zoroastrian religious calendar as official in the empire under Artaxerxes I demonstrates a clear and henceforth continuing commitment to fundamental Zoroastrian beliefs.

As in belief, so in ritual practice, with one exception: there is good evidence to suggest that from Darius onwards the Achaemenid kings were good Zoroastrians as that religion was then defined. First, while fire has never actually been worshipped by Zoroastrians, Zoroaster had emphasized the purity and importance of fire, and had attempted to make the use of fire the key to ritual practice. Now fire was central to Persian royal religious practice. The king is regularly depicted worshipping in front of a sacred fire; such scenes appear on all royal tombs. Within the sacred precinct at Pasargadae, the only structure in the Achaemenid homeland whose function is clearly religious is a large stone fire altar facing a stone platform. It is clear from the tomb reliefs that the Great King stood on this platform and conducted religious rituals in the presence of a sacred fire. Second, the complete absence of any indication of animal sacrifice at the Achaemenid court is further evidence of good Zoroastrian ritual behaviour. In pre-Zoroastrian times animal sacrifice had been an important part of Iranian religion, and it had been thoroughly condemned by Zoroaster as anathema. In the Persepolis texts we have abundant evidence for the use of wine, beer, wheat and flour in ritual, all of which would have been entirely satisfactory to the prophet. Finally, on at least one count, the Achaemenid kings were not good Zoroastrians in their ritual behaviour. The prophet had roundly condemned the ancient Iranian religious practice of drinking the intoxicant *haoma*, yet there is abundant textual and archaeological evidence from Persepolis for the widespread practice of the *haoma* cult in Achaemenid times. In sum, in terms of both theology and ritual, Darius and Xerxes were probably good Zoroastrians of their day, and from Artaxerxes I onwards the Achaemenids were certainly Zoroastrian. No attempt, however, was made to impose early Zoroastrianism on the Medes and Persians, or, indeed, even on the functionaries of the court. The Persepolis Texts make it clear that the worship of a wide range of Iranian, and even non-Iranian, deities was tolerated regardless of the Great King's own beliefs.

As is clear, our primary evidence on Iranian religion in Achaemenid times focuses almost entirely on the beliefs and practices of the king. We know next to nothing about the religion of the common people.

What is important, however, within the history of Zoroastrianism is that the message of the great reforming prophet, at least as it was understood in the fifth and fourth centuries BC, was probably legitimized and preserved by its acceptance at the Achaemenid court. Had this not been so, one wonders whether this great religion would have survived to become the orthodoxy of Sasanian times.

Art and Architecture

Achaemenid art is one of the great legacies of ancient West Asia. It is a blend of two elements: first, the artistic and architectural experiences of the Iranians on the Iranian plateau in the several centuries prior to the rise of Cyrus the Great; and, second, the arts of ancient Mesopotamia, Greece and, to a lesser extent, Egypt.

Turning first to architecture, we see immediately that we are dealing with imperial art on a grand scale. The artists and the materials they worked with were brought from practically all the lands ruled by the Great King. Thus it has often been argued that Achaemenid architecture and its adorning art are nothing but an eclectic blend of artistic elements from earlier and contemporary cultures. That this is not so can be demonstrated by a close look at the architecture of Pasargadae and Persepolis.

At Pasargadae, founded in the 540s BC by Cyrus the Great, while we recognize definite Egyptian and Mesopotamian forms in much decorative detail, and while there is clear Greek influence in the style and craftsmanship of column bases, relief drapery, stone-cutting and building techniques, the layout and conception of the whole is entirely original. The Dasht-i Morghab, or 'Plain of Pasargadae', is well watered by the Pulvar River. This river is the key to understanding the layout of the site, in which we find the tomb of Cyrus, the main gate, two major palaces, two pavilions, a bridge, the so-called Zendan, the sacred precinct and the hilltop platform, the Tall-i Takht. All the principal structures are clearly oriented to a style of life directed towards open space, and the various water channels feeding off from the river and running among the buildings make it clear that the site was essentially a great park rather than a city – our first example of a Persian paradise. This conception – a park with bridges, gardens, colonnaded palaces and open columned pavilions – is distinctively Achaemenid.

The ancient interpretation of the name Pasargadae as meaning 'encampment of the Persians', while certainly incorrect, is nevertheless understandable. The overall impression of the site is of a tent encampment transferred into stone and mud brick – appropriate as the foundation of a Great King who, in a short period of time, rose from leadership of a tribe to mastery of a vast empire.

That imperial authority is even more forcefully expressed in the art and architecture of Persepolis and Susa. Of the two sites, Persepolis is much the grander, and in many ways represents the example *par excellence*

The Apadana staircase at Persepolis. It demonstrates how the main vehicle of Achaemenid art was relief sculpture.

of Achaemenid monumental architecture and sculptured relief. Its foundations are a large platform carved and constructed at the western foot of the Kuh-i Rahmat, or 'Mountain of Mercy'. The platform itself, its waterworks, the Apadana (or large audience hall) and sections of the Treasury were built by Darius I. Late in the reign of Darius, and early in that of Xerxes, the platform was expanded and the private palace called the Tacara, a second section of the Treasury, some of the fortifications, the main stair and the Gate of All Nations were built. Xerxes also constructed a large private palace, the harem, an enlarged treasury and at least laid foundations for a new audience hall, the Hall of 100 Columns. Most of the fairly limited further construction at the site took place during the late fifth century BC, in the reign of Artaxerxes I.

As at Pasargadae, the characteristic feature of Persepolis is the columned hall, and these halls are the legacy of Iranian experiences on the plateau prior to Achaemenid times. The prototypes of the Apadana and the Hall of 100 Columns clearly lie in the column structures of Hasanlu V and IV (1400–800 BC) and the columned hall of Median Godin II and Nush-i Jan (eighth–seventh centuries BC).

A closer look at the reliefs which adorn these buildings also reveals a strong overall Persian conception, regardless of the extent to which foreign styles and motifs were borrowed. A recent detailed study demonstrates that the cutting and carving was done by teams of artisans: a master craftsman working with lesser artists and apprentices, each assigned special elements of each figure. In short, the reliefs were created in an almost assembly-line manner. This makes it clear that the master artist(s) was not the carver of the reliefs, but the man who designed their purpose, overall conception and final layout. That master artist was clearly a Persian, for the story he tells, and the way that he tells it, is an original contribution by the Achaemenids to the art of the ancient world.

The first thing we note is that the reliefs are entirely unhistorical; unlike the reliefs of the Egyptians and the Assyrians, they tell no developing story. Rather we are presented with a static picture of something done, something accomplished, something that already exists. Second, the king is the focus of almost all these reliefs, and his depiction is not a portrait. We do not confront Darius or Xerxes or Artaxerxes. Instead of the image of a particular king, we have the abstract depiction of 'kingly glory' or *khvarna*. Clearly the ultimate goal of the artist who stood behind this monumental architecture and art was to put before the world the concept of *pax persica* – the picture of a king who contained within his person and office the welfare of a harmonious and peaceful empire.

Curiously enough, royal Achaemenid sites have produced almost no objects from foreign cultures. It seems that Persians preferred their own products. Stone and pottery vessels, one of the great aesthetic achievements of the period, are relatively plain, with an emphasis on crisp shapes derived from metal prototypes. Birds and animal heads were cleverly used for decoration, particularly on vessel handles. While the cutting of stone seals achieved high artistic levels, metalwork and jewellery were the triumphs of the Achaemenid craftsmen. The emphasis in metalwork was on intricate, repetitive and highly geometric decorative elements, though animal motifs, a long tradition on the Iranian plateau, were commonly used.

The monumental quality of the smallest Achaemenid art objects is best seen in jewellery and tableware. Here we find delicate gold earrings, which in their design and craftsmanship represent some of the highest achievements in ancient metalwork. Silver spoons, whose handles end in ducks' heads, demonstrate the equal skill of the silversmith.

Thus Achaemenid art, while displaying the eclectic character one might expect of so vast and diverse an empire, is nevertheless in conception and execution thoroughly Iranian. The Achaemenids blended the art of others with the architectural and artistic traditions they had developed on the plateau for 1,000 years prior to Pasargadae and produced an original art which, like their empire itself, marks the end of the ancient world and the beginning of something new.

The Parthians (247 BC–AD 226)

E. J. Keall

History

A fresh chapter in world history began in 330 BC when the last Persian ruler, Darius III, was assassinated in Central Asia. No power based in West Asia had ever controlled so much of Europe. When Alexander the Great returned to Babylon he was master of everything from Greece, through Turkey and Egypt, to India. Throughout the area the man himself became a legend.

We are so accustomed, however, to reading about Alexander's brilliant military exploits and the far-reaching implications of a Hellenized West Asia that we tend to forget that, for many, the Macedonian king was simply a butcher. He literally destroyed the Persian empire of the Achaemenids. Texts written in West Asia, as opposed to western sources, state that 'he killed many magi [priests]', 'slew many teachers' and 'quenched many [sacred] fires [of Zoroastrianism]'. In a society where historical and religious traditions were transmitted orally, the impact must have been crippling. It says something for the resilience of these people, and Iranian culture as a whole, that after a century and a half of Hellenic domination another group emerged to champion the cause of Iran for a further 500 years, followed by another for 400 more.

The Iranian Revival

It would be misleading, however, to imply that these two national monarchies repeated the same formula for empire as had the Achaemenids, even accounting for the changing circumstances of world history. There were, however, three fundamental common denominators: namely, Iranian languages, Iranian culture and the physical boundaries of an Iranian empire. In terms of the last category at least, it is something of a misnomer to talk of empire at all. For instance, in the new realms there were many levels of vassaldom and some cities originally founded by Alexander still enjoyed a degree of local autonomy centuries after the loss of actual Graeco-Macedonian political control of Iran.

Those who emerged after the Hellenistic period to control Iran – known to the west as the Parthians – ruled from around the mid-third century BC. Obscurity actually bedevils the origins of the Parthians. Parthia, south-east of the Caspian Sea, together with the district of Hyrcania, formed a satrapy in Darius I's empire. Yet their name nowhere appears in the Old Testament, not even in the late apocryphal texts; neither do they appear in the annals of Assyrian history. The Parthian people are brought to our attention through the recording of their country's name – Parthava – in various royal inscriptions commemorating the accomplishments of Darius, including the subjugation of an abortive Median revolt of 521 BC which was supported by 'Parthia'. A Parthian force fought on the Persian side in 331 BC at the battle of Arbela, but appears to have offered no major resistance to the subsequent Graeco-Macedonian invasion of their homeland.

During the fourth century BC, there were numbers of Iranian-speaking tribes living beyond the fringe of Seleucid authority, particularly in the north-east. These included a small group called the Parni who, as part of the Dahae confederation, were related through kinship to the more famous and widely scattered Saka or Scythian groups of tribes, and spoke an Iranian language, one of the group of related languages within the Indo-European family. By the beginning of the third century BC, the Parni may well have settled in the province of Parthava, where they adopted the variant Iranian dialect and culture of the 'Parthian' residents.

It is generally accepted that one of these Parni took it upon himself to wrest control of the province from the Seleucid governor, who himself may already have turned rebel against Seleucid authority. The Parthian counter-rebel was called Arshak (Arsaces in Greek), and he founded the first, albeit modest, government which was the beginning of over four centuries of Arsacid or Parthian rule, lasting from 247 BC to AD 226. The neighbouring province of Hyrcania was soon annexed by the Arsacids to Parthia.

There were attempts by the Seleucids to restore their authority on the eastern frontier, but in the long run it proved impossible, from so far away as Syria, to stifle the ambitions of either the governors of the eastern provinces or their rebellious residents. In 212 BC Antiochus III mounted an extended but ultimately unsuccessful campaign against Bactria, which had also successfully broken away from Seleucid control. In the process of protecting himself from a rear attack, Antiochus was forced to recognize Parthia as an independent state.

Beginning around 171 BC, under Mithridates I, the Parthians established a power that the Seleucids were never again able to suppress. Though Media was still technically in Seleucid hands, by 141 BC Mithridates had captured the capital of Seleucia-on-the-Tigris in Babylonia and dramatically restored Iranian control to most of central Iran. Of course, the Parthian holdings were not nearly as extensive in the west as they were in the heyday of the Achaemenids, and the administrative structure imposed does not really merit the term 'empire'. But by virtue of his successful campaigns between 171 and 138 BC, Mithridates came to hold sway over a wide variety of vassal kings and subject nobles.

Following Mithridates' death there was some erosion of control. These reverses inspired a Seleucid bid, under Antiochus VII Sidetes in 130 BC, to regain territories

Chronology

BC

c. 247–217 Arshak, or Arsaces I, seizes power from Seleucids in province of Parthava

212 Unsuccessful expedition of Antiochus III to reclaim Bactria

190 First independent state of Armenia under Artaxiad I

141 After dramatic conquests, Mithridates I captures the Seleucid capital of Seleucia-on-the-Tigris

121 Over-strikes of Characenian coins, indicating Parthian control of former independent state

115 Zhang Qian succeeds in bringing back from Ferghana to China horses, alfalfa and grape vines, heralding significant contact with Central Asia

c. 80–70 Political chaos in Parthia

66 Tigranes II (the Great), by uniting 'Lesser' and 'Greater' Armenia, creates a larger realm, but is drawn into conflict with Rome's Pompey

53 Orodes II's brilliant general, Suren, defeats the Romans on the plains of Syria at the battle of Carrhae but the king murders him out of jealousy

39–2 Phraates IV agrees to negotiate terms for the return to Rome of legionary standards lost at Carrhae

2 BC–AD 4 Phraataces and Musa, mother and son, rule as co-regents

A silver coin of Mithridates I, the first Parthian king. He struck coins to celebrate the revival of Iranian power.

AD

First century Hippalos, the legendary Greek, 'discoverer' of the monsoon winds which became common knowledge and fostered oceanic trade

10–38 Artabanus II successfully counters Roman attempts to place hostage princes upon Parthian throne but has to face challenges from his own nobility for the right to rule, especially in 36, when Tiridates II was installed for a while

43 End of civil war in Seleucia-on-the-Tigris marks loss of independent status of the old Macedonian colonies in Parthia

53 Nero's campaign to remove the Parthian candidate from the throne of Armenia reaches a compromise and Tiridates I (of Armenia) founds an Arsacid line of Armenian kings that lasts several centuries

77–*c.* 110 Struggles to gain throne
In 110 Vologases II 'sells' kingdom of Osrhoene, signalling flexible attitude towards management of the Parthian territories

97 Chinese diplomatic mission to Roman Syria, outflanks Parthia, but only reaches Characene

114 Trajan, the Roman emperor, embarks on conquest of Parthia in order to establish direct link with India, but retreats after finding his extensive conquests untenable

138 Ambassadors from the Syrian caravan city of Palmyra send delegation to an independent Elymais

164 Campaign directed by Avidius Cassius establishes Roman rule in the caravan city of Dura Europos for remainder of Parthian period

c. 213–24 Rebellion against Artabanus V in Pars province by Papak sets stage for Sasanian takeover of Iran

recently claimed by the Parthians. However, in spite of early gains, the Seleucid expedition was disastrously unsuccessful. Parthian fortunes improved once more when Mithridates II (*c.* 123–87 BC) came to power and repeated the expansive policy of his namesake, re-establishing military control over a wide range of territory, reaching from well east of the Caspian Sea to the River Euphrates in the west. In fact, his annexation of the principalities of Adiabene, Gordyene and Osrhoene, as well as interference in the running of Armenia, precipitated the rebirth of the old great West Asian-European conflicts, this time with Rome. The wide-ranging campaigns included the reclaiming of Characene, a principality that had maintained itself as an independent state at the head of the Persian Gulf following the weakening of Mithridates I's command. In 121 BC the act of over-striking coins issued originally by Hyspaosines of Characene by Mithridates II dramatically documents the success of the new campaign.

Those who prefer to be critical of the Parthian monarchy may see the failure after Mithridates II to establish full authority over the entire territory for centuries to come as a sign of weakness. Indeed, following the era of Mithridates II, the difficulties that numismatists have in identifying rulers' portraits on their coins, and therefore the timing of their successions, echoes the chaotic political scene in mid-first-century BC Parthia. After about 90 BC, the kings are known to us largely only because of their names — Orodes I (*c.* 80 BC), Sinatruces (*c.* 77 BC) and Phraates III (*c.* 70 BC). In 58 BC Phraates III was murdered by two rival sons. The one who prevailed was Orodes II, a figure who was to gain international notoriety for the humiliating defeat of the Roman general Crassus at the battle of Carrhae in 53 BC.

A Divided State

It must be acknowledged, however, that in spite of a decisive victory in the battle, the energies of the Parthian monarchy appear to have been involved more with self-preservation than with imperial expansion. It appears that Suren, a feudal lord from the east and the battle of Carrhae's brilliant Parthian tactician, was murdered by royal order; and Orodes is said to have mounted repressive campaigns against other Parthian aristocrats. Notwithstanding these moves, Orodes in turn was murdered around 40 BC by his own son, Phraates, whom he had already appointed as his successor. Phraates IV (38–32 BC) took preventive measures to ensure that the same fate did not happen to him, executing his brothers as well as his own son. Even so, Phraates was forced to concentrate his attention on diffusing the grievances of the Parthian aristocracy.

In addition, when Rome emerged with a united empire after years of civil war, Parthia found itself once more facing the threat of interference on its western borders. The emperor Augustus was able to put sufficient pressure on Parthia that it acknowledged

The Parthian and Sasanian empires.

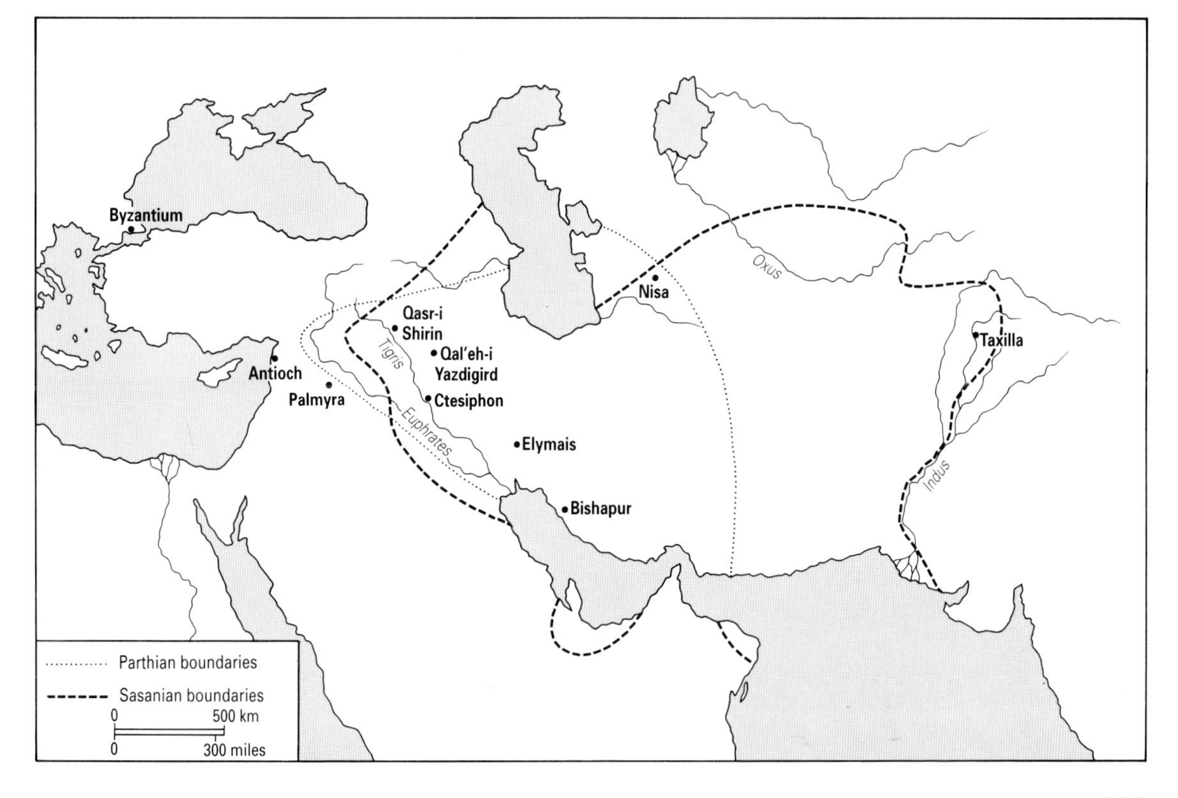

Armenia as a Roman possession, and also released the legionary standards that the Parthians had held since the battle of Carrhae. In return, the Romans acknowledged the Euphrates as the western border of Parthia. Perhaps as a sign of good faith, though conceivably also out of fear of potential patricide, Phraates sent four of his sons to Rome as guarantors of the peace. Augustus had recognized that political manoeuvring might be just as effective against Parthia as a military campaign. The Pandora's box component of the treaty was the gift to Phraates of Musa, a slave girl who became the Parthian king's favourite wife. She bore Phraates a son, Phraataces. Eventually Musa poisoned the old king and took the throne herself, along with her son. On the coins Musa is shown as co-regent (2 BC–AD 4).

The Musa–Phraataces years were marked by increasing Roman attempts to manipulate Parthian affairs. During yet another squabble over the question of ownership of Armenia, Rome forced Phraataces to relinquish once again any claim to that territory, in return for Roman recognition of the latter's right to be Parthian sovereign. When he died, and his successor Orodes III enjoyed only a brief reign (4–7), Augustus engineered the return of one of the four 'hostage' sons of Phraates IV. But the son he sent, Vonones, was not acceptable to the aristocracy, whose reaction to the 'effete' foreigner is succinctly reported by Tacitus. The Parthian aristocrats' own candidate accepted the invitation to bid for the throne, was successful and became Artabanus III (10–38). The exiled Vonones fled to Armenia.

Artabanus' attempt to consolidate power in his own hands, however, brought about a backlash from his supporters, as well as a reaction once more from Rome. Artabanus had also removed the native kings of Media, Elymais, Persis and Characene, substituting his own viceroys. There are also grounds for suggesting that he attempted to reduce the strength of the barons, the people who had put him in power. Becoming dissatisfied with their candidate, the barons negotiated with Rome to send another of the sons of Phraates IV back to Parthia. When the nominee died *en route*, a second candidate, a grandson, was sent. The replacement was successfully installed in the capital, Ctesiphon, as Tiridates III of Parthia around 36. Artabanus was expelled. However, as with his predecessor, Vonones, the expatriate king soon lost favour and the disenchanted nobility invited Artabanus back again.

Artabanus and his successors continued to be preoccupied with Armenia. Only twice in the next 100 years was there a peace that lasted as long as a generation (beginning in 37 and 67). At home there were serious social upheavals, and the city of Seleucia-on-the-Tigris was in a state of rebellion that was only finally put down in 43, after a seven-year insurrection, an event marked by the final loss of civic autonomy for this former Graeco-Macedonian colony. Artabanus appears to have often relied upon minority groups for support, such as when he entrusted the control of southern Babylonia to two Jewish robber barons. Distrust of Rome made the Jews obvious potential supporters of the Parthian throne.

The Decline of Parthia

Patterns of fraternal strife and attempted manipulation of the throne in Armenia continued to plague Parthia. Its evident confusion may have been largely instrumental in convincing the Roman emperor Nero that it was feasible to reclaim Armenia, though his campaign under Corbulo was indecisive. But the fact that an embassy from the province of Hyrcania reached Rome serves to underline the fact that the former heartland of Parthia scarcely belonged to the Parthian monarchy any more. Characene too had regained its independence. In 45 the Parthians no longer had control of the city of Susa in Khuzistan, if one can judge correctly from the coin evidence.

During the first century it appears that two monarchs sometimes struck coins in the capital from the same mint. While these actions have often been interpreted as indications of civil war, it may be just as reasonable to suggest that there was some degree of power-sharing from time to time. In 110 Pacorus II (77–115) even put the kingdom of Osrhoene up for sale. Such a move would tend to suggest that he was forced to return to a policy of decentralization, after a bold show of strength during the middle of his career, when he was portrayed on his coins in a victory pose.

The figure of Osroes who struck coins intermittently between 89 and 127, never claimed the old title King of Kings, yet it was he who was the main protagonist against the emperor Trajan when the latter invaded Armenia. Just as it is unclear whether or not Osroes' opposition to Trajan represented political opportunism, so the actual Roman aggression may well have been motivated by a number of different ambitions, of which the settlement of Armenia was only one. Trajan invaded Armenia in 114, and did not hesitate to kill Pathamisirsis, the Parthian candidate for the throne. He then went on during two successive campaigns to take the Parthian capital, reaching the Persian Gulf before the end of 116.

In spite of these reverses, Parthia escaped this time with little more than a swift and brief invasion, because Trajan died suddenly in 117 and Hadrian realized that the eastern conquests were untenable. Yet before the end of the Parthian era the Romans invaded Armenia three more times and tried to manipulate affairs to suit their own purposes: under Avidius Cassius, directed by the emperor Lucius Verus, in 163, when Dura Europos fell into western hands; under Septimius Severus in 199; and under Caracalla in 217, although the latter's assassination once more left Parthia largely unscathed.

However, the increasing number of divisions within the realm, and a chronic lowering of silver standards in the coinage, give a clear indication of how badly Parthia was in decline. Already by this time the Persian prince Papak had begun a rebellion which was eventually to lead to the Parthians' overthrow. Moves by the last Parthian king, Artabanus V (*c.* 213–24), failed to dislodge the upstart, and two years later Ardashir, Papak's son, was crowned king of all Iran.

War and External Relations

Parthia's external affairs were dominated by two factors: national security and international trade. The most persistent border disputes were in the extreme north-eastern and north-western segments of the realm. Since the origins of the Parthians themselves had been in that north-eastern section, it is hardly surprising that there should be further pressure by tribal groups of the same kind operating in that area. Following the death of Mithridates I in 138 BC, two kings in turn suffered fatal reverses fighting to resolve the question of territorial rights of the Śaka tribes along the eastern border of Iran. The tribal threat was quietened for a while when the Śaka moved into the province of Drangiana, where they settled straddling the modern Iran–Afghanistan border, giving the area the name of Śakastene (the modern province of Seistan). But while the political settlement in Śakastene reached by Mithridates resolved the Śaka problem for the Parthians, it paved the way for the establishment of a largely independent kingdom (known to numismatists as 'Indo-Parthia'), whose subsequent history was often more bound up with India than it was with Iran. The fluctuating nature of Parthia's eastern borders, then, confirms that it is misleading to speak of an empire.

Later, towards the end of the Parthian period, another group, known to us as the Kuṣāṇas, came for a while to dominate the reaches on both sides of the Hindu Kush, present-day Afghanistan and northern Pakistan. They formed one of the many tribal groups, as already described, who filled a vacuum in Central Asia and northern India after the demise of the Seleucids, establishing West Asia's link with China. Since the art of sailing the open ocean had not yet been mastered, these land links from western China to the narrower seas of the Persian Gulf and the Gulf of Aden were pivotal in any early east–west contacts.

A Chinese version of the 'Parthian shot'.

Contacts with China

The existence of China was unknown during the lifetime of Alexander the Great. Not for another two centuries would the first Chinese envoys travel westwards in order to find allies against the Xiongnu, the Huns. Then an alliance was made with another nomadic people, the Da Yuezhi, who themselves had been pushed westwards by the Xiongnu. Though this piece of diplomacy was not without its perils – ambassador Zhang Qian endured a decade of Xiongnu captivity before returning to China in 126 BC – the encounter was fortuitous and may be looked upon as a catalyst for the development of transcontinental traffic along what was later to be called the Silk Road.

The beginnings of this trade lay with China's interest in acquiring superior horses, the fabled Ferghana stock. Zhang Qian's reports of 'blood-sweating' horses caused the Han emperor Wu Di to connect them with an oracle about the 'heavenly horse'. On his second mission, in 115 BC, Zhang Qian brought back not only horses but also a wide range of plant products, including the grape vine and alfalfa. The initial diplomacy, prompted by questions of national security, paved the way for the growth of long-distance trade. His explorations represent the first beginnings of regular communications between China and Iran.

A second highly significant mission from China was dispatched westwards in AD 97. It is thought that the Chinese were trying to make direct contact with Rome so as to overcome problems with the Parthians, who sought to impose very heavy customs duties on the silk trade. Quite possibly the political troubles in Parthian Iran also affected the security of the trade routes in the Euphrates corridor. During the first century, the 'secret' of the monsoon winds had become common knowledge, and the opportunity to outflank Parthia by sea became possible, using the predictability of the seasonal winds. At this point, the Nabataeans of Petra were still independent of Rome, maintaining a link across Arabia, which permitted caravans from the port of Gerrha to reach the Mediterranean, staying out of Parthian control.

The Chinese mission of 97 reached Characene, at the head of the Persian Gulf, near modern Basra in Iraq. However, by now, this important entrepôt appears to have been subsumed again by Parthia, for the Chinese reported that the former principality was ruled by a Parthian governor. The absence of Characenian coins between 73 and 101 may well corroborate this position. And the mission seems to have been deterred from proceeding beyond this point by the tales of the horrors to be encountered on the way if they attempted to round Arabia.

To a certain extent, there was probably a genuine element of truth in what appear as exaggerated tales.

Until public knowledge of the phenomenon of the seasonal winds was widespread, craft could rarely cross open water, except for blind dashes across large bays or stretches of open sea. The Red Sea had never been easy for sailing craft, due to the prevalence of coral reefs and sandbanks close to the shore, and the lack of reliable winds in the northern half. The work of Ptolemy in the second century did much to advance cartography, but there were still no practical maps or charts to make navigation completely safe. Boats and their steering mechanisms were relatively primitive, so they had to stay close to the coast, where the off-shore winds were not always predictable. They could sail only by day, if they hoped to avoid the reefs. As a consequence, long-distance communication was slow. Overland trade, using camels, was often the preferred alternative. Even though ships sailed to India, they did not yet navigate as far as China. One overland route from China operated by way of the Pamirs, connecting with the mouth of the Indus and ships that plied the Red Sea and the Gulf. Land routes across the Arabian peninsula formed the western leg of this lengthy and complicated journey. Goods transported were precious commodities for which a high return on volume and weight could be guaranteed. The *Periplus of the Erythraean Sea*, a first-century merchant's guide to the Indian Ocean fringe, lists silk, pepper, cinnamon, perfumes, medicines, cotton and sugar cane as goods shipped from India in exchange for gold and glass beads.

As the Roman empire developed into a money economy, eastern spices and perfumes were purchased in large quantities, but the bulk of the trade remained raw silk thread. Stoic Roman writers lamented extravagant tastes and deplored the passing of a simple way of life. The moralist Seneca wrote: 'I see garments, if one may call them garments, in which there is nothing to cover either the wearer's body or her shame.' The monetary costs were also considerable. Commenting on what he saw as a devastating imbalance in foreign trade, Pliny complained that in one year India drained the Roman treasury of 550 million sesterces: 'In exchange for trifles, our money is sent to foreign lands and even to our enemies.' Eastern goods imported into Rome brought prices 100 times higher than their original cost, with the result that the gold aureus was exchanged for these luxuries in such large quantities that supplies of the precious metal were being exhausted in Rome. Archaeology attests to the export of manufactured glass and metal objects eastwards, but it is obvious that there was a serious deficit in the Roman economy. The colossal trade imbalance may have been one of the reasons for the emperor Trajan's invasion of Parthia in 114. But as with other conflicts in this border area, events are almost inextricably bound up with the history of Armenia and Parthian and Roman attempts to establish firm control there.

The Armenian Question

The frontier had been a bone of contention ever since Rome's expansion into West Asia under Pompey in the first century BC. The creation of Armenia as a state had been one of the consequences of Rome's defeat of the Seleucids in 190 BC, with the resulting recognition of Armenian independence under the dynasty of Artaxiad I (190–159 BC). Later, following the successful campaign of the Parthian Mithridates II in the general area of eastern Turkey, the then crown prince, Tigranes, was sent to Iran as a hostage in 105 BC – a condition of the peace terms. But on the death of the old king, Artavazd I (123–95 BC), Tigranes was allowed to return to Armenia and take his legitimate throne.

It should be emphasized that the Armenians were not Iranians, though their language was Indo-European and many of them spoke both Iranian and Greek besides their native tongue. It was Tigranes II (95–55 BC) who first established a firm territorial identity for his people, uniting a number of smaller Transcaucasian principalities into the kingdom of Greater Armenia, roughly centred around Lake Sevan and Lake Van to the south of it. For his efforts, he earned the title 'Tigranes the Great'. The original capital of Artaxata, near Mount Ararat, was replaced by his new seat at Tigranakert, close to the headwaters of the Tigris, near the modern Turkish-Syrian border. In addition, Tigranes II's annexation of territory west of the Euphrates added a large part of the area generally known later as Lesser Armenia to the main body of the country.

To the west of Armenia lay the kingdom of Pontus, along the shore of the Black Sea, which had absorbed the northern part of Lesser Armenia. There, the ambitious ruler was Mithridates VI, who secured his eastern holdings by making Tigranes his son-in-law, and then trying valiantly in 88 BC to drive the Roman forces out of Asia Minor. However, in the inevitable Roman counter-attack Mithridates lost so much that he was forced to seek refuge in Armenia, this inadvertently bringing Tigranes into the conflict with Rome.

As a result of the Roman general Pompey's subsequent campaign in Armenia in 66 BC, Rome came face to face with Parthia. This initiated a century of rivalry between the two great powers, almost always involving attempts to manipulate Armenian affairs to their respective advantage, although Armenia remained, technically, an independent state. Many of republican Rome's great figures dreamed of eastern conquest as a way of establishing their reputations and their personal fortunes: Mark Antony's desperate failure in Armenia is a classic example of such often rash adventures. For the emperor Augustus political considerations were more important than personal gain. He recognized the potential danger for Roman interests of an Armenia allied with Parthia, although he did not feel inclined normally to go further than arrange for pro-Roman members of the royal family to take the throne. With the end of the Artaxiad line at the turn of the millennium, opportunities increased for political manipulation of the country by outsiders.

No native son of Armenia appeared capable of challenging the constant intervention from outside. This was true even when the country actually rebelled in

53 at the idea of being ruled by Rhadamistus, a despised member of the Iberian royal family, who had moved into Armenia to assassinate Mithridates, the preferred Roman candidate. (The Iberians were located further to the north, in the Caucasus.) The ensuing Parthian intervention, taking advantage of Armenian discontent, resulted in the installation of Tiridates, the younger brother of the Parthian king. Although challenged by Nero, whose veteran general Corbulo waged a long and sometimes difficult campaign, a peaceful compromise was arrived at whereby the Parthian Tiridates travelled to Rome in 66 to be crowned by the emperor in recognition of his vassal status. Notwithstanding his subservience, though, Tiridates I (53–75) founded the Arsacid line of Armenian kings, which furnished a number of rulers before the line was finally terminated in the early fifth century.

Indeed, in spite of being reduced briefly to provincial status under Trajan in 114, subjected to invasion in 163 by Lucius Verus and viciously attacked by Caracalla in 212, Armenia retained its largely independent status right down to the Sasanian takeover of Iran, which began technically in 226. Caracalla's successor, Macrinus, who was forced to sue for peace with the Parthians, was prepared to recognize Tiridates II (217–52) as lawful heir to the throne, and the latter maintained his loyalty to the Arsacid line by siding with the emperor Severus Alexander in his stand against the Sasanian Ardashir's attacks on Roman territory. But Ardashir's campaign was brilliant, and Armenia found itself completely defenceless following the Roman retreat, though it may not have actually been subjugated by the Sasanians during Ardashir's lifetime.

The Struggle against Rome

The first real direct confrontation with Rome had begun innocently as a minor territorial squabble along the upper Euphrates in 66 BC, when Pompey invaded Armenia. Although Pompey allowed Tigranes to stay on the throne of Armenia as a client king, representing a *détente* of sorts, the Romans occupied Gordyene – the upper Tigris region previously claimed by Parthia's Mithridates II. Knowledge of an internal struggle for control of Parthia may have allowed another Roman to fantasize about a glorious conquest of West Asia. In 55 BC the pro-consul Crassus methodically set about using his impending governorship of Syria to stage an invasion of Parthia. By 53 BC he had a large force of 40,000 legionary soldiers assembled, although there were few cavalry troops. The cavalry he expected to raise from the principalities of northern Mesopotamia and Armenia, where the Parthian king Orodes went to face his expected attack.

Being told that one of the Parthian contingents was in retreat, Crassus made the mistake of striking out from the Euphrates in pursuit across the open Syrian steppe (in Roman eyes, a 'trackless waste'), towards the town of Carrhae. Completely outmanoeuvred by repeated attacks from mailed horse-lancers and mounted archers, half of the Roman force was lost. Crassus himself fled, but he was pursued and killed; 10,000 men were taken prisoner, along with their legionary standards. As a result, the Parthians acquired instant international notoriety for their spectacular prowess as cavalrymen, in spite of the fact that the Roman attack was ill-conceived by an ageing politician and completely mismanaged because of inappropriate tactics.

The Parthians, however, were unable to take advantage of the situation as a result of internal wrangling. Similar domestic political feuding prevented the Parthians from exploiting another heavy Roman defeat – this time Mark Antony's loss in 36 BC of almost one-quarter of the 100,000 troops with which he was planning to invade Media. Interestingly, as in the case of Crassus' campaign, it was the desertion of the Armenian contingent that made the Roman attack no longer viable. It was Augustus who finally seized the initiative and drew up peace terms favourable to Rome.

In 12 the failure of the Parthian Vonones to acquire the confidence of the aristocracy in Iran forced him to flee to Armenia, where Augustus installed him temporarily on the throne, until pressured by Artabanus III to remove him. Vonones went into the custody of the Roman governor of Syria. Artabanus, meanwhile, attempted to place one of his own sons on the Armenian throne, which in turn prompted the new emperor, Tiberius, to counter by dispatching his general Germanicus. The latter's resolution of the power vacuum in Armenia was to install another foreign king, this time from Pontus, who adopted the title of Artaxias III. Later, Tiberius continued his attempt to turn events his way, inciting Pharasmanes, king of the Iberians, to take control of Armenia, before replacing him with his brother Mithridates. Artabanus' attempts to resist and place his own candidate on the throne resulted in a disastrous rout of his forces, eventually forcing the Parthian king into exile. After further manoeuvring a treaty was agreed with Rome which recognized the *status quo* in Armenia and the line of the Euphrates as the frontier of Parthia.

Yet again, in 53, the Parthians took steps to install a protégé in Armenia. This time it was the murderous rule of the Iberian Rhadamistus, son of Pharasmanes, which served as the excuse for the Parthian Vologases I to place his younger brother, Tiridates, on the Armenian throne. Naturally, this caused consternation in Rome, where Nero mounted a campaign, led by his general Corbulo, to restore Roman authority in the east. Vologases was distracted by the rebellion of his son Vardanes, but much more serious than this was an uprising in the north-eastern province of Hyrcania. This event is famous for the embassy sent by the Hyrcanians which reached Corbulo in Armenia and returned by way of the Red Sea in order to circumvent the Parthians. For all its initial success, however, the Roman campaign lost momentum. Eventually the deadlock was resolved: Nero agreed to allow Tiridates to stay on the throne, on condition that the investiture took place in Rome. Tiridates' strict observance of

A Parthian sculpture from Hatra, a city often the subject of dispute between Parthia and Rome.

Zoroastrian custom on the journey serves to remind us that Armenia at this time was still predominantly influenced by eastern culture.

Of course, the convenient truce between Rome and Parthia did not last. The next pretext for overt action in Armenia occurred when Osroes, himself possibly a Parthian pretender, deposed the incumbent Armenian king and placed the crown upon the head of his own designate, Axidares, another member of the Arsacid royal family. This act prompted a hostile reaction from Trajan, who in Athens rejected Osroes' embassy and offer to substitute Parthamasiris on the throne instead. Trajan's own invasion of Armenia in 114, during which he deposed the Arsacid Parthamasiris, was followed by his conquest of all of Mesopotamia during the next two years' campaigns. Whatever its other motives, in all likelihood the invasion was seen as necessary to balance the Roman foreign debt, by taking the Indian trade directly into Roman hands. Following this line of argument, Trajan set out to conquer Parthia as a way of avoiding the heavy taxes placed on goods from India and China traded across Iran. The opportunity to establish direct links with India was made possible by the emergence there of the major independent force of the Kuṣāṇas. Rome's annexation of Nabataea in 106, as the province of Arabia, provided the western link in the chain.

By 116 Trajan had created the provinces of 'Armenia', 'Mesopotamia' and 'Assyria', taken Ctesiphon, the Parthian capital, and reached the Persian Gulf. The war prompted ancient writers to suggest that Trajan may have aspired to emulate Alexander and conquer the whole of Asia. However, as it turns out, the Romans were severely limited in their ability to hold the invaded territory. A significant revolt was brewing in northern Mesopotamia even before Trajan completed his campaign. Recent scholarship has suggested that although the Mesopotamian uprising was quelled, the pressure of Jewish revolts which followed in Palestine and Africa made Trajan's distant eastern conquests untenable. Whatever the explanation, Trajan withdrew from northern Mesopotamia and died *en route* to Italy in 117 without having consolidated any of his Parthian conquests. His successor, Hadrian, recognized the dangers of having to defend the too far-flung extremities of the Roman empire and abandoned the briefly held provinces of Mesopotamia and Assyria without resolving Rome's eastern trade imbalance.

After Hadrian, international trade along the Silk Road corridors actually increased. However, neither of the two great powers appear to have been the recipients of the real benefits of the commerce. The winners in the new scheme of things were the merchants of Palmyra, and other Syrian and Mesopotamian desert cities, such as Dura Europos. Trade inscriptions attest to the fact that caravans returned regularly from Characene to Palmyra, by way of the emporium of Vologesias, the customs post established by the Parthians to control trade along the Euphrates. There was a resident community of Palmyrene merchants in Charax itself, as well as at Alexandria in Egypt.

In 138 Palmyrene ambassadors visited the authorities in Elymais, an Iranian kingdom on the edge of the Iranian highlands which was independent of the Parthian King of Kings. These diplomatic moves circumventing Parthian Iran were matched by practical measures, which included the protection of the middle reaches of the Euphrates by Palmyrene mercenaries. Eventually, because of the peaceful conditions fostered as a result, caravans to Palmyra were able to pass directly from Babylonia across the desert to Syria, avoiding the Euphrates and the Parthians altogether. These merchant principalities flourished, while Parthia became an increasingly ineffective state, unable to maintain even token unity or control of the trade. In the end, Rome was able to take Dura Europos, and it was Rome, not Parthia, that dealt the merchant kingdom of Palmyra its death blow in 270. When Roman dominance finally ended, it was not because of a Parthian resurgence but because of the Sasanians.

Life and Society

Western scholars, as *aficionados* of Hellenic civilization, have tended in the past to see West Asia after Alexander the Great as a region gradually reverting to barbarism. The agonies experienced by his troops, because the terrain was different and the climate unlike that at home, are described at length. They encountered vast tracts of desert, impenetrable mountain ranges, saline rivers, severe extremes in climate and often enormous distances between cultivated, inhabited regions.

Speaking of the campaign in India, Curtius talks of the desolation of the landscape and the 'pathless solitude' which terrified the soldiers. However, it is wrong to view West Asia from this European standpoint. After all, the Persian empire of the Achaemenids had functioned for many years before Alexander's arrival. There were administrators and farmers, artisans and scribes, and effective lines of communication connecting the extremities of the provinces. The representatives of distant provinces presented themselves regularly at official ceremonies in the royal capital. If one can interpret the scant archaeological evidence, these contacts promoted international commerce.

Of course, the impact of Alexander's conquest of West Asia cannot be ignored. He founded cities peopled with veteran soldiers and artisans, leaving abiding centres of Greek culture scattered from the Mediterranean right across West Asia. Greek ideals in the arts and sciences, religion, political thought and law became universal expressions, irrespective of geography or national boundaries. Yet without detracting from the impact Alexander, or rather his successors, had upon the area, it is important to define West Asia from an internal perspective. The problem is that the most accessible texts are those written from the viewpoint of Rome, Iran's enemy, so even apart from any deliberate attempt to distort original sources now lost, the writers would have been outsiders, with all the scope for misunderstanding that entails.

The Parthian Identity

Unfortunately, there is an abysmal lack of substantive, contemporaneous source material concerning the history of the 500 years of Parthian history written by West Asians. What does exist is often either very obscure in topic or virtually indecipherable except by language specialists, which really makes meaningful interpretation of the subject matter very difficult. At very best, a few nuances have to serve as the framework for characterizing an entire society. Often the references are to the rulers alone; we may get little sense of the common populace or even of the aristocrats just below the level of the royal family. And the Sasanian rulers of the subsequent 400 years seem to have made distinct efforts to suppress the history of their Parthian predecessors. The Iranian dialect spoken by the Parthians ceased to be used in official inscriptions by the end of the third century, and Middle Persian became the sole language of state. Because the Zoroastrian religious traditions of earlier centuries were not formally written down until the later Sasanian period, including translations of the much earlier hymns of the prophet Zoroaster himself, the erroneous impression is given that the Parthians did not care very much about their national religion.

Islam's preoccupation with its own destiny meant that the details of Iran's history after Alexander never became part of a widespread scribal tradition that could perpetuate, as it did in Europe, a memory of the past. Although there are historiographic traditions from Islamic times regarding the Iranian past, much of it glorifies the exotic and the bizarre, thus excluding the vast majority of people and most aspects of ordinary life. The challenge of trying to reconstruct a picture of Parthian Iran from a variety of different and obscure sources is compounded by apparent regional disparities.

In spite of the fact that the Seleucid settlement of West Asia had far-reaching impact, provincial governors retained considerable powers, which may have fostered the separate development of local religious and linguistic traditions. This would explain, for instance, the growth of different but related languages as an expression of Iranian culture. Admittedly, the kings continued to mint coins in Greek denominations, if not strictly in the purest of Greek styles, and with Greek inscriptional formulae. Also, the persistent use of the royal title Phil-Hellene neatly illustrates a continued desire on the part of the rulers to accommodate the Greek communities within the new Parthian state. From inscriptions, it seems that Greek was used in Iran for formal administration, but this should be seen as helping ensure loyalty from the minority Greek population and their assistance in running the state. Anyway, the continued use of what amounted to an archaic language for official purposes probably did not affect the lives of ordinary people any more than the use of Latin in modern law reflects our own today.

On the other hand, astute or not, the Iranian populace may not have been too keen on these foreign intrusions. For instance, the adoption of the honorific titles of *theos*, or 'god', and *theopator*, meaning 'descended from the gods', must have been intolerable to a conservative Zoroastrian priesthood. The Zoroastrian response to the adoption of the old Seleucid royal titles by the Parthian kings on their coins is also unknown. Similarly, it is hard to judge the extent of the reaction to the way in which the Greek settlers after Alexander set up anthropomorphic representations of their gods when they arrived. Indeed, it has been suggested during the late Achaemenid period that the Zoroastrian priesthood deliberately promoted the formal cult of fire, as the religion's most visible sign of worship, in order to counter the increasing veneration for man-made icons. In the Parthian period, a subtle difference may have permitted easier assimilation of the Greek practice. There was nothing in the Greek custom that prevented the transfer of a new meaning to the original form. Thus an identifiable Zeus or Apollo, a Nike or a Heracles, could be used to represent the Iranian equivalent of Ahura Mazda or Mithra, Ashi or Verethragna. By being willing to adapt in this way, Zoroastrianism may also have ensured its survival at this difficult time.

Another example of how the Zoroastrian clergy of the Parthian period appear to have been willing to accommodate change relates to consanguineous marriage. Ever since the time of Cambyses, it had been a perfectly acceptable, if not positively desirable, practice for kings to engage in *khvaetvadatha*, or 'next-of-kin marriage'. In underlining how orthodox Zoroastrianism would have seen this as an abnormal practice, it is argued that the custom may reflect Zoroastrian willingness to accept an element of strong matriarchal culture from religious traditions still surviving from the old Elamite (second millennium BC) period in Iran.

In Parthian Iran, most business transactions were in Aramaic, a Semitic language that had been the *lingua franca* of West Asia since Achaemenid times. With the increased independence of the various components of Parthian Iran, different scribal schools began to use their own versions of the Aramaic script for their Iranian language. Different languages like Median (in Azerbaijan), Parthian (in Turkmenistan), Sogdian (in Tajikistan) and Khwarezmian (in Uzbekistan) began to develop. At first, local words appeared scattered as foreign intrusions in the Aramaic texts. Ultimately, the Aramaic words were used as ideograms, so that their shapes were Aramaic but the words were pronounced as Parthian ones, or other Iranian equivalents.

Using the standard historical sources, however, it is hard to find a way to characterize the Parthian populace. If one tabulates the list of events known to us, the impression gleaned is one of an endless round of minor confrontations with Rome. When a peace treaty was drawn up, the wars were interrupted for a short generation or so and some semblance of order was established. But political wrangling then ensued within the country. So, the Parthians could be argued to be their own worst enemies. A pattern of fratricide and patricide plagued the royal family for almost a century and diverted energy away from significant international issues. Though there were frequent skirmishes with the Romans west of the Euphrates, the Parthians were often unable to capitalize politically upon their military successes, even when Rome was experiencing civil war.

There is a danger in focusing exclusively on the royal family in Parthian history, for it obviously excludes the question of what was actually happening in broader social and cultural terms. For example, tensions in the city of Seleucia-on-the-Tigris, which culminated in a seven-year civil war beginning in 38, may well have stemmed from the different backgrounds and aspirations of the city-dwellers and the Parthian barons, who were trying to control the throne of Parthia. The existence of these groups, which can be postulated from a study of numismatic and textual evidence, must surely have resulted in different cultural expressions for which we have little tangible evidence.

Owing to the paucity of original source material and frequent adulation of the achievements of Alexander, western historians have had a tendency to evaluate the Parthian state by focusing upon the foreign elements that became part of its culture. Nowhere is this better seen than in the dramatic reports surrounding the death of Crassus, the Roman pro-consul who lost his life during the botched attempt to invade Parthia during the mid-first century BC. News of the dramatic success in halting the invasion reached the ears of the Parthian king Orodes while he was being entertained at the Armenian court. According to Plutarch, the royal party was watching a performance of Euripides' *Bacchae* when the severed head of Crassus was brought on stage, representing the mutilated remains of the play's victim, Pentheus. The fact that two royal Iranian figures were watching a Greek play is, of course, immensely revealing. It is also remarkable that over two centuries after Alexander's death, a Greek play should be performed in a country like Armenia, which must have received few new Greek speakers, apart from those in the garrison towns founded by Alexander. Few writers have been able to resist the temptation, however, to treat this gruesome stage prop as another example of eastern barbarity.

Setting parochialism aside, there are some useful pointers to be found in the report, thus indicating how the small details of a story can be used to establish broader principles, and help identify what might be termed a national character. The fact that Orodes of Iran and Artavasdes of Armenia were watching a play together is innocent enough, until one is reminded that Crassus had arranged for Artavasdes to provide him with 30,000 troops in the event of the Romans choosing the Tigris route to the Parthian capital by way of the mountainous terrain of Armenia. The theatre performance, in fact, was part of the festivities celebrating the new alliance between Iran and Armenia, which was sealed with the marriage of Orodes' son to Artavasdes' sister. Although there is nothing remarkable by itself in such an arranged marriage, it underlines how easily the eastern and western borders of Parthian Iran might fluctuate through alliances of this kind when common Iranian heritage existed. At times it is hard to discern what is really Parthian territory and what is not.

Ancient Iran encompassed territories that now lie within the borders of different nation states, including Iraq, the former Soviet Union and Afghanistan. From time to time, parts of the Arabian peninsula were also occupied. Because of contemporary Iranian national interests, Iranian studies have often been focused upon the history and culture of the Iranian heartland, the area of modern Iran itself. As future studies generate more and more information about life in southern Arabia and Central Asia, this will be found to be a slightly biased ethno-centric position, and conclusions will need to be modified. For the moment, however, the central Iranian focus is the only vantage-point for which there is sufficient published evidence to substantiate our ideas.

Levels of Authority

One of the reasons for our uncertainty over the exact territorial extent of the Parthian realm is the lack of administrative documents or official inscriptions which might provide evidence. While a single reference may list the groups of people comprising Parthia, and the kings may have claimed grandiose titles for themselves, it is not apparent that the machinery of imperial government was ever put in place, after the initial annexation of a given territory following conquest. There was no standing army in Parthia and no central bureaucracy. Typifying this apparently fundamental lack of strong centralized control, it appears that towards the end of Mithridates II's reign in the first century BC, a senior governor he had previously honoured, a certain Gotarzes, took the opportunity to declare himself king in Babylonia. But it may be wrong to imply that this was simply incompetence or, at best, weakness. The adoption, around 109 BC, of the old title 'King of Kings' by Mithridates II signals the fact that the Parthian monarch did also have aspirations to be seen as heir to Achaemenid authority and might have wished to become more powerful. This move may be seen, of course, as no more than a clever ploy on the part of the king to acquire legitimacy in the eyes of those Parthian conservatives who might have still seen the Arsacid family as upstarts.

In the political climate of the contemporary world, when the concept of empire itself has ceased to be the ideal way to approach the administration of vastly disparate territories, it may be possible to see the Parthians' somewhat loose formula for administration as a successful system of government over the Iranian realms. The formula for this kind of fluid, non-centralized state had really been inherited from the Achaemenids. While there can be no denying that frequent power struggles around the Parthian throne took place, and different principalities even distanced themselves from the royal Parthian capital, it is questionable to what extent such actions should be viewed as simple rebellion. A minor king could strike a coin without necessarily being a rebel. One might argue that, at times, there appears rather to have existed a mutual acceptance of varying degrees of independence. It is also true that during what seems to be a particularly weak period from the point of view of centralized authority some of the most vital developments in the arts occurred. There was, in fact, an Iranian cultural revival. The problems surrounding the throne at that time may not necessarily have interrupted other developments.

We get a tantalizing glimpse of the ranks below the level of king in the colourful description of Parthian battle tactics. Crassus' failed campaign, which brought unprecedented national disgrace to Rome, is famous for the unique manoeuvres that the Parthians practised in battle. English literature has created a colourful metaphor from the devastating hit-and-run tactics of the Iranian mounted archers, 'a Parthian shot', which has come to mean the stinging remark left by a parting lover. Parthian archers would ride towards the stationary infantry, discharging arrows at full gallop, and then, wheeling around as though to withdraw, turn in the saddle and fire more arrows before pulling away to a safe distance, where they re-armed from camel trains.

One may also extrapolate from another vivid episode some sense of the Parthian barons' preferred lifestyle. The occasion was the return to Iran of a Roman-backed nominee for the Parthian throne in 8–9, Vonones. He had been educated in Rome as an expatriate Parthian and brought his Roman habits with him when he was installed as king. Tacitus records how he was carried in a litter when he travelled and preferred to recline when dining. The aversion of the barons towards this odd foreigner resulted in their issuing a counter-invitation to a more distant member of the royal family. The new candidate, Artabanus, was an aristocrat from Hyrcania, in north-eastern Iran. It is reported that when the invitation came, Artabanus was out hunting. It is possible to deduce that the barons' lifestyles must have continued to include the kind of hunting and banqueting that had been illustrated in royal art since Assyrian times.

Art and Architecture

Perhaps the greatest impact that the Graeco-Macedonian conquest had upon Iran was in the visual arts, and by extension in the field of religious expression. What remains to be resolved is whether the impact was more than superficial. Discussion invariably resorts to the tangible symbols of a regime to identify its character. In this way, monuments, statues and coins are treated as silent expressions of the past. Yet in the case of Parthian Iran, this may cause a distortion, for there is a tendency to judge these works of art simply by gauging their closeness to a western classical norm.

A Parthian figure from Hatra, probably a votive offering.

Also, regardless of how accurately or not the artist chose to portray the anatomical details of the human figure, did the use of these images extend beyond the nobility? We do not really know how the religious authorities formally responded to the increasing use of sculptures to portray individuals.

Judged by world standards, there is not much Parthian art that has survived. A variety of small objects exists, though the lack of sound dating evidence tends to reduce their interpretive potential. Immensely valuable information comes from Parthian coins because of the portraits they bear of the kings. Artistic conventions changed as the era progressed. But the coins are not without their own special kinds of drawbacks, particularly because, until the middle of the first century, the king was identified only by the generic title 'Arsaces' and not by his individual name. The known corpus of Parthian artefacts also includes a limited variety of inscriptions, but here again the evidence is obscure, and no literature from the period has survived in its original form. There are a few inscriptions on small objects, particularly the wine records from Nisa in Turkmenistan, though those from other sites are often more famous for the challenge they present the linguist than the meaningful substance of their contents.

Architecture provides us with the richest legacy, though even here the evidence is confusing. The realm was fragmented, and there were no such things as 'imperial' standards. Also, because of the variety of terrain it is natural to find a range of different building materials used, from sun-dried brick to stone rubble. The majority of the 'name' sites fall in the western and north-eastern extremities of the area, and most lie outside the boundaries of modern Iran. If this inquiry is limited to territory controlled by the Parthian monarchy, one must exclude the Punjab (sites like Taxila), northern Afghanistan (Bactrian sites like Surkh Kotal), Turkmenistan (Nisa, the original capital of the Parthians), Armenia and Asia Minor (Nimrud Dagh), Syria (Palmyra and Dura Europos) and north-western Iraq (Hatra). By around 60, even Kuh-i Khwaja (in Sistan) and Shahr-i Qumis (Hecatompylos, a former Parthian capital, in Gurgan province) lay outside the domain of territory controlled from Ctesiphon. In the west, the famous site of Hatra was built by an Arab principality which maintained only nominal ties with the Parthian crown. Dura Europos fell into Roman hands in 164, and its artwork should be viewed in a special light. As for Palmyra, it was never a Parthian possession, yet it is often cited in the great debate about the nature of Parthian art by those whose background is centred on the classical Mediterranean. Even closer to home, in the foothills of the Zagros mountains at sites such as Qal'eh-i Yazdigird (in Media), and Masjid-i Sulaiman and Bard-i Nishandeh (in Elymais), these monuments were sponsored by figures who were in direct confrontation with the Parthian ruler or who, at very best, paid him only token allegiance.

An Artistic Upsurge

Interestingly enough, the economic factors which were beginning to cripple the empire may actually have fostered the development of the arts. The dimensions of international trade in the first century were such that huge wealth could be accumulated in certain segments of society. It is reasonable to suppose that these *nouveaux riches* were particularly active in the area of sponsorship of the arts, building palaces and monuments to the glory of their own names, and dedicating shrines to the gods for their successful business dealings. By the end of the second century we may even be dealing with a kind of democratization of the arts, as individual economic prosperity permitted the expanding mercantile class and the proliferating petty nobility to indulge in classic manifestations of success but expressed in a new style.

It became fashionable, at least from the evidence of the western reaches of Parthia, for private individuals to have themselves portrayed in life-like sculptures. Albeit sometimes crudely done, these portraits were not idealized in the way Greek artists would have produced them. There can be no denying that, from the middle of the first century onwards, artistic expressions no longer bear the same kind of relationship to Hellenistic models that they did before. In the later period, the artist placed more importance on the personal trappings of the individual than on the beauty of the subject's form. Details of dress may indicate a person's rank or social background.

At Hatra, which is now known to have been a sacred sanctuary rather than a palace, as was once thought, the site's most distinctive artwork is the votive statuary. Here, religion seems to be merely the vehicle for an individual's self-display. One cannot help but think of the way in which deification of the emperor had become part of the Roman consciousness following Augustus. In one sense the Hatra statues are no more religious in essence than a rock relief depicting the king handing out a fiefdom or receiving a conquered vassal.

Whether the changes that the new building plans and sculptural traditions reflect represent a deliberate and intellectual turning away from the old Hellenistic models or something much more practical, such as the unsponsored emergence from obscurity of long-standing, indigenous artistic practices, is hard to judge. Given the fact that at least some of the ancient temples of Babylonia appear to have functioned along traditional lines until as late as the Christian era, it is hardly surprising to see the survival of many motifs and symbols from earlier times. Mother-goddess figurines, of a type scarcely distinguishable from those of centuries earlier, appear in contexts alongside the very latest in imports from the west. Strange beasts reflect the ancient Mesopotamian fondness for hybrid monsters.

In architecture, there emerged the dramatic concept around the middle of the first century of creating a completely open-fronted, barrel-vaulted room on one or more sides of a courtyard. This vaulted *iwan* replaced the archaic Greek *megaron* type of hall where two columns were placed in the portico.

The Parthian use of four *iwans* facing an inner courtyard also appeared at this time. Flanking walls were decorated with articulated façades, decorative stucco in buildings enjoying a tremendous vogue under the Parthians. Readily available as a resource and easily worked, stucco became the standard ornament for buildings constructed from a variety of base materials. The speed with which it could be laid tended to encourage a wallpaper effect, where linked designs covered surfaces in an all-over pattern. Possibly the development occurred in close association with the idea of hanging rugs in a dwelling. It may not be unreasonable to see the nomadic origins of the Parthians playing a role here, providing a tradition where textiles were used, as well as accommodating the need for climate control. However, the design principle of breaking up a wall surface in this way may also have been inherited from ancient Mesopotamian architectural practices, though the architectonic elements used in the decorative scheme reflect the infusion of Hellenistic forms.

Unfortunately there is no archaeological evidence to show how these spaces were used. One can only surmise that the positioning of the *iwans* was in response to the climate, providing alternate shade or sun, depending upon the season. The idea of receptions, dining and entertainment all taking place in a common area is an acceptable extrapolation from traditional West Asian practices. A peristyled court within the palace at Ashur is a good example of the Hellenistic impact on West Asian architecture, though, and in the same complex the appearance of a tetrastyle hall in Achaemenid vein shows how Parthian architects borrowed indiscriminately from a variety of traditions.

Houses, as well as a large ceremonial complex, in the citadel at Nippur, which overlies the city's once-famous ziggurat enclosure, contain halls which feature as *iwans* in groundplan. By contrast, in the contemporaneous temple, the architects deliberately employed an archaic layout, where the use of a sequence of transverse halls leading up to an inner shrine gives a markedly different feeling from that of a longitudinal *iwan*. The Nippur structures are built almost entirely of huge sun-dried bricks, with the occasional fired brick recycled from older structures. The awkward solutions called for in bonding bricks at the corners reflects experimentation, if not incompetence.

Massively buttressed wall systems which preceded the construction of the temple at Waka in the early second century, perhaps as at Nippur, were designed more for their imposing presence than for actual defence purposes. The temple itself, built of fired bricks, retains the sense of an ancient Babylonian temple, with a series of transverse halls leading up to the inner shrine. But the eclectic use of composite orders in a blind façade, with entablatures and arches surmounting the pilasters in between, reflects the same kind of free use of Mediterranean-derived forms observed in the small temples at Hatra, the capital city of an Arab principality whose artwork none the less is often considered to represent the epitome of Parthian architecture.

Chronology

AD

226–40 Ardashir I's conquest of Iran includes take-over of extensive Kuṣāṇa territory in north-east
At the end of his reign he abdicates in favour of Shapur, the crown prince

240–70 Shapur I acquires suzerainty over Armenia in 244 when Philip the Arab's bungled campaign puts the Romans on the defensive in Syria

259 Ignominious defeat of Valerian in 259 and capture of 70,000 Roman prisoners at Edessa match the count of 60,000 taken three years earlier at Antioch

270 In response to the dramatic rise in the fortunes of Palmyra, the Roman emperor Aurelian annexes Queen Zenobia's famous caravan city
After the death of Shapur I, who had been sympathetic to the teachings of Mani, the Zoroastrian prelate Kartir savagely persecutes unorthodox practices

276–9 Romans make inroads back into Mesopotamia while Bahram II is king

293–302 Successful challenge for throne from outside of royal family
Adoption of Christianity in Armenia in 294
In 297 treaty with the Roman emperor Diocletian establishes single transfer point in Syria for entry of raw silk from China, encouraging Sasanian trade monopoly
Death of usurper Narseh in 302

309–79 During Shapur II's long reign the state acquired a centralized bureaucracy
The king showed sympathy for Zurvanism, which challenged the tenets of orthodox Zoroastrianism
In 360, Syrian silk weavers transplanted to south-western Iran

399–420 Reputation for being tolerant of Christians earned by Yazdigird I

420 Accession to throne of Bahram V, who was educated in Arab principality of Lakhmids and celebrated by later Islamic tradition as a great hunter who earned the title of 'Gur' (Wild Ass)

438–57 Yazdigird II attempts to make Armenia Zoroastrian and fails, but the resistance in 451 provided the country with a famous martyr, Vardan

469 Peroz is forced to pay the Huns a ransom for his own release
The King also gave them Kavadh, his son, as a hostage of the peace

488 Installed on the throne of Iran with the aid of the Huns, Kavadh I introduced radical reforms known as the Mazdakite movement, which preached social equality

531 After obliterating the Mazdakites and introducing fiscal reform, Khusrau I undertook yet another successful attack on Antioch in 540 but opted for a truce with the Byzantine emperor Justinian after failing to take Edessa
In 562 Sasanian alliance with the Turks ended the threat of the Huns but paved the way for Turkish intrigues with Byzantium
In a face-off against Byzantium in the Red Sea in 575, the Sasanians oust the Ethiopians from Yemen and install their own governor there

591–628 The Byzantine emperor Maurice backs Khusrau II against the pretender Bahram Chobin
In 609 the Sasanians take Edessa for the first time
Dramatic victories in Palestine and Egypt include the sack of Jerusalem (614) and the capture of Alexandria (619)
After rebuilding the Byzantine army and navy, in 622 Heraclius penetrated deep into Iran by way of the Black Sea but stops short of the capital, Ctesiphon
The murder of the king by his own men heralds an era of chaos and weakness

641 The Sasanian dynasty flees into exile following defeat in the third pitched land battle against the invading Muslim army

A gold coin of Ardashir I, the first Sasanian king. He abdicated in favour of his son Shapur in 241.

The Sasanians (226–651)

E. J. Keall

History

During the last half-century of the Parthian era the western edge of Iran was subjected to numerous Roman invasions, encouraged by the increasing fragmentation of Parthian rule. In the end, however, it was an internal *coup* that spelled the end of the old regime rather than conquest by foreigners. The Sasanians came to power in the early third century, ruling Iran until the Islamic conquest in the middle of the seventh century. Their fame reached from Rome to China. Yet in spite of colourful folk-lore about the beginnings of the Sasanian dynasty, factual details are as scanty as they were for the origin of the Parthian dynasty. It is difficult to establish a firm chronology for events, partly because records were maintained using only an individual ruler's regnal years and not a continuous calendar; discrepancies may occur regarding the actual start of a reign.

Throughout their history, as far as can be judged from the meagre sources, the Sasanian monarchs were far more imperial in their aspirations than the Parthians, eventually even taking over parts of the Arabian peninsula in attempts to control the eastern world's maritime trade. The self-styled Kings of Kings held centre-stage in a global struggle, first with Rome and then with Byzantium, which came to replace Rome as the power of Europe. Zoroastrianism, the religion, experienced the benefits of state support. Agricultural and engineering projects were organized on a scale that far outstripped those of their distinguished Achaemenid predecessors. But Sasanian kings also remained remote from their subjects, emerging only rarely from within the confines of their palaces to appear before the public. Much of what we know about them concerns their military confrontation with Europe.

The Sasanian Empire

It is possible to gain some sense of the Sasanian kings' own view of themselves by examining their published genealogies. Although to the outside world both Parthians and Sasanians were Iranians, within the context of Iran itself there was a distinct difference. Both adopted Ctesiphon, the area around Baghdad, as their capital. But the Parthians represented the north-east, and there was always a sense of a strong link to their past on the steppes of Central Asia. The Sasanians, however, hailed from the south-west, and it is no mere coincidence that the most extensive public display of cultural monuments is to be found in Pars province (former Persis, the Achaemenid homeland, and later Fars under the Arabs).

The Parthians fabricated a genealogy which traced their descent back to the Achaemenid Artaxerxes as a way of establishing their right to rule Iran. Outdoing them, the Sasanians cleverly played with the name of Vishtaspa, the father of Darius, and created a link simultaneously with the mythical, original founder of the Kayanian line of legendary Iranian kings. According to that same legendary tradition, Vishtaspa was also the prophet Zoroaster's patron. This revisionist version of history also maintained that the Parthian period was simply an interlude in the history of Iran after the invasion of Alexander the Great.

The foundation of the Sasanian regime is distinguished from that of the Parthian takeover of Iran by the fact that this was a revolution against fellow countrymen rather than an uprising against foreign intruders. Also, both parties were Zoroastrian, although the Sasanians were the more aggressive proselytizers of that religion. The similarities of both eras are underlined by the fact that the new Sasanian monarchs became entangled in further confrontations, first with the Roman and then with the Byzantine empires. And eastwards, too, incursions by nomadic tribes caused the Sasanians considerable headaches, as with the Parthians before them, including the exile and death of more than one king. Nevertheless, the Sasanian era is usually considered to be quite different from that of its Parthian predecessor.

The revolution began in Fars province. There are conflicting interpretations of how the first king, Ardashir, came to power, depending on whether one follows the Arabic version in the chronicles of the historian Tabari or the Persian literary tradition. All agree that Papak was the first rebel, some two decades before the formal founding of the Sasanian era around 226. He is claimed by some to have been a priestly guardian at the temple of Anahita (situated at Istakhr, near the old capital of Persepolis) who took it upon himself to wrest control of the region from the resident ruler. For some, Papak is simply the father of Ardashir; for others, he is the grandfather who adopted Ardashir when the latter's real father, Sasan, died shortly after the birth. Another tradition makes Papak's daughter marry a shepherd descended from the Achaemenids, from which union Ardashir was born. Whatever the real family tree, Sasan is said to have been the figure who brought royal blood into the line by virtue of his ancestry, hence the name of the dynasty which Ardashir founded.

Ardashir's coins show him wearing different crowns, and this has been taken to reflect different stages in his rise to ascendancy over all of Iran. His first capital was in Fars province, at Firuzabad, where he founded a fortress and city called Ardashir-Khvarrah, or 'the glory of Ardashir'. The first expansion of his territory took place between the lower Euphrates, in southern

Iraq, and Kerman, on the western edge of the central Iranian desert. Following the decisive victory over the Parthian Ardavan in 226, the course of his conquests took him through the eastern provinces that flank modern Afghanistan, and then up into the north-eastern frontier zone of Central Asia. Exactly how far is difficult to judge, because here again there are conflicting references, depending on whether the inferences are drawn from contemporaneous inscriptions or later chronicles.

Tabari's tenth-century account speaks of the defeat of the Kuṣāṇas by Ardashir in the area straddling the Amu Darya, on the River Oxus. Little understood because of their peculiar admixtures of Iranian culture, Buddhist religion and Roman-Hellenistic art, these Kuṣāṇas had nevertheless furnished for a while a political stability in the Indus valley which made promotion of the trans-Asian caravan trade feasible. The Sasanians were to benefit from the network of settlements and lines of communications which the Kuṣāṇas had established.

In the meantime, nominal Parthian resistance continued in the region surrounding the old Parthian capital of Ctesiphon, in Iraq, where Vologases V struck coins as late as 228. But the city fell shortly afterwards to Ardashir, and he then felt free to assume the old title of King of Kings. His new capital there was called Veh Ardashir, meaning 'Ardashir's good deed'.

Following the inception of Sasanian rule, Ardashir made it clear to the Romans that he wished to see them withdraw from what was for them their eastern holdings. He made moves against their various territories in Syria, though the counter-attacks by Alexander Severus were initially successful. After that Roman emperor's assassination in 235, however, the Sasanians were able to take the upper plains area between the rivers Tigris and Euphrates, notably the frontier towns of Carrhae and Nisibis. These fortified cities were strategic for holding up any move against the Mesopotamian heartland. Yet Carrhae and Nisibis counted immediately for less than the anarchy brought about in the Roman empire by military rivalry. So determined were the legionaries to have emperors to their liking that their squabbles raised and pulled down twenty rulers in as many years. In these confused circumstances the Sasanian advance in Syria went unchallenged for the next half-century. Also, the capture by the Sasanians of the previously impregnable city of Hatra in 238 was an extremely important event in the extension of Iranian control into the reaches of the upper Euphrates, since it eliminated one of the strongest Arab groups in the region and a potential ally of Rome in any attempt to drive a wedge between Iran and Armenia.

Coins issued around this time reveal that Ardashir abdicated the throne shortly before his death. His son, the future Shapur I (241–72), is represented alongside him in a double-profile portrait, as crown prince. Later, Shapur appears alone, but without the crown of full kingship, suggesting the period before his actual formal coronation. Like Ardashir, Shapur found that the north-eastern and north-western frontiers were at one and the same time vulnerable as well as tempting for conquest.

Perhaps because of distractions on his north-eastern borders, Shapur I found himself defending the north-western frontier zone very quickly against an invading force led by Timesitheus, an able Roman general acting on behalf of the boy emperor Gordian III. The Romans penetrated down the Euphrates, but their leader died. He was replaced by Philip the Arab, who soon murdered the eighteen-year-old Gordian but lost a decisive battle in 244 against the Sasanians at Meshik, west of present-day Baghdad. In order to make good his own claim to the title of Roman emperor, Philip was obliged to withdraw, pay a large indemnity and cede suzerainty over Armenia. To celebrate their victory, the Sasanians added the epithet Peroz Shapur, 'Shapur victorious', to the town of Meshik.

Assassination in 252 of the Arsacid Armenian king, Khosrov, and the subsequent flight of his son Tiridates to Rome were the precursors to other acts of Sasanian aggression against Roman Syria, which included the sack of Antioch and the capture of its bishop, Demetrianos, who was deported as a prisoner to Iran. Some 60,000 Roman prisoners were claimed to have been captured by the Sasanians at the battle of Barbalissus, east of the famous city, in 256, and thirty-seven other cities were listed in the victory announcement in Shapur's grand inscription superimposed on the walls of the so-called Ka'ba of Zoroaster, an old Achaemenid monument at Persepolis. The event was also commemorated by the foundation of a new city, Veh Antiok Shapur – literally 'Shapur's superior Antioch' – east of the southern Tigris in Khuzistan.

There are discrepancies between dates cited by different sources, so there is some confusion regarding the precise movements of Shapur's third campaign in Syria, but his pressure on Edessa, to the north of Carrhae, in the old kingdom of Osrhoene, prompted in 259–60 another abortive Roman counter-offensive. In a battle fought at Edessa, the Roman emperor Valerian suffered an ignominious defeat, and again Shapur's victory inscription celebrates the capture of 70,000 people and the plundering of thirty-six cities in what amounts to the foothill area flanking the Taurus mountains.

Notwithstanding this dramatic success, as with the earlier Parthian campaigns in Syria, the Sasanians

A silver coin of Shapur I (241–72), the conqueror of Roman Antioch.

failed to impose any formal control over the region, which they looked upon as a source of plunder rather than a place of settlement. This was a particularly weak time for the Roman empire, often spoken of as its 'third-century crisis', when military anarchy prevailed and there was little to stop a concerted effort at settlement of the territory formerly held by the Romans. Perhaps one of the fundamental reasons for the Sasanian lack of interest may have been the fact that the inhabitants were not Iranians. Its residents spoke dialects of Aramaic, a Semitic language rather than an Iranian one. It is clear that there was an overwhelming leaning towards monotheistic faiths too, including Judaism, and Christianity by the third century. None of these tendencies would have found particular favour with Sasanian officials. Possibly Shapur became distracted in his later years by ambitious building projects in the Sasanian homeland of Fars, and by sympathy for the radical preaching of the prophet Mani.

Renewed Roman Pressure

At first it was the Arab kingdom of Palmyra, based in the Syrian desert, which felt motivated to reduce the effectiveness of the Sasanian hold on the region. As a caravan city that had experienced remarkable prosperity as a result of international trade, Palmyra stood to lose a great deal if the Iranians were allowed to dominate Syria permanently. Harassment of the Sasanian army of occupation forced a retreat, leaving the Palmyrenes a relatively free hand in the absence of any effective Roman presence. Queen Zenobia, following her husband's death, set out deliberately to extend Palmyrene influence even more. Unfortunately for her, Rome was then being revitalized by the emergence of strong military commanders and the adoption of a policy of maintaining mobile frontier forces rather than static infantry forces. In 270 the emperor Aurelian had started on the recovery of lost territories in a series of systematic campaigns, culminating with the capture of Zenobia herself and the plundering of Palmyra when the city incautiously rebelled in 273 after its defeat. It established once more Roman control in the upper reaches of the Euphrates.

Even though the destruction of Palmyra brought the Romans back into the Syrian desert, Iran still had considerable holdings. After he had become supreme monarch, somewhere between 240 and 243, Shapur adopted the more elaborate title of 'King of Kings of Iran and non-Iran', an explicit reference to his control of territory beyond the strict limits of Iranian-speaking inhabitants. The trilingual inscription on the Ka'ba at Persepolis in Greek, Parthian and Pahlavi (Sasanian Persian) allows us to see the territorial conquests which gave him grounds to claim such standing. His possessions can be grouped regionally for convenience: in what is the Tigris–Euphrates corridor, the territories of Khuzistan, Maishan, Asuristan, Adiabene and Arabistan; in the Zagros mountains of western Iran, Fars, Elymais, Media and Azerbaijan; in the Caucasus region, Balasgan, Albania, Malechonia, Georgia and Armenia; on both sides of the Elburz mountains of northern Iran, Patishwagar, Gorgan, Abarshahr and Parthia; west and north of the Hindu Kush, Aria, Merv and Kushanshahr; in the land flanking the lower reaches of the Indus, Seistan, Turan, Makran and India. Finally, the possession of part of Oman, in Arabia near the Straits of Hormuz, meant Sasanian control in the third century included both sides of the Persian Gulf, as far as the Arabian Sea.

Ruling these vastly disparate lands had proved impossible for the Seleucids, the Graeco-Macedonian dynasty which followed the division of Alexander's conquests. Even a reduced amount of territory had been difficult for the Parthians, because of the endless fragmentation caused by the presence of local hereditary dynasties of varying strength. The Sasanian attempt to solve the problem involved installing members of the royal family, who ruled the provinces with the title of Shah, or 'King'. The fact that heirs to the throne were often given authority over the more important, larger regions such as Armenia or the Kuṣāṇa territories, with the title 'Great King', is in marked contrast to Parthian times, when paranoid fratricide seems to have often gripped the throne and prevented sharing of authority unless it was claimed by a local dynast through personal strength. Although many of the noble families still survived from Parthian times, the responsibilities for administration and military preparedness lay in the hands of appointed officials, rather than with the nobility, as under the previous more feudal system. This is not to say that Sasanian monarchs ruled only on the basis of their own authority. Undoubtedly the house of Sasan was held in great awe by both the priesthood and the aristocracy, but it was felt that each occupant of the throne should rule by virtue of *khvarnah* – the 'divine majesty' that alone gave him the right to command. Without it, another member of the royal family might be substituted instead.

From time to time the nobles were instrumental in establishing their own preferred candidates on the throne. Following the death of Shapur I, there was a rapid succession of kings, including Bahram I (273–6), who was not a primary heir to the throne. It was during Bahram's reign that the chief prelate, Kartir, assumed the right to control many of the affairs of state by his religious pronouncements. The priest proudly announced in a public inscription his persecution of minority religions.

After their sorry performances against Shapur I, the Romans turned the tables and twice made successful inroads into northern Mesopotamia. Bahram's son, Bahram II (276–9), was so distracted by his own brother's revolt in eastern Iran that he was forced to relinquish territory to the Romans. And it was indeed an internal challenge to the royal line of succession that weakened for a while the Sasanian empire, and threw up the figure of Narseh (293–302). This noble appears to have deposed Bahram III. The adding of

Narseh's name to an earlier rock relief of Bahram I, as well as a prostrate form of a defeated figure beneath the king's horse (probably Bahram III), graphically draws attention to the challenge. At another site further north in the Zagros mountains, beyond Ctesiphon, Narseh's victory monument at Paikuli lists the names of rulers who appear to be those who backed him. It is noteworthy that many of the names previously present in Shapur's earlier dedication were not there this time. The notable absences include the rulers of the central kingdoms, and the great 'feudal' families of the Parthian era. It is generally concluded that Narseh's support must have come largely from the fringe areas of the realm, including Khwarezm beyond the border in the far north-east, and Arab Lakhmid territory in the desert region to the west of the Euphrates. With his position consolidated, Narseh turned his attention to Armenia, but his efforts there backfired. The Romans emerged as the eventual victors and the Sasanians were forced to cede territory in northern Mesopotamia for a generation.

Following the death of Hormizd II (302–9), there was again a contest for the throne, based on a challenge by the nobility to install the young Shapur II, who actually went on to rule for a large part of the fourth century. In fact, it was the strong authoritarian rule of Shapur II that restored centralized cohesiveness to the realm, a principle that lasted almost unchallenged until the end of the dynasty and allows for the identification of the Sasanians as rulers of powerful bureaucracies.

It was during Shapur's reign (309–79) that the Roman empire became Christian and witnessed the birth of Constantine's new capital city at Constantinople: otherwise known as Byzantium. This shift eastwards once more brought the two great powers into conflict, partly because of the threat perceived by the Sasanians in the fact that Armenia had already officially adopted Christianity. Shapur battled with the Byzantines over northern Mesopotamia on three occasions, though he was forced to be absent once for five years, between 353 and 358, when he faced the threat of invasion by the Huns in the north-east of Iran.

Captives transplanted from Antioch by Shapur I included many Christians, so their new communities in Khuzistan provided potential sources of revolutionary activity now that they could identify with a political force in Europe. Christians were subjected to harsh taxes for their faith, and were persecuted when they resisted paying. As Jews and Manichees were also persecuted for their beliefs, it is clear that Shapur's policy aimed at establishing state orthodoxy, and was not simply political wrangling with the Byzantines.

Following the death of Shapur, his successors' reigns are obscure, although it is known that the Armenian

The Perso-Roman border: successively disputed by Roman, Parthian, Sasanian and Byzantine armies.

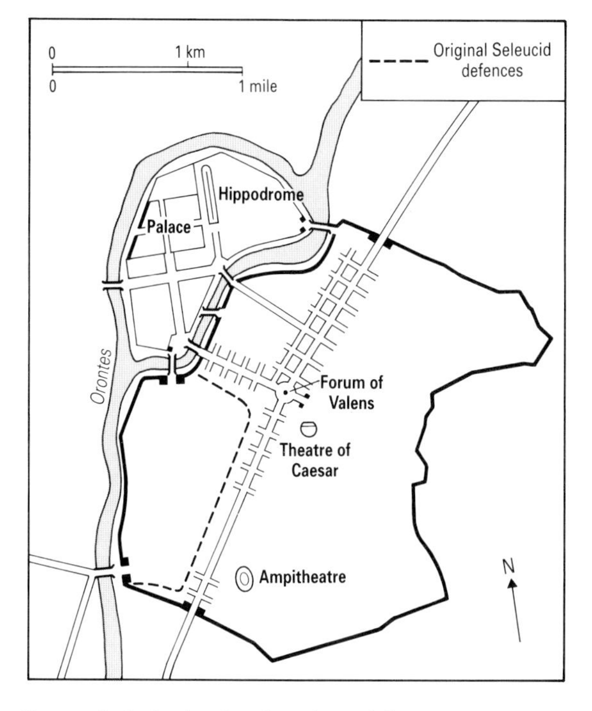

Roman Antioch, showing the colonnaded streets running through the centre of the grid. Founded by Seleucus I in 300 BC, the city became critical in Roman times for the defence of the eastern frontier. On several occasions the Persians carried off its inhabitants as prisoners.

situation continued to be contentious, and Iran itself was still threatened by the Huns. In addition, both Iran and Byzantium began to feel the threat of incursions through the Caucasus. At the end of the fourth century, Yazdigird I is most famous for the epithet he earned among Zoroastrians of 'sinful', on account of his reputed initial tolerance of the Christians. Perhaps on this account the nobility challenged the succession to the throne by one of his sons, substituting their own royal candidate. But a counter-challenge came from another of Yazdigird's sons, Bahram, who was successful in claiming the throne. Around him, Bahram V (420–38), have been woven the most colourful legends in the traditions of Persian literature and the arts. His campaign to claim the throne began on the western fringe of the realm, where he had been sent as a boy to be brought up by the Arab (Lakhmid) vassal king of the area west of the lower Euphrates. His skill at hunting earned him the epithet Bahram Gur, or 'wild ass', and he is frequently portrayed in later Islamic art performing virtuoso acts with his bow and arrow. For his actual exploits, particularly military campaigns against the Huns, we have much less detail. Highly significant, however, was the return of the old Armenian issue, which surprisingly resulted in the 422 declaration of freedom of worship for Christians in the Sasanian empire. As a result, the Persian church came to see itself as an independent entity.

The change of attitude should not be read as a sign of weakness of resolve on the part of the Sasanian state religionists, but a sign that both Byzantium and Iran were beginning to be concerned about incursions from the north. That tolerance of the Christians was politically motivated is supported by the fact that early in Bahram's reign there had been persecutions of Christians. Also, it was under Bahram that the prime minister, Mihr-Narseh, made a number of pious public statements in support of Zoroastrianism and built a series of fire temples. Subsequently, under the next king, Yazdigird II (438–57), Mihr-Narseh's attempt to convert the new Sasanian province of Greater Armenia to Zoroastrianism resulted in a rebellion that was put down in 451 with such force that the battle is still commemorated by Armenians for the martyrdom of the cause's champion, Vardan, and his supporters.

It was only after a series of disasters on the eastern frontier against the Huns that the Sasanians made any real concessions towards freedom of religion in Armenia. This occurred in 484, the same year that the Christian church of Iran declared its support for the Nestorian doctrine, thus allowing it to be seen by the Sasanian state as entirely separate from the church of Byzantium.

The eastern border of Iran proved to be particularly difficult for the next Sasanian kings to maintain, partly because of increasing pressure by the Huns, but also because there were a number of internal disputes over who should inherit the throne. King Peroz (457–84) had been forced to leave his son Kavadh as a hostage with the Huns, as well as pay ransom for his own release, the first time he was defeated, in 469. His death in a second engagement only caused further tribute to be paid by the Sasanian state to the Huns. The latter were also instrumental in deposing Peroz's immediate successor and helping Kavadh ascend the throne.

Kavadh's interrupted reign (488–96 and 498–531) is to be explained by his sympathy for the revolutionary movement of Mazdakism, which can be seen as a threat to some of the privileges enjoyed by the nobility. Because his forces were divided in meeting rebellion from different quarters, and because he felt constrained to challenge Byzantium's refusal to support the mutual defence of the north-western borders, Kavadh found himself unable to cope with the determined opposition of the nobility and the orthodox Zoroastrian clergy, and he fled for his life into temporary exile with the Huns. Order was finally restored to the Sasanian empire by Khusrau, a younger son of Kavadh. As Khusrau I (531–79), this energetic ruler settled territorial rights in the Caucasus with Byzantium so that he could be free to deal with the reconstruction of his realm. The Mazdakite movement had caused serious disruption to the established practice of Sasanian fiscal and legal policy. However, recognizing that Kavadh's sympathy for the Mazdakites may have stemmed from genuine concern over the serious inadequacies in property and product assessments, Khusrau initiated administrative reforms which established an effective state-taxation policy, whose principles continued to be used long after the end of the dynasty. A major innovation was the levying of crop taxes in cash on the basis of an average yield, a move that ensured the state had a surer way of estimating revenues in advance. The creation of a professional army – previously it had been necessary to rely on the private armies of the great nobles – had an immediate impact upon Sasanian success against the Byzantines, as well as reducing the potential power of the old nobility.

Khusrau's most effective campaign in Syria started in 540 with a savage attack upon Antioch, from which vast spoils were drawn. Following the earlier example of Shapur, Khusrau ordered the construction of a new city near the Sasanian capital called Veh Antiok Khusrau, or 'Khusrau's superior Antioch'. Also he followed the usual Sasanian practice of populating the foundation with war captives. Though Khusrau launched further campaigns, he failed to achieve total mastery over the reaches of the upper Euphrates, just as previous Sasanian kings had failed to dominate this Arab and now Christian territory.

With Edessa stubbornly unsubdued, Khusrau decided to conclude a truce with the Byzantines and turn his attention to the eastern frontier, where in 562 he enjoyed a dramatic victory over the Huns. In this bloody engagement the Sasanians were aided by the latest tribal group to arrive in Transoxiana, the Turks.

The truce with the Byzantine emperor Justinian was supposed to last for fifty years. But a number of different intrigues threatened to break it, including Turkish moves to end their alliance with Iran and to side with Byzantium instead. Imperial Sasanian aspirations, including a desire to keep Byzantine interests out of southern Arabia, where Europe could trade directly with India, were responsible around 575 for a positive response to a request for help by the Yemenis against Ethiopian occupation. The Persians moved in to hold Yemen as a province. In Armenia a local uprising of 571 had resulted in the slaughter of the Sasanian governor, and this became the pretext for Justinian's successor to renege upon the terms of the existing Sasanian-Byzantine truce. This prompted a return to active campaigning, with losses on both sides, but no clear-cut winner before Khusrau died.

Sasanian Decline

That same year, 579, the Byzantine army, under its commander Maurice, waged an effective campaign against Khusrau's successor, Hormizd IV. This unhappy monarch was also plagued by his people's perception that he was weak in his approach to the Christians. This apparent failing opened the way for one of the rare occasions when a contender for the Sasanian throne based his claim to legitimacy upon a lineage that did not come through the royal family of Sasan. Rather, Bahram Chobin was an Arsacid from the region of the Elburz in the north. As a Sasanian general he had been particularly successful in stemming the tide of defeat that his country had experienced in the north-east, where he penetrated beyond the Amu Darya and successfully battled with the tribes there. But, according to a Byzantine source, when Bahram Chobin was transferred to the western frontier, Hormizd moved to have him demoted, an action that turned Bahram Chobin into a rebel.

After Hormizd was murdered in 590, his unpopularity soon transferred itself to his son, another Khusrau, who attempted without success to challenge the rebellious general. The seasoned campaigner proved too strong for Khusrau, who was forced to seek the protection of the Byzantine Maurice, now an emperor himself. Both Sasanian parties sent delegations to the court in Byzantium, promising concessions over territory and indemnities in the hopes of buying his support. In the end, Maurice backed Khusrau, and Bahram Chobin was defeated because of the overwhelming force of two Byzantine armies that was sent against him. Khusrau took the throne in 591, although some of the rebels did manage to set up a principality that survived on the north-eastern frontier for a number of years. As Khusrau II (591–628), the new king kept his promise and gave to the Byzantines territorial rights in the Caucasus, which hardly justifies the epithet Parvez, or 'victorious', by which he is generally known.

His victories came about because Maurice himself was assassinated in 602 during a military *coup*, and Khusrau turned that unexpected event into an excuse to resume the offensive. By 609 Khusrau had found

Possibly the emperor Maurice, the Byzantine backer of Khusrau II (591–628).

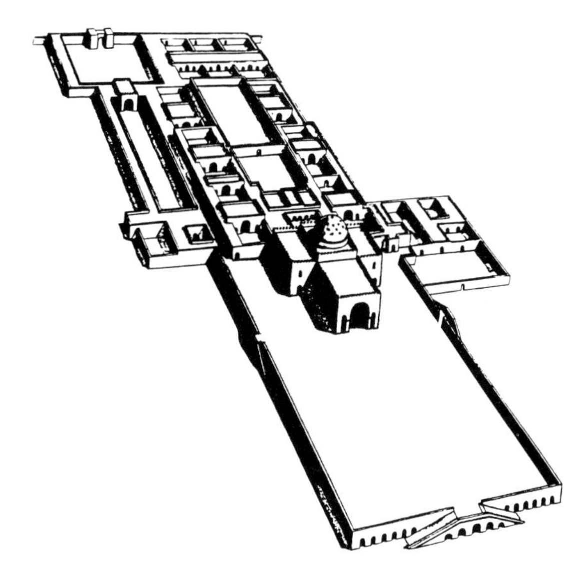

Khusrau II's palace at Qasri-i-Shirin.

more success in northern Mesopotamia than either Ardashir or Shapur. The spoils of war included the capture of Edessa, which had often been able successfully to resist Sasanian attacks. The city had been the principal military base of the Byzantines in the area since the fourth century. Then, with no fear of a hostile force at their rear, the Sasanians were able to take Antioch again in 611. Controlling Edessa became the pivot of success. From there, Khusrau went on to take Palestine and lower Egypt as well. Jerusalem was captured in 614, and the Holy Cross taken as spoil; Alexandria fell in 619. In the meantime a Sasanian army reached the Bosporus and threatened the existence of Byzantium itself.

But at the very moment all seemed beyond hope, the Byzantines discovered in Heraclius, son of the governor of Africa, a commander capable of restoring confidence in the army and planning a campaign to win back the lost lands. The struggle between the Sasanians and the Byzantines, which lasted from 622 to 628, has been called the first fully-fledged crusade

Two gold coins of the Byzantine emperor Heraclius and his son, first as a youth and later as a young man. They were struck between 613 and 631.

of the medieval world. It was accompanied by feverish religious enthusiasm and hatred on the Christian part. In 622, via a seaborne expedition, Heraclius was able to strike at Armenia from the Black Sea. He penetrated southwards as far as the Zagros mountains, where Adur-i Gushnasp, one of the three Sasanian national shrines for fire worship, was sacked in revenge for the desecration of Jerusalem. In 627 another southern thrust took Heraclius within easy reach of Ctesiphon, which he failed to attack only because of the onset of winter.

By 629 the Sasanians were ready to sue for peace. The son of Khusrau, Kavadh II, who had ascended the throne after angry generals killed his father, relinquished all claims to recently conquered territories in order to stop further hostilities. In the ensuing years a series of assassinations brought a number of rulers to the throne in quick succession, including a woman, about all of whom very little is known. At the end of the dynasty, it was a grandson of Kavadh, Yazdigird III, who faced the overwhelming challenge of nascent Islam. Possibly Yazdigird's only compensation in defeat was the knowledge that restored Byzantine power was also in a state of collapse. For Arab armies conquered Syria in 636, Mesopotamia in 639 and Egypt and Iran in 640 and 641 respectively. While the Sasanian army made a valiant attempt to fight this new tide of invaders, the people of Iran had no spirit to resist.

Religious Beliefs

The Sasanians are generally associated with Zoroastrianism, which they successfully promoted as a state religion. At the same time, however, there were also intense intellectual debates about the nature of god, reflecting the complexity of a religion that had been developing for over a millennium. Mysticism and the eastern sects of Christianity also began to make inroads on the national religion. Ironically, in the end, this complex religion was eclipsed by the relatively simple but vigorous message of Islam. But, there is a counterviewpoint. Whether Iran was really overthrown by military prowess on the part of the Arabs or by their religious zeal continues to be an issue that divides historians today. Judgement, then, on the effectiveness of Sasanian empire hangs in the balance. On one hand, Iran stands for a rich country overthrown brilliantly by successful military tactics and effective proselytizing; on the other, Iran is held to be jaded and receptive to Islam simply because it had grown tired of an obscure liturgy and a distant leadership. By the same token, no one denies that Iranian culture endured and made a strong contribution to the development of Islamic culture itself.

To some extent, the perceived differences between the Parthian and Sasanian eras are due to the tangible, physical imagery surviving in the form of rock reliefs and other representations in the minor arts. Collectors and museum curators have little difficulty distinguishing generally between 'Parthian' and 'Sasanian' works of art. Also, the Iranian language was evolving. We may speak of a change from a 'Parthian' language to 'Middle Persian', and ultimately to 'Pahlevi', which survived beyond the Sasanian era itself. Yet the fundamental reason behind the differences lies more in the subtle area of doctrinal issues. This involves what can be perceived as a deliberate attempt to establish Zoroastrianism as a state religion, along with a suppression of other religions. Thus we think of the Sasanians first and foremost as Zoroastrians and fire-worshippers.

An Imposed Orthodoxy

A rock relief on the mountainside near Istakhr, at Naqsh-i Rustam, which illustrates Ardashir's triumph when he founded the Sasanian state, vividly reveals the new regime's view of itself. The huge relief at the end of a dramatic promontory housing tombs of former Achaemenid kings depicts Ardashir on horseback, his hand held victoriously by the opposing mounted figure of Ohrmazd (formerly Ahura Mazda). Beneath both horses lie trampled the respective enemies of both god and king. Ohrmazd carries the sacred bundle of *barsom* twigs in one hand, and offers a diadem of sovereignty to Ardashir with the other. While a trilingual inscription in Greek, Parthian and Middle Persian links the scene with the official traditions of the preceding era, the deliberately close identification of the king with the supreme deity reflects the authoritarian stance of the new rulers.

The suppression of heterodoxy best characterizes the difference between the Parthian and Sasanian states. Apparently, Ardashir claimed the right to suppress variant traditions that had become incorporated into the religious history contained within the Avesta, the scriptures of Zoroastrianism. It was the Parthian Volgases I who had earlier arranged for these oral traditions to be compiled as written texts. But different traditions survived in different parts. The rare preservation of a unique document illustrates very neatly how the new single doctrine was instituted. Appropriate nuances can be extrapolated from this copy of correspondence written by Tansat, the *herbad*, or 'chief priest', the highest religious authority in Iran during Ardashir's reign. In a letter addressed to a king named Gushnasp, and one of the former Parthian vassals, Tansar was attempting to justify Ardashir's shedding of blood in promulgating the new orthodoxy. The claim that Ardashir had full licence to abolish whatever he liked, because of the errors of his predecessors, has an ominous ring for any student of political science.

But it would appear that in founding the Sasanian state, Ardashir introduced a policy for the suppression of idolatry, even in his native Fars. All cult images were outlawed and, with the king's blessing, fire was promoted as the appropriate object of worship. The veneration of images had been initiated by the Achaemenid Artaxerxes II, at a time when the Babylonian cult of Ishtar was being assimilated into that of goddess

Thought to be a portrait of the prophet Zoroaster, from a Mithraeum excavated at Dura, the Mesopotamian city known as Europos by the Greeks.

Aredvi Sura Anahita. But iconoclasts held that cult images were inhabited by the demons who misappropriated the offerings laid before them. Well before the death of the last Achaemenid king in 330 BC, priests had praised fire worship as a means of combating such notions.

Alongside Ardashir's promulgation of new doctrines went the establishment of a new calendar. This proved to be a less successful move than the abolition of statue cults, and its failure underlines the complexity of Iranian heritage at this point. As with all other ancient calendars, the question of the intercalation of varying amounts of time to keep the months synchronized with the natural seasons remained a headache for officials. The old Zoroastrian calendar of the Achaemenids had involved a cycle of 360 days, with the intercalation every six years of an extra month. Perhaps following the Roman example (of the Julian calendar), Ardashir introduced an extra five days at the end of each year. Ordinary people became confused. The traditional day-long acts of veneration at the end of the old year, when the *fravashi*, or 'spirits of the dead', were welcomed back into the household, now had to be stretched out over six whole days, until the beginning of No Ruz, the New Year. The reforms failed to simplify the calendar. Rather than give up their old practices, people honoured the new calendar but celebrated their traditional festivals on the old dates as well. Curiously, because the Parthian New Year had begun in autumn, following the Graeco-Macedonian practice, Ardashir's New Year followed suit. It was only later that the Sasanians reintroduced the spring equinox No Ruz, which is still celebrated in modern Iran.

The Elevation of Fire Worship

Under Ardashir's successor, Shapur I, the name of Kartir became synonymous with religious persecution. This influential Zoroastrian cleric attacked Jews, Buddhists, Hindus, Manichees and Christians alike. Within his own faith he was responsible for replacing cult images with sacred fires. As he put it himself, 'Images were destroyed, the lurking places of demons demolished and the abodes of angels established.'

Once the Sasanians had fully adopted this new doctrinal stance, fire played a vital part for promotional purposes of both church and state in Iran. At the king's coronation a fire was consecrated in his name. Most coins issued by the Sasanian monarchs bear images on the reverse face that are variations on a theme of two attendants flanking an altar, with an inscription that identifies the fire on it by the name of the king. The discovery of similarly proportioned altar fragments in excavations at the site of Takht-i Sulayman in western Iran attests to the fact that the altars depicted on the coins represent not just metaphysical expressions of an idealized altar but a physically known type. These same

A Sasanian fire altar in Fars.

excavations have exposed the walls of a simple, square monument – a pavilion conveniently called a *chahar taq* from the four open, arched sides – which has become recognized as the standard form of the main shrine in a fire-temple complex of Sasanian times.

An altar was positioned centrally on the floor beneath the dome of the *chahar taq* sanctuary. Eighteen *bullae* found in a storeroom at the rear of the complex carried stamps identifying them with the Mobadh-i Adhur-i Gushnasp, or the 'Priest of the Sanctuary of the Warriors' Fire'. This, in fact, was one of the three great national shrines of Sasanian Iran.

The oldest of the three was the great Parthian fire, Adhur-i Burzen Mihr, somewhere in the Parthian homeland of north-eastern Iran. The Sasanians did not feel inclined to denigrate this fire but, in keeping with their national policy, they designated it as 'the fire of

A Sasanian fire temple in Fars. Fire worship became important under the cleric Kartir.

herdsmen and farmers'. The Adhur-i Farnbag, 'the fire belonging to the priests', was in the Sasanian homeland of Fars. This particular label included a clever play on words, since the term *khvarenah/farr* holds a connotation of the divine grace enjoyed by kings. The 'warrior' fire, in Media, at least after the fourth century, was particularly associated with royalty. This shrine became the appropriate place for the newly crowned monarch to make a pilgrimage or to give thanks after victory. In turn, the fire sanctuary was also visited by ordinary pilgrims.

In spite of the often authoritarian stance of Ardashir and his successors, the Sasanian era was to be plagued by religious debate. So much so that R. C. Zaehner refers to the Sasanians finding themselves in search of an orthodoxy, to counter rising dogmas that threatened national stability. Persecutions of heretics reached a climax in the fourth century, particularly when Christians became too closely identified with Iran's enemy, Rome, following the conversion of the emperor Constantine. It was only following the split in the Christian church, after the Council of Chalcedon (525), that Nestorian Christians were no longer thought of as potential fifth columnists within Iran.

Manichaeism was also a heresy that threatened those who felt a need for national uniformity. Its prophet, Mani, was born as a Persian under the Parthians, but he grew up under the Sasanians in an ascetic community in Babylonia. His teachings and worldly withdrawal were influenced by the beliefs of a number of faiths, including those of Christianity, as well as orthodox Zoroastrianism. He should not be thought of as a Zoroastrian reformer, but rather as an ecumenicalist. He was aware of the teachings of Buddha. His appropriation of the names for the Zoroastrian deities may have been why the Zoroastrian clergy considered him to be such a dangerous heretic.

Mani's fame today is due in large part to the fact that, in contrast to the largely oral tradition of ancient Zoroastrianism, his teachings were written down as texts. It has been suggested that Mani's upbringing in Babylonia, where there had been such a long tradition of document-writing, may have underlined the value of the written word for the promulgation of the Manichaean faith. Large numbers of Manichaean writings have been recovered (some disgracefully pillaged around the turn of this century) from the ruins of old monasteries in Chinese Turkistan. It was here that the original Manichees found refuge from Iran. For, although Mani had found a sympathetic ear in Shapur I and spent time at the royal court, he was the target of the widespread campaign of persecution conducted by the prelate Kartir. Reference has already been made to Kartir's role in the suppression of image cults during the late third century. It was at his insistence that Mani was put to death.

But Zoroastrianism also exhibited a number of profound intellectual divisions. Our knowledge of them is derived largely from Armenian religious commentaries. Soul-searching of this kind paralleled the then current debate in the eastern Mediterranean that was dividing Christianity over the nature of Christ's human and divine natures. For Zoroastrians the key question was the origin of evil. One school of thought held that Zurvan, best rendered as 'Time', existed before the creation of heaven and earth. According to this philosophy, Ohrmazd (Ahura Mazda) and Ahriman (Anru Mainyu) were the twin sons of Zurvan. Whereas Ohrmazd had created the world, Ahriman added its evil. The Zurvanite separation of good from evil had its origins in the Achaemenid period, when Zurvan was embellished to the point where he took on the role of a divine entity which could control time, in addition to providing its outlines. Part of the rationale was clearly an attempt to resolve the issue of how a good god can be responsible for bad things as well. But by making good and evil originally equal, the Zurvanites had lessened the nature of Ohrmazd, even though he was considered responsible for all subsequent acts of creation. Orthodox Mazda-worshippers believed Ohrmazd to be the only creator, so that Zurvanism was looked upon as a heterodox point of view, if not actual heresy.

The tomb of Cyrus the Great at Pasargadae.

Zurvanism apparently found favour with some members of the Sasanian royal family, especially Shapur II, who named one of his daughters Zurvandukht, or 'Daughter of Time'. Mihr-Narseh, the pious minister of the fifth century, called a son Zurvandad, or 'Gift of Time'. Zurvanism was treated as a serious heresy only in the sixth century, during the period when Khusrau I initiated his programme of purges after the Mazdakite movement had severely challenged the basis of Sasanian rule. The Mazdakite doctrine combined ideas of social equality with religious beliefs that were based partly upon the ecumenical tenets of Manichaeism. There is some suggestion too that the Mazdakites supported the individual rights of women, who hitherto were held to be no more than the property of their nearest male relative. By treacherously contriving to have Mazdak and his followers murdered at a banquet, Khusrau acquired the epithet of Anoshirvan (of immortal soul), because of his efforts on behalf of orthodox Zoroastrianism. Subsequently, the state religion did not falter until the political machinery itself had been felled by Islam.

Foreign Trade and Ideas

The Parthians had earlier enjoyed the benefits of long-distance caravan traffic which connected the Mediterranean world with China, by way of a number of circuitous paths across the high reaches of the Pamirs or across treacherous deserts, using the hardy Bactrian camel. Although often dangerous, and easily exploited by bandits, these land routes were preferred to sea

The tomb of Xerxes, the invader of Europe, at Persepolis.

The winged symbol of Ahura Mazda, originally the Persian god of prophetic revelation. As Ohrmazd, he later became the source of all creation.

routes because of inadequate maps and charts, as well as inadequate sailing craft, for the open sea. The transcontinental route flourished in particular during the Kuṣāṇa period. But even then, because of the political realities of a rival Parthia, the Kuṣāṇa route followed the Indus down to its delta, and then crossed by sea to Arabia rather than travelling directly through central Iran.

Of course, local navigation had probably flourished for 3,000 years or more. But this does not mean that the Arab and Indian sailors were part of any organized trade system. The disjointed patterns of communication began to change radically under the Sasanians, when territorial control was more extensive and secure than under the earlier Parthians. That trade was a matter of concern to both the Sasanians and the Romans can be seen in the agreement of 297 for the establishment in Syria of a single transfer point for silk, at a fixed price. Essentially the Sasanians held a monopoly over the eastern passages because of their control of the maritime routes towards the Arabian and Red Seas, exporting raw silk to what was now Byzantium, Egypt and Syria. Byzantine attempts to outflank them were prevented by tribes to the north of the Caucasus and along the Danube, and by the Ethiopians in Africa. Cosmas Indoplasticus, a sixth-century Indian navigator, reports Arab and Persian merchants trading as far away as the island of Sri Lanka.

In 360 Shapur II seized some of the Syrian craftsmen and resettled them in Khuzistan, where they formed the nucleus of the nascent Sasanian silk industry, using raw imported Chinese silk. In 408 and 562 there were further treaties between Iran and Byzantium concerning the importation of silk. The emperor Justinian attempted to enrich his treasury by establishing an imperial monopoly in silk-brocade production, which caused a further number of craftsmen to flee to Iran in order to escape the restrictions. But it was also Justinian who is reputed to have been the first ruler to receive live silkworms, which marks the beginning of Europe's own sericulture.

Byzantium's fortunes were enhanced by the emergence in Central Asia of an Iranian group whose identity is associated with the name of the province of Sogdia. They were Iranians, but separate from the Sasanian state. Just as the Kuṣāṇa state had represented a stable force which permitted trade to flourish, so now the Sogdians acted as a spur to the development of trade following the unsettled years of the previous centuries. Sogdian rulers deliberately encouraged trade, and their merchants visited China itself, introducing grape wine to the Tang court. These traders were followed by Christian missionaries, the Chinese emperor Tai Zong welcoming himself in the 630s a Nestorian monk. But it was the Buddhist monasteries in Sogdia that provided havens for merchants on their travels, and served as the exchange points for goods and ideas. It is said to have been Christian monks who brought the first silkworms to Justinian. By the end of the sixth century, Byzantium resorted to other tactics in order to gain an advantage, allying with the Turks to the north of the Caucasus, in order to circumvent the Iranian hold over the central silk routes. In the meantime, Sasanian Iran maintained direct contact with China, receiving numerous embassies from the middle of the fifth century onwards.

The remains of the Sasanian capital at Ctesiphon.

According to Chinese sources, there were at least ten official diplomatic exchanges between Iran and China between 445 and 521. Apart from this formal contact, it is apparent that there was a large exchange of goods and ideas between the two countries via Sogdia. Not to be forgotten is the timely refuge provided by the Tang court for the descendants of the last Sasanian king, who in 651 fled from the advancing Arabs. For a while the disinherited crown prince, Peroz, made a last futile attempt to restore the *status quo*, establishing a garrison state in China's 'Western Regions'.

Iran and China

At the height of its glory, Chang'an prided itself on being the capital of China with a population of 1 million people. An Iranian presence there is recorded in many Chinese texts, suggesting that the expatriate community may have grown to its size of several thousands largely as a result of an influx of refugees. But there is no reason to suppose that their presence was not already felt during the actual Sasanian period. Chinese silk, of course, was the product most extensively traded westwards. What is remarkable is that in the Sasanian period China actually imported silk fabrics that had been made in Iran with Chinese silk.

Reference has been made above to the settlement of Syrian craftsmen to Iran. These and other weavers produced what was known as 'Persian brocade', their manufacturing technique being very different from that of the Chinese workshops. Sasanian brocades are characterized by the tightness of the spun thread and a compound twill weave. Motifs are frequently depicted in a weft-based pattern which is carried within pearl-bordered medallions; favourite devices were a boar's head or a standing bird in profile. Such animals are usually shown with bands of ribbons tied around the neck, while the bird often holds a pearl necklace in its beak. The figures are quite different from the designs found in Chinese art, but they are comparable with similar designs found in Central Asian wall-paintings and silver vessels of Sasanian and post-Sasanian times in Central Asia.

Sasanian silver and gold vessels also became particularly popular with the Chinese. It is possible that some of these vessels may actually have been made by Iranian craftsmen resident in China. Sasanian cut glass was also in demand. While many of the artefacts in

Sasanian style may have been buried after the fall of the dynasty, a reflection of the influx of royal refugees, there have been numerous finds made by archaeologists which indicate that Sasanian products were being traded there from at least the fourth century onwards. Additionally, Chinese archaeologists have in recent years unearthed thousands of coins. The earliest date from the time of Shapur II, and they extend over the reigns of twelve kings, down to the time of the last Sasanian monarch. The largest group dates from that of Khusrau II, a monarch who was obliged to issue many new coins in order to meet the growing demands of trade. When mint marks are discernible, it is apparent that the coins found in China were struck both in the central as well as in the eastern sections of Sasanian Iran.

The artefacts and coins confirm what we know about the history of the period from the sparse written texts. Of course, the Sasanian experience in Central Asia was not all one-sided, and political reverses may have been just as instrumental in the spread of Sasanian works of art as was trade. Coins and precious objects often changed hands as booty, not to mention ransoms.

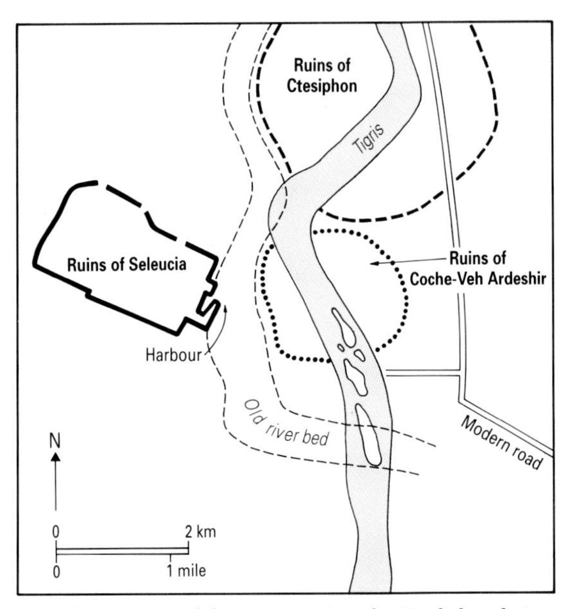

The adjacent sites of three great cities: the Greek foundation of Seleucia, Parthian Ctesiphon and Sasanian Coche-Veh Ardeshir.

The Art of Building

The Sasanian period is known for the entrenchment of architectural innovations begun under the Parthians, massive barrel-vaulted chambers surrounded by corridors as a buttressing device continuing to appear. On the Iranian plateau, round domes in solid masonry over square chambers were erected, but these are rare in Mesopotamia. The increased use of columns allowed for the opening up of internal spaces, giving open fronted halls a basilica look which may have been due to the influence of Rome. Numerous engineers and architects are known to have been captured by the Sasanians in the wars with both Rome and Byzantium. Hardly surprising, therefore, was the renewed interest in western decorative devices, although indigenous building techniques continued, particularly the use of blind-façade decoration.

The Sasanians were responsible for the foundation of several new cities, often on the occasion of decisive victories abroad. Perhaps because they were no more than the grand gesture of a monarch, few of them have survived with visible monuments. Excavations at the site of Coche have revealed an urban block of buildings and part of the round city wall of Ctesiphon, the Sasanian capital. Coche had actually become stranded on the west bank of the Tigris after the river changed course during the fifth century, leaving it rather derelict. Late in the sixth century Khusrau II moved the seat of government to Dastagird, but little survives there except a single massive wall of baked brick. The rest of Ctesiphon is known to us through the unearthing of a variety of stucco decorations and the Iwan Kisra, 'the hall of Khusrau'. The archaeological history of this great vaulted monument remains difficult to interpret because of the ongoing dispute over the date of its construction: either during the reign of Shapur I (241–72) or of the two Khusraus (531–79 and 590–628). The notoriety that the structures received at the time of the Muslim conquest of 637 also tends to cloud the issue.

Archaeological work has invariably concentrated on restoration of the monument. One-third more of the structure was still standing in 1888, when the flooding

A commemorative stone arch at Taq-i-Girra. The Sasanians used Roman captives on such public works.

Tigris took away the north wing of the main façade. The style of the articulated façade that flanks the great *iwan* hall is linked very closely with that of the Parthian version found at Ashur, which makes a third-century date feasible. A pre-Islamic literary tradition tends to confirm this. Many western commentators have found subtle differences between the façades of the two structures, supporting their argument that the Ctesiphon version must post-date the sixth century, and have produced examples from the eastern Mediterranean as comparative models which they feel must have existed first. This is not satisfactory, though. Pending more extensive excavations, the question as to the date, and therefore the significance, of the Iwan Kisra remains open.

At Kish excavations have unearthed structures that reflect the growing pretensions of the nobility. Two palace courts include ornamental pools, while the triple-aisled *iwan* in one of them, together with an apse at the rear, allows for interpretation as an audience chamber with throne hall. The extensive decorations in stucco found at Kish are similar to those recovered from fifth- and sixth-century Ctesiphon. The style is characterized by extensive use of heraldic figures and symbols, together with human busts.

A rock-cut scene of Shapur I's triumphs against Rome. The huge reliefs at Bishapur, southern Iran, continue an ancient kingly tradition in West Asia.

While we are dependent upon ecclesiastical records, often compiled centuries after the events they describe, for interpretation of beliefs and attitudes, inscriptions and other archaeological remains are direct attestations of the formal provision made for the veneration of fire throughout the land. In fact, from the record of fire temples present on the landscape of Iran, there is a tendency to imagine that the Zoroastrian religion involved little other than fire worship.

During the 1930s, when archaeological studies were beginning to expand, a number of theories were formulated regarding the Sasanian fire temple. These deductions were partly based upon observations of the groundplans of then contemporary fire temples in Iran. Discoveries of numerous *chahar-taq* buildings in Fars province now allow us to observe a variety of physical arrangements for these fire sanctuaries. It is clear that many of the square, domed structures were originally surrounded by a corridor on all four sides, rendering implausible the notion of a holy beacon blazing on the horizon to inspire the faithful. Rather, one must imagine more discreet ceremonies conducted inside the building, where the sacred fire was shielded from the elements. Altars located on the nearby open hillside appear to have served the need for more public display. Other enclosed kiosks within these complexes may have served as sanctuaries for the fire, where it could be purified and sustained.

There is a tantalizing statement recorded by the

tenth-century writer Tabari, who claims that, in the fifth century, Mihr-Narseh, the prime minister of Bahram Gur, the king, founded four villages in a single valley in southern Iran, each with a fire temple. One was dedicated in his own name; the others were for fires named after three sons who were high officers in the Sasanian realm. The mention of fields and orchards connected with the villages must imply that Mihr-Narseh made financial arrangements for the maintenance of these shrines. His piety is attested to by the fact that the dedicatory inscription on a bridge in the area states that it was the work of Mihr-Narseh, at his own expense, for the benefit of others and the blessing of his soul.

This concern with public image, albeit piously expressed in the case of Mihr-Narseh, is typical of the way the Sasanian monarchs created new settlements after significant victories, adding epithets connected with 'glory' to the name of a city. Unfortunately, since the archaeological work required to investigate these settlements takes such vast amounts of time and money, most of what we know about the cities comes from written texts. As a result, commentaries tend to concentrate on the striking differences between rectangular grid-patterns and circular city-plans, concluding that the different layouts reflect the importation of Roman prisoners who were responsible for the western, rectangular solution to city-planning. Until more archaeological work is completed, however, it is difficult to be sure that these interpretations are soundly based. For instance, the round city of Darabgird in the province of Fars was often thought to represent the prototype for the first Sasanian capital city, of Ardashir-Khvarrah, at Firuzabad. The fact that Darabgird has even been claimed to be post-Sasanian in date serves only to highlight the under-developed state of Sasanian archaeological studies.

Better documented are the irrigation systems and canal networks of the Mesopotamian plains in Sasanian times. These vast schemes, the result of significant capital outlays by the state, resulted in large-scale irrigation agriculture, which was perhaps motivated as much by a desire to increase the state's revenues as by concern for feeding the populace. These agricultural networks, including systems of communication, were to remain viable after the fall of the dynasty. Without administrative systems for the distribution of water and the collection of the crops, and without the engineering skills fostered by the Sasanians for the maintenance of the barrages and canals, it is unlikely that Islam's ninth-century capital city of Baghdad could ever have fed its people and sustained its culture.

IMPERIAL INDIA

Bull capital of an Aśokan pillar at Rāmpurvā, dating from 244 BC. Seven such columns, surmounted by sculptured symbols, have been preserved. Five have lion capitals, one a bull capital and one an elephant capital.

Chronology

BC

Protohistoric Period

c. 563–483	Siddhārtha Gautama, the Buddha (traditionally 623–543)
c. 540–468	Vardhamāna Mahāvīra, the Jina (traditionally 600–528)
c. 546–494	Bimbisāra, king of Magadha
c. 520	Darius, Achaemenid ruler of Iran, conquers part of north-west India
c. 494–462	Ajātaśatru, king of Magadha
c. 484–468	Ajātaśatru's war with the Licchavis
5th C. BC–4th C. AD	The *Mahābhārata* and the *Rāmāyaṇa*
c. 380–325	Śiśunāga and Nanda dynasties
326–325	Invasion of Alexander the Great of Macedon

Mauryan Period

4th C. onwards	South Indian Kingdoms of the Cōḻas, Cēras and Pāṇḍyas
c. 322–298	Candragupta Maurya
c. 305	Seleucus I Nicator's incursion into the Punjab
c. 302	Megasthenes arrives at Pāṭaliputra as Seleucus' ambassador
c. 298–272	Bindusāra
c. 268–232	Aśoka
261–260	Conquest of Kaliṅga, followed in 257–255 by the fourteen rock edicts and the Kaliṅga edict, and in 242 by the pillar edicts
3rd–1st Cs.	Sāñcī and Bhārhut *stūpas*
c. 183	Last Mauryan king, Bṛhadratha, murdered by his commander, Puṣyamitra Śuṅga

The Age of Invasions

3rd–1st C.	Bactrian Greeks in Gandhāra and the Punjab (*c.* 155–130 Menander, king of the Punjab)
c. 182–72	Śuṅga dynasty; overthrown by the Kaṇvas (*c.* 72–27)
mid-1st C.	Khāravela, ruler of Kaliṅga
c. 58 BC – AD 90	Śakas and Pahlavas in Punjab and Sind
c. 50 BC – AD 250	Sātavāhana dynasty in the Deccan (Buddhist caves in the western Deccan)

AD

1st C.	Kuṣāṇas, under Kujula Kadphises, invade north-west India and conquer Taxila
c. 78–101 (?)	Kaniṣka (Gandhāra and Mathurā art)
late 1st C.	Aśvaghoṣa, author of the *Saundarananda* and the *Buddhacarita*
c. 130–388	Śaka satraps at Ujjain
c. 150	Earliest known Sanskrit inscription erected by Rudradāman I
1st–2nd Cs.	Arikameḍu, a Roman trading station The emergence of Mahāyāna Buddhism
2nd C.	The Lawbook of Manu compiled

Gupta Period

320–*c.* 335	Candragupta I, founder of the Gupta dynasty
c. 335–76	Samudragupta
c. 360	Embassy from Meghavarṇa, king of Sri Lanka
c. 376–415	Candragupta II (perhaps patron of Kālidāsa), who conquered western India *c.* 395
c. 405–11	Travels of Fa Xian in India
c. 415–54	Kumāragupta I
c. 454	First Hūṇa invasion, repelled by Skandagupta as prince
c. 454–67	Skandagupta
late 5th C.	Excavation of the Ajaṇṭā caves under the Vākāṭakas
c. 495	Second Hūṇa invasion, under Toramāṇa
499	Āryabhaṭṭa, the mathematician, wrote his main work
6th C.	Varāhamihira, the astronomer Gupta temple at Deogaṛh
c. 533	Yaśodharman finally defeats the Hūṇas under Mihiragula
mid-6th C.	End of the Gupta dynasty

Imperial India (500 BC–c. AD 550)

John Brockington

History

Before the end of the sixth century BC Darius had extended the Achaemenid empire of Iran to the Indus and annexed Taxila. Bimbisāra and his son Ajātaśatru, the rulers of Magadha, in southern Bihar, may have been inspired in their ambitions by the Achaemenid example. Certainly, Magadha in the fifth century was becoming the most important state in north India. Bimbisāra (*c.* 546–494 BC, according to Buddhist sources) annexed the neighbouring state of Aṅga, with the wealthy river-port of Campā, while Ajātaśatru (perhaps 494–462 BC) acquired Kāśī in a war with Kosala and, after a long-drawn-out campaign, around 483 BC defeated the powerful tribal confederacy north of the Ganges led by the Licchavis. Together these ensured Magadhan control of the Ganges basin.

We know little about the later part of Ajātaśaru's reign, since the Buddhist and Jain texts give meagre information about events occurring after the deaths of their founders, but he undoubtedly created the most powerful empire India had known until then. Buddhist sources place his death twenty-four years after the Buddha's at the hands of his son, Udayabhadra, who founded the new capital of Pāṭaliputra (modern Patna). Magadha continued to expand in the century and a half after Ajātaśatru's death, first under later members of his dynasty, then under the Śiśunāgas and Nandas. The founder of the Nanda dynasty is variously named (probably Mahāpadma) but was of low birth, it is generally agreed. After some kind of *coup*, he proceeded to unify north India under a centralized government, being an energetic and ambitious ruler. The Nandas are widely remembered for their great wealth, having perhaps increased taxation greatly to support their imperial ambitions; certainly the last Nanda, ruling when Alexander invaded, is described by Greek writers as having vast armies and as the king of powerful peoples beyond the Beās.

At this period the north-west was split up into several independent states, some with monarchic constitutions, others with oligarchic or quasi-democratic constitutions. Āmbhi, king of Taxila, had already made overtures to Alexander out of hostility to Porus, who ruled the area between the Jhelam and Rāvi rivers. After campaigning against various minor states, in 326 BC Alexander crossed the Indus and was warmly welcomed in Taxila by Āmbhi. He next marched eastwards to attack Porus, taking with him 5,000 troops provided by Āmbhi and appointing a satrap at Taxila to secure his rear. Alexander defeated Porus' troops, but only with great difficulty, following a surprise crossing of the Jhelam. After leading one elephant-charge in person, Porus was captured but then reinstated as a vassal. According to the story this was because Alexander was impressed by his bearing and boldness, but in reality, no doubt, it was because this magnanimity offered Alexander the best chance of retaining some degree of control over the territory. Despite revolts in the newly conquered areas and the assassination of one of his satraps, Alexander pressed on with his Indian campaign, but when he reached the Beās his troops became mutinous and he was forced to retreat.

To salvage something from this situation, Alexander decided to take his army down the Indus River to the sea, and in late 326 BC the army set out, some on boats and the rest accompanying them along the banks. Revolts had started even before his departure and, following Alexander's death in 323 BC, his successors in effect recognized the area's independence. If any Greek troops remained in the Punjab, they were soon to be driven out or destroyed by Candragupta, the founder of the Mauryan dynasty.

The Mauryan Dynasty (c. 322–183 BC)

European sources record a meeting between a young Indian named Sandrocottus, or Candragupta, and Alexander, but the story must originate from Indian sources, as does much that they record about him. According to both Greek and Indian traditions, Candragupta was of low birth – a son of the last Nanda king by a low-born woman – but Buddhist tradition more plausibly makes him a member of the Moriya clan. There is a widespread but unsubstantiated tradition linking Candragupta with the brahmin Cāṇakya, reputedly his chief minister and the real power behind the throne.

Candragupta rose to power around 322 BC, but details of his conquest of the Nanda empire and of the north-west are lacking. Probably he seized Magadha first, before advancing on the Punjab, where Alexander's campaigns had weakened the local rulers, enabling Candragupta to conquer them and annex their territories. Possibly from there he moved southwards into central India, where by 313 BC he had occupied the area round Avanti. Plutarch says that Candragupta 'overran and subdued all India with an army of 600,000 men'. Whatever the exact size of his army, Candragupta clearly relied on it, since his empire (comprising the Punjab, the Yamunā and Ganges valleys, and the land as far as Kaliṅga) was built and consolidated largely through force of arms.

About 305 BC, Seleucus I, the successor to Alexander's eastern provinces, set about regaining control over the easternmost areas and reached the Indus, but was eventually defeated by Candragupta and compelled to withdraw. In the peace concluded in 303 BC Seleucus ceded Aria, Arachosia and Paropamisadae (the areas

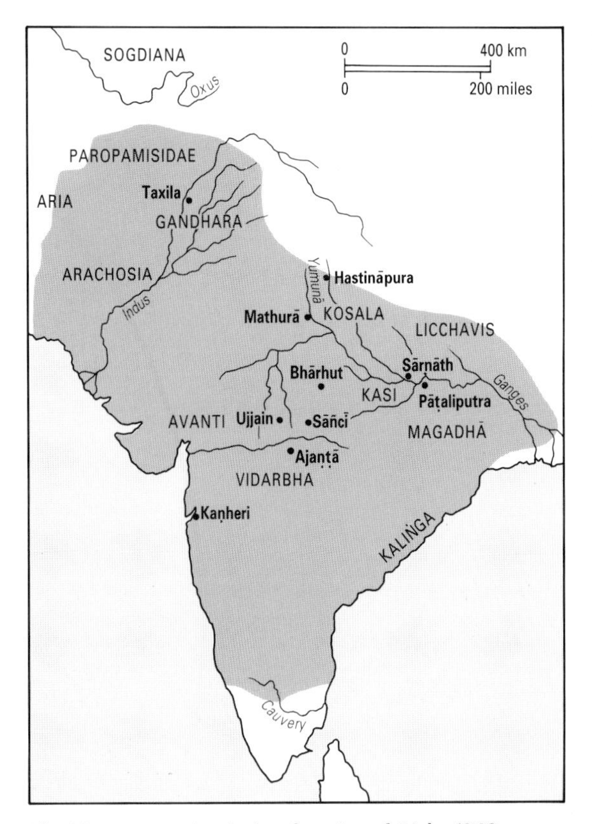

The Mauryan empire during the reign of Aśoka (268–232 BC).

round modern Herat, Kandahar and Kabul respectively) and probably part of Gedrosia (modern Baluchistan) in return for 500 elephants to use in his wars in the west, and a marriage alliance was arranged, although its exact nature is uncertain. Mauryan rule of the ceded provinces was clearly effective, for several inscriptions of Aśoka, Candragupta's grandson, have been found in modern Afghanistan. Seleucus also sent Megasthenes as ambassador to Candragupta's court around 302 BC, and while there Megasthenes compiled a valuable account of the Mauryan court and administration.

A very late Jain tradition says that Candragupta was converted to Jainism towards the end of his reign, renounced the throne in favour of his son, and went to south India, there ending his life by deliberate starvation in the orthodox Jain manner. The same source mentions a twelve-year famine in Magadha and this point is perhaps confirmed by two early Mauryan inscriptions which deal with relief measures during such a catastrophe. The Purāṇas, ancient collections of religious and historical texts, merely indicate that Candragupta was succeeded by his son Bindusāra around 298 BC, after a reign which lasted twenty-four years.

The names by which the Greeks called Bindusāra suggest significant conquests but their details must be deduced. Candragupta seems never to have campaigned in the south and we know that Aśoka's only conquest was to be Kaliṅga, but the Mauryan empire later included the Deccan (the area of modern Andhra and Karnataka), which was presumably conquered by Bindusāra. Aśoka, who was evidently not the crown prince, first served as Bindusāra's viceroy at Ujjain. He was then transferred to Taxila as viceroy, in place of his eldest brother, to quell a revolt against the oppression of the higher officials, which had got out of his brother's control. The interval of four years found in the records between Bindusāra's death and Aśoka's installation could indicate a long contest over the succession, but more probably results from discrepancies in the reckonings. However, Aśoka (268–232 BC) evidently had to struggle to reach the throne, and some Buddhist texts even assert that he secured it only after killing ninety-nine brothers.

The Kaliṅga War in the ninth year of Aśoka's reign, 261–260 BC, was a turning point. Two years earlier he had come into contact with Buddhism, been impressed by the doctrine and become a lay follower. Nevertheless, Aśoka continued his preparations for war against Kaliṅga, a part of modern Orissa. After inheriting control over the Indus and Ganges basins and probably much of the Deccan, he was led by economic as well as strategic motives to incorporate the nearby independent coastal state of Kaliṅga into the Mauryan empire. After this short but bloody war, Aśoka's interest in Buddhism increased and he was filled with remorse for the bloodshed, resolving to abandon all warfare and to devote himself to *dhammavijaya*, or 'conquest through righteousness'. However, this acquisition conveniently rounded off his empire and his remorse did not lead to a return of the conquered state to its former rulers. Indeed, the term *dhammavijaya*, with its implications of gaining supremacy over others by moral superiority, suggests that he had simply turned to other forms of conquest; significantly Aśoka claims that 'this conquest has been won repeatedly'.

In 259 BC Aśoka undertook a tour throughout his empire, calling it a journey to promote *dhamma*, or moral principles, in contrast to the pleasure trips of earlier rulers. Buddhist sources state that in 258 BC the king had entertained monks at Pāṭaliputra in order to celebrate his foundation of monasteries, but Aśoka dedicated caves in the Barābar hills to the Ājīvikas two years later and clearly did not restrict his generosity to the Buddhist Saṅgha (the order of monks and nuns). Next came the creation of the post of officers of *dhamma*, who were responsible for the moral welfare of the people. Aśoka also sent envoys to propagate *dhamma* at home and abroad, including to five named Hellenistic rulers, as he records in his thirteenth rock edict.

The fourteen rock edicts are important not only for giving information on his reign but also for indicating the extent of Aśoka's territory, since they are placed near the borders of the empire. Thus there are several in the south (around the Raichur Doāb) and in Afghanistan. The edicts would not have been read by the population at large but recited and explained by Aśoka's officials. They cover a wide range of matters, starting

A rock edict of Aśoka (268–232 BC). Such inscriptions are testimony to the Mauryan king's concern for peace, following the bloody Kaliṅga War of 261–260 BC.

with two edicts concerning the slaughter of animals and the provision of medical and welfare services, continuing with the policy of *dhamma* and its application, and ending with the history of the Kaliṅga War and its effects. The pillar edicts were then issued in his twenty-sixth and twenty-seventh regnal years and are primarily concerned with various aspects of the policy of *dhamma*. There are no further major edicts in the last ten years of Aśoka's reign. There are, though, several stories in Buddhist sources about Aśoka's later years which seem to indicate that he began to lose control over the government of the empire, coming unduly under the influence of one of his queens. There is possibly some confirmation in the queen's edict, a short inscription added later to the series of edicts engraved on the Allahabad pillar, in which Aśoka orders that all donations of the second queen must be carefully recorded to her credit.

Aśoka had plenty of sons to succeed him, but the various texts do not agree on the details. The usual interpretation of this conflicting evidence is that on Aśoka's death the empire was divided into western and eastern halves. The capital of the western part was perhaps moved from the north to Ujjain; this part was threatened by the Bactrian Greeks in the north-west and later by the rising Sātavāhana power in the northern Deccan. The succession of the main line in the eastern half, ruling from Pāṭaliputra, starts on this view with Daśaratha, securely known from three short inscriptions in the Nāgārjunī hills on caves which he gave to the Ājīvikas, a heterodox sect which espoused determinism. Subsequently the empire was reunited around 223 BC by Samprati, who had come to power in the west and whom Jain texts regard as a powerful ruler, treating him as a patron of Jainism almost in the same way that Buddhist texts treat Aśoka. In reality, however, the empire had already begun to disintegrate. To the west, the Bactrian Greeks had broken away from the Seleucids and were poised to occupy the north-west, and several areas beyond the Indus may already have broken away while Samprati was busy establishing himself at Pāṭaliputra. Gradually the area controlled shrank to Magadha alone and the later Mauryas hung on there, unable to prevent the breaking away of more distant parts of the empire. By 206 BC the Seleucids, seeking to re-establish their control, were again in the north-west. According to Polybius, Antiochus III renewed his alliance with Sophagasenus, 'king of the Indians' – perhaps some local chief taking advantage of the decline of the Mauryas to establish himself in the Kabul valley, but perhaps a Maurya, in which case the alliance that was renewed may be the treaty between Seleucus I and Candragupta or more generally the friendly relations between Aśoka and Antiochus II.

Bṛhadratha was the last of the dynasty, assassinated around 185 BC by his general Puṣyamitra, the founder of the Śuṅga dynasty, who perhaps favoured a more hawkish line against the Greek incursions in the north-west. The brevity of the later reigns may be one factor in the decline of the Mauryas, or it may itself be a symptom of their weakness. The partition of the empire into two after Aśoka's death, if it did indeed occur, may have been a more direct cause, preventing effective opposition to the Greeks and disrupting the internal organization of the empire. After the partition, the eastern part would have retained the imperial organization based on Pāṭaliputra, leading to a top-heavy system with an excessive bureaucracy inadequately supported by a reduced economy. The western part, on the other hand, would have needed rapidly to expand a provincial organization to cope with a larger area and so might well have had little time to be concerned about the Greek threat.

Śuṅgas and Kaṇvas

Puṣyamitra, having murdered the last Maurya ruler, apparently extended his sphere of influence over Vidarbha by intervening in dynastic disputes there and certainly clashed with the Greeks in the Punjab. He also twice performed the horse-sacrifice, the elaborate ritual by which kings asserted claims to paramountcy.

Buddhist tradition depicts Puṣyamitra as a terrible persecutor of Buddhism. Buddhists may have resented his action in overthrowing a dynasty under which they had flourished, while in the Punjab they seem to have allied with the Greeks. There may thus have been political factors at play here, but the religion as such did not suffer; major Buddhist monuments, such as the *stūpas* at Sāñcī and Bhārhut, continued to receive both private and royal support. (These tumulus-like structures contained relics of the Buddha or others revered by Buddhists.) Although our knowledge of the Śuṅga dynasty is sketchy, its role was significant. Puṣyamitra stemmed the tide of foreign invasion and maintained his authority widely, checking for a time the disintegration of the Magadhan empire, which throughout the century of Śuṅga rule extended as far as Vidiśā in Madhya Pradesh, if not further to the west. The Śuṅga period saw a revival of brahminical influence and the early stages of Krishna-worship; it also witnessed a revival in art, especially in central India. The Purāṇas record the overthrow of the last king at the hands of his minister, Vasudeva, who became the first of the Kaṇva dynasty, perhaps around 72 BC.

Like their predecessors, the Kaṇvas were also brahmins belonging to an ancient Vedic family, but they probably controlled Magadha alone, for the Greeks had already occupied the Punjab. Most of the Ganges basin west of Magadha was divided among various 'Mitra' kings, another line of Śuṅga vassals ruled at Mathurā and Śuṅgas still held Vidiśā. We know almost nothing of their history, beyond the record in the Purāṇas of their subjection of neighbouring kings and the overthrow of the last ruler by Simuka, the first Sātavāhana ruler, *c.* 27 BC. This invasion did not result in any permanent occupation, to judge by the lack of coins or inscriptions. After the withdrawal of the Sātavāhanas, Magadha lapsed into obscurity for over three centuries.

Khāravela of Kaliṅga

An inscription engraved on the Hāthīgumphā cave in the Udayagiri hills, near Bhubanesvar in Orissa, provides our only information about Khāravela, a member of the Cedi dynasty, which seized Kaliṅga from the Mauryas at some time after Aśoka's death. This important king most probably ruled in the middle to later part of the first century BC. Much of the inscription is taken up with a detailed account of his career for thirteen years after his installation and lists his military exploits against the Sātavāhanas and other minor powers to the south and to the north in the Ganges basin. Despite this military activity, Khāravela was a devout Jain who excavated a number of caves for Jain ascetics in the area. Unlike the Buddhist remains associated with the Śuṅga and Kaṇva dynasties, the many caves linked with this dynasty are all Jain. However, Khāravela claims to have repaired the temples of all the gods and shown equal honour to all sects. The end of the dynasty is obscure and not long after Khāravela's reign the country split into a number of smaller kingdoms.

South India

Much further south, from 300 BC onwards, kingdoms appeared under three main dynasties, the Pāṇḍyas, Cēras and Cōḻas, and this political division stayed unchanged for some centuries. The Cēras had their capital at Vañci and their territories roughly corresponded to modern Kerala. The Cōḻas, with their earliest capital at Kāvērīpattinam, held the region round Tiruccirāppalli. The Pāṇḍyas had their capital at Madurai, while their territory stretched to the south of the Cōḻa kingdom as far as Kanyākumārī.

These kingdoms developed largely independently of the north, from which they were cut off by jungles and the nomadic tribes living in them, although the earliest inscriptions do indicate that Jainism and Buddhism had penetrated into the region. Overseas contact, however, was considerable, with strong trade links with both the Roman empire and Han China. The decline of these two empires contributed to a decline in the economic prosperity of south India, an important factor in the eclipse of the three ancient kingdoms. This earlier period was brought to an end in the fifth century AD by the Kaḷabhras, who assumed control of the south till about 550. This interregnum was in turn ended by the emergence of two more stable kingdoms: a revived Pāṇḍya kingdom and a newer dynasty, that of the Pallavas, whose capital was Kāñcīpuram, near present-day Madras.

The Greeks in Bactria and India

Diodotus, the founder of the Hellenistic kingdom of Bactria, was for a long time satrap there under the Seleucids before becoming independent in 239 BC. Soon afterwards he was succeeded by his son, also named Diodotus, who made an alliance with the Parthian ruler Arsaces. Diodotus II's reign ended before 210 BC, when with a large army Antiochus III was reasserting Seleucid suzerainty, since Euthydemus was then ruling Bactria, having ousted the previous rulers. Euthydemus capitulated and handed over his war elephants, while Antiochus, after contact with Sophagasenus, returned westwards, leaving Euthydemus effectively independent. Near the end of his reign (between 200 and 190 BC), Euthydemus may have gained control over southern Afghanistan, the adjoining area of Iran and parts of north-western India.

Demetrius, Euthydemus' son and successor, launched a thrust into India, probably soon after Puṣyamitra's overthrow of the Mauryas, in which one army went south-east as far as Ujjain, while his son-in-law Menander at the head of another army pushed towards the Ganges, capturing Śākala, Mathurā and Sāketa successively, before besieging Pāṭaliputra. Demetrius' conquests in India and his resulting absence from Bactria led to the revolt there of Eucratides around 171 BC, a revolt unmistakably referred to in an Indian astrological work. Menander, a Buddhist sympathizer figures in Buddhist literature, which places his capital at Śākala, although his coins show that the focus of his kingdom was at Puṣkalāvatī (modern Charsada,

Silver coin of Menander, the greatest of the Indo-Greek kings and a convert to Buddhism. Struck before 130 BC, the coin shows Menander and, on the reverse, has Athena armed with a thunderbolt.

near Peshawar). A tradition that he built a *stūpa* at Pāṭaliputra seems to refer to a second Greek invasion of Magadha under Menander's leadership towards the end of the second century BC, which led to the transfer of the Śuṅga capital from Pāṭaliputra to Vidiśā and to the alliance between the Śuṅga ruler and the Greek Antialcidas against Menander.

Demetrius' own hold over India was brief, but Eucratides was ruling over parts of India for much of his reign. From the start Eucratides had to fight not only Demetrius and his family but also the people of Sogdia – the Bokhara region, probably already controlled by Central Asian peoples. Subsequently, the Parthian king Mithridates (*c*. 171–136 BC) attacked Bactria and annexed two districts (probably the Herat and Kandahar areas) and before long Eucratides' son had to relinquish the rest. After the loss of Bactria, the Greeks continued to rule in Afghanistan and the north-west, but their rule in these regions is characterized by internecine fighting among the Euthydemids and Eucratidids, more than thirty of whose names are known from coins. Basically, it seems, the house of Euthydemus ruled mainly in the eastern Punjab until it was supplanted by the Śaka king Azes I around 58 BC, while the house of Eucratides ruled in the region west of the River Jhelam, with capitals at Puṣkalāvatī, Taxila and in the upper Kabul valley. However, Greek involvement with Indian politics did not end with the establishment of Śaka and Kuṣāṇa supremacy, for there must still have existed petty states under Indo-Greek chiefs.

Central Asian Invaders

The Scythians, or Śakas, were the first of a series of Central Asian peoples who, pushed westwards by events behind them, arrived in the Afghanistan area and from there pushed on into India in the next century or two. The Śakas themselves seem to have migrated more or less southwards from Bactria to Seistan (Śakasthān) and thence through the Bolan or neighbouring passes into the lower Indus basin; from there they then expanded into the Punjab and Gandhāra. Little is known of them beyond their names, although the second of them, Azes I, is linked with the era commencing in 58–7 BC, known later as the era of Vikrama. They were followed briefly by a group of Parthian, or Pahlava, rulers. Gondophares (19–46) seems to have ousted the last Greek king of the upper Kabul valley and ruled an extensive area covering Seistan, Gandhāra and other Indus territories. Later Pahlavas, however, were restricted to Arachosia and Seistan. The significance of both groups of rulers is cultural more than political, since they provide the connecting link between the Greek kingdoms in Bactria and India and the Kuṣāṇas – the most successful of the Central Asian invaders.

Chinese sources, which identify the Kuṣāṇas as a branch of the Central Asian people, the Da Yuezhi, record that towards the middle of the second century BC, under pressure from the Xiongnu, they migrated westwards, and occupied the Śaka territories, driving the Śakas before them into Bactria. Later the Da Yuezhi themselves crossed the Oxus, dispersed the Śakas and conquered the whole region up to the Hindu Kush. Unlike the Hunnish Xiongnu, the Da Yuezhi were not just pastoral nomads even in their original home and in the fertile valley of the Oxus and its tributaries more of them settled to agriculture. However, trade soon

The major powers of the post-Mauryan era, showing their power bases.

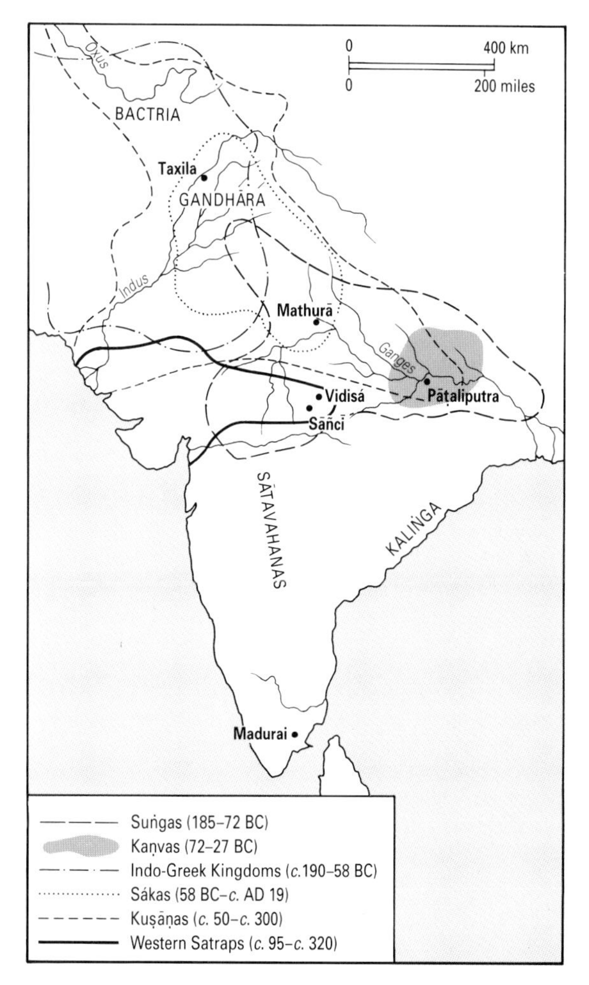

A headless statue of Vīma Kadphises, an early Kuṣāṇa king. According to the inscription, the more than life-size work was executed in 150, as a posthumous honour.

became the most important feature of their economy. Connections with India and West Asia had already been established and links with China now developed. The Sogdian and Bactrian traders certainly stepped up their commercial activities, and the Da Yuezhi as rulers took advantage of the boom.

One of the five clans of the Da Yuezhi, the Kuṣāṇas, came to dominate the others, hence the name generally used for this people. Early in the first century AD Kujula and his son Vīma Kadphises between them gained control of north-west India. Vīma may have been associated with his father in the latter part of his reign and have helped him substantially with his conquests. His own short reign was taken up with the advance into India. Taxila and the Punjab were annexed early on and before the reign's end the Kuṣāṇa empire had probably reached Mathurā, already an important cult centre on the Yamunā River. He became a zealous convert to the Śaiva faith on the evidence of his coins.

Kaniṣka, his successor, assumed power in 78 (the

Gold coin of King Kaniṣka (78–106), who ruled over the cosmopolitan Kuṣāṇa empire.

most plausible of several postulated dates), possibly after an interval. Since he controlled what is now Afghanistan, Gandhāra and the mouth of the Indus, he was in a position to divert the silk trade from China through the Khyber Pass down to the Indus delta. From there merchandise could go the safer and cheaper way by sea up the Persian Gulf to Characene, the kingdom which controlled the Tigris–Euphrates delta. Much of the Kuṣāṇa power was undoubtedly built on their role as successful intermediaries in this trade. Kaniṣka ruled his empire through subordinate rulers known as satraps, as had the Parthians and Śakas. The prosperity of the Kuṣāṇa empire increased under Kaniṣka, as his many beautiful gold coins indicate, while the legends on them illustrate the cosmopolitan nature of his empire. The large number of deities on Kuṣāṇa coins is noteworthy: Hindu, Buddhist, Zoroastrian, Elamite, Sumerian, Greek and Roman deities are all represented, with Zoroastrian or Iranian deities forming the largest group. Certainly Kaniṣka's possessions outside India were at least as important as his Indian territories. The Chinese annals record that a Kuṣāṇa king, who is probably Kaniṣka, demanded the hand of a Han princess in marriage and was soundly defeated for his arrogance by the general Ban Chao, who at the end of the first century campaigned as far as the Caspian. Kaniṣka is believed to have died fighting in Central Asia, according to one story murdered by his officers who were weary of continual campaigning.

The next king, Huviṣka (106–*c.* 40) had a prosperous reign, as shown by the large number of his gold and copper coins. The Kuṣāṇas were now becoming naturalized, and his successor, Vāsudeva (known dates 142–76) has a purely Indian name; the coinage declines in standard during his reign. The number of rulers within a short period implies succession from brother to brother, a system known to have been practised among some other tribal peoples of Central Asia. Later Kuṣāṇa rulers include a third Kaniṣka and a second Vāsudeva, ruling probably over the extreme north-western parts of India.

The later Kuṣāṇas clashed with the powerful Sasanid empire of Iran, which seems to have conquered some western Kuṣāṇa provinces. Although Kuṣāṇa kings continued to rule in the area north of the Hindu Kush, they probably had to acknowledge the supremacy of the first Sasanian king, Ardashir (*c.* 212–41). In the break-up of the Kuṣāṇa empire from about 240, most of the territories within India were lost to the growing power of various Indian chiefs. Shapur I, in his inscription at Naqsh-i Rustam of 262, lists part of the Kuṣāṇa empire among the eastern Sasanian provinces, and Shapur II campaigned against Kuṣāṇas in 356–7. Thus later Kuṣāṇa rulers may simply be Sasanian viceroys in the old Kuṣāṇa empire, or viceroys of some of its western provinces lost to Sasanid control, or independent Kuṣāṇa kings, ruling a much diminished territory, influenced by Sasanian culture and linked at times by marriage alliances with the Sasanians.

The Kuṣāṇa empire probably reached the height of its power under Kaniṣka. Positive archaeological evidence for prolonged Kuṣāṇa presence comes from only five main districts: Mathurā, Taxila, Peshawar, Begram and Surkh Kotal. Direct evidence for briefer Kuṣāṇa presence also comes from Kauśāmbī, Vārāṇasī, Śrāvastī and Vidiśā. The presence of the Kuṣāṇas can also be traced throughout Gandhāra, the Swat valley and the Kabul region. Literary evidence strongly indicates their presence in Kashmir and Balkh. In Iran the Kuṣāṇas as invaders could hardly pretend to be successors of the Achaemenids but they probably attempted to present themselves as upholders of Iranian values and even imitated certain Achaemenid practices. In India their situation was different: they could not claim to be the successors of the Mauryans or upholders of Indian identity, but they patronized Indian religions, Buddhism and Hinduism, and used local Indian languages, respecting the culture and religion of their subjects to the point of conversion.

A Greek-influenced statue of the Buddha from Gandhāra, whose artistic centre was situated at modern Peshawar.

Western Satraps and Sātavāhanas

Rule by satraps was introduced into parts of western and central India during Śaka and Pahlava rule and became well established under Kuṣāṇa rule. The earlier of the two groups known in western India consists of two members of the Kṣaharāta family, while the later group of the Kārdamakas comprises a large number of satraps, starting with Caṣṭana. The first Kṣaharāta ruler, Bhūmaka, ruled only briefly and was probably appointed to administer their westernmost conquests during Kuṣāṇa rule, although he may already have been ruling as the satrap of the Pahlavas when the Kuṣāṇas took over. His successor, Nahapāna (*c.* 95–125), ruled from the Ajmer region of Rajasthan in the north to the Nasik region of Maharashtra in the south, where his son-in-law Uṣavadāta was viceroy; an inscription at Nasik records Uṣavadāta's endowment to support twenty Buddhist monks living in a nearby cave.

Nahapāna was defeated, and probably killed, by the Sātavāhana ruler Gautamīputra Śātakarṇi, who annexed the southern parts of the Kṣaharāta territories in or soon after 124–5. Gotamī Balaśrī, Gautamīputra's mother, boasts in a later inscription that her son not only destroyed the Śakas, Yavanas (Greeks) and Pahlavas but also uprooted the Kṣaharātas. Another inscription of Gautamīputra himself records the grant to certain monks of land in a village previously in the possession of Uṣavadāta (evidently Nahapāna's son-in-law). The Sātavāhana dynasty had been ruling large parts of the Deccan since the end of the first century BC, when the first ruler Simuka had ended Kaṇva rule in Magadha; they were particularly prosperous early in the first century AD, when they controlled the north-western Deccan and benefited from the Roman trade, but then underwent a temporary eclipse owing to the incursions of the Western Satraps.

Even after the loss of the southern provinces, Śakas appear to have retained the northern provinces (although the Kṣaharāta family itself was probably wiped out) and reconquest of the area from the west began through the Kārdamakas, already ruling in Sind as satraps of the Kuṣāṇas. Caṣṭana won early success against the Sātavāhanas and established a dynasty which continued without interruption down to 304, issuing coins giving not only the name of the ruling king and that of his father but also, after 180, the date in the Śaka era. Caṣṭana's reign ended somewhere between 140 and 150. His son died before him and he was already reigning jointly with his grandson Rudradāman in 130. It is likely that by 150 the Western Satraps had recovered most, if not all, the northern parts of the Sātavāhana conquest.

Indeed, Rudradāman extended his rule over an area comprising the lower Indus valley in the north-west, central India in the east, and the entire coastal region of Kathiawar, Gujarat and the Konkan. Several areas had formed part of Gautamīputra's dominions and Rudradāman claims in his Junāgaḍh (Girnar) inscription of 150 that he had twice defeated Śātakarṇi but spared him because of their near relationship; this presumably is Gautamīputra's son and Rudradāman's son-in-law, Vāsiṣṭhīputra Puḷumāvī. After being ousted again from the north-western Deccan, in the late second century the Sātavāhanas centred their attention on the eastern Deccan and from there developed extensive trade with South-East Asia, which resulted also in some colonization. However, early in the following century the Sātavāhana empire seems to have been split up under different members of the dynasty and before long had passed into other hands.

From the degradation of the coinage, it is clear that after the middle of the third century the prosperity of the Western Satraps gradually declined, due in part to the expansion of Sasanian power towards the east. Power was usurped in the first half of the fourth century by another line. Then, in the second half, the restored house of Caṣṭana came under pressure from the Guptas until the last ruler (whose last known date is 397) was defeated and his territory annexed by Candragupta II.

The Gupta Dynasty (320–c. 550)

The Guptas had been an obscure feudal dynasty which, during the period of Kuṣāṇa supremacy, gained control of the former imperial capital, Pāṭaliputra. Candragupta I, the first important ruler, initiated the Gupta era, beginning in 320, to commemorate his accession or installation. Candragupta I's marriage with a princess Kumāradevī of the Licchavi tribe figures prominently in his son Samudragupta's Allahabad pillar inscription, and elsewhere Samudragupta proudly described himself as the son of the daughter of the Licchavis. The importance of this marriage is also shown by a series of gold coins, depicting on one side the names and figures of Candragupta and Kumāradevī and on the other a goddess seated on a lion with the name of the Licchavis beside it. Apparently the Licchavis had carved out a new kingdom, in the absence of any strong central control, and were powerful again in northern Bihar. It is interesting to note their re-emergence like this so long after their defeat by Ajātaśatru, when they were ruling as a tribal state at Vaiśālī. Candragupta himself ruled over Sāketa (Oudh), Prayāga (Allahabad) and Magadha.

Coin of the second Gupta ruler, Samudragupta (*c.* 355–76). During his reign Pāṭaliputra again became the centre of a great empire.

Under Candragupta's successor Samudragupta (*c.* 335–76), Pāṭaliputra again became the centre of a great empire. The Allahabad inscription, a eulogy composed by the courtier Hariṣeṇa and engraved on the already 600-year-old Aśokan pillar (which probably came originally from Kauśāmbī) is our main source of information. It describes Samudragupta's selection as heir to the throne by his father, Candragupta I; apparently Candragupta then abdicated in favour of Samudragupta, who by implication was not the obvious heir and may have had to face a revolt by other brothers on his accession. Perhaps more probably the emphasis on Samudragupta as the grandson of the Licchavi ruler suggests that he was entitled to succeed his maternal grandfather and thus his succession to Candragupta I kept the two kingdoms together.

Samudragupta undertook a remarkable string of military campaigns. His conquests, listed in the Allahabad inscription, are grouped according to their political status in the Gupta empire. First, several rulers in north India were eradicated, including two members of the Nāga dynasty, who had set up kingdoms at Padmāvatī (Pawaya, Gwalior), Vidiśā and Mathurā. The next categories of less complete conquest were five frontier kingdoms and nine tribal peoples; the warlike tribes to the west merely rendered him homage and rulers of the forest states are said to have been reduced to servitude. Thirdly, twelve rulers south of the Vindhya mountains were defeated and captured, among them the ruler of Kosala (the Raipur area) and Viṣṇugopa of Kāñcī (younger brother of the Pallava Siṃhavarman, ruling *c.* 332–44). The order of listing implies an advance through the eastern and southern parts of Madhya Pradesh to Orissa and then along the east coast as far as the Pallava kingdom. This southern campaign was not really conquest, for the defeated kings were reinstated on giving homage and tribute and, though nominally vassals of Samudragupta, were probably little affected by the change of status. Finally, more distant peoples are said to have offered their service: those listed here are the Daivaputraṣāhis, Ṣāhānuṣāhis, Śakas and Muruṇḍas, Sinhalese and 'all dwellers in islands'. The first four are Iranian or Central Asian peoples, either in north-western or western India, where the Western Satraps had been in power for over 200 years and still controlled Mālwā and Kathiawar, although there is a significant gap in their coinage between 351 and 360. Less likely is Samudragupta's

claim that Meghavarṇa of Sri Lanka (*c.* 352–79) was his vassal. In fact, Meghavarṇa sent a mission to Samudragupta with rich presents to ask for permission to build a monastery and rest-house for Sinhalese pilgrims at Bodh Gayā, the place where the Buddha attained enlightenment. Samudragupta evidently regarded this as paying tribute.

Samudragupta's power or influence thus extended over most of northern and central India and approached in scope Aśoka's empire, the memory of which was still vivid. The Guptas seem deliberately to have imitated their Mauryan predecessors and the identity of name between Candragupta I and Candragupta Maurya is probably not coincidental. Similar motives no doubt underlay Samudragupta's choice of one of Aśoka's columns for this enumeration of his own conquests. Even Aśoka's palace at Pāṭaliputra was not destroyed until 411.

Besides listing his martial achievements, the inscription also praises Samudragupta's moral character and his interest in the arts; indeed, the inscription is evidence of this, since it is composed in the manner of classical Sanskrit poetry. According to Hariṣeṇa, Samudragupta was not only a great patron of learning but was himself a great poet and musician. Nothing survives to show whether he deserved the title of 'king of poets' but his love of music is suggested by one type of his gold coins, showing him seated cross-legged on a couch and playing a *vīṇā*, or seven-string lute. Inscriptions of his successors refer to Samudragupta as having restored the horse-sacrifice, or *aśvamedha*, a kingly rite that had long been in abeyance; this is supported by coins depicting the sacrificial horse. Kumāragupta issued a similar type of coin.

There is a story that on the death of Samudragupta the Śakas succeeded in shaking the Gupta empire and forced a weak king named Rāmagupta to conclude a dishonourable peace. This episode formed the plot of the drama *Devīcandragupta* by Viśākhadatta, which is our main source for the story. Unfortunately, the drama survives only in fragments, but the basic plot was apparently as follows:

Samudragupta was succeeded by his son Rāmagupta, whose wife was Dhruvadevī. During a war with the Śakas he was besieged and placed in such a difficult position that he agreed to surrender his queen to the Śaka king in order to save his people. His younger brother Candragupta protested against this and offered to go to the enemy's camp disguised as Dhruvadevī and kill the Śaka king, which he duly did. The incident increased his reputation with the people and the queen at the expense of Rāmagupta's, the brothers fell out, and Candragupta had to feign madness to preserve his life. Ultimately Candragupta succeeded in killing his elder brother and so acquiring his kingdom and his wife.

Although Rāmagupta may not have been an historical king, Candragupta II (376–412 or later) certainly annihilated the Śaka satraps in western India after a long campaign. The details are not known but

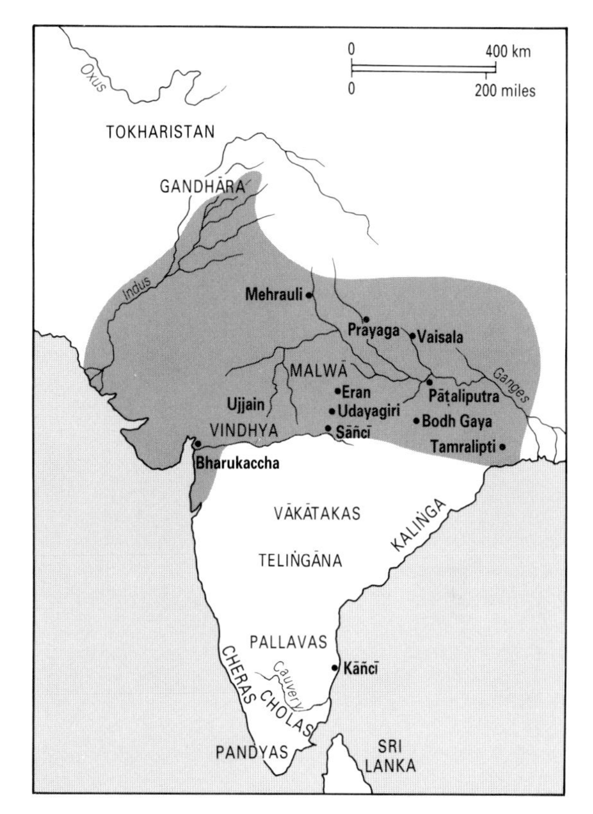

The Gupta empire during the reign of Candragupta II (376–*c.* 412).

the dating and location of some inscriptions indicate that he made a prolonged stay in Mālwā, possibly from soon after 388 until almost 400, during which time the ancient city of Vidiśā assumed particular importance. However, not only were the satraps defeated but their kingdom was annexed. The Gupta empire now stretched from coast to coast. Indian legends tell of a great and good king, Vikramāditya, who, having driven the Śakas out of Ujjain, reflects the popular image of Candragupta: this king ruled over the whole of a prosperous India and was a munificent patron of literature. Candragupta's reign marks the culmination of ancient Indian culture, which carries over into the reign of his son Kumāragupta. The Mehrauli iron pillar records that a certain Candra, identified as Candragupta II, 'defeated a confederacy of hostile chiefs in Vaṅga and, having crossed in warfare the seven mouths of the Indus, conquered the Vāhlīkas'. Vaṅga (eastern Bengal) is virtually identical with Samataṭa, one of the frontier kingdoms tributary to Samudragupta in the Allahabad inscription. Either there was a rebellion there or else Candragupta decided to bring the area directly under the control of the central government; we know that a Gupta ruler was ruling in this area early in the sixth century and it was probably, therefore, as a result of this campaign that direct rule

Mehrauli iron pillar, now located in the Quwwat-ul-Islam mosque, south of Delhi.

was established. The Vāhlīkas must designate Balkh (Bactria); the Kuṣāṇas ruling here seem to have acknowledged the supremacy of Samudragupta, so presumably again Candragupta was asserting closer control.

Candragupta II had several queens, one of whom allied him with the Nāga families defeated by his father. Candragupta himself joined the Vākāṭaka and Kadamba kingdoms of the Deccan to the Gupta political system by marrying his daughter, Prabhāvatīguptā, to the Vākāṭaka Rudrasena II and his son (or perhaps himself) to a daughter of the Kadamba ruler. The Vākāṭaka dynasty probably originated as vassals of the later Sātavāhanas, becoming powerful on their decline and then extending control over Central India. Late in the third century, Pravarasena I had secured his position to the north by a marriage alliance with the powerful Nāga dynasty and, by the time he died, early in the fourth century, the Vākāṭaka empire may have extended from Bundelkhand in the north to Telingāna in the south. His kingdom was then divided, one part under the descendants of his son Gautamīputra, with their capital in Nagpur district, and one part under another son Sarvasena and his successors, with their capital at Vatsagulma (modern Basim in the Akola district). The Vākāṭakas were apparently ousted from their central Indian possessions by the Guptas, and Rudrasena II's marriage to Prabhāvatīguptā was probably arranged in order to check the Gupta advance towards the Deccan. The Vākāṭakas now became subordinate allies of the Gupta emperors, helping them in their struggle against the Śaka satraps. The early death of her husband, Rudrasena II, thrust Prabhāvatīguptā into the position of regent and so secured a further increase in Gupta influence. Prabhāvatīguptā exercised power in a regency of at least thirteen years. She was a vigorous woman who lived for a century, as stated on a copper plate issued in the nineteenth regnal year of her third son Pravarasena II.

The Buddhist complex of cave monasteries and shrines at Ajaṇṭā.

Kumāragupta I, Candragupta II's son by his chief queen, Dhruvadevī, had a long reign of about forty years (*c.* 415–54). No specific military campaigns are known but, since he celebrated a horse-sacrifice, he must at least have kept intact the empire inherited from his father. Samudragupta and Candragupta II had issued 'tiger-slayer' and 'lion-slayer' coin types, which are sometimes thought to indicate their conquests over Bengal and Kathiawar respectively. By analogy, the 'rhinoceros-slayer' type issued by Kumāragupta has been taken to commemorate his conquest of Kāmarūpa (Assam), of which the rhinoceros is characteristic, but there is no supporting evidence. Kumāragupta's reign is marked by further cultural development, facilitated by the peace and prosperity already established. However, at its very end, the Gupta empire suffered a severe blow from the incursions of an enemy whose identity is unclear but who must have been connected with the migrations of the Hūṇas, known in Europe as the Ephthalites or White Huns.

Originally the Hūṇas migrated west of Khotan, establishing themselves in an area stretching from Tokharistan to the borders of Iran. But in the middle of the fifth century they founded a large but short-lived empire corresponding roughly to that of the defunct Kuṣāṇa empire. At first the Hūṇas did not occupy any part of India and were resisted by the Sasanian ruler Peroz, but his death in 484 after a defeat by them paved the way for their expansion in eastern Iran, where they made Herat their headquarters. They next overwhelmed Gandhāra, making it their base for the conquest of north India.

The prince Skandagupta was sent against this enemy and, although the Gupta forces met with serious reverses, he finally turned the scales to inflict a crushing defeat on them. An inscription says that the enemy had 'great resources in men and money', that during the campaign 'to restore the fallen fortunes of his family' Skandagupta passed a whole night on the bare ground, and that his victory was sung in every region 'by happy men, even down to the children'. Altogether, the picture is of a very formidable enemy. During the war, Kumāragupta died and Skandagupta assumed power; although he was probably not the son of the chief queen, he must have profited by

Frescos from the entrance of Cave 17 at Ajaṇṭā. Here the usual narrative sculpture has been replaced by painting.

Sāñchī. The episodes depicted on the outer façade of the north gate include the Buddha's first sermon, when he set in motion the 'wheel of enlightening doctrine'.

the special responsibility he had been given by his father.

Skandagupta (*c.* 455–67) had to face an even greater danger almost immediately after his accession, but he was again successful and won a complete victory over the Hūṇas, who were so deterred that they left the Guptas alone for over forty years. Successful though these campaigns were, they taxed the resources of the empire and this was clearly a period of some financial strain (the gold content of the coins was reduced and only three types were issued). Even so, considerable public works were carried out, while the Junāgaḍh inscription of 458 indicates that early in his reign Skandagupta's control was fully exercised far to the west. However, there are no inscriptions after 466 and the break-up of the empire known to be occurring in the 470s may have begun before the end of his reign, although it was more probably triggered off by his death.

No sons of Skandagupta are known, and the later Guptas trace their descent from Kumāragupta I through an older son, Purugupta, completely ignoring Skandagupta. Purugupta may have ruled briefly, probably after Skandagupta (having perhaps also contested the throne on Kumāragupta's death), since the imperial line was continued by his sons. Gupta central control now weakened and local governors became feudatory kings with hereditary rights: for example, the Maitrakas became hereditary rulers of Kathiawar about 470 and the Parivrājaka Mahārājas were independent in Bundelkhand by 475. After about a decade of disorder following Skandagupta's death, Purugupta's son Budhagupta (known dates 477, 495) ruled for twenty years or so. Inscriptions indicate that he had firm control of the dynasty's heartland in the lower Ganges basin, while inscriptions from Bengal cite the authority of his governor. However, an inscription of 484 at Eran, while acknowledging Budhagupta's suzerainty, is mainly devoted to eulogizing the local ruler, and this area is obviously in the process of breaking away; and an inscription from Mandasor refers to the period between 436 and 472 as full of troubles and seeing the rule of other kings, although the exact implication is not clear. Budhagupta's death was certainly followed by a further period of troubles for the Guptas, of whom five are known in the period around 500–570.

About 495 came the second Hūṇa invasion. Toramāṇa, the Hunnish chief of Śākala in the Punjab, established himself in eastern Mālwā, probably on the death of Budhagupta. His rule at Śākala probably began about 460, with Skandagupta's death enabling him to occupy central India. He seems to have flanked the main Gupta territories and kept west of the Yamunā to attack the area between the Kālindī and Narmadā rivers. Toramāṇa annexed at least a part of the Gupta empire, but his rule over the Eran area was relatively brief. Before 515 the Aulikara Prakāśadharman, a Gupta vassal, defeated Toramāṇa (who seems to have been forced to retreat to Gwalior), greatly enhancing the prestige of his dynasty. Around 515 Toramāṇa was succeeded by his son Mihirakula, who made his capital at Śākala. At this point the Hūṇa empire extended from Balkh to Gwalior and he was still ruling Gwalior in the fifteenth year of his reign. However, Yaśodharman, also of the Aulikara dynasty, defeated Mihirakula before 533 and went on to achieve further conquests, mainly no doubt at the expense of the Guptas. Yaśodharman's career is known from a single record at Mandasor, dated 533–4, which claims that he ruled all north India, being lord of the countries not possessed by the Guptas or the Hūṇas, and that he surpassed the prowess of the Guptas, while 'obeisance was made at his feet by even the mighty king Mihirakula', who had never before bowed to anyone except Śiva. Yaśodharman's period of prominence seems to have lasted only a decade (*c.* 530–40), but it dealt a major blow to the prestige of the Guptas. However, with the combined aid of his vassals, Narasiṃhagupta eventually defeated Mihirakula and destroyed Hūṇa power in India. Mihirakula was forced to retreat to Gandhāra, where he continued to rule for about a decade. But the collapse of Hūṇa power in India was followed by the defeat of their central power on the Oxus by the combined forces of the Turks and Iranians between 563 and 567. Besides the Hūṇas we know of at least one other invasion: the Vākāṭaka Hariṣeṇa from the Deccan invaded Mālwā and established his authority there. Hariṣeṇa, of the branch Vākāṭaka line founded by Sarvasena, is especially associated with the great Buddhist cave-complex at Ajaṇṭā. Soon afterwards, however, this dynasty was eliminated by powerful neighbours, while the main Vākāṭaka line ended their rule by the middle of the sixth century.

Narasiṃhagupta's successors, Kumāragupta III and Viṣṇugupta (*c.* 535–70), continued to issue gold coins but their further debasement reveals the swift decline of the Gupta empire under these two rulers. However, some vestiges of their power remained: we know that the rulers of Valabhī paid nominal allegiance to the Guptas till about 550 and Gupta suzerainty was acknowledged in Kaliṅga as late as 569. Direct control was presumably limited to Magadha and before the end of the century all trace of the Guptas had vanished.

War and Foreign Affairs

For Indians throughout most of their history India itself has been a complete world and, although there were periods when their horizons extended beyond the subcontinent, Indian rulers usually thought of foreign affairs in terms of their neighbouring and rival rulers. Relatively little survives that directly records either warfare or diplomacy in action, although there is a considerable amount of theoretical description.

Nevertheless, it is clear that warfare was endemic and, indeed, often ritualized. The institution of the horse-sacrifice was already well known in the Vedic period and persisted at least till the Gupta empire. Its whole ethos revolved around the proclamation of his paramountcy by the ruler making the sacrifice: the stallion was let loose to roam at will (except that it was denied access to mares) for a year before it was sacrificed and the ruler's sovereignty was held to extend to all the territory it covered, with its attendant warriors ready to give battle to any who denied it free passage. The claims to power (symbolized in the horse itself and transmitted to the chief queen in ritualized intercourse with the horse when sacrificed) are obvious, as is the pride with which so many rulers record their performance of this elaborate ritual.

In the Sanskrit epics the *Mahābhārata* and the *Rāmāyaṇa*, which probably reflect the traditional pattern from about the middle of the first millennium BC, combat was the privilege of the political élite. The armies are composed of members of the aristocratic warrior class, the *kṣatriyas*, who individually maintain horses, chariots and elephants, bringing them with them in the event of war. The *Mahābhārata* contains several statements that death at home, in bed with the illnesses of old age, is a disgrace for members of the ruling class, just as it is to return from battle without wounds. The great set-piece duels central to both epics are fought by warriors mounted on the two-wheeled chariots which had been typical of Vedic warfare: in the *Mahābhārata* Arjuna has Krishna as his charioteer; and in the *Rāmāyaṇa* the gods send Indra's chariot and charioteer to assist Rāma when his own chariot is destroyed. Similar chariots are known to have been used unsuccessfully by Porus against Alexander, but over the period of composition of the epics they decline in importance compared with elephants. Elephants were actual combatants in battle, using their trunk or tusks against opponents, although by the Mauryan period archers were mounted on an elephant. Cavalry, though listed as one of the four 'limbs', or components, of an army in the epics, was not equal to elephant and chariot forces in prestige or importance. The more humdrum infantry gets relatively scant recognition in the epics. The main weapons were the bow and arrow (of various shapes), after which came spears, javelins and the like; but clubs and maces were also used, as well as swords and battle-axes. Rules of fair combat were agreed between the two sides before the conflict, although they were at times breached during it; such rules of warfare gained general currency in classical India and included a ban on fighting at night, immunity for non-combatants and especially envoys, appropriate signals for surrender and the concept that duels should be only between warriors who were similarly armed.

The Advent of Professional Armies

The Purāṇas regard the reign of Mahāpadma, the first Nanda king, as marking a decisive downturn in Indian history. As the destroyer of the old aristocratic class, he inaugurated an era in which for the most part rulers were low-born and unrighteous. The end of the *kṣatriya* class implies the demise of traditional, heroic armies. If combined with traditions of the Nandas' great wealth and wide taxation, this may mean that Mahāpadma instituted an army of professional soldiers paid for by a large treasury, a supposition perhaps supported by the high numbers of the Nanda army, which Alexander learned of in 326 BC during his invasion: 20,000 horses, 200,000 infantry, 2,000 chariots and 4,000 elephants. Even under the Nandas Magadha had grown to be a large imperial state, underpinned by its military strength, but the enlargement of this empire by Candragupta Maurya undoubtedly necessitated further changes. Not only did Candragupta regularly deploy 600,000 infantry but he could also put into the field 30,000 cavalry and 9,000 elephants. Clearly war was a professional concern.

Our two main sources for the description of the Mauryan state, including its military aspects, both have limitations. Megasthenes' account belongs precisely to the reign of Candragupta (since the Ionian was Seleucus I's ambassador to Candragupta) and, although written by an interested and well-informed foreigner, is extant only in extracts quoted by later authors, with the attendant risks of distortion and misunderstanding. The *Kauṭilīya Arthaśāstra* is an extensive Indian work on politics but, quite apart from problems of dating, it is theoretical and in no sense a manual of current practice at any period. The identification of Kauṭilya, to whom it is attributed, with the legendary Cāṇakya, Candragupta's minister, arose much later than the text. The context also makes this traditional attribution untenable, since the *Arthaśāstra* refers to peoples and places which would not have been known in Mauryan times and envisages a later political set-up, though one which is certainly earlier than the Gupta period. It was probably compiled from earlier treatises on different aspects of the subject during the first or second century AD.

According to Megasthenes, the Mauryan army was organized under a committee of thirty, divided into subcommittees which controlled the corps of infantry, cavalry, chariots, elephants, navy and commissariat; this seems to be modelled on his description of the administration of Pāṭaliputra and is not confirmed by any other source. According to Arrian, the fighting class, who numerically were second only to the peasantry, led a life of great freedom and enjoyment, having only military duties to perform. Others made their arms and supplied them with horses, and they had people to wait on them in camp, to groom their horses, to clean their arms, to drive their elephants and to prepare and drive their chariots. As long as they were required to fight they fought, and in peacetime they gave themselves up to pleasure, the pay which they received being so liberal that they could easily maintain themselves and others as well. Thus the evidence deriving from Megasthenes shows a huge, centrally paid and fully professional standing army.

Like most Greeks, Megasthenes appears to have been very impressed with the elephants, and his accounts of their capture and breeding are remarkably accurate. In the peace treaty of 303 BC, Candragupta gave Seleucus 1,500 elephants, which is an enormous number for any one ruler to own and maintain, still more to give away. However, besides emphasizing the size of the territory ceded by Seleucus to Candragupta, it confirms Megasthenes' report about the Mauryan government's monopoly on elephants, horses and arms, by which they controlled these important components of their formidable war machine. Incidentally, Megasthenes also credits the queen of the Pāṇḍyas in the far south with an army of 500 elephants, 4,000 cavalry and 13,000 infantry.

The *Arthaśāstra* gives detailed instructions on the control of the state and the conduct of war, many of which seem to reflect Mauryan conditions despite some later features. The officers of state and the army were to be well paid, requiring a large state income. Such linking of taxation, administration and military power was crucial to the establishment of a centralized empire, but probably even under the Mauryas the influence of the state was not quite so all-pervasive as the system propounded in the *Arthaśāstra*.

The *Arthaśāstra* defines the sphere of an emperor's rule as the whole of India from the Himālayas to the Indian Ocean. It also enumerates the important tribal states and discusses the means by which such tribes can be reduced to subordination by an ambitious king – the main method being to sow dissension among the leading tribesmen so that their assembly loses its unanimity and the tribe is divided against itself. The emergence of the Mauryan empire had marked the definite triumph of the monarchical state over other forms, so this is possibly an archaic feature; on the other hand, though, some of these tribal states had retained their individuality and survived the Mauryan empire to re-emerge as independent units, although they remained subject to strong monarchical influences, which tended to make them give up election in favour of hereditary office.

A notable witness to Aśoka's military activity in Orissa is the site of Śiśupālgaṛh, where there is an enclosure 3/4 mile square, with two entrances set symmetrically in each side, obviously implying a grid-plan on the Hellenistic model. The earliest defences consisted of massive clay ramparts over 25 feet high. From the occurrence of black-and-red ware in the first occupation layer contemporary with the rampart, it can be assigned to *c.* 300–200 BC. With regard to diplomacy, the thirteenth rock edict records that Aśoka ordered his envoys to propagate *dhamma* at home and abroad and that they were sent 'even as far away as 600 *yojanas*, where the Yavana king Antiyoka rules, and even beyond Antiyoka in the realms of the four kings named Tulamaya, Antekina, Makā and Alikasudala, and to the south among the Cōlas and Pāṇḍyas as far as Sri Lanka'. These Hellenistic rulers can be identified as Antiochus II Theos of Syria (261–246 BC), Ptolemy II Philadelphus of Egypt (285–247 BC), Antigonus Gonatas of Macedonia (276–239 BC), Magas of Cyrene (300-?250 BC) and Alexander of Epirus (272–255 BC). There is, however, no record of the arrival of these embassies.

The role of envoys was well established in classical India, but as a messenger rather than a permanent ambassador. The *Arthaśāstra* recognizes three types: one with full powers to negotiate with the foreign ruler, one with definite instructions from which he could not deviate and one who was just a courier. The inviolability of the envoy is recognized both by the *Arthaśāstra* and by the didactic portions of the *Mahābhārata*, and was generally observed. Apart from Aśoka's sending of envoys to the Hellenistic rulers, information on such diplomatic exchanges comes almost entirely from outside India. Inscriptions of the second century AD from Palmyra, an oasis strategically situated midway between the Euphrates and Damascus, mention direct relations with the Kuṣāṇa-controlled region around the mouth of the Indus. We also learn of various Indian embassies, of which the earlier ones were probably Kuṣāṇa, visiting the Roman emperors Trajan (98–117), Hadrian (117–38), Antoninus Pius (138–61), Heliogabalus (218–22), Aurelian (270–75), Constantine (323–53) and Julian (361–3), while two more Indian embassies were probably sent to Byzantium in 520 and 532. But some could have come from southern India, where the site of Arikamedu has revealed extensive evidence of Roman trade in the first and second centuries.

Other forms of contact in the period between about 200 BC and 200 AD shed some light on the developments in the techniques of war. In later parts of the *Mahābhārata* the excellence of the horses and the horsemanship of the Yavanas, or Greeks, is their most often mentioned characteristic, along with their fine armour of damascened steel and brass. Neither the horses nor the armour were products of Greece; their use had been learned in the Iranian highlands and in India. The heavy weapons and armour of the Indo-Greek cavalry would require powerful horses, often represented on Bactrian and Indo-Greek coins. The cavalry charge was a spectacular military tactic of the Yavanas. We also find mounted archers in the Kuṣāṇa period.

The Handling of Foreign Affairs

Seemingly as a reflection of the period of its compilation in the first or second century, the *Arthaśāstra* conforms to the traditional, rather artificial Indian idea of foreign policy. The theory of the *maṇḍala*, or 'circle', turns the fact that neighbouring states are often hostile to each other into an article of faith and automatically assumes that the neighbour is an enemy, the state beyond him an ally, and so on. The constant struggle between survival and expansion is, according to this theory, acted out in concentric circles, in which the intending conqueror (*vijigīṣu*) and his state are surrounded by potential and often actual enemies, who are ringed by their enemies (allies of the *vijigīṣu*) and again by their enemies (allies of the *vijigīṣu*'s enemies). The circle of friends and a further circle of friends' friends are together counted as one of the seven factors or constituents of the Indian state (ruler, officials, province, forts, treasury, army and ally). In addition, in a modification of the pattern, there is the 'middle' state adjoining both the hostile states, able to aid but also to defeat them if they are disunited, while the 'non-involved' state lies beyond the area of these three; it is stronger and able to defeat them if they are disunited. Each of these states has circles of allies and their allies' allies, so that the political systems of the *vijigīṣu*, his enemy, the 'middle' and 'non-involved' kings together total seventy-two factors. Both the *Arthaśāstra* and the *Mahābhārata* devote some attention to classifying the different types of allies, according to their motives.

In relations with a foreign ruler, another classification developed was that of the so-called six strands: peace, war, sitting, marching, alliance and duplicity. These six are part of a larger pattern: the factors or constituents are the basis of the circle of states, which in turn is the basis for the six strands, which are the basis for ease and effort, while these two are the basis for acquisition and security, which form the goal. Alongside the six strands there is the concept of usually four 'means' – conciliation, gifts, dissension and force – which are listed in order of declining value, for conciliation is the best route to political success and force the worst (since the outcome of war is always uncertain); the ideal conquest is thus attained without a fight.

The whole purpose of the *Arthaśāstra* is to make its king the universal monarch, starting from parity with the neighbouring kings. The land is visualized as divided into territories, each originally belonging to a particular tribe. These are separated by extensive forests inhabited by fierce forest peoples, who are difficult to conquer by military means. In the intermediate stage are a few powerful, armed tribal oligarchies, which have to be defeated ruthlessly by any means available. The *Arthaśāstra* is concerned only with success and advocates deceptive tactics whenever they are called for. The *Mahābhārata* and later texts seek to inculcate codes of proper conduct but still allow deceptive measures to save the state; when the survival of the dynasty is threatened, actions that would otherwise be unrighteous could be righteous, and vice versa. The aim of all political moves is to increase the size and status of one's own state. The ultimate goal of every ruler should be to rule the world as universal sovereign. Three types of conquest are enumerated: righteous conquest, in which the defeated king is forced to render homage and tribute; conquest for greed, in which enormous booty is demanded; and demonic conquest, in which the conquered territory is annexed and its

Krishna and his brother Baharama with the cowherds in the forest. In the *Mahābhārata* Arjuna has the divine Krishna as his charioteer.

corporate existence destroyed. The order in which the methods of conquest are listed is interesting and typical: 'Intrigue, spies, winning over the enemy's people, siege and assault are the five means to capture a fort.' If the defeated king is killed in the war, the victor should install his enemy's son as the successor. Righteous conquest was the ideal throughout the classical period.

The Gupta Period
The Guptas employed heavy cavalry extensively, chariots having by now largely been abandoned, except as a means of transport – this is one legacy of the Indo-Greeks and Kuṣāṇas. The import of horses through the north-west increased during the Gupta period, evidently to provide the considerable numbers employed in warfare (it seems impossible to breed horses of suitable quality in India). Elephants usually carried two or three soldiers in addition to the mahout and were often protected with leather armour. A tendency was developing to place excessive reliance on the elephant corps in combat, perhaps partly because of problems with the supply of adequate horses for the cavalry. Gupta inscriptions mention ten different ranks of officer in their army, which was organized on the traditional four-limb model, while the Allahabad inscription of Samudragupta mentions a wide range of weapons: battle-axes, bows and arrows, swords, spears, pikes, javelins and lances.

In the Gupta period many titles lost their full meaning and became honorific marks of rank or prestige. The multitude of titles in inscriptions and literature occurs with very little information on what these officials actually did, especially since states no doubt differed from each other in their administrative pattern. The primary duty of the frequently mentioned *sāṃdhivigrahika* was the conduct of foreign affairs, but he is also often mentioned as being entrusted with drafting land grants. Hariṣeṇa, for example, the composer of the Allahabad inscription, terms himself the *sāṃdhivigrahika* of Samudragupta. Nevertheless, except when external events compelled attention, inter-state policy was regarded as secondary to administration of the state's internal affairs.

Life and Society

The earliest model of society, that of its division into four *varṇas*, or 'classes', is still the pattern found in the epics and the earliest texts of Buddhism and Jainism. The group with the greatest prestige were the brahmins, who were the religious specialists and the guardians in general of tradition (although many have always engaged in other occupations). Next came the *kṣatriyas*, the aristocratic élite, who had developed out of the Vedic warriors. They were followed by the *vaiśyas*, the merchant and artisan community, which had developed from the peasantry. The fourth *varṇa*, the *śūdras*, originally little more than serfs, were now predominantly agriculturalists. It was still by no means uncommon for individuals to marry outside their *varṇa* (when the children took the father's *varṇa*), although this became steadily less usual and was ultimately frowned on. This underlies the practice of referring to one's brahmin mother (first found in the *Śatapatha Brāhmaṇa*, and frequent in inscriptions from Uttar Pradesh), for when the father's status alone decided the child's status, it was a matter for pride to be able to indicate brahmin ancestry on the mother's side too. This persisted down to the first century, as the names of several Sātavāhana kings refer to their mothers by their brahmin clan names, revealing the same brahminical influence evident in the dynasty's activities.

The emergence of monarchical states in north India, of which Magadha was the most prominent, led to considerable changes in the whole social pattern, with the decline of the older kinship ties and their replacement by more impersonal governmental organization. The growth of trade also meant an increase in the economic importance of the *vaiśyas*, not matched by their ritual status, and saw the rise of guilds as a significant feature of urban life, where they often had a large measure of self-government. There was a highly organized bureaucracy under the Mauryas. Most areas lost their independence and were included within its extensive political and economic system, although states lying on the borders of the empire naturally maintained a looser relationship with the Maurya throne. The imperial structure was provided with a base through the spread and establishment of an agrarian economy. Land revenue had been recognized as a major source of state income even before the Mauryas – the proverbial wealth of the Nandas was derived from the revenue collected from the fertile middle Ganges – and they saw to its correct assessment and collection, but other activities were also controlled and supervised by the state so that they would yield the maximum revenue.

Between 302 and 291 BC Seleucus' ambassador Megasthenes lived at Pāṭaliputra and travelled extensively in India. He was clearly an interested observer, although he may not always have interpreted his information correctly. Megasthenes states that 118 distinct nations or tribes were said to exist in the whole of India. He relates a story that the Pāṇḍya kingdom was founded by the daughter of the Greek hero Heracles, which perhaps reflects the matrilineal society of early south India. Megasthenes notes seven castes in India – philosophers, farmers, soldiers, herdsmen, artisans, magistrates and councillors – and comments: 'No one is allowed to marry outside his own caste or exercise any calling or art except his own.' He remarks that there was no slavery for free Indians. He correctly distinguishes orthodox and heterodox religious trends under the terms *bragmanoi* and *śramanai*, and recognizes that the latter group is very diverse, recording four classes among them of 'forest-dwellers', healers, diviners and reciters of charms. Buddhist texts agree with Megasthenes in contrasting the *śramana* teachers with the brahmins.

Administration and Control

Megasthenes outlines a highly organized bureaucracy in charge of all the Mauryan administration, consisting of three groups: district officials, town officials (for Pāṭaliputra and perhaps other cities) and officials to administer the armed forces. The district officials supervised irrigation and land measurement, hunting, the various industries connected with agriculture, forestry and timber-working, metal foundries and mines, and lastly maintained the roads. Pāṭaliputra was administered by a committee of thirty members divided into six subcommittees; the main committee collectively had charge, in addition to their special departments, of all matters concerning public welfare, including the repair of public works, the maintenance of markets, harbours and temples, and the regulation of prices. The responsibilities of the six subcommittees were industrial arts, care of foreigners, registration of births and deaths, trade and commerce (including supervision of weights and measures), supervision of manufactures, and collection of a tithe on the price of articles sold. Indian sources do not mention these committees, although each had its equivalent official in the list of superintendents given in the *Arthaśāstra*. The second subcommittee was to provide lodgings for foreigners and keep watch on them through people who were ostensibly helping them, as well as to escort important ones when they left the country. This, like the registration provisions, indicates the close surveillance exercised by the Mauryas.

Megasthenes also describes the grandeur of the Mauryan court. When he appeared in public the king was either carried in a golden palanquin or mounted on an elephant with gorgeous trappings; he was dressed in fine muslin embroidered with purple and gold. Within the palace precincts, the ruler was protected by a bodyguard of armed women. The harem was on an extensive scale and carefully guarded; the king dared not risk either sleeping in the daytime or occupying the same bedroom two nights in succession, and nothing passed into or out of the harem without a permit. On the other hand, Megasthenes also describes Candragupta receiving complaints and discussing matters of state even while being massaged, which is paralleled by Aśoka declaring that, no matter where he was, no member of the ministerial council should be debarred from seeing him. Megasthenes greatly admired Candragupta for his energetic administration of justice, which he presided over personally in open assembly. Megasthenes speaks of Indians as remarkably law-abiding and states that crime was very rare: while he lived in the imperial camp, with a population of 400,000 people, the daily thefts reported did not exceed 200 drachmae in value. On the other hand, he notes that death was the penalty for injury to an artisan in royal employment and for evasion of the municipal tithe on goods sold.

The machinery of government described in the *Arthaśāstra* may also to some degree reflect Mauryan practice. Every activity was liable to taxation by the state. Practically every professional and skilled person was registered and ultimately controlled by a superintendent. The officers of state and the army were to be well paid, requiring a large state income. Such linking of taxation, administration and military power was crucial to the establishment of a centralized empire, but probably even under the Mauryas the influence of the state was not as all-pervasive as the system propounded in the *Arthaśāstra*.

The seven constituents of the state were king, officers, provinces, towns, treasury, army and allies. The two main officers at the centre were the collector-general and the treasurer. The former supervised the collection of revenue in the whole kingdom; he was responsible for the collection of revenue from fortified towns, land, mines (including pearl fisheries and salt pans), irrigation works, forests, cattle and other livestock, and trade routes by land and water. The collector-general also controlled expenditure, which went mainly on the king and his court, the maintenance of members of the royal family, and the salaries of ministers and other officials. The treasurer oversaw the construction of treasuries, warehouses, armouries and prisons as needed in different localities; he was also responsible for the building of royal trading houses, courts of justice and offices of ministers and secretaries, and guarded all revenue realized in cash or kind. The accounts branch had an elaborate organization and expenditure was carefully classified.

Each administrative department was under a superintendent, subordinate to the collector-general, and their duties covered the entire range of social and economic life in the community, although it is not clear whether these superintendents operated centrally or were part of each provincial government. (The latter is more likely.) The departments specifically mentioned in the *Arthaśāstra* are treasury, mines, metals, mint, salt, gold, storehouse, trade, forest produce, armoury, weights and measures, land survey, tolls, spinning and weaving, agriculture, alcohol, slaughterhouses, prostitutes, shipping, cattle, horses, elephants, chariots, infantry, passports, pastures, elephant-forests, spies, religious institutions, prisons and ports. Thus it appears that in Mauryan times every aspect of an individual's life was supervised by the government to the best of its ability.

The provincial administration was no doubt similar, but exact details are not known. The revenue and general administration in rural areas was entrusted to two grades of official, of which the lower had charge of five to ten villages, where he supervised the maintenance of boundaries, registered gifts, sales and mortgages, and kept an accurate record of the population and their material resources. The towns were administered on similar lines, the lower officials having charge of a fixed number of families in a town instead of a number of villages. Village elders are often mentioned in the *Arthaśāstra* and they must have played a considerable part in guiding the people in day-to-day affairs. The work of officials was controlled not only by inspection and audit from higher officials but also by the regular employment of spies and *agents provocateurs*. The frequency of inspections and the existence of spies must have imparted the flavour of a totalitarian state, although they also served the king as a means of gauging public opinion.

The rather sketchy information on the administration that can be gleaned from Aśoka's edicts broadly confirms the combined evidence of Megasthenes and the *Arthaśāstra*. His major officials were called *mahāmātras*. Several of them would be based in the large cities, from where they administered both the city and the surrounding province. The 'officers of *dhamma*' were his own creation. The regional administration in Suvarṇagiri was headed by the senior prince and those in Ujjain, Tosalī, Taxila and a place in the central Deccan by other princes. Local officials clearly had considerable latitude in decision-making. Aśoka (*c*. 268–232 BC) undertook to send out several different officers on tour through their assigned territory every five years, and the princes in Ujjain and Taxila were to arrange something similar every three years. The Rummindei inscription is the only Aśokan edict to make a precise reference to taxation, for we are told that because Lumbinī was the birthplace of the Buddha, Aśoka exempted it from taxes and required only an eighth share of the produce, but it is not clear whether the latter is a reduction on or a continuation of the normal amount paid.

There is a sentence in one edict which may suggest that Aśoka abolished the traditional, orthodox practice of grading punishments according to caste, but it is unlikely that such a major innovation was put into practice. While it might be seen as following through the principles of *dhamma*, it would also have been likely to cause considerable upheaval in society and to antagonize both the brahmins and the *kṣatriyas*, who in combination might well have been difficult to keep under control. On the other hand, Aśoka may well actually have abolished the death penalty.

The Development of the Classes

In the next period (*c*. 185 BC–AD 320), the arrival of outsiders, the Yavanas, Śakas, Pahlavas and Kuṣāṇas, posed a serious social challenge to the existing *varṇa* system, for their rulers already enjoyed the status of aristocrats but not the hereditary qualifications. It is interesting to see how the great legal theoretician Manu deals with this situation, writing as he most probably was in the second century in the immediate aftermath of this series of invasions. In the part of his textbook dealing with the four classes he recognizes not only the emergence of the numerous occupational groups, former tribal groups and other small social units which were evidently the forerunners of the modern *jātis*, or 'castes', but also assigns these rulers of foreign origin a place in the scheme of things, in both cases making use of what one can only call a legal fiction. He explains the many 'mixed castes' as originating from a miscegenation between the basic four *varṇas* that produced a large number of separate groups, with their relative ranking being dependent on the parents' status and in particular those of lowest rank coming from the union of a woman of higher status with a man of lower status. The device he uses to account for the discrepancy between the actual and the notional status of foreign rulers is to assert that they had in fact once been resident within India, when they had the status of *kṣatriyas*, but became 'degraded' as a result of their wandering away. Thus their status is open to change, since if they are purified of their degradation – by suitably lavish ceremonies with their attendant gifts to the brahmins and recognition of their supremacy in religious matters – and so recover their former position in the hierarchy, everything will be as it should. We see here an excellent example of accommodation of theory to reality under the guise of affirming the *status quo*, something that the legal theorists were to practise extensively later.

Another social change which is already apparent in this textbook of Manu is the decline in the status of women, resulting, it seems, from the lowering of the age of marriage. The pattern which was applicable to boys of the first three *varṇas*, by which they underwent a period of celibate studentship in their teens (the precise age varied from one class to another) as a necessary preliminary to membership of adult society, and at the beginning of it received the sacred thread, seen as a kind of rebirth and marking their admission into adulthood, was no longer followed for girls, who were standardly married at or before the onset of puberty. This had a twofold result: first, girls no longer took part in the higher levels of education associated with study under a *guru*, or 'teacher', and second, they no longer received the sacred thread and so technically were not full members of their class. Thus women joined *śūdras* and outcastes as groups ineligible to hear the recitation of the Vedic hymns. This decline in the status of women continued steadily in the theoretical literature and, so far as our rather sporadic information goes, also in reality, although there is no real evidence for the seclusion of women in India until much later.

Consolidation under the Guptas

The industrial and commercial guilds so characteristic of the earlier economic organization continued to flourish during the Gupta period (320–*c*. 550), although there is also evidence of *śūdras* as artisans and traders playing a more significant role. The head of a guild often had considerable influence locally or in the municipality. Various inscriptions indicate the functioning of the guilds as corporate bodies and also their use as a kind of bank. We have little direct evidence of rates of interest prevailing at this period, although there is plenty of theoretical literature on the subject, which gives rates ranging from 1.25 per cent on secured loans to 20 per cent on capital for high-risk ventures such as voyages overseas.

The picture of administration that we get is generally one of mildness and benevolence. The administrative system of the Guptas was much more decentralized than that of the Mauryans. Unlike the Mauryans, the Guptas accepted a number of vassals, many of whom were rulers of large territories. In general, the degree of autonomy granted to these lesser rulers was related to the distance between their own states and the Gupta capital. The nearest ones were treated more or less as imperial officers and their powers were considerably restricted, but those on the periphery were practically independent and might have vassals of their own. The department of the chief foreign minister was instituted to keep a close watch on their activities. Significantly, Samudragupta's Allahabad inscription is almost silent about the administrative organization of the provinces, which we know from other records to have existed.

There was a growing tendency for kings to donate entire villages for religious and charitable purposes. In these cases the donee not only acquired the right to receive a certain amount of the royal revenues but, on some occasions, also enjoyed all kinds of royal dues which are often specifically recorded in the inscriptions. There thus arose a new class of intermediary between the king and the actual farmers, and certain broad features of feudalism, such as the granting of cultivated land, the gradual emergence of a self-sufficient local economy, the relative paucity of coins, the decline in trade, and decentralization in administration as a result of grants of revenues to brahmins and later to officials begin to be noticeable from the Gupta period onwards. There is, however, a marked difference between the land grants in the Guptas' own territories and grants in the dependent states: in their own territories land grants required the consent of the king, but the subordinate rulers on the periphery made land grants on their own with only a respectful mention of their overlord.

The chief feature of the land system was its partial feudalization as a result of the grant of cultivated land to temples and brahmins in central India, Bengal and Bihar. The central India grants were made by Gupta vassals, who not only gave away villages free of taxes but also provided administrative immunities. Royal ownership of mines, which was an important sign of sovereignty, seems to have been transferred to the brahmins, who, according to several grants of the fourth and fifth centuries, were allowed to enjoy mining rights in the villages granted to them. Equally important was the development that the donor abandoned the right to govern the village's inhabitants. We have at least half a dozen grants of apparently settled villages made to brahmins by the king's vassals, in which the residents, including cultivators and artisans, were expressly asked by their respective rulers not only to pay customary taxes to the donees but also to obey their commands. Nevertheless, the inscriptions of the fifth century show that the ruler generally retained the right to punish thieves, which was one of the main bases of state power. The Gupta emperors presumably made grants on the same kind of terms as their vassals in central India; little firm evidence remains, but the Bihar stone inscription of Skandagupta, dated 489, leaves the impression that whole villages were granted by the Gupta emperors on such terms.

An interesting independent picture of life in the Gupta empire is provided by the Chinese pilgrim Fa Xian, who noted the decline of Buddhism and the growth of vegetarianism and of untouchability, all of which point to the re-emergence of orthodoxy in a form much closer to modern Hinduism. Fa Xian left China in 399 and travelled to India by land. From the Punjab he travelled right across the Gupta empire to reach his destination of Magadha, including Pāṭaliputra. The state of law and order was such that a solitary foreign pilgrim could travel freely without fear of molestation by robbers. Fa Xian left India in 414 for Sri Lanka and spent two years there, collecting and copying Sanskrit texts. He describes the central part of north India as follows:

> It has a temperate climate, without frost or snow, and the people are very well off, without poll-tax or official restrictions. Only those who till the royal land have to pay so much on the profit they make. Those who want to go away may go; those who want to stop may stop. The king governs without corporal punishments; criminals are merely fined according to the gravity of their offences. Even for a second attempt at rebellion the punishment is only the loss of the right hand. The king's personal attendants, who guard him on the right and left, have fixed salaries.

The notable absence of close supervision is in decided contrast to the earlier Mauryan system. Fa Xian also comments on the absence of slavery. But the deserted condition of some of the most sacred sites associated with the Buddha's life upset him. Elsewhere he observes:

> Throughout the country the people kill no living thing, nor drink wine, nor do they eat garlic or onions, with the exception only of the Caṇḍālas [outcastes]. The Caṇḍālas are named 'evil men' and live apart from others; if they enter a town or market, they sound a piece of wood in order to separate themselves; then men, knowing who they are, avoid coming in contact with them. In this country they do not keep swine nor fowls, and do not deal in cattle; they have no slaughterhouses or liquor-stores in their market-places. In selling they use cowrie shells. Only the Caṇḍālas hunt and sell flesh.

This is obviously an over-simplified account, but it does point to the widespread nature of these customs. Meat and wine had long been avoided by most brahmins, but the wider observance of such a ban may well owe a great deal to the concept of *ahiṃsā* (non-injury to all living beings), although the imitation of the customs of the brahmins as a prestige group was clearly a factor. Fa Xian's mention of untouchability is the first precisely datable reference to its practice. This is the corollary of the much greater emphasis on purity for the 'twice-born', a term which by now refers almost exclusively to the brahmins.

This period also saw a growth of city life, with the opening of new routes and a rise in the political status of provincial areas. Archaeological evidence and descriptions in contemporary literature show that the standard of living was high and that urban dwellers lived in prosperity and comfort with a variety of luxuries in the way of jewels and clothes. A picture of the life of a fashionable man about town is given in Vātsyāyana's *Kāmasūtra*, in which we see the gentle indulgence in the refinements of life by an accomplished young man with ample wealth and leisure at his disposal. When a man has finished his education and entered the life of a householder with the help of self-acquired or inherited property, he should take himself to a large or small town and there build and furnish a suitable house; comfortable if not luxurious surroundings should be provided to harmonize with moods conducive to poetry and painting, music and literary discussion. The young man was also expected to be trained in the techniques of amorous dalliance, for which the evening was regularly set aside. The courtesan was a normal feature of urban life, neither romanticized nor treated with contempt, but a member of a demanding profession; in order to act as a cultured companion to her clients, the *Kāmasūtra* expected her to undergo a thorough training.

Material Culture

It was once thought that the use of iron came from Iran and was popularized if not introduced into India by the extension of Achaemenid power to the Indus. However, the now generally agreed date for the introduction of iron technology is around 800 BC, although the use of coinage was perhaps a result of this Achaemenid intrusion. The epics, while fully aware of the use of iron, in their earlier portions still refer more commonly to copper; equally, although they mention various cities, the descriptions make clear that these are simply larger than usual settlements and that real urbanization has scarcely begun.

A more or less uniform culture, whose hallmark is a black lustrous ware, first appears around 500 BC, extending from the lower Ganges to the Punjab. The control of firing and temperature required to produce this pottery indicates use of a sophisticated kiln, which by inference involved a separate fire-chamber with a good draught control. Black pottery is found in great quantities in the early Iron Age mounds of the Doāb, especially Ahicchatrā, Hastināpura and Kauśāmbī. The culture thus provided the background for the early cities of classical India, which find repeated mention in the accounts of the life of Gautama the Buddha and Mahāvīra the Jina, as well as for dynasties such as the Nandas and Mauryas. The pottery associated with the Mauryan period consists of many types of ware but the black is especially characteristic.

One factor in the dominance of Magadha over the other states may well have been its possession of iron mines in its southern hilly areas not too far from the Ganges. In many ways Magadha was ideally suited for the founding of a state. The land was fertile and naturally irrigated, the forests of the Rajmahal hills would provide timber and elephants and to the south were located the major iron ore deposits of the region, while it was well placed in relation to the major routes for trade.

The Mauryan capital of Pāṭaliputra goes back to the fifth century and Ajātaśatru's founding of a fort at the confluence of the Ganges and Son rivers to keep the Licchavis in check. Much of the area is now covered by the city of Patna and neighbouring villages. Almost 150 years later Megasthenes describes Pāṭaliputra as being over 9 miles long and nearly 2 miles wide (extending along the bank of the Ganges like modern Patna) and surrounded by a timber palisade. Part of these massive wooden fortifications have been excavated south of Bulandībāgh. This exceptional type of fortification agrees with Megasthenes' remark, 'Towns which are down beside rivers or the sea are made of wood, since towns built of brick would not hold out against rain and flood, but towns built on elevated sites are made of brick and clay.'

Carpentry was long established – early Buddhist texts refer to woodwork, including boat-building, house-building and the making of carts, chariots and machines of various types. The skill in carpentry of the Mauryan period (322–185 BC) is attested by the timber fortifications of Pāṭaliputra and by the earlier stages of the imperial palace, which include seven massive wooden platforms which probably belong to Candragupta's reign, while the sculpture of Aśoka's reign presupposes a long tradition of carving in wood and ivory. Alexander's admiral Nearchus noted that wealthy Indians wore ivory earrings and elaborate, built-up shoes, while cotton was in general use for clothing.

Stone-cutting was also highly developed. One of the best specimens of the pre-Aśokan period is the massive stone coffer exhumed from the Piprāhwa *stūpa*, containing an inscribed relic casket, which is a large monolith in fine grey sandstone carefully hollowed out. In addition, the relic casket of rock crystal, with a hollow fish-shaped handle which it contained, and another casket of beryl from Bhaṭṭiprolu of somewhat later date constitute two of the finest examples of the stone-cutter's art. Terracotta objects of various sizes, often mould-made, have been found at Mauryan sites extending from Pāṭaliputra to Taxila. Many have stylized forms and are technically very advanced, having well-defined shapes and clear ornamentation. Terracottas from Taxila consist of crude images, votive reliefs with deities, toys, dice, ornaments and beads; toys were mostly wheeled animals, the elephant being a particular favourite, while among the ornaments were round medallions.

A wide range of metals was known in the Mauryan period. Antimony-rods and nail-parers in copper were found at Hastināpura and other copper and bronze objects came from the Mauryan levels at the Bhir Mound, Taxila; then there are the copper bolt from the Rāmpūrvā pillar (barrel-shaped and over 2 feet long) and the cast copper coins of the Mauryan period. The demand for iron seems to have increased during the Mauryan period, for iron objects at the lower levels of the Bhir Mound are limited to adzes, knives and scrapers, but the later level shows a wider use of iron, including weapons, tools, agricultural implements and household vessels. Lead, silver and gold were also used.

Economic motives for Mauryan expansion into the Deccan are provided by its gold-fields, which were being worked to depths as great as 250 feet early in the Christian era. Although the first discovery of the gold-bearing reefs probably goes back to ancient times, the tools available then would have limited work mainly to the surface. This would have changed with the arrival of iron and steel, which perhaps coincided with the imposition of Mauryan rule and its capacity to dragoon a labour force. Certainly a strong central power would be needed to maintain work under these conditions, and the rule of the Mauryan and later Sātavāhana empires seem the most probable. It is significant that Aśokan inscriptions are found at five sites in the area (including the minor rock edict at Maski actually on the gold-field) and they probably reflect a very material interest in the area.

Aśoka's edicts include provision for wells at regular intervals along major routes, supplementing the concern all through the Mauryan period for the construction and maintenance of roads. Indeed, the inscriptions of rulers over the centuries often mention public works. Provision for the water supply, both for human use and for the irrigation of crops, was widespread from an early date. The history of one project in Kathiawar can be traced over more than seven centuries, through several changes of ruling power. The Junāgaḍh inscription of Rudradāman (150) records the repair of the dam – over 100 feet thick at its base – of the Sudarśana lake, originally constructed by order of Puṣyagupta, Candragupta Maurya's provincial governor, and later provided with conduits by Aśoka's governor, the Yavanarāja Tuṣāspha; the repair was supervised by Rudradāman's governor, the Pahlava Suviśākha, and Rudradāman met the cost out of his privy purse. The Sudarśana dam again gave trouble and burst in the first year of Skandagupta's reign (*c.* 455–67). Despite external difficulties and in addition to many other public works undertaken during his reign, Skandagupta had it reconstructed by Parṇadatta, governor of Surāṣṭra, and his son Cakrapālita, the local magistrate.

The Growth of Trade

Few traces remain of the Hellenistic civilization established by the Greeks in Bactria and the north-west. However, Aï Khanum, close to the Oxus River, shows a typically Greek layout; one of the water-control systems discovered belongs to the period of the Graeco-Bactrian town and remained in use until the beginning of the Kuṣāṇa period. At Charsada (ancient Puṣkalāvatī) the oldest settlement was succeeded by a Hellenistic settlement laid out on a grid-plan at Shaikhān Ḍheri, apparently under Menander towards the middle of the second century BC. Many beautifully executed coins of these Greek rulers have been discovered. They are generally of silver and bear the names as well as the busts of the rulers who issued them. The Bactrian issues show a Greek legend only, but the Indian coins have on the reverse a Prakrit rendering of the Greek legend. This system of issuing bilingual coins in two scripts was followed by the Śaka and Pahlava rulers and in general Indo-Greek coinage influenced the design of much later coinage.

Indian trade with the Roman empire reached its peak under the Kuṣāṇas and their south Indian contemporaries. Perhaps the most striking testimony to this trade in the south is the Roman settlement at Arikamedu, the so-called Jain mound, on the outskirts of Pondicherry, but large quantities of Roman coins have also been found inland. Arikamedu seems to have been developed as a sizeable trading port with a small foreign quarter and extensive warehouse accommodation and was in existence in the first and second centuries AD. The market towns were mainly located along the Cōḻa coast; at the time of the *Periplus of the Erythraean Sea*, a first-century geography, exports included 'fine pearls in great quantity'. Early Tamil literature makes several references to Yavanas, who were clearly inhabitants of the Roman world and who helped to introduce elements of Greek science and Roman technology to blend with indigenous knowledge, including the Tamil tradition in astronomy.

The Silk Road, linking the Mediterranean with China, is known to have existed since the beginning of the Christian era, while trade between the Mediterranean and Bactria well before the Christian era is proved by finds of coins from the sixth to the fourth century BC in the region of Kabul. Two main roads led out of Bactria to India, one following the fertile Bāmiyān valley and the other following the valley of the Qunduz River; the two roads met again near the rich city of Begram to continue to Kabul and the Indus valley. Mathurā too undoubtedly owed its prosperity at this period to its pivotal position as a trade centre with good links both to the north-west and to the western coast through Ujjain. Particularly important was the trade in ivory, especially in finished articles, one example of which was discovered as far away as Pompeii, in southern Italy. Other major exports were pearls (mostly from Sri Lanka), many kinds of precious and semiprecious stones, perfumes and spices, cotton and various woods, including teak, ebony and sandalwood.

Although Indian trade with the Roman empire declined significantly after the third century, there is ample evidence, particularly in the finds of Roman coins in south India, that it continued on a reduced scale for at least another two to three centuries. But trade relations with western Asia were flourishing throughout this period and the considerable trade between China and western Asia must also have passed through India. Chinese pilgrims attest the existence of regular commerce between the fourth and the seventh centuries, linking Tāmralipti (Tamluk, the seaport of Bengal) and Sri Lanka with Indonesia and Indo-China. The period also saw a growth in city life with the opening of new trade routes and the rise in the political status of provincial areas. Archaeological evidence and descriptions in contemporary literature show that the standard of living was high and that urban dwellers lived in prosperity and comfort.

After Candragupta II's conquest of the Western Satraps in the third century the Gupta empire stretched from coast to coast and thus, to a large extent, controlled Indian trade with the western world. About this time, in 408, Alaric the Goth spared Rome in return for a ransom which included 3,000 pounds of pepper, a good indication of the size of this trade, which was heavily in India's favour. Cosmas Indicopleustes informs us that in the middle of the sixth century the ports on the east and west coasts of India were linked via Sri Lanka which, as a result of its central position, became the main entrepôt in the Indian Ocean. He also mentions a number of important trading ports on the west coast of India, including Sindus, Kalyāṇa and no fewer than five ports of Malabar. Arab and Persian ships trading with China must have passed through Indian ports *en route*. According to Cosmas, aloes, clove wood and sandalwood were dispatched from the east coast via Sri Lanka to the western ports and even to Iran and Ethiopia; pepper was exported from the five ports of Malabar. From the extensive references in literature of this period to sandal and other fragrant woods, it is clear that these were extensively traded between their places of origin in south India and the rest of the subcontinent. Saffron was a product of the north-west, while horses were also imported from this part of India, as well as from Arabia, Iran and Afghanistan. Other main items of trade were pearls, coral, silk and ivory; pearls came from south India, coral was found in the sea between India and Sri Lanka, silk must have come from China by land routes through Central Asia as well as by the sea routes. Metals and gems were also traded over considerable distances.

A wide range of industries depended on and promoted this still extensive trade. The remarks of the Chinese pilgrims show that the textile industry was highly developed in the Gupta period, with manufacture of certain types of textile concentrated at various centres, some of them of considerable antiquity, such as Vārāṇasī with its high-quality silk-weaving. Production of highly ornamented furniture formed one part of the output of the ivory-carvers, usually in the form of plaques decorated in relief attached to such articles. Metallurgy was highly developed. A notable example is the Mehrauli iron pillar, belonging to Candragupta II's reign. Now installed in the Quṭb Masjid at Mehrauli, south of Delhi, but originally erected on a hill near Ambālā, this pillar is over 23 feet high and consists of a single piece of iron, which shows no sign of rusting, since the iron is chemically almost pure; technologically it is a most impressive piece of work. Its lotus-shaped capital demonstrates the persistence of the Aśokan model for such free-standing columns (though not for architectural ones), since the form of the lotus is relatively close to Mauryan ones; above the topmost square block, an emblem of Vishnu would have completed the capital. The high quality of Indian steel was known to the Greeks and the Iranians, but we have no records of the method of production.

Coinage is among the best of the minor arts of the Gupta period and exhibits a high standard of simplicity, refinement and elegance. The early Gupta gold and silver coinage was undoubtedly based on Indo-Greek and Kuṣāṇa models, not only in design but also in treatment and execution. There is a notable coin of Candragupta II, showing the king killing a lion, in which the king's figure echoes the tense curve of his bow and the whole design seems a miniature version of such Gupta carvings as the relief at Gwalior. Another well-known coin is that of Kumāragupta attacking a rhinoceros. The subjects of these two and other similar coins are intended as symbolic references to the might and invincibility of the king. With the later weakening of the central Gupta authority, the coinage shows a downward trend, not only in purity but also in artistic merit. Apart from Kumāragupta, the Gupta rulers issued only a few copper coins; indeed, Fa Xian commented that cowries still formed the common medium of exchange. Even allowing for the fact that copper is more liable to corrode than precious metals, the comparative rarity of Gupta copper coins suggests that the money economy was becoming weaker at this time. This can be linked, on the one hand, with the decline in internal trade and the resulting need to produce commodities locally to meet local needs, and, on the other, with the weakening of the central power, which gradually adopted the method of paying officials by grants of revenues or in kind.

In connection with his western conquests, around 388 Candragupta II moved his court from Pāṭaliputra to Ujjain. This had repercussions for the history of Indian science, for Ujjain was in close touch with west-coast ports such as Broach, through which Indian scholars gained further knowledge of Greek astronomy. Evidence of this is seen in the Sanskrit words for hour and diameter and in the Indian names for the days of the week. When Varāhamihira, the sixth-century astronomer, gives star positions, he notes them for Alexandria as well as Ujjain. However, the Indians of the Gupta period did not just copy this astronomical information but combined it with their own knowledge, for in algebra and arithmetic Indian scholarship was ahead of the Greeks. Thus the noted mathematician Āryabhaṭṭa, writing in 499, as well as being noted for his abilities in algebra (by this time regarded as a separate discipline), combined Indian mathematics with Greek astronomy to make major advances.

Religion and Ideas

By the start of the fifth century BC the shape of the Indian religious scene for the next millennium had to quite an extent already been determined. The Vedic literature was largely complete, with the earlier Upaniṣads laying the groundwork both for the more impersonal aspects of later Hindu philosophy and for the emergence of more devotional forms of religion. Siddhārtha Gautama, the Buddha, and Vardhamāna Mahāvīra, the Jina, on their usual dating (which assigns the Buddha to 563–483 BC and the Jina to 540–468 BC) were already preaching the ideas which established Buddhism and Jainism as major challenges to brahminical orthodoxy. It is, therefore, the developments in all three – Buddhism, Jainism and Hinduism, as the Vedic religion was to become – that are relevant.

Early Developments

Traditionally the First Buddhist Council was held immediately after the Buddha's death in order to collect his teachings together. A century or so later at Vaiśālī a second council was held, at which, according to the monastic tradition of Theravāda, a schism occurred over points of discipline between the Sthaviravādins, the party of the elders, and the Mahāsaṃghikas, the party of the majority. However, other sources assign the split to a council held at Pāṭaliputra some decades after the Vaiśālī council, on the issue of the status of the *arhat*, 'one who has achieved enlightenment for himself'. Subsequently, the two sides began to differ on several other matters, among which was the Mahāsaṃghika teaching of the 'supramundane Buddha', an exaltation of the Buddha which mirrored the lowering of the status of the *arhat*.

Seated Buddha from Sāñcī, whose original *stūpa* was built during Aśoka's reign. However, Buddhist monks appear to have been in occupation of the site prior to the *stūpa*'s construction.

The Theravāda sources record a Third Buddhist Council held at Pāṭaliputra and called by Aśoka, although Aśoka himself does not mention it; possibly a local council was held at Pāṭaliputra, with which Aśoka had little or no connection. Following it, monks are supposed to have set out in all directions to and beyond the borders of the Mauryan empire. This was quite separate from Aśoka's sending of envoys to foreign rulers. On the whole the Buddhist missions were sent to much nearer areas than Aśoka's envoys and were probably not a coordinated enterprise. However, it may well be true that a mission led by the monk Mahinda, who was a son (or younger brother) of Aśoka, took Buddhism to Sri Lanka; the history of Buddhism in Sri Lanka is reckoned from his arrival at Devānaṁpiya Tissa's court.

At this period the propagation of Buddhism through the Saṅgha, the order of monks and nuns, was fairly widespread; the monks preached the law during the hot and cold seasons, returning to their monasteries during the rainy season. Instead of elaborate sacrifice, Buddhist ritual centred round *caityas* and *stūpas*, buildings for worship and mounds enclosing relics of the Buddha respectively; very often a monastery was built in association with one of them. The column, possibly the survival of a phallic emblem or a megalith, was perhaps another feature of the Buddhist cult; certainly, Aśoka used pillars for his edicts.

Aśoka's patronage of Buddhism must have been important, and he probably did more than any other individual to facilitate its spread, although the picture of him as an enthusiastic adherent found in Buddhist literature is exaggerated. As ruler, he supported all religions and pleaded in his inscriptions for toleration among all sects, 'for they all seek mastery of the senses and purity of mind'. He put on record his personal Buddhist faith, however. He had contacts with the Saṅgha and visited at least one of its centres, and in his capacity as a ruler whose traditional duty it was to see that corporate bodies could function properly, he advised on discipline. Under his patronage the Buddhist community at Pāṭaliputra may have grown rich and attracted adherents from less-favoured groups, Ājīvikas and others, who began to disturb community life. This has been suggested as the context in which he appointed the so-called moral guardians, who were not only to look after the Saṅgha but also to foster the preservation of its unity. However, Aśoka appointed these officials for all the religious communities and, when listing their duties, in effect classified all the religions of his empire into five: the Saṅgha, the brahmins, the Ājīvikas, the Jains and 'other sects'.

Aśoka's donations to the Ājīvika sect, to whom he gave in all three caves, confirm his own broad-mindedness, for both the Ājīvikas and the Jains were disapproved of by Buddhists. His stress on *ahiṃsā* (non-injury to all living beings) as a major virtue was due less to the influence of Buddhism than to a general religious trend in this period, for an increasing emphasis on non-violence was developing more or less simultaneously in most religious groups. His approach here as elsewhere was basically pragmatic. Aśoka no doubt realized the harm that sectarian conflict could produce and one motive in pleading for toleration was no doubt political. This aspect of the policy of *dhamma* may perhaps be seen in his threats to the forest tribes and in his distrust of festive gatherings, probably because they could form a focus for discontent.

Aśoka sums up his aims for himself and his empire in the term *dhamma*, the Pāli form of Sanskrit *dharma* – 'duty, morality, religion'. For him it was a way of life, based on social ethics and civic responsibility, which he saw in terms of practical everyday life, rather than abstract theory. *Dhamma* is of course a fundamental Buddhist concept, but Aśoka openly asserts that *dhamma* is cultivated in all religions and sects and that he wishes to promote it in all men, whatever their religion. By holding out the possibility of heavenly bliss and similar rewards, he tried to encourage the idea of responsibility, investing it with a certain spiritual significance. Aśoka attributes his own interest in morality to repentance for the violence of the Kaliṅga War. Basically, he preached *dhamma* because he realized that no real unity would be possible unless founded on a common way of life; he was trying to reform the narrow attitudes of religious teaching, to encourage harmony, and to promote throughout his empire a sense of social responsibility so universal that no cultural group could object to it.

In the period of considerable ferment in the north-west following the Mauryan empire, when Hellenistic rulers were followed in rapid succession by the Śakas, the Pahlavas and the Kuṣāṇas, Buddhism and other less orthodox religious movements were able to make considerable headway among the newcomers. Kaniṣka's reign (78–123) is traditionally associated with the appearance of the Mahāyāna form of Buddhism, which was to be carried by Indian traders into Central Asia and from there spread into China and ultimately Japan. This form of Buddhism is marked by a number of features which are usually held to be a response to the needs of such non-Indian converts and which certainly gave it wide popular appeal.

Among the Greeks in India there was interest both in Buddhism and in the newly emerging cult of Krishna, the Bhāgavata cult, which is the oldest form of Vaiṣṇavism. Demetrius' descendant Agathocles (*c.* 180–165 BC) issued coins showing Vāsudeva and Saṃkarṣaṇa. An ambassador from Antialcidas (ruling around 100 BC) erected a stone memorial pillar at the ancient city of Vidiśā in honour of Vāsudeva, or Krishna. Various officials are known to have erected Buddhist *stūpas*. Most notably, though, the ruler Menander figures in the *Milindapañha*, named after him, which originated in north-west India around the beginning of the Christian era. It begins with an idyllic description of Milinda's capital, Śākala (modern Sialkot), where the Buddhist monk Nāgasena expounds the major concepts of Buddhism to the eager Greek inquirer Milinda, starting from the kind of issues that seem appropriate to a non-Indian. The last book of the Pāli recension (concluding a later extension of the text) claims that at the end of the dialogue Milinda was accepted as a lay Buddhist and, after entrusting the throne to his son, embraced the religious life and became an *arhat*. But at the end of the earlier portion there is a different conclusion: satisfied by the replies given him, Milinda expresses a longing to join the order but regrets that political considerations rule it out. There is some evidence that Menander did become a Buddhist, but it is far from conclusive.

Mahāyāna Buddhism

Around the beginning of the Christian era, a new form of Buddhism emerged, claiming to offer universal salvation and so calling itself the Mahāyāna, 'the Great Vehicle', in contrast to the older Buddhism, which it dismisses as the Hīnayāna, the Lesser Vehicle. The Mahāyāna was not a sudden phenomenon with a single geographical or intellectual origin; it developed over a period as an alternative and distinctive view of the nature of Buddhism, and its early development saw the evolution of a new canonical literature, the *Mahāyāna sūtras*. These claimed to represent the complete teachings of the Buddha, revealed only to the chosen, while the earlier doctrines were merely preliminary ones. This new literature comprises a shifting mass of teachings with little or no central core. The one common factor is a desire to identify itself as the Mahāyāna, the superior way to religious fulfilment. Many early *Mahāyāna sūtras* emphasize the superiority of the Bodhisattva – one who has conceived an intention to become a Buddha – and the Bodhisattva path, adopting a contemptuous attitude towards monks following the older path to individual release, while a number stress the importance of the laity. They were evidently produced by monks who were sensitive to

An early image of the Buddha from Ellora.

the aspirations of the laity and who used lay people in the texts to heighten their criticisms of the monks they saw as conservative or élitist.

There are two types of Bodhisattva: earthly and transcendent. The first are human beings, recognizable as Bodhisattvas only by their universal compassion and their resolve to strive for the salvation of others. Transcendent Bodhisattvas are those who have attained the liberating wisdom but remain within the universe, so that they can continue to work for the benefit of others. They are no longer subject to rebirth but can at will assume any bodily form which is appropriate for the help they give. Bodhisattvas seem mainly to have arisen through personification of the different virtues and attributes of the Buddha's personality, with certain epithets applied to him being converted into the names of Bodhisattvas. The Bodhisattva became a living symbol of compassion, while the concept of *karma* itself was transformed. Through countless lives of self-sacrifice, the Bodhisattva acquires a virtually infinite store of merit, which he can distribute to the otherwise unworthy devotee. Whoever calls on a Bodhisattva in faith will be reborn in a paradise – not through his own merits but through those of the Bodhisattva.

The spiritual perfection of a Buddha could not be gained in one life but only over many. Thus the theory was evolved of the successive stages in the Bodhisattva's career, which were then equated with *pāramitās*, or 'perfections'. Theravādin texts enumerate ten perfections, while six are recognized throughout the Mahāyāna. A Bodhisattva has to fulfil them in all three degrees of their intensity over several births in the ten stages in order to attain enlightenment. The being who will become the next Buddha, Maitreya, is already far advanced as a Bodhisattva; he is the only celestial Bodhisattva accepted by all Buddhist traditions. Life under Maitreya represents nothing less than the Buddhist millennium. Like Gautama before his final birth, Maitreya now dwells in the Tuṣita heaven waiting for the right moment to descend to the world.

The Buddha may have been revered as superhuman even in his own lifetime. Although in theory the Buddha had completely left the universe, the formula of the 'Three Refuges', which early on became the Buddhist profession of faith, might well have encouraged some kind of belief in his continued presence. The

A reconstruction of the great *stūpa* at Sāñcī.

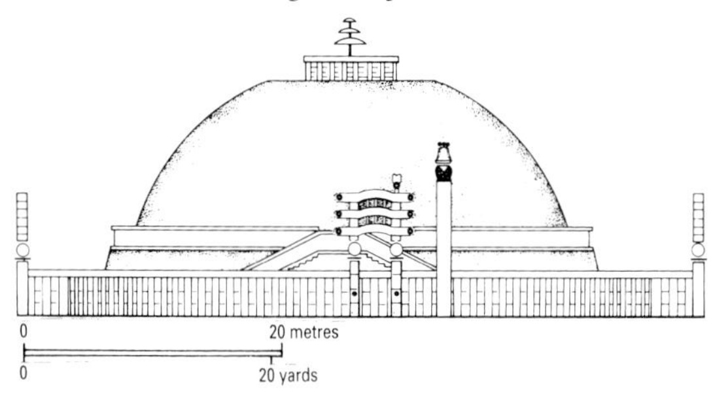

Fresco of the Thousand Buddhas at the Ajaṇṭā caves in Mahārāṣṭra. The painting technique involved the application of colours to a lime-coated layer of clay mixed with rice husk and gum.

Buddha is said himself to have declared that all who had faith in him and devotion to him would obtain rebirth in heaven. Although the cult of Buddhas and Bodhisattvas originated in popular devotionalism, it also reflected an ethical tension. While the Buddha emphasized both compassion and the need to follow 'the Eightfold Path', the Saṅgha seemed to be turning its back on compassion to concentrate exclusively on individual salvation. Critics of a narrow monastic ideal recalled that the Buddha himself was tempted by Māra to disappear into Nirvāṇa without preaching the saving doctrine.

Eventually the doctrine of 'the three bodies' (so-called because it defines and coordinates the three aspects of the Buddha) was formulated; it not only brought into relation popular and philosophical Buddhism but also unified the manifestations of Buddhahood. The Buddha exists on three levels: a fictitious, transformation body, a communal or 'enjoyment' body and a *dharma* body (*dharmakāya*). The fictitious body is the one which people can see at any given time, that is a historical Buddha, while the *dharma* body is both the corpus of his teachings and the true nature of things. The contrast of the Buddha's physical form with his *dharma* body meant that those opposed to the innovations of the Mahāyāna could be accused of sticking too rigidly to the physical Buddha rather than to the *dharma*, which the Buddha himself had said would lead the community after his death. The second, glorified body provided a justification for the *Mahāyāna sūtras*, which could be traced to its activities; it is the body in which the Buddha appears to superhuman beings and to celestial Bodhisattvas in Buddha Fields which his merit has created and where he personally preaches the law to them. Within the vast expanses of the Buddhist cosmos some universes are known as Buddha Fields, where a Buddha exerts his spiritual influence. The main function of a Buddha is to teach sentient beings in his Buddha Field. However, the Buddha Field is not just the place where the Buddha appeared, but rather the place which the future Buddha, during his career as a Bodhisattva, purifies through his great compassion and turns into an area where he can nurture individuals who are reborn there.

Alongside this more popular element of devotion, the Mahāyāna also developed a much more philosophical aspect, notably in the Madhyamaka system founded by Nāgārjuna around 150 and noted for its concept of emptiness (*śūnyatā*). From the fact that entities have causes, the Madhyamaka considers that they do not exist independently of other entities and that therefore they lack a nature of their own. This emptiness has three implications. First, things are not born or destroyed, because empty things born of empty things are in reality not born at all and so cannot be destroyed; secondly, since things are neither produced nor destroyed, they are originally calm and in a complete state of Nirvāṇa; and thirdly, since all things are equally calm, they are all equal and admit of no duality. In China the concept of emptiness was to become intermingled with Daoist ideas.

Classical Hinduism

The more popular form of Hinduism from the Gupta period (320–*c.* 550) onwards has often been called Purāṇic Hinduism. The Purāṇas, though composed and edited by brahmins, are very much a manifestation of popular religion; they show that the brahmins have maintained their position as guardians and transmitters of Hinduism only by being receptive, even if reluctantly, to any innovations which achieve a real popular following. The word *purāṇa* appears in literature from the *Atharvaveda* onwards and is often linked with the term *itihāsa*. Just as *itihāsa* refers to the stories which have been elaborated to form the epic, the Vedic *purāṇa* must refer to the stock of 'antiquities' which came to constitute the Purāṇas.

Conventionally there are eighteen major Purāṇas and the same number of minor ones; an attempt to link a third of the number each with Brahmā, Vishnu and Shiva is even more artificial. The Purāṇas and the

Vishnu Anantaśayin, 'Vishnu recumbent on the serpent Endless'. The great god of the Hindu pantheon shown at rest on Ananta in Daśāvatāra Temple, Deogarh, Bihār.

epics share a number of similarities of background, suggesting that the Purāṇas too were originally less strictly religious than their present form implies. Traditionally the five topics of a Purāṇa are emanation of the universe; destruction and re-emanation; the reigns and periods of the Manus, who were the legendary progenitors of mankind; the genealogies of the gods and sages; and the genealogy of the solar and lunar dynasties – essentially king-lists. Later, other related topics were added, such as the duties of class and stage of life, sacred sites and pilgrimage, worship of images and construction of temples. Belief in the power of pilgrimages to holy places and bathing in holy rivers to destroy the effects of even the gravest sins is an important innovation, as is the introduction of numerous observances or vows. A characteristic theme is to declare how great rewards and results can be secured with little effort and to emphasize their accessibility to women and *śūdras*, the lowest class.

The first three topics amount to a full presentation of Hindu cosmology. In relation to the other two topics of genealogies, they represent the universal as against the particular. Their elaborate cosmology, with its immense cycles of time repeating themselves indefinitely, tends to reduce the significance of the particular. The world perpetually undergoes a cycle of emanation from a state of non-differentiation through a series of ages to its dissolution back into the unevolved state, from which the whole cycle starts again; the timescales and other details vary but in each case work down from an astronomical figure. Alongside the whole cyclical theory there evolved a view of the degeneracy of the current age. Each age is divided into four periods, characterized by ever-decreasing duration and ever-declining moral and physical standards, and a progressive decay of all that gives value to life. The world is now in the middle of the last of these ages, the Kaliyuga; popularly held to have begun with the *Mahābhārata* war, it will end when Kalki, Vishnu's tenth *avatāra*, or incarnation, overthrows the foreign, heretic and *śūdra* rulers of the time and inaugurates a new great age, beginning with its first, ideal age.

The king-lists give a clue to the dating of the Purāṇas. They divide into two groups, of which the first runs from Manu, the mythical ancestor of the human race, to the immediate descendants of the heroes of the *Mahābhārata*, probably early in the first millennium BC, and was placed in dynastic order before the third century BC. Subsequent genealogies are presented as prophecies of the future (perhaps reflecting their addition to established texts) but were undoubtedly written afterwards. This second series ends either with one of the Gupta rulers or with one of the foreign tribes who preceded the Guptas in north-west India – the Śakas, Yavanas, or Hūṇas.

The *kṣatriya* background of the Purāṇas can be recognized both in the royal genealogies and in the numerous legends shared with the epics. Tradition also reflects it by attributing the Purāṇas to the same Vyāsa

A scene from a medieval version of the *Rāmāyaṇa*. Rama gives the monkey chief Hanumān his ring.

who is recognized as the author of the *Mahābhārata*, or by declaring that they were expounded by bards. But early on the brahmins appropriated them, filling them with precepts, didactic material and hymns. A third stage in their development (the descriptions of pilgrimages and of temples) incorporates components of local cults, suggesting that the Purāṇas had become the preserve of individual religious communities. These materials are juxtaposed rather than organized; the *Bhāgavata Purāṇa*, for instance, reveals its lateness by the very fact that it is relatively structured. The Purāṇas are largely dedicated to the task of synthesis, not only between differing religious trends but also between religious and more secular aspects of tradition.

When the major Purāṇas reached their present form, nearly every major and minor Hindu deity was dealt with in this literature, sometimes on a vast scale. Krishna and Rāma, the two great incarnations of Vishnu, figured already as heroes in the dynastic histories typical of the epic. The Purāṇas, like the epics, include material which suggests that around the start of the Christian era worship of Brahman was common, but around the fifth century Brahman had faded out, and Vishnu and Shiva come to the fore. The Purāṇas, as compendia of Hindu mythology, by means of particular myths bring into relationship with the two major

A medieval illustration of the ten incarnations of Vishnu. 'When order, justice and mortals are endangered,' the god remarked, 'I come down to earth.'

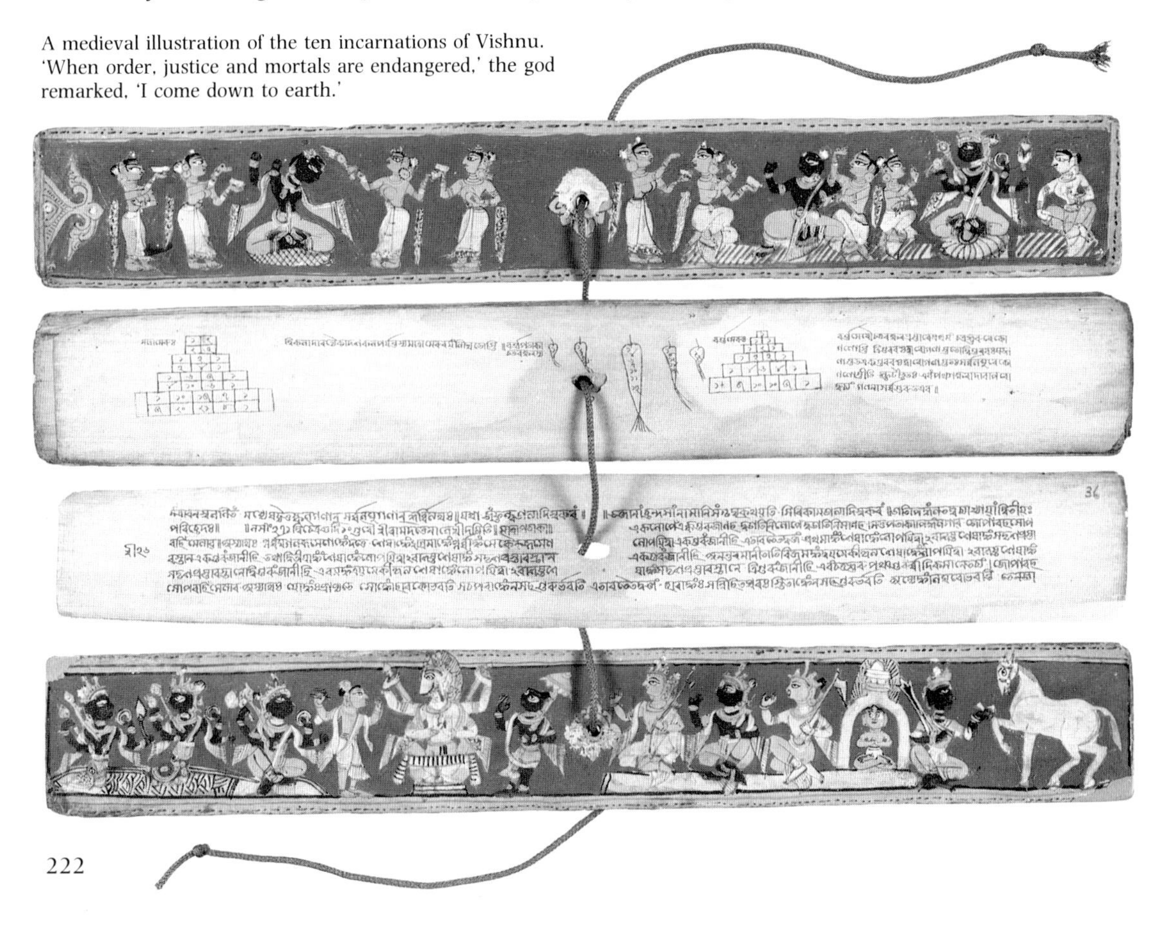

CXX

deities, Vishnu and Shiva, many local deities as incarnations of Vishnu or members of Shiva's ever enlarging family circle. The system of providing each deity with an appropriate mount (usually an animal) is another mechanism by which the Purāṇas and the traditional Hinduism derived from them assimilate into the framework of a developed religion the multiplicity of local cults, which have always been a feature of Indian religion.

The Purāṇas also included material on the worship of images and construction of temples. In fact, almost the first Hindu temples come from the Gupta period and thus are roughly contemporary with the compilation of the earlier Purāṇas. The earliest shrines were just a four-square cell, but soon this was normally raised on a plinth and surmounted by a *śikhara*, or 'spire', whose name identifies it with the sacrificial flame and the mountain peak. Although temples and image worship displaced the Vedic ritual, their earliest symbolism was derived from it. The shrine on its plinth was equivalent to the Vedic altar and the flames leaping up from it, or was identified with the world-mountain, Meru. The Purāṇas also give the first clear prescription concerning images: making them, installing them in the temple and the patterns of their worship.

The Six Systems

The six systems of orthodox Hindu thought are traditionally grouped into three complementary pairs (Nyāya and Vaiśeṣika, Sāṅkhya and Yoga, Mīmāṃsā and Vedānta), although this does not necessarily reflect the original situation. Since they were all coming into existence over basically the same period, it is not surprising that there was considerable mutual influence.

The links between the Nyāya and Vaiśeṣika systems seem to have existed from the start. Nyāya is primarily a school of logic and epistemology, and the system's proponents are firm realists. The school's supposed founder is traditionally assigned to the third century BC, but the *Nyāyasūtra* attributed to him is no earlier than the first century AD. The first extant commentary on the *Nyāyasūtra* is that of Vātsyāyana (probably of the fourth century), which, in explaining the text in detail, formulates a coherent system out of its rather varied parts. Almost from the start the school was in conflict with Buddhist epistemology. An important logical topic, where Nyāya ideas were borrowed by other schools, was that of the 'means of <valid> knowledge'. The Nyāya system accepts four, in descending order of validity: perception, inference, analogy and verbal testimony. Perception, originally meaning just sense perception, later covered all forms of immediate apprehension, including yogic insight. Inference rested on a generalization based on a quality of 'pervasion', analysis of which led to theories of universals and particulars. Analogy, or comparison, is a weaker form of inference through which we come to know something from its similarity to another previously known object. Verbal testimony originally denoted information accepted on the authority of others, the weakest source of knowledge; subsequently, it covered the authority of scripture, in orthodox thought the strongest.

A scene from the great Hindu epic the *Mahābhārata*, the longest poetic composition in the world.

The Vaiśeṣika system was primarily interested in physics. The earliest text, the *Vaiśeṣikasūtra* (around the first century) propounds the view that nature is atomic, a view occurring with some variation of detail in Buddhist, Jain and Ājīvika doctrines. An individual atom is devoid of qualities but possesses potentialities, realized when it combines with others of the same type to form molecules of the four elements (earth, water, fire, air); the fifth element, ether, is a single, all-pervasive substance. Each element has unique particularities, which distinguish it from the four other non-atomic substances (time, space, soul, mind). The atoms are eternal and indivisible and creation or re-creation of the world consists in the combination of all the separate atoms into the elements. Praśastapāda's *Padārthadharmasaṃgraha* (*c.* fifth century) is an independent explanation of the basic views of the system, remodelling it to take account of Buddhist ideas and elaborating the atomic theory, only sketched in the *Vaiśeṣikasūtra*. In the creation of the world the atoms first combine into dyads and these then group into triads, which are the basic molecules and are identified with the small dust particles that can be seen floating in a shaft of sunlight.

The earliest phases of the Sāṅkhya and Yoga systems are visible in the Upaniṣads and in the didactic portions of the *Mahābhārata*, which preserve something similar to the basic texts of other schools, but the earliest surviving text of the Sāṅkhya as a separate school is relatively late; this is Īśvarakṛṣṇa's *Sāṅkhyārikā* of probably the fourth or fifth century. Taking as its starting point the fact of human suffering, it then introduces its basic concepts of matter or nature (*prakṛti*) and the spiritual principle (*puruṣa*), the first and the last of its twenty-five categories. The evolution of the world is due to the inherent nature of *prakṛti*, not to any outside agency; this implies that the whole world, including human beings, evolved through individuation from matter and consequently that the spiritual is superfluous. The last category, *puruṣa*, should have no connection with the world, yet it does in some way become involved. The individual souls comprising this category can achieve release by realizing their essential difference from matter. Although the world does not derive from the spiritual, everything functions for its sake. Ultimately, however, matter is unconscious and, since the system is centred on consciousness, which belongs to *puruṣa*, the world itself is irrelevant apart from acting as a means of escape from itself.

Another Sāṅkhya concept, widely used in Indian thought, is that of the three *guṇas*, or 'strands', constituting matter. They both subsist in its unmanifest form and pervade the whole manifest world. As the world unfolds, the previous equilibrium between them is disrupted and one or another predominates in different entities; after an enormously long period there is a reabsorption of the universe, until the inherent nature of the *guṇas* breaks the equilibrium and the process starts all over again. The *sattva guṇa* is related to what is good, pleasant and truthful, *rajas* to what possesses energy or passion, and *tamas* to what is dark and inert. Broadly, there is an opposition between *sattva* and *tamas*, with *rajas* as the active force; they are associated with the colours white, red and black. At times they are brought into some relationship with the concept of the twenty-five categories, but basically the theories of the categories and of the strands remain separate explanatory systems.

The Yoga system is first expounded separately in the *Yogasūtra* of Patañjali (sometimes assigned to the second century BC but in its present form composed much later), which has probably been built up into a relatively coherent pattern from several separate texts, showing different starting points and stages of procedure in the progress from impurity to isolation; these presumably originated in separate schools of Yoga. Yoga also absorbed most of the Sāṅkhya cosmology as it developed, and thus the yogin was considered to reverse the process of evolution detailed in the Sāṅkhya and to return to the original unevolved, unitary state.

A god closely associated with Yogi was Shiva, shown here in a sacred pillar, a lingam. From a cave at Udayagiri.

The text distinguishes eight 'limbs' or stages in the technique of Yoga. The first five concern the training of the body and the last three the perfecting of the self. The first stage is self-control or restraint, which regulates the yogin's external activities. The second, observance, consists of five regulations for personal behaviour: purity, contentment, austerity, study of the scriptures and devotion to the Lord or Īśvara. However, this Īśvara is not active or creative – indeed, essentially he is distinct through never having become involved with the ills of the world – and so is not an object of true devotion but an aid to meditation. The third stage, posture, which begins the typically Yoga practices, is little emphasized in the *Yogasūtra*, where it is just a matter of assuming a suitable position. Next, in breath-control, the involuntary process of breathing is brought under the control of the will and regulated, originally perhaps to secure mastery of time, equated with the rhythm of breathing. Then follows withdrawal of the senses from their objects, eliminating their contact with the external world, which is what binds one to *saṃsāra*, or 'the cycle of rebirth'. One method is to concentrate on a single point until everything else disappears from consciousness and then to transfer the attention from an object to a mental image. The remaining three stages tend to shade into one another. The sixth is fixing the thoughts without the aid of the senses, whose operation has been suspended. The stage of meditation is reached when the *puruṣa* remains stably directed to one point without distraction. The last stage of ecstasy, or trance, is reached when one is no longer conscious even of meditating and arrives at an identification of subject and object; it cannot be described in words but is a state of transcendent bliss, leading to the attainment of isolation.

As the yogin proceeds through the stages, signs of success begin to appear, which by the later stages become various magical feats such as levitation. There is no agreement whether these feats are purely subjective or objective activities. However, they are an integral part of Yoga as indicators of successful practice but also function as temptations, into which the yogin may be diverted away from his real goal of achieving release, just as ecstasy is not an end in itself but must be transcended to reach release.

These four schools were only gradually taken into the orthodox synthesis, but the remaining two were always orthodox and directly religious. Indeed, the Mīmāṃsā system began not as a school leading to release but as a means to ensure the correct interpretation of the Vedas. Its basic standpoint is that the Vedas, being eternal and uncreated, possess absolute authority and that the Vedic commands constitute man's entire duty. The function of Mīmāṃsā, 'inquiry', is to interpret these commands systematically and to deduce logical principles for their consistent application. The earliest text, Jaimini's *Mīmāṃsāsūtra* (*c.* second century BC), is earlier than the basic texts of other schools but still presupposes a long history of Vedic interpretation. The *Mīmāṃsāsūtra* describes the different sacrifices and their purposes, and elaborates the theory of a power produced by correct performance of a ritual which subsequently produces the result promised, often after the death of the sacrificer. Jaimini regards deities as redundant and irrelevant to his central concern, the discussion of religious duty (*dharma*); belief in the eternality of the Vedas precludes their divine authorship. The first extant commentary on Jaimini's work by Śabara (probably sixth century) develops these arguments, as well as defining *dharma* more exactly as consisting of sacrifice, libation and giving, of which the common factor is the transfer of possession from oneself to another; there is a limited role here for deities as notional recipients of the sacrifice. However, effectively Mīmāṃsā became atheistic through a fundamentalist concentration on the scriptures themselves.

The Vedānta system is regularly coupled with Mīmāṃsā, but the relationship here is one of succession rather than complementarity. Whereas Mīmāṃsā deals with ritual acts and bases itself on the Brāhmaṇas, Vedānta is concerned with knowledge or insight and is based on the Upaniṣads. But, since Vedānta also relies on the authority of the Vedas, it accepts study of Mīmāṃsā as a necessary preliminary. Its basic text is Bādarāyaṇa's *Brahmasūtra* or *Vedāntasūtra*, written early in the Christian era as a deliberate synthesis of the Upaniṣadic views, largely in the original wording and sometimes therefore obscure. It affirms Brahman, the impersonal Absolute, as the goal of inquiry and the source of the universe, asserts the identity of Brahman and *ātman*, or 'the individual self', expounds the means for the realization of Brahman, and gives a detailed account of the successive stages of spiritual ascent until the final merging with Brahman in liberation.

Literature and the Arts

The core of both the early Sanskrit epics, the *Mahābhārata* and *Rāmāyaṇa*, was composed in the fifth to fourth centuries BC, no doubt on the basis of earlier bardic material, but then underwent a long period of development and expansion which to a large extent was completed early in the Gupta period (320–*c.* 550). They belong in their origins to the culture of the *kṣatriya* aristocracy and were originally secular works, recited at courts by bards attendant on the kings, but over time their transmission and amplification passed into the hands of the brahmins and much other traditional and especially religious material was incorporated into them. Both Krishna and Rāma came to be seen as incarnations of the great god Vishnu and so ultimately both epics became religious works. They are composed mainly in a simple narrative metre, the *śloka*, and the various episodes that cluster around their main stories have provided plots for many works of classical Sanskrit literature. The *Rāmāyaṇa* is somewhat more unified and sophisticated than the *Mahābhārata* and is probably slightly later in origin, but a summary of it is included with the developed *Mahābhārata*, suggesting that it was substantially complete and well known at an earlier date.

The *Mahābhārata* centres on the war for possession of the kingdom between two sets of cousins, Dhṛtarāṣṭra's 100 sons and Pāṇḍu's five. Yudhiṣṭhira, the oldest of Pāṇḍu's sons, is tricked out of the kingship in which he is being confirmed. Along with his brothers and Draupadī, the wife they all share, he is exiled to the forest for twelve years and spends a further year in disguise; their return to claim back the kingdom leads eventually to the great war and its sad aftermath. In the *Rāmāyaṇa*, the central plot is based on Rāma's exile for fourteen years when he is about to be installed as co-ruler with his father, the seizure of his faithful wife, Sītā, by the demon king, Rāvaṇa, the search for her abductor and the assistance rendered by Hanumān and the other forest-dwellers, the siege of Rāvaṇa's capital, Laṅkā, and his defeat, and the triumphant return to Ayodhyā. The inclusion in the *Mahābhārata* of the *Bhagavadgītā*, Krishna's sermon to Arjuna as the great battle is about to start, marks an early stage in Krishna's rise to prominence, while the didactic material included in the twelfth book contains important information on the emergence of the Bhāgavata movement, the devotional cult centred on Krishna and certain related figures. A supplement to the *Mahābhārata*, the *Harivaṃśa*, belonging to the early centuries AD, then gives a fuller account of the life of Krishna. In it Krishna is fully divine, although the other characters act for most of the time as though unaware of this, and the setting is the pastoral one of the cowherds in Vṛndāvana which increasingly dominates the Krishna mythology.

The earliest surviving Sanskrit literature in the classical style is that of the Buddhist poet Aśvaghoṣa, who may belong to the end of the first century. He wrote a poem on the legend of the Buddha's conversion of his half-brother, the *Saundarananda*, and the better known *Buddhacarita*, a kind of biography of the Buddha, as well as three dramas on Buddhist themes, extant only in fragments. The earliest complete dramas are the group of thirteen plays usually ascribed to Bhāsa, which probably date to the second or the third centuries. They show various archaic features, such as an unusual form of prologue, brevity and depiction of violence on stage. The best of them, the *Svapnavāsavadatta*, is drawn from the legends about the king Udayana and focuses on his self-sacrificing queen Vāsavadattā. The Junāgaḍh (Girnar) inscription of Rudradāman from 150, though not of great literary merit, is important as the earliest datable example of ornate Sanskrit prose composition. The inscription refers to the king's skill in the composition of prose and verse, which can be taken as evidence of the early interest in Sanskrit culture evinced even by a king of foreign origin.

Also to the same period belongs the earliest Tamil literature, the Caṅkam poetry, so called from a tradition of a series of *caṅkams*, or 'literary academies', controlling the literary and cultural life of ancient

Tamilnad, in the south-east. Unlike the oldest literature in north India, this is predominantly secular in tone; it is also characterized by highly individual conventions (indicating a sophisticated audience) which permit great economy of expression. There are two genres: *akam*, consisting of love poems, and *puṟam*, all other poems, usually about war. One of the most distinctive features of the love poetry is the convention which sets it in one of five regions, each presided over by a deity and named after a characteristic flower or tree, and each associated with an appropriate phase of love. The characters involved in the poems are limited in number and are not named, for the inner world here being expressed is archetypal and universal. By contrast to the relatively brief *akam* poems, much *puṟam* poetry consists of longer, bardic material in which one of the main purposes is eulogy of a patron, normally a local ruler, whether directly or indirectly. This attractive and sophisticated poetry is extant in two collections of anthologies, arranged according to metre, genre or setting (or some mix of these). In the next phase of Tamil literature, in the third to the sixth centuries, the two most important works, the *Cilappatikāram* and the *Maṇimēkalai*, are longer narrative poems; the second of these is set in the three ancient south Indian kingdoms of the Cōḻas, Pāṇḍyas and Cēras and seems indeed to be a celebration of Dravidian identity.

Classical Sanskrit Literature

Classical Sanskrit literature consists essentially of two major genres, the so-called *mahākāvya* and the drama, to which may be added a third form consisting of shorter pieces, including lyrics and epigrammatic verses. Although the term *kāvya*, applied to all three forms, is often translated as 'poetry', which is indeed the commonest form in Sanskrit literature, the term can equally be applied to prose works and designates rather 'literature' in contrast to technical writing. Of the considerable body of literature which must once have preceded the major writers now preserved, who belong to the Gupta period onwards, very little remains; most has been lost owing to the popularity of the later masterpieces (and to the rigours of the Indian climate), and only the surviving works of Aśvaghoṣa and Bhāsa are left to give some indication of this background.

Later literary theorists recognize ten distinct types of drama, of which the most frequent is essentially a heroic romance based on a traditional, often epic, story presented at suitable length, while two other common forms are the secular romance, based on an invented plot and with a more worldly hero, and the farce. The hierarchical ordering of society is reflected in the convention that the characters speak different languages according to their status: the hero, his advisers and others of high status, including brahmins, speak Sanskrit, while those of lower status or education speak stylized forms of 'natural' language, the dramatic Prakrits. There is also a blending of verse and prose, with the majority of verses in the plays being in Sanskrit, while the Prakrits are used mainly for prose passages; the verses carry the emotive content, whereas the prose communicates ideas and events directly. The characters are not so much individuals as personifications of types, partly because the doctrine of *karma* – that one's status in this life results from one's actions in a previous one – means that character and action are necessarily related, which also accounts for the popularity of the curse or a similar motif as a way of introducing the element of the unexpected without compromising the basic nobility of character of the hero or heroine. The *mahākāvya* should, like the heroic romance, be based on a plot taken from traditional material and include various stock elements, such as descriptions of cities, of the seasons, of the heroine's beauty and of nature, accounts of marriages and love-making, embassies, campaigns and battles; there were also various conventions about its form.

Kālidāsa, the greatest of India's poets and dramatists, is traditionally associated with Vikramāditya (usually identified with Candragupta II) as one of the nine jewels at his court, and from internal evidence it is likely that he wrote during the period 350–450. In one of his poems, the *Raghuvaṃśa*, he describes the lives and exploits of successive rulers of the Ikṣvāku or Solar dynasty, to which Rāma belonged, but it also contains a number of verses which seem to allude to events in the reigns of Samudragupta and Candragupta II. Three of his plays have survived. The *Mālavikāgnimitra* is a comedy of harem intrigue, set in the Śuṅga period, its hero Agnimitra being Puṣyamitra's son. The *Vikramorvasīya* is based on a story going back to the *Ṛgveda* of the love of the king Purūravas for a celestial nymph, Urvaśī. His most famous work is the other play, the *Abhijñānaśakuntala*, whose plot is drawn from the *Mahābhārata* and centres on the mutual attraction of king Duḥṣanta and Śakuntalā, foster-daughter of the sage Kaṇva; the plot is given dramatic tension when Śakuntalā loses the ring given her by the king, so that he fails to recognize her when she follows him to court (the result of a curse pronounced on her for a trivial fault by another notably irascible ascetic). The idyllic setting of the lovers' first meeting in Kaṇva's hermitage gives ample scope to Kālidāsa's descriptive skills. Kālidāsa also wrote two *mahākāvyas*, the *Raghuvaṃśa* already mentioned and the *Kumārasambhava*, which describes the courtship and marriage of Shiva and Umā and the birth of Kumāra or Skanda, the war god, but which, although its theme and characters are religious, is basically secular in outlook. In both of these, as in most examples of this genre, the story is unimportant by comparison with the descriptions and the elaboration of ornament in style and language.

Śūdraka, probably an approximate contemporary of Kālidāsa, is known from one drama, the *Mṛcchakaṭika*, or 'The Little Clay Cart', which is of the secular romance type. Its hero is a now penniless young merchant of Ujjain and its heroine a courtesan who falls in love with him, while the plot to quite an extent is built around errors of identity and at times is distinctly melodramatic. Political plots were, however, favoured by Viśākhadatta, writing probably in the sixth century, in his two known plays: the fragmentary *Devīcandragupta* and the *Mudrārākṣasa*, or 'Rākṣasa's Ring', which depicts the machinations of the unscrupulous Cāṇakya on behalf of Candragupta Maurya to secure the loyalty of Rākṣasa, the high-minded minister of the now defeated Nanda king. This play is unusual in having no significant female part and thus no love interest, while the contrasting characters of its two protagonists are finely presented. A notable example of the third genre is to be found in the work of Bhartṛhari (fifth century), who, though primarily a grammarian and philosopher, also wrote three collections of 100 stanzas on politics, love and renunciation respectively; the expression in these is concise and powerful, genuinely revealing, it seems, his own internal struggle between the opposing goals of the world and of release from it.

While it is not known directly whether any of these writers were patronized by the Gupta dynasty (even Kālidāsa's link is a matter of legend and inference), there is ample evidence that they did stimulate a flowering of literature and also of art; the redaction of the two great Sanskrit epics into something like their present form is probably to be ascribed to this period, as is the development of the extant Purāṇas. Their allies, the Vākāṭakas, were also patrons of art and literature. Besides Pravarasena II, author of the *Setubandhakāvya* in Mahārāṣṭrī Prakrit, two other members of the family are credited with literary works, while the gentler and simpler *vaidarbhī* style of Sanskrit composition was so called because it flourished at the court of the Vākāṭakas in Vidarbha.

Mauryan Art and Architecture

Although most extant examples of Mauryan art come from Aśoka's reign (*c.* 268–232 BC), monumental building was in vogue from the start of the dynasty. A Roman description of Candragupta's palace, following Megasthenes, is distinctly reminiscent of Iranian originals; excavated remains include a column capital of Achaemenid pattern and a large hall whose ceiling was supported by eighty or more monolithic columns, plain but highly polished in the Iranian fashion. Aśoka supposedly constructed hundreds of stone buildings throughout the empire. Most of his *stūpas* no longer survive, while others were so much enlarged later that none of their original structure is visible, although they remain as the brick cores of later stone structures.

The most notable monuments are the Aśokan columns. Some cruder examples may belong to Bindusāra's reign (*c.* 298–272 BC), as is suggested by the order issued early in Aśoka's reign that 'wherever there is a stone pillar, this edict is to be engraved on that pillar'. There were originally at least thirty columns, of which ten bear Aśokan inscriptions. Their plain monolithic shafts support a lotus-shaped capital, topped by an abacus supporting a large sculpture, usually an animal in the round; the total height may reach 50 feet. Although the Sārnāth lion capital shows Achaemenid influence, the lion was already a royal emblem in India.

Lion capital of Aśokan pillar at Sārnāth. Despite the king's pacifism, the carving does reflect Mauryan imperial aims.

The stone elephant at Dhauli does not belong to the same tradition as the animal capitals and was probably carved by local craftsmen; the impressive image of the elephant emerging from the rock was no doubt meant to draw attention to the Aśokan inscription below.

Seven rock-cut caves in the Barābar and Nāgārjunī hills (the earliest known examples, executed in granite) are Mauryan. The Barābar caves show the Iranian polish of the stone but closely imitate local structures in timber and thatch. The Lomas Ṛṣi cave, an oblong vaulted hall, is entered by a doorway obviously based on a wooden model, carved with a fine relief band of elephants. The cave is unfinished and so perhaps late,

Elephant carved from a rock at Dhauli, Orissā. Its Aśokan rock edict can be dated to 257 BC.

The great *stūpa* at Sāñcī, enlarged by the Śuṅga kings. A *stūpa*'s interior is a compact heap of earth, pebbles or stones enclosed by a mantle of brick, the brick being faced with a covering of polished stone.

but the adjacent cave was excavated by Aśoka for the Ājīvikas and is identical apart from its doorway. Another cave, the Sudāma, encloses a circular 'thatched' shrine with walls simulating planking, again with a high polish.

Other items have been assigned to the Mauryan period because of their use of the same Chunār sandstone as most of the columns and their high polish, but are in fact somewhat later, as shown by inscriptions. They include two *yakṣa*, or 'tree-spirit', statues from Patna, a statue of a female tree-spirit with yak-tail fan from Didārgañj (a suburb of Patna) and a larger than life-size statue from Pārkham. The *yakṣī* from Didārgañj is artistically the best, although the sculptures are still conceived as two reliefs placed back to back and the figures are often somewhat crude and stiff. The production of cult statues and terracotta figurines continued without any break from the Mauryan into the Śuṅga period. However, completely moulded plaques largely replace modelled figurines and in their subjects and treatment the terracottas often echo the monumental sculpture.

Śuṅga Art

The major monuments of the Śuṅga period are all Buddhist. The most important is the now ruined *stūpa* of Bhārhut, about 100 miles south-west of Allahabad. The *stūpa* must have been over 67 feet in diameter, with a processional path about 10 feet wide surrounded by the great railing. This railing (*c.* 150–100 BC) had openings towards the four cardinal points at which an L-shaped screen extended out, blocking a direct approach; the enclosure thus formed a huge swastika. The gateways were added about fifty years later. An inscription on the eastern gateway records its erection during the reign of the Śuṅgas, but others mention donations by several queens of the Mitra dynasty of Mathurā, rich merchants, artisans and others from all over the subcontinent. As elsewhere, the gateways imitate in stone the wooden gates of early Indian towns, while the railing imitates a post-and-rail fence. The figure sculpture on the uprights is archaic in character, with the individual figures flattened against the background to which they are attached, and the railing medallions are basically similar.

At Sāñcī, important through its closeness to the city of Vidiśā, the simple Stūpa 2 is the earliest Śuṅga monument. Its sandstone railing is notable for the medallions carved on the uprights of the interior and more elaborate rectangular panels on the entrance posts. The figures of tree-spirits in bold relief resemble those at Bhārhut, while the decorative panels are richer in composition. Under Śuṅga patronage, the Great Stūpa, Stūpa 1, built in brick by Aśoka before his accession, was doubled in size around 100 BC and encased in stone, while balustrades were erected on the platform and at ground level. Additions continued to be made to the *stūpas* during the following period of Sātavāhana rule. The sculptural decoration of Stūpa 1 is concentrated on the gateways, added around the beginning of the Christian era under the Sātavāhanas. The southern gateway is the earliest and is notable for its lion capitals, probably copied from the adjacent Aśoka column. Each gate, supported by elephants, stands on two rectangular pillars and is covered with reliefs. The three architraves are surmounted by a carving of 'the Wheel of the Law' and their projecting ends are supported by fine *yakṣī* figures, which are still not fully in the round.

The Western Deccan

During the period when the Sātavāhanas and Western Satraps were vying for domination in the western Deccan, a series of remarkable Buddhist caves were excavated along the Western Ghats, largely by private patronage, just off the major trade routes through the passes. Among the earliest is that at Bhājā (excavated early in the first century BC), where the *caitya*, or 'prayer hall', shows clear evidence of the development from wooden prototypes in the inward slope of its octagonal columns and generally simple interior. The two early prayer halls at Ajaṇṭā show some development, both in the elaboration of their façades and in containing traces of painted ornament. The largest and most impressive of these prayer halls is that at Kārlā (probably second half of the first century AD), where the plan has been further elaborated by an outer screen with free-standing columns beyond it. The capitals of the pillars are now particularly elaborate and the various elements of the composition are well integrated. The most extensive group of caves is that at Kaṇheri (about 25 miles from Bombay), where the prayer hall further elaborates on the plan of Kārlā and the total number of caves is at least 128 (excavated over a period up to the end of the second century AD).

Gandhāran Art

The Kuṣāṇas were great patrons of art and their early rulers fostered not only the Hellenistic art of Gandhāra but also the indigenous art of Mathurā. The craftsmen who served the Kuṣāṇa religious establishments in Gandhāra were probably at first Roman craftsmen from eastern Mediterranean sites, although Bactrian Greek remains probably kindled Kuṣāṇa interest in the style. Gandhāran art extended from the first to the fifth centuries AD in two distinct phases and over two areas. In the earlier phase, up to the third century, the medium was stone (mostly schist), which was abundant in the plain of Peshawar and the Swāt valley. In the second phase, from the third century onwards, the sculptures were done in stucco or lime plaster and clay, often painted in gold and polychrome, and the main sites are spread over a much wider area.

The representation of Buddhas and Bodhisattvas becomes common in Gandhāra and Mathurā art. King Kaniṣka traditionally constructed an enormous *stūpa*

Interior of an early rock-cut Buddhist cave (No. 2) at Ajaṇṭā. Monks lived in cells on three sides of this once highly painted prayer hall.

near Peshawar (Shāhjī-kī Ḍherī, literally 'the mound of the king'), described by Chinese pilgrims as the 'highest tower' in the whole of India. The façades of the plinth were decorated with Buddha figures in stucco between Indo-Corinthian pilasters and the relic-chamber contained a famous gilt relic-casket, on the lid of which is one of the earliest Buddha figures. Several coins of Kaniṣka bearing Buddha figures with descriptive legends beside them suggest that the developments in the Buddha image were not concurrent but rather that Gandhāra follows the lead of Mathurā. In the earliest Buddhist art, the Buddha was usually represented symbolically or, more accurately, was not shown at all, to symbolize the fact that he had attained Nirvāṇa, although there are occasional literary references to much earlier representations.

The earliest Buddhas combine various elements drawn from the repertoire of the foreign craftsmen employed. As Indian carvers steadily took over the work, the Buddhas underwent a process of Indianization. The images become more rigidly frontal and the drapery, as in the Roman provincial art of Palmyra, is reduced to a schematic pattern of string-like loops, while the face assumes a mask-like character, which becomes standard in Central and East Asia, as Buddhism spread to these areas in the wake of trade. During its earlier phases, Gandhāran art expresses the ideals of the early Buddhist schools and portrayals of the Buddhas of the Mahāyāna pantheon are rare. One indication of the gradual predominance of Mahāyāna views is the appearance of the colossal image, the most notable examples of which are those in the Bāmiyān valley in Afghanistan. Gandhāra also produced an enormous number of bas-reliefs. Some decorated the bases of statues or even the risers of a staircase, but most were placed on small and medium-sized *stūpas*. They are often quite small and are devoted entirely to scenes from the present or past lives of the historical Buddha.

The stucco school must have been as important as the stone-carving school, but the material was perishable and most has disappeared. Cheap, plentiful and easy to work, stucco was used in conjunction with stone at various places or, where stone was scarce, on its own. The technique must have come from the region of Alexandria; it was transmitted from there to Iran and north-western India, and pieces found at Taxila show that it had reached the Indus basin in the first century AD. The subjects depicted were broadly the same as in the stone school but the fragility of the material prevented the creation of single figures and so large images and groups were given support – either the wall of the *stūpa* or the shrine – and were not made entirely of stucco but built up over some kind of core. Moulds were used in conjunction with freehand modelling and the sculpture was normally painted.

In the excavations of the Kaniṣkan palace at Begram (ancient Kāpiśa), some 40 miles north of Kabul, two walled-up storerooms were discovered, filled with objects from all over the world: fragments of Chinese lacquer boxes, Graeco-Roman statuettes in bronze, a rich collection of Roman glassware and a large number of fine Indian ivory carvings. These ivories represent a variety of techniques and periods – some have analogies to the Sāñcī carvings, while others are related to tree-spirits in the Mathurā style of about the second century. This treasure, especially the number and variety of Graeco-Roman imports, confirms the close commercial and cultural relations between the Kuṣāṇas and the Roman empire and also the Kuṣāṇa taste for Graeco-Roman art.

The Buddha from the Mathurā school, patronized by the Kuṣāṇa kings.

Mathurā Art

Mathurā must have been the centre of Kuṣāṇa power within India and the area is one of the most significant in the history of Indian art, for large quantities of sculpture have been found dating from the Śuṅga to the late medieval period, identifiable as the product of local workshops from the stone used, a red sandstone with buff spots. The massive proportions of Mathurā images, with their suggestion of weight and inner vitality, are clearly connected with the *yakṣa* and *yakṣī* statues of popular Mauryan and post-Mauryan art, though showing more sophistication. The faces, by contrast with Gandhāran images, have an open expression. The influence of its characteristic style was pervasive: at Sārnāth, local copies were made of imported specimens, and at Kanśāmbī what appears to have been a local school is basically a variant of the Mathurā school.

Many other subjects besides Buddhas and Bodhisattvas are represented. A richly decorated stone railing from a *stūpa* at Bhūteśvara, near Mathurā, bears reliefs of voluptuous women in casual poses, while amorous couples dally on balconies above. At its peak around the time of Kaniṣka, sculpture from Mathurā is excellent and shows a naturalistic style, but it seems to decline twenty or thirty years after Kaniṣka, when stereotyping becomes frequent and no further works on a monumental scale were produced, while influences from Gandhāra intrude. Later Mathurā sculpture of the Kuṣāṇa period often consists of Jain images, which are relatively crude and debased in style.

Gupta Art and Architecture

The Gupta period marks a turning point in the development of Hindu temple architecture, but unfortunately its major monuments have disappeared and what survive, often covered by the jungle of central India, are provincial shrines from the southern fringes of the Gupta empire, mostly from late in the Gupta period. With increasing use of stone, an elaboration of structure followed. A clearly defined iconography also developed and in the representations of the gods a system of symbolic postures, gestures, weapons and

A Gupta depiction of Vishnu, as the boar (varaha) incarnation, saving the earth. Cave 5 at Udayagiri.

attendants was adopted which served to indicate their attributes. Both religious and secular figures were represented in an apparently natural manner, but in fact were studied works of art. This classical style first really developed at the court of Candragupta II at Ujjain at the beginning of the fifth century, for in the reigns of Candragupta I and Samudragupta a rather harsher imitation of the Mathurā school was prevalent. A striking example of this new development is to be found in the Udayagiri caves, in which the style is undeniably powerful if sometimes a little clumsy, as in the huge relief of the boar incarnation of Vishnu raising the earth (Cave 5), where the pose of the central figure is standard for the depiction of this *avatāra* as a boar-headed man: the left knee bent as he steps forward and upward, the goddess held up in the crook of the left arm, the right hand placed on his hip in an exultant pose of power and achievement. The Udayagiri caves are the only monuments closely associated with a Gupta ruler; one was donated by a minister of Candragupta II and another inscription records the pious gift of a local ruler made in 402. All the caves are Hindu, except for one Jain cave, which contains the only inscription of Kumāragupta's reign, in 426. The elaborately carved doorways of the Gupta style first appear here.

With the reign of Kumāragupta the style found general acceptance, but also became gentler and even somewhat mannered. The Buddha statues found at Mathurā and Sārnāth are typical of this trend, without, however, losing a sense of spirituality. Four matching seated Buddhas round the Great Stūpa at Sāñcī (in place before 450) show the general elegance of the mature Gupta style. All are slender, the soles of the feet turn upwards and particularly the eastern and southern ones have drooping shoulders. The Buddhas from Sārnāth are in many ways the greatest achievement during the Gupta period in the visual arts; the First Sermon was a favoured subject, since it had actually occurred here. Three Sārnāth Buddhas bear clear dates (one 474, the other two 477) and are all in the mature Sārnāth style. In addition to the substantial Buddhist production centred at Mathurā and Sārnāth, an enormous amount of carving, both Hindu and Buddhist, was done all over India. In the representation of deities an interesting convention was adopted to indicate flying through the air, which is shown by the direction of the legs and the upturned feet and by the upward swirling lines of the billowing scarf which is often worn.

The Bhītārgāon temple (early fifth century) is the only Gupta brick temple to survive, but little remains of its superstructure. Architecturally, the temple incorporates an unusual feature: true rather than corbelled arches and vaulting in the porch and shrine chambers. The richly decorated pilasters and cornices are of carved brick and the many relief panels are modelled in terracotta. The terracotta sculpture is more flowing than the carved brickwork, for the medium encourages rapid modelling.

Narasimha, the man-lion incarnation of Vishnu, who saved the world from a demon king.

Perhaps the best example of Gupta architecture is the temple at Deogaṛh, dating to the sixth century. The central shrine, consisting of a cubic block of masonry surmounted by a pyramidal tower about 40 feet high, was surrounded by four porticoes, three of which merely served to protect the inset reliefs. The platform on which the temple is raised was originally decorated with a frieze showing events from the *Rāmāyaṇa* and an extensive Krishna cycle. The main shrine is a square of slightly more than 18 feet, occupying the central one of the nine squares into which the platform can be divided. The façade on the west has particularly varied and graceful ornamentation, and the main doorway of the temple is highly ornate. In either corner of the architrave are reliefs of the river goddesses Gaṅgā and Yamunā, common motifs on buildings of the Gupta period. Each of the remaining three walls is provided with a niche containing an exquisitely carved scene from Vaiṣṇava mythology: on

The façade of Cave 19 at Ajaṇṭā anticipates the shape of the *stūpa* within. Its elaborate carving is typical late devotional work at this Deccan site.

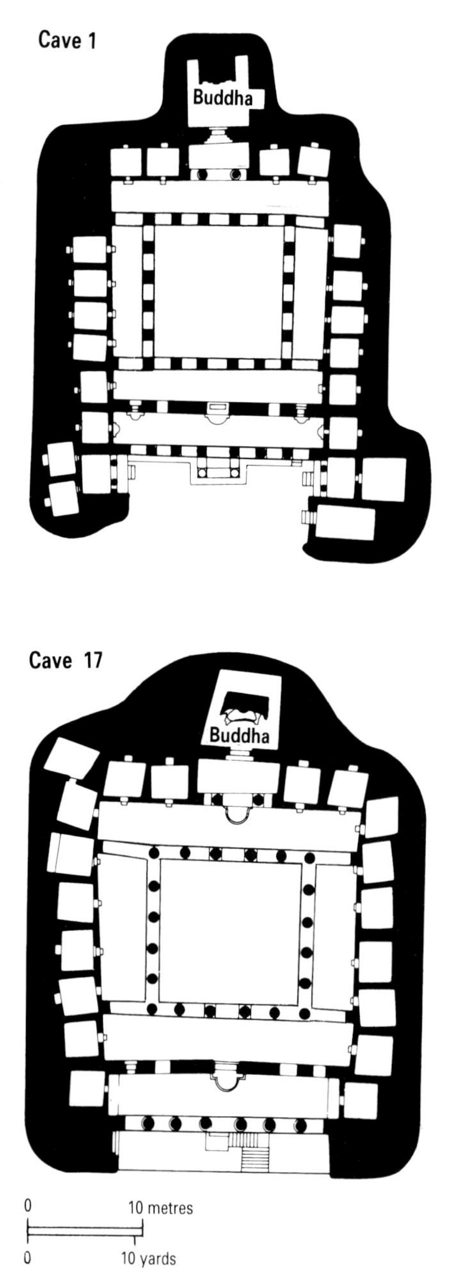

the south Vishnu sleeping on Śeṣa, on the east the penance of Nara and Nārāyaṇa, and on the north the deliverance of the elephant by Vishnu. In all Gupta temples the decorative carving is confined to the doorways, windows and panels, where it provides a rich contrast with the otherwise plain walls. The columns are much more complicated than previously and varying shapes are used.

Buddhist cave monasteries were very common in the Deccan and were regularly embellished with paintings (often called frescoes, which technically they are not) of considerable merit. The walls and ceilings are painted with scenes from the lives of the Buddha, with celestial Buddhas and Bodhisattvas, and also with dancers, musicians, amorous couples and the like. At Ajaṇṭā the early caves are found roughly at the centre of the curving scarp which forms their setting and the later caves flank them on either side. The branch Vākāṭaka line of Vatsagulma (modern Basim in the Akola district) is especially associated with the Ajaṇṭā caves and their brilliant mural paintings; their capital, Vatsagulma, is hardly 100 miles north-east of Ajaṇṭā. Indeed, caves 16 and 17 bear inscriptions showing that they were excavated during the reign of Hariṣeṇa of the Vatsagulma line at the end of the fifth century. Architectural elements at Ajaṇṭā are highly decorated and are closely related to contemporary Gupta work, though executed under the Vākāṭakas, but the sculpture is less good. The most famous paintings at Ajaṇṭā are in cave 1 and originally covered the entire interior. Although the painting does not form a complete or unified scheme, large portions are parts of a single concept; the two colossal painted figures of Bodhisattvas on either side of the niche at the back of the hall form a trinity with the Buddha image there. The paintings show a wide variety of pigments, all of which, with the exception of black (lamp-black), are of mineral origin; lapis lazuli was the only import. The outlines were drawn first in red ochre and then, after the local colour was applied in different tones, the outline was redrawn in brown, red or black.

Two cave temples at Ajaṇṭā from the fifth century (caves 1 and 17).

THE UNIFICATION OF CHINA

Inlaid wine vessel. Scrolled and geometric designs remained popular right down to the imperial unification in 221 BC under the Qin dynasty.

Chronology

BC

479	Death of Confucius
438	Death of Mo Zi
356	Shang Yang's reforms begin
338	Execution of Shang Yang
300	Qin builds wall to resist nomads
288	Death of Mencius
260	Battle of Chang Ping
256	Deposition of last Zhou king
247	Li Si arrives in Qin
246	Chengkuo canal opened
233	Han Fei Zi dies in Qin
223	Qin annexes Chu
221	Qin unites all China
	Accession of the First Emperor
219	First Emperor tries to obtain elixir of immortality
214	General Meng Tian ordered to build the Great Wall
213	Li Si advises the First Emperor to burn the books
212	460 dissident scholars killed
210	The far south annexed
	The First Emperor dies on a tour of inspection
209	The Second Emperor purges the imperial family
208	Execution of Li Si
207	Suicide of the Second Emperor; the eunuch Zhao Gao fails to gain the throne
206	Liu Bang captures Xianyang, the Qin capital
202	Official accession of Liu Bang as the Han emperor Gaozu
200	Gaozu almost captured by the Xiongnu
195	Death of Gaozu
154	Rebellion of the eastern kings
136	Confucianism recognized as state cult
126	Zhang Qian returns from Central Asia
119	State monopoly declared over iron and salt industries; merchants forbidden to own land
111	Nan Yue incorporated in the empire
110	Princess Lu Xijun marries Kazakhstan chieftain
104	Death of Dong Zhongshu
101	The Western Regions declared a Chinese protectorate
99	Li Ling surrenders to the Xiongnu
87	Death of Wu Di
81	Debate on iron and salt industries

AD

9	Usurpation of Wang Mang
23	Green Woodsmen rebellion
	Death of Wang Mang
25	Accession of Later Han emperor Guangwu Di
40	Rebellion of Vietnam
70	General Ban Chao in Hami
75	Death of Ming Di
100	Death of Wang Chong
105	Manufacture of paper announced
139	Death of the inventor Zhang Heng
159	Suicide of Liang Ji
168	Death of Huandi
184	Yellow Turbans rebellion
189	Massacre of the palace eunuchs
215	Surrender of Zhang Lu
220	Death of Cao Cao
	Deposition of last Han emperor
234	Death of Zhu Geliang
263	Fall of the Shu kingdom
265	Sima Yan founds the Western Jin dynasty
280	Fall of the Wu kingdom
291	The Disturbance of the Eight Princes
316	Collapse of Western Jin power

A portrait of Dong Zhongshu, the Former Han philosopher who made Confucianism the state ideology.

The Unification of China (481 BC–AD 316)

Arthur Cotterell

History

The determining influence on early Chinese civilization was its isolation from other centres of development in the ancient world. Well over a millennium of history had passed before the Chinese realized in the Former Han period (206 BC–AD 9) that there were any other civilizations. We can still catch something of the amazement of the envoy Zhang Qian when in 126 BC he returned to Chang'an, the imperial capital, and reported that in what is now Afghanistan there were 'cities, mansions and houses as in China'. It was in fact the recently conquered Graeco-Buddhist state of Bactria, a remnant of Alexander's dominions in Asia, but Zhang Qian does not seem to have appreciated that the former kingdom had been on the fringe of the Hellenistic world. No cultural exchange occurred between China and the Graeco-Roman west; Chang'an became aware of other civilized peoples, but the only foreign influence at this early stage was to come from India, in the form of Buddhism.

What interested the Han emperor Wu Di (140–87 BC) in Zhang Qian's account of his travels were the large horses he noticed in Xiyu, 'the Western Regions', since they could be used to carry heavily armed men against the nomadic Xiongnu, who rode the smaller Mongolian pony. By the reign of Wu Di nomad incursions were again a serious problem for the Chinese empire, and in 138 BC Zhang Qian had been dispatched westwards to stir up the Da Yuezhi, enemies of the Xiongnu in Central Asia. The discovery of a different breed of horse there was an unexpected bonus for the Chinese, who soon established good relations with horse-breeding tribes. One chieftain living near Lake Balkhash, in modern Kazakhstan, asked for the hand of a Chinese princess and sent 1,000 horses as a betrothal present. The chieftain was given Liu Xijun, a princess of royal blood, who in 110 BC set off with a large retinue for the distant land. Ever since the homesickness of the princess has proved a fascinating subject for both painters and poets: she who yearned 'to be the yellow swan that returns to its home'.

Liu Xijun's sacrifice aside, Wu Di had found a method of strengthening the northern defences, whose parlous state preoccupied Chinese rulers throughout the classical age. Although victories won by his new cavalry

The Warring States (481–221 BC).

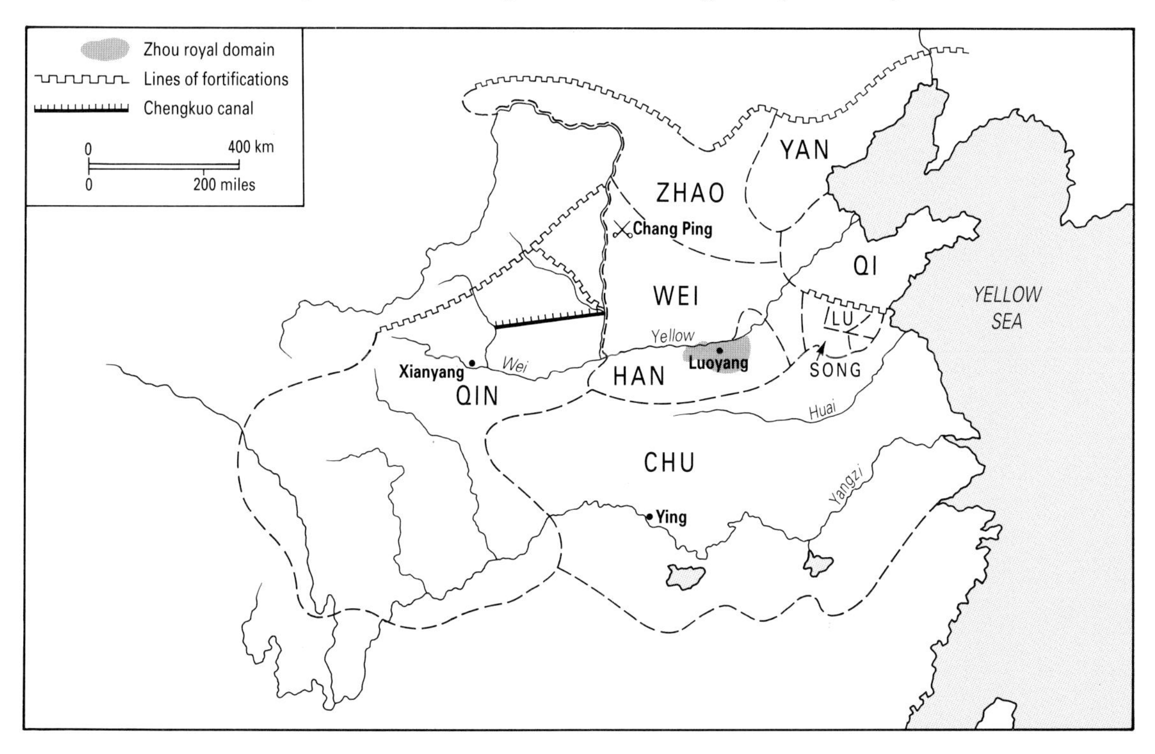

reduced for a while the nomad danger, Wu Di overburdened the imperial exchequer with continuous campaigns, so a compromise was later tried with the Xiongnu, probably the Huns who invaded the Roman empire in the fifth century AD. During the Later Han period (25–220) Chinese armies could achieve victories on the steppe only with the active assistance of nomad allies. Eventually the Western Jin dynasty (265–316) found it impossible to cope at all with friendly barbarians settled inside the imperial frontier. As a result of their involvement in civil disturbances, nearly all the provinces north of the Yangzi watershed fell after 316 temporarily under Tartar domination.

The Warring States Period (481–221 BC)

The greatest of China's philosophers, Confucius (551–479 BC), was in no doubt that a similar barbarian conquest had been averted in the seventh century BC by the energetic campaigns of Huan, duke of Qi (684–642 BC). Had this leading nobleman not dealt decisively with the northern nomads, Chinese civilization would have been unable to evolve in its own distinct manner. 'But for him,' Confucius remarked, 'we should now button our clothes down the side and wear our hair down the back.'

Confucius.

A section of the Great Wall, near the Gobi desert. It shows the rammed-earth core of the original defences.

The terracotta statue of an infantry general from the pits near the First Emperor's tomb. No other figure excavated so far has equalled his height.

The various measures adopted during the Warring States period to protect *Zhongguo*, or the 'Middle Kingdom', as China was then called, from nomad incursion constituted more than a military exercise. The rammed-earth walls built along the northern frontier, the precursors of the Great Wall itself, were intended to signal a divide between the steppe and the sown. They marked a line of cultural and economic division. The unifier of China and the builder of the Great Wall, the First Emperor, who reigned supreme from 221 to 210 BC, was equally determined to halt any movement of population to the north in case the farmers of the northern outposts abandoned tillage and took up stock-rearing, so enhancing the nomad economy. The decision in 214 BC to join up existing defences into a single wall meant his own subjects were to be kept under control and his enemies shut out. For the same reason the Chinese had been scandalized in 307 BC by the desperate measure adopted by Zhao, the northernmost of the Warring States. Its ruler went so far as to allow the barbarian fashion of wearing trousers for his newly formed light cavalry. This imitation of nomad horse tactics proved useful on the borders of the steppe, where high speed was needed to counter sudden raids, but it did little to assist Zhao in confronting the heavily armoured infantry and the crossbowmen of rival Chinese states.

During the two and a half centuries prior to the unification of China in 221 BC warfare was endemic. With the collapse of the feudal system, the nominal king of China, the Son of Heaven, was reduced to a figurehead with ceremonial functions within a small domain surrounding the city of Luoyang. In theory the rulers of the other territories which constituted the Middle Kingdom owed allegiance to the reigning Zhou king at Luoyang; in practice, however, these feudal lords exercised authority within independent states. A few were almost the size of a modern province, though along the Yellow River valley several older ones still survived as small units. But the tendency for the more powerful states to swallow up their weaker neighbours was the dominant trend of the Warring States period, when only seven of them were able to marshal adequate resources for war. Powerless, the Son of Heaven watched as two great powers, Qin and Chu, gained territory through the quarrels of their neighbours. By 221 BC the strength of Qin was sufficient to destroy all its rivals and unify the whole of China in one empire. The last Zhou king was rudely pushed from his throne by Qin troops in 256 BC.

A part of the great Buddhist complex at Dunhuang, where the Silk Road left China proper for the 'Western Regions'.

Bronze wine vessel, or *hu*, used in the ritual of ancestor worship. Probably Warring States period (481–221 BC).

Because the core of contending armies consisted of highly trained and well-equipped regular soldiers, rulers were loath to waste in unprofitable campaigns what was a considerable investment. Sun Zi's *Art of War* (*Bingfa*), the oldest-known military treatise in the world, cautions the eager commander about taking unnecessary risks with his forces. Never press an advantage too hard, Sun Zi warns: 'Always leave a way of escape, or your foe will be forced to fight to the death.' The realism of this fifth-century BC strategist stems from an appreciation of logistics, and their burdensome cost. Succinctly he notes:

> If a campaign is protracted, the resources of the state will prove unequal to the strain. When your weapons are dulled and morale is weakened, your strength exhausted and your treasure spent, other rulers will take advantage of your plight. Then no adviser, however clever, will be able to save your state.

Sun Zi also makes clear the severity of the discipline in these largely professional armies. He relates how a Chu officer succeeded in taking a pair of Qin heads prior to an attack, and was beheaded for his daring exploit. In explanation, the Chu commander commented: 'I am confident he is an officer of ability, but he is disobedient in leaving our lines.' Yet it was the state of Qin which effectively broke the power of the hereditary aristocracy in the army by, after 350 BC, promoting only the brave and the able to the highest ranks. Thereafter the Qin army was a war machine with no scope for noble display, like head-hunting. Its ruthlessness on the battlefield could be disguised no longer; 'blood for the drums' ceased to be the ceremonial execution of a handful of prisoners after the fight when, in 260 BC at Chang Ping, the Qin generals ordered the wholesale slaughter of Zhao prisoners. Horrifying though this extreme act seemed to many people at the time, it was to be some years before the ultimate downgrading of the military in Chinese society took place – a later achievement of Confucianism, especially under the Former Han emperors.

Driving the Qin juggernaut along its relentless path to victory was a radical series of reforms introduced by Shang Yang (390–338 BC). A new spirit of government was abroad, but no one applied so effectively the harsh tenets of Legalism as this minister, who discovered in the Qin ruler a man indifferent to the restraints of traditional morality. In 350 BC Shang Yang introduced a law code which elevated the throne, weakened the nobility, broke up powerful clans, freed the peasantry from bondage and directed the whole energies of the state to agriculture and war. It had to be made worse for someone to fall into the hands of the police than go to war. 'Those who occupy themselves with trade,' he declared, 'shall be enslaved, along with the destitute and lazy. Those of noble lineage who have no military value shall lose their noble status.'

Shang Yang's single-mindedness in the application of the law, a notable characteristic of Legalist thinkers, made him unpopular and, like Li Si, the First Emperor's chief adviser, he did not long survive his master's death. Inhumanity was the accusation most often levelled against him by the followers of Confucius, who were quick to see the totalitarian dangers in subjugating the state entirely to the ruler's wishes. For, on the contrary, they held the welfare of the people to be the objective of politics, and regarded ethics as the standard of life. When asked about government, Confucius said: 'Let the prince be a prince, the minister a minister, the father a father, and the son a son.' Officials were obliged to obey a ruler's commands only so long as they were ethical, which meant displaying an independence of mind that put morality before personal safety.

Such scruples had no place in Shang Yang's order of society: improvements in agricultural productivity and battle readiness alone were what carried Qin to complete domination of China. Zheng, the victorious Qin ruler, chose in 221 BC to celebrate the great event of unification by adopting a new imperial title. He was called Qin Shi Huangdi, First Sovereign Qin Emperor, in order to show his supremacy over the rulers he had overthrown.

Qin Unification (221–207 BC)

As the sole survivor of the Warring States period the Qin ruler found himself in an unprecedented position.

The final version of the Great Wall, faced by stone.

Han bas-relief showing an assassination attempt on the First Emperor in 227 BC. It greatly increased his anxiety about dying.

With no rivals left he could justly insist, 'We are the First Emperor, and Our successors shall be known as the Second Emperor, Third Emperor, and so on, for endless generations.' Indeed, there was in all probability a definite reference to divine favour, even divinity, in the character (*di*) chosen for emperor. Already a very old and complex word by 221 BC, it had been used by Daoist philosophers as a means of elevating the semi-divine figures they wished to claim for their own inspiration. Steadfast opponents of Confucian philosophy, they looked wistfully back to a golden age which was said to have preceded the development of feudalism. Its great sage was the Yellow Emperor, Huang Di, who ascended into the sky as an immortal after an exemplary reign. Personal contact with Daoist magicians may have encouraged the First Emperor's own superstitions, since he tried to communicate with the immortals first in 219 BC, so as to acquire the elixir of life.

In the administration of the newly united empire two notions powerfully coalesced, a Legalist emphasis on conformity and the First Emperor's anxiety about orderliness. Although the Han historian Sima Qian (145–79 BC) admitted a pressing need to sort out the muddle of inherited practices and customs once unification had taken place, he also made plain official preoccupation with standardization.

> Black became the chief colour for dress, banners and pendants, and six the chief number. Tallies and official headgear were 6 measures long, carriages 6 measures wide, one pace was 6 measures, and the imperial carriage had 6 horses . . . In order to inaugurate Qin's element, water, it was believed that there must be firm repression with everything determined by law. Only ruthless, implacable severity could make the five elements accord. So the law was harsh and there were no amnesties.

Obedience to the letter of the law was demanded, and the politeness of everyday manners condemned as an unnecessary hindrance to the smooth running of the state. It was not surprising, therefore, that in 213–212 BC books should be burned and scholars buried alive when Confucianists dared to express reservations about the harsh tendency of imperial policy. That their warnings were ignored cost the Qin dynasty dear, for the first peasant rebellion of Chinese history arose to end its supposed 'endless generations' within two decades. Quite simply the Legalists overestimated the level of bullying that the people would stand.

In 221 BC, however, nothing seemed capable of denting the programme of Qin reform. Such was the determination of the First Emperor that his brief reign represents a turning point in Chinese history, as the bureaucratic form of government he established became the model for the future empire, which was to last until modern times. In his drive for uniformity the First Emperor had to rely on military force. Feudal holdings were abolished and noble families compelled to take up residence in Xianyang, now the capital of all China. The peasants received greater rights over their land but became liable for taxes, labour on public works and military conscription. Weapons were also

A standard Qin measure of volume. Many of the convicts who laboured on the First Emperor's tomb at Mount Li had been condemned for ignoring such regulations.

brought to the capital, where they were melted and cast into twelve colossal statues. The empire was divided into administrative districts, garrisons planted at strategic locations, and a body of inspectors was set up to audit accounts as well as check on the administration of justice. There was standardization of weights and measures, coinage, axle wheels and the written script. A national road network was built and canals improved for the supply of the army, and as a counter to the Xiongnu nomads the Ordos desert region was annexed and defended by the construction of the Great Wall, which stretched for almost 1,000 miles between the upper reaches of the Yellow River in the west and the Liaodong peninsula in the east. Something of the enormity of the programme can be glimpsed in Sima Qian's account of the guilt felt by the builder of the Great Wall. Tricked into committing suicide in 210 BC, following the First Emperor's sudden death, the Qin general Meng Tian reconciled himself to his fate by accepting the crime of its construction. 'I have made walls and ditches,' he said, 'over more than 10,000 *li*. In this distance it is impossible not to have cut through the veins of the earth.'

When, in 213 BC, the First Emperor discovered that there was criticism of his policies, he followed the advice of Li Si (280–208 BC) and burned all books except those on medicine, forestry, agriculture and divination. 'These scholars,' said Li Si, 'learn only from the old, not from the new, and employ their learning to oppose your rule and confuse the people.' Extreme though the proscription of study was, this burning of books was not unique, Shang Yang having destroyed among other classics the *Book of History* (*Shu Jing*), a collection of documents covering the early feudal age. But the result of the First Emperor's edict was more profound. When, in 206 BC, a rebel army burned Xianyang, the conflagration engulfed the imperial library and in many cases destroyed the sole surviving copies. The loss caused a definite break in consciousness, for when, under the patronage of the Han emperors, ancient texts were painfully reconstructed from memory and the badly tattered copies hidden in 213 BC at great personal risk were unearthed, the feudal age seemed historically remote. It also gave later scholars a lasting revulsion against the Qin dynasty, although this fact did not entirely prevent censorship in imperial China.

Further criticism in 212 BC goaded the First Emperor to conduct a purge of scholars, some 460 being condemned to a lingering death. Crown prince Fu Su was banished to the Great Wall to oversee its completion as a punishment for his protest at the purge. His departure from the capital, and subsequent death in the same plot that eliminated Meng Tian, removed the most vigorous and able member of the imperial family at a critical moment. Popular risings started in 210 BC as the crushing burden of Qin rule became even more intolerable. Li Si's motive in plotting against Fu Su appears to have been grounded in personal anxiety, a weakness skilfully played upon by the chief eunuch,

Li Si, chief adviser to the First Emperor.

Zhao Gao. The First Emperor's growing concern about his own death gave the plotters a chance to install Hu Hai, the worthless second son. Being told by his Daoist advisers that his efforts towards immortality were being frustrated by a malignant influence at court, he decided to protect his own divinity by restricting access to his person. To keep his movements secret, the First Emperor 'gave orders for the 270 palaces and pavilions within 200 *li* of Xianyang to be connected by causeways and covered walks ... and made disclosure of his whereabouts punishable by death'.

The circumstances of the First Emperor's illness in 210 BC played into the conspirators' hands. While on a tour of inspection he dreamed of a sea god, which was interpreted as an evil spirit keeping him from making contact with the immortals. The First Emperor roamed the shore of Shandong province until he dispatched what was most likely a stranded whale with a repeater crossbow. Afterwards he sickened and died, but Li Si and Zhao Gao hid the event and brought the

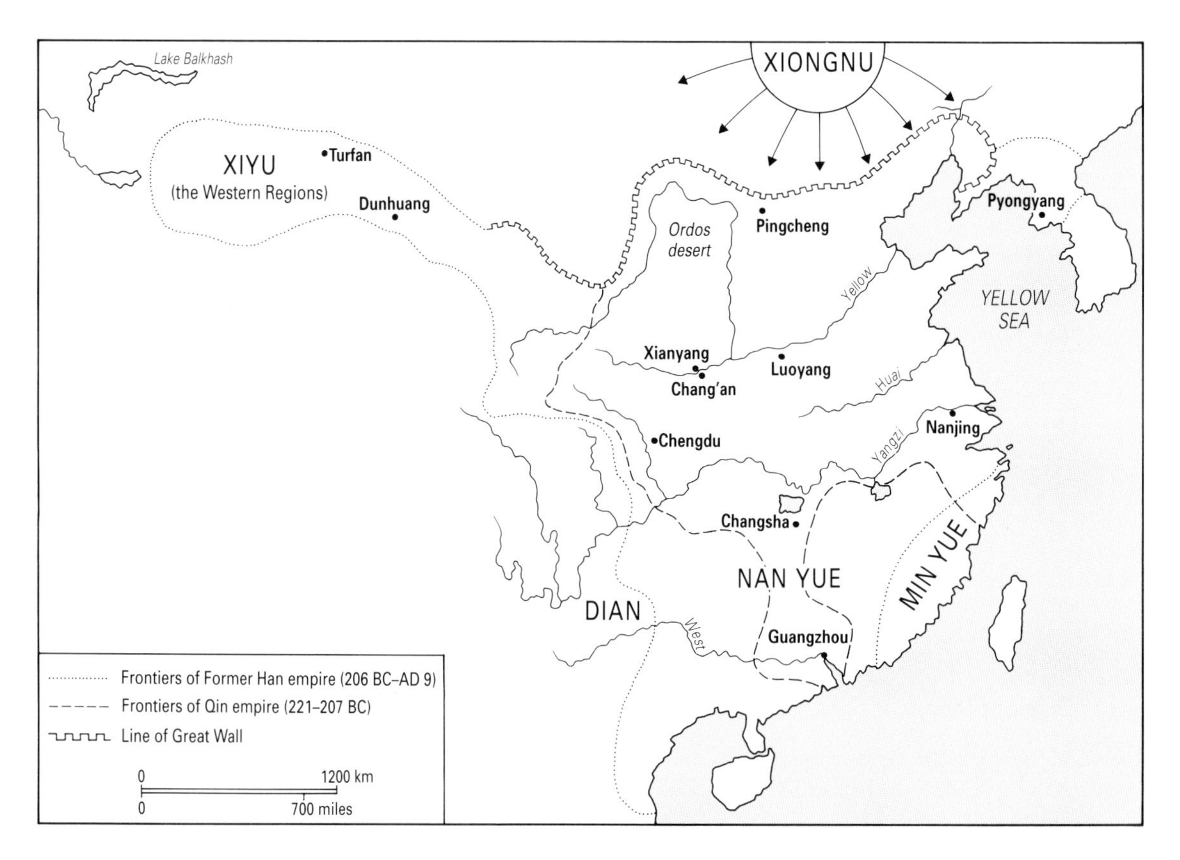

Imperial unification: the Qin and Former Han empires.

body back to Xianyang, where they proclaimed Hu Hai as the Second Emperor, Ershi Huangdi. Sima Qian drily remarks:

> The coffin was borne in a litter escorted by the emperor's favourite eunuchs, who presented food and official reports as usual and issued imperial commands from the covered litter ... But it was summer and to disguise the stench the escort was told to load a cart with salted fish.

Thus it was that the unifier of China, Qin Shi Huangdi, the would-be immortal, returned to the imperial capital, following a cartload of mouldering fish. Such was the terror inspired by his title that there was no one to question this final indignity, or to prevent forged orders being sent to Fu Su and Meng Tian demanding their suicides.

Neither of the conspirators gained permanently from their actions. Zhao Gao engineered Li Si's execution in 208 BC and the next year forced the Second Emperor to take his own life, but the usurpation of the throne then attempted by the scheming eunuch was effectively blocked. However, the end was already near for the Qin empire, as more and more of the oppressed Chinese rose against its forces, Xianyang receiving the torch in early 206 BC. 'Palaces and houses were looted and fired. The burning lasted for several months. So it was,' Sima Qian tells us with a certain satisfaction, 'that the power of Qin was overthrown.'

Former Han (206 BC–AD 9)

The complicated struggle between the insurgent leaders for the honour of replacing the Qin dynasty was eventually won by Liu Bang (247–195 BC), a man of the people. Tradition relates that in 209 BC, having lost several convicts from a group he was conducting to Xianyang, Liu Bang released the others and put himself at their head. While the popular insurrection against Qin rule started as an attempt to restore feudalism, the old aristocracy soon showed itself incapable of undertaking the task of government and, faced with the prospect of protracted conflict, the Chinese put their trust in the ordinary men who had risen to prominence during the course of the revolt.

Ban Gu's *History of the Former Han (Han Shu)* is at pains to emphasize the supernatural support shown for Liu Bang, but its narrative of the dynasty's foundation cannot disguise the peasant background of the first Han emperor. According to Ban Gu (32–92), the First Emperor even remarked on the presence of a rival to the throne: 'In the south-east there is an emanation of a Son of Heaven,' he said, dispatching troops unsuccessfully to capture Liu Bang. The emanation took the form of the mist, red inside and yellow outside, which appeared when a future emperor, or an emperor, was approaching. Because of this manifestation of divine approval, Liu Bang was once traced by his wife to his mountain hide-out. When the fugitive asked how she had managed to find him, he was told, 'There is always a mist. So we follow after it and always find you.' Pleased though his supporters were by the news, the fact remained that Liu Bang was illiterate and not a little intolerant of scholars. Prior to his final victory over all other rebel leaders in 202 BC, he displayed his dislike for the excessive ceremony attached to learning. When some scholars came to him in costume, wearing their elaborate hats, he snatched one of these pieces of headgear and urinated in it. But Liu Bang was moderate in comparison with his aristocratic rivals for power, who thought nothing of boiling opponents alive.

The mildness of the first Han emperor Gaozu, or 'High Ancestor' as Liu Bang styled himself, was a welcome trait in a very violent age. People felt he would govern in their interests, unlike the absolute rulers of Qin. On the throne Gaozu neither aped aristocratic manners nor slackened his concern for his poorer subjects, and his habit of squatting down, coupled with an earthy vocabulary, unsettled polite courtiers and accentuated the kindly feeling people felt towards him. Yet he had the wit to appreciate the value of learned and cultivated advisers and assistants. To bring order to the daily life of the palace, which was built at Chang'an, 'Forever Safe', on the opposite bank of the Wei River from Xianyang, Gaozu commissioned the arrangement of a new court ceremonial for his boisterous followers. His only instruction was, 'Make it easy.'

By turning to scholars untarnished with the excesses of Legalism, Gaozu paved the way for the ultimate 'Confucianization' of a bureaucratic empire. But imperial patronage of learning did not happen all at once, as this exchange between the emperor and his chamberlain indicates. So often did the official quote from the *Book of History* that Gaozu became annoyed and said:

'I conquered the empire on horseback. What is the good of these quotations from books of old?'

Chamberlain Lu Jia replied, 'That is correct, but Your Majesty will not be able to govern it on horseback ... If Qin had governed with humanity and righteousness, if it had followed the precepts of the ancient sages, then Han would not have gained the empire.'

At this the emperor blanched and said, 'Explain to me the reasons for the fall of Qin and the rise of Han, as well as what it was that won and lost kingdoms of old.'

In obedience to Gaozu's wish, Lu Jia wrote a book about statecraft, in twelve chapters. When the emperor listened to his chamberlain reading aloud his book, he praised his ideas strongly.

In a similar manner the teaching of Confucius on rites became the pattern at court, the emperor assuming responsibility for rituals belonging to the state worship of Heaven. The transformation of China into a unified state run on Confucian lines was a slow process because the early Han emperors settled for a political compromise after the repression of Qin. Certain

One of the standard weights introduced throughout China by the Qin dynasty.

feudal houses were restored, but their diminished holdings were intertwined with districts controlled by imperial officials.

A rebellion among the eastern vassals in 154 BC was used by emperor Han Jin Di (156–141 BC) to alter the laws of inheritance. Henceforth all sons were to be coheirs of their father, with land divided between them, an amendment which did much to quicken the breakdown of large territories into little more than substantial estates. Emperor Han Wu Di completed the dispossession of the old aristocracy prior to 100 BC by means of harsh officials who moved against overpowerful families, whether of ancient lineage or recent origin. His most zealous agents were accused of subordinating everything in Legalist fashion to the imperial will. Because he wanted to rule as well as reign, Wu Di ended the initial Han compromise of shared power with the aristocracy and recruited as his ministers scholars who would execute his policies. Gaozu had summoned such men to the capital to assist with administration, but Wu Di was the first emperor to set examinations for would-be officials. The total size of the imperial bureaucracy, from ministers down to minor officials, in 5 BC was recorded as 135,285 men, a figure thought to be slightly higher than in Wu Di's time.

Although popular hatred of Qin ruled out any return to Legalism, the authoritarian character of Wu Di necessitated a revision of Confucian conceptions about the ruler. A less ceremonial role was envisaged, not least because in tackling the problems facing the Former Han dynasty the emperor evolved into something like the chief executive of a bureaucratic state. As even the philosopher Dong Zhongshu (179–104 BC) had to concede, the burdens of empire required more than a display of imperial virtue. But, having persuaded Wu Di to proclaim the state cult of Confucius in 136 BC, he reasserted the theory of the heavenly mandate (*tianming*): 'Heaven bestowed a mandate to rule on Han, for the reason that Qin had grown tyrannical. So Han was able to overthrow Qin. The one in possession of Heaven's favour smote the one lacking it.' Thus, Dong Zhongshu argued, a ruler's position of authority was granted and taken away by Heaven, whose agents for affecting change could be humble men like Liu Bang, virtuous individuals supported by the mass of the people.

This theory of Heaven's limitation of imperial power formed the basis of the Chinese constitution until the twentieth century. Imperial unification was, of course, intimately connected with technical advance, but the ability of a dynasty to endure also related to the acquiescence of the governed and the means by which they could effect political changes. It happened in China that offensive weapons were always superior, the crossbow before the lifetime of Christ having already ruled out any domination by armoured imperial troops.

While Wu Di would not accept Dong Zhongshu's belief that heavenly disapproval was shown in natural phenomena such as floods or drought, he understood how delay in mounting adequate relief measures must inevitably encourage peasant rebellion. Just as agriculture needed to be sustained through the maintenance of extensive water-control works, so speculation in foodstuffs could not be allowed to disrupt the economy, and in 115 BC public granaries were established to stabilize prices. Provincial officials were ordered to buy when prices were low and sell in times of shortage, a system known as the *pingzhun*, or 'leveller'. The economic difficulties of Wu Di's reign were exacerbated by the long war against the Xiongnu, which dragged on from 114 to 91 BC. Even though Chinese foreign policy was dictated by the requirement to contain nomad pressure, it was obvious that the empire could not remain on a permanent war-footing. Victories did not win the war and an uneasy peace along the northern frontier was eventually paid for by substantial imperial gifts to the Xiongnu.

Mounting problems in the production and the distribution of basic commodities, the worsening condition of the peasantry, the growing wealth of merchants and inflation caused by the private minting of coin called for drastic action. To meet immediate financial commitments Wu Di was advised to sell titles and call in privately minted coins by issuing treasury notes made from the skin of a rare white stag. In 119 BC, the same year that merchants were forbidden to own land, a state monopoly was declared over the iron and salt industries, the control of which was given to senior officials, until their incompetence compelled the recruitment of professional salt boilers and iron masters. Despite the disdain of many Confucian ministers, the arrangement became a part of imperial policy, though the monopoly on the production of alcohol declared in 98 BC was replaced by the payment of tax. The iron and salt monopolies were simply too lucrative to be dropped. The *Yantielun* (*Discourses on Salt and Iron*) records the philosophical debate over this extension of public control in 81 BC, when the issue was reopened after Wu Di's death. The main aim of the monopolists was to achieve the greatest exploitation of the empire's resources and the most effective distribution of its products. They justified the imposition of controls on the grounds that they ended private profit, stabilized prices and ensured fair distribution of iron tools to the peasantry. Against the advocates of monopoly, the traditionalists argued that government regulation would be seen as harsh and oppressive, besides pointing out the poor quality of the tools actually produced by the imperial iron agency.

Glazed pottery model of a watchtower, an important feature of the Han defence system along the Great Wall.

Still impoverished though the empire was after the long struggle with the Xiongnu, the smooth succession of Zhao Di (87–74 BC), Wu Di's youngest son, gave

China a welcome respite. The political complications which undermined his successors arose in the imperial palace through rivalry between consort families, especially the newly ennobled relatives of the empress and the entrenched relatives of the emperor's mother. The family of Wang Mang had been influential at court through marriage for two decades prior to his usurpation of the throne. His brief dynasty, the Xin, was closely bound up with recurring economic problems and the renewed activities of the Xiongnu.

The Usurpation of Wang Mang (AD 9–23)

The Han dynasty is divided into two parts, the Former and Later Han, by the so-called usurpation of Wang Mang. Had he founded a lasting dynasty, Chinese historians would have accorded him the heavenly mandate and detailed with sympathy the policies of his reign. But with the collapse of his administration and his violent death, Wang Mang automatically became a usurper who was blamed for a whole series of bungled decisions. The bias of Ban Gu is obvious:

> Wang Mang by nature was touchy and hot-tempered and could not bring himself to let things alone. Every time there was something that he initiated or invented, he always tried to justify it by reference to ancient custom ... But his new measures for currency ... buying and selling ... price control ... and state monopolies ... caused hardship and suffering ... And when the wealthy were not able to protect themselves and the poor had no way of keeping themselves alive, they arose and became thieves and robbers ... Before Wang Mang was executed, the population of the empire had been reduced by half.

This telescoped version of the disruption apparently caused by Wang Mang's interference indicates the obstacle we have to overcome in making any assessment, not least because it comprises virtually the sole account of the period.

Yet within Ban Gu's memoir of the hypocritical rise of Wang Mang to supreme power we are given the real reasons for his subsequent fall. While there can be no doubt that his determined programme of reform stimulated opposition, the imperial bureaucracy remained a firm supporter of Wang Mang almost to the end of his reign. Ultimately, it was widespread peasant unrest that brought about a change of allegiance, and then only after the abortive imperial campaign of 23 against the Green Woodsmen, a rebel army at large in Hebei province. The sending of 400,000 troops into a famine area turned the rebellion into a disaster, for the empty state granaries there obliged the hungry soldiers to relieve the peasantry of what little food was left. In the confused fighting which ensued, the success of the then popular Green Woodsmen gave encouragement to anti-Wang movements elsewhere.

The spectre of hunger haunted Wang Mang's reign. Severe droughts occurred in the five years prior to his fall, the price of grain in 21 rising twenty-five times above its normal level throughout the northern provinces, where most of the empire's 58 million inhabitants lived. The floods caused a decade earlier by a shift in the course of the Yellow River seem to have been less a factor in rural distress than the prolonged absence of rain. As Ban Gu records, 'At this time ... there had been a famine and drought for several years, so that bandit bands gradually became large enough to defy government forces sent against them.' But there was worse trouble with the Xiongnu. In 19 we are told how 'the nomads made a great raid. As soldiers in this emergency Wang Mang enrolled convicts, prisoners and domestic slaves ... and he temporarily taxed both officials and ordinary people, taking one-thirtieth of their property.' The counter-attack worked and Chinese border fortifications were held, although once again the heaviest burden pressed down on the poorest peasants.

Wang Mang fell, therefore, because of the knock-on effects of drought, a factor which his efforts at famine relief could not alleviate. Other actions he took may have contributed to social disharmony, but over the weather he had no control. Because Wang Mang endeavoured to intervene so energetically in affairs he could influence, it is possible to decry the depth of the crisis he certainly faced. At the centre of his reforms was a redistribution of land aimed at curbing the power of substantial landowners and relieving peasant distress. The process of land concentration had started during the early years of the Former Han and, while it helped to feed a growing urban population, the advent of speculation in the countryside offered nothing to smaller farmers. A bad harvest, higher taxation, official corruption, an imperial requisition, rebellion, a nomad incursion – any of these events spelled debt and ruin for the peasant who lacked financial reserves. So the buying and selling of land as well as slaves was banned by Wang Mang, and small families in possession of large estates were forced to surrender part of their holdings for reallocation to those who had none. Government loans at low interest were offered to poor peasants for the purchase of tools and seed, the finance for this regeneration of the countryside coming from state monopolies. The latter were the same as those introduced by the Han emperor Wu Di, except that Wang Mang adopted a more systematic approach to their enforcement. Where he appears to have gone beyond his predecessors is in measures aimed at price stabilization. Products included for the first time were 'hempen cloth, silk cloth, silk thread and silk wadding'. Stockpiles of these items commonly used in the making of clothes were formed in government storehouses in five cities.

Another innovation of Wang Mang's was the restriction also placed in the first year of his reign on slavery. The measure mainly affected wealthy families that kept domestic slaves. The lowest group in society, the enslaved were never a significant feature of Chinese civilization in the classical period, unlike the case in the Graeco-Roman world. Exactly how many slaves existed during Wang Mang's reign is impossible to calculate from surviving evidence, but that the number was low is not a matter of debate. In 44 there were

100,000 government slaves, the majority of whom were engaged in looking after livestock. Only convicts are mentioned as working in iron mining and manufacture. Convicts, unlike slaves, were sentenced to servitude for a definite period of time. Compulsory labour on public works provided the manpower necessary for large-scale water-conservancy projects, grain transportation, even the constant repair of fortifications along the northern frontier. Scholars frequently complained about the uselessness of government slaves who 'idle with folded hands', in contrast to the hard-working peasants. For slaves possessed civil rights and could not be killed at will: Wang Mang had no hesitation in ordering his middle son to commit suicide for such a crime. In 17, however, he abandoned as unworkable the prohibition on buying and selling slaves, and instead imposed a stiff annual tax on each slave owned.

Slavery continued under the Later Han, despite further edicts of manumission. Even so the continued fighting on the steppe did little to change the total number of slaves in China. Captured enemies were usually enslaved, but never those who voluntarily surrendered, not least because the return of honourable prisoners was an important part of border diplomacy. And the Chinese habit of periodic release of convicts and slaves for military service, as evident in Wang Mang's call-up to meet the threat posed by the Xiongnu, also helped to keep the pool of those under restraint well drained.

Later Han (25–220)

In the restoration of the Han dynasty it is notable that the chief target of Wang Mang's reforms, the large landowners, played a decisive part. The debt that the first Later Han emperor, Guangwu Di (25–58), therefore owed to the gentry made it difficult to interfere with land tenure again. As one of his strongest supporters said: 'In present times, it is not only the sovereign who selects his subjects. The subjects select their sovereign too.' These are the words of Ma Yuan, whose generalship later saved the empire from Tibetan attack and secured the far south through the annexation of northern Vietnam. A member of an influential north-western family, he suffered posthumously in the fall of his relatives in the factional struggles at court. The general's body had to wait six months for a proper burial, following death from fever in 48 while on campaign.

The enthronement in Luoyang of Guangwu Di did not put an end to civil strife. Eleven others claimed the right to imitate Wang Mang and, though by 27 the struggle began to go his way, the last pretender was removed only in 36 with the reconquest of Sichuan province. The ability of this part of the empire to resist for so long reflected a profound economic change. The transfer of the seat of the imperial government downstream from Chang'an to Luoyang, on the lower course of the Yellow River, was a tacit acknowledgement of the shift in the national centre of gravity. The Huai and the Yangzi river valleys had overtaken the province of Shaanxi, the old centre of Qin and Former Han power, as the most developed region in the empire. The temporary break-up of China during the Three Kingdoms period (222–65) can be seen as a continuation of the same process in that the southern kingdoms of Shu and Wu were sufficiently strong to challenge for many years the northern state of Wei, the rump of the Han empire.

This economic transformation is reflected in the census of 140: the northern provinces registered a fall in population, as land close to the northern frontier was abandoned under nomad pressure, but figures for all the southern provinces showed steep increases. Population in Sichuan rose by 50 per cent, in Jiangxi and Hunan it doubled, and for Guangdong in the far south the returns indicate it trebled. Migration southwards from the lower Yellow River valley was precipitated by more than Xiongnu incursion, however. The 11 million drop in population here was abetted by movements in the course of the river itself, just before and just after Wang Mang's usurpation. First the Yellow River split into two branches, no longer entering the sea only at Tianjin; it kept the old northern course and in addition sent a new southern arm to join the Huai River. Then the Yellow River largely ceased flowing on either of these courses and entered the sea just to the north of the Shandong peninsula, the position today. The disruption caused by these sudden changes would have been far-reaching and beyond the scope of the government to handle with any speed. The dikes along the new river course were not brought up to a satisfactory standard again until 70.

With the end of the civil war in 36, Guangwu Di set about restoring the old order, even to the extent of reinvesting subordinate kings. From the point of view of a centralized empire, this was a retrograde step, even though the territories they held were minuscule in comparison with the situation prior to the rebellion of the eastern vassals in 154 BC. Malcontents in these royal courts, nevertheless, plotted separatist movements: three of Guangwu Di's own sons were accused of treason, and two of these ended their lives by their own hands. One was Liu Ying, the ruler of a small kingdom in present-day Shandong province. His sponsorship of Buddhism is the earliest documented case of the new religion in China. In 65 the second Later Han emperor Ming Di (58–75) addressed his half-brother Liu Ying as one who 'recites the subtle words of Daoism and respectfully performs the gentle sacrifices of Buddha'. This characteristic mixture of the two beliefs derived as much from the circumstances of Buddhism's arrival in Han China as from the purposes to which its doctrines were initially put. Eclecticism was forced upon the classical Chinese by a shortage of scriptures, the small number of converts who could read them in the original Indian language, and competition between the different Buddhist sects. To overcome these problems Chinese pilgrims like Fa Xian later travelled to India in order to receive instruction and collect manuscripts. In 399, he took the overland route along the Silk Road, descending on to the north Indian plain from modern Afghanistan. His return journey by ship from the Ganges delta brought him home via Sri Lanka and Sumatra before landing in 414 on the coast of Shandong province.

That Liu Ying was interested in both Daoism and Buddhism, and surrounded himself with adepts as well as monks, clearly shows that his goal was not the throne but longevity or immortality. He was denounced for magical activities in 70, and Ming Di received a strong official recommendation that his half-brother should be executed for treason. The emperor refused the advice, but demoted Liu Yin and exiled him to the Yangzi valley, where he committed suicide a year afterwards. Thousands of his supposed adherents were arrested and executions continued until the end of Ming Di's reign. It is almost certain that the conspiracy existed in the mind of a suspicious emperor alone.

The capital from which Ming Di watched for signs of rebellion appears modest, almost frugal in comparison with that of the Former Han. But with a walled area of more than 7 square miles, Luoyang was, after Chang'an and Rome, the third largest walled city in the world. Like other classical Chinese cities, Luoyang was approximately rectangular in shape and oriented

Two bronze wrestling figures, dating from the fourth century BC.

Later Han Luoyang, a smaller capital than Chang'an. The main government offices were in the Southern Palace.

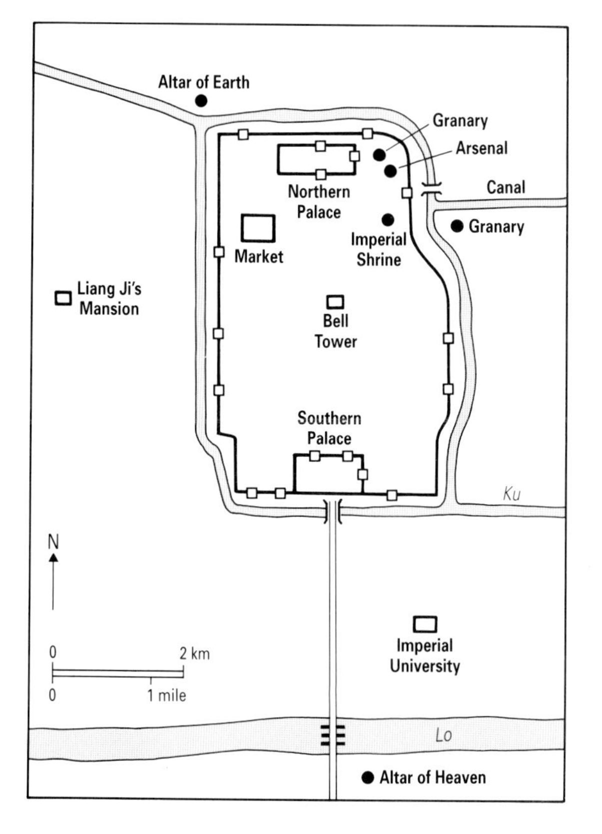

on a north–south axis. Its streets formed a rough grid and around each of its wards were walls with gates for controlling the movement of people. At a certain hour the drum tower in the centre of the city signalled the closure of these gates for the night. Although the rigidity of town planning was often relaxed, as a result of population growth or enforced movement during war or a weak dynasty, the classical Chinese city never succeeded through trade and industry in becoming sufficiently independent to challenge political, legal and religious ideas. It was never a centre of social change, for the good reason that a more deliberate pattern of foundation always left the authorities firmly in control. The same word, *cheng*, was in fact used to denote a city and a city wall. Outside Luoyang's city wall there was also a moat. The two walled palace compounds, located at opposite ends of the city, reinforced the impression of imperial authority.

Beyond the moat were sprawling suburbs, divided into wards. The total population of Luoyang was probably 500,000, of whom 30,000 were students of the imperial university. The density of population was high, and even the wealthy had a rather restricted living area, though every courtyard, no matter how small, became something of a garden by use of plants and small trees in pots. A sense of seclusion was preserved by house design, based on a central courtyard, referred to as the 'well of Heaven'. Substantial family dwellings would be laid out around two or more such courtyards. The richest inhabitants maintained a residence within the walled city as well as a mansion in the suburbs, where, among the less built-up areas, were to be found official altars, shrines, parks and the imperial tombs. Later Han Luoyang survived until 189, when, following the assassination of a general by the palace eunuchs, his troops sacked and looted the city for several weeks. The loss of the imperial library was almost as serious as the book-burning at the end of the Qin dynasty. Luoyang's ruin was so complete that the Wei dynasty (220–64), the creation of another general's son, had to rebuild everything from the ground up with the exception of the rammed-earth city walls.

None the less, the first emperors of the Later Han enjoyed the support of powerful families. This dominant group owed their influence in part to their connections with the government, whether through marriage to the imperial clan or the holding of office. But another, and more important, source of their strength was an unchallenged position on their own estates. Gradually as the central government weakened during the second century and could no longer guarantee famine relief or order in the countryside, these local élites used their armed retainers to assume more independence. After the Yellow Turbans rose in 184 they were often the sole authorities in the provinces, an incipient regionalism also reflected in the power of local religious movements. Such an upsurge in eastern China constituted the two-year struggle of the Yellow Turban rebellion, which arose at a moment when predictions of the end of the world and the coming of a new era were rife throughout the empire. The three magicians who led the rebels proclaimed the Taiping, or 'Great Peace', as a return to justice and plenty. Their enthusiastic supporters were the depressed peasantry, starving refugees remote from the prosperity enjoyed by the large landowners. While the religious inspiration of the Yellow Turbans remains obscure, the Daoist origin of the parallel Five Pecks of Grain movement (*Wudoumi dao*) is transparent. The first heavenly teacher of this sect was believed to have acquired immortality when in 156 he suddenly disappeared, leaving only his clothes behind. His successor, Zhang Lu, organized from the 180s the peasants living on the borders of Sichuan and Shaanxi provinces into a small, semi-independent state. The area was administered with such fairness by Daoist officials that on its recapture in 215 the warlord Cao Cao went out of his way to praise the good intentions behind this quasi-religious experiment. He even arranged for the ennoblement of Zhang Lu and five of his sons.

Jade was highly esteemed by the classical Chinese, as this finely carved *bi* indicates. It comes from a Later Han burial.

The progressive decline of the Later Han dynasty was not unconnected with the growth of eunuch power, itself the result of a series of child-emperors and weak adults occupying the throne. A number of powerful families vied to dominate the imperial palace, but under emperor Shundi (124–44) the Liang had acquired unprecedented power. First noted for its involvement in Ma Yuan's posthumous humiliation, this rival north-western family overcame factional reverses to ally itself through marriage to Shundi.

In 141 the emperor appointed his brother-in-law Liang Ji to head the imperial administration, an appointment which allowed him to remain supreme for nearly two decades. Not until the death of emperor Huandi's consort Liang Nuying in 159 did the all-powerful minister lose his vital ally in the imperial palace. Well before he came of age Huandi (146–68) had also been married to a member of the Liang family. Gripped by panic, Liang Ji resorted to murder and intimidation during the uncertain summer of 159. Having identified the eunuchs he could trust, the emperor commissioned them to surround Liang Ji's mansion in the western suburbs and secure the palace against a counter-attack from his kinsmen. A force of over 1,000 men surprised the minister, who chose suicide rather than disgrace. All his relatives were killed and their property confiscated. The Liang family never recovered from this blow, for which Huandi depended primarily on eunuch aid. Once the emperor showed his gratitude by formally granting all eunuchs the right to hand down noble titles and land to adopted sons, the situation was set in Luoyang for a period of eunuch rule, which lasted almost without interruption till 189.

A chance to dislodge the eunuchs in 179 was missed through the overconfidence of powerful families. Their slowness to respond to the death of an emperor without a designated heir gave the eunuchs time to gain control over the capital and place upon the throne a suitable prince. Hardly had the young Lingdi (168–89) been enthroned when a general purge was initiated against those whom the eunuchs feared. Hundreds of officials were executed and even more dismissed from office for life; many of them were exiled to Vietnam. A career in the imperial bureaucracy was henceforth a gift belonging to the eunuchs, who even insinuated their own candidates into senior military positions. But it was reluctance on the part of the armed forces to be drawn into the eunuch network of influence that led to the massacre of 189.

Later Han armies still relied on conscription for the overall defence of the empire, but professional troops were deployed for the protection of Luoyang and strategic points along the northern frontier. And local magnates supplemented with their own troops the imperial garrisons stationed in the provinces, especially after the wave of peasant uprisings from the late 170s onwards. Gone were the glorious days of Ban Chao's tenacious campaigns to reassert Chinese influence in Central Asia. For thirty years (73–102) the general had fought his way into the Western Regions as a means of keeping the military initiative on the steppe. His conquests were lost through Xiongnu attack in the 150s, the same decade as pressure was steadily applied to the north-eastern defences by the Xianbei. These nomads of Tartar descent appear to have shaken themselves free of Xiongnu subjection towards the end of the first century. 'After 168,' a chronicler sadly notes, 'no year passed without a nomad incursion.' In such uncertain circumstances it soon happened that several wealthy land-owning families produced military commanders capable of bidding for supreme power themselves. The killing of one of their number by the eunuchs, a few months after Lingdi's death in 189, finally drew the army into politics. The immediate response of the murdered general's troops was to storm the palace and slaughter every eunuch in sight.

The ultimate beneficiary of this *coup* was the soldier-poet Cao Cao (155–220), who from 196 assumed authority in all but name. The situation was almost a repeat of the Warring States period, with the Son of Heaven fulfilling a ceremonial role at Luoyang. The fiction of the Later Han was continued as long as it was politically expedient. But when in 220 Cao Cao's son Cao Pi deposed the puppet emperor and founded the Wei dynasty, his military rivals set up ruling houses of their own – Shu in the south-west at Chengdu and Wu in the south at Nanjing. With the foundation of these kingdoms, the edifice of empire began to crumble.

The Crisis of the Chinese Empire (220–316)

The forty-five years of rivalry between Wei, Wu and Shu is celebrated in the famous novel *The Romance of the Three Kingdoms* (*Sanguo Yangyi*), written in the fourteenth century by Luo Guanzhong. To the Chinese the period has always appeared romantic and legendary, so much so that from one of its generals they have derived Guan Di, the Confucian god of war. However, he was neither bloodthirsty and cowardly like Ares, nor an implacable foe like Mars; on the contrary, he was a deity who sought to prevent war. Guan Di is still regarded as the antithesis of Cao Cao, whose famous epigram was 'I would rather betray the whole world than allow the world to betray me.'

That Cao Pi was never to receive from historians an acknowledgement of legitimacy for his dynasty would probably have called forth an equally cynical remark. The Chinese preoccupation with a legitimate succession, as evident in an unmistakable transfer of the heavenly mandate to rule, led later commentators to regard the king of Shu as the true successor of the Han. He was after all a member of the deposed imperial clan, and his regime in Chengdu endured almost as long as its rivals, not falling to Wei attack until 263. By then Cao Cao's descendants were as impotent as the last Later Han emperors, the dominant family in northern China being the Sima. In 265 Sima Yan actually declared himself the founder of a new dynasty, the Western Jin.

Before the rise of the Sima family, and its temporary reunification of China, a triangular struggle took place between the Three Kingdoms. Despite its relative weakness in terms of population, Shu pursued an aggressive policy towards both its southern neighbour Wu and Wei, the strongest state of the three. Behind its early successes lay the genius of Zhu Geliang (181–234), an inventor as well as a man of action. His ability to master apparently insoluble problems has made him something of a legend. Three examples should suffice to illustrate his quick-wittedness. When in 222 the Shu king chose to ignore Zhu Geliang's advice and launch an ill-prepared attack on Wu, the minister is said to have built on the line of his inevitable retreat a wonderful city, modelled on a battle array. The maze-like construction baffled the victorious army of Wu,

Liu Bei's chief minister, Zhu Geliang, whose efficiency in war and diplomacy ensured the survival of the Shu state. He was also a distinguished mathematician and inventor.

which turned back rather than risk disaster in exploring its layout. Five years later, after the collapse of the Shu army during an invasion of Wei, Zhu Geliang saved the day by means of a similar ruse. He ordered the gates of the city into which his men had fled to be thrown open, while conspicuously on the undefended battlements he strummed a lute. So at odds with the military situation was the joy of the music that the Wei commander decided to withdraw in case a trap was being set. The difficult northern campaign had been made possible only by a third instance of Zhu Geliang's ingenuity, the invention of the wheelbarrow. These 'wooden oxen and running horses' had permitted the transport of military supplies over mountainous terrain.

The struggle between the Three Kingdoms was ended in 280 by the Western Jin dynasty through the defeat of Wu. The first Western Jin emperor, Sima Yan, was another northern general in the mould of Cao Cao, but he outdid him by briefly achieving the reunification of the whole country. Under his direction, the ancient heartland of China, the original Middle Kingdom, reasserted its political authority over the newly developing areas in the south and south-western provinces. What facilitated this triumph was a greater concentration on agricultural productivity and water transport as a means of strengthening military power. Extra manpower also came from barbarian migrants who were permitted to settle in large numbers within the Great Wall. This policy of barbarian settlement was to have at last the dire consequences it had for the western provinces of the Roman empire. But by waging a war of economic attrition alongside an orthodox military campaign the Western Jin was able to emerge victorious.

The Western Jin dynasty lasted only till 316, the year in which most of the northern provinces passed into the hands of people from the steppe, and the remnants of Sima Yan's line fled southwards to Nanjing, where they founded the Eastern Jin dynasty (317–420). A combination of pressures caused this breakdown of the empire and ensured that China was divided for almost three centuries. Encroachment from nomads had worried Chinese emperors from the start of the Former Han, but the more conciliatory policy forced upon the Later Han really opened the frontier to invaders, because the price of employing friendly barbarians as allies was often their settlement of key areas within the empire itself. A name given to some of these peoples in the Later Han period indicates their purpose: they were *baosai*, or 'frontier-guarding barbarians'. As far as possible the various tribes were dispersed into small groups, each under the supervision of a Chinese official, but in times of civil strife opposing sides were tempted to call upon friendly barbarians for support. This happened during the so-called Disturbance of the Eight Princes, a struggle between members of the Sima family which continued without remission from 291 till 306. It proved the undoing of the dynasty once Xiongnu, Xianbei, Qiang and other nomadic peoples joined the fray. In 311 Luoyang was sacked and Sima Yan's successor captured, and then in 316 the last Western Jin emperor was taken prisoner on the fall of Chang'an.

Sima Yan himself must bear some responsibility for the disaster, since he had made the fatal error of allowing his twenty-five sons to govern separate territories. These princes had imperial officials in their courts and they were supposed to come forward, like other governors, with an army in support of the central authority whenever a crisis occurred. A number of them, however, forged alliances beyond their territories as part of the intrigue surrounding the throne after Sima Yan's death in 290. Their mutual antagonisms weakened the imperial system to such an extent that it fragmented into a number of separate states. Nevertheless, the surviving imperial house at Nanjing, the Eastern Jin, held its own against further nomad advance at the battle of Feishui. There in 383 the better discipline and equipment of a small Chinese army secured a decisive victory over an infantry force of 600,000 accompanied by 270,000 horsemen. This engagement drew a line of partition along the northern boundary of the wet-rice growing area, countryside unsuited to the mobile tactics of the nomads.

War and External Relations

China's attitude towards its neighbours was essentially defensive. The Great Wall came to epitomize a state of mind which regarded war as a necessary evil. 'An army is kept for 1,000 days to be used on one,' went an old saying. Down to 221 BC the crescendo of fighting between the feudal states kept rising, but once central power had been won on the battlefield the unity of the empire was maintained as much by a preference for peace as by the readiness of the army. The daring overthrow of the Qin dynasty in the first peasant rebellion of Chinese history owed something to the countryman's distaste for the military. Qin despotism miscalculated the degree of oppression the people would stand. It had also chosen to ignore the non-violent doctrines of Confucianism. A prince should attain his ends without violence, Confucius always maintained. This optimistic belief in the effect of a ruler's virtuous conduct on his subjects made any resort to force an admission of failure. Hence the salutory influence of Confucian officials on the progress of imperial campaigns. Such wars were not easy to glorify because ideally they should never have taken place. For this reason the cynicism of Cao Cao rankled at the end of the Later Han dynasty. The warlord in 196 showed utter contempt for the sufferings caused by his forcible takeover of power. 'Unexpectedly,' a chronicler notes, 'Heaven showed no regret for his evil-doing, and one disaster followed another.'

An Intensification of Warfare

As the name suggests the Warring States period (481–221 BC) witnessed an unprecedented bout of internecine conflict among the feudal powers which then constituted the Middle Kingdom. That this rivalry also gave rise to the oldest surviving military treatise in the world is a sign of the intense contemporary preoccupation with armed solutions to the political problem of instability. In his *Art of War* (*Bingfa*), Sun Zi was indeed the first known person to formulate a rational basis for the planning and conduct of military operations. Because war was of vital importance to a state, Sun Zi wrote a systematic guide for feudal rulers in much the same way as philosophers offered advice on administration and justice. But in spite of the belligerence of the times, the *Bingfa* makes plain how an engagement on the battlefield is only one part of warfare and not even the preferred part. The aim of the skilled strategist is rather the overcoming of an opponent without the clash of arms. For Sun Zi's restraint stems primarily from an understanding of the variety of factors involved in any campaign: material, psychological and economic. 'Numbers alone,' he shrewdly comments, 'confer no advantage.'

The singular emphasis placed on morale in the *Bingfa* was doubtless intended as a check on a commander's readiness to accept casualties. Reliance on force, no matter how energetically delivered, led to an unacceptable tally of slaughter and destruction. It fell far short of the ideal victory, the surrender of an enemy with little loss of life, or even none at all. 'A victor always defeats a demoralized foe.' Apart from the risk of frittering away a state's armed forces in unnecessary battles, the most economical means of attaining a military advantage is praised because excessive violence might endanger the feudal order itself. Although the mannered skirmishes of the aristocracy had already given way to a complexity of siege and manoeuvre, Sun Zi never believed that large-scale operations should be allowed to end in carnage. The business of war was simply too difficult and too dangerous to be left to amateurs.

The professionalization of command, the feature of the Warring States period so well documented by Sun Zi's treatise, ran parallel to the increased size of armies. Both the large states of Qin and Chu were capable of putting 1 million soldiers into the field. Battles turned into massive infantry engagements, with armoured columns of foot-soldiers supported by crossbowmen, spearmen, cavalry and chariots. The archaeological excavations at Mount Li, the site of the First Emperor's mausoleum, have revealed how elaborate arms and armour became. Several thousand life-sized terracotta warriors and horses were placed there between 221 and 209 BC in subterranean chambers, apparently disposed in battle formation. Columns of infantrymen are modelled wearing iron-mail coats, even the heads of the rivets being shown. Such armour represented a major improvement on the padded jackets or treated sharkskin and animal hide used in the lifetime of Huan, the early defender of China praised by Confucius. Most significant of all, though, is the vanguard of the terracotta army – three ranks of crossbowmen whose weapons had an estimated range of 600 feet. The heavy arrows they fired would have swiftly turned into colanders the shields carried by contemporary Indian, Macedonian or Roman soldiers.

Crossbowmen from the front rows of the terracotta warriors in Pit No. 1 at Mount Li. They wore lightweight clothing.

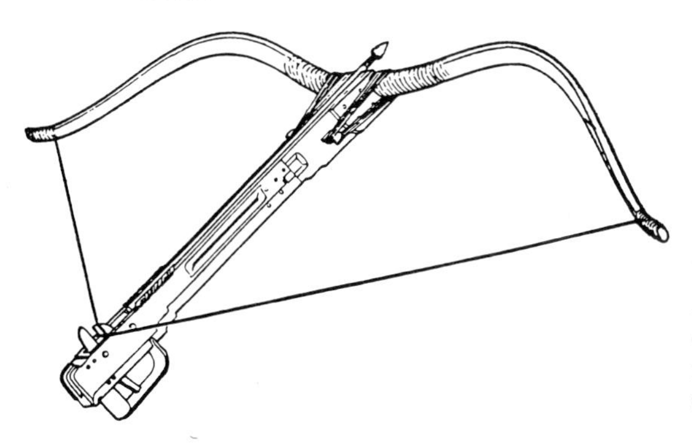

Chinese crossbow.

The sharpshooters in the infantry pit at Mount Li are shown wearing light cotton clothes, because they acted as fast-moving, long-range fighters – the classical Chinese equivalent of artillery. They would have dispatched their arrows from a safe distance, keeping well away from hand-to-hand engagements, once contact with the enemy had been made. The three ranks would have taken turns at firing, so as to keep up a continuous stream of arrows. Having thus disrupted the enemy front rank, the armoured infantry immediately behind the crossbowmen would have gone into the attack. According to chronicles,

> Qin foot-soldiers wore no helmets and charged opponents with untold ferocity. Whereas the infantry regiments of the other feudal states when they joined battle wore heavy armour which was clumsy and impeded their movements, Qin soldiers threw away their coats of mail and rushed straight into the thick of the fighting.

A toggle near the left shoulder of their armoured jackets obviously permitted this swift removal of the plated iron, as soon as the enemy was so close that continued crossbow fire became impossible for either side.

In Pit No. 1 at Mount Li the crossbowmen and armoured infantry seem to have been directed by non-commissioned officers riding in six chariots a short way back in each column. They were pulled by four terracotta horses and manned by a charioteer and a guard in addition to the junior officer. The guard would have wielded a long bamboo lance in order to stop any enemy soldiers cutting off the heads of the horses. Two of the six chariots, however, had a special function. They were command vehicles, equipped with drums and bells to signal any change necessary in tactics. Referring to the urgent need to keep control of forces during an engagement, Sun Zi comments: 'Gongs and drums, banners and flags are employed to focus the attention of troops. When soldiers are united by these signals, the bravest cannot advance alone, nor can the cowardly withdraw. This is the art of handling a host.'

Disciplined and well-trained regulars formed the nuclei of Warring States armies, and from their ranks were drawn the shock troops who spearheaded the attack in the increasingly bitter battles which took place right down to the triumph of Qin in 221 BC. The harsh military code of the times entitled an officer to behead any soldier. The clear expectation was that discipline would be accepted by the peasant levies called upon for every campaign. But it did not always mean that rulers were as controlled themselves in the management of warfare.

In one famous instance, the final triumph in 223 BC of Qin over its great rival Chu, the veteran general Wang Chien had to contend with an anxious and impatient ruler. The future First Emperor had almost brought Qin to the brink of disaster by entrusting a previous campaign against Chu to an inexperienced general, for no other reason than that he promised to win with an army of 200,000 men, one-third of the number which Wang Chien said was required. The mauling suffered by the expeditionary force compelled the strong-willed ruler to beg the old soldier for help. When the veteran agreed to come out of retirement on condition that the size of his army should be 600,000 men, the news of Wang Chien's appointment attracted as many to the colours within a matter of days. Even then the future First Emperor accompanied the commander on his march south and, after he crossed into Chu, sent letters every day to urge his success. This pressure was quite at odds with his strategy because Wang Chien knew that in defending their homes Chu soldiers would prove most formidable on the battlefield. He just could not risk an uncertain decision on enemy soil. Taking a leaf out of the *Bingfa*, therefore, Wang Chien decided to fain indifference to action. He accordingly entrenched his army in a strongly fortified camp, and there behaved as though his men had not come for the serious purpose of war, but rather for a prolonged holiday. They swam, sang and feasted. In the meantime, the Chu army began to look with contempt upon the invaders, slowly slackening its discipline and losing its alertness. As soon as Wang Chien perceived the moment to strike had arrived, he sent his forces crashing into the relaxed Chu army and secured an overwhelming victory. As Sun Zi believed, 'Those skilled in war avoid the enemy when his spirit is keen and attack him when it is sluggish and his soldiers homesick.'

An imperial tally. Qin armies would accept an order only when both parts of a tally fitted together.

Although the ruthlessness of Qin in warfare was a factor in the unification of China, the drive of the First Emperor cannot alone explain the falling behind of Chu in the race for supremacy. Chu was a state endowed with a mild climate, better suited to intensive agriculture – a considerable advantage when the call-up of peasant armies could have an adverse effect on the production of foodstuffs. Yet, there was not in Chu any determined exploitation of this basic resource. Possibly the loess soil of northern Qin, with the consequent importance of irrigation, comprised the lever by which its ruler moved the people as a united force, whereas the ruler of Chu required less social cohesion in order to secure a reliable agricultural surplus. With a feudal order as shallowly founded as in Qin, Chu also inclined towards Legalist doctrines, but no Shang Yang appeared to give the great southern state an organization robust enough to withstand the political storms raging at the time. Though not until after the conquest of Chu in 223 BC could Qin be certain of final victory, the growing strength of its forces was signalled in a series of defeats inflicted on Chu during the earlier campaigns of 280 and 278 BC, which resulted in the annexation of large tracts of the middle Yangzi valley.

The intensification of warfare described so far has concerned the extension of Qin power over China till, in 221 BC, it incorporated all the feudal states within a unified empire. The Warring States period, however, saw another equally important increase in military activity, aimed at the consolidation of the northern frontier. Again it is the First Emperor who is associated with the Great Wall, built to separate the steppe from the sown, but the defences he commissioned were really a rationalization of the rammed-earth walls already thrown up by the feudal states. Many walls had been built between them, and especially along the northern frontier against the nomads. It can indeed be argued that the First Emperor largely joined together the frontier walls belonging to conquered states. The patent exception was the pushing north of the northern defences to include the Ordos desert, a great task accomplished by Meng Tian shortly after 214 BC. Argument still continues over the exact line this general's new defence took, and there is even a suggestion that he repaired an existing wall built by the state of

Zhao. The remorse felt by Meng Tian himself four years later, on his own death, for having injured the earth by his wall-building would suggest otherwise. 'Indeed I have a crime for which to die,' he said when he eventually complied with the forged order of the recently deceased First Emperor and committed suicide.

The Defences of the Han Empire

One of the first acts of Gaozu, the founder of the Han dynasty, was to proclaim a general amnesty, together with a demobilization of troops. The edict of 202 BC was intended to win the loyalty of a people exhausted by the civil war which had followed the overthrow of the Qin empire. It effectively put China on the defensive, a military stance soon reinforced by the *heqin* policy: namely, 'friendly and peaceful relations' with the Xiongnu nomads who dominated the steppelands beyond the northern frontier. This change of approach from the Qin offensive was necessitated by the near disaster at Pingcheng, where in 200 BC Gaozu was lucky to escape capture, after his forces numbering over 300,000 men were encircled by the mobile nomads. The realization that the Xiongnu could not easily be defeated in a set-piece battle beyond the line of the northern defences led the Former Han emperors to develop policies that sought to contain the threat by a mixture of diplomacy and force. Essentially it meant the establishment of stable foreign relations, the payment of subsidies to unaggressive nomad kings and the tolerance of international trade. One reason for the Chinese acceptance of an armed truce with the nomads was the unity achieved by the Xiongnu, through the rise of a supreme ruler, the so-called *shanyu*. There was at this moment no scope for the Later Han policy of playing one tribal group off against another.

A ceremonial brooch derived from a nomad design. Such brooches were presented as gifts to Xiongnu chieftains by the Former Han emperors.

The *heqin* policy was not a lasting success. Hostilities continued while it was in effect and, by the accession of Wu Di in 140 BC, it was accepted that conciliation would have to be abandoned. The annual gifts of silk, wine, rice and silver were no longer being balanced by commensurate saving on military expenditure. Nomad raids still cost the imperial exchequer dear. In 134 BC Wu Di tried without success to ambush the *shanyu* and full-scale war followed soon afterwards. The emperor (whose name means 'Warrior Ruler') launched a series of campaigns designed to outflank and ultimately crush the Xiongnu. The Ordos was cleared, the Xiongnu driven deep into the Gobi, and then Han forces moved westwards into the Tarim basin. In 121 BC General Huo Quling (died 116 BC) captured, after a six-day advance across the steppe with a cavalry force, the *shanyu* and 40,000 of his followers. But such victories were gained at an enormous cost in terms of human and animal losses. Some 100,000 Chinese soldiers died and twice as many horses, while the Xiongnu seemed for ever capable of reviving as a potent enemy. A part of the problem for the imperial armies was the terrain on which the campaign was fought. Supplies of food, weapons and fuel to deal with the winter cold proved impossible in the quantities necessary to sustain a long campaign.

The difficulty of keeping a force going on the steppe is graphically illustrated in the surrender of one of the best Han field commanders, Li Ling. Bereft of cavalry support, Li Ling managed with only 5,000 infantrymen to keep at bay a vastly superior force of nomads. He positioned his crossbowmen behind a wall of shields and spears so that their arrows could outrange those shot from Xiongnu bows. The effect was devastating, and Li Ling almost showed that properly armed foot-soldiers could defeat horse-archers. But without adequate food provisions and with crossbow bolts running out, he ordered his men to find their way back to the Great Wall as best they could. Only 400 soldiers reached the safety of its gateways, Li Ling himself being taken prisoner. When Wu Di heard of this in late 99 BC he was furious that the commander had not fallen in battle. Sima Qian wrote a memorandum defending Li Ling, pointing out how the general had fought as long as possible, but the emperor was encouraged by the historian's rivals at court to regard the opinion unfavourably; the result was the charge of attempting to deceive the throne, a perfunctory trial and castration. A year later, Wu Di recognized that he had been to blame for not sending a relief column to aid Li Ling, and he sent for the general, but the latter would not return to China. Eventually Li Ling's family were exterminated.

The expansion of Han China to Central Asia was a direct result of conflict with the Xiongnu. In a search for nomad allies and horses, Chinese forces pressed westwards, reaching Ferghana in 101 BC. There Wu Di found the larger mounts he was seeking for his armoured cavalrymen, and a protectorate was declared over the whole of the Tarim basin. Known as Xiyu, 'the Western Regions', the area remained friendly to the Chinese as long as they kept the upper hand over the Xiongnu. The maintenance of influence in this remote area involved a heavy outlay of resources, for earthern defences had to be extended far beyond the limits of the Great Wall built in the reign of the First Emperor. The new line led westwards as far as Dunhuang, almost 1,800 miles west of the Yellow Sea. In the Western Regions themselves the Han yoke appears to have been light.

> Those who were submissive from the very beginning received gifts and official seals as an imperial favour, but those who surrendered after a fight were punished. Agricultural garrisons were set up in fertile places and post-stations built on the main highways. Messengers and merchants travelled freely, and commerce flourished ... [along what became known as the Silk Road.]

The oasis states of the Tarim basin were left to their own devices, provided they gave no aid to the Xiongnu.

In the north-east a more direct approach was tried, a number of commanderies being formed on the Korean peninsula between 109 and 106 BC. But the military objective remained the same – the denial of supplies to the Xiongnu. Intervention in Korea was justified on the grounds that the local rulers were harbouring too many Chinese rebels. Certainly the first Korean state, Choson, would seem to have been strengthened by an influx of settlers; its throne was occupied by descendants of a Chinese refugee named Wei Man, in Korean Wiman. The introduction of an iron industry by Wiman gave Choson a distinct advantage over rival kingdoms to the south, a situation the Han emperors were at first content to tolerate. Fear of an alliance between Choson and the Xiongnu caused Wu Di to act in 109 BC. Following the surrender of its capital at Pyongyang, the core of Choson became the commandery of Lolang, with a population of over 400,000.

Yet no emperor could afford a prolonged war lest the burden on the people caused a rebellion like the one that overthrew the Qin dynasty. Chinese foreign policy was always dictated during the early empire by the need to contain the northern nomads, never by any ambition for foreign conquests. By 91 BC even Wu Di had to admit that further campaigning was beyond the capacity of the imperial exchequer. Thus the Xiongnu raid of 87 BC, the year of Wu Di's death, was not followed by an offensive on the steppe. Instead of conducting a punitive strike, the troops stationed along the Great Wall were merely set to renewing the defences, repairing watchtowers and fortresses. Relief was not to come from these bastions, however. In 53 BC the Xiongnu were so divided by tribal antagonisms that the *shanyu* chose to make peace with the Han emperor, a welcome state of affairs that was destined to endure for nearly half a century.

While foreign relations on the northern frontier returned to the presentation of gifts, in a revived version of the *heqin*, the authority of the Han emperors was more easily imposed elsewhere. In the far south Nan Yue became part of the empire. Despite the brevity of its rule, the Qin dynasty had advanced into the West River valley, and in 196 BC Gaozu confirmed the client status of the kingdom of Nan Yue established there, in what is now Guangdong province. In 113 BC the queen dowager, herself a Chinese married to a prince who had attended the imperial court at Chang'an, endeavoured to negotiate the admission of Nan Yue to the empire on the same basis as the feudal kingdoms that had existed since the foundation of the Han dynasty. The reaction of the local aristocracy against this move, however, cost the queen dowager her life, a provocation Wu Di could not leave unanswered. In 112 BC imperial armies swiftly overran Nan Yue, which was then divided into four commanderies and administered directly. Four other commanderies were also established as a result of the campaign, covering the present-day Chinese borderlands with Vietnam, a substantial part of north Vietnam and the island of Hainan. But the two off-shore commanderies proved beyond the power of the Han; they were abandoned in 82 and 46 BC respectively.

One reason behind the queen dowager's attempted amalgamation of Nan Yue with the Chinese empire was the warlike activities of the neighbouring state of Min Yue, located to the north-east in the modern province of Fujian. Shut off from the interior of China by mountain ranges, the people living in Min Yue were able to maintain their independence throughout the period of the Han empire. Only internal dissension in Min Yue saved Nan Yue from an all-out assault. To the south-west the petty kingdoms along the edge of the Tibetan highlands offered a lesser threat to both Nan Yue and the Han empire. The most notable power, Dian, submitted to the Son of Heaven and became a subject ally. Centred in the eastern part of the Yunnan plateau, the Dian king ruled over a diverse population, including among its constituent tribes the ancestors of the modern Thai. An abortive military expedition sent to these parts by the feudal state of Chu between 339 and 328 BC had ended with the establishment of Dian as an independent kingdom under a Chinese house. One of the officers who accompanied the Chu force stayed on to rule from a capital sited on the shores of Lake Dian.

The recent discovery of a solid gold seal, in all probability the one Wu Di granted to the Dian king, is evidence of standard Chinese practice in foreign affairs. The acceptance of a seal inscribed in Chinese characters, acknowledging the authority of one's right to rule, was part and parcel of the tributary system gradually built up along the imperial borders. But *gong*, or 'tribute', was not understood narrowly as the presentation of foreign products to the imperial court as a token of political submission, because the Chinese themselves were also regarded as tributaries through the taxes they paid. Rather the exchange of royal gifts between Dian and Chang'an was intended to bind the client state to the empire in an orderly manner. Although Chinese emperors did not seek to interfere with the domestic affairs of vassals as a rule, imperial envoys were often passing from one ally to another, so that the imperial court was kept informed of any dangerous developments. After the turmoil of the Warring States and the Qin periods, the Han occupants of the dragon throne in general desired peace, with the notable exception of Wu Di. Though the *heqin* may have become a synonym for appeasement, Wu Di's continuous campaigning was always a byword for a policy of unrestrained warfare which brought the empire almost to ruin.

Because the Later Han faced very different external problems to the Former Han there was an opportunity for foreign policy that avoided appeasement as well as militarism. In spite of the Xiongnu taking advantage of the civil strife that followed the fall of Wang Mang in AD 23, and causing in consequence a serious depopulation of borderlands in what today is Shanxi province, the nomads soon permanently split into two mutually antagonistic groups, known as the northern and southern Xiongnu. This fortunate occurrence for China brought the southern Xiongnu into the tributary system, thus forming a buffer state immediately beyond the Great Wall. Inside or on the northern frontier the Later Han emperors in fact settled a number of barbarian peoples besides the Hunnish Xiongnu. These included the Wuhan, who spoke an Indo-European language, their cousins the Qiang, and the Xianbei Tartars. Thus the immediate concern at Luoyang was not to advance the imperial borders but how to embrace all these semi-sinicized tribesmen within the empire without disturbing the peace. Guangwu Di, the first emperor of the Later Han, refused to countenance military operations on the steppe, telling his generals that China had enough internal troubles to worry about without adding foreign wars to the cost of reconstruction. Wherever feasible, border troops were stationed as agricultural garrisons (*juntian*), self-supporting units capable of holding the first line of defence until reinforcements arrived. This method of control had been tried in the Western Regions under the Former Han (206 BC–AD 9), but for the Later Han (25–220) these outposts proved too remote to hold. Only

Xiyu, the Western Regions.

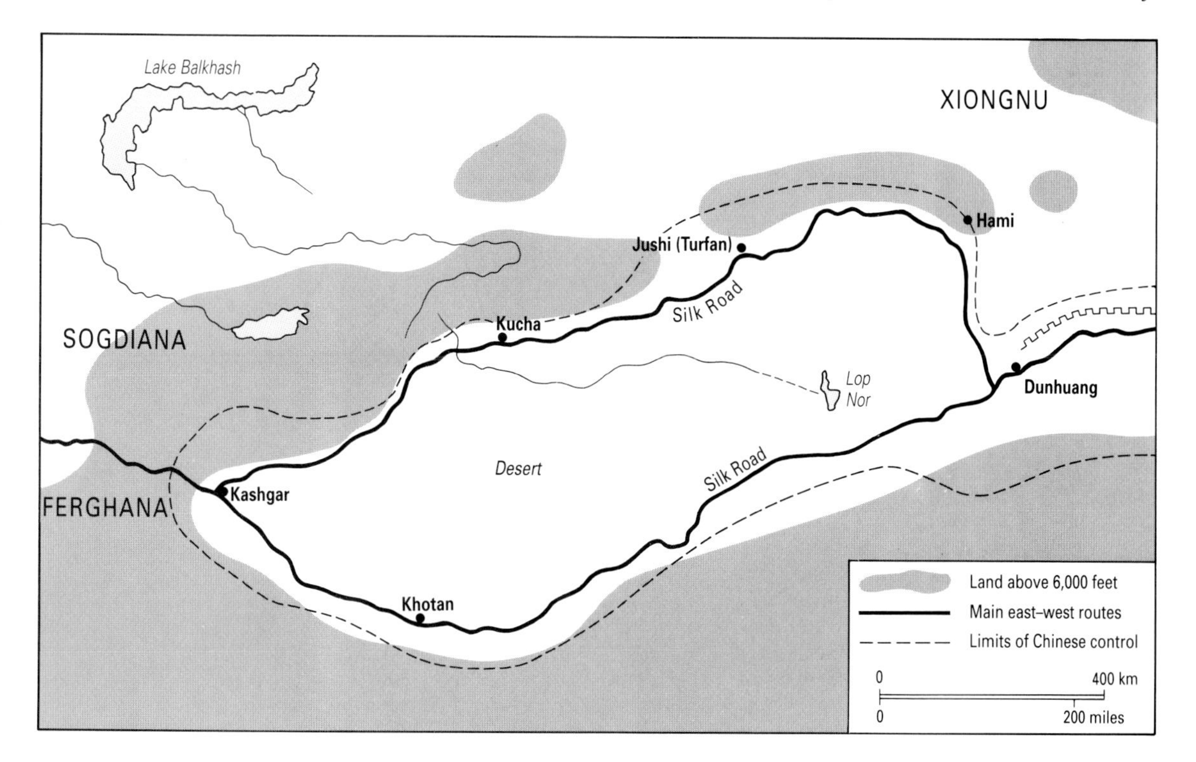

the fertile lands around Hami were able to support a large enough force, although even this oasis was never continuously in Chinese hands.

General Ban Chao, the brother of the historian Ban Gu, had to reassert Han authority at Hami in the 70s. For thirty years Ban Chao used diplomacy and, when necessary, military action to impose Chinese suzerainty over the oasis states of the Western Regions. He relinquished the post of protector-general (*duhu*) only at his own request in 102, months before he died. During his tenure of office Ban Chao had to deal not only with nomads and local rulers but also, in 90, with the Kuṣāṇas, who had just carved out a great realm extending from north-west India to Sogdia. Following his victory over the Kuṣāṇas, Ban Chao advanced from his headquarters at Kucha with an army to the eastern shores of the Caspian, the closest the Chinese ever got to the Roman empire. Contact between China and Rome was never direct in the classical era, notwithstanding the so-called Roman embassy of Marcus Aurelius. Its members in 166 were presumably merchants from Da Qin, Roman Syria, and the gifts they presented at Luoyang – elephant tusks, rhinoceros horn and tortoise shell – aroused little admiration, since the Chinese imported these commodities regularly from South-East Asia. Although few Roman merchants can have reached Han China, silk was an article of luxury apparel in Rome from the early days of the empire. The Chinese seem to have been aware of the potential value of exported surplus silk, which they also knew passed through the hands of the Parthians. These determined middlemen made sure that direct trade contacts between the Mediterranean and East Asia never evolved. But the Parthians could not disrupt the sea route via India, which acted as an entrepôt for east–west trade in luxuries. The merchants who ostensibly arrived from Rome in 166 took this route, buying their exotic presents in one of its ports.

A curious incident at Jushi, possibly Turfan, may have been the only occasion on which Chinese and Roman soldiers met face to face. There in 36 BC an imperial force captured a fortification in which a Xiongnu leader had taken refuge. Ban Gu records how

> from a distance the Chinese army could see the coloured banners of the *shanyu* and several hundred armed men positioned on the walls. More than 100 horsemen had emerged from the gate and were galloping back and forth in front of the defences. More than 100 foot-soldiers, lined up on either side of the gate in a fish-scale formation, were practising military drill.

It is suggested that the 'fish-scale formation', the only known use of the term *yulinjen* in Chinese documents, was the Roman *testudo*, the locking of legionary shields as a protection from arrows and spears. If this were so, then the mercenary detachment of Romans at Jushi could have been survivors of the 10,000 prisoners taken by the Parthians in 53 BC at the battle of Carrhae. Some of these soldiers are known to have been settled in the eastern territories of Parthia. A clinching piece of evidence is said to be the 'double palisade of wood' surrounding Jushi, a standard feature of Roman fortification. After its capture, the Chinese themselves resettled the surrendered Romans, if such they were, in another frontier town. They had stopped fighting, as professional soldiers did in classical times, when their Xiongnu employer fell.

Whatever the truth behind the story, the policy of redeploying the captives prefigured the Later Han tactic of *yiyu fayu*, or 'using the barbarians to attack the barbarians'. Not entirely a new method of defence, the Later Han emperors came increasingly to rely upon friendly tribesmen to garrison stretches of the northern frontier. Towards the end of the Han empire and in the era of the Three Kingdoms (221–65), they even played an important role in civil conflicts. Yet for a century or more the *yiyu fayu* policy gave China a respite from nomad attack. When the Xianbei Tartars defeated the northern Xiongnu in 88, a memorial to the throne could congratulate the emperor for having won a war without losing a single Chinese soldier. What the writer of the official praise tactfully did not mention was the bestowal of imperial largesse expected by the Xianbei leader as a reward. Until 150 the balance of power on the steppe favoured China, and the domination of Central Asia by the two empires of the Han and the Kuṣāṇa guaranteed the safety of caravans along the Silk Road. That year, however, a resurgent Xiongnu wrested the Western Regions from Chinese control.

Imperial Decline

The collapse of dynastic power at the close of the Han empire was brought about by a number of factors, one of which was the rise of regional warlords. Although the rebellion of the Yellow Turbans (184–6) was put down, it left the empire sorely disrupted and the dynasty weakened. More than at the restoration of the Later Han, following the usurpation of Wang Mang, the emperor was dependent upon the support of powerful families, whose armed retainers maintained order in the countryside. A typical tomb find of this period is a terracotta model of a fortified house, a prerequisite for the survival of a land-owning family. After 190 the existence of the dynasty was merely nominal, and power lay with regional commanders, who organized increasingly for civil war. The fragmentation of China into the Three Kingdoms resulted from the struggle between the most successful of their number: Cao Cao (155–220), Liu Bei (161–223), a relative of the imperial family, and Sun Quan (185–252).

The immediate crisis for the Later Han in 189 was the selection of a successor to Lingdi, the emperor placed on the throne by the eunuchs over two decades earlier. Any prince would be a focal point of conflicting interests: those of the eunuchs, the empress's family, Lingdi's mother, the officials, and the warlords. In the event a thirteen-year-old was briefly enthroned as Shaodi. Not even the support of generals stationed close to Luoyang was enough to keep Shaodi safe from the eunuchs, who dared to behead the senior commander himself in late 189. Possibly they intended to repeat their seizure of power on the accession of Lingdi, but the situation in the capital was not the same as in 168. This time the soldiers were in no mood to obey any orders issued by the eunuchs in the young emperor's name. They stormed the imperial palace, putting 2,000 eunuchs to the sword. The fugitive emperor was found hiding in the mountains north of Luoyang by Dong Zhuo, one of the regional commanders responsible for defeating the Yellow Turbans. Taking the wretched Shaodi with him, Dong Zhuo marched on Luoyang and drove off his military rivals. Within days he had deposed Shaodi and set up the eight-year-old Xiandi (189–220) in his stead. The last Later Han emperor thus became a creature of warlords rather than eunuchs.

Opposition was centred in the commanderies to the east of the capital. There several commanders, including Cao Cao, gathered soldiers together and formed a loose coalition against Dong Zhuo. What should happen after his defeat does not seem to have been decided beforehand. A restoration of Shaodi was impossible because Dong Zhuo took the precaution of killing him in early 190. Emperor Xiandi had already been sent to the old capital Chang'an, Dong Zhou's regional base. Attacks by coalition forces, however, overcame the emperor's captor, who was killed in 192. Once Dong Zhuo was removed from the scene, his opponents had nothing to unite them any longer, and they manoeuvred for power themselves. Only the existence of a legitimate bearer of the imperial title deterred the warlords from founding new dynasties. On his return to Luoyang in 196 Xiandi was quickly taken into custody by Cao Cao. Realizing the time was not right for his disposition, Cao Cao let the Later Han dynasty continue in name, while he built up his own military position. The warlord did this by settling soldiers on agricultural land in exchange for regular payment of grain as taxes. Ostensibly a servant of the emperor, Cao Cao used the grain surplus to make himself master of north China. In 208 he was strong enough to move south against Sun Qian, whose power was centred in the lower Yangzi River valley. But at the battle of the Red Cliffs the superior nautical skills of the southerners won the day; Cao Cao's ships were burned and his troops defeated.

The reverse restricted the authority of Cao Cao to the north, leaving the south in Sun Qian's hands and the south-west in those of Liu Bei. When in 220 Cao Cao's son finally deposed Xiandi and founded Wei, Sun Qian set up the rival kingdom of Wu and Liu Bei that of Shu. The half-century of conflict between these Three Kingdoms was a continuation of warlord politics, a chaotic state of affairs that hardly ceased during the Western Jin dynasty, which saw in 280 the temporary reunification of the empire. Quarrels among the imperial princes eventually opened the way for a nomad takeover of north China. Like small-scale warlords, all twenty-five of them had been invested with territories to govern.

With almost continual fighting from 189 onwards, there could be no question of any far-reaching foreign policy. The northern frontier was saved from serious attack by the westward movement of many Xiongnu tribes, whose eventual arrival in Europe as the Huns did so much to destroy Roman power. Except for minor border raids, the security of north China appeared at first to be assured, but an internal threat was forming in the growing employment of barbarian auxiliaries. Xianbei and Xiongnu contingents fought out their tribal animosities as allies of contending warlords, till in 316 they dominated great tracts of the empire in their own right. That year the cities of Chang'an and Luoyang both fell to their arms.

On the southern frontier the situation was somewhat different. A Vietnamese rebellion in 40 had been followed by the abolition of the native aristocracy and the substitution of Chinese customs of ownership for what appears to have been a system of matrilineal inheritance. General Ma Yuan appreciated that the southern frontier could not be made secure without economic progress. 'Wherever he passed,' the records relate, 'Ma Yuan promptly set up prefectures and districts to govern walled towns and their environs, and dug ditches to irrigate the fields in order to sustain the people living in those places.' Garrisons of soldiers protected the imperial officials who were directly responsible for implementing the regulations by which Ma Yuan bound the Vietnamese people to the empire. The result was that they came more and more under Chinese cultural influence, and many intermarried with the flood of Chinese immigrants then pouring into the frontier commanderies. But the influence of China penetrated no further south than Hué, until an independent Vietnam much later started to expand in that direction at the expense of the Indianized kingdom of Champa. This loosely organized state first attacked the Chinese commandery of Rinan in 399.

Economy and Society

The social and economic developments of the Warring States period (481–221 BC) which laid the foundation for the Chinese empire took place on a regional scale in a number of independent states. But the nature of these changes was such as to encourage unification and the evolution of a centralized state run on bureaucratic lines. In place of a feudal structure, with sharp divisions between a hereditary nobility and the peasantry, a more complex society developed, so that all sections became the emperor's subjects, likewise divided, but by less insurmountable barriers than birth. Under the Former Han (206 BC–AD 9) the last vestiges of feudalism disappeared and the political structure began to assume a pattern that was to serve China down until 1911, when the empire was overthrown and a republic set up. The twin pillars of this new society, which supported

A liquid container in the form of a ram. It was excavated during the 1970s at Xianyang, the site of the Qin capital.

the world's largest enduring state, were a progressively more privileged bureaucracy, closely connected with the land-owning class, and the great multitude of farmers, no longer tied to a feudal lord but now liable to taxation, labour on public works and military service.

Improvements in Agriculture

Notable changes in the countryside, the core of the Chinese economy, were caused through the introduction of iron implements and the application of animal power to cultivation using the plough, together with the widespread development of flood control and irrigation works. Although the importance of iron-working was recognized by the government under the Former Han emperors, there were misgivings among Confucian officials about the state monopoly introduced in 119 BC by Wu Di. This exchange of views is recorded in the *Yantielun, Discourses on Salt and Iron.*

GRAND SECRETARY: Now the government manufactures agricultural implements so that the people can pursue the fundamental occupation of tillage, and not engage in secondary occupations. Thus the problem of hunger is overcome. Consider then the harm to the empire of abolishing the monopoly?
WORTHIES: Agriculture is the great enterprise of the world, and iron implements are the great appliances of the people. When tools are easy to use, the necessary toil is less and the results better. The farmer enjoys his work and harvests are bountiful. When tools are inadequate, the fields are wasted and the results miserable. Labour is expended but nothing grows properly. Therefore the convenience of having good tools, as opposed to the inconvenience of not having good tools, will increase agricultural production tenfold. Of the iron implements cast and supplied by the government, most of them are large tools made to meet official quotas. They are not suitable for the people's use. Implements used by the people are so dull and worn out that grass cannot be cut. As a result the farmer struggles to no real purpose.

Of course, the issue here turned on more than quality control, for the followers of Confucius identified the extension of state control with Legalism. The Worthies were concerned to prevent any return to the strict regulation of the previous Qin dynasty, something that the determination of an emperor like Wu Di could well bring about. An effective rejoinder from the Grand Secretary, however, drew attention to the dangers that tended to arise whenever families became too wealthy. He noted how

iron implements and soldiers' weapons are vital in the service of the empire and should not be made a source of profit. Formerly great families, aggressive and powerful, obtained control of the revenues derived from the mountains and the sea, mined iron and smelted it, and made salt. One family would collect a host of over 1,000 men, mostly exiles who had left their homes and abandoned the tombs of their ancestors. Attaching themselves to a great house and collecting in a mountain fastness or a barren marsh, they built up its power to a dangerous height. Their readiness to break the law was also great. But through the opening up of office to capable men, and the careful selection of administrators, it has become possible for the people to enjoy peace and plenty without any abolition of state monopolies.

These quotations appear at length for the reason that they show the extent of official concern about the economy. Scholars might staff the imperial bureaucracy, but they were heirs to a tradition of princely control over key industries. Merchants were never allowed in classical China to become an influential force in society.

The early perfection of the collar harness, first invented during the Warring States period, permitted greater traction than the throat-and-girth harness used

Iron mould for casting a bronze axe. This late fifth-century BC implement reveals the long-standing Chinese concern with metallurgy.

A water-powered blowing-engine for blast furnaces and forges, which led to the early perfection of the iron- and steel-making process in China.

for animals elsewhere. As a result the Chinese wagon was much larger than its counterpart in other classical civilizations, and remained ahead till the Middle Ages in Europe. Zhu Geliang's invention of the wheelbarrow also eased the lot of the porter, who could steer heavier loads piled each side of a large centrally placed wheel. It is a singular feature of Chinese history that labour-saving devices have never been rejected because of the fear of technological unemployment. On the contrary, they have always received official encouragement as a means of exploiting more effectively the resources of the country. Wheelbarrows were even fitted with masts and sails in order to take advantage of the wind.

Dominating life in the countryside, however, was the problem of the proper use and regulation of water. Once again the initiative was taken by the authorities, even though the water-control schemes built during the Warring States period were small in comparison with those commissioned by Qin and Han emperors. One of these early projects, none the less, was considered by Sima Qian to have been decisive in the rise of Qin and, in consequence, the foundation of the Chinese empire. While the Han historian understood the fundamental importance of the increase in agricultural productivity and the supply potential for maintaining military supremacy, Sima Qian's attention was caught by the intrigue surrounding the construction of the Chengkuo canal. He relates

> how the ruler of [the feudal state of] Han wished to prevent the eastern expansion of Qin by exhausting it with projects. He therefore sent the water engineer, Cheng Kuo, to the king of Qin to convince him that a canal should be dug between the Jing and Luo rivers. The proposed canal would be 300 *li* long and used for irrigation. The project was half finished when the plot was discovered. The Qin ruler was stopped from killing Cheng Kuo only by the engineer's own argument: 'Although the scheme was intended to injure you, if the canal is completed, it will be of great advantage to your state.' The work was then ordered to be completed. When finished it irrigated 40,000 *ching* of poor land with water laden with rich silt. The output of the fields rose dramatically and Qin grew rich and strong until it finally conquered the whole of China. The canal was named after Cheng Kuo, who built it.

The additional grain from this vast area in the Wei River valley supported extra soldiers, while the strategic advantage of the east–west canal was much improved communication. The Chengkuo canal, opened in 246 BC, turned the Qin homeland into the chief economic area, a place where agricultural productivity permitted a supply of grain-tax so superior to all other places that the ruler who controlled it could control all China.

Not until the Later Han (25–220) would the Huai and Yangzi River valleys begin to challenge the economic position of the Wei and middle Yellow River valleys. The transformation of the southern provinces into the granary of China was a still later development, however. It was connected with the shift of population southwards, a process which began in earnest following the nomad partition of the empire in 317. A point to note in Sima Qian's story is the assumption of the Han king about the willingness of Qin to adopt public works on a scale larger than any other feudal state. A reputation for innovation must have been a legacy of Shang Yang's reforms.

Pottery model of a grain silo from Xianyang, the Qin capital. Greater harvests brought about by the Changkuo irrigation scheme allowed the state of Qin to spend more time on war than its feudal rivals did.

In sympathy with the Legalist emphasis on agriculture was Chao Cuo, an official charged by the Han emperor Wu Di with the task of raising technical levels in the countryside. Around 100 BC, as *sousu duwei*, or 'grain superintendent', Chao Cuo pioneered a system of ploughing in ridges and trenches that aided planting, irrigation and soil renewal. A further elaboration of this system was known as the pit-farming method, which consisted of an intensive concentration of labour and fertilizer within small pits evenly spaced across a field. The purpose of pit farming, other than excellent yields, was to counteract drought and cultivate marginal land too small and inconvenient for regular ploughing. The use of night soil as a fertilizer was inevitable in an agriculture which neither kept grazing animals nor allowed land to lie fallow. Farmers also turned to the cultivation of leguminous crops to restore field fertility.

According to the historian Ban Gu, conditions in the countryside had become critical because of Wu Di's long campaign against the Xiongnu. Presumably it was the steady decline in yield caused by the diversion of manpower to war that led the emperor to issue an edict saying, 'The most urgent task of today is to strengthen agriculture.' Immediate improvements occurred in the environs of the capital, but Chao Cuo's system of ploughing even spread to border towns. Thus, Ban Gu notes, the grain superintendent 'taught the people farming'. It is notable that the agricultural crisis which Chao Cuo overcame was centred in the northern provinces, since the improvement he introduced was suited only for dry-land crops such as millet. In the Yangzi valley rice cultivation remained efficient with 'fire-tilling and water-hoeing', a refinement on slash-and-burn farming. A piece of land was burned, then water tapped into the paddy where the rice was to be sown. Weeds and rice grew side by side until the rice seedlings reached a certain height, at which point the grass was cut down and more water tapped into the paddy to drown the grass roots, which soon died. Both the cut grass and the roots rotted underneath the water and nourished the rice.

Classical Chinese buildings. Note that none of the walls was weight-bearing, because of earthquakes.

That grain was the staple can be seen from *geng*, a favourite dish of the Han dynasty; it was a stew that included cereals, pieces of meat or fish and vegetables. From tombs excavated in 1974 at Mawangdui, near Changsha, Hunan province, we can reconstruct the diet of a noble family living shortly before the accession of Wu Di in 140 BC. Set out for the deceased in forty-eight bamboo baskets were prepared meats and fruits, as well as fifty-one pots containing cereals, vegetables and cakes. On small bamboo slips were recorded for each the details of preparation methods and ingredients. Appreciation of cookery arose early in Chinese civilization and, though the cuisine did not reach its peak during classical times, the art of blending fine flavours and slicing ingredients into the thinnest slivers was already looked upon as the hallmark of excellence. A Han feast always began with wine, then came stew, followed by a series of dishes culminating in grain and followed by fruit. The same pattern persists in the modern Chinese banquet, where fried rice or noodles is invariably the penultimate dish.

Apart from sustaining the people with its plenty, land became in itself a source of wealth. The first tax based on the amount of land held was instituted in 594 BC by Lu, the feudal state in which Confucius was born. The rate was 20 per cent of the total yield. This innovation marked a turning point in land tenure, for peasant farmers were entrusted with manorial land as a means of securing a regular surplus. Until the rise of strong rulers towards the close of the Warring States period, it is doubtful if the taxes collected by noble landlords were all passed on to state granaries and treasuries. There is evidence, even in Lu, for the nobility treating their dependants differently. Tax rates would therefore seem to have been set by manorial lords rather than state governments, prior to the advent of the bureaucracies which foreshadowed the centralized empire. In theory at least, the Zhou king owned every piece of land, but with the run-down of the feudal system the right of possession was disputed between, and within, the Warring States themselves. Strife decimated the hereditary aristocratic houses and widened the land-owning class to include the families of new office-holders, successful soldiers, reclaimers of waste-land and merchants. Well before Shang Yang's reforms of 356–338 BC in Qin encouraged the private ownership of land, the peasantry was already on its way to becoming owner-occupiers. Critics of Shang Yang, however, blamed on his agricultural policy the concentration of land ownership and the widening gap between rich and poor.

The Expansion of Trade

Shang Yang himself was very aware of the dangers involved in land speculation – we have already seen how he ordered that 'those who occupy themselves with trade shall be enslaved, along with the destitute and lazy'. But not even the fully-fledged Legalism he espoused was capable of holding back the expansion of trade during the Warring States period. Several factors abetted its rapid progress. First, the increasing area controlled by individual rulers gave the merchant more territory in which he could safely trade. A second factor was the general improvement in communications, both on land and water. Roads and canals, of course, were greatly advanced under the Qin and Han dynasties. Although the vast network of roads commissioned by the First Emperor had a military purpose, its shaded routes were soon speeding merchants on their far-flung business, once peace returned under the Han emperors. As Sima Qian comments on the commercial boom that ensued: 'Barriers and bridges were opened, and restrictions relaxed over the use of mountains and marshes. Therefore, rich traders and great merchants travelled freely throughout the empire. No commodity was unavailable so that everyone could buy what he wanted.' For last and not least, different regions became more interdependent because of specialization of local production. This was inevitable, Sima Qian thought, because 'various products rare in one part of the empire were plentiful in another part'.

Despite the discriminatory laws that the first Han emperor Gaozu enacted to impede the activities of merchants, many large-scale enterprises were operational by the end of his reign in 195 BC. They dealt successfully with foreign trade, iron smelting, fish, grain, salt, livestock, credit, moneylending and distribution. Not untypical of the new entrepreneurs were the Cho and Jen families, both of whom became 'outstanding and unusually wealthy'. The former originated in the most northerly feudal state of Zhao, where they were iron-smelters. When Zhao fell to Qin arms in 228 BC, the Cho were dispossessed of their property and resettled in another part of China. 'The husband and wife,' reports Sima Qian, 'were compelled to make this move alone, pushing their belongings in a cart.' Instead of attempting to bribe the officials and find a new home not far distant from their place of birth, they elected to be sent to a distant location in the west. There they discovered a mountain which yielded iron ore, and began smelting once again, so that within a few years they dominated local industry in what is now the northern part of Sichuan province. 'Mr Cho grew so rich that he owned 1,000 slaves, and the pleasures he indulged in among his fields and lakes were like those of a nobleman.'

Less ostentatious, but no less rich, were the Jen, once an official family hailing from the old feudal state of Han. Its ancestor was in charge of an imperial granary on the banks of the Yellow River. When the Qin dynasty was overthrown, 'Mr Jen quietly dug a hole and stored away the grain that had been under his care.' Later, when the prolonged struggle between the rebel leaders prevented the people in that area from ploughing and planting their fields, the price of grain rose astronomically and the Jen fortune was founded. Wise purchases of agricultural land and a frugal lifestyle not only enriched the family but earned for it the grudging respect of the imperial authorities. Though the Jen still dealt in grain, and were therefore technically merchants, direct involvement in the fundamental activity of farming did a great deal to ameliorate their social standing.

None of the examples Sima Qian cites of successful 'money-makers' enjoyed any official titles or government privileges, nor can they be said to have obtained their wealth by fraudulent means. 'They simply guessed what events would happen and acted accordingly, keeping a sharp eye out for extra profit as the occasion allowed. They gained money from secondary occupations and held on to it by investing in land.' Thrift and hard work clearly made a contribution to the prosperity of the Cho and Jen families, but this was not enough to endear them to a centralized empire. The Former Han government was far from friendly to merchants, who were subject to special taxes and regulations. They were forbidden to wear silk or ride in carriages, and no access was permitted to official appointments. This denial of social advancement to merchants and their descendants was the really effective curb, since a poor scholar without any official position would prefer farming to trade as a means of livelihood, lest he spoil any future opportunity of a civil-service career. During the Later Han, however, commerce and industry were not subject to as much political interference as they had been down to the usurpation of Wang Mang. The restored imperial house was naturally in a weaker position, and for a brief period even the iron and salt monopolies were found impossible to enforce.

A voice raised against the luxury of the times was that of Wang Fu (90–165), a scholar who was too honest to pursue an official career and chose instead to spend his life in honourable seclusion. 'Nowadays,' he lamented, 'people are extravagant in clothing, excessive in food and drink, and fascinated by clever language ... At Luoyang the clothing, food and drink, carriages, adornment, and houses of the rich all exceed what is prescribed for kings.' In particular, Wang Fu complained about lavish funerals, a Later Han social trait that fills the display cases of museums today with artefacts. On the other hand, that there was poverty in the countryside among the smaller farmers cannot be doubted. Government measures to cope with rural distress were aimed at preventing rebellion, something they were progressively unable to do from the 160s onwards. The first reports of serious famine date from the previous decade, when impoverished peasants are also reported to have subordinated themselves to large landowners.

A Society in Transition

A sense of loss haunted many of the philosophers of the Warring States period. In the centuries of turmoil down to imperial unification under the Qin dynasty, it was not unnatural to look back with nostalgia to an earlier age in which feudal society was supposed to have been in good order. But the conviction that an ideal had been lost and civilization was in decline reflected more than the change in political realities; much of its strength was drawn from the great social upheaval which accompanied the demise of feudalism. Alongside the process of centralization that led to the foundation in 221 BC of a single empire organized by an efficient bureaucracy, an equally significant social revolution was taking place.

During the Warring States period, in fact, the four famous estates of Chinese society were first recognized. In order of precedence these were the *shi*, 'the lesser nobility' or gentry, knights and scholars; the *nong*, 'the peasant farmers'; the *kong*, 'the artisans'; and the *shang*, 'the merchants and traders'. The low social position of those involved in manufacture and commerce was a consequence of economic development down to 221 BC, because princes had always assumed responsibility for industry, and especially metal-working.

Out of the conflict between states and within states arose a new social class, just below the feudal hierarchy. This was the *shi*. With the blurring of feudal distinctions and the demand for skilled administrators, the rights of birth seemed to count for less than ability and talent. A growing surplus of younger sons, educated but without rank, took advantage of whatever opportunities offered themselves. This usually meant service with a state or a noble family. The special training these upwardly mobile scholars received in preparation for their administrative and political duties came from a new institution, the school. It is generally held that the first school was established by Confucius, when he allowed his disciples to live in his household. Their education took the form of listening to, and arguing with, the philosopher.

According to his own testimony, Confucius was of humble origin, once served as an accountant and at another time had charge of some pasture land. Tradition would make him the descendant of a feudal house, but it is likely his ancestors were *shi*, stewards who served a noble family. His own studies seem to have been part of his preparation for higher office, something he never attained, possibly because of his own disinclination to flatter and conduct intrigues. In the last years of his life, approximately from 500 to 479 BC, Confucius had obviously given up this ambition and devoted himself entirely to teaching. The only criteria for admission to his school were virtuous conduct, intelligence and a willingness to study. The moral emphasis of the philosophy he impressed on his followers gave them a dependable character, which was appreciated by rulers, who had reason to worry about less ethical officials. It could be said that Confucius elevated the virtues of the *shi* into a successful moral code, since the stress on honesty and loyalty made Confucian scholars excellent recruits for a bureaucracy.

However, the practical doctrines of Confucius were essentially feudal, so later adaptation converted them into a philosophical system only suited to a centralized empire. For at the very moment he endeavoured to reform China the whole structure of feudalism was in terminal decay. The traditional charisma of rulers and the ruling class was no longer acknowledged, and respect for the past was being replaced by attention to present expediency. That the old familial bond between the ruler and his officials had given way to a more contractual relationship patently concerned Confucius, who regarded the advent of written law codes as an unnecessary break with tradition. As he astutely reminded progressive princes, the setting down of laws was a dangerous step for the nobility to take. He said that the code of punishments inscribed on a tripod by a ruler in 513 BC would be learned and respected by ordinary people above all else. Those in authority could never again evoke the past in order to declare that their judgements were correct. But not for a moment was Confucius suggesting that arbitrary decisions were to be justified. Without a proper understanding of propriety (*li*), a correct judgement could never be reached.

The *nong*, the peasant farmers, were always well regarded and overworked. Their poverty was a constant complaint, though rulers were sensitive about rural unrest and sought to protect the honest countryman. Of particular concern to Mencius (372–288 BC), the greatest follower of Confucius, was the lot of the peasantry caught up in a money economy. He advocated a return to the well-field system (*jintian*), which may have existed prior to the Warring States period. This form of land tenure would hopefully remove pressure from the peasant farmer, whose accumulating debts forced him to sell out and become either a tenant or a sharecropper. The well-field system is supposed to have contained nine squares of land, the central square belonging to the ruler, and the remaining eight cultivated by each family. Such an attempt to recover rural self-sufficiency was doomed to failure, not least because a farmer was dependent on the *kong*, the artisan. He could not supply his own cloth, cooking pots or implements, but relied upon people in other occupations, whom he in turn supplied with grain.

Wang Mang's abortive land reform in AD 9 also harkened back to the well-field system. Its nationalization of land was aimed at solving the basic economic and social problem of classical China, the steady acquisition of land by powerful families. Former Han emperors had already sent out commissioners to deal with overbearing clans but, though they killed the worst offenders and confiscated their property, others soon replaced them. In 127 BC a policy of removal was tried, when 'powerful and awe-inspiring persons of the various commanderies and kingdoms and those of great wealth were moved to the site of Wu Di's mausoleum', some 25 miles north of Chang'an. The idea behind the move was to strengthen the economy of the greater capital and eliminate dangerous influences elsewhere. Amnesties were naturally used by removed families to seek another home, and these not infrequent events meant government action against the wealthy was at best spasmodic. Even a disgraced official is known to have escaped punishment, returned to his place of birth, grown rich through land speculation and then taken advantage of a general amnesty.

During the Later Han the scope of powerful families was almost unrestricted until the eunuchs brought down the Liang family in 159. For thirty years the eunuchs maintained a grip on government appointments, and Luoyang was little more than their private kingdom, but away from the capital local magnates continued to exercise power. The latter became critical for the maintenance of order at times of peasant rebellion, such as the Yellow Turban uprising of the 180s. So independent did these large landholders become that they were said to

> possess several hundred houses, which are joined together, and extensive fertile land stretching all over the countryside. Their retainers are numbered in thousands and those who depend on them cannot be counted. They dispatch wagons and ships to make trade in all directions, while their agents handle enough goods to fill whole cities. Precious jade and valuable objects overflow their storerooms; horses, cattle, sheep and pigs are too many to be enclosed in a valley.

The status of such a family can be in no doubt. Poor farmers could neither rival this prosperity nor hope to be treated as equals. As an official commenting on the discrepancy between the legal position and social esteem of farmers and merchants said, 'Now the law despises merchants, but merchants have become rich and powerful; it esteems farmers, but the farmers have become poor and impotent.'

Clay model of a fish pond, found in a Later Han tomb. Models of complete farmyards were often buried with the dead.

The toil of the peasant was considered productive and fundamental, for it supplied society with food. The work of artisans and traders, on the other hand, was thought to be non-productive and secondary. But social reality did not correspond with the ideal. Artisans could earn in a single day enough money to live for five days, whereas farmers might labour the year round and still be unable to feed themselves. Squeezed between the tax collector, the moneylender and the weather, the hard-pressed countryman could not survive without periodic state relief. Once governmental interference with trade slackened, though, merchants were able to amass wealth and enjoy the respect of their neighbours. They undoubtedly played a critical part in backing the southern regimes of Shu and Han during the Three Kingdoms period.

Whatever the class or rank of society, humility was the expected pattern of behaviour for women in classical China, since they were held to be naturally inferior to men. Its most famous woman, Ban Zhao (48–117), sister of the historian Ban Gu, based her *Lessons for Women (Nujie)* on this principle. She wrote:

> *Yin* and *yang* are not of the same nature; men and women behave differently. Rigidity is the virtue of the *yang*; yielding the function of the *yin*. Strength is the glory of men; weakness is women's good quality ... Thus it is that the way of compliance is the proper behaviour [*li*] for a woman.

Subordination was shown in women's obedience to their fathers when they were children, their husbands when they married and their sons when they were widowed. The ideal age for a girl to marry was fifteen, but wedlock could not be countenanced between persons of the same surname, lest the couple have a common ancestor. This taboo originated in the Warring States period, when social upheaval gave rise to family names, and its influence has not entirely disappeared among modern Chinese. There were seven grounds for divorcing a wife: namely, disobedience to parents-in-law, barrenness, adultery, jealousy, incurable disease, loquacity and theft. It needs to be noted, however, that in classical China a man could have only one wife. Concubines were not regarded as full members of the family and the status of a concubine was always inferior to that of a wife. Unfortunately for women, Ban Zhao's recommendation that they should receive the same education that she enjoyed was generally ignored. Because of her own Confucian learning she was able to complete her brother's history of the Former Han dynasty on his early death. And she was also appointed as a tutor to the empress and her ladies-in-waiting, a rare event celebrated by Gu Zaizhi (345–406) in one of the earliest surviving Chinese paintings.

Administration

The Chinese genius for government first became apparent during the period of the Han emperors, and the bureaucratic arrangements evolved at that time formed the model for all subsequent imperial administrations, down to the early decades of our own century. In reaction to the authoritarianism of the brief Qin dynasty, which unified China in 221 BC, Han government was based on the principle that no person should have unlimited authority, and that all actions, including those of the emperor, should be open to scrutiny.

The Growth of Bureaucracy

The dim beginnings of this administrative system, one of the most enduring human creations, are to be found in the Warring States period. No longer did a feudal state appear to be an enlarged household, with the familial ties so dear to Confucius, but rather its court acted as the centre of government for a more consolidated administration. Rulers were reluctant to share power with local lords and, instead of granting land to relatives and favourites, they appointed officials to govern the districts of each state. Such an administration grew automatically from conquest, since reliable governors were needed to administer annexed territories. Although these officials were awarded noble titles, as vassals they did not inherit their offices, so that vacancies were simply filled by the sons of other prominent families. In the state of Qin, for instance, it was common practice to rotate officials between such governorships. Thus the control of state government over local administration was much tighter, and the selection of post-holders tended to be made on criteria other than noble birth. The *shi*, the educated gentry, was thus given its chance to rise in the social order by means of service in this nascent bureaucracy. It produced in time a new kind of minister, a career official who saw his role as a servant of the ruler, and not a noble rival like previous members of a feudal court.

The consolidation of state governments during the Warring States period raised issues of official conduct that exercised the minds of both administrators and philosophers. A quest for efficiency without regard to traditional morality characterized the policies adopted by most administrations. It was a trait usually blamed on Shen Buhai (*c.* 400–337 BC), a man of humble origin who served as chief counsellor of the feudal state of Han for many years. His fragmentary writings are concerned with the promotion of effective government. The later philosopher Han Fei Zi summarized Shen Buhai's theory of administration as appointing officials according to ability, demanding that they perform the duties of office, examining the worth of all ministers and keeping control of justice. While Shen Buhai stressed the authority of the ruler, he advocated the use of neither naked power nor harsh punishments, unlike the full-blooded Legalist Shang Yang, but the strictness with which penalties were applied in Han remains chilling. When on one occasion the ruler got drunk and fell asleep in a cold place, the crown-keeper put a coat over him. Coming to, the prince asked who had covered him and being informed, punished the coat-keeper but put the crown-keeper to death, on the principle that stepping outside the duties of an office was worse than negligence.

For the state of Qin, however, the more rigorous reforms of Shang Yang were deemed to be necessary for the strengthening of its military power. Shang Yang must have made a thorough study of administration before he fled from his native state of Wei to Qin in 356 BC, impressed its ruler with his political theories and later put them into practice. A descendant of the princely house of Wei by a concubine, Shang Yang seems to have hurriedly quit Wei on the death of his patron, the premier. This official's final advice to the ruler of Wei is supposed to have been to appoint Shang Yang in his place or execute him.

Sensing the impatience of the Qin ruler with his conservative advisers, Shang Yang recommended a complete break with the past:

> A wise man creates laws, but a worthless man is controlled by them; a man of talent reforms rites, but a worthless man is enslaved by them. With a man who is controlled by laws, it is useless to discuss change; with a man who is enslaved by rites, it is useless to discuss reform. Let your Highness not hesitate.

Given a free hand by the grateful ruler, Shang Yang introduced a new law code that weakened the nobles and elevated the throne. 'Those of ancient lineage who had no military value,' a chronicle recounts, 'lost their noble status.' Implementation of such regulations was by no means easy, though dissension did not outlast the shaming of the heir to the throne. When the crown prince transgressed one of the new laws, Shang Yang demanded that he should receive at least token punishment. So it was agreed that the prince's guardian be downgraded and the face of the prince's tutor tatooed, presumably on the grounds that these nobles shared responsibility for the prince's misbehaviour.

Not surprisingly, Shang Yang fell from power on the succession of this prince. But the new ruler chose not to abolish a programme of reform aimed at fostering a centralized state, a disciplined bureaucracy and a strong army. By hastening the tendency of the age, Shang Yang turned comparatively backward Qin into the most powerful of the feudal states, and ultimately the unifier of China.

When in 221 BC the First Emperor accepted the recommendation of Li Si, his own Shang Yang, to divide the newly unified empire into thirty-six commanderies (*jun*), each comprising several subprefectures (*xian*), he was merely extending Qin administration to the whole of China. Each commandery was under the authority of a civil administrator and a military governor. The activities of the civil administrator were supervised by an inspector, who reported direct to the central administration. This new post would seem to have been added to the provincial system of government in order to keep the capital informed about local developments, including the enforcement of edicts. At the head of each subprefecture was an official known as *ling*, best translated as 'prefect'. This centralized bureaucracy left no place for feudalism, something even the cautious Han emperors were soon obliged to recognize as inheritors of the Qin unification. The removal of 120,000 noble families to the capital in 221 BC had effectively deprived the nobility of its territorial and hereditary privileges and made it subject to the law and a hierarchy of merit.

The Han Administration

The turmoil that accompanied the overthrow of the Qin dynasty in 207 BC tore the empire apart and necessitated the compromise of early Former Han government. Thus the new imperial administration started as a dual system of commanderies and feudal holdings, but the diminished fiefs awarded to old families, supporters of the first Han emperor Gaozu, and his own relatives were carefully intertwined with territories controlled by imperial officials. A rebellion among the eastern domains in 154 BC upset the administrative balance, which subsequently tilted towards a purely bureaucratic state under central control. Quite apart from the measures introduced to break up large holdings after the suppression of the rebellion, there is evidence to suggest that few of the 150 families Gaozu rewarded with land for services rendered in the foundation of his dynasty survived for long. The great majority were brought to an end naturally by the absence of a successor or by the crime of the individual holder of the title. They rarely outlasted the fourth generation.

The structure of the Han empire has been likened to a pyramid, with the emperor at the apex, the officials immediately below, and the people at the base. Notwithstanding Gaozu's dislike of the ceremony attached to scholarship, the critical dividing line in classical Chinese society was determined by literacy. It marked the difference between the rulers and the ruled, between the educated gentry, from whom the officials were drawn, and the peasants, who could not read or write. The ruling class, however, was neither closed nor unchanging. Conscious efforts were made to recruit suitable candidates for office throughout the empire, a quota system being designed to permit the rise of humble men who had made a local reputation for themselves. The principal method of recruitment was by recommendation of provincial officials or ministers in the central government. They were required to find candidates for office who combined intelligence with integrity. The guidance for initial selection spoke of them as 'capable and virtuous' (*xianliang*), 'sincere and upright' (*fangzheng*), 'highly talented' (*xiucai*) and 'frank and unflinching in speech' (*zhiyan jijian*).

Although Later Han emperors responded to the southwards movement of population by issuing edicts recommending the preferment of southerners, the northern provinces continued to dominate the central administration. The colonial commanderies in Vietnam must have found compliance with this order very difficult, although provincial officials in the Yangzi River valley seem to have discovered that suitable candidates were more readily available. But despite the various devices tried to extend the area of recruitment, almost all the senior appointments during the Later Han went to members of influential families who lived within a radius of 400 miles of Luoyang. A high proportion came from Nanyang, a city less than 200 miles south of the capital. Nanyang was the home of Guangwu Di, founder of the Later Han dynasty, and situated there were the estates of old family friends of the imperial house. The philosopher Wang Chong (27–97) was certain that recommendations depended on favouritism rather than merit. According to him, the problem with the civil service was its capacity for self-perpetuation. He lamented how

> officials in childhood become accomplished at calligraphy without reciting the classics, or learning of benevolence and principle. When they grow up and assume office they employ their skill with words to enrich themselves and gain power. They accept gifts when making investigations, and they take what they can when put in charge of the people ... It is not that their nature is bad; it is that their habitual practices are in opposition to the classical teachings.

Even more discouraging to an upholder of simple morality like Wang Chong was the growing influence of wealth on the distribution of posts, titles and honours. Had he been alive during the ascendancy of the eunuchs (159–89), the philosopher would have been appalled at the way in which money ruled Luoyang. It is said that a tariff was publicly displayed, giving the price of a dukedom, a governorship, a prefectship and so on.

But prior to the decline of the civil service in the last years of the Later Han, the recruitment system laid the foundation of China's famous imperial examinations, which reached maturity under the Tang and Song dynasties, from the seventh to the thirteenth centuries. In comparison to their future operation, the Han method of attracting talent was crude and corrupt. Yet somehow it provided the government with enough competent candidates, and for nearly four centuries officials fulfilled their duties effectively. Under an energetic emperor such as Wu Di the primitive tests set were even used to offer appointments to persons whose ideas he liked. The emperor's concern extended to grades for individual answers and he would revise the pass list whenever he spotted someone interesting. This involvement is hardly surprising in the context of his personal style of administration, which could function only with a reliable and subservient civil service. Such a candidate was Gongsun Hong, to whom Wu Di entrusted in 125 BC the reorganization of finance and education. The emperor would not accept the low grade awarded to Gongsun Hong, who was so poor that he supported his family by breeding pigs. Even as a high official Gongsun Hong's frugality was famous: he made do with old clothes and gave all his salary to poor and deserving strangers, for whom he maintained a kind of hostel in the capital.

Above the central administration stood the emperor,

the Son of Heaven, the unique source of temporal authority and leadership. He owed his position to his own merit as the chosen occupant of the throne. He alone, in theory at least, was in receipt of divine approval, the so-called heavenly mandate to rule (*tianming*). In the business of government, of course, the emperor was assisted by a senior group of officials, to whom he delegated the necessary authority to act on his behalf. Out of deference to Confucian ethics, the senior official in the empire was the Grand Tutor (*Taifu*), who had charge of the throne's moral guidance. While the Former Han emperors often left the post unfilled, the first Later Han emperor appointed a Grand Tutor soon after he had ascended the throne, and his successors followed this precedent. But they seem to have paid only lip service to the notion of a mentor, not least because they also neglected to fill the post once it fell vacant – an early event in each reign as those appointed were usually elder statesmen.

The main responsibility for central government rested with two of the Three Excellencies (*Sangong*), who might be termed first minister and head of the civil service. They were called the Grand Counsellor (*Chengxiang*) and the Grand Secretary (*Yushidafu*) respectively. The third member of this top group of officials was the Grand Commandant (*Taiwei*). When the post was filled, he was in charge of military affairs. During the Later Han the duties of the Grand Commandant were extended to the general supervision of officialdom. Along with the other two Excellencies he had a censorial and advisory role over the provincial government. When one of his officials was dispatched to the provinces on a special errand, he was known as a *Qingzhaoshi*, or 'Messenger with a Pure Edict'.

Below the Three Excellencies there existed nine major offices of state, or ministries, each with well-defined powers. The Grand Master of Ceremonies (*Taiching*) was in charge of rites, astrology, medicine, learning and the imperial tombs. Following the example of the First Emperor, an ancestral temple and a settlement were built at the site chosen for the grave of every Former Han emperor. From 43 BC onwards jurisdiction over the tomb towns was transferred to the appropriate provincial authorities, but the Grand Master of Ceremonies still sent his own staff to inspect the imperial graves. As the Later Han abandoned the practice of building ancestral temples at the imperial graves, and instead located two shrines within the walls of Luoyang, this section was drastically cut to forty-six officials and guards. One of the chief tasks of this ministry, however, was the supervision of official education, and especially the Grand School (*Taixue*), the name by which the imperial university was then known. The cleverest provincial students came to the capital to attend this institution, studying the classics alongside the sons of high officials. The number of students enrolled was restricted to fifty under the Former Han emperor Wu Di, but this increased steadily until it reached 10,000 during Wang Mang's usurpation and yet more under the restored Later Han emperors. An ideal candidate of the imperial university was said to be distinguished by abundant talents, respect for the family, loyalty to the emperor, moral rectitude and deep learning. When in 130 BC the Grand Master of Ceremonies gave Gongsun Hong the lowest grade in the imperial examinations, an enraged Wu Di moved the poor scholar up to first place.

Somewhat different from the duties of the Grand Master of Ceremonies were those discharged by the Superintendent of the Imperial Household (*Guang Lushun*). He was responsible for security within the public parts of the imperial palace and for protecting the emperor on his excursions outside its walls. In the private apartments the emperor was protected by the eunuchs, a division of duties undoubtedly designed to prevent a single official from gaining physical control over the emperor's person. It may have been enough to stop the chief eunuch Zhao Gao's bid for the throne in 207 BC, once he had forced the suicide of the second Qin emperor. As Sima Qian states:

> No official would accept his usurpation, and when he entered the audience chamber, three persons offered him harm. Realizing that Heaven had refused to grant him the empire, and that the officials as a whole would not cooperate with his desire, he summoned a nephew of the First Emperor and reluctantly handed over the imperial seal.

While this was the only occasion on which an individual eunuch tried to usurp the throne, the eunuchs as a group enjoyed great power towards the end of Later Han, after the fall of the minister Liang Ji in 159.

Part of the earliest surviving Chinese scroll, *Admonitions of the Instructress to the Court Ladies*, by Gu Zaizhi (345–406).

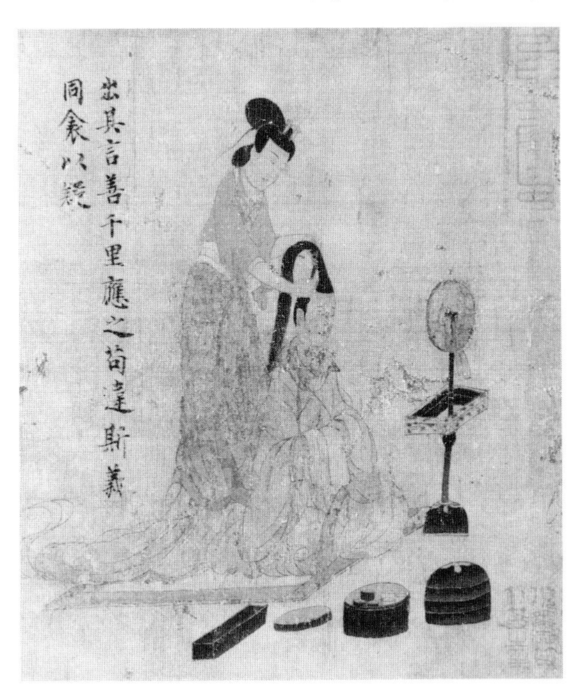

Another minister who commanded armed men was the Commandant of the Guards (*Weiwei*). During the Former Han his ministry was located within the palace precincts, but at Luoyang it appears to have been moved to a position in the city itself. The reason for this change is unknown, since the Later Han emperors still relied on the Commandant of the Guard's 3,000 conscripts for the control of palace gates, walls and passageways. On completion of their one-year term of duty the conscripts were feasted by the emperor, then sent home. A system of tallies ensured that only authorized persons could enter the palace. Permanent residents identified themselves with iron tallies, the other halves of which were kept at the gate designated for their use. Non-residents were issued with wooden credentials, and officials on business were also announced by attendants. In an emergency the tallies were collected, which meant entry could be effected only by force. Although the Grand Coachman (*Taipu*) was primarily concerned with the imperial stables, records show that some of his grooms took part in the downfall of Liang Ji. They were among the force which surrounded the minister's residence in the western suburbs.

The administration of the law was under the control of the Commandant of Justice (*Tingwei*), who ruled personally on the most difficult cases. Before becoming the Grand Secretary, Chang Tang made his mark in this post by anticipating the throne's desire in almost Legalist fashion. If he knew that the emperor wanted a person condemned, Chang Tang would turn the case over to the harshest judges; when, on the other hand, the emperor wanted to let someone go free, he was careful to choose mild judges for the case. Sima Qian describes an attack launched on the conduct of the Commandant of Justice in front of Wu Di himself. Another minister declared:

> People say that petty clerks with brushes and scrapers have no business becoming high officials. How right they are! It is men like Chang Tang who have turned the empire into a state where men are afraid to look each other in the eye or to put one foot down beside the other for fear of breaking the law!

Unimpressed though the determined emperor was with this Confucian viewpoint, he respected the tradition of open discussion allowed in the court, and did no harm to the accuser. Whereas this official eventually retired, in 116 BC Chang Tang was obliged to commit suicide as a result of corruption. On hearing how Chang Tang's mother was so put out by his sudden fall that she forbade a decent funeral, Wu Di commented, 'If she weren't that kind of mother, she could not have borne that kind of son!'

What had angered officials of the Confucian persuasion most about Chang Tang was his readiness to enhance the power of the throne. Both as Commandant of Justice and Grand Secretary he had used the law with the utmost severity, forcing feudal rulers into positions of guilt, and bringing about estrangement between the emperor and his own blood relations. The reduction of these surviving houses was in fact achieved partly by deliberate design and partly by exploiting opportunities such as a ruler's rebellion or his death without a successor. The larger territories were split into smaller units, and members of the imperial clan were installed in them very much on sufferance. The beginning of the end for the remnants of the old feudal order was the rebellion in 154 BC of the eastern vassals. It was led by the ruler of Wu, then aged sixty-two. His distaste for Han rule was long-standing, because his own son and designated heir had been murdered at Chang'an following a quarrel over a game of chess with the imperial crown prince, who became the fifth emperor of the dynasty, Jin Di (156–141 BC). The rebellion was far larger than any previous uprising and took several months of hard fighting to master.

Over relations with these humbled princes the Grand Herald (*Dahonglu*) exercised control. His staff were responsible for the orderly inheritance of noble titles and fiefs, the scrutiny of annual accounts and the conduct of business on behalf of the central administration. When the feudal rulers presented themselves for an imperial audience, the Grand Herald welcomed them in the suburbs. A similar function was discharged by this minister for barbarian rulers who had acknowledged the suzerainty of the Son of Heaven. In order to assist him in the maintenance of satisfactory foreign relations there was an office of interpreters at hand. Though the Former Han first established a number of dependent states (*shuguo*) along the northern frontier, as a buffer between China and the nomadic Xiongnu, the system was greatly expanded under the Later Han to help defend the outlying parts of the empire. Each dependent state had to heed the advice of a Chinese official, rather like the native rulers and their residents in British colonial possessions. Wherever possible the empire sought to coexist with its barbarian neighbours: diplomacy was always preferred to warfare.

Despite his title, the Grand Minister of Agriculture (*Dasinong*), was the government treasurer. The retention of this archaic designation until the end of the Later Han reveals the fundamental importance of grain-tax in classical China. The Grand Minister of Agriculture did not collect the poll and land taxes but stored them, whether in kind or in cash. His staff oversaw the great granary within the walls of the capital, which served the needs of the palace and the bureaucracy. They also looked after provincial granaries, and especially those involved in price-stabilization arrangements. The so-called Ever Full Granary in the suburbs of Luoyang must have been used for this purpose. A ceremonial duty clearly designed to remind the keeper of the imperial purse of the ultimate source of prosperity was the *gengji*, on 'spring ploughing'. Emperors were to turn the first furrow down to modern times, and so impressed were eighteenth-century European philosophers by this royal gesture of solicitude for the people's welfare that in 1756 Louis XV, at the suggestion of the encyclopedist François Quesnay made through the Marquise de Pompadour, enacted the Chinese ritual at Versailles.

The so-called Privy Treasurer (*Shaofu*) headed the biggest ministry, but was one of the least influential of the nine ministers. Once the emperor's private purse was amalgamated in the Later Han with the public purse administered by the Grand Minister of Agriculture, the Privy Treasurer's role shrank to superintendence of the emperor's well-being: running the palace, keeping order in the harem and seeing to the upkeep of the imperial parks. Although not castrated himself, many of his subordinates were eunuchs. The ease with which the eunuchs seized power during the Later Han can be traced back to the authoritarianism of Wu Di. Refusing to allow the power of the Three Excellencies to curtail his own, Wu Di governed increasingly through a secretariat (*shangshu*) within the palace precincts, staffed by officials and eunuchs belonging to the Privy Treasurer's ministry. Only documents and reports deemed by this inner administration to be worthy of the emperor's eyes were selected, and in consequence it could under certain circumstances actually shape policy. Being so close to the emperor, its members were readily able to ignore their nominal master, the Privy Treasurer. They came over time to form an imperial cabinet which rivalled the power of all the ministers. But it was the Later Han emperor Ming Di who set the scene for the rise of eunuch power when, in the late first century, he expanded the number of palace attendants and established a secretariat to which only eunuchs were appointed.

The ninth and last of the nine ministers was the Director of the Imperial Clan (*Zongzheng*), who was always a member of the imperial house himself. He kept a regularly updated register of all those who belonged to the Liu family, the imperial clan. He was also responsible for any punishment due for crimes committed by its members, although the emperor always had to confirm his decision.

Provincial government under both Han dynasties was divided between two types of administrative unit – commanderies and fiefs. In 200 BC there were fifteen commanderies and ten feudal regions. By the usurpation of Wang Mang most of the fiefs had been reduced in size or split into several smaller units. As a result the number of commanderies had increased considerably, and this growth was further augmented by the creation of new commanderies on the empire's expanded borders. The eighty-three commanderies and twenty fiefs then in existence were divided into 1,577 subprefectures, each about the size of an English county. Subprefectures inhabited by barbarian peoples were called *dao*, or 'marches', rather than the usual *xian*. It was at this level of provincial government that the real work was done, because the official (*ling* or 'prefect') in charge of a subprefecture had to enforce law and order, register individuals and property, collect taxes, store grain against times of famine, mobilize labour for public works, supervise schools, and judge civil and criminal cases. Each subprefecture consisted of a walled city, surrounding villages and farmland. Minor officials assisted the prefect down to the headman of a hamlet, but the cement binding society together at the lowest level was the collective responsibility of every five or ten families for one another's conduct. A legacy of Shang Yang's reforms, the Former Han emperors were never comfortable with its dreadful implications for fathers, mothers, wives, children, brothers and sisters. The wholesale slaughter or banishment involved was stopped for a number of years in 178 BC. Its eventual revival in the face of serious crime seemed to justify the classical Chinese notion that merely punishing a criminal himself was not an adequate deterrent. The arrest and punishment of relations and friends with him was thought to increase the mental burden of the criminal so that he would hesitate to break the law. Extermination was used again in 163 BC, during the reign of the same emperor who had ordered its abolition. The crime was treachery, the very charge brought by the eunuchs in AD 159 against the prominent Later Han family the Liang.

A vital responsibility of the subprefecture was the upkeep of communications, without which a far-flung empire could not operate effectively. Roads were policed by a corps of postmasters who oversaw the coaching inns and stables placed at regular intervals along main roads. Urgent dispatches as well as routine mail were carried from one coaching inn to another on horseback, while officials on government business progressed via these chains of resting places. It was as a humble Qin postmaster that Liu Bang, the first Han emperor, began his career.

The authority of the civil governor (*taishou*) and the military commander (*duwei*) of a commandery was so great that it was essential to supervise their activities. A body of inspectors (*cishi*) travelled throughout the empire every year, and from 145 BC onwards included both commanderies and fiefs in their tours of inspection. They examined the honesty and competence of provincial officials, their obedience to central government, justice, and the treatment of prisoners and convict labourers; they also looked at local conditions and the abuses of powerful families. During the Later Han the inspectors no longer set out annually from the capital on their tours of inspection, because they were transferred to the provincial administration. Inspections thereafter occurred in the eighth month of each year, a report being sent to Luoyang in time for the New Year, when a portion of the taxes arrived at the capital. This tribute (*gong*) helped to support the central administration, whose officials were paid partly in grain and partly in cash. The whole amount was calculated in *shi*, roughly translated as a bushel. Until the creation of a 10,000-*shi* post in 8 BC, the scale varied from over 4,000 *shi* per annum for the Three Excellencies to 100 *shi* for a junior official. In the provinces a prefect would have received between 1,000 and 600 *shi*, according to the size of his *xian*.

The Decline of Government

Problems of training, as cited earlier by Wang Chong, led during the Later Han to a decline in the quality of official recruitment. Too often candidates were appointed on the basis of fame and reputation, not to say family connections. Their supposed talents were not carefully examined and in consequence both the central and provincial administrations began to fill up with less than dedicated officials. 'Accomplishing nothing for the dynasty, showing no benevolent concern for the people, they monopolize their offices almost like kings and consume vast revenues.' The transfer of the inspectorate to the provincial administration did nothing to alleviate the situation, although the weakened position of the restored dynasty needs to be recalled too. Emperor Guangwu Di was unable to survive without the support of his backers, not least because the long campaign he fought for military supremacy made him vulnerable to any criticism from powerful families. Well might he endeavour to raise administrative standards, but in reality he still had debts to repay. In 35 an official ventured to suggest that 'in filling official posts men of outstanding talent and good character from all over China should be selected. It is not a good thing to employ only Nanyang men.' The emperor agreed, but the preference for Nanyang candidates persisted.

The use made of eunuchs by Guangwu Di's successors as a counterbalance to the influence of powerful families only undermined officialdom even more. As one commentator remarked:

> The fate of the dynasty was in the hands of eunuchs with whom scholar-officials were ashamed to associate. Ordinary persons expressed resentment, and scholars living in seclusion gave full expression to the popular discontent, naming incompetent ministers without fear or favour. Trenchant criticism became commonplace.

This Confucian barrage failed to halt the decline of the Han administration, which continued apace under the Wei dynasty of Cao Pi. By the 240s only a handful of officials were competent at literary composition, a sure sign of the falling away of scholarship. Daoism had come to replace the teachings of Confucius as the preoccupation of the ruling class, with the new faith of Buddhism not far behind. The full recovery of government bureaucracy had to await the reign of Tai Zong, the second Tang emperor (626–49). The fame of this ruler's relationship with his ministers, a subject dear to subsequent ages, was not unconnected with the return of Confucian officials to the halls of government after an absence of more than three centuries.

Religion and Philosophy

Prior to the arrival of Buddhism from India in the first century AD, China was isolated from the beliefs and ideas of other classical civilizations. Indeed, so late was the arrival of this new faith that its advocates found the conversion of the Chinese hard going, little headway being made until the chaotic years following the fall of the Later Han dynasty in 220. The civil disturbances of the second century not only put the empire into temporary eclipse but also undermined the Confucian orthodoxy upon which imperial power supposedly rested. It was the loss of the ancient heartland of China, after nomadic peoples overran the north in 316, that raised doubts about traditional beliefs and encouraged scholars to open their minds to Buddhist ideas. The upsurge of monastic Buddhism falls outside the scope of our period, but attention will be given to its early rivalry with Daoism, the indigenous 'way' of personal salvation.

The dominant position Confucianism was to attain under the Han emperors could not have been foreseen even as late as the Qin unification of China. The burning of the books and the killing of scholars in 213–212 BC were intended to end Confucian criticism of imperial policy once and for all. No longer would opponents of the regime be able to 'use the past in order to discredit the present', a reference to the yardstick of tradition always applied by followers of Confucius. The author of the book burning, Li Si, was by temperament and conviction a Legalist minister who believed the newly united empire could not endure without strict obedience to the will of the ruler. That the First Emperor himself was fascinated by another strand of classical Chinese thinking was not ignored by Li Si, however. His exemption from the flames of works on divination was calculated, given the First Emperor's interest in the spirit world, which had already led to the dispatch of embassies up mountains and overseas in the hope of establishing contact with the immortals.

The events of 213–212 BC thus bring into focus the three main schools of thought in classical China: Confucianism (*zujia*), Daoism (*daojia*) and Legalism (*fajia*). Although the first two were to have lasting importance in Chinese history, and especially Confucianism, the most powerful influence down to the collapse of the Qin dynasty in 207 BC was Legalism. It might even be said of the Han Chinese that they were Daoist in private and Confucian in public, while those who entered the civil service always felt the lingering influence of the administrative concepts of Legalism. In reaction to this accommodation of inherited beliefs Wang Chong (27–100) attacked both the superstitions of his time and the use to which corrupt officials put Confucian precepts. By no means the first rationalist, Wang Chong was distinguished by his refusal to accept statements of fact on trust, and his insistence on an intellectual explanation of anything he was asked to believe. Wang Chong's vision of a universe operating on the basis of systematic principles led to the scientific and technological innovations of scholars such as Zhang Heng (78–139), the inventor of the first practical seismograph. This 'earthquake weathercock' could not furnish a scientific explanation for seismic disturbance, but at least it gave the emperor immediate notice of a disaster and its direction from the capital. The theory of the Mandate of Heaven and the corresponding benevolence of Shang Di, the high god of Heaven, made the throne sensitive to the interpretation of natural phenomena or marvels (*zaiyi*). This explains the political importance of the observatory Zhang Heng ran as Director of Astrology (*taishi ling*). In 133 he declared that a particularly severe earthquake indicated heavenly disapproval of eunuch power in the imperial palace. His memorial called for the restoration of authority to the place where it belonged – the Son of Heaven.

The profound sense of mystery that Zhang Heng obviously retained in the universe as an astrologer-scientist should warn us about overestimating the contemporary influence of Wang Chong's scepticism. Like the Roman philosopher and poet Lucretius, he was concerned to disprove more than the absurdities of popular belief: his rational approach was an attempt to liberate the mind from false and disturbing opinions. But Wang Chong's *Lun Heng (Discourses Weighed in the Balance)* was largely ignored as an irrelevant attack on official ideology. Not until after the disaster of 316 would scholars be prepared to countenance any trenchant criticism of Confucianism. This disinclination to question orthodox belief needs to be borne in mind when considering classical Chinese philosophy, since it reveals the strength of the religious foundation underlying the various schools of thought.

The Spirit World

Classical China recognized a multiplicity of divinities and spirits. There were popular cults which placated two types of spiritual being, known as the *shen* and the *gui*. Whereas the former tended to be associated with particular places or activities, the latter were usually identified as the spirits of the dead. *Gui*, translated 'devils', were ghosts who had returned to plague the living, the hungry ghosts still feared by some Chinese today. Against this dread Wang Chong argued that there was no evidence at all for anything surviving the corruption of the body. He pointed out the scarceness of supposed sightings. If indeed the dead could become spirits and be observed, then instead of appearing in ones or twos, there would be ghosts thronging the roads in great numbers. No less ridiculed by Wang Chong, but not so malevolent in character, were the *shen*. These spirits often took hybrid forms with human heads and the bodies of dragons, snakes, horses, birds or oxen. The dragon (*long*) was essentially a benevolent divinity as the rain-bringer, the lord of waters, clouds, rivers, marshes, lakes and seas. Extremely versatile, he could make himself as tiny as a silkworm or become so big that he overshadowed the world.

Associated with the imperial throne from 221 BC onwards, the dragon may have had a special significance for the First Emperor, whose lucky element was water. Though correctness in everything was a feature of Legalist philosophy, its ruthless enforcement during his reign seems to have owed something to the theory of the Five Elements (*wuxing*) as well. According to this cyclical view of events, the previous dynasties of China, legendary and historic, had already depended in turn upon the elements of earth, wood, metal and fire. As a text from the Warring States period (481–221 BC) predicted:

> It will be the energy of water that displaces fire, and Heaven in advance will make a display of water, so that it will come into the ascendant. When this occurs, the new ruler will single out black for prominence among colours and model action on water.

Thus the First Emperor was said to have extinguished the energy of fire supporting the Zhou kings and unified China into a single state. To celebrate the victory of his own element he renamed the Yellow River 'the Powerful Water'.

As already observed, the superstitious character of the First Emperor was a factor taken into account by his chief minister, Li Si, in the selection of books for the bonfire. Two incidents should suffice to illustrate this marked disposition. The first occurred in 219 BC, when the First Emperor was struck by a gale as he crossed the Yangzi River. Blaming the local *shen* for

Cross-section of a Later Han tomb, excavated near the capital, Luoyong, during 1991. It shows the typical brick structure and the position of murals.

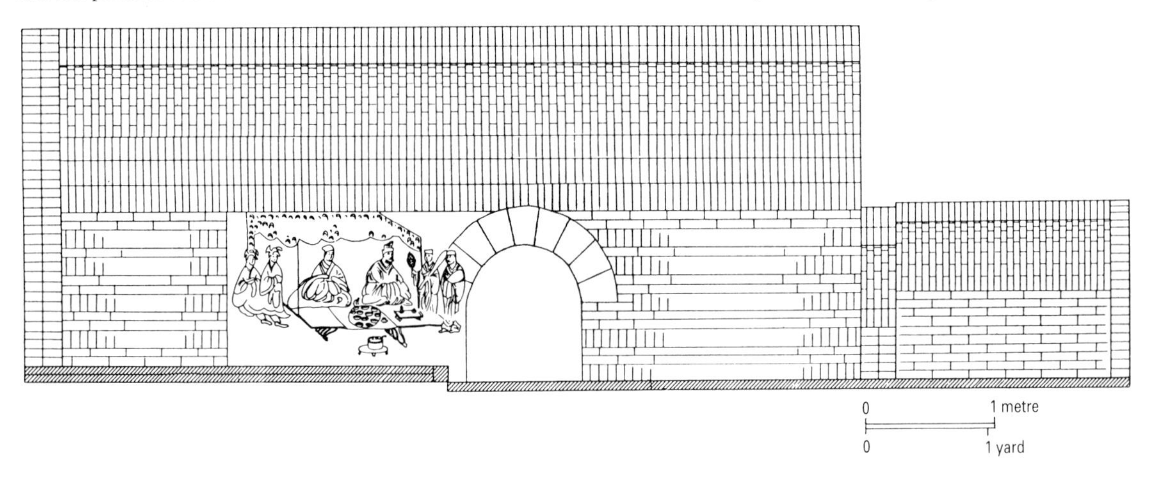

Terracotta warriors from Pit No. 1, Mount Li. These fierce infantrymen acted as the personal guard of the First Emperor in the afterlife.

the wind, he ordered 3,000 convicts to fell in retaliation all the trees on a nearby mountain, the site of a temple dedicated to the river goddess. The second incident probably contributed to the First Emperor's death in 210 BC. Interpretation of a dream he had on a tour of the eastern commanderies led to a prolonged stay on the seashore, where he may have caught pneumonia and died. The First Emperor felt obliged to hunt with a repeater crossbow another troublesome *shen* there, because he was told that a certain sea god was preventing him from meeting the immortals.

Superior to these divinities were the *di*, the gods of various portions of the universe, and *tian*, Heaven itself. More is known about them for the reason that it was the prerogative of the ruler to organize their worship. As the Son of Heaven (*tianzi*), a title reserved for the Zhou king prior to the unification of China in 221 BC, the emperor was expected to be the chief worshipper of the principal powers. The Han empire, however, was also an age of religious synthesis, when many diverse ancient cults were amalgamated in accordance with an elaborate cosmology. This process began to affect imperial rituals in earnest towards the close of the Former Han dynasty. The renewed worship of Heaven as the controller of human destinies from 31 BC onwards marked the establishment of an imperial sacrifice that was to last till 1911. It resolved at the same time an inherited ambiguity over the relationship between Heaven and Shang Di, 'the high god of Heaven'. The former derived from the founding ancestor of the Shang dynasty, the original historic house which the first Zhou king overthrew about 1027 BC. It was only natural that the victorious Zhou should not have been interested in making obeisance to their opponents' ancestor, yet they did not simply want to drop the idea of an awesome power in the sky. Because Heaven was also worshipped in their religion, they identified this earliest ancestor with Shang Di, a sky god whom they already revered. Gradually but unmistakably, the heavenly realm became remote from the everyday world of man, in particular when marginalized Zhou kings tried to assert their position as Heaven's chosen rulers. The collapse of feudal order during the Warring States period ruled out a priest-king claiming to hold any heavenly mandate. It was only after the consolidation of Han rule that political circumstances allowed the revival of a cult dedicated to the celebration of divinely conferred authority within a unified state.

Instrumental in bringing this about were the teachings of Dong Zhongshu (179–104 BC), a leading Confucian official. He argued that Heaven exercised a benevolent influence upon the affairs of mankind, but kept a close watch on the conduct of the ruler. As tyranny was not a heavenly characteristic, a tyrannical emperor could never hope to enjoy an orderly reign. First, Heaven would send forth calamities and prodigies as a warning. Should these omens be ignored, then heavenly support would be withdrawn and, in the last resort, a violent end overtake an intransigent dynasty. 'The Zhou,' Dong Zhongshu contended, 'received a mandate to rule. Yet after many years their house became corrupt and degenerated into insignificance, losing all control over the people. The great lords were always rebellious and employed cruel punishments to achieve their aims.' The reference to the harshness of Legalism was doubtless intended to remind the emperor Wu Di of the dangers he ran himself through a determination to have everything his own way. While this headstrong ruler was largely unimpressed by the threat of omens, he recognized the value of Dong Zhongshu's philosophical justification for imperial power. Wu Di also seems to have been astute enough to realize that it would be best anchored in the minds of the people by means of impressive rites. In addition to the cycle of sacrifices instituted in the capital to Houtu, 'the Earth Queen', and Taiyi, 'the Grand Unity', he therefore journeyed in great state three times to the sacred mountain of Taishan in modern Shandong to engage in private worship of Heaven.

Victories over the Xiongnu nomads were celebrated with great pomp in Chang'an immediately before Wu Di's first ascent of Taishan in 110 BC, an indication of official concern to associate the terrestrial achievements of the emperor with his role as a religious dignitary.

But there was a superstitious trait in the make-up of Wu Di that also inclined him towards such an undertaking. By no means as preoccupied with magic as the First Emperor, Wu Di was still sufficiently moved by the discovery of an ancient bronze tripod cauldron to believe he could use it to communicate with the spirit world. He was even persuaded that the sacrifices to be made on Taishan would permit him to acquire powers comparable to those of Huang Di, the wise king earlier revered by the First Emperor.

One of the *di* who really fascinated Chinese rulers was Huang Di, personified as 'the Yellow Emperor'. Especially favoured by the Daoists, this monarch was regarded as the ancient sage from whom their teachings had descended. According to one account of his end:

When Huang Di had a special tripod cauldron cast for the brewing of elixirs, a celestial dragon came down from the sky to collect him. On to this creature stepped Huang Di, along with seventy other people, both officials and palace ladies. Then the dragon carried them upwards, disappearing into the clouds.

Interestingly combined in this account of Huang Di's ascent as an immortal are the rituals of Confucian ancestor-worship in the form of the sacrificial vessel, and the Daoist pursuit of the elixir of life. The practice of worshipping four major *di* of different colours – white, green, yellow and red – seems to have arisen before the reign of the First Emperor. The founding Han emperor Gaozu added a fifth *di*, a black one. Until 31 BC the worship of these five principal powers may have formed the core of religious ceremonies at the capital. Ceremonies addressed to the Grand Unity commenced in 113 BC, a year after Wu Di offered animal sacrifices to the Earth Queen on a circular mound. But from 31 BC onwards worship of Heaven took pride of place in the imperial cults.

A singular classical belief concerned the *xian*, or 'immortal beings'. Until the arrival of Buddhism the Chinese entertained no ethical ideas in respect of the afterlife. There was neither a paradise for the worthy nor a hell for those deserving torment. On death the two souls that were believed to inhabit every person simply quit the body. The *hun* soul returned to the sky, while the *po* soul fell back into the earth. In cases of violent death the two souls sometimes failed to separate, even though they had left the corpse. Remaining together like this allowed them to retain the power of assuming another bodily form, and thus exact vengeance for the violence practised on the body they had formerly inhabited.

Normally, though, the *hun* and the *po* would part on

The tomb of Qin Shi Huangdi at Mount Li, Shaanxi province.

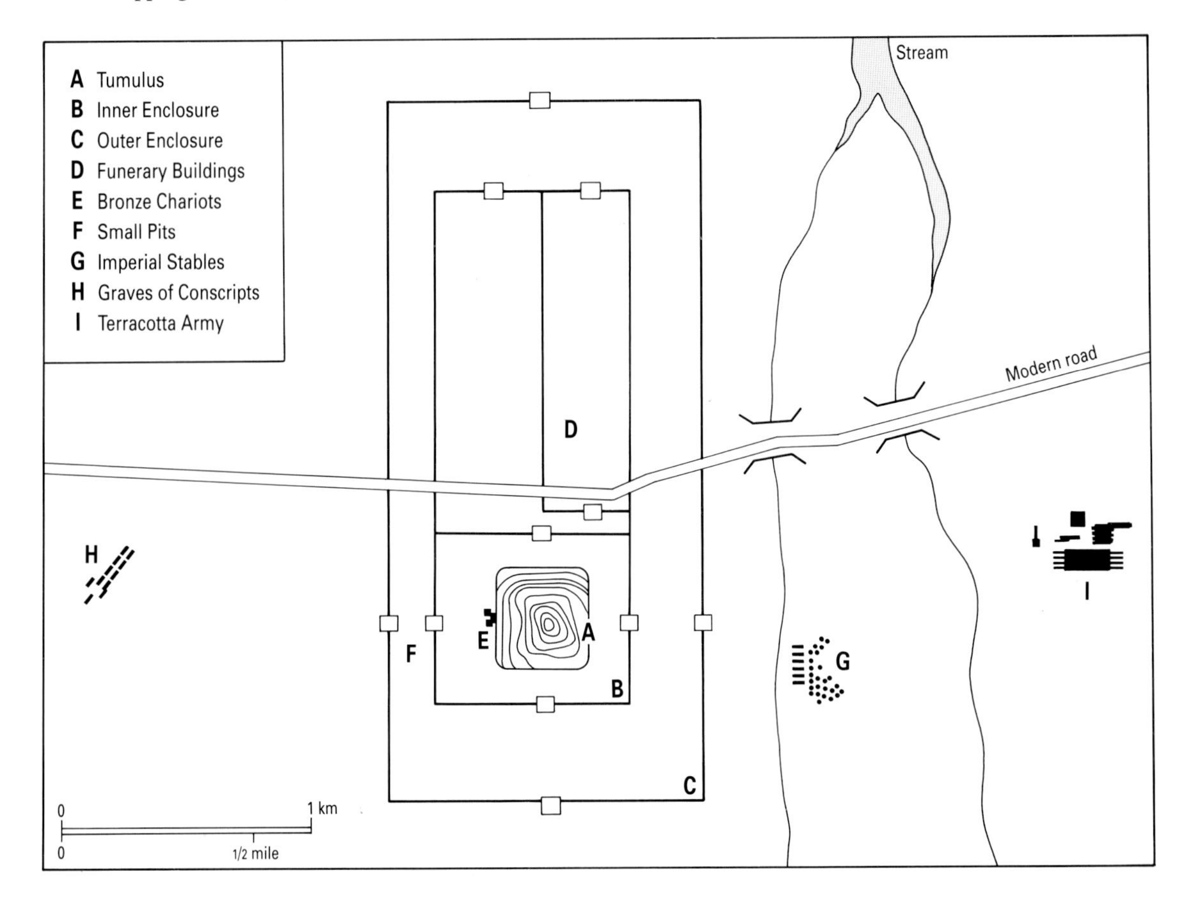

death. Excavation of Han tombs indicates some of the destinations envisaged for both souls, but it should be stressed that no systematic explanation of the afterlife survives. From funerary gifts a certain anxiety about the *po* soul can be deduced. As long as adequate nourishment had been provided by the descendants of the deceased, it was expected to remain a satisfied companion of the corpse. Hence the gastronomic pleasures of the three intact tombs found in 1974 at Mawangdui, a suburb of Changsha, in Hunan province. Built between 186 and 168 BC for prominent members of the local aristocracy, besides decorated wooden coffins they contain an astonishing array of foodstuffs. By means of these enticements it was hoped that the *po* soul would be appeased and benevolent, so as to prevent its appearance as an evil-minded *gui*.

Another line of defence for the living was the provision of equipment for the Yellow Springs (*huangchuan*), an unattractive abode ruled by the Earth Queen somewhere underground. Its location was thought to be close enough to the surface to worry miners digging out metals. In case the *po* soul was drawn to this dismal place, a tomb was furnished with miniature houses, farmyards, granaries and stoves, together with more personal belongings. Evidently the vast preparations made at Mount Li for the First Emperor's own mausoleum were driven by a similar desire to preserve in the shadowy afterlife below at least a semblance of his exalted position as the sole ruler of China. Apart from burying a life-size terracotta army close to the tomb, it is recorded how

> 700,000 conscripts laboured for more than a decade. They dug through three underground streams; they poured molten copper for the outer coffin; they filled the burial chamber with models of palaces, towers and official buildings, as well as fine utensils, precious stones and rarities. Artisans were ordered to fix automatic crossbows so that grave robbers would be slain. The waterways of the empire, the Yellow and the Yangzi rivers, and even the great ocean itself, were represented by mercury and were made to flow mechanically. Above, the heavenly constellations were depicted, while below lay a representation of the earth. Lamps using whale oil were installed to burn a long time.

But not to be overlooked was the strenuous effort made by the First Emperor to attain simultaneously another means of overcoming death – namely, by joining the select band of the immortals in the manner of the Yellow Emperor.

The quest for immortality would appear to have depended upon the fate of the *hun* soul, not least because its function was the exercise of spiritual and intellectual faculties. The *po* soul merely enabled the body to move and operate efficiently. After burial of the deceased, the destination of the *hun* soul in the sky was probably identified with the home of the *di*. Unlike the Yellow Springs, this was a place of delight for which nothing was required other than the right of entrance. One tradition suggests a difficult ascent via numerous stairways, guarded by ferocious beasts such as horned serpents of inordinate length. Paintings on

The sheer scale of Mount Li is impressive. No two heads of the several thousand terracotta warriors so far unearthed are alike; each one is an individual portrait.

the Mawangdui coffins refer to this perilous journey and were doubtless intended to prevent the *hun* soul from being devoured. By the Later Han (25–220), the location of paradise had started to shift from the sky to the far west. There the fortunate were said to live under the rule of the Queen Mother of the West (*Xixangmu*), whose chief attribute seems to have been the ability to confer immortality on her chosen subjects.

Another way of sharing eternal life with the greater gods, including Heaven itself, was through herbs of immortality (*buxi cao*). This typical Chinese notion of the continuance of the individual person with an etherealized body on earth arose as a practical alternative to the usual fates of *hun* and *po* souls. Since there was no ethical polarization of the afterlife before the coming of Buddhism, everybody went to one or the other destination, including the mountainous dwellings of the mysterious *xian*. These immortals were believed to enjoy earthly imperishability because of the elixir of life, a drug still sought by alchemists in Europe long after the Buddhist doctrine of reincarnation had ousted this Daoist idea from the Chinese mind. So convinced was the First Emperor of its efficacy that ambassadors were sent up mountains and across the sea to acquire the magic herbs from the immortals themselves. Even the otherwise practical Han emperor Wu Di once remarked, 'Ah, if only I could become like the Yellow Emperor, I can see myself leaving behind my women and their children as lightly as casting off a sandal.' Wu Di was in fact highly susceptible to the claims of Daoist adepts, who held out the hope of longevity, if not immortality.

Many Daoist thinkers of Wu Di's reign gathered at the court of Liu An, the subject ruler of Huainan. Though ordered to commit suicide for sedition in 122 BC, this southern king was responsible for the publication of a major collection of texts on cosmology and alchemy. Much to the chagrin of the emperor, Liu An was rumoured to have ascended into the sky as a *xian*, along with his family and their pets. All had taken a draft of a particularly potent elixir.

Bronze wine vessel (*hu*), used during the lifetime of Confucius in the rites of ancestor worship.

The Regulation of Man

That Wu Di was influenced by the spirit world, even in the construction of public monuments, can be observed at the tomb of Huo Quling, who died at the age of twenty-four in 116 BC. General Huo Quling conducted a series of brilliant campaigns against the Xiongnu, thereby opening China's route to Central Asia. In recognition of this achievement, a grateful emperor accorded the general the honour of a state funeral adjacent to the imperial tombs, north of Chang'an. On an artificial hill raised above the grave were placed a variety of stone carvings, executed by the imperial workshops. The purpose of these fabulous beasts, monsters and horses trampling nomads was the perpetuation of Huo Quling's victories through the attraction of benevolent spirits. Wu Di is known to have been advised by Daoist adepts that if he wished to communicate with the spirit world he must portray the strange forms taken by the gods on the buildings he commissioned.

While he never ceased to believe in the influence of the spirit world on earthly affairs, Wu Di ruled an empire progressively more rational in its ideology and conduct of government. The slow transformation came about through the acceptance of Confucianism as the ethical basis for imperial rule. In contrast to the natural philosophy of Daoism and the authoritarian tenor of Legalism, the teachings derived from Confucius and his disciples placed stress on *li*, 'propriety', and *jen*, 'benevolence'. Often translated as rites, the character for *li* tells us exactly what Confucius had in mind, since the strokes represent a vessel containing precious objects as a sacrifice to the ancestral spirits. The rite of ancestor-worship thus became a moral code in which proper social relations were clearly defined: the loyalty a minister owed to a prince was the same as that owed to a father by a son. Filial piety (*xiao*) became in effect the basis for all of the other human virtues. As Dong Zhongshu asserted in defence of social regulation, since human nature possesses only the beginnings of goodness, society can be saved from barbarism through the institutions of kinship and education alone. Three relationships were critical: those between ruler and subject, father and son, and husband and wife. At Dong Zhongshu's suggestion, in 136 BC Wu Di made Confucianism the recognized state ideology, but this did not deter the determined emperor from embarking on a vigorous foreign policy. Despite the omens Dong Zhongshu drew to the throne's attention, Wu Di disregarded these heavenly warnings until unrest among the peasantry indicated an exhaustion he could not afford to ignore. It was not until the final years of the Former Han that Dong Zhongshu's ideas on the unitary nature of the worlds of heaven, earth and man may be said to have been fully accepted. The acceptance of Heaven's power to issue warnings to its son, the Chinese emperor, represents nothing less than the triumph of Confucianism in political theory. Thereafter Daoism was forced to concentrate on the spirit world, while Legalism gradually declined into a number of administrative techniques.

Confucius in conversation.

But this ultimate victory was by no means predictable during the Warring States period (481–221 BC). Rulers then appeared indifferent to anything but personal gain. Only the glibbest advisers could expect to make careers for themselves and avoid miserable ends. Even a successful policy-maker like Shang Yang could find that execution awaited him at the end of his service in 338 BC. The political troubles were lamented by scores of philosophers who keenly felt their own marginal influence on contemporary events. Their frustration called forth an intellectual ferment unmatched in the later monolithic unity of the Chinese empire. Confucius himself was compelled to write books because no king would listen to his advice. In the final years before his death in 479 BC Confucius seems to have despaired at the collapse of feudalism.

The Warring States period was the time of the so-called Hundred Schools, when roving philosophers offered advice to any lord who would listen or collected followers in order to establish a body of teachings. Apart from Han Fei Zi (280–233 BC), who was a prince of the royal family of the small feudal state of Han, the philosophers seem to have been *shi*, members of the scholar-gentry and administrative class. Their social position entitled them to a freedom of thought and movement that was denied to the nobleman above, as it was to the peasants and artisans below them. Though later commentators have sought to dignify Confucius, his family were almost certainly *shi*. It was indeed his lack of personal preferment that caused him to turn to the teaching of ethics. So profound an appreciation of the role of moral upbringing in maintaining a civilized society did Confucius give to the classical Chinese that subsequent philosophers never ceased to refer to this underlying principle. Of the Daoists, Confucius said: 'They dislike me because I want to reform society, but if we are not to live with our fellow men, with whom can we live? We cannot live with animals. If society was as it ought to be, I should not be seeking change.' It was a point echoed down the ages by Confucian scholars, whose outlook rested on a deeply felt concern for the welfare of mankind. Since they viewed the state as a large family, or a collection of families, the virtue of obedience also found a place among the characteristics that defined the relationship between the ruler and the ruled. Commenting on government, Confucius said: 'Let the prince be a prince, the minister a minister, the father a father, and the son a son.'

Just as the subordinate people in these relationships had a duty of submission, so those in authority were required to act with benevolence. The ideal was embodied in the old concept of *junzi*, usually translated as the 'superior man'. It means literally 'sovereign son', a reference to both character and status. Confucius himself appears to have deliberately shifted the meaning away from birth and towards behaviour. Without entirely dropping the notion of social position, he asserted that the superior man had to deserve the authority which he inherited. 'Such a person, having valour without righteousness, will be guilty of insubordination; one of the ordinary people, having valour without righteousness, will commit robbery.' For, Confucius said, 'There has never been a mean man who was a man of benevolence.'

What was primarily intended here was a rebuke to the feudal aristocracy, whose own shortcomings contributed so greatly to the general breakdown of authority. Power had come to count for more than family background in an age where physical force could utterly suppress the exercise of hereditary privilege. The steady extinction of old families raised the vexed question of whose hands actual political power should pass into. Unless there was a class of cultivated and competent officials who were prepared to administer affairs of state in the best interests of the people, then the Middle Kingdom was doomed to the ceaseless strife of ambitious rivals for power. This new ruling class, the *shi*, not only failed to emerge by the end of Confucius' own life but, to the equal frustration of his followers, its later appearance hardly moderated the harshness of politics down to the imperial unification of China in 221 BC, or afterwards during the short ascendancy of the Qin emperors.

The teachings of Confucius seem to have had a more immediate effect in the field of religion. The moral emphasis placed on the rites of ancestor-worship began a process by which superstition was by and large contained. His own attitude to the spirit realm was practical. 'I stand in awe of the spirits,' Confucius said, 'but keep them at arm's length.' This was neither an anticipation of Wang Chong's rationalism, nor a rejection of the microcosmic–macrocosmic correspondences developed by Dong Zhongshu, but rather a warning that the ways of Heaven were beyond human comprehension. They were not to be readily interrogated via divination. As Confucius never tired of repeating:

> Heaven decrees life and death; wealth and rank depend on the will of Heaven. If a superior man attends to his duties with courtesy to others and follows the rules of ritual, then all within the Four Seas are his brothers.

A not dissimilar objective, universal love, preoccupied Mo Zi (c. 468–376 BC). Harking back to the perfection of the legendary rulers of the past, when people were said to have treated each other as members of a single family and looked upon all children as their own, Mo Zi condemned the Confucian stress on lineage as socially decisive. In particular, he detested the ease with which so many Confucian scholars settled for comfortable careers as advisers on ritual. But where Confucius and Mo Zi were really in total disagreement was over the role played by the supernatural.

According to Mo Zi, vengeful *gui* were the guardians of justice. 'If the fact that spirits reward the worthy and punish the evil can be made the cornerstone of policy in a state,' he said, 'it will provide a means to bring order to the state and benefit to the people.' The later disappearance of Mo Zi's thought under the Han emperors may have been a result of the affluence then enjoyed by educated men. Stable political conditions led to a growing sophistication which, with the triumph of Confucianism, had much less interest in the spirit realm. This was instead appropriated by Daoism, the enduring opponent of Confucian ideology and, until the arrival of Buddhism, its most subtle challenger.

The founder of Daoism was Lao Zi, the so-called Old Philosopher. An older contemporary of Confucius, he was keeper of the archives at the Zhou court. Access in Luoyang to records more ancient than anything available to Confucius in the eastern states of Lu, Song and Qi may have persuaded him of the falseness of traditions glorifying the feudal past. Lao Zi was convinced that the causes of disorder in the world lay not in the shortcomings of feudal institutions but rather in the fact that they were themselves an unsatisfactory method of achieving order. Benevolence and righteousness, Lao Zi argued, usually acted as a mask for princely ambition. The book associated with his name, *The Way of Virtue, (Daodejing)*, sets the rivalry of feudal houses in a cosmic perspective:

> Who would prefer the jingle of jade pendants,
> Once he has heard stone growing in a cliff?

Man's rootedness in nature, an inner strength that made all men wiser than they knew, was looked upon as the means to salvation. The artificial demands of feudal society had so disturbed the innate abilities of the people that instead of following the natural way (*dao*) of living, they were circumscribed through man-made codes of honour, love and duty. Daoist quietism was practised by a number of Lao Zi's followers, one of whom, Zhuang Zi (350–275 BC), rejected the premiership of the southern state of Chu. As he succinctly commented: 'A thief steals a purse and is hanged, while another steals a state and becomes a prince.' In the turmoil of the Warring States period, the only sensible policy for the sage was to live the life of a recluse.

Later Han censer in the shape of a hill. It was probably used by Daoist priests.

Such an attitude was, of course, anathema to Confucian and Legalist thinkers alike, as they could not conceive of life without some form of social organization. Along with Mo Zi, the Legalists placed the state first and imposed on the people a set of well-defined obligations. The problem for the Daoists was that in classical times China had no popular institutions on a par with those that arose in Greece; there was nothing for them to use in the furtherance of a fundamentally democratic philosophy. Withdrawal from service in government, or becoming a hermit, was almost inevitably little more than a political protest. Though the idea was to prove attractive during periods of disturbance or foreign conquest, scholarly retreat could never advance political development beyond the imperial system. The only revolutionary glimmer to survive at all was in popular Daoist religion, a transformation of the philosophy largely brought about by the need for solace among the peasantry when crisis overtook the empire in the third century. In 215 the strength of Daoism in the countryside caused the warlord Cao Cao to treat with dignity the defeated leader of the Five Pecks of Grain movement. The peasants who had lived under its rule enjoyed a degree of justice then unknown in the tottering Han empire.

That the tomb of Lao Zi was also unknown indicates more than an unConfucian indifference to ancestor worship. It shows how Daoism was always connected with the pursuit of the elixir of life. The followers of Confucius were convinced that the Daoists were entirely misguided in their concentration on Nature, and they marvelled that they could waste time on the study of apparently useless things. In fact this detached outlook proved to be important for the development of science in China, since it has been plausibly argued that Daoist observation and experiments in alchemy equal the dim beginnings of scientific method. Yet not everyone shared a Confucian scepticism, the First Emperor alone spending vast sums on seeking for himself the elusive herbs of immortality.

Notwithstanding the superstition of the First Emperor, it was the school of Law which provided the philosophical basis for enforcing strict obedience. The oldest meaning of *fa*, the fundamental concept of Legalism, is 'standard'. Initially connected with standard measures of weight, length and volume, *fa* was extended to mean the general regulation imposed by an all-powerful ruler. First apparent in the policies of Shang Yang, Legalism claimed that the only model for conduct was the law of a state, which would determine punishments and rewards. Law thus became the regulator of all human action, entirely replacing traditional notions of morality. This notion of a law devoid of any religious sanction was unique in a classical civilization.

What Shang Yang (*c.* 390–338 BC) aimed at, through the 'unification' of punishments and teachings, was to make sure that 'the gate to riches and noble status has its approach in soldiering; then, when the people hear of war, they congratulate each other and, whether at work or at rest, at times of drinking or eating, they will sing songs of war.' That total militarization was the object of Shang Yang's reforms is evident in his advocacy of war service for every adult in a state. He bluntly says:

> One army should be formed of able-bodied men, and one of able-bodied women, and one of old and feeble men and women. These are called the three armies. Command the able-bodied men, with adequate supplies and sharp weapons, to deploy against the enemy. Command the able-bodied women, with adequate supplies and ramparts at their backs, to dig earthworks, construct obstacles and clear the ground of useful materials, so that an invading force will acquire nothing that can assist its attack. Command the army of the old and feeble to guard the livestock, and to collect food from the fields, thereby ensuring supplies for the able-bodied men and women.

Elsewhere Shang Yang confirms that war must be waged not only to achieve hegemony but, even more important, to prevent the development of humane culture. 'If a state is strong and war is not waged, the poison will be carried into its territory; rites and music and the parasitic functions will arise and dismemberment will be inevitable.'

The cultural tradition espoused by Confucius was of course the poison for which the sole antidote remained war. It was not, therefore, an accident that in 213 BC books should be burned when Confucian scholars dared to express reservations about the harsh tendency of imperial policy. The destruction was nothing more than a thorough implementation of the Legalist idea of stupefying the mind of the people. Though Han Fei Zi, Shang Yang's greatest follower, was less extreme in stressing war, he was just as firm on the dangers inherent in learning:

> In the state of an enlightened ruler there is no literature written on bamboo slips, but the laws serve as the teaching. There are no sayings of the ancient kings; magistrates act as teachers. And there is no valour through private swords; instead courage will be shown by those who behead the enemy.

Like all Legalist thinkers, Han Fei Zi's philosophical advice was addressed exclusively to feudal rulers. The only goal was to instruct the ruler how to survive and prosper in the present world. For only a comprehensive law code backed by inescapable punishments would safeguard the state. 'If the laws are weak,' Han Fei Zi insisted, 'so is the power of a prince.' Above the law himself, the ruler had to keep a tight rein on his bureaucratic subordinates and their activities. 'The ruler alone should possess the power, wielding it like thunder and lightning.'

So impressed by such totalitarian advice was the future First Emperor that he said if he could once converse with Han Fei Zi, he would die without regret. The meeting took place in 233 BC, and proved fatal for the philosopher, not the Qin ruler. At the suggestion of Li Si, the chief minister, armies had been prepared for an attack on the state of Han, a declared enemy of Qin since the building of the Chengkuo canal. On the eve of hostilities in 234–233 BC, the anxious ruler of Han sent Han Fei Zi to the Qin court as a friendly ambassador. According to Sima Qian:

> Zheng, the ruler of Qin, was delighted with the ideas of Han Fei Zi, even though he did not yet trust him enough to follow his advice. Therefore, Li Si did him injury and slandered him, saying, 'Han Fei Zi is a prince of Han. At present Your Highness wishes to annex the lands of the feudal lords. Han Fei Zi is bound to side with Han. Such is human nature ... The best thing to do is to hand him over to the law officers for investigation.' After the arrest had taken place, Li Si sent poison to Han Fei Zi, who eventually swallowed it in despair at his captivity. Later Zheng sent an official to release the philosopher, but by that time only a corpse remained in the cell.

Neither Li Si's motive nor the reason for Han Fei Zi's acquiescence in his suicide is explained. The most likely cause of the philosopher's death was the insecurity of the minister, a personal trait cunningly exploited by the eunuch Zhao Gao under the weak Second Emperor. Quite possibly Li Si was prepared to sacrifice a fellow Legalist because, in the cut and thrust of the Qin court, he could not cope with such an eminent rival.

Indeed, Li Si's own execution in 208 BC signalled the practical limits of Legalism. The Second Emperor had soon lost touch with daily reality. His own relations were frightened for their lives, his most competent ministers were silenced, and the only group regularly about his person were the eunuchs. Li Si himself was always introduced by Zhao Gao into the imperial presence on the most inconvenient occasions. In prison Li Si is supposed to have lamented, 'For an unprincipled ruler, how can one make any plans?' The Qin dynasty was doomed along with Legalism. In reaction to the unprecedented interference with everyday life, the Chinese people ended totalitarian rule in the first nationwide revolt and, through the compromise of the Former Han settlement, supported a system of government that was founded upon a principle of responsibility for the country's welfare. Never again would an emperor or a minister possess absolute authority.

The Coming of Buddhism

The phenomenal rise in the popularity of Buddhism following the fall of the Western Jin dynasty in 316, and the abandonment of north China to nomad invaders, should not be permitted to obscure the period of preparation that was essential for this remarkable event. Two complementary processes were at work from the second century AD onwards. One comprised the decline of imperial government and its ideology, in particular the Confucianism associated with the bureaucracy and state-sponsored learning. The other process was the adaptation of Buddhism into a faith accessible and intelligible to the Chinese.

The many-sided struggle for power around the weakened Later Han throne became so intense that it effectively put an end to any unified state. Warlords

Bronze brazier dating from the Later Han period.

might later temporarily hold sway over the whole of China, but lasting reunification was not achieved for another three centuries. In these early years of crisis, Chinese scholars speculated on what had befallen their state and society, on the insecure and unhappy lives they led. They endeavoured to reinterpret Confucianism in a less scholastic way, turning to the long-neglected works of Daoist philosophy for inspiration. In the middle of this profound reassessment of traditions and ideas, Buddhism entered the consciousness of Chinese thinkers. The infiltration of the new faith among the educated élite was the work of scholars involved in the Daoist revival who believed they found a reflection of their own concerns in the doctrines of Mahāyāna Buddhism. The first translations of Buddhist texts into Chinese are indeed full of Daoist expressions: for instance, *bodhi*, 'enlightenment', was rendered as *dao*, 'way', while *nirvāṇa*, 'ultimate release', became *wuwei*, the 'non-action' of the sage. Such usage at first led Buddhism to be looked upon as a sect of Daoism.

Daoist communities may have served to spread certain Buddhist symbols and cults, thus playing a role analogous to that of the Jewish communities which helped to spread early Christianity in the eastern provinces of the Roman empire. But eclecticism was born as much from the circumstances of the faith's arrival from India as from the ability of the Chinese mind to hold a number of different propositions simultaneously without apparent distress. The earliest Buddhist converts had few texts, depended on the testimony of foreigners, and had scant knowledge of the society in which the Buddha had preached. Mahāyāna, the Great Vehicle, was the form of Buddhism carried to China and this more evolved version of the faith already had many opposing schools. At a congress called by the Kuṣāṇa ruler Kaniṣka (78–123), a gathering held in the Punjab and known as the Fourth Buddhist Council, the representatives of no fewer than eighteen Buddhist sects were in attendance.

Under these circumstances the task of translation proved very difficult. The first translators were of Central Asian origin, like the Parthian An Shihkao, who settled in Luoyang around 148. With the assistance of both Central Asian and Chinese converts, An Shihkao translated works connected with meditation, techniques of breath-control, and psychology. Though within the imperial palace sacrifices were made in 166 to the Buddha, this worship was entwined with Daoism, as Lao Zi received honour at the same time. Not for another century would translations begin to free Buddhism from the Daoist embrace, and its central doctrine of *sunyata*, 'emptiness', make a powerful challenge to the this-worldly approach of Confucianism. Instrumental in the emancipation of Buddhist thought was Dharmaraksa, or Fa Hu, a man born of a Da Yuezhi family long resident at Dunhuang. As Fa Hu had spoken Chinese from birth at this western outpost, he was able to translate over 100 sacred texts. Before his death in Luoyang around 310, Fa Hu gave China what was to become its most treasured *sutra*, the *Lotus of the Good Law*, which promised salvation to all who sought enlightenment like the Buddha.

The spread of the Buddhist faith among the peasantry was yet to occur. Much of its initial impetus, like the philosophical speculation of the scholars, derived from an association with Daoism, then enjoying a great revival in the countryside as a popular religion. Out of movements such as the Five Pecks of Grain developed a community of believers who, in rivalry with Buddhism, would eventually constitute the Daoist church. In the third and fourth centuries, however, the collapse of order encouraged both Daoists and Buddhists to concentrate on individual happiness, usually envisaged as an escape to some form of paradise. The distinctive character of salvation in Chinese Buddhist belief came primarily from the teachings of Hui Yuan (334–416), whose spiritual progress is reminiscent of St Augustine's. His early training was in the Confucian classics, which in old age he felt still contained the flower of Chinese thought. But along with this scholarship he developed a strong interest in Daoist philosophy, mastering its texts before his first exposure to Buddhism. Converted to the new faith, Hui Yuan became a monk, studied and began to preach. About 380 he settled on a mountain in the Yangzi valley and formed around him a community worshipping Amida Buddha, in whose paradise of the Pure Land they sought to be reborn.

While Buddhism carried all before it until the reunification of China under the Sui and Tang emperors (589–906), its advocates had to accommodate a tradition which took for granted a powerful throne as well as strong family obligations. The choice of the Confucian expression *xiaoshun*, or 'filial obedience', as a translation for the Buddhist concept of morality helped to deal with the charge of indifference to society. But useful though this was in justifying the pursuit of individual salvation, the first steps had been taken along a path that would lead to the transformation of the Buddha into the epitome of the dutiful Chinese son.

Further Reading

Hellenic Civilization

Adcock, F.E. *The Greek and Macedonian Art of War*, Berkeley, 1957
Allan, D.J. *The Philosophy of Aristotle*, Oxford, 1970
Andrews, A. *The Greeks*, London, 1967
Annas, J. *An Introduction to Plato's Republic*, Oxford, 1981
Boardman, J. *Athenian Red Figure Vases: The Archaic Period*, London, 1975
– *Greek Sculpture: The Classical Period*, London, 1985
– *Athenian Red Figure Vases: The Classical Period*, London, 1989
Burkert, W. *Greek Religion*, trans. J. Raffan, Oxford, 1985
Davies, J.K. *Democracy and Classical Greece*, Hassocks, 1978
Dodds, E.R. *The Greeks and the Irrational*, Berkeley, 1951
Dover, K.J. *Aristophanic Comedy*, London, 1972
Ehrenberg, V. *The Greek State*, London, 1969
Gagarin, M. *Early Greek Law*, Berkeley, 1986
Gould, J. *Herodotus*, London, 1989
Harris, H.A. *Sport in Greece and Rome*, London, 1972
Hooker, J.T. *The Ancient Spartans*, 1980
Hornblower, S. *Thucydides*, London, 1987
Hussey, E. *The Presocratics*, London, 1972
Kerferd, G.B. *The Sophistic Movement*, Cambridge, 1981
Lesky, A. *Greek Tragedy*, trans. H.A. Frankfort, London, 1985
Murray, G. *Aeschylus: The Creator of Greek Tragedy*, Oxford, 1940
Phillips, E.D. *Greek Medicine*, London, 1973
de Romilly, J. *A Short History of Greek Literature*, trans. L. Doherty, Chicago, 1985
Carne-Ross, D.S. *Pindar*, New Haven, 1985
Stockton, D. *The Classical Athenian Democracy*, Oxford, 1990
Swaddling, J. *The Ancient Olympic Games*, London, 1980
Tomlinson, R.A. *Greek Architecture*, Bristol, 1989
Vlastos, G. *Socrates: Ironist and Moral Philosopher*, Cambridge, 1991

The Hellenistic Age

Bell, H.I. *Egypt from Alexander the Great to the Arab Conquest*, Oxford, 1948
Casson, L. *Travel in the Ancient World*, London, 1974
Ferguson, W.S. *Hellenistic Athens*, London, 1911
Finley, M.I. *Classical Slavery*, London, 1987
Fraser, P.M. *Ptolemaic Alexandria*, Oxford, 1972
Green, P. *Alexander the Great*, London, 1970
– *Alexander to Actium: The Hellenistic Age*, London, 1990
Griffith, G.T. *The Mercenaries of the Hellenistic World*, Cambridge, 1935
Hammond, N.G.L. *Epirus*, Oxford, 1967
– *Alexander the Great: King, Commander and Statesman*, Princeton, 1980
– *The Macedonian State: The Origins, Institutions and History*, Oxford, 1989
Jones, A.H.M. *The Greek City from Alexander to Justinian*, Oxford, 1940
Larsen, J.A.O. *Greek Federal States*, Oxford, 1968
Lloyd, G.E.R. *Greek Science after Aristotle*, London, 1973
Long, A.A. *Hellenistic Philosophy: Stoics, Epicureans, Sceptics*, London, 1974
Narain, A.K. *The Indo-Greeks*, Oxford, 1957
Nock, A.D. *Conversion: The Old and New in Religion from Alexander the Great to Augustine of Hippo*, Oxford, 1933
Pollitt, J.J. *Art in the Hellenistic Age*, Cambridge, 1986
Pritchett, W.K. *The Greek State at War*, Berkeley, 1971–91
Scullard, H.H. *The Elephant in the Graeco-Roman World*, London, 1974
Shimron, B. *Late Sparta and the Spartan Revolution, 23–146 BC*, Buffalo, 1972
Tarn, W.W. *Hellenistic Military and Naval Developments*, London, 1930
– *The Greeks in Bactria and India*, Cambridge, 1966
Walbank, F.W. *Philip V of Macedon*, Cambridge, 1940
– *The Hellenistic World*, London, 1981

The World of Rome

Alfoldi, A. *Early Rome and the Latins*, London, 1965
Birley, A.R. *Marcus Aurelius*, London, 1987
Brown, P. *Augustine of Hippo: A Biography*, London, 1967
– *The Making of Late Antiquity*, Chicago, 1978
Brunt, P.A. *Social Conflicts in the Roman Republic*, London, 1971
Campbell, J.B. *The Emperor and the Roman Army, 31 BC–AD 235*, Oxford, 1984
Chadwick, H. *The Early Church*, Harmondsworth, 1967
Crawford, M.H. *The Roman Republic*, London, 1978
Crook, J.A. *Law and Life of Rome*, London, 1967
Fraenkel, E. *Horace*, London, 1957
Gardner, J.F. *Women in Roman Law and Society*, London, 1986
Griffin, J. *Latin Poets and Roman Life*, London, 1985
– *Virgil*, Oxford, 1986
Harris, W.V. *War and Imperialism in Republican Rome, 327–70 BC*, Oxford, 1979
Hopkins, K. *Conquerors and Slaves*, Cambridge, 1978
Levick, B. *Claudius*, London, 1990
Liebeschuetz, J.H.W.G. *Continuity and Change in Roman Religion*, Oxford, 1979
Martin, R.H. *Tacitus*, London, 1981
Millar, F.G.B. *The Emperor in the Roman World*, London, 1977
Ogilvie, R.M. *The Romans and Their Gods in the Age of Augustus*, London, 1969
Potter, T.W. *Roman Italy*, London, 1987
Salway, P. *Roman Britain*, Oxford, 1981
Sear, F. *Roman Architecture*, London, 1982
Stockton, D. *Cicero: A Political Biography*, Oxford, 1971
– *The Gracchi*, Oxford, 1979
Syme, R. *The Roman Revolution*, Oxford, 1939
Wacher, J. *The Roman World*, London, 1987
Wells, C.M. *The Roman Empire*, London, 1984

The Empires of Persia

The Achaemenids
Burn, A.R. *Persia and the Greeks*, London, 1962

Cook, J. M. *The Persian Empire*, London, 1983
Culican, W. *The Medes and the Persians*, London, 1965
Frye, R. N. *The Heritage of Persia*, Cleveland, 1963
Olmstead, A. T. *The History of the Persian Empire*, Chicago, 1948
Porada, E. *The Art of Ancient Iran*, New York, 1965
Root, M. C. *The King and Kingship in Achaemenid Art*, Leiden, 1979
Schmit, E. F. *Persepolis*, Chicago, 1953–70
Stronach, D. *Pasargadae*, Oxford, 1978
Zaehner, R. C. *The Dawn and Twilight of Zoroastrianism*, London, 1967

The Parthians and the Sasanians

Boyce, M. *Zoroastrians: Their Religious Beliefs and Practices*, London, 1979
Colledge, M. A. R. *The Parthians*, London, 1967
Downey, S. *Mesopotamian Religious Architecture*, Princeton, 1988
Ettinghausen, R. *From Byzantium to Sasanian Iran and the Islamic World*, Leiden, 1972
Gage, J. *La montée des Sassanides*, Paris, 1964
Ghirshman, R. *Iran: Parthians and Sassanians*, London, 1962
Gobl, R. *Sasanian Numismatics*, Wurzburg, 1971
Harper, P. O. *Silver Vessels of the Sasanian Period*, New York, 1981
Hayashi, R. *The Silk Road and the Shoso-in*, New York and Tokyo, 1975
Hermann, G. *The Iranian Revival*, Oxford, 1977
Hopkins, C. *Topography and Architecture of Seleucia-on-the-Tigris*, Ann Arbor, 1972
Rosenfield, J. *The Dynastic Art of the Kushans*, Los Angeles, 1967
Schlumberger, D. *L'Orient hellenisé*, Paris, 1970
Segal, J. B. *Edessa*, Oxford, 1970
Sellwood, D. *An Introduction to the Coinage of Parthia*, London, 1971
Ward Perkins, J. B. *The Art of Dura-Europos*, Oxford, 1973

Imperial India

Agrawal, A. *The Rise and Fall of the Imperial Guptas*, Delhi, 1989
Auboyer, J. *Daily Life in Ancient India, from approximately 200 BC to AD 700*, London, 1967
Basham, A. L. *A Cultural History of India*, Oxford, 1975
Bhattacharji, S. *The Indian Theogony*, Cambridge, 1970
Brockington, J. L. *The Sacred Thread: Hinduism in Its Continuity and Diversity*, Edinburgh, 1981
Dutt, S. *Buddhist Monks and Monasteries in India*, London, 1962
Harle, J. C. *Gupta Sculpture*, London, 1975
Jaini, P. S. *The Jaina Path to Purification*, Berkeley, 1979
Lienhard, S. *A History of Classical Poetry*, Wiesbaden, 1984
Ling, T. *The Buddha: Buddhist Civilization in India and Ceylon*, London, 1973
Miller, B. *Theater of Memory: The Plays of Kālidāsa*, New York, 1984
Mitra, D. *Buddhist Monuments*, Calcutta, 1971
O'Flaherty, W. *Hindu Myths*, Harmondsworth, 1965
Schwartzberg, J. E. *A Historical Atlas of South Asia*, Chicago, 1978
Smith, V. A. *Aśoka, the Buddhist Emperor of India*, Oxford, 1901
Thapar, R. *Aśoka and the Decline of the Mauryas*, Bombay, 1973
Warmington, E. H. *Commerce Between the Roman Empire and India*, Cambridge, 1928
Weiner, S. L. *Ajaṇṭā: Its Place in Buddhist Art*, Berkeley, 1977
Williams, J. G. *The Art of Gupta India*, Princeton, 1982
Williams, P. M. *Mahayana Buddhism: The Doctrinal Foundations*, London, 1989
Zimmer, H. *Philosophies of India*, New York, 1952
Zvelebil, K. V. *Tamil Literature*, Leiden, 1975

The Unification of China

Bodde, D. *China's First Unifier: A study of the Ch'in Dynasty as seen in the Life of Li Ssu (280–208 BC)*, Leiden, 1938
Chang, K. C. *The Archaeology of Ancient China*, New Haven, 1977
Chu, T. T. *Han Social Structure*, Seattle, 1972
Cotterell, A. *China: A Concise Cultural History*, London, 1988
Creel, H. G. *What is Taoism? and Other Studies in Chinese Cultural History*, Chicago, 1970
de Crespigny, R. *Northern Frontier: The Policies and Strategy of the Later Han Empire*, Canberra, 1984
Dubs, H. H. *The History of the Former Han Dynasty*, Baltimore, 1938–55
Duyvendak, J. J. L. *The Book of Lord Shang: A Classic of the Chinese School of Law*, London, 1928
Elvin, M. *The Pattern of the Chinese Past*, London, 1973
Giles, H. A. *The Travels of Fa-hsien (399–414 AD) or Record of the Buddhistic Kingdoms*, Cambridge, 1923
Griffiths, S. B. *Sun Tzu: The Art of War*, Oxford, 1963
Hsu, C. Y. *Han Agriculture: The Formation of the Early Chinese Agrarian Economy (206 BC–AD 220)*, Seattle, 1980
Kierman, F. A. and Fairbank, J. K. *Chinese Ways in Warfare*, Cambridge, Mass., 1974
Lau, D. C. *Mencius*, Harmondsworth, 1970
Loewe, M. *Crisis and Conflict in Han China*, London, 1974
– *Ways to Paradise: The Chinese Quest for Immortality*, London, 1979
– *Chinese Ideas of Life and Death: Faith, Myth and Reason in the Han Period (202 BC–AD 220)*, London, 1982
Maspero, H. *La Chine antique*, Paris, 1927
Munro, D. J. *The Concept of Man in Early China*, Stanford, 1969
Smith, D. H. *Confucius*, London, 1973
Waldron, A. *The Great Wall of China: From History to Myth*, Cambridge, 1990
Waley, A. *The Analects of Confucius*, London, 1938
Watson, B. *The Basic Writings of Mo Tzu, Hsun Tzu and Han Fei Tzu*, London, 1967
– *The Records of the Historian (Sima Qian)*, New York, 1969
Yu Ying-Shih, *Trade and Expansion in Han China: A Study in the Structure of Sino-Barbarian Economic Relations*, Berkeley, 1967

ACKNOWLEDGEMENTS

The publishers of this book would like to thank the following for granting permission to reproduce illustrations. Every effort has been made to trace all copyright owners. The publishers apologize if the acknowledgement proves to be inadequate; in no case is such inadequacy intentional.

American Institute of Indian Studies: 20 (top left), 221, 226, 234
The Ancient Art & Architecture Collection: 1, 8, 47, 53 (all), 54, 104, (bottom left and right), 121 (both), 122, 130, 134, 138, 164, 205, (bottom), 255 (top), 275
Archaeological Museum of Thessaloniki: 44 (both)
Archaeological Survey of India: 193
Archivi Alinari: 40, 81
Asian Art Archives, University of Michigan: 231, 232, 235
Bildarchiv Foto Marburg: 114
Bildarchiv Preussischer Kulturbesitz: 24
The British Library: 222, 223, 224
The British Museum: 26, 55 (both), 56 (top two), 58, 60, 61 (bottom), 63, 91, 93, 100, 101 (top), 111 (bottom), 118, 119, 132 (top), 150, 153, 176, 178, 199, 200 (top right), 202, 237, 243, 248, 251, 252, 267, 270, 278 (top), 280, 282
Dr J. L. Brockington: 230 (top left)
Ny Carlsberg Glyptotek, Copenhagen: 69
J. Allan Cash: 27 (bottom left), 57, 140
Peter Clayton: 183 (bottom), 188 (bottom)
Douglas Dickens: 197, 204, 229, 230 (top right)
The Fitzwilliam Museum, University of Cambridge: 56 (bottom)
Werner Forman Archive: 210, 241 (bottom), 242
Sonia Halliday: 35, 36 (all), 103 (bottom), 158
Robert Harding: 6, 74, 99, 103 (top), 104 (top), 161, 187 (both), 188 (top), 191, 201, 205 (top), 206, 220 (top), 241 (top left and right), 244 (bottom), 247, 256, 262 (both), 263 (bottom), 277
J. C. Harle: 218, 233
Hirmer: 9, 10, 16, 20 (bottom left), 23, 25, 28, 30, 41, 62, 73 (both), 80 (both), 84, 101 (bottom)
E. J. Keall: 170, 174, 185 (both), 190
Leeds City Museum: 131 (bottom)
The Mansell Collection: 12, 15, 31, 75, 76 (both), 94, 95, 96, 107, 129 (top), 131 (top), 133, 137, 142
Meridian: 238, 240, 244 (top), 253, 257, 263 (top) (line drawings from *China: A Concise Cultural History*, Arthur Cotterell, 1988)
Musées Royaux d'Art et d'Histoire, Brussels: 79
Musei Vaticani: 89 (bottom)
Museo Nazionale, Naples: 29
Penguin Books: 21, 72 (line drawings from *Greek Architecture*, R. A. Tomlinson, 1984); 27 (top left and right), 108 (bottom), 220 (bottom) (line drawings from *The Penguin Encyclopedia of Ancient Civilizations*, Arthur Cotterell, 1988); 101, 108 (top), 129 (bottom), 135 (line drawings from *Roman Imperial Architecture*, J. B. Ward-Perkins, 1981)
The Royal Ontario Museum, Toronto: 147, 159
SCALA: 4, 112, 182
Roger Viollet: 78
Yale University Art Gallery, Dura Europos Collection: 184

INDEX